Book of Country Walks

edited by Nicholas Albery

(assisted by Hugh Kelly)

updates provided by the members
of the Saturday Walkers' Club

D0415409

Published by Time Out Guides Ltd, a wholly owned subsidiary of Time Out Group Ltd.

Time Out and the Time Out logo are trademarks of Time Out Group Ltd.

© Time Out Group Ltd and Nicholas Albery Foundation 2005

Sketch maps copyright © Nicholas Albery Foundation 2005

Nick Temple prepared and typeset this edition for the Nicholas Albery Foundation

Previous editions 1997, 1998, 1999, 2001, 2003, 2004

10 9 8 7 6 5 4

This edition first published in Great Britain in 2005 by Ebury

Ebury is a division of The Random House Group Ltd, 20 Vauxhall Bridge Road, London SW1V 2SA

Random House Australia Pty Limited, 20 Alfred Street, Milsons Point, Sydney, New South Wales 2061, Australia

Random House New Zealand Limited, 18 Poland Road, Glenfield, Auckland 10, New Zealand

Random House South Africa (Pty) Limited, Endulini, 5A Jubilee Road, Parktown 2193, South Africa

Random House UK Limited Reg. No. 954009

Distributed in USA by Publishers Group West, 1700 Fourth Street, Berkeley, California 94710

Distributed in Canada by Penguin Canada Ltd, 10 Alcorn Avenue, Toronto, Ontario, Canada M4V 3B2

For further distribution details, see www.timeout.com

ISBN 978-1-904978-88-6

A CIP catalogue record for this book is available from the British Library

Colour reprographics by Icon, Crowne House, 56-58 Southwark Street, London SE1 1UN

Printed and bound in Great Britain by Cox & Wyman Ltd

Papers used by Ebury Press are natural, recyclable products made from wood grown in sustainable forests

All the walks in this book have been checked at least ten times (most recently in 2004/5) but neither the editor nor the publisher can accept responsibility for ANY problems encountered by readers. The maps are sketches only and are not to exact scale. The self-organising Saturday Walkers' Club is an initiative of the editor, and is entirely independent of *Time Out*.

Please e-mail all updates to walks@alberyfoundation.org. Access all updates and other news about the Saturday Walkers' Club at: www.walkingclub.org.uk. To sign up for club walks and for last-minute changes, e-mail walks@alberyfoundation.org

The editor is grateful to Hugh Kelly, who walked – and did the initial write-ups for – ten walks in this book and helped check others; to Mike Taylor, who helped with the checking and updating; to Andrew Murphy for running the website; to Lindesay Irvine, Merlyn Albery, Richard Doust and Phil Buckley who helped with computerising the maps; to Richard Monkhouse for the dates; and to all the other walk checkers who are credited on page 425. Thanks also to Alana Black for her editorial help. All the editor's royalties from this book go to the Institute for Social Inventions, a project of the Nicholas Albery Foundation, regd. charity 1091396 (see page 425 for more information). The Institute for Social Inventions developed the concept for the book and club, laserset and laid out the book and designed the maps.

Contents

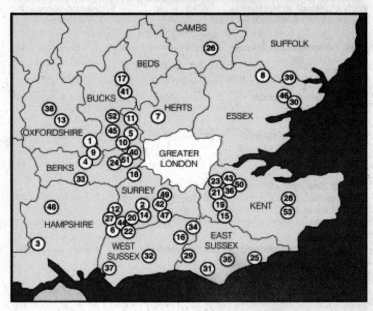

Walk	Length	Toughness (out of ten)	County	Page
Walk 6 Liphook to Haslemere Shulbrede Priory & its woods	15km (9.3m)	5	Hants & Surrey	50
Walk 7 Garston to St Albans River Ver, Moor Mill & Verulamium	13.6km (8.4m)	1	Herts	57
Walk 8 Bures to Sudbury Gainsborough country	16km (10m)	4	Essex & Suffolk	65
Walk 9 Shiplake to Henley River Thames, Rotherfield Greys & Greys Court	17.25km (10.7m)	4	Oxon	73
Walk 10 Beaconsfield (round walk) Milton's cottage & a Quaker hamlet	19.5km (12.2m)	4	Bucks	80
Walk 11 Tring to Wendover Reservoir nature reserves & Wendover Woods	21.5km (13.5m)	6	Herts & Bucks	89
Walk 12 Farnham to Godalming River Wey, Waverley Abbey & Peper Harrow park	19.9km (12.3m)	6	Surrey	98
Walk 13 Oxford (round walk) Port Meadow, the river, canal & colleges	15.2km (9.4m)	1	Oxon	105
Walk 14 Gomshall to Guildford Medieval Shere, Blackheath & River Wey	14.8km (9.2m)	3	Surrey	111
Walk 15 Leigh to Tunbridge Wells Penshurst Place & Medway Valley	17.5km (10.8m)	5	Kent	118
Walk 16 Balcombe (round walk) The gardens of Nymans & the ruins of Slaugham	17.5km (10.8m)	5	West Sussex	127
Walk 17 Bow Brickhill to Woburn Sands Woburn, its park & abbey	17.5km (10.8m)	6	Bucks & Beds	137

Contents

Walk	Length	Toughness (out of ten)	County	Page
Walk 30 Wivenhoe (round walk) To Rowhedge by ferry across the River Colne	14km (8.7m)	1	Essex	237
Walk 31 Glynde to Seaford Alfriston & the Seven Sisters	23km (14.5m)	8	East Sussex	245
Walk 32 Arundel to Amberley Arundel Park, River Arun & Burpham	18.8km (11.7m)	7	West Sussex	254
Walk 33 Mortimer to Aldermaston The Roman town of Calleva	13.1km (8.2m)	3	Berks & Hants	262
Walk 34 Balcombe to East Grinstead Wakehurst Place, Priest House & Weir Wood	16.5km (10.3m)	7	West Sussex	269
Walk 35 Crowhurst to Battle Battle of Hastings & its abbey	19km (11.7m)	4	East Sussex	278
Walk 36 Borough Green to Sevenoaks Plaxtol, Ightham Mote & Knole House	15.5km (9.5m)	4	Kent	287
Walk 37 Southbourne to Chichester A Chichester Harbour walk	15.5km (9.5m)	3	West Sussex	294
Walk 38 Hanborough to Charlbury Blenheim Palace & Cornbury Park	21km (13m)	6	Oxon	303
Walk 39 Manningtree (round walk) River Stour – Constable country	15km (9.3m)	4	Essex & Suffolk	312
Walk 40 Gerrards Cross to Cookham Bulstrode Park, Burnham Beeches & Spencer	14.8km (9.2m)	2	Bucks & Berks	321
Walk 41 Bow Brickhill to Leighton Buzzard Greensand Ridge & River Ouzel	13.8km (8.5m)	2	Bucks & Beds	328

Contents

Introduction

The walks in this book grew out of the experiences, over the previous six years or so, of a group of young and middle-aged Londoners, friends and friends of friends, who went walking together every Saturday.

We called our group various names over time, from the Never Ending Walking Talking Perpetual Motion Encounter Group and the Gourmet Walkers to the Adventure and Romance Agency – indeed, the walks led to several romances.

We came to the conclusion that there is no better way to have an inexpensive party each week than for a dozen or so people to go for a walk together in beautiful country-side, with the walking stimulating conversation and an anarchic spirit. We would take a whole day to do about seven to 13 miles: walking to the pub, having lunch, walking to a cream tea somewhere, and taking the train home, sometimes giving each other foot massages on the way back.

Using Ordnance Survey maps, we chose walks which looked interesting – those with National Trust land or buildings on the route, or those which led through woods and along streams. We were surprised how few walkers were out in these lovely places.

Thinking of all the Londoners and tourists of all ages who would really enjoy getting out of London for the day, I was prompted to do this book.

I started taking walk notes one Saturday, in the snow, when nobody else from the group turned up.

I realised I needed to find a hardier bunch of winter walkers. And so it is that our group has now merged with the self-organising Saturday Walkers' Club (see page 13) and I have found readers who share my enjoyment of walks in all weathers. In fact the club has developed into a social network of regulars who go on outings and holidays together.

The train journey

Walks go from mainline railway stations to stations that are, on average, an hour outside London. Some routes require coming back from a different station. And some even return to a different station in London. In such cases we have found that, in practice, ticket inspectors are normally prepared to accept a cheap day return to the further away station, if you explain you've been out walking, even if the stations are on different routes. I have never once been charged extra in many years of walking, but you may prefer to play safe by getting two singles.

If you have a Network Railcard, at weekends (or after 10am on weekdays) up to three adults can travel with you, and all of you get a third off the ticket price – with a further reduction if you show the ticket office a tube Travelcard. Fares for the train journeys required by the walks in this book are between £5 and £12 with a Network Railcard (2004 prices). A Network Railcard costs £20 for a year. Up to four adults and four children can travel on a Network Railcard; children receive a 60% discount on the fare (see www.railcard.co.uk for further information).

GroupSave tickets are also now available for many of the walks in this book (but not yet, for instance, for the ones from Waterloo or Victoria). These tickets allow four people to travel for the price of two – a greater reduction than from using a Network Railcard, except that they do not give you an extra amount off for using a Travelcard.

If the walk is too long for you and the Ordnance Survey (OS) map shows no obvious short cuts, you can always walk just to the lunchtime pub and ask for their help in calling a taxi to take you back to the station. Likewise, at the end of a non-circular walk, you may need to call a taxi if you came by car. You could phone one of the local pubs whose numbers are in this book to get the number of a taxi firm, text yell.co.uk on 80 248, or you could ask Scoot on 0800 192 192.

Beware that, on Sundays, some pubs do not serve food and there is often engineering work on the railways – although normally an alternative bus service is provided. If the station is closed on a Sunday, you may need to catch a taxi or bus from the nearest possible station. The stations in this book currently closed on Sunday are: Bow Brickhill, Hever, Holmwood, Ockley, Warnham and Woburn Sands. Those with only a very irregular service on Sundays are: Charlbury, Gomshall and Hanborough.

Further, on any day of the week you should carefully check your return train times from Charlbury, Gomshall and Warnham.

For **train times** phone the 24-hour phone number 08457 48 49 50 (charged as a local call), although the phone information given is only about 80 per cent reliable. The best website for train times is Railtrack's (at: www.nationalrail.co.uk ; click 'plan my journey'); otherwise try Virgin Trains' nationwide information (at: www.virgintrains.co.uk/); or try www.thetrainline.com

For information on rail disruptions in the UK, at present the best site is www.nationalrail.co.uk/realtime/fs_realtime.htm

Many of the walks in this book use South West Trains and Connex. Their websites are www.swtrains.co.uk and www.connex.co.uk

Note that stations sometimes ignore the existence of connections. Although your desired station may not appear on a station departure board (or even in the printed timetable) it may still exist. A free map entitled 'Rail services around London & the South East' is available at stations.

Note that Thameslink rail stations are sometimes geographically separate from mainline stations – for example, King's Cross Thameslink has its own exit tunnel from the underground, and is situated 200 metres to the east of the mainline station, on the corner of Caledonian and Pentonville Roads.

Bus information is best obtained from Traveline, the new national enquiry service, on 0870 608 2608 (charged at national call rates), which is open daily from 7am to 8pm. It provides detailed information about country buses – or indeed about any buses, coaches, ferries or trains.

Gear needed

Some walkers have boots costing £100 and other fancy gear. I don't. I only take a rucksack if I need to carry my rain gear.

Before the walk, in order to decide what to take, I look up Ceefax on BBC1 (pages 401 and 403) and Teletext on ITV (page 154) to see how wet and cold it is likely to be (or you can call the relevant Weathercall or Weather Check regional number in the phone directory). Many websites will also give you a five-day weather forecast for the main cities in the UK. Try for instance: www.bbc.co.uk/weather/

The clothes and equipment I can select from include: a lightweight poncho mac (£5) that packs away small; a pair of waterproof trousers (£11) – these make a crucial difference to the enjoyment of a long walk in the rain; a small rucksack (£8); a fleece jacket (£28); scarf, hat (sunhat in summer) and gloves; a pair of boots for walking (try the excellent Shoefayre chain, tel 020 8951 4028); and, if it's very wet weather, you may need gumboots or at least a change of socks.

The cheapest camping shop I could find which does credit card phone orders is Tarpaulin & Tent Ltd, PO Box 350, Esher, KT10 8DZ (tel 020 8873 3797); another camping mail order supplier is Culverhouse in Hertfordshire (tel 01923 252 805); Millets is dearer and does not do mail order, but has various branches, such as 98 High Street, Putney, SW15 (tel 020 8788 2300); dearer still is the YHA Adventure Shop (tel 0115 950 5172). Shopping around ensures success.

Finding the way

I have often witnessed people getting lost trying to follow walk books, so I have tried to make the directions in this book very full – but the principal changes of direction (when the direction is other than straight on, or following a clear or signposted footpath) are in *italics*, in case you are able to manage just with these.

My hope is that, if some landmarks have changed since the publication of this book, if the footpath signs have been vandalised, or if there is snow on the ground and no clear path, there will often be enough other information to keep you on the right track. But do get the book's updates before you set off, from www.walkingclub.org.uk

Exclamation marks in square brackets – **[!]** – mean 'pay careful attention to the route here, it is easy to go wrong'. Numbers in square brackets – eg. **[7]** – refer to numbers on the maps.

For direction finding, it is reassuring, although not essential, to have the relevant Ordnance Survey (OS) Landranger map. This can increase your options for detours and short cuts.

Maps can be bought from Edward Stanford (12-14 Long Acre, WC2), ordered over the phone by credit card (tel 020 7836 1321), or online (www.stanfords.co.uk). If you want to buy all the main OS maps used in this book, ask for numbers 165 to 167, 176, and 186 to 188. Other maps used less often are numbers 152-155, 164, 168, 175, 177-179, 189 and 196-199. Explorer maps with orange covers are now available for all the walks in this book.

Their scale is 4 cm to 1 km (as opposed to 2 cm to 1km for Pathfinder maps) so you would need many more maps – they are probably an unnecessary luxury. Useful, however, is a plastic folder to keep your map dry, with the folder attached to a cord which can be slung round the neck. You can make one of these, or they can be bought for about £5.

This book often gives the direction in degrees, when a change of path is encountered, so it might be worth buying a compass with a swivelling rim marked in degrees (about £7) – although most novice walkers checking drafts of this book managed perfectly well without referring to either a map or a compass. (A compass is, however, particularly useful for Walk 17, as an aid to finding your way through Woburn Abbey's park.) It is surprising how many people find a modern compass difficult to understand. One simple way to use it is as follows. If in the book it says 'head for the edge of the wood, your direction 250 degrees', swivel the outer arrow until it lines up with 250, and then turn the whole compass, keeping it level, until the inner casing's arrow is on top of the compass needle's north (the red or black end of the needle, not the white). Proceed in the direction now shown by the outer arrow.

Some compasses have a millimetre ruler along one edge, which is useful – 2mm on the OS Land-ranger map equals 100 metres on the ground. I therefore often give approximate distances in metres – as a tall person, I find that 80 of my paces are about 100 metres, on level

ground. (Incidentally, where the directions say 'in xx metres', this always means 'in a further xx metres from the previous spot where the number of metres was stated'.)

For winter walks, it might be worth taking a tiny (one AA battery) torch in case you get lost in the dark. Walks 50 (Yalding to Borough Green), 51 (Henley to Pangbourne) and 52 (Princes Risborough to Wendover) always seem to end up in the dark. You may want the added safety of wearing bright-coloured clothes on these walks. When walking on roads, it is usually best to walk on the right so as to face the oncoming traffic.

Lyme Disease

Fact Sheet No 15 from the Ramblers Association (available for an SAE to their address on page 413) warns that Lyme Disease is 'a rare illness but has recently started to occur more frequently and the risk of infection cannot be ignored. It is caused by bacteria carried by ticks. People who walk in the countryside though rough vegetation (especially bracken) are most at risk especially from April to October'.

Symptoms often include a red blotch or a circular rash several centimetres across in the bite area. This appears between a week and a month after the bite occurred. Flu-like symptoms such as tiredness, aching and fever might occur. Serious neurological problems or chronic arthritis can also develop in some cases.

The Ramblers' Association state that the tick needs to be attached to the body for at least 24 to 36 hours in order to transmit the bacteria, but recent research (at: www.dis.strath.ac.uk/vie/LymeEU) suggests that the bacteria may be transmitted in less time than this.

Remove the tick with tweezers or long nails, and wash hands and the bite area afterwards with disinfectant. Grasp the tick firmly as close to the skin as possible and pull it steadily out without squashing it. Others recommend covering the tick with petroleum jelly for 10 to 15 minutes, then, using tweezers, to remove it and to clean the site with a disinfectant. (For a tick remover costing about £5 pounds including p&p, phone SJH Products on 01948 780 624. 'It removes the entire tick,' they claim, 'so reducing the risk of disease transmission.') Take the tick with you to the doctor for analysis.

To guard against ticks keep your trousers tucked into your socks or wear insect repellant. Examine your body for ticks in the backs of the knees and groin, under the arms and on the scalp.

In Britain it seems that 30 per cent of ticks carry the *Borrelia burgdorferi* bacterium which causes the disease. The hotspots are areas where deer are common, such as the New Forest, Exmoor, Richmond Park, Scotland and Thetford Forest, but evidently the infected ticks can be found elsewhere.

A year later, despite antibiotics, Angela Knight was still not sure whether all her symptoms would eventually disappear.

An article in New Scientist (October 9th 1999) suggested that it is pheasants which mainly carry the parasite in the UK and that if the rearing of pheasants in artificially high numbers for shooting were banned then Lyme Disease 'would almost certainly disappear from the UK within a year'.

Other problems

Previously walks have been affected by the Foot and Mouth crisis and by severe flooding. For information at such times, call DEFRA's Helpline on 08459 335577 or the Environment Agency's Floodline on 0845 988 1188. See also their websites at, respectively, www.defra.gov.uk and www.environment-agency.gov.uk.

Volume 2

The Saturday Walkers' Club (see next few pages) have devised and written a new walking guide with 30 new walks, all an hour's train journey from London. The book will follow the style and format of this one, but also including more short options, round walks, and photos. It has its own separate walking groups set up, also part of the Saturday Walkers' Club.

So if you like this book, do look out for its sequel in the shops, e-mail walks@alberyfoundation.org for more information/ordering, or check recent information on the website: www.walkingclub.org.uk

Saturday Walkers' Clubs

For those who would like to try – at their own risk – the popular, self-organising Saturday Walkers' Clubs (which are independent of *Time Out*), simply choose one of the clubs described below.

Find out the time of the train that most nearly matches (*before or after*) the starting time suggested in this book. In the rare instance when the train *before* is scheduled at exactly the same time difference from the suggested time as the train *after*, take the later train. For the exact train times – both outwards and for the return – and for any recent walk updates, see www.walkingclub.org.uk; for any last minute changes, train news, engineering works etc, see the site, or e-mail walks@alberyfoundation.org. The outward train times can also be found in *Time Out* magazine's Sports section (with a smaller selection in the Around Town section and with the Drawing, Writing and Photography Walk in the Books section).

Club walkers are required to have a copy of this book. So as to share Network Card reductions with fellow walkers, meet up 15 minutes before the departure time, in the advance ticket queue (these tend to be shorter queues where you can nevertheless buy tickets for the same day) or, if there isn't an advance ticket queue in evidence, then in the main ticket office's ticket queue furthest to the right-hand side or in its single file queuing system. If you are late, it is a worthwhile risk to buy a Network Card cheap day return ticket from a machine, on the assumption that you will find fellow walkers on the train who have a Network Card. Club walkers tend to congregate for the journey in whichever seems to be the middle carriage of the train.

The categories that follow replace those in earlier versions of this book.

If there are more than 25 people on any of these walks, consider splitting into slow and fast groups to avoid overwhelming the lunchtime pub; or consider trying one of the other clubs another week. It is also quite acceptable to set your own pace and go apart, if you find at any stage that the group that day, or individuals within it, are not suited to your mood. There are no leaders.

Main / Nature

The Main Walk is the most popular walk, and the one on which the chart on page 13 is based. It is for people wishing to share their interest in tree, bird and wild flower identification. Turn to the chart. For example, if you were planning to go walking on Saturday July 28th in the year 2007, the Nature Walk for that week is Walk 30.

Vigorous

For those wanting to join the Vigorous Walk (a fairly fast pace), turn to the chart on page 15 to see which number chart walk it would be for the Saturday of your choice and add one. For example, if you were planning to go walking on Saturday July 28th in the year 2007, the chart walk for that week is Walk 30. Your Vigorous Walk would therefore be 30 plus 1 – Walk 31.

Relaxed

For those wanting to join the Relaxed Walk (a less fast pace), turn to the chart on page 15 to see which number chart walk it would be for the Saturday of your choice and subtract one. For example, if you were planning to go walking on Saturday July 28th in the year 2007, the chart walk for that week is Walk 30. Your Walk would therefore be 30 minus 1 – Walk 29. This walk also has an interest in identifying trees and birds. At present it tends to set out earlier than the times suggested in this book. Normally catch the train closest to one hour before the time given. But if the time given is before 9.30am (but not before 9am) then catch the train closest to 30 minutes before the time given. If the time given is before 9am, however, simply catch the same train as the other walks.

Creative

This Drawing, Writing & Photography Walk is for people willing to stop for half an hour to do their artistic thing, maybe sharing the results later – it's the walk I most enjoy going on. Turn to the chart on page 15 to see which number chart walk it would be for the Saturday of your choice and add two. For example, if you were planning to go walking on Saturday July 28th in the year 2007, the chart walk for that week is Walk 30. Your Walk would therefore be 30 plus 2 – Walk 32. As of 2005, this group is dormant, but could be started up again by an enthusiast.

Midweek

The club also run some midweek day walks (usually on a Wednesday), for those who work at weekends.

In the spring and summer, there are also often midweek evening walks in London, run by members of the club. For details of these, and the day walks above, check the website at www.walkingclub.org.uk

Substitute

If the walk number is impossible any particular week, because of a railway breakdown or for any other reason, club walkers should do the reserve substitute walk, the last walk in the book – Walk 53.

A Final Note

The Saturday Walker's Club is self-organising, and based solely around this book. There are no prescribed leaders, and *all* the information you need is in this publication. You join the club at your own risk, and are simply asked to respect others, and treat them in the manner in which you would expect to be treated. With these simple rules, the SWC has provided years of walking pleasure to many, and we hope it will continue to do so for many more.

Nicholas Albery (Editor)

	2005	2006	2007	2008	2009
Walk 1	1 Jan	7 Jan	6 Jan	5 Jan	3 Jan
Walk 2	8 Jan	14 Jan	13 Jan	12 Jan	10 Jan
Walk 3	15 Jan	21 Jan	20 Jan	19 Jan	17 Jan
Walk 4	22 Jan	28 Jan	27 Jan	26 Jan	24 Jan
Walk 5	29 Jan	4 Feb	3 Feb	2 Feb	31 Jan
Walk 6	5 Feb	11 Feb	10 Feb	9 Feb	7 Feb
Walk 7	12 Feb	18 Feb	17 Feb	16 Feb	14 Feb
Walk 8	19 Feb	25 Feb	24 Feb	23 Feb	21 Feb
Walk 9	26 Feb	4 Mar	3 Mar	1 Mar	28 Feb
Walk 10	5 Mar	11 Mar	10 Mar	8 Mar	7 Mar
Walk 11	12 Mar	18 Mar	17 Mar	15 Mar	14 Mar
Walk 12	19 Mar	25 Mar	24 Mar	22 Mar	21 Mar
Walk 13	26 Mar	1 Apr	31 Mar	29 Mar	28 Mar
Walk 14	2 Apr	8 Apr	7 Apr	5 Apr	4 Apr
Walk 15	9 Apr	15 Apr	14 Apr	12 Apr	11 Apr
Walk 16	16 Apr	22 Apr	21 Apr	19 Apr	18 Apr
Walk 17	23 Apr	29 Apr	28 Apr	26 Apr	25 Apr
Walk 18	30 Apr	6 May	5 May	3 May	2 May
Walk 19	7 May	13 May	12 May	10 May	9 May
Walk 20	14 May	20 May	19 May	17 May	16 May
Walk 21	21 May	27 May	26 May	24 May	23 May
Walk 22	28 May	3 Jun	2 Jun	31 May	30 May
Walk 23	4 Jun	10 Jun	9 Jun	7 Jun	6 Jun
Walk 24	11 Jun	17 Jun	16 Jun	14 Jun	13 Jun
Walk 25	18 Jun	24 Jun	23 Jun	21 Jun	20 Jun
Walk 26	25 Jun	1 Jul	30 Jun	28 Jun	27 Jun
Walk 27	2 Jul	8 Jul	7 Jul	5 Jul	4 Jul
Walk 28	9 Jul	15 Jul	14 Jul	12 Jul	11 Jul
Walk 29	16 Jul	22 Jul	21 Jul	19 Jul	18 Jul
Walk 30	23 Jul	29 Jul	28 Jul	26 Jul	25 Jul
Walk 31	30 Jul	5 Aug	4 Aug	2 Aug	1 Aug
Walk 32	6 Aug	12 Aug	11 Aug	9 Aug	8 Aug
Walk 33	13 Aug	19 Aug	18 Aug	16 Aug	15 Aug
Walk 34	20 Aug	26 Aug	25 Aug	23 Aug	22 Aug
Walk 35	27 Aug	2 Sep	1 Sep	30 Aug	29 Aug
Walk 36	3 Sep	9 Sep	8 Sep	6 Sep	5 Sep
Walk 37	10 Sep	16 Sep	15 Sep	13 Sep	12 Sep
Walk 38	17 Sep	23 Sep	22 Sep	20 Sep	19 Sep
Walk 39	24 Sep	30 Sep	29 Sep	27 Sep	26 Sep
Walk 40	1 Oct	7 Oct	6 Oct	4 Oct	3 Oct
Walk 41	8 Oct	14 Oct	13 Oct	11 Oct	10 Oct
Walk 42	15 Oct	21 Oct	20 Oct	18 Oct	17 Oct
Walk 43	22 Oct	28 Oct	27 Oct	25 Oct	24 Oct
Walk 44	29 Oct	4 Nov	3 Nov	1 Nov	31 Oct
Walk 45	5 Nov	11 Nov	10 Nov	8 Nov	7 Nov
Walk 46	12 Nov	18 Nov	17 Nov	15 Nov	14 Nov
Walk 47	19 Nov	25 Nov	24 Nov	22 Nov	21 Nov
Walk 48	26 Nov	2 Dec	1 Dec	29 Nov	28 Nov
Walk 49	3 Dec	9 Dec	8 Dec	6 Dec	5 Dec
Walk 50	10 Dec	16 Dec	15 Dec	13 Dec	12 Dec
Walk 51	17 Dec	23 Dec	20 Dec	20 Dec	19 Dec
Walk 52	24 Dec	30 Dec	29 Dec	27 Dec	26 Dec

Nature Walk dates

	2010	2011	2012	2013	2014	2015	2016
Walk 1	2 Jan	1 Jan	7 Jan	5 Jan	4 Jan	3 Jan	9 Jan
Walk 2	9 Jan	8 Jan	14 Jan	12 Jan	11 Jan	10 Jan	16 Jan
Walk 3	16 Jan	15 Jan	21 Jan	19 Jan	18 Jan	17 Jan	23 Jan
Walk 4	23 Jan	22 Jan	28 Jan	26 Jan	25 Jan	24 Jan	30 Jan
Walk 5	30 Jan	29 Jan	4 Feb	2 Feb	1 Feb	31 Jan	6 Feb
Walk 6	6 Feb	5 Feb	11 Feb	9 Feb	8 Feb	7 Feb	13 Feb
Walk 7	13 Feb	12 Feb	18 Feb	16 Feb	15 Feb	14 Feb	20 Feb
Walk 8	20 Feb	19 Feb	25 Feb	23 Feb	22 Feb	21 Feb	27 Feb
Walk 9	27 Feb	26 Feb	3 Mar	2 Mar	1 Mar	28 Feb	5 Mar
Walk 10	6 Mar	5 Mar	10 Mar	9 Mar	8 Mar	7 Mar	12 Mar
Walk 11	13 Mar	12 Mar	17 Mar	16 Mar	15 Mar	14 Mar	19 Mar
Walk 12	20 Mar	19 Mar	24 Mar	23 Mar	22 Mar	21 Mar	26 Mar
Walk 13	27 Mar	26 Mar	31 Mar	30 Mar	29 Mar	28 Mar	2 Apr
Walk 14	3 Apr	2 Apr	7 Apr	6 Apr	5 Apr	4 Apr	9 Apr
Walk 15	10 Apr	9 Apr	14 Apr	13 Apr	12 Apr	11 Apr	16 Apr
Walk 16	17 Apr	16 Apr	21 Apr	20 Apr	19 Apr	18 Apr	23 Apr
Walk 17	24 Apr	23 Apr	28 Apr	27 Apr	26 Apr	25 Apr	30 Apr
Walk 18	1 May	30 Apr	5 May	4 May	3 May	2 May	7 May
Walk 19	8 May	7 May	12 May	11 May	10 May	9 May	14 May
Walk 20	15 May	14 May	19 May	18 May	17 May	16 May	21 May
Walk 21	22 May	21 May	26 May	25 May	24 May	23 May	28 May
Walk 22	29 May	28 May	2 Jun	1 Jun	31 May	30 May	4 Jun
Walk 23	5 Jun	4 Jun	9 Jun	8 Jun	7 Jun	6 Jun	11 Jun
Walk 24	12 Jun	11 Jun	16 Jun	15 Jun	14 Jun	13 Jun	18 Jun
Walk 25	19 Jun	18 Jun	23 Jun	22 Jun	21 Jun	20 Jun	25 Jun
Walk 26	26 Jun	25 Jun	30 Jun	29 Jun	28 Jun	27 Jun	2 Jul
Walk 27	3 Jul	2 Jul	7 Jul	6 Jul	5 Jul	4 Jul	9 Jul
Walk 28	10 Jul	9 Jul	14 Jul	13 Jul	12 Jul	11 Jul	16 Jul
Walk 29	17 Jul	16 Jul	21 Jul	20 Jul	19 Jul	18 Jul	23 Jul
Walk 30	24 Jul	23 Jul	28 Jul	27 Jul	26 Jul	25 Jul	30 Jul
Walk 31	31 Jul	30 Jul	4 Aug	3 Aug	2 Aug	1 Aug	6 Aug
Walk 32	7 Aug	6 Aug	11 Aug	10 Aug	9 Aug	8 Aug	13 Aug
Walk 33	14 Aug	13 Aug	18 Aug	17 Aug	16 Aug	15 Aug	20 Aug
Walk 34	21 Aug	20 Aug	25 Aug	24 Aug	23 Aug	22 Aug	27 Aug
Walk 35	28 Aug	27 Aug	1 Sep	31 Aug	30 Aug	29 Aug	3 Sep
Walk 36	4 Sep	3 Sep	8 Sep	7 Sep	6 Sep	5 Sep	10 Sep
Walk 37	11 Sep	10 Sep	15 Sep	14 Sep	13 Sep	12 Sep	17 Sep
Walk 38	18 Sep	17 Sep	22 Sep	21 Sep	20 Sep	19 Sep	24 Sep
Walk 39	25 Sep	24 Sep	29 Sep	28 Sep	27 Sep	26 Sep	1 Oct
Walk 40	2 Oct	1 Oct	6 Oct	5 Oct	4 Oct	3 Oct	8 Oct
Walk 41	9 Oct	8 Oct	13 Oct	12 Oct	11 Oct	10 Oct	15 Oct
Walk 42	16 Oct	15 Oct	20 Oct	19 Oct	18 Oct	17 Oct	22 Oct
Walk 43	23 Oct	22 Oct	27 Oct	26 Oct	25 Oct	24 Oct	29 Oct
Walk 44	30 Oct	29 Oct	3 Nov	2 Nov	1 Nov	31 Oct	5 Nov
Walk 45	6 Nov	5 Nov	10 Nov	9 Nov	8 Nov	7 Nov	12 Nov
Walk 46	13 Nov	12 Nov	17 Nov	16 Nov	15 Nov	14 Nov	19 Nov
Walk 47	20 Nov	19 Nov	24 Nov	23 Nov	22 Nov	21 Nov	26 Nov
Walk 48	27 Nov	26 Nov	1 Dec	30 Nov	29 Nov	28 Nov	3 Dec
Walk 49	4 Dec	3 Dec	8 Dec	7 Dec	6 Dec	5 Dec	10 Dec
Walk 50	11 Dec	10 Dec	15 Dec	14 Dec	13 Dec	12 Dec	17 Dec
Walk 51	18 Dec	17 Dec	22 Dec	21 Dec	20 Dec	19 Dec	24 Dec
Walk 52	25 Dec	24 Dec	29 Dec	28 Dec	27 Dec	26 Dec	31 Dec

Walk 1

Henley-on-Thames (round walk)

Temple Island, Hambleden & the Great Wood

Length 15.8km (9.8 miles), 4 hours 30 minutes. For the whole outing, including trains, sights and meals, allow 7 hours 50 minutes.

OS Landranger Map No.175. Henley-on-Thames, map reference SU 764 823, is in **Oxfordshire**, 10km north-east of Reading.

Toughness 2 out of 10.

Features Route-finding is easy on this mainly flat walk along the Thames, or up on the wooded geological terrace above it. The walk starts in Henley (famous for its rowing regatta in late June or early July) and goes along the Thames towpath, with rowing instructors on bikes shouting instructions to their crews, past Temple Island with its neo-folly, to the 250-metre footbridge over the weir at Hambleden Mill, where canoeists practise in the stormy waters. From there it is northwards to the suggested lunchtime pub in the well-preserved hamlet of Hambleden, which has a huge church out of all proportion to the population. After lunch, the walk for the next 2.5km is through the Great Wood, the endlessness of which gives an inkling of how most of Britain must once have been. From the village of Fawley with its church and mausoleum, the walk returns to Henley and its many tearooms, past the manor of Henley Park, along the Oxfordshire Way.

Shortening the walk You could get a bus back to Henley from Mill End (there are about three buses each hour) or a taxi from the pubs in Hambleden or Fawley.

History Henley, with its 300 listed buildings, is said to be the oldest settlement in Oxfordshire – a Roman grain store and skeletons of 97 supposedly unwanted children were excavated at **Mill End** in 1911.

Fawley Temple, the neo-folly on Temple Island, is maintained by the Henley Regatta on a 999-year lease. It was built by James Wyatt in 1771 for a local landowner, Sambrooke Freeman, and has Etruscan-style murals inside.

Hambleden Mill, mentioned in the *Domesday Book*, was used for grinding corn until 1955.

Hambleden means 'village in a valley'. Charles I spent one night at the manor house in Hambleden whilst fleeing from Oxford to St Albans in 1646.

St Mary the Virgin Church, Hambleden, has a memorial with alabaster figures representing Sir Cope D'Oyley (who died in 1633), his wife and their ten children – with the children shown carrying skulls if they died before their parents. To the left of the monument is the oak muniment chest used by the Earl of Cardigan in Balaclava, where he led the ill-fated Charge of the Light Brigade in 1854. And to the left of this chest, tucked in an alcove, is a reusable stone coffin. The churchyard contains the grave of the bookseller WH Smith, who became (posthumously) Lord Hambleden.

The village of **Fawley** (Old English for 'clearing') is listed in the *Domesday Book* as having 13 villeins, one cottager and five slaves. In 1086 it was given to a Norman, Herbrand de Sackville, as a reward for guarding his master's estates in Normandy during the invasion of England. The churchyard in Fawley contains a large circular neoclassical **mausoleum** built by John Freeman for his family around 1750.

Saturday Walkers' Club Take the train nearest to **10.05am** (before or after) from **Paddington** Station to **Henley**. You will need to change at Twyford. Journey time 56 minutes. Trains back from Henley run about once an hour.

Lunch The suggested lunch pub is the **Stag & Huntsman** (tel 01491 571227) in Hambleden, which serves gourmet food (for instance garlic snails) from midday to 2pm daily.

Tea The Henley tea place I suggest is **Crispins** (tel 01491 574232) in Hart Street, opposite the church, which serves cream teas and other food until 7pm daily. My second preference is the upstairs Asquiths **Teddy Bear Tearoom** (tel 01491 571978) in New Street (last serving 5pm daily, 4pm Sundays; closed Mondays). Other tea places include **Old Rope Walk** (tel 01491 574595) in Hart Street (open until 5.30pm daily) or **Henley Tearooms** (tel 01491 411412) in Thames Side, facing the river (open until between 5pm and 6pm daily).

WALK DIRECTIONS

[1] [Numbers refer to the map.] Coming out of **Henley Station**, turn right, your direction 305 degrees, and walk 50 metres to the main road. Here, *with the Imperial Hotel opposite you, turn right on the road*, your direction 45 degrees, towards the Boats for Hire place 125 metres away. Continue along the riverfront, with the River Thames to your right. In 250 metres, *cross the bridge*.

40 metres from the other end of the bridge **[2]**, *turn left on a footpath signposted Thames Path, then take the left fork* beside the tollgate, on a tarmac lane with a concrete bollard guarding its centre, your direction 350 degrees.

In 55 metres, you come to the river and turn right, with the river on your left-hand side, your direction due north.

After 1.75km **[3]**, you come to a footpath sign to the right. You may wish to go through the wooden swing gate and take a detour of 100 metres here to see **Remenham's St Nicholas Church**, but only the exterior and churchyard can normally be seen, as its doors are kept locked nowadays because of burglaries.

Back on the towpath, in 500 metres you pass **Temple Island**. Keeping to the towpath for 1.25km (or, by the large white mansion on the other side of the river, heading east across the often very wet open land), you reach **Hambleden Lock [4]**, a cluster of houses with street lamps. Here you pass through a wooden kissing gate and, in 70 metres, *go to the left over the far*

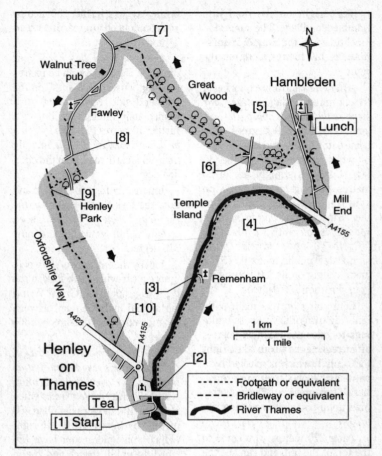

[7]

Walnut Tree
pub

Great
Wood

Hambleden

[5]

Lunch

Fawley

[8]

[6]

Mill
End

A4155

[9]

Henley
Park

Temple
Island

[4]

Oxfordshire Way

[3]   Remenham

A423

[10]

A4155

1 km

1 mile

Henley
on
Thames

[2]

Tea

- - - - - Footpath or equivalent
- - - Bridleway or equivalent
River Thames

[1] Start

lockgates (following the public footpath sign). Then you are on a tarmac path on the right-hand side of the lockhouse, your direction 60 degrees, which, in 30 metres, leads to the footbridge *over the weir*.

At the other end of the bridge go straight on, staying on the tarmac and bending left with it to the A4155, with Old Millgate Cottage, **Mill End**, on your left-hand side. *Turn right on the A4155*, your direction 115 degrees. In 30 metres, by the bus stop, *turn left, on a road signposted Hambleden*, heading northwards.

In 350 metres, where a car road goes right to Rotten Row, take a signposted *footpath through a wooden kissing gate on the right-hand side of the road, to go straight on*, parallel to your previous road. Continue for 600 metres, heading for a stile about 20 metres to the left of the small flint bridge ahead. Cross this stile, cross the earth road and continue on over another stile, heading towards **Hambleden Church**. In 500 metres, the path comes out by a metal kissing gate beside another small bridge.

Turn right on the road into Hambleden village. The suggested lunchtime pub, the **Stag & Huntsman**, is 140 metres along on the right.

After lunch and any exploring of the church and village, *retrace your steps on the village's approach road*, your direction 210 degrees. You come to the bridge and kissing gate by which you first entered the village. Continue straight on, in 20 metres passing cottage no.57 on your right-hand side, and in a further 35 metres, *you come to the main road. This you cross, slightly to the left, to go up a tarmac path*, signposted public footpath **[5]**, a metal railing on its left-hand side, your direction 195 degrees.

Continuing on this main path, ignoring turn-offs, you pass buildings to enter the wood. 25 metres after entering the wood, take a right fork uphill (which is marked by a white arrow on a tree), your direction 190 degrees, and keep to this main uphill path, following the white arrows.

After 270 metres, you come to the top of the hill, and can see the Thames ahead of you. In 15 metres, ignore a path to your right, to carry straight on downwards, your direction 240 degrees.

In a further 160 metres, and *20 metres before the edge of the wood* (marked by a wooden swing gate at the exit) *turn right on a bridleway*, your direction 285 degrees.

Your route is straight on thereafter: in 165 metres, you ignore a fork to the right and, in 75 metres, another going very sharp right, and, in 125 metres, you leave the wood to continue along a tree-lined bridleway. In a further 250 metres, you come out on to an earth car road T-junction.

Turn right on this road, your direction 350 degrees, in 55 metres passing houses nos.6 and 7 on the left-hand side. Ignore a left turn immediately after these, but in a further 10 metres **[6]**, *turn left, on a bridleway marked HA37a*, initially a car-wide earth road, your direction 285 degrees.

Ignore the fork to the left and take the fork that keeps *near the right-hand edge of the field*, soon steeply uphill, your direction now 310 degrees.

Just by the entrance of the wood, ignore a car-wide earth fork to the right, to go uphill into **Great Wood** (as marked on the OS map) between dilapidated posts, your direction 305 degrees.

Your route is more or less straight on through this wood, ignoring all turn-offs, for over 2km, following relatively clear *white arrows* when in doubt. But in more detail: In 450 metres, by a way off to the right (which you ignore) you have finished the uphill stretch and are on the terrace land above the Thames. Ignore more ways off (in 210 metres, one to the left; in a further 45 metres, one to the right; and, in a further 120 metres, one to the left). But then, in 90 metres, *bear left for 30 metres, following white arrows on trees*, before regaining your direction (now 325 degrees).

In 250 metres, ignore a fork sharply to the left and, in 85 metres, one to the right. When the wood ends on your left-hand side, continue on the path, a fence on your left-hand side and **Roundhouse**

Farm (so marked on the OS map) visible ahead of you, slightly to the left. This is a potentially muddy stretch of narrow bridleway, particularly in winter.

In 500 metres, you come to a bench by **Orchard House**, from which you have a fine slopes view.

In 90 metres, continue on along an earth driveway. In 100 metres **[7]**, you come out on to *a tarmac road by the Round House, where you turn left*, your direction 190 degrees.

Keep to this road, ignoring all turn-offs, for 1.5km. In 270 metres, you pass (what was) the **Walnut Tree** pub, **Fawley Green**, on your right-hand side. In a further 220 metres, ignore a left turn signposted to Marlow. At the next T-junction in 280 metres, keep on, following the sign to Henley. In 80 metres, you come to the lychgate of **St Mary the Virgin Church**, **Fawley**, which is worth a visit.

Continuing on the road, ignore a footpath to the left by a house called Mavoli. In a further 250 metres **[8]**, *take a public footpath signposted earth road to your left, by a yellow water marker* (H100/2), your direction 145 degrees.

You pass Five Gate House on your left-hand side. In a further 175 metres, you pass the gates of Homer House on your left-hand side, and, in a further 40 metres, you come to an out-of-place set of overwrought high iron gates by a field on your right-hand side, and just to their right, by a three-armed footpath sign, you *take the footpath branching right* from your road. Your new direction is 230 degrees, with llamas

in the field on your left-hand side. In 140 metres, you go through a metal barrier, cross a tarmac road and continue straight on uphill, a field fence on your left-hand side, crossing over a stile in 15 metres. In 80 metres, you go over a stile and onwards. In a further 140 metres, you go over another stile and a car lane (reservoir gates on the left) then over a stile to continue on.

In a further 200 metres, *go over a stile to a T-junction with a gravel car road* **[9]**, *where you turn left*, your direction 150 degrees.

Thereafter, it is more or less *straight on all the way to Henley.* But in more detail: In 300 metres, you come to a white post announcing 'Henley Park Private', but you carry straight on. In 270 metres, you pass **Henley Park**, a white manor with a crescent driveway on your left-hand side. In a further 100 metres, you leave the car road, which bears left, to go through a wooden kissing gate, marked **Oxfordshire Way** (a metal fieldgate on its left-hand side), to continue straight on, through a pig farm, a field fence on your left-hand side, your direction 150 degrees.

In 450 metres, go through a metal kissing gate to continue straight on, your direction 165 degrees (the path may not be clear at this point and may well be cow-churned). In 500 metres, you pass through a metal kissing gate to go down into the wood.

In 430 metres, ignoring all other ways off, *you come out on the A423* **[10]**, *and turn left*, your direction 135 degrees.

In 50 metres, you pass the **Old White Horse** pub on your left-hand side. In a further 250 metres, at the roundabout, keep straight on. Then, in 220 metres, you come to New Street, with the **Teddy Bear Tearoom** on the corner, but keep straight on, along Bell Street. In 100 metres, *turn left into Hart Street*.

There, in 75 metres, you pass the **Old Rope Walk** tea place on your right-hand side, and, in a further 35 metres, Café Rouge on your left-hand side, and, in a further 40 metres, the (usually locked) **Parish Church of St Mary the Virgin**.

10 metres beyond the end of the church, before the bridge and across the Red Lion Hotel, you come to **Crispins** on your right-hand side, the suggested tea place.

After tea, turn right out of Crispins and immediately right again, along the riverfront, retracing your morning steps – in 50 metres passing **Henley Tearooms** on your right-hand side – to the Boats for Hire, where you bend right with the road, taking the second left to **Henley Station**, by the Imperial hotel.

Walk 2

Wanborough to Godalming

Watts Gallery & Chapel

Length 11.5km (7.2 miles), 3 hours 30 minutes. For the whole outing, including trains, sights and meals, allow at least 8 hours 40 minutes. In winter, it's best to be on your way from Watts Chapel by 3pm, so as to reach Godalming before dark.

OS Landranger Map No.186. Wanborough Station, map reference SU 931 503, is in **Surrey**, 6km west of Guildford.

Toughness 2 out of 10.

Features Note that there are no trains to Wanborough on a Sunday. You may need gumboots – one path in particular is like a flood drain in wet weather. I was enchanted by this walk – first by Wanborough Manor and its tiny church, then by lunch in Compton at the tea shop with its 50 varieties of tea, but, above all, by Watts Gallery and Chapel, the monuments left by Mary Fraser-Tyler to honour her husband George Frederick Watts, a Victorian painter and sculptor, 'England's Michelangelo' ('though that's a bit rich,' I overheard one visitor comment). Later, the walk is along the River Wey followed by tea in Godalming, an ancient town, the centre of which is virtually car-free.

Shortening the walk The hourly Godalming-Guildford No. 46 bus service from the Watts Gallery car park goes at about 10 to the hour (not on Sundays). The Watts Gallery staff may also be able to help you call a taxi.

History Wanborough ('bump-barrow') may be named after a Bronze Age burial site on the Hog's Back. A Wanborough manor and chapel are said to have belonged to King Harold's brothers and to have been ransacked by William the Conqueror's army marching up the Hog's Back. The present **manor house** was built in the eighteenth century. During the war it was a training centre for 'the members of the European Resistance Movement who served behind enemy lines in special operations, facing loneliness and unknown dangers in the cause of humanity'.

Wanborough Church, one of the smallest in Surrey, was rebuilt by the Cistercian monks of Waverley Abbey in 1130, and was visited by pilgrims passing along the Pilgrim's Way.

When Surrey County Council wanted to build a by-pass through the Watts property, Mary Watts refused, then finally agreed – if the **bridge** were to be designed by Lutyens. The original railings of oak, cantilevered out, had to be replaced by metal safety rails, but the two crosses over the Pilgrims Way have been renewed.

Watts Gallery, Down Lane, Compton (tel 01483 810 235, admission free). In summer the gallery is open 2pm-6pm on Monday, Tuesday, Friday and Sunday; 11am-1pm and 2pm-6pm on Wednesday and Saturday. In winter (October 1st to March 31st) the gallery is open 2pm-4pm on Monday, Tuesday, Friday and Sunday; 11am-1pm and 2pm-

4pm on Wednesday and Saturday. It is closed, apart from Thursdays, on Good Friday, Christmas Eve and Christmas Day. This gallery is how all galleries should be: wonderfully intimate, eccentric and on a human scale. There's a vast sculpture of Watts' lifelong friend Tennyson, allegorical paintings of Time, Death and Judgement, political paintings of hunger, and some coy nudes. Watts' most famous painting is the Rossetti-like portrait of the actress Ellen Terry, called 'Choosing' (would she give up the stage for him?). Their marriage, in 1864, is said never to have been consummated. He was 46 and she was 17.

Watts Chapel was the project of his second wife, Mary, who designed this Celtic, Byzantine, art nouveau masterpiece without previous architectural or building experience, inspired by the Home Arts and Industries Association, and with the help of local villagers. Every interior surface is covered with what Mrs Watts called 'glorified wallpaper' – angels and seraphs made out of gesso, a material which her husband used when rheumatism meant he could no longer handle wet clay. He is buried in the cloister behind the chapel. Admission is free, and it's open dawn to dusk daily.

Godalming is thought to mean 'field (-ing) of Godhelm' (the putative first Saxon to claim the land). On the north side of the churchyard of St Peter and St Paul in Godalming, there is the **Phillips Memorial Cloister** designed by Thackeray Turner in 1913, with a garden by Gertrude Jekyll. Phillips was the chief wireless operator of the Titanic, who went down at his post on the ship.

Saturday Walkers' Club Take the train nearest to **9.40am** (before or after) from **Waterloo** Station to **Wanborough**, changing at Guildford. Journey time 50 minutes. There are trains back from Godalming several times an hour. Journey time 45 minutes.

Lunch The suggested lunch place is the **Tea Shop** (tel 01483 811 030; groups should phone in advance), Compton, open 10.30am to 5.30pm daily (closed Xmas to New Year). Eat there early if possible, before looking around Watts Gallery, as there tend to be queues at lunch. It offers good food at reasonable prices and sells about 50 varieties of tea. There is no room for large groups – an alternative would be the **Withies Inn** (tel 01483 421158) Withies Lane, Compton, later on in the walk, which serves food daily from midday to 2.30pm (groups of 15+ should book).

Tea The suggested tea place is **Pizza Piazza** (tel 01483 429 191), 78 High Street, Godalming, open daily till 11pm. Also, **Bay Tree** (tel 01483 427 337), just a few doors down, offers a good selection of tea and light supper items.

WALK DIRECTIONS

[1] [Numbers refer to the map.] Turn left out of **Wanborough Station** and, in 80 metres, *turn right on the main road*, in a southerly direction for 200 metres, to the junction where the main road continues, but you *turn left on to Flexford Road*.

In 50 metres, opposite Little Hay Cottage, **[2]** *take the public footpath to the right*, your direction 160 de-

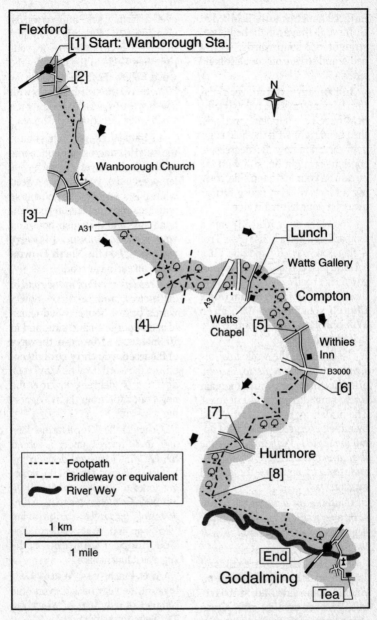

Flexford

[1] Start: Wanborough Sta.

[2]

N

Wanborough Church

[3]

A31

Lunch

Watts Gallery

Compton

[4]

A3

Watts
Chapel

[5]

Withies
Inn

B3000

[6]

[7]

Hurtmore

[8]

- - - - - Footpath
- - - Bridleway or equivalent
~~~~ River Wey

1 km

1 mile

End

Godalming

Tea

grees, over a stile with a metal fieldgate on its left-hand side, into a field where you go on a potentially very muddy path between fences

towards a little concrete bridge and stile visible some 200 metres away.

Go over the stile and continue on, your direction 150 degrees, for a further 200 metres, to the field hedge. Go through the gap in the hedge and straight on, southwards, with a hedge and stream on your left-hand side.

In 400 metres, you go over a stile, then left for 30 metres, following the field edge on your left-hand side, then bend right with the field edge, your direction now 215 degrees, to continue straight on, still with the stream on your left-hand side, passing a black wooden house further away on your left-hand side.

You reach a car road **[3]** with a footpath sign and a house (Pear Tree Cottage) on your left-hand side. *Turn left on to this road and, in 150 metres, go left on a road with a footpath sign*, directing you to **Wanborough Church**, your direction 100 degrees. **Wanborough manor house** is to the left of the church.

To continue the walk *take the signposted bridleway just to the south of the church* (back towards the main road), your direction 140 degrees. The bridleway is soon overarched by mixed evergreens, and goes uphill *to the A31. With care, cross the first carriageway, slightly to the left, and straight on*, over the second carriageway.

Continue on a signposted footpath, over a stile, your direction 130 degrees, *along the left-hand edge of the field*.

In 300 metres go over a stile and straight on, still with the hedge on your left-hand side, and, in 100 metres, go over another stile. Cross over a farm track, and over the next stile, to go half right across a small field, your direction 135 degrees, to a stile near a cow barn. 15 metres brings you to another stile, and then

over a farm track; and onwards, your direction 130 degrees. Continue beyond a golfcourse tee on your right-hand side to the fence by the wood. Follow the fence to the left for 30 metres to wooden gateposts with a yellow arrow, where you enter the wood, your direction 165 degrees.

In 100 metres, you come out of the wood to go across the golfcourse (golf balls coming at you from your left-hand side), your path between white posts, and exit the golfcourse with huts and chickens on your left-hand side and a largish house on your right, *to a T-junction* **[4]** *where you turn left* on the **North Downs Way**, an earth car road.

Keep left at a fork in the road in 20 metres, and carry on downwards past a house called Questors on your left-hand side, and in 100 metres, at a crossing of the ways in the wood, you carry straight on, still on the North Downs Way, your direction 65 degrees, towards the noise of traffic from the A3, ignoring ways off.

Go under the A3 on a tarmac lane and, in 40 metres, under a second **bridge** (this is the one designed by Lutyens), to keep straight on, ignoring forks to the left, to a road T-junction. *Turn left on the road, and, in 40 metres, turn right*, at a sign saying 'Tea Shop and Watts Gallery'. The **Tea Shop** in **Compton** is the suggested lunch place.

After lunch, visit **Watts Gallery**, at the very back, beyond the complex of buildings of which the Tea Shop forms part.

To get to Watts Chapel (which is recommended), *return to the car road and turn left along it*, your direction 230 degrees. In 160 metres, you pass Coneycroft Farm on your left-hand side and, in 100 metres beyond the farm, you reach the cemetery, with **Watts Chapel** up above you on the hillside.

Coming out of the cemetery, turn right and, in 100 metres, turn right at the footpath sign – just before Coneycroft Farm – and keep to the right edge of the barn beyond the farm; following the path left at the end of the barn, then through a metal fieldgate and, in 10 metres, right through another metal fieldgate, following arrows.

You are now on a concrete road, your direction 110 degrees.

Ignore ways off. At the end of the concrete, in 200 metres, by a fieldgate, *turn right over a stile, and then ignore the stile immediately on your left, to continue on a path due south*. In 40 metres, you have the edge of the wood on your left-hand side and, in 120 metres, you *go over a stile and left, still with the edge of the woods on your left-hand side*, your direction 145 degrees.

In 135 metres, you go over a stile and into the wood, straight on, ignoring ways off. In a further 450 metres, you come out of the wood by a footpath sign, *on to a tarmac lane* **[5]**. *Turn left. In 10 metres, you turn right*, past some houses on your left-hand side (one of them is called Waterhaw), your direction now 200 degrees.

You pass the **Withies Inn**, a sixteenth-century pub. At the main road, the B3000, called *New Pond Road, go straight over (slightly to the right)* and continue on a lane called The Avenue, fringing the wood on its right-hand side, your direction 200 degrees.

In 250 metres **[6]**, *take the first right, an unsignposted bridleway*, to go into the wood, due west, on a car-wide earth road.

[!] *In 30 metres, ignore the blue bridleway arrow to the right in 30 metres, but, in a further 5 metres, fork right (away from the house drive) on a mud track. In a further 10 metres, take the bridleway to the left*, between hedges, running parallel to the track, your direction 220 degrees.

You pass a house on your left-hand side in 80 metres, and your way merges again with the farm track, to carry straight on, your direction 220 degrees.

In a further 125 metres, *at a white fieldgate* (with a large old ash tree on the left-hand side of the gate) instead of going straight on uphill to the wood 400 metres away, *turn right*, just before the gate, on a clear path, with the field hedge now on your left-hand side, your direction 265 degrees.

In 120 metres, follow the path as it bends sharp left to go due south, with the field hedge still on your left-hand side, and a fence on your right-hand side.

At the top of the field in 350 metres, turn right, and keep the edge of the wood on your left-hand side, on a footpath going due west.

In 380 metres, turn right with the path for 15 metres, and then left again, to continue in your previous direction, now 215 degrees, into the wood on a wide path.

In 120 metres, you pass a large house on your right-hand side, and, 200 metres past it, you come out into its driveway and go straight on between houses – with Broomfield

Manor on your right-hand side. 100 metres past this manor, *you come to the main road, ignoring a yellow marked footpath alternative uphill to your left* **[7]**, *and go straight over on to another bridleway*, your direction 250 degrees.

200 metres down this path (which is like a flood drain in wet weather) you *go straight across another car road on to another path*, your direction 220 degrees, soon between wooden fences on both sides.

After 250 metres, you come to the end of the fence on your left-hand side, and carry straight on downwards (ignoring a left turn).

In a further 60 metres, *at a T-junction, go left*, following a blue bridleway arrow, due south. *Then in 15 metres, ignore a yellow arrow footpath uphill to your left* (which goes off at 130 degrees) to *keep on due south, still downwards, along a wide path*.

In 450 metres, you pass a drystone wall on your right-hand side, with a lovely mansion house with varied window styles beyond it. *Just past this house* **[8]**, *turn left on a tarmac lane*, your direction 145 degrees.

In 80 metres, you go through a wooden swing gate (a wooden fieldgate and the entrance to Milton Wood on its right-hand side). In 150 metres, go through a metal barrier, now alongside the **River Wey**.

In 500 metres, go through another metal barrier. In 40 metres, *1 metre before the start of a tarmac road, follow the signpost right*, marked 'Public Footpath to Godalming', your direction due south.

In 75 metres, you go over a concrete bridge, straight on. In 15 me-tres, *turn left under the pylons*, your direction 140 degrees, with the River Wey on your right-hand side.

In 30 metres, you *pass under more pylons and fork left*, your direction 170 degrees.

In 40 metres, continue to the left, your direction 100 degrees, *alongside the River Wey on your right-hand side*.

In 120 metres, you again go under pylons; and do so again in 55 metres.

In 120 metres, by a bench, yours becomes a tarmac path. In 55 metres, you cross the stream on a bridge. In a further 280 metres, you cross a bridge with scaffolding pole railings. In 5 metres, you go through a metal barrier, *across an entrance drive to offices on your right-hand side, and straight on*, with the stream still on your left-hand side.

In 65 metres, *at a tarmac road, go right*, your direction 170 degrees. In 20 metres, *go under the railway line. 10 metres after the bridge, fork right, on a signposted public foot-path*. In 110 metres, having kept parallel to the road, you cross the river on a wooden bridge with wooden railings.

In 35 metres, you are *back on the main Borough Road, going straight on*. In 65 metres, by the entrance to the Church of St Peter and St Paul, *go left up Church Street* (which is a car road made up of bricks), signposted 'To the High Street', your direction 125 degrees.

Going uphill, in 130 metres, *turn left into the High Street*, **Godalming**. In a further 140 metres, you come to the suggested place to have tea, **Pizza Piazza** at no.78.

Coming out of Pizza Piazza after tea, *retrace your steps to the church* – in other words, turn right into the High Street. In 140 metres, by the Old Town Hall, turn right, down Deanery Place, to go back down to the church – *but then straight on, to pick up a passageway leading to the station*, again straight on. Once you are at **Godalming Station**, go under the subway for trains back to London.

Walk 3

Netley
to Botley

Southampton Water
& the River Hamble

Length 14km (8.7 miles), 4 hours
15 minutes. For the whole outing,
including trains, ferry, sights and
meals, allow 9 hours 45 minutes.
Allow an extra 30 minutes in summer if visiting the Netley Chapel
centre and the Manor Park farm.

OS Landranger Map No. 196.
Netley, map reference SU 464 086, is
in **Hampshire**, 5km south east of
Southampton.

Toughness 1 out of 10.

Features I much prefer this walk
which replaces the Dunbridge to
Romsey walk that appeared in previous versions of this book. The
walk goes down through the Royal
Victoria Country Park, past the
Netley Chapel, down to the shore at
Southampton Water, with a dra-
matic view of the vast Fawley oil
refineries opposite. Then the way is
along the stony beach for a couple
of kilometres (or, for part of the
way, parallel to the beach, in and
out of the scrub woodland if preferred) followed by an inland path
through the woods and Hamble
Common to the ferry in the delightful village of Hamble. The Warsash
Ferry (tel 01489 572840) returns to
Hamble every ten minutes or so and
costs 75p per person, with room for
12 people maximum (closed Christ-

mas week). On the other side of the
river, the walk continues up alongside the River Hamble, with its ma-
rinas for yachtsmen and mudflats
for birds – every variety from Grey
Herons and Kingfishers to
Redshank and Lapwing (binoculars
are worth bringing). Lunch is in
Lower Swanwick. Then it is up the
other side of the river and through
woodlands and fields to Manor
Farm, an open farm run for visitors
by the council, with its own tearoom
(in summer). The route ends in a
pleasant footpath called Lovers'
Lane over a stream and up into
Botley, where there is a fine tea
room. It is then a kilometre along
the main road to the station, with a
good pub opposite the station.

Shortening the walk Take one
of the hourly trains (seven days a
week, summer and winter) from
Bursledon station after lunch, either via Southampton or Fareham.
Or much earlier in the walk, you
could get one of the regular buses
from Hamble (Nos. 16 or 16a) to
Netley station or to Southampton
town centre.

History Netley Chapel (tel 023
8045 5157) in the Royal Victoria
County Park was at the centre of the
Royal Victoria military hospital that
opened in 1863 and was demolished
in 1966. It now houses an exhibition
and a shop and allows visits to the
top of the tower. But it is only open
from about April to October.

    Manor Farm (tel 01489 787055)
with its wheelwright, blacksmith's
forge and tea-room, is only open
Monday to Friday from Easter to
October 31st (till 5pm); from November 1st to Easter (and during
February half-term) open on Sun-

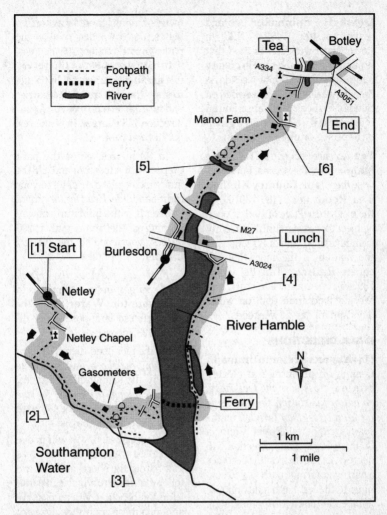

Key:
- - - - Footpath
▪▪▪▪ Ferry
━━ River

Botley

Tea

A334

Manor Farm

[5]

[6]

End

A3051

M27

Lunch

Burlesdon

A3024

[1] Start

Netley

[4]

River Hamble

Netley Chapel

N

Gasometers

[2]

Ferry

Southampton
Water

[3]

1 km

1 mile

day only (till dusk). The building of
the parish church next to the farm
started in 1282. The church was damaged by a tree that fell in the 1700's.

Saturday Walkers' Club Take
the train nearest to **8.15am** (before or after) from **Waterloo** Station to **Southamton Central** that
will allow at least 8 minutes to
change for Netley, your morning's
destination (I normally buy a cheap

day return to Netley, which ticket
inspectors seem to accept, despite it
not being entirely correct.) Journey
time approximately 1 hours 37 minutes. Return from Botley (trains run
at 25 minutes past each hour on
Saturdays) changing at Eastleigh
if you want a faster train. You can
also go via Fareham and Havant at
30 minutes past each hour from the
far platform at Botley, if you miss
the Basingstoke direction train.

Lunch The **Spinnaker** pub and restaurant (tel 01489 572123) in Lower Swanwick serves food that is slightly above average in quality and price, until 2.30pm weekdays, 3pm on weekends. It is crowded on Sundays so book in advance, and on other days as well if you are a group of 10 people or more.

Tea An early tea can be had at the **Manor Farm** in season, but otherwise there is the **Country Kitchen Tea Room** (tel 01489 789161) in the pleasant village of Botley, open 'subject to weather' until 5pm daily (Sundays until 4pm only). Opposite the station is the more-than-adequate **Railway Inn** (tel 01489 799746), open until late daily, and serving food from 6pm on weekdays and all day at weekends.

WALK DIRECTIONS

[1] [Numbers refer to the map.] Coming off platform 2 at **Netley Station**, *cross over the footbridge, go out of the station the other side for 20 metres, then turn left* on the road signposted Royal Victoria Country Park, your direction 145 degrees. In 120 metres this becomes a narrower tarmac path as you continue to the left-hand side of house number 30, past a 'No Cycling' sign, soon with a steep wooded valley below to your right-hand side.

200 metres down this narrower path, *turn right on a tarmac road*, your direction 235 degrees, past No. 4 Fermain on your left-hand side. In 100 metres, near a notice board with a map of the Royal Victoria Park, *take the middle fork road*, slightly to your left, bearing a 'No Entry' sign, your direction 165 degrees, marked 'Police and Residents Only'. In 120

metres, having ignored ways off, go between two wooden post on the path, your direction 205 degrees, with the tower of Netley Chapel visible ahead to your south. In 65 metres, go through a wooden barrier and *turn left on a tarmac road*, your direction 145 degrees. In 60 metres, *take a right fork*.

In 80 metres, enter the park proper, with a tearoom and YMCA hut (which opened in 1940) to your right-hand side. *Head for the chapel*, due South, with a miniature railway running parallel to your path. In 200 metres, you come to the **Netley Chapel**.

From the front of the chapel, head straight on for 140 metres to **Southampton Water**, down the path between lampposts, your direction 235 degrees.

At the pier head there **[2]**, *turn left along the shore*, and, in 80 metres, by the sailing club entrance, *continue along the beach for the next two kilometres*, to the pier with pipes and crane in the distance.

From the beach, you will in due course see ways up into the trees that border the shore, and you can follow paths there which run parallel to the beach, if you so prefer – although these are rather zigzaggy paths that can be difficult to follow.

On reaching the oil refinery fencing, you will need to leave the beach up steps. You then follow the concrete path next to the fence, along the shoreline.

Go under the pier with its oil pipelines. *At the end of the fence, continue on for 100 metres (ignoring earlier ways off to the left, including one marked 'Solent Way').*

You then go half left off from the beach up a wide grassy path, your direction 65 degrees. In 20 metres you come to a Hamble footpath post (marked 'Hamble Common Circular Trail' and with a green arrow) at a T-junction and *go left* on the footpath **[3]**, your direction 330 degrees, back towards the oil refinery.

In 40 metres, ignore a kissing gate on your right-hand side. In 25 metres, by a post, bear right with the path over an open grassy area, your direction 20 degrees. In 50 metres, the path is again clear and you follow the trail signs.

In 70 metres, cross over a two-plank footbridge. In 45 metres, *fork left* with the main trail. In a further 80 metres, *by a three-armed footpath sign, go right* (signposted 'Hamble Village'), your direction 175 degrees.

Stay with this main trail, in 150 metres walking on wooden boards to the tarmac road. *Turn left* on this road, your direction 20 degrees.

In 40 metres, turn right, on a footpath signposted 'Hamble Village', your direction 120 degrees.

In 80 metres, ignore a 'Hamble Point' sign to the right. In a further 85 metres, keep straight on over wooden boards, then bear left, now beside the **River Hamble**.

In 50 metres, bear left with the path and over boards. Ignore a kissing gate to your left-hand side and keep going through a copse, even when the path thins.

In 150 metres, go over boards past a noticeboard and *follow the car track onwards*. In 40 metres, *by the No Entry signs for cars, turn right downhill* on the road passing Oyster Cottage

and other **Hamble Village** houses, your direction 75 degrees.

By the water's edge, *go left towards the white metal pier*, at the end of which you catch the **Warsash Ferry**.

Once over on the other side, *turn left* and *follow the riverside causeway, heading north, for three kilometres*, through the mudflats, ignoring ways off and passing the **Crableck Marina [4].** (To get through this boatyard, turn right just before a large shed on your right-hand side – a shed with its side facing the water painted blue – going on a path alongside it. Carry on for 30 metres beyond the shed and between the yachts, until you reach the main road through the centre of the yard, where you turn left. In 60 metres go the left of the one-storey building with a veranda which has a flagpole to its right-had side, and go through a wooden gate to rejoin the riverside path.)

At the end of the three kilometres, you come *to a tarmac road where you go left*, your direction 340 degrees, still along the riverbank and soon passing Swanwick Shore Public Hard to your left-hand side. Ignore ways off and you come in due course *to the main road, the A27*, where you cross the road and *turn left*, your direction 305 degrees. In 200 metres you come to the **Spinnakker** pub and restaurant on the other side of the road, the suggested lunchtime stop.

Coming out of the pub, continue on the main road. In 150 metres, go over the bridge, and then under the railway bridge. (Those ending the walk here can turn left to **Bursledon Station**, opposite the

Yachtsman's pub.) The main walk *turns right here, up Blundell Lane*, your direction 50 degrees.

In 250 metres, where the tarmac public road goes left, carry straight on, through **Brixedone Farm** (a boat repair yard). Soon you go *under the motorway and you immediately fork right over a stile*, your direction 50 degrees, to keep alongside the shore. In 80 metres go over another stile.

In 80 metres, pick up the footpath *forking half left diagonally across the field*, your direction 20 degrees. In 200 metres, you are now beside a channel of water to your right-hand side, one that links up with the river, your direction 330 degrees. In 80 metres, go through a potentially muddy hedge gap and in 50 metres, *go over a stile on your right-hand side, to cross the channel* **[5]**.

At the other side, in 40 metres, *at the T-junction, turn right*, your direction 140 degrees. In 90 metres, *by a fork, turn left on a path*, your direction 50 degrees, following the yellow ringed wooden posts and occasional signs for Manor Farm.

In 600 metres, you path opens up and there is now a car wide track, with a wooden fence and field to your right hand side, your direction 30 degrees.

Ignoring ways off, in one kilometre you come to Manor Park Farm, to bear leftwards through the farm (ignoring the right fork with the large Manor Park sign), downhill, marked 'No Unauthorised Vehicles', past a post with blue and yellow bands, your direction 25 degrees, with buildings to your right hand side. Soon you pass the fieldgate to the **Manor Farm** entrance on your

right-hand side, and then the wheel-wrights on your left-hand side, and soon a pond on your right-hand side, to emerge *through a wooden gate onto an earth road* **[6]**. **St Bartholomew Church**, the old Botley parish church, is to your right-hand side. You *head left* on this road, your direction 15 degrees.

In 60 metres, y*ou come to a T-junction with the tarmac road, where you go left*, your direction 300 degrees. In 120 metres, just 30 metres past the Old Rectory on your right-hand side, *go right on a signposted footpath*, your direction at this point 30 degrees.

In 300 metres, ignore a metal kissing gate to your right-hand side. In a further 50 metres, *turn half right* on a broad way across fields, your direction 65 degrees.

This brings you through an old metal kissing gate and in 75 metres down onto a tarmac road. *You turn right for 10 metres, and then left on a footpath* through a metal kissing gate, your direction 35 degrees, on a path that is known as **Lovers' Lane**.

In 40 metres, you cross water on a concrete bridge with metal railings and go up the other side; in a further 100 metres coming *to a road, where you turn right*, heading eastwards.

In 30 metres, *turn left by the 'No Entry" sign*, to go northwards, on Church Lane, into the centre of **Botley**, reaching the main road in 200 metres.

On the other side of the road is the **Country Kitchen Tea Rooms**, the recommended tea stop.

Coming out of the tea room, turn left on the main road, the A334, your direction 105 degrees, and follow it for 1km over the stream and past Botley Mills Craft and Business Centre on your left-hand side, to **Botley Station**, ignoring the A3051 right turn. By the station is the **Railway Inn**, a possible tea stop.

The near platform is for Basingstoke, Winchester and London, although the far platform can get you to London via Fareham.

Walk 4

Pangbourne
(round walk)

River Thames &
Crays Pond

Length 13.5km (8.4 miles), 4 hours. For the whole outing, including trains and meals, allow 7 hours.

OS Landranger Map No.175. Pangbourne, map reference SU 633 766, is in **Berkshire**, 8km west along the Thames from Reading.

Toughness 3 out of 10.

Features Pangbourne and its companion Whitchurch, on the other side of the Thames, are delightful villages, spoilt only by too much traffic. Passing on a tollbridge over the river, you come to St Mary's Church, with the route continuing along part of the Thames Path National Trail (which opened in 1996) past Coombe Park, to a wood with views down to the Thames. From there it is up through a nature reserve and Great Chalk Wood, to a pub for lunch by Crays Pond. After lunch you pass Great Oaks manor, now a preparatory school, and go through woods and fields back down to a tearoom in Pangbourne.

Shortening the walk The first third of the walk is perhaps the most interesting – you could catch a bus at lunchtime from the pub in Crays Pond back into Pangbourne.

History The earliest mention of **Pangbourne** is in a Saxon charter of 844 as Paegingaburnam (meaning 'streams of sons of Paega'). In 1919, DH Lawrence stayed in Pangbourne, commenting: 'Pleasant house – Hate Pangbourne – Nothing happens.' Kenneth Grahame, author of *The Wind in the Willows*, lived in Church Cottage, Pangbourne.

An act of parliament in 1792 allowed the building of **Whitchurch Toll Bridge**, to replace the ferry. The ten proprietors were given the right to charge tolls – for instance, one halfpenny for every sheep and lamb. The present iron bridge of 1902 replaces two previous wooden tollbridges.

St Mary's Church in Whitchurch dates from the twelfth century. St Birynius is said to have landed at the ferry crossing at Whitchurch and, on seeing how fine the place was, decided to build a church there.

Saturday Walkers' Club Take the train nearest to **9.30am** (before or after) from **Paddington** Station to **Pangbourne**. Trains run back about twice an hour. Journey time about one hour.

Lunch The suggested lunchtime pub is the **White Lion** in Crays Pond, which serves large portions at reasonable prices but can be slow. Food times are: midday-2pm Monday to Friday; midday-2.30pm Saturday and Sunday (groups of 30+ people should phone 01491 680 471 to book).

Tea The suggested tea place is **The Ditty** (tel 0118 984 3050) 11 Reading Road, Pangbourne, open Monday to Saturday until 5pm, which also serves hot food. There is also

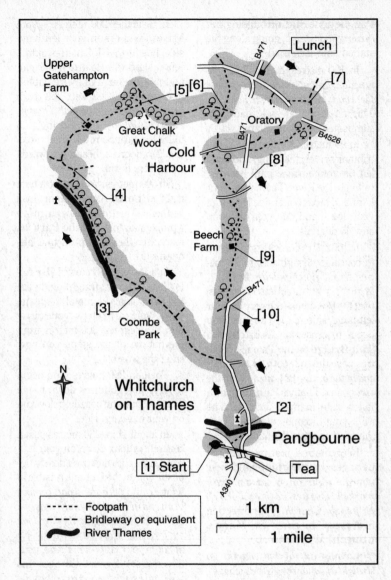

Upper Gatehampton Farm

[5] [6]

Great Chalk Wood

Oratory

Cold Harbour

[7]

B471

B4526

[8]

[4]

†

Beech Farm

[9]

[3]

Coombe Park

B471

[10]

Whitchurch on Thames

[2]

†

Pangbourne

[1] Start

†

A340

Lunch

B471

Tea

N

----- Footpath
- - - - Bridleway or equivalent
▬▬▬ River Thames

1 km

1 mile

the **Copper Inn** on the A329 just before the station, or the nearby **George Inn**.

WALK DIRECTIONS

[1] [Numbers refer to the map.]
From the platform, go down into the tunnel and turn left towards the carpark and way out. On exiting

Pangbourne Station building, *you turn right downhill*, going along the station approach road.

In 100 metres, *at the A329 T-junction, Shooters Hill, cross over the road to continue straight on*. This is a gravel car-wide road and a signposted public footpath.

In 90 metres, you cross a small tributary river, the Pang, and bend left on your tarmac path between railings, the River Thames on your left-hand side, Waterside House on your right-hand side, your direction now 45 degrees.

In 100 metres, cross a gravel road to continue straight on. In 25 metres, *at a T-junction with the B471, turn left*, your direction 55 degrees, past the Boathouse Surgery on your left-hand side. In 110 metres, you begin to cross the **Whitchurch Toll Bridge** on the Thames. 5 metres past the tollbooth *at the other end of the bridge* **[2]**, *turn left* on the signposted Thames Path, through a fallen gate marked 'Private. The Mill', your direction due west, with the river on your left-hand side.

In 65 metres, just past Church Cottages on your right-hand side, you *go right on a tarmac path marked Thames Path and 'Footpath to the Church'*, your direction 5 degrees, to enter **St Mary's Church, Whitchurch**.

Coming out of the church, go straight ahead through the lychgate, and straight on, now a tarmac road, your direction 20 degrees. In 100 metres, this road, having bent to the right, leads you *back on to the B471, where you turn left*, your direction due north, in 35 metres passing the Greyhound pub on your right-hand side.

In a further 200 metres, ignore Manor Road off on your left-hand side. In a further 155 metres uphill, ignore Hardwick Road to your right, and in a further 110 metres uphill (having veered left with the road) *turn left on a signposted Thames Path bridleway* ('to Goring, 3.5 miles'), a tarmac road, your direction 275 degrees, heading towards Long Acre Farm.

In 500 metres, you ignore a turn right to **Long Acre Farm**. In a further 350 metres, you begin to get a proper view of **Coombe Park** (as marked on the OS map) on your left-hand side.

In a further 650 metres **[3]**, follow blue arrows straight on (to the left-hand side of a metal fieldgate) down wide earth steps, your direction 325 degrees. 300 metres from the bottom of the steps you now enter the wood.

Then, in 250 metres, you begin to have fine glimpses down to the Thames, running parallel below you on your left-hand side.

In about 1km, 230 metres past a concrete pillbox down on your left-hand side, with a church nearly opposite you on the far bank (visible in winter), and *with the wood coming to an end in 5 metres, and a massive beech tree overhanging the way, look out for a stile visible 20 metres steeply uphill to your right-hand side*, your direction 20 degrees. Go over this stile and exit the wood over the stile into **Hartslock Nature Reserve**, the enterance an iron gate clearly marked 'Nature Reserve', which covers 11 acres of chalk grassland.

Now continue on the path ahead, your direction 60 degrees, over a small hill from which there are fine upstream views of the river. In 200 metres, you exit the reserve by a gate **[4]** and *turn left on an earth road*, your direction 285 degrees.

In 150 metres, *turn right on a tarmac road*, which is also a bridleway, your direction 30 degrees, heading uphill. In 400 metres, *go left over a stile*, your direction 70 degrees. In 20 metres, go over another stile, to pass wooden stables on your right-hand side. *In another 35 metres, just before a wooden fence and private garden, turn left*, your direction 335 degrees, with a wooden fence on your right-hand side and a lorry trailer [for now] on your left.

Go over a stile and on between fences, your direction now 70 degrees, and with **Upper Gatehampton Farm** (so marked on the OS map) on your right-hand side.

In 40 metres, go over another stile, look for the pole with the yellow arrow, to *turn left slightly back on yourself, going round a high earth pile to regain your path*, your direction 65 degrees. 40 metres beyond, just after crossing an earth farm track leading into the lorry park, head half left *diagonally across the field* towards a stile visible by the far woods, 230 metres away, your direction towards it 60 degrees.

Once over the stile into **Great Chalk Wood** (so marked on the OS map) *go half right on to a footpath*, your direction 85 degrees, in 35 metres ignoring a turn to the right. In a further 150 metres, just after a yellow arrow on a post on your right-hand side, cross a grassy car-wide track **[5]** to continue.

In a further 125 metres, *at a T-junction with another footpath, go right* (virtually straight on), your direction now 115 degrees. In 45 metres, *turn left downhill* (by hinges for a missing swing gate) following a blue bridleway arrow, your direction 5 degrees.

In 105 metres, at a multiple path junction *at the edge of the wood, go straight on, soon veering right*, your direction 100 degrees.

In 400 metres, you need to go through a wooden swing gate marked **Bottom House Farm** and, in 100 metres, just past a wooden horse stable on the right-hand side in a paddock, you go through another wooden swing gate, in 80 metres passing the farm cottage on the left-hand side, to continue on the tarmac driveway, your direction 75 degrees.

In 450 metres, and *5 metres before a bridleway up to the right, go left uphill* **[6]** *on a footpath* signposted as GH18, your direction 35 degrees. (This footpath comes just before a large house visible uphill on your left-hand side, in case you've gone too far.) In 15 metres, follow the yellow waymark, keeping right of an old gate (ignoring another possible fork off to the left). Continue up, with the fence on your left-hand side, bending round with the path (the large house is now off to your right) until you settle down to a path between hedges, your direction 20 degrees. In 160 metres, at the end of the hedges, continue on a clear path across fields, your direction 345 degrees. In 250 metres, you come out under a wooden barrier *on to a tarmac road, the B4526, and turn* *right*. (You may need to walk up and over an earth barrier across the path).

In 500 metres, you come to a road junction, with a pond on your right-hand side. The **White Lion pub**, **Crays Pond**, is just off to your left. This is the suggested lunchtime stop.

Coming out of the pub on to the tarmac road, turn left and, in 50 metres, *turn left on to the B4526*, your direction 130 degrees. In 225 metres, ignore a footpath to the right (by a sign for Oratory Preparatory School). In a further 90 metres (10 metres beyond a metal barrier on your left-hand side), *you come to a footpath sign to your left, and take this path*, following a white arrow on a tree, into the wood, your direction 80 degrees.

In 300 metres, there is a suggestion of a fork, with the right fork leading to a heap of rubble. You go left, your direction 30 degrees. In 70 metres, *you come on to a T-junction path where you turn right*, your direction 135 degrees; *in a further 20 metres, you come on to a car-wide earth road* **[7]**, *where you turn right*, your direction 200 degrees – in 40 metres passing the heaped rubble on your right-hand side.

Keep straight on, *in 200 metres crossing the B4526 to take the public signposted footpath straight on*, signed Whitchurch Hill, your direction 200 degrees.

In 30 metres, you come to an open space with a concrete base. Cross this, in 40 metres picking up your onward path straight on (the middle of two possible paths), its direction 235 degrees (the one to the left being a mossy green path, heading 110 degrees).

In 40 metres, you ignore a fork to the left to keep on, now with a rusty metal fence on your right-hand side. In 180 metres, you ignore another fork to the left to continue with the metal fence. You can briefly see to your right the rather fine timber-framed building that is now **Oratory Preparatory School**, although it is still sometimes marked as Great Oaks on the OS map.

The original path has overgrown, so turn left into the open field until the end, then walk through a gap to the right of a metal gate into a wide path. It will lead out on to a car-wide farm track, your direction now due west.

In 100 metres, you pass a timber-framed house on your right-hand side. In a further 40 metres, *cross the B471, to continue on a tarmac road opposite*, your direction 260 degrees.

In 125 metres, you pass under mini-pylons. In a further 200 metres, ignore a bridleway to the right by Laurel Cottage. Then in 85 metres, by the entrance to Coldharbour Farm on the right-hand side, *go over a stile on your left-hand side and take the left fork footpath, signposted Whitchurch* (GH20), your direction 165 degrees, heading left of the clump of trees and between the two houses visible in the distance ahead.

In 300 metres, go over a stile to continue through the next field. In 245 metres, you go through a narrow gate and come out on a tarmac road opposite a house called Pine Paddock **[8]**.

Turn right on the road, your direction 250 degrees. In 75 metres, *turn left by the footpath sign*, still to

Whitchurch, down an earth car-wide road, your direction 175 degrees, through the gate of Boundary Farm. (It is labelled 'no bikes')

In 100 metres, you pass the farm, guided by yellow arrows, to *take a footpath, no.27, to the left into the wood* (25 metres before a hay barn) your direction 145 degrees.

In 85 metres, keep left by an uprooted tree and, in a further 15 metres, take the pronounced right-hand fork, following a white-painted arrow up on a tree (the left fork clearly leads, in 10 metres, to a private garden), your direction 235 degrees. Your onward path may not be very clear, but keep roughly in the middle of this strip of wood, heading southwards.

In 140 metres, at a T-junction (a 'Private. Danger' sign on the tree 15 metres ahead of you), go left, your direction 145 degrees, now going near the left-hand edge of the wood.

In 135 metres, leaving the wood via a metal kissing gate, continue with the field fence on your right-hand side, your direction here 170 degrees.

In 100 metres, go through a wooden swing gate and over the driveway, with **Beech Farm** (so marked on the OS map) **[9]** on your right-hand side, to follow the wooden fence on your right-hand side, your direction 195 degrees.

In 35 metres, go through a metal kissing gate (with a metal fieldgate In a further 260 metres, go through another metal kissing gate (also with a metal fieldgate on its left-hand side) to continue with the field edge on your right-hand side.

In 500 metres, by a mini-pylon on your left-hand side, go through a metal swing gate and keep to the right. In 75 metres, you come down on to the B471 [10] with Stoneycroft House on your right-hand side. Continue on the B471 into Pangbourne, your direction 190 degrees.

In 40 metres, you pass Whitchurch war memorial on your right-hand side and a short distance beyond this you can pick up the path parallel to the B471 and above it, on the left-hand side, for 350 metres. Then you are on the B471 itself, downhill. You pass the interesting **Modern Art Gallery** on your right-hand side (tel 01189 845893; they are open to walkers dropping in and are tolerant of muddy boots) retracing the morning's start of the walk as far as the tollbridge. In 750 metres, you again cross the tollbridge.

Keep on the main road, to pass Pangbourne Working Men's Club on your right-hand side, and go under the railway bridge. *50 metres past the bridge, turn left by the George Hotel.* In 35 metres you come to **The Ditty** on your left-hand side, the suggested tea place.

Coming out of the tearoom, turn right and in 125 metres you come to the **Copper Inn**. *Here you turn right on the A329.* In 145 metres, just before the bridge, *turn left up the lane* to **Pangbourne Station**. You need platform 2, on the other side, for trains to London.

Walk 5

Great Missenden to Amersham

Through the Chilterns
to Little Missenden

Length 14.25km (8.8 miles), 4 hours 30 minutes. For the whole outing, including trains, sights and meals, allow 7 hours 45 minutes.

OS Landranger Map No.165. Great Missenden, map reference SP 893 013, is in **Buckinghamshire**, 8km north-west of Amersham.

Toughness 3 out of 10.

Features This walk, in the chalk downs of the Chilterns, only 40 minutes by train from London, makes an easy brisk winter outing – although it can be slightly muddy in places. The route takes in woods, fields, four interesting churches and the ancient village of Little Missenden; it comes to a lunch pub by the common in the village of Penn Street; and ends up for tea in Amersham's surprisingly unspoilt Old Town. Then it is a 20-minute walk up through the wood after tea to reach the station.

Shortening the walk You could call for a taxi from any of the pubs en route, whether in Little Missenden, Penn Street or Coleshill. There is an hourly bus from outside the Squirrel pub in Penn Street to Amersham. The walk also passes a bus stop in Coleshill, which has buses every two hours to

Amersham. For details phone Travelline on 0870 608 2608.

From Little Missenden there is a quicker footpath route to Amersham, running parallel to (and about 300 metres to the right of) the A413. This shorter route (4.5km as against the 12km of the suggested route) starts 150 metres beyond the Crown pub in Little Missenden. See the OS map for details.

History The **Parish Church of St Peter and St Paul** in Great Missenden was built mainly in the fourteenth century. It has a marble monument to a certain Lady Boys, for which the sculptor Nicholas Stone was paid £30 in 1638.

St John the Baptist Church, Little Missenden, has a giant thirteenth-century mural to St Christopher carrying the Christ child across the waters. Part of the church was built in the tenth century. The gatepost is in memory of Dunkirk in 1940.

All Saints Church in Coleshill is a neo-Gothic church designed by Street, whose work was praised by Betjeman. The stone for the church, built in 1866, was brought by river to Windsor and then by cart.

The building of the **Parish Church of St Mary**, Amersham, started in the early 1100s. The window glass is mainly from the nineteenth century.

Saturday Walkers' Club Take the train nearest to **9.55am** (before or after) from **Marylebone** Station to **Great Missenden**. Journey time 42 minutes. Check on whether a combined Travelcard and train ticket would be your cheapest option. Trains back from Amersham to

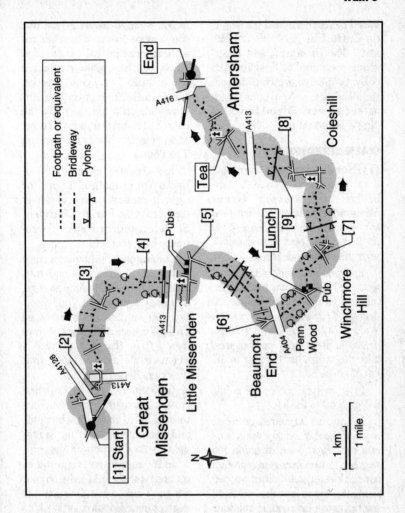

Marylebone run about twice an hour. Journey time 39 minutes. From the same platform you can also get twice hourly direct tubes to Baker Street, if your ticket covers this.

Lunch The recommended lunch-stop is the **Squirrel** pub (tel 01494 711 291) in Penn Street, which serves food from midday to 2pm daily; booking is advised, as is removing boots before entry. An alternative is the nearby **Hit or Miss Inn** (tel 01494 713 109) which has a broader and more gourmet menu but less atmosphere, and serves food from midday to 2.30pm daily; groups of more than six should phone to book.

Slow walkers or late starters should use the **Red Lion** pub (tel 01494 862 876) in Little Missenden, which serves food from midday to 2.15pm daily; groups of more than 20 should ideally phone to book to eat here.

Tea The recommended tea stop is the **Caffé Uno** (tel 01494 729 749) at 27 The Broadway, Old Amersham, open until at least 10.30pm daily; or take your own pick from the other cafés or local pubs – such as the **Saracen's Head Inn** or the **Nag's Head** pub.

WALK DIRECTIONS

[1] **[Numbers refer to the map.]** Coming off the train, cross the footbridge and, *leaving* **Great Missenden Station** *building, turn left*, your direction 20 degrees. *At the T-junction, turn right downhill*, your direction 65 degrees.

In 60 metres, at the next T-junction, the High Street is to the right, but you *go left*, your direction 320 degrees. *In 25 metres, turn right* on Walnut Close, your direction 50 degrees. At the bottom, in 60 metres, take the tarmac path going to the left of house no.18.

In 40 metres, ignore the public footpath off to the left.

In a further 90 metres, *go over a wooden barrier serving as a stile and turn right*, your direction 160 degrees, in 40 metres going through a metal kissing gate (with a wooden fieldgate next to it on the left). In 10 metres, cross the road, to continue straight on, signposted South Bucks Way and public footpath, your direction 165 degrees, with a green open space on your right-hand side.

In 60 metres, a tarmac path begins, with the sign 'Give way to pedestrians'. In 280 metres, you come to Oldham Hall on your left-hand side and a tarmac road **[2]**. *Turn right, heading 160 degrees and, in 30 metres, head for the metal four-armed footpath sign 25*

metres straight ahead of you (the sign may be obscured by a bush; if so, head for a flint wall), *to go left on this tarmac road uphill*, signposted South Bucks Way, your direction 115 degrees. The sign on your left-hand side on a tree says 'To the church'. The first cottage you come to on your left-hand side is called The Pound.

In 210 metres, ignore the South Bucks Way footpath off down to the right, to continue on a bridge over the A413 to the **Parish Church of St Peter and St Paul** – the entrance is to your left.

Coming out of the building, turn right, go up the steps and turn right following the building's edge, and then downwards, your direction 200 degrees. In 20 metres, *go through a metal kissing gate and turn left in the field* towards a pylon visible in the distance, your direction 75 degrees.

In 450 metres, go over a stile and cross a car road with grass down the middle, to go over another stile and continue straight on, gently uphill, your direction 100 degrees.

In 250 metres, go over a stile to continue with the field hedge on your left-hand side, your direction 130 degrees (marked 'Circular Walk').

In 230 metres, you pass under pylons and, in 250 metres, over another stile, straight on, with the hedge on your right-hand side, your direction 100 degrees.

In 160 metres, go over a stile and straight on (ignoring a possible arrow to the left) – there is a metal fieldgate on your right-hand side in 10 metres and a house visible some 250 metres away.

In 100 metres, go over a stile on your right-hand side, your direction now 95 degrees, in 10 metres coming to a garage shed on your right-hand side. 20 metres past this, you come out on a tarmac road opposite Rowen Farm [3] and turn right, still *following the Circular Walk arrow*, your direction 200 degrees.

You pass the flintstone timber-framed Chapel Farm, with lighthouse lamps as décor, on your right-hand side. 15 metres beyond the farm, turn left on a concrete road signposted Circular Walk, your direction 100 degrees.

In 160 metres, veer left downhill with this concrete road, in 120 metres ignoring an earth road forking off to the left. 15 metres later, *ignore a stile and the Circular Walk going off to the left, and bend uphill with your lane, which ceases to be concrete at this point*, your direction now 125 degrees.

In 180 metres, ignore a stile and footpath off to your left and *take a waymarked path right*, 10 metres before a T-junction. This path leads into the wood, with a wire fence to your right-hand side, and leaves the wood by a stile after 60 metres.

Cross the stile and turn right, along an earth road, with the wood on your right-hand side. In 80 metres, at the end of a manure heap, *where the wood begins to jut out, veer right* for 3 metres on an indistinct path, to continue just inside the wood, with the field edge to your left hand side, for 50 metres. This brings you *back to the earth road, where you turn right*, to come, in 15 metres, to a wooden post.

Here, fork left on a car-wide strip between fields, towards the wood on the other side, your direction 130 degrees. In 60 metres, by a wooden post with arrows, go right, with the field edge on your left-hand side, your direction 215 degrees.

In 470 metres, you stay on your way upwards into the wood, past a car-wide wooden barrier, your direction due south. In 200 metres, you come to a crossroads [4] with a sign, 40 metres ahead, saying 'Strictly private. No thoroughfare', and large farm sheds beyond. At this crossing you turn right, on a car-wide earth path, your direction 215 degrees.

In 275 metres, ignore a fork off to the right, to go straight on, still mildly downhill, your direction due south initially.

In 170 metres, by a car-wide wooden barrier, turn right to go on a footbridge over the railway, your direction 200 degrees. From the other side of the footbridge, carry straight on, along a path downhill, just to the left of the first mini-pylon, your direction due south.

In 150 metres, go over a stile to cross the A413, and over a stile the other side, to continue on, parallel to mini-pylons. In 90 metres, cross a streambed on a concrete bridge.

In 140 metres, you go over a stile and *turn left on a tarmac road* to Little Missenden's **St John the Baptist Church**, which is well worth a look inside.

Coming out of the church, turn left, to continue on the tarmac road, in 60 metres keeping straight on, ignoring a car road to the right to Holmer Green; and in a further 15 metres, ignoring Taylors Lane to your left. In a further 85 metres, you come to a sixteenth-century inn, the **Red Lion**.

Continue on, in a further 170 metres passing the front gate of Missenden House on your left-hand side. In a further 25 metres, ignore a stile and footpath on your right-hand side. Then, in 230 metres, you come to the **Crown** pub **[5]** on your left-hand side (serving sandwiches, ploughmans and pies from midday to 2pm Monday to Saturday) – but *5 metres before the Crown pub, turn right on the public footpath and bridleway*, between Jug Cottage and the village hall, your direction 175 degrees, in 55 metres passing Tobys Lane Farm on your left-hand side, then continuing straight on uphill along a bridleway.

In 400 metres, ignore a stile on your right-hand side. In 180 metres, ignore a possible path right (downwards with the wood to its left) and, in 35 metres, ignore a fork to the right (which 10 metres after the fork goes between two wooden posts, its direction 215 degrees).

In a further 100 metres, there is no longer a wood on your right-hand side. 250 metres later, ignore a stile on your left-hand side to bend right with the bridleway, which still runs between hedges, your direction 205 degrees.

In a further 440 metres, you pass under pylons. Then, in 230 metres, you pass under more pylons. In 350 metres, ignore a footpath which you cross, with stiles to the left and right of you.

In a further 250 metres, at a footpath crossing, *take the stile and footpath to your right*, between fields, your direction 250 degrees, your

path parallel to the A404 away on your left-hand side.

In 250 metres, cross a stile and continue on past Finchers Lodge on your left-hand side. 160 metres past this house, you come on to a driveway between houses, leading, in 90 metres, to a tarmac road **[6]** (with the gates of Beamond Lodge ahead of you). *Turn left on this road*, your direction 195 degrees.

In 70 metres, go straight on (at the junction where sharp right goes to Holmer Green). Then, in 50 metres, *cross the A404, slightly to your left, to enter* **Penn Wood** (so marked on the OS map) by a wooden kissing gate, your direction straight on, 155 degrees.

In 55 metres, you come to an oak tree with painted arrows offering a left fork or straight on. Go straight on. In 80 metres, ignore a fork to the right, to follow white arrows straight on. In 850 metres, ignore a fork to the right. 150 metres beyond this, *turn left when you reach the tarmac road and head for the* **Squirrel** *pub*, the suggested lunchtime stop, visible 130 metres to your left (due east from you).

Coming out of the pub, turn left on the car road and, in 40 metres, turn left on the road signposted Winchmore Hill and Amersham. In 30 metres, turn left on a signposted footpath (unless you wish to detour to the **Hit or Miss** pub, in which case continue up the road for a further 100 metres).

Your footpath's direction is due east, with, in 85 metres, a wooden stile (a metal gate to its left). 175 metres straight on beyond the stile, having passed a yard with timber roof frames on your right-hand side, you go over a stile to continue straight on, in 25 metres going under some mini-pylons.

In a further 30 metres, you go over a stile and through a kissing gate on your left-hand side, and follow the fence to your right-hand side. In a further 100 metres, you enter a wood and go straight on, with the edge of the wood nearby to your right, your direction 125 degrees.

In 380 metres, you exit the wood by a metal kissing gate to go half right, your direction 150 degrees, across a field.

In 135 metres, go over a wooden stile and through a metal kissing gate, to go straight on. In 165 metres, you come to a tarmac road, with a bus shelter opposite **[7]**, and *cross the road to continue straight on up an open space* of green grass, keeping the hedge to your left, your direction 145 degrees, parallel to the driveways of houses on your left-hand side.

In 160 metres, you carry on, now on a tarmac road, in a further 100 metres passing the Memorial Hall on your left-hand side.

At **Winchmore Hill**'s *common, turn left and, in 2 metres, turn sharp left again*, going down a road called The Hill, your direction 5 degrees, past the Plough Inn and Windsor Restaurant on your right-hand side.

In 75 metres, *opposite the Methodist Church on your left-hand side, turn right on a signposted footpath*, your direction 80 degrees.

In 135 metres, keep straight on, the field edge on your right-hand side, ignoring a fork downwards to your left.

In a further 180 metres, go on under mini-pylons and keep straight on. Then, in 300 metres, go under main pylons. 125 metres from these, you enter the wood and keep straight on, your path now a car-wide earth track, ignoring all turnings off, your direction due east.

Likewise at the other end of the wood, in 60 metres, ignore all turnings off to keep straight on towards the right-hand edge of a copse, 125 metres ahead across the field.

From there it is 125 metres, on a potentially muddy path, to go over a stile and onwards, your direction 110 degrees, with a wooden fence to your left and blackberries rather too close on your right-hand side. In 200 metres, ignore a path to the left marked by a white arrow to follow the other white arrow straight on over a stile, towards a church visible in the distance, your direction 115 degrees.

In 155 metres, go over a stile to keep on along a gravel drive, in 75 metres going through a white fieldgate, which in 60 metres leads to a tarmac road.

Go left on this tarmac road for 20 metres to enter the church gate and to visit **All Saints Church** *in* **Coleshill**.

Coming out of the church door, *turn left, and exit the churchyard on to a two-lane car road, where you turn left*, your direction 15 degrees. Ignore a left turn in 50 metres by the memorial cross. In 480 metres, you pass a bus stop and Village House on your right-hand side and Coleshill Cottage on your left-hand side. In a further 150 metres, *you come to a multiple junction at which you fork right with the main road, Tower Road*, your direction 45 degrees.

In 40 metres, fork left up a concrete road [8], signposted public footpath, parallel to a driveway to its left, your direction 30 degrees.

In 155 metres, when the concrete ends, fork slightly right to continue straight on, along a path between fences, your direction still 30 degrees. In 50 metres, you pass an elliptical concrete fenced stockade on your left-hand side and, in 15 metres, you go over a stile to continue on, Amersham soon visible below and ahead of you.

In 150 metres from the stile, you go over another, in 45 metres passing under pylons [9] on your path – which has bent slightly to the right – and keeping the field edge on your right-hand side, your direction 60 degrees.

In 155 metres, ignore the field ridge off to your left, to carry straight on, passing under mini-pylons (on the right-hand side of the pole). Continue, your direction 50 degrees, with the bank (leading up to the field above you) on your left-hand side.

In 200 metres, this bank comes to an end and your onward path is somewhat to the left, your direction 10 degrees, *aiming just to the left of the church*.

In 450 metres, go over a stile. Deep in the cutting *below you is the A413. Your onward path is almost straight ahead of you (about 40 metres to your right)*, but to get to it you have to turn left, your direction 255 degrees, with the field hedge on your left-hand side.

In 115 metres, the path leads down to the A413. Cross it to pick up the public footpath visible on the other side (slightly to the right) by the footpath post. Go up the road's embankment, your direction 55 degrees. In 125 metres, cross a stile on your left-hand side, and then go half right, your direction 15 degrees. In 90 metres, go over a stile and, in a further 20 metres, another stile, to come out on a road opposite Amersham General Hospital.

Turn right on this road, your direction 45 degrees, and ignore all ways off. In 220 metres, you pass the Saracen's Head Inn on your right-hand side. In a further 70 metres, you pass the Nag's Head pub on your left-hand side. Then, in 60 metres, you get to a T-junction. Turn right and go 75 metres to the suggested tea place, on the other side of the road, the **Caffé Uno**.

Coming out of the tearoom, turn right and in 100 metres turn right again, picking up the footpath that passes Amersham's **Parish Church of St Mary** on your left-hand side, your direction 15 degrees. In 70 metres, *you come to a tarmac lane and turn right*, with the stream on your left-hand side, your direction 75 degrees.

In 50 metres, you come to a T-junction with a cemetery beyond it. *Turn left, your direction 315 degrees, and, in 30 metres, turn right* on a tarmac path uphill, with the cemetery wall to your right and allotments to your left, your direction 25 degrees.

In 250 metres, you enter **Parsonage Wood** and keep straight on, ignoring all turn-offs and keeping some 25 metres from the edge of the wood and the road on your left-hand side.

In 450 metres, *with the railway bridge visible some 100 metres ahead, take the right fork*, a short cut marked with a yellow arrow on a post, your direction 30 degrees, heading down towards the railway embankment fence.

In 100 metres, *at the fence, turn right* and follow the embankment, your direction 100 degrees, on a tarmac lane with houses standing on your right-hand side.

In 70 metres, *go left under the railway bridge, and turn right for* **Amersham Station**, just 60 metres away. The platform for trains to London is then the one nearest to you.

Walk 6

Liphook to Haslemere

Shulbrede Priory & its woods

Length 15km (9.3 miles), 4 hours 30 minutes. For the whole outing, including trains and meals, allow 6 hours 30 minutes.

OS Landranger Map No.186. Liphook, map reference SU 842 309, is in **Hampshire**, 15km south of Farnham. Haslemere is in **Surrey**.

Toughness 5 out of 10.

Features This walk can be muddy, especially the part after lunch, and has plenty of relatively mild uphill and downhill sections. It is almost entirely through full-grown mixed woods – mainly oak, beech and chestnut trees. After passing Shulbrede Priory in the middle of the woods, you come to the pub and church by the village green in Fernhurst. In the afternoon, you cross streams in the forest, before passing through Valewood Park and up into Haslemere, a town surrounded by beautiful countryside.

Shortening the walk There is an hourly bus service from Fern-hurst (the halfway-mark lunchtime village) to Haslemere (the bus goes from the top of Hogs Hill Road in Fernhurst, along the A286).

History Shulbrede Priory is the remains of a priory for Augustinian regular canons dating from about 1200. It was dissolved in 1536, with the King's Commissioner alleging that 26 whores were found at the priory, and it is now a private house. The prior's chamber, above a vaulted undercroft, contains sixteenth-century wall paintings. The priory is open to visitors by appointment (tel 01428 653 049) and also on the Sunday and Monday of the late May and August bank holidays (admission is about £3).

In Tudor and Stuart times **Haslemere** was a centre for the iron industry. With the coming of the railway in the mid-nineteenth century it became a popular spot for literary people. The poet Tennyson's house, Aldworth, is on the slopes of Black Down where he loved to walk; and George Eliot wrote *Middlemarch* in Shottermill.

The town has an interesting **museum** some way further up the High Street beyond Darleys tearoom. The museum is open 10am to 5pm Tuesday to Saturday, and has a fine explanatory display of local wild flowers in the foyer. Other highlights include an Egyptian mummy showing the toes of one foot and an observation beehive.

Saturday Walkers' Club Take the train nearest to **9.20am** (before or after) from **Waterloo** Station to **Liphook**. Journey time 57 minutes. Get a day return ticket to Liphook. Trains back from Haslemere run about twice an hour. Journey time 52 minutes.

Lunch The suggested lunchtime stop is the **Red Lion** pub (tel 01428 643 112), by the village green at Fernhurst, offering quality home cooking. It serves food until 2.30pm

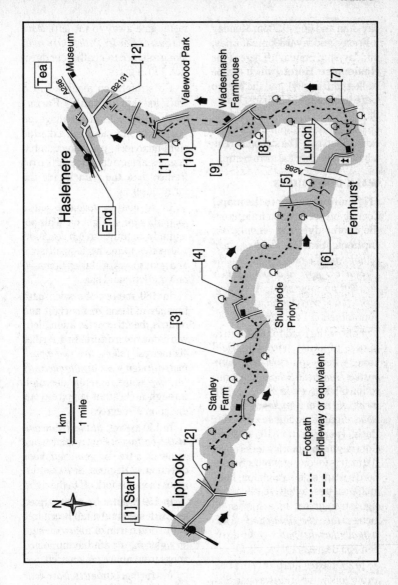

Museum

Tea

[12]

Valewood Park

Wadesmarsh Farmhouse

A286

B2131

[11]

[10]

[9]

[8]

Lunch

[7]

A286

Fernhurst

Haslemere

End

[5]

[4]

Shulbrede Priory

[3]

[6]

Stanley Farm

1 km
1 mile

[2]

N

Liphook

[1] Start

Footpath
Bridleway or equivalent

daily. Groups of more than 20 people should phone to book.

Tea The suggested tea place is **Darnleys** tearoom (tel 01428 643 048) on Haslemere High Street, which closes at 5pm. The easiest

alternative is the **Pizza Express** (tel 01428 642 245) next door, open till at least 10pm daily. The **White Horse Hotel**, also in the High Street, offers reasonably priced food and tea (its serving times are: midday-3pm and 6pm-9.30pm Monday to Friday; midday-9.30pm Saturday; midday-9pm Sunday). There is the **Haslemere Hotel** (which can be walker-unfriendly), and the **Metro Café** (tel 01428 651 535) just before the station. This café is open till 6pm weekdays (5pm Saturdays; closed Sundays). The station is a ten-minute walk from the town centre.

WALK DIRECTIONS

[1] [Numbers refer to the map.] Coming off the London train, cross the footbridge. *On leaving the* **Liphook Station** *building, turn right under the road bridge into the station carpark and immediately turn left up some steps. At the top, turn left and cross the railway bridge*, your direction 140 degrees.

Follow the road for 600 metres to the junction with Highfield Lane, where you *turn left, sign-posted Highfield School*, your direction 50 degrees. In 20 metres [2], *turn right on to a bridleway into the wood*, signposted **Sussex Border Path**, your direction 105 degrees. Go straight on, ignoring forks off, in 100 metres following another Sussex Border Path sign straight on; then, in 230 metres, follow another such sign straight on. In a further 40 metres, *take the right-hand of two virtually parallel paths*, your direction 105 degrees.

In 280 metres, at a post with a blue arrow, follow the bridleway and Sussex Border Path left, uphill, your direction 50 degrees.

In 100 metres, go straight on along a broad track which has come in from behind you on your left-hand side. In another 140 metres, at a three-armed footpath sign (with a

metal gate away to the left), *leave the Sussex Border Path to turn right* along a signed footpath, your direction 130 degrees.

Go straight on along a broad track for 1km to **Stanley Farm**.

Pass these farm buildings on your left-hand side, and take the right-hand fork, your direction 100 degrees, along a car-wide earth road (rather than the path beside the farmhouse).

In 40 metres, *follow a public footpath sign* straight on. This potentially muddy stretch leads, in 130 metres, to another footpath sign, and good views of Marley Common on your left-hand side.

In 180 metres, the wide path finishes its bend to the right and returns the other way, a long leftward downward turn. In a further 40 metres, *follow the two-armed footpath sign, (one arm broken off) forking right*, steeply downhill through a chestnut coppice, your direction 95 degrees.

In 150 metres, *at the T-junction at the bottom* follow a faint white arrow on a tree by *going left*, your direction 40 degrees. In 70 metres, ignore a vague fork off to the right.

In 150 metres, by a two-armed footpath sign and a tall beech tree with a dozen trunks, follow the sign straight on, a path having joined yours from above on your left.

In a further 80 metres, *leave your main path to follow the public footpath sign by forking right*, your direction 80 degrees.

In 120 metres [3], you pass a house and garden, keeping their wooden fence on your right-hand side. Then in 20 metres, *by a three-*

armed footpath sign, go through a wooden fieldgate and turn right, with the house fence still on your right-hand side, your direction 150 degrees. In 25 metres, go over wooden planks and through two fenced wooden fieldgates to go down a wide grassy path, your direction 95 degrees – and the far continuation of this path is visible.

Ignore all turn-offs and, in 400 metres, you come to the edge of the wood (that has been felled recently) and a two-armed footpath sign, which you follow by turning left, your direction 70 degrees, on a car-wide earth track.

In 40 metres, cross a stream. In a further 70 metres, ignore a footpath off to the right, to continue towards **Shulbrede Priory** (as marked on the OS map) visible ahead of you.

In 125 metres, *at the tarmac road T-junction, turn left*, your direction 355 degrees, passing Shulbrede Priory on your right-hand side. *50 metres beyond the white gates to the priory, turn right on a car-wide earth road*, marked 'Please keep dogs on a lead', with Keepers Cottage on your left-hand side.

In 200 metres, go over a stream and bend sharp right with your earth road, your direction 140 degrees.

In 150 metres **[4]**, you go through a gate and immediately – *by the three-armed footpath sign – turn left gently uphill into* **Greenhill Wood** (so marked on the OS map), your direction 45 degrees.

In 130 metres, ignore a fork off to the left (marked 'Private') to keep straight on, uphill.

In 150 metres, *by a three-armed footpath sign, take the right-hand*

fork, your direction 95 degrees. In 350 metres, ignore a fork left (marked 'Private') to follow the footpath sign straight on.

In 220 metres, whilst going steeply uphill, ignore a fork off to the left to follow the footpath sign to the right, your direction 140 degrees. Stay on this main path (on the edge of the wood). In 230 metres, you cross a path to follow the footpath sign straight on.

In 200 metres, by a three-armed public footpath sign, ignore a fork to the right to keep straight on, your direction now 100 degrees.

In 450 metres, ignore a fork to the right (marked 'Private'), to keep straight on, following the footpath sign.

In 180 metres, you come to a stile, with a metal fieldgate to its left then to a four-armed footpath sign. A few *metres beyond the stile, go right downhill on a path*, your direction 140 degrees.

In 50 metres **[5]**, you come out on to a tarmac road by Updown Cottage. *Go to the right down this road*, your direction due south, and, in 350 metres, having passed Crabtree Cottage, Cartref Farm and Manor Farm, you come *to an old house and garden called Thrae* (on your left-hand side).

100 metres beyond Thrae's entrance **[6]**, *take the footpath signed to the left* through the green open space with oak trees, your direction 150 degrees.

In 50 metres, another footpath sign leads you into the woods proper and down steps across a stream and up the other side (ignoring turn-offs, and now with gardens on your right-hand side) for some way. *Go across the main road (the A286), straight over and down Hogs Hill Road*, keeping to this tarmac road for 400 metres down to the **Red Lion** pub, which is the suggested lunchtime stop.

After lunch the route is relatively gently uphill for the first 2.5km, on bridleways that can be very muddy. *Turn left out of the pub and left again down the side of the pub* and alongside its back garden, *following the footpath sign*'s direction (your direction 85 degrees), in 20 metres passing Manesty Cottage on your right-hand side, and in a further 40 metres entering the woods, by a gap next to a wooden barrier on its right-hand side.

Continue on the main path. In 115 metres, you cross a stream and in a further 30 metres you ignore a fork off to the right. In a further 105 metres, ignore two metal fieldgates and a stile off to your left-hand side.

In a further 225 metres **[7]**, bend right with the main path to cross a stream where the water falls down from a storm pipe, with the stream soon on your left-hand side.

In 165 metres, *at the next T-junction, with a wooden barn opposite, turn left*, following the footpath sign, on a car-wide earth track, your direction 30 degrees.

In 80 metres, at a crossing of paths, marked by a zero-armed post with yellow arrows on it, take the car-wide *left fork uphill*, your direction due north, a fairly muddy path.

380 metres further uphill, at a crossing of paths, follow the public footpath fork to the right, still uphill, your direction 60 degrees.

In 150 metres, with low-cut woodland ahead and to your right, fork left, following the footpath sign, your direction 345 degrees.

In 340 metres, with a ditch stream on your right-hand side, ignore a fork down to the left, to keep straight on.

In 150 metres, you come to a bridleway T-junction. Take the level way to the left, virtually straight on, your direction 315 degrees (the grass avenue uphill to its right is marked 'Private'). Ignore all ways off and in 120 metres, at a major crossroads, take the fork, not straight on, but slightly to the right, signposted bridleway, your direction 350 degrees (again the grass avenue uphill is marked 'Private').

Keep to this path and, in 150 metres, you come to a wooden fence on your left-hand side, with a thatched converted barn beyond.

In 200 metres curve right with the path uphill, and in a further 200 metres, by a two-armed footpath sign, fork left, your direction 15 degrees, down to a tarmac road 20 metres below.

[8] *Cross straight over the tarmac road to take the signposted footpath downwards*.

[!] In 120 metres, by an easy-to-miss post on your left-hand side with a yellow and blue arrow, follow the yellow arrow by *going very sharp right on a faint footpath steeply uphill*, climbing over the fallen Beech tree, your direction due east.

In 100 metres, you come to a fence and follow the footpath sign left, with the fence on your right-hand side. In 30 metres, go over a stile and turn right, a wooden fence on your right-hand side, your direction 355 degrees. In 100 metres, go over a stile and straight on.

In 200 metres, at the far right corner of the field, go over a stile and follow the footpath sign on a path with fences on both sides, your direction 95 degrees.

[9] In 100 metres, cross another stile to come out on to a tarmac road by **Wadesmarsh Farmhouse**.

Cross over the road, slightly to the left, to continue on a bridleway, your direction 10 degrees. In 30 metres, you enter the National Trust's **Valewood Park**. There are good views of **Black Down** on your right-hand side.

Keep straight on for 500 metres, [10] *until you come to a large and isolated oak tree with a three-armed footpath sign leaning against it, at which point you leave the main track to fork left*, your direction 330 degrees.

In 100 metres, go through a kissing gate into the wood. Keep to the main way straight on. In 300 metres, ignore a fork to the right and, in a further 35 metres, one sharply to the left. In a further 125 metres, by a three-armed footpath sign, and, *40 metres before a building with many outhouses, turn right downwards on the Sussex Border Path*, your direction 50 degrees. Go on a series of planks over a potentially muddy zone, to veer left with the path at the bottom of the hill, and continue with the stream on your right-hand side.

In 75 metres, go on two planks over the stream and, in 25 metres, you come out on to *a road junction*, [11] *where you take, not the imme-diate right marked Valewood Farm House, but the further right, which goes past Stedlands Farm*, your direction 40 degrees.

Then go past the entrance drive on your right that leads to a large new brick house with diamond-paned windows. *At a fork in the track marked with a footpath sign, take the bridleway uphill to the left*, your direction 20 degrees. Then go fairly steeply uphill, ignoring turn-offs. In 500 metres, *you come to a tarmac road at the top* with a house called Littlecote on your left-hand side. *Turn left and, in 20 metres, turn right again* up a tarmac path marked 'Neighbourhood Watch Area', with an anti-motorbike barrier at its start, the direction 20 degrees, and soon with playing fields on your left-hand side.

In 300 metres, *cross another tarmac road but keep straight on*, down a path with steps between high hedges, *to the main road, the B2131.* [12] *Turn left and then in 200 metres turn right* into **Haslemere** High Street. In 40 metres, you pass the **White Horse Hotel** on your right-hand side. And, 100 metres beyond this, you come on your left-hand side to the suggested tea place, **Darnleys** tearoom.

Coming out of Darnleys, turn right and in 25 metres, turn right again *down West Street, signposted to the police station*. In 120 metres, where the main street curves to the right past the police station (which is on your right-hand side), *take the street straight on to the fire station*, but then *not* the tempting path straight on, but rather *turn left in front of the fire station* and take the footpath that goes *down the left-hand side of the fire station* signposted 'to the station', your direction 315 degrees.

Follow this path, with a stream to your right and, later, a playground to your left, till you come *out on to a tarmac road* with Redwood Manor opposite. *Turn left and, in 40 me-* *tres, turn right on to the B2131, leading in 260 metres to* **Haslemere Station** on your right-hand side. **Darnleys Café Central** is on your right-hand side just before the station and **Haslemere Hotel**, with its bar, is opposite the station. The London platforms (2 and 3) are over the footbridge.

Walk 7

Garston to St Albans

River Ver, Moor Mill & Verulamium

Length 13.6km (8.4 miles), 4 hours 10 minutes. For the whole outing, including trains, sights and meals, allow at least 6 hours.

OS Landranger Map No.166. Garston, map reference TL 118 999, is in **Hertfordshire**, 2.5km north of Watford Junction.

Toughness 1 out of 10.

Features This walk, although not the most beautiful in the book, is surprisingly unspoilt by twentieth-century 'civilisation', despite being close to London, squeezed between Watford and St Albans, the M1 and the M25. From Garston – (on Sundays, there is no train to Garston, but you can go the short distance from Watford Junction by bus) – the walk is through Bricket Wood Common to Lord Knutsford's park and manor at Munden, passing the impressively converted Nether-wylde Farm, to go along the River Colne and River Ver to Moor Mill Inn, the suggested lunchtime pub. The walk follows Ver Valley Walk arrows almost all day. After lunch the walk is through woods and blackberries, beside lakes, up to a mobile home park, and then along the River Ver and into the Roman town of Verulamium (which derived its name from the river) – and so to St Albans Cathedral

and its cloisters; then either back into the cathedral grounds, down to the Roman walls and Abbey Station, or through the old town to the Thameslink station.

Shortening the walk You could order a taxi from any of the pubs mentioned in the lunch details below. Or take a train from Park Street Station. Or, at the asterisk **[*]** below, near the end of the walk, you could go to Abbey Station without sightseeing in St Albans.

History **Munden House** is owned by Lord Knutsford.

Moor Mill, built in 1762, was a working mill until 1939. A mill has stood on this site for over 1,000 years, know as Moremyll in Norman times. For 500 years, it was under the control of the abbots of St Albans and was rebuilt in 1350 for £11. Its giant revolving waterwheel has recently been restored.

In its heyday, the **River Ver** once powered 11 waterwheels and sustained the Hertfordshire watercress industry. Steps are being taken to increase its flow once more.

The **Catuvellauni** tribe, in the Ver Valley, were defeated by Julius Caesar in 54BC. **Boadicea** destroyed Verulamium in 61AD, while the Roman legions were in north Wales. In 209AD, the Roman **Alban** was beheaded for refusing to sacrifice to the Roman gods, on the orders of Geta Caesar, son of Emperor Severus, during the latter's visit to Britain to put down a rebellion.

St Albans Abbey (tel 01727 860780) and its monastic buildings were completed in 1088 with bricks from the Roman town (dismantled because it had become a hiding place for robber gangs). In 1381, its **Great Gateway** was besieged during the Peasants' Revolt – it was later used to imprison the rioters. In 1455, during the War of the Roses, **Henry VI** was wounded in the neck by an arrow and took refuge in the abbey, while drunken Yorkists ransacked the town. The abbey, now a cathedral, is open daily to 5.45pm; outside these hours, you can enter for evensong at 5pm weekdays, 4pm Saturdays, 6.30pm Sundays.

Saturday Walkers' Club Take the train nearest to **10am** (before or after) from **Euston** Station to **Garston**, changing at Watford Junction to platform 11. Journey time 32 minutes. Trains back from St Albans Abbey Station run about once an hour. Or there are trains from St Albans Thameslink station to King's Cross Thameslink station at least three times an hour. For walk directions to St Albans Thameslink see the double asterisk **[**]** below.

Lunch The suggested lunchtime pub is **Moor Mill** (tel 01727 875 557). Groups of more than 10 people should phone to book. This is due to become a Whitbread Out and Out chain eatery. Meals are served between midday and at least 10pm daily. A later alternative is the **Overdraught** pub, on the A5183 at Park Street, which serves meals midday to 3pm daily (tel 01727 874 280). Or near the start of the walk, there is the **Old Fox** pub, which serves meals midday to 8.30pm daily – except to 2pm Sunday (tel 01923 673 083).

Tea The suggested tea place is **Abigails**, The Village Arcade, near St Albans Cathedral (tel 01727 856 939), which opens till 5pm daily. An alternative is the cafeteria (just inside the cathedral), open until 4.30pm or 5pm (6pm on Sundays).

WALK DIRECTIONS

[1] [Numbers refer to the map.] Coming out of the train at **Garston Station**, head *leftwards off the platform on a tarmac path*, signposted towards 'The Gossamers', down between fences, your direction 30 degrees, with the railway track on your left-hand side.

In 150 metres, you come down *to the car-road T-junction* by the traffic lights. Cross the road here and *turn right*, your direction 85 degrees.

In 35 metres, *turn left on the road, Falcon Way*, signposted as public footpath no.16, your direction 70 degrees. Keep on this road, ignoring turn-offs.

In 180 metres, when this road comes to an end, continue straight on. In 10 metres, you go *through a tunnel under the M1*.

The other side of the tunnel, *take the tarmac lane fork up to your left*, your direction 70 degrees.

Ignore ways off and, in 360 metres, you pass the **Old Fox pub** on your left-hand side, and keep on your tarmac road.

45 metres beyond the pub, *fork left on a signposted public footpath*, your direction 10 degrees.

In 70 metres, cross a gravel drive keeping ahead past cottages on your left-hand side, and then slightly to the right of a gated driveway.

After a further 40 metres, you pass through a metal barrier to continue straight along a tarmac lane, with a thatched cottage and pond

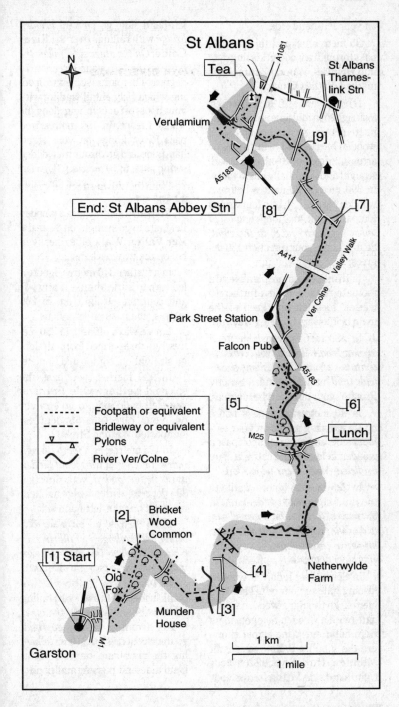

St Albans

Tea

St Albans Thameslink Stn

Verulamium

[9]

End: St Albans Abbey Stn

[8]

[7]

Valley Walk

A414

Ver Colne

Park Street Station

Falcon Pub

A5183

[5]

[6]

Lunch

M25

Footpath or equivalent
Bridleway or equivalent
Pylons
River Ver/Colne

[2]

Bricket Wood Common

[1] Start

Old Fox

[4]

Munden House

[3]

Netherwylde Farm

1 km

1 mile

Garston

M1

on your left-hand side.

35 metres beyond this cottage, pass through a wooden kissing gate into **Bricket Wood Common** (as marked on the OS map).

Ignore ways off. In 40 metres, fork right at a multiple junction and, in 10 metres, go straight on past a wooden barrier, following a yellow arrow marked no.48 – along a broad, straight and potentially muddy way. In 390 metres, 20 metres before a wooden barrier **[2]**, by a four-armed footpath sign, *take the signposted public bridleway no.8, to the right*, School Lane, your direction 120 degrees.

In 15 metres, ignore planks and a footpath to the left. In a further 10 metres, fork left and keep to the main bridleway, ignoring ways off.

In 380 metres, you come *to a tarmac road, which you cross to continue straight on, along a car-wide road* marked 'Munden. Strictly Private', your direction 140 degrees.

In 40 metres, you pass house no.18, ignoring a stile on your left-hand side, and go straight on past a wooden fieldgate and cattle grill *on bridleway no.9, a car-wide road.*

In 285 metres, ignore a stile to the right signposted Aldenham. In 55 metres, *fork left on a gravel car-wide road, which is signposted as a bridleway and footpath*, your direction 95 degrees.

In 85 metres, ignore a wooden kissing gate to your left. Then in 5 metres, go though a wooden swing gate (with a wooden fieldgate to its right-hand side), the arrow showing the number 9, and soon with **Munden House** visible on your right-hand side. With a ford on your left-hand side, go *on to a wooden bridge* with railings over the **River Colne**. *On the other side, follow the path to the left*, your direction 70 degrees. This path is subject to flooding which may entail wading with your boots off or climbing along the wooden fence. In 150 metres, you pass River Lodge on your right-hand side and go through a wooden swing gate. In 10 metres **[3]**, *go left on bridleway no.22*, your direction 40 degrees.

In 40 metres, you pass a wooden fieldgate to go straight on. Note the **Ver Valley Walk** blue river symbol on the waymark disk.

In a further 340 metres, ignore a left turn to Little Munden Farm **[4]** and continue straight on. In 200 metres, you pass under pylons.

Ignore ways off and, in 350 metres, by a three-armed footpath sign, go straight on, signposted Radlett.

In 900 metres, you pass the splendid **Netherwylde Farm** on your left-hand side to go straight on, your direction 55 degrees, signposted Watling Street.

In 125 metres, *by a footpath sign marked no.54, at times half-hidden in the hedge, go left*, your direction 305 degrees, with a hedge and tennis court on your left-hand side.

In 55 metres, go *on a wooden bridge with railings over the river. In 6 metres, follow the footpath sign marked no.54, to the right*, due north.

In 145 metres, go over a two-plank bridge (with a wooden railing on its left-hand side). *At the other end of this little bridge, go right*, your direction 45 degrees, following the riverbank on your right-hand side and passing under electricity cables in 10 metres.

In a further 165 metres, you pass a pumping station on your right-hand side (situated on the other bank). In a further 40 metres, *turn 90 degrees to your left, following the yellow no.54 arrow, with the ditch on your right-hand side*, your direction 330 degrees.

In 500 metres, go over a stile and *follow the blue arrow no.6 to the left, on an earth car road*, your direction 295 degrees.

In 180 metres, you come to a tarmac road, which you cross to *enter the tarmac driveway signposted bridleway and Moor Mill*, your direction 345 degrees.

In 160 metres, you come to **Moor Mill Inn**, the suggested lunchtime stop. After lunch, *coming out of Moor Mill, turn right, retracing your steps. In 135 metres, you are back to the car road T-junction. Here you turn right over the bridge*, your direction 260 degrees. 5 metres beyond the bridge, *turn right on a signposted public footpath* – the Ver Valley Walk – your direction 340 degrees.

In 375 metres, *cross the M25* on a footbridge. From the other end of the bridge, *follow the arrows to the right*, down alongside the motorway. In 35 metres, *follow the arrow on a post for way no.35, to the left*, your direction 345 degrees – in a further 35 metres with the edge of the wood on your right-hand side.

Ignore a fork right downhill in 100 metres, and another 400 metres **[5]** later. Then in 180 metres, follow the fence and the path to the left, your direction 300 degrees, then going round the lake that is to your

right hand side, *following the Ver Valley Walk signs*. This involves going right and right again with the path, now between two lakes, your direction 115 degrees. Then in 110 metres, at the end of the lake on your right-hand side, *turn left on path 26*, the Ver Valley Walk. You are again between two lakes, your direction 340 degrees, on a path of fine gravel.

Ignore ways off. In 250 metres, *your way rejoins the River Colne on your right-hand side. There, with only three rows of poplars remaining ahead of you on your left-hand side, fork right, with the Ver Valley Walk path, hugging close to the river on your right-hand side, towards a closely packed town of mobile homes* with aerials, your direction 30 degrees.

In 60 metres, go over a three-plank bridge and follow the river-bank, ignoring other ways off.

In 220 metres, you come to the A5183 (with the Old Red Lion pub on the other side of the bridge).

Turn left on this A road, your direction 340 degrees. In 145 metres, you pass the **Overdraught pub** at **Park Street** on your left-hand side. In 90 metres, you come to the **Falcon** pub on your left-hand side. Here you *turn right to go down Burydell Lane*, opposite the pub, a tarmac road, your direction 45 degrees. In 85 metres, you go over the **River Ver** on a brick bridge.

In 100 metres, by Toll Cottage, *follow the public footpath sign sharply to the left*, your direction 340 degrees, with allotment fences on your left-hand side.

In 100 metres, at the end of the allotments, go through a latched metal kissing gate to *follow the Ver Valley Walk arrow* straight on, across open fields, your direction 350 degrees, a line of thorn trees on your right-hand side.

In 110 metres, you come to a post with arrows, at which you go right, your direction 60 degrees.

In 80 metres, *ignore a fork off to the left to keep on, following the telegraph poles*. The simplest route, so as to keep dry, is to follow the telegraph poles for about 200 metres, until you can clearly see the arch of the bridge in the far left corner of the field, 200 metres away. And then to *head north towards this bridge* – although any not-so-wet route you can find towards the bridge will do.

Go through a metal kissing gate (to the right of a metal fieldgate) to *cross the bridge*, then follow the path with the river now to your right-hand side.

In 35 metres, *go under the A414.* In 25 metres, go through a metal kissing gate (with a metal fieldgate to its left). In 80 metres, ignore a stile straight on to *go back over the river on a concrete bridge* with scaffolding pole railings. *Follow the river walk arrow to the left*, with the river on your left-hand side, your direction 30 degrees.

In 500 metres, go through a metal kissing gate. In 100 metres you come to a tarmac road, with a wooden barn on your right-hand side. **[7]** *Go left on this road, Cottonmill Lane*, your direction 320 degrees.

In 10 metres, you go over water, and in a further 35 metres, over a brick bridge. Ignore Butterfield Lane to your left and keep on up through the estate, your direction now 325 degrees.

In 270 metres, ignore Old Oak Road to your right. You can now see the cathedral ahead.

In 290 metres, *by house no.59, take the tarmac lane to your right* **[8]***, signposted Sopwell Mill Farm*, your direction 70 degrees.

In 65 metres, *fork left* to go on a path parallel to yours, with a children's playground to its left, *following the river walk arrow. At the end of the playground fence, go half left*, your direction 20 degrees, *towards the far corner of the playing field*, 130 metres away. Once there, *continue on the path to the next waymark post* 30 metres ahead, by a concrete sluice, where you *go left*.

In 20 metres, you pass under a bridge and continue on a potentially muddy way, staying on the riverside path, ignoring all ways off.

In 470 metres, you come up *to a tarmac road* **[9]***, by St Peters School. Go across the road and over the bridge, to continue on the river walk*, with the river and allotments now on your left-hand side.

In 190 metres, follow the river walk arrow by forking right, away from the river, your direction 295 degrees, rejoining the river in 125 metres. In 30 metres, *go over the river* on a metal bridge with scaffolding pole railings, to continue with the river now to your right-hand side.

In 80 metres, you come *to the main road* (**[*]** going left here would take you, in 200 metres, to St Albans Abbey Station). The suggested route is to go *right, over a bridge*, your direction 20 degrees.

In 25 metres, *turn left, on a tarmac road, just before the Duke of Marlborough pub*, your direction 300 degrees initially.

In a further 35 metres, you pass the left turn into Pondswick Close; then in 45 metres, *turn left onto Lady Spencer's Grove*, a footpath lined with horse chestnut trees.

In 150 metres you reach Abbey Orchard. Here you *turn right up the hill towards the Abbey* (or you could go straight on for coffee at the Fighting Cocks, reputedly the oldest pub in Britain). In 210 metres *turn right* along the modern outcrop of **St Albans Abbey**, coming, in 7 metres, to the entrance. *After visiting the cathedral, come out by this same door and turn left. Follow the cathedral building all the way round to the other side.* Then *go uphill, away from the cathedral*, your direction 40 degrees, past Radio Days restaurant on your left-hand side. In 30 metres you come to the suggested tea place, **Abigails**, above the green, on your right-hand side.

Coming out of the tearoom, go right down the arcade. In 45 metres you come *to the High Street, where you turn left.* In 30 metres, you come to the **Clock Tower** on the other side of the road. (If you have time, the Clock Tower is a good starting point for a wander through the alleys of the old town, starting with French Row to its left.)

(For directions to St Albans Thameslink station see the double asterisk **[**]** below.)

To get to St Albans Abbey Station continue along the High Street. In 45 metres you come *to the Tudor Tavern. Go straight on, to the left-hand side of this.* In 100 metres, *fork left on a tarmac road signposted 'Cathedral West Gate'.*

In 110 metres, go through the **Great Gateway** of the monastery. Carry on *down Abbey Mill Lane.* In 150 metres *take the left fork*, with a house on your left-hand side.

In 80 metres *turn right to pass the front door of the Fighting Cocks pub.* The water is on your left-hand side. 30 metres beyond the pub, *turn left over the bridge*, your direction 245 degrees, with the ponds to your right. (25 metres beyond the bridge, turning right leads to the museum.) The suggested route is straight on, along the edge of the pond on your right-hand side, *carrying on beyond the ponds for 30 metres to the remains of the* **Roman wall**.

Turn left along the line of the Roman wall, your direction 185 degrees. In 85 metres, *cross a tarmac path to carry straight on*, your direction now 120 degrees, on a tarmac path. You pass a sports ground on your right-hand side. In 300 metres, you come *to a tarmac road, a large leisure centre complex ahead, where you go left, your direction 100 degrees. Follow the line of the road, but just inside the park railings.*

In 260 metres, exit the park by the main road T-junction. *Cross the road to the Abbey Tavern and turn right on the main road.* The entrance road to **St Albans Abbey Station** is in 30 metres on your left, under a yellow metal gate.

[**] To get to St Albans Thameslink station from the Clock Tower, *go to the left of the Clock Tower*, with the Fleur de Lys pub now on your left-hand side, going up French

Row, your direction 30 degrees. In 75 metres, *go right through the archway* (Lamb Alley), next to a hairdressers, your direction 130 degrees.

In 40 metres, *cross the main road to go straight under the archway into the Maltings*. In 250 metres, exit the Maltings, with café bar on your right-hand side, and *turn right on the main road, downhill*, your direction 105 degrees.

In 650 metres, you *go over the railway bridge. Before the bridge ends, go down the steps to your left*, to **St Albans Thameslink** station. The platform (no.1) for trains to London is on this side.

Walk 8

Bures to Sudbury

Gainsborough country

Length 16km (10 miles) 4 hours 50 minutes. For the whole outing, including trains, sights and meals, allow at least 9 hours 30 minutes.

OS Landranger Map No.155. Bures, map reference TL 903 338, is in **Essex**, 13km north-west of Colchester and 8km south of Sudbury, which is in **Suffolk**.

Toughness 4 out of 10.

Features This walk has few hills and some pleasant scenery. It should be quite easy going, with simpler route-finding once a couple of farmers en route have been persuaded to maintain their overgrown footpaths. Sudbury lies at the heart of the Stour Valley, designated as an Area of Outstanding Natural Beauty. On the final approach into this historic town, you cross the Sudbury Common Lands, a traditional pastoral landscape which has the longest recorded history of continuous grazing in East Anglia, where the painter Thomas Gainsborough is said to have played as a child, to tea in a converted millhouse on the banks of the river. Note that the train from Marks Tey to Bures and Sudbury does not run on Sundays in winter (September 29th to June 1st) and is irregular on Sundays in summer.

Shortening the walk If you are not having lunch in the suggested pub, you can avoid the detour to Bulmer Tye by carrying on northwards up the road at point **[5]** to rejoin the route, in 200 metres, at the asterisk **[*]** below. Or, if you have a map and are confident at route-finding, you could head due north along the footpath from the church at Great Henny **[4]**, rejoining the walk at **[6]** below. There is a regular bus service from Halstead into Sudbury, which stops outside the Fox pub in Bulmer Tye at approximately 90-minute intervals.

History St Mary's Church in Great Henny has a tower with parts dating back to the late eleventh century, although most of the church was rebuilt in the middle of the fourteenth century.

Thomas Gainsborough, the eighteenth-century portrait painter, was born in Sudbury in 1727, the youngest son of a wool manufacturer. He studied in London under Gravelot and Francis Hayman. On his marriage in 1746, he moved to Ipswich, where he remained until his move to Bath in 1760. **Gainsborough's House** (tel 01787 372 958) in Sudbury is now a museum with the most extensive collection of his paintings, drawings and prints in the world (the house is open until 4pm daily in winter; otherwise until 5pm daily; closed Monday).

Saturday Walkers' Club Take the train nearest to **9:15am** from **Liverpool Street** Station to **Bures**. Trains back from Sudbury run about once an hour. Change at Marks Tey on both the outward and return journey. Journey time 1 hour 13 minutes going out; a little longer on the return.

Lunch The suggested lunchtime place is the **Fox** pub (tel 01787 377 505) in Bulmer Tye. Under the new management, food is served either at the bar until 2pm daily or in the carvery sometimes for a further 20 minutes or so. This was closed for refurbishment in 2005, so a packed lunch might be a good option.

Alternatively, you could have lunch very early in the walk, in Lamarsh, at the **Red Lion** pub (tel 01787 227 918) which serves food midday to 2pm weekdays, 2.30pm weekends.

Tea The suggested tea place is the **Mill Hotel** (tel 01787 375 544) in Sudbury. Tea is served 2pm to 5pm, with scones, pastries and toasted tea cakes on offer. You may find an open fire and a luxurious sofa and the prices are not unreasonable. Alternatives open later include the **Anchor** pub (tel 01787 372 680) in Friars Street, Sudbury, open till at least 10.30pm daily, serving tea and coffee; and the **Eastern Café Bar** (tel 01787 374 241) on Station Road, just before the station, which is open daily for food and drinks from midday to 8pm.

WALK DIRECTIONS

[1] [Numbers refer to the map.] *Coming out of* **Bures Station** *turn left on The Paddocks road.* In 50 metres, you come *to a T-junction* where you *turn right* into Station Hill, due east. In 100 metres, you pass Water Lane on your left-hand side. 40 metres further on, the **Swan Inn** is on your right-hand side, just before the T-junction. *Opposite the pub, turn left off the road and follow the public footpath sign* down the wide gravelled lane along the left-hand side of a building, your direction 20 degrees.

Keep following the high wall on your left-hand side, ignoring other ways off. In 180 metres, the path comes to the end of the hedge on your left-hand side, where there is a wooden post with public footpath arrows on it. *Follow the Stour Valley Path* along a car-wide track to the left of the hedge ahead of you, your direction 350 degrees.

Follow this path for the next 1km until it brings you down to the River Stour. As it approaches the river, the path becomes much narrower as it enters a clump of trees. Ignore a bridge with metal railings away to your right-hand side. 40 metres further on, the path wends its way down to a stile, which you cross over into a field. Ahead of you is the **River Stour**.

Once over this stile, *turn left and follow the riverbank*, keeping close to the fence on your left, your direction 280 degrees. In 300 metres, you will see a concrete pillbox down by the river, and directly ahead a wooden stile. Cross over the stile, which leads you on to and over the railway track and over a stile the other side. 70 metres up the footpath ahead, there is a wooden telegraph pole on your right-hand side, with footpath signs on it. Take the footpath going straight ahead along the car-wide track, heading in the same direction as before.

In 370 metres you come out on to a road. *Turn right along the road*, in 40 metres passing the **Red Lion** pub, **Lamarsh**, on your left-hand side. In 150 metres follow the road as it curves around to the right, past the turning on the left sign-posted

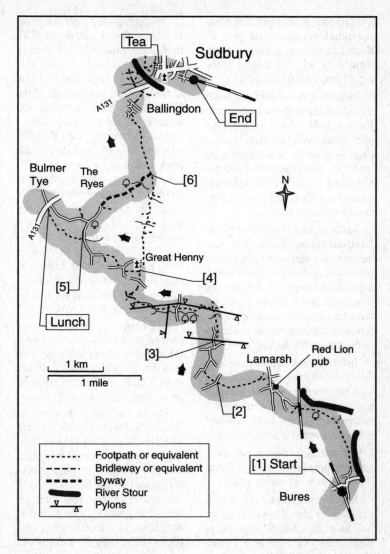

Tea

Sudbury

A131

Ballingdon

End

Bulmer Tye

The Ryes

[6]

N

Great Henny

[4]

[5]

Lunch

[3]

Red Lion pub

Lamarsh

[2]

1 km

1 mile

[1] Start

Bures

- - - - - Footpath or equivalent
- - - Bridleway or equivalent
▬▬▬ Byway
🔴 River Stour
▽△ Pylons

Horne's Green. In 110 metres you pass a turning on the left signposted to Alphamstone and Pebmarsh. Continue straight on for Sudbury and Henny.

250 metres further on, there is Lamarsh Village Hall on the right-hand side, and a house called Green Hills on your left-hand side. 10 me-

tres beyond, *turn left off the road*, following the direction of a concrete public footpath sign down a car-wide track to the right-hand side of the house, your direction 260 degrees. In 270 metres, walking up-hill with a field on your left-hand side and a large house with tennis courts on your right, the path takes a sharp turn to the right, following the right-hand edge of the field. 50 metres further on, it takes a sharp turn to the left, still following the right-hand edge of the field.

In 200 metres you come to a small dip where the path goes down into the next field. Follow the left-hand edge of this field, your direction 250 degrees initially. In 200 metres go under the overhead cables into the next field and follow the left-hand edge of this field, in the same general direction as before.

In 350 metres you come to the far left-hand corner of this field, and out on to a country lane [2]. On the other side of the lane, you will find a public footpath sign; follow its directions going gently uphill (in the same general direction as before, now 310 degrees) on a vehicle-wide grassy track.

In 80 metres you pass a wooden fieldgate on your right-hand side and go straight ahead beneath some overhead cables, now with hedges to your left-hand side and a fence to your right-hand side.

180 metres further on, you come to the corner of the field, and go over a wooden stile into the next field.

In 70 metres, cross over a stile on to a country lane. *Turn right up the hill*, your direction 50 degrees. In 300 metres you come *to a T-junction* at the top of the hill, with a farm building on the right-hand side. *Turn left*, your direction 355 degrees. In 150 metres you come to another T-junction, signposted left to Twinstead, and right to Lamarsh. Go straight over the road, following the public footpath sign, though gateposts and in 10 metres over a stile.

You then go *half right across the field*, your direction 20 degrees [3]. In 30 metres the field dips sharply downhill. Aim for the wooden stile which is now visible ahead of you, in the far right-hand corner of the field. 130 metres down the hill, you go under some overhead cables. 20 metres further on, cross over the stile, and *turn left along the car-wide track*, your direction due north. In 130 metres *fork to the right*, your direction 350 degrees, towards the farm.

In 100 metres you go directly past the farmhouse. Beware of a boisterous dog at this point. 45 metres further on you go over a stile (with a metal fieldgate to its left-hand side) and walk straight ahead, following the left-hand edge of the field, your direction due north.

In 140 metres, before you reach the end of the field, cross over the three wooden planks on the left, then over the stile with a public footpath marker on it, and finally over three more planks across a small stream.

On the far side, *turn right, following the direction of the footpath along the bank of the stream*. In 30 metres the stream turns sharp right, but you continue straight ahead across and up the field, towards a stile on the far side, your direction due north (away from the sun). The path takes you directly under electricity cables on pylons. 65 metres beyond the pylons, you come to the top of the field, to go up the bank and over the stile at the top.

Turn left, following the yellow pointer on the post for the Stour Valley Path, your direction 280 degrees. The path now follows the direction of the electricity pylons. In 140 metres cross over another stile and follow the path on the other side in the same direction as before. Keep as close as possible to the hedge on your left-hand side and, in 150 metres, you come to a car-wide track.

Turn left to follow the track round the side of the house. *In 10 metres leave the track and turn right into the field.* Follow the edge of the garden for 25 metres, until you come to its far corner, under electricity cables. Branch right, diagonally across the field, *following the line of the pylons*, your direction roughly 265 degrees. When you reach the first pylon, the field splits into two levels (originally two fields, with the bank as the hedge). *Follow the edge of the lower field*, along the foot of the bank.

340 metres further on, you come to the far end of the field. The official route down onto the tarmac road is to *go left down the ridge, parallel to the road on your right-hand side, and then down on to the road itself. Cross over it to go up a car-wide gravelled way*, following the public footpath sign, in the same general direction as previously (320 degrees). In 25 metres, you pass a wooden fieldgate on your right-hand side, with a 'Private' sign next to it. A wooden fence borders the path on your right-hand side, as it takes you back underneath the overhead cables. Ignore the Loshes Meadow path to your left and, 20 metres further on, you come out into a field. Follow the left-hand edge of the field.

In 300 metres you come to the far left-hand corner of the field, where you go over a couple of wooden posts laid across the ground, and across a missing stile (you can still see its foundations). Then ignore the stile on your left, with 'Private' painted on it, and continue straight on along the left-hand side of the field, your direction 280 degrees. 500 metres further on, you come to the far left-hand corner of the field. Cross the stile, a metal fieldgate on its right-hand side, and *turn right up the hill*, your direction 20 degrees, with a wooden fence on your right-hand side. In 80 metres, keep to the fence and the path as they veer right. **[!]** *In a further 150 metres, where the fence does a four-metre dog-leg left, you go left uphill on a potentially very overgrown path*, your direction 50 degrees. Keep the line of conifer trees on your left.

In 100 metres you come to the end of the trees and to a crossroads with another path.

Go straight on up the hill, ignoring paths to the side, and carry straight on, aiming always for the church spire (your interim destination) with your direction 15 degrees, soon keeping the wooden fence to your left-hand side.

In 60 metres, where the wooden fence goes sharp left, carry straight on downhill along the right-hand side of the field, towards the spire which you can soon see in front of you. 120 metres further on, you come down on to a road. *Turn right along the road and, in 40 metres, turn left* uphill, following the public footpath sign towards the spire. You pass **Great Henny Rectory** on your right-hand side.

150 metres further on, you come to a wooden fieldgate. On its left there is a smaller wooden gate. To visit **St Mary's Church**, **Great Henny**, go through this gate into the churchyard.

[4] To continue the walk, *turn left before the gate*, your direction 275 degrees. In 15 metres, the hedge on your right-hand side goes sharp right. But you *head straight on across the field*, on what may be a clear path (depending on the time of year) and *aiming for the two houses on the far side*. In 250 metres you come *to the perimeter fence around the houses*. Although my map indicates that you should be able to cross a stile here and follow a way between houses on to the road (coming out at a fingerpost and waymarker), this path appears to be either permanently obstructed or diverted. Therefore the suggested route is: *turn left along the fence*, with the hedge on your right-hand side; *veer right when it does* and so come, in a further 40 metres, out on to the road.

Turn right along the road. In 60 metres, you pass The Thatched Cottage on your right-hand side and, 15 metres further on, ignore a turning to the right signposted 'Henny Church. No throughway'. *Follow the road as it curves around to the left*, past Henny Parish Room on your right-hand side. 140 metres further on, *turn right*, following a public footpath sign along the right-hand side of the field, your direction due north.

In 300 metres [!] *you come to a live oak, then a large oak stump*, where you have a clear view across the field to The Hall (screened by trees; marked on the OS map). *Go to the right of the stump, across a ditch and then left, following the right-hand edge of a line of trees*, your direction 295 degrees. In 200 metres you pass a farmhouse on your left-

hand side and, 30 metres further on, go straight over into the next field. Walk along the edge of this field in the same direction as before. [!] *In 40 metres turn left over the ditch*, then *turn right along the car-wide track*, continuing in the original direction.

In 30 metres ignore a bridleway on your left-hand side. 200 metres further on, you come out *to a T-junction*, and *turn right into* **Little Henny**. In 160 metres you pass a house on your left-hand side called Pitfield Green. 200 metres further on, the road curves around to the right, heading towards some trees. Just 5 metres beyond the curve, there is a public footpath sign on the left-hand side of the road.

[5] *Turn left off the road and* [!] *follow the direction (300 degrees) of the concrete footpath signpost across the field, which could be a very poorly maintained and scarcely visible path. In 150 metres, halfway across the field, the offical route is to turn a quarter right towards the footpath post visible through a gap in the hedgerow ahead*, 150 metres away on the far side of the field (further to the left than you might imagine – keep well away from the car road away to your right-hand side – unless you get lost at this point, in which case the road will lead you to the pub, if you turn left when you reach the A131).

By this post marked with yellow arrows, cross over two wooden planks into the next field. Continue straight on across the field, your direction 315 degrees.

In 150 metres you come to the far side of the field, where there is another wooden footpath post. Cross on two planks over a ditch to go straight across the next field, in the same direction as before, for 250 metres, **[!]** *aiming for the trees with a long red-brick building behind them. Once at these trees, turn right, following the left-hand edge of the field*, with the trees on your left-hand side.

150 metres further on, *turn left through the trees*, through a small wooden swing gate, following the direction of the wooden footpath post [NB - if this is closed, follow an alternative route to the main road]. Cross the small wooden three-plank footbridge and then *turn right*. Follow the signs through the trees, past the house on your left, and out on to a driveway. 40 metres further on, this leads you down on to the main road, the A131. *Turn right along the road* and, in 50 metres, you come to the **Fox** pub, **Bulmer Tye**, which is the suggested lunch place.

Coming out of the pub after lunch, *turn right along the road*. In 100 metres you pass Church Road on your left-hand side. 70 metres further on, *turn right into Ryes Lane*, which takes you back to Little Henny. *Walk down Ryes Lane for 1km*, until the road enters some trees and curves sharply around to the right. Directly opposite is the entrance to The Hall.

Turn left on a road at this juncture, **[*]** *following the sign for 'The Ryes School'*, your direction 55 degrees. In 60 metres you pass Lodge Farm on your left-hand side. 100 metres further on, where a small postbox faces you, *take the left-hand fork* which is signposted public byway. Walk straight down this car-wide track, your direction 35 degrees, past two brick cottages on

your left-hand side.

In 800 metres the path leads down and out of the trees, and on your right-hand side there is a wooden post with various yellow footpath markers on it. Ignore this and continue straight on along the existing path.

[6] In 600 metres, having gone down the hill and up the other side, at the crest of this hill you have a fine view out to Great Henny Church; and at this crest you come to a four-armed footpath sign (where the path straight on goes through trees). *Turn left* along the car-wide public footpath, going due north. This car-wide track takes you steadily downhill. In 500 metres you come to the foot of the hill (where there are extensive farm buildings off to the right of the path) and to a footpath sign. Ignore the way to the right and go straight ahead along a car-wide track, due north. 200 metres further on, you come to the top of the rise and pass the stile into the next field. Walk straight over this field towards the far side, your direction 340 degrees. From here, you have a good view of Sudbury away to your right-hand side. In 250 metres, you come to the far side of the field and exit the field by a post with footpath arrows on it.

Follow the path left through some trees, your direction 300 degrees, as it makes its way downhill. You are now on the outskirts of **Sudbury** and can see some houses down on your right-hand side. Ignore ways off and, in 120 metres, the path takes you up to the back of a row of houses, and you *follow the path sharp right down the hill*, parallel with the row of houses.

In 100 metres you come out on to a residential street, by a public footpath sign. *Turn right down the street*, your direction 60 degrees. In 100 metres, you come down to the bottom of Pinecroft Rise and *turn left*. In 100 metres *follow the road as it curves around to the right*, past Hall Rise on your left-hand side. 70 metres further on, you come to the bottom of Meadowview Road, where you reach a T-junction with the main road.

Cross over the main road and on the far side go through a wooden kissing gate near a sign saying Kone Vale. Go straight ahead down the path through lawns and into the trees. In 250 metres *take the right-hand fork* in the path, next to a Babergh District Council sign. 15 metres further on, fork left up the slope with metal railings on to the disused railway line. At this point, those in a hurry to catch the train can turn right and follow the path directly to the station.

For those making their way to the Mill Hotel for tea, and a walk through the town, *turn left on the track,* your direction 310 degrees initially. In 50 metres a bridge takes you over the main road. 80 metres further on, continue straight on over a metal bridge. 200 metres beyond that, you come to a brick bridge with a metal railing and *take the steps (with a wooden banister on their right-hand side) down to the right* before the bridge. Go round the wooden barrier at the bottom and head straight across the field towards the bridge across the river ahead, your direction 80 degrees. In 150 metres cross the bridge and, on the far side, *turn half left*, heading towards the Mill Hotel (the large white building to the right of the church tower), your direction 60 degrees. In 300 metres you come across the field to a gate leading on to a brick bridge, going alongside a large duck pond, and out to the **Mill Hotel, Sudbury**, on your left-hand side, the suggested tea stop.

Coming out of the Mill Hotel, go straight up to the top of Walnut Tree Lane. Turn left on the main road, going into town. In 200 metres ignore the way left to Bury St Edmunds and Colchester. Carry on down Gainsborough Street. 170 metres down on your left-hand side is **Gainsborough's House**. 100 metres further on, you come out *into the Market Square*. To get to **Sudbury Station**, *turn sharp right* and, in 40 metres, with the **Anchor** pub on your right-hand side, *turn left into Station Road*. At the bottom of Station Road, the **Eastern Café Bar** is on your left-hand side, but follow the signs straight across for **Sudbury station**.

Walk 9

Shiplake to Henley

River Thames, Rotherfield Greys & Greys Court

Length 17.25km (10.7 miles), 5 hours 15 minutes. For the whole outing, including trains, sights and meals, allow 8 hours 45 minutes.

OS Landranger Map No.175. Shiplake, map reference SU 776 797, is in **Oxfordshire**, 9km north-west of Reading.

Toughness 4 out of 10.

Features This walk is a bit like the scenery in a cowboy film: as soon as you are more than a few feet up, you have magnificent views over the unspoilt Thames valley. From Shiplake Lock the route follows the Thames, then up to the church beside Shiplake College, and through bluebell woods beside Crowsley Park (the grandiose site for the BBC's listening masts), to the church and pub in Rotherfield Greys. The cherry trees and cricket green in the hamlet of Greys Green lead on into the National Trust estate of Greys Court, and from there into the beechwoods of Lambridge, and past Friar Park, the estate of the late Beatle George Harrison, with its splendidly over-opulent Gothic gatehouse, to a teahouse in Henley beside the church and river bridge.

Shortening the walk After lunch at the Maltsters Arms pub in Rotherfield Greys, you could take a direct footpath to Henley (see the asterisk **[*]** below: map and compass needed), and so avoid the extra 4km involved in visiting Greys Court; or you could call a taxi from the pub. Earlier in the walk, on Shiplake Row, there are hourly buses from near the White Hart pub into Henley or Reading.

History Shiplake was as close as the Vikings could get their ships to their main encampment in Reading – hence, possibly, the name 'Ship lack'. There were vineyards on the riverside slopes during Tudor and Stuart times.

Shiplake College was built in the 1890s by a stockbroker; it was used by the BBC in World War II; and became a school in 1959.

Shiplake Church dates from the eleventh century and contains stained glass from the Abbey of St Omer in France. The poet Tennyson was married here in 1850 – he wrote: 'The Peace of God came into my life before the altar when I wedded her.' Four times a week Shiplake College uses the church for its assemblies.

St Nicholas Church in Rotherfield Greys contains the ornate tomb of Robert Knollys, Elizabeth I's treasurer who took charge of Mary Queen of Scots during her imprisonment; and of Robert's wife Katherine, a first cousin to Elizabeth I; and the effigies of their 16 children. The church curate reported in 1738 that, so poor were his parishioners, of the 'Absenters from ye Church… there are a great many yet come but seldom… [for] want of clothes'. Whilst the church's Revd J Ingram wrote of his experiment in 1823 to create jobs by cultivating opium: 'From its purity it was found of superior efficacy to that bought from Turkey or the East Indies, and I obtained a high price for it from the Society of Apothecaries Hall.'

Greys Court (tel 01491 628 529), owned by the National Trust, is a sixteenth-century house of brick, flint and stone, erected in the ruins of a vast mansion that was castellated by the first Lord Grey in 1347 – with a licence from Edward III, in recognition of loyal service at the Battle of Crécy. The house is today the home of Lady Brunner, a granddaughter of the actor Sir Henry Irving. The estate has a maze, two possibly Tudor towers, ruins and a large donkey wheel and horse wheel that were used for pumping up water. (The ground floor of the house is open from April to the end of September on Wednesdays, Thursdays and Fridays, 2pm to 6pm; the gardens are open at these times and on Tuesdays, Saturdays and bank holiday Mondays; admission £4.60).

Henley, with its 300 listed buildings, is said to be the oldest settlement in Oxfordshire.

Saturday Walkers' Club Take the train nearest to **9.05am** (before or after) from **Paddington** Station to **Shiplake** (change at Twyford). Journey time 51 minutes. Return from Henley Station. Journey time 58 minutes. Buy a cheap day return ticket to Henley.

Lunch The suggested lunchtime pub is the **Maltsters Arms** (tel 01491 628 400) in Rotherfield Greys, serving food daily from midday to 2.30pm. It is often crowded, so phone to reserve your tables. However, this pub is 10.3km from the start of the walk, so, if you think that you will not get there in time, the suggested

alternative is 4km earlier on: the thatched pub in Binfield Heath called the **Bottle & Glass Inn** (tel 01491 575 755), where food is served from midday to 1.45pm daily.

Tea The Henley tea place I suggest is **Crispins** (tel 01491 574232) in Hart Street, opposite the church, which serves cream teas and other food until 7pm daily. My second preference is the upstairs Asquiths **Teddy Bear Tearoom** (tel 01491 571978) in New Street (last serving 5pm daily, 4pm Sundays; closed Mondays). Other tea places include **Old Rope Walk** (tel 01491 574595) in Hart Street (open until 5.30pm daily) or **Henley Tearooms** (tel 01491 411412) in Thames Side, facing the river (open until between 5pm and 6pm daily).

WALK DIRECTIONS

[1] **[Numbers refer to the map.]** Coming off the train at **Shiplake Station**, *head left towards the end of the platform (away from Henley) and go down steps with white railings*, your direction 250 degrees. In 3 metres, go through a white swing gate and *straight on*; and in 75 metres, *turn left on a tarmac road*, your direction 160 degrees.

Ignore ways off. In 425 metres, by a brick postbox, *take a road to the left, marked Lashbrook Farm and Thames Path* (with Crowsley Road going off to the right), your direction 120 degrees. In 15 metres, go over the stream, and in a further 20 metres, *turn right on a footpath* signposted to Shiplake Lock, your direction 165 degrees, down steps and over a stile.

In 45 metres go over a stile and straight on, with a fence on your

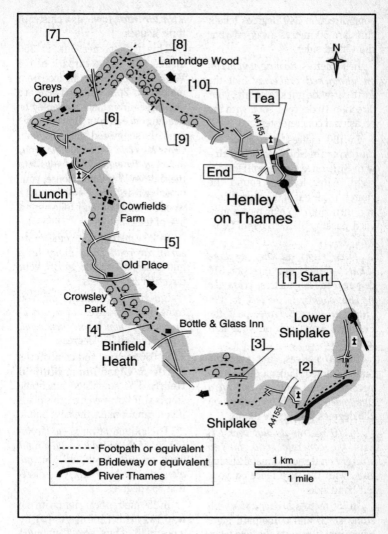

[7]

[8]

Lambridge Wood

Greys
Court

[10]

Tea

A4155

[6]

End

Lunch

[9]

Henley
on Thames

Cowfields
Farm

[5]

Old Place

[1] Start

Crowsley
Park

Lower
Shiplake

Bottle & Glass Inn

[4]

[3]

[2]

Binfield
Heath

A4155

Shiplake

- - - - - Footpath or equivalent
- - - Bridleway or equivalent
River Thames

1 km

1 mile

right-hand side. In 150 metres, go over another stile and, in 40 metres, *to a grave road opposite Millhouse, where you go right*, your direction 250 degrees. In 20 metres, *turn left* on a tarmac lane, *following a Thames Path signpost*, your direction 195 degrees.

In 35 metres *go over a stile on your right-hand side*, with **Ship-**

lake Lock and the River Thames on your left-hand side, your direction 245 degrees.

In 1km **[2]**, *you come to a small bridge on your left-hand side, but you stay on this side of the river, about 20 metres from the bank, to take the car-wide gravel path straight on, that has the Shiplake College Boathouses on its right-hand side,* your direction 240 degrees (chalk cliffs are 50 metres away on your right-hand side).

In 90 metres, *turn right uphill on an unmarked bridleway* (not the earth car-wide track to its left), your direction 10 degrees, soon with the occasional concrete step.

In 150 metres, you *enter the churchyard* of **Shiplake Church** – with **Shiplake College** off to your right. After looking round the church, come out of the church door and turn right, to exit the churchyard, passing by the cedar of Lebanon.

Turn right on the car lane (Church Lane), your direction 310 degrees. In 250 metres, *cross the A4155, slightly to the left, to continue on Plough Lane*, past the Plowden Arms pub on your left-hand side.

In 200 metres, just past the timber-framed Tudor Cottages on your left-hand side, *go left on a signposted footpath*, your direction 230 degrees (a concrete road).

In 40 metres do not veer left with the concrete road, but go straight on through a metal kissing gate, with the field fence on your left-hand side.

In 350 metres *go over a stile* with stone steps and a footpath sign, where you *turn right*, the field fence on your right-hand side.

In 150 metres you come to a two-armed footpath sign, where you follow its direction left, your direction 220 degrees.

In 85 metres, *by the first of two copses and by a mini-pylon, ignore the footpath sign straight on and turn very sharp right, due north, on a tractor track*, towards a cluster of three houses.

This way comes out, in 350 metres **[3]**, to the carpark of the **White Hart** pub (serving food from midday to 2pm daily). There are also buses from here to Henley or Reading once an hour. However, this is not the suggested lunchtime pub. *Cross the road, slightly to the right, to pick up the signposted footpath* to the right of Waylands House, your direction 5 degrees, going through a wooden fieldgate and following a line of telegraph poles.

In 200 metres you come *to an earth car road (Kiln Lane)* by a bungalow, where you *go left*, your direction 260 degrees.

Ignoring all turnings off, you come, in 760 metres, *to a car T-junction, at which you turn right*, your direction 350 degrees.

In 650 metres, you come to the **Bottle & Glass Inn** in **Binfield Heath**. The suggested lunchtime stop is still 4km away: try this place if you cannot make the next pub.

To continue onwards – *as if coming out of the pub door – turn right on a car-wide track and continue along the narrower path*, your direction 360 degrees.

In 250 metres bear right with the way. In a further 100 metres **[4]**, by a post with a blue arrow left and a yellow arrow right, follow the *blue bridleway arrow to the left*, into the wood, your direction 295 degrees. Keep to the main path.

Ignore all turnings off and follow the arrows on trees. In 350 metres you cross an earth car-wide track marked with 'No horses' signs. In 250 metres, bear right, your direction now 345 degrees, with the battered iron railings of the BBC's **Crowsley Park** (with its listening masts) on your left-hand side.

Ignoring ways off, in 300 metres you cross the drive to Keeper's Cottage. In a further 250 metres, you exit the wood *to a car road T-junction, where you turn left*, your direction 255 degrees. You pass a timber-framed mansion, **Old Place** (as marked on the OS map), on your right-hand side, to *take the road right at the end of the building*, your direction 355 degrees. *In 85 metres fork left with the road*, still uphill, your direction 320 degrees.

In 550 metres, by Kingsfield House, ignore a footpath sign off to the left.

In a further 110 metres, *by house no.2, do not go left with your road, but fork right, following the footpath sign* to go over a stile (a metal field-gate to its left), your direction 70 degrees, on an earth car-wide road.

[!] *In 25 metres, by the back of the garage, by a concealed yellow arrow on a post, go left over the stile* **[5]** and straight on, your direction 20 degrees, with the wooden field fence on your left-hand side.

In 135 metres, go over another stile and straight on, across a grass road and then between fences. In a further 200 metres, leave the paddocks through a line of trees and go straight on across open fields.

In 125 metres, go over a stile and onwards, with the field fence on your right-hand side. In a further 425 metres, go through a fieldgate with **Cowfields Farm** (so marked on the OS map) on your right-hand side. In a further 50 metres, go

through another fieldgate and straight on.

In 25 metres, follow the yellow arrow half left, 325 degrees, on a tractor way, heading just to the right of St Nicholas Church, which is visible in the distance. You *come out on to a road and cross it, straight on.* In 10 metres this brings you *to a road T-junction, where you turn left,* your direction 290 degrees (you can see Greys Court House 1.5km ahead of you, at 340 degrees).

In 360 metres, you come to **St Nicholas Church** in **Rotherfield Greys** and, 35 metres beyond the church, to the **Maltsters Arms**, the suggested lunchtime stop.

Coming out of the pub door after lunch, turn right and, *just past the church, opposite it,* go through a wooden kissing gate (and **[*]** take the right footpath signposted Henley, but only if you want the short cut mentioned in the introduction above; compass and map advised if doing the shortcut). The main walk involves taking *the left of the two signposted footpaths,* your direction 20 degrees. In 135 metres go over a stile and straight on into a wood, following a clear path, your direction 35 degrees.

In 170 metres *exit the wood over a stile and turn left,* your direction 305 degrees, and walk with the edge of the wood on your left-hand side.

In 120 metres you pass a stile, with an ex-vicarage on your left-hand side.

In 80 metres go over a stile. In a further 120 metres, you come *to a minor car road* **[6]**, *where you turn left,* due south, in 35 metres passing Green Place House on your right-hand side. 60 metres beyond the house's driveway, *at a T-junction, go right*, your direction 295 degrees.

In 100 metres, by a war memorial, you join a more major road, straight on, signposted Nettlebed (the road is lined with cherry trees).

In 240 metres *you pass the wooden village hall of* **Greys Green** on your left-hand side. *20 metres beyond the village hall turn right on an earth car road*, due north, with the cricket green on your left-hand side.

In 85 metres pick up a *signposted footpath to the right*, your direction 65 degrees. In a further 50 metres, you pass a stile and go down into the wood on a clear path.

In 50 metres you pass another stile. In 60 metres, you exit the wood over a stile, to go straight on, your direction 45 degrees, towards Greys Court, visible across the valley. In 80 metres you pass under cables. In 40 metres *go across a tarmac road and straight on*; in a further 20 metres entering **Greys Court** land over a stile, your direction 55 degrees.

In 40 metres join a tarmac drive to go straight on. In a further 160 metres, a left turn leads to the horse wheel and donkey wheel and main house. But the public footpath is straight on, past the manor on your left-hand side, protected by its ha ha (wall). You *pass the ticket kiosk, to go half left*, following yellow arrows, your direction 15 degrees.

In 100 metres go over a stile to continue with pine trees on your left-hand side.

In 120 metres cross a stile (a small wooden gate and a wooden fieldgate on its left-hand side) and continue; in a further 75 metres, go over a wooden bridge structure with a wooden railing. Then, in 35 metres, ignore a yellow-arrow path up some steps to the left.

In a further 45 metres, *go over a stile (with a wooden fieldgate on its left-hand side and a farm shed ahead of it) to go right*, to continue in your previous direction, 50 degrees, with the fence on your right-hand side.

In 130 metres, you come *to a tarmac lane and ignore the two sets of onward footpath arrows visible* **[7]**, *to turn right downhill* on a lane, your direction 105 degrees.

In 55 metres you come *to a tarmac road T-junction* by Broadplat Croft, where you *go left uphill and, in 10 metres, take the footpath right*, signposted Lower Assenden, your direction 55 degrees, into the beechwood marked on the OS map as **Lambridge Wood**.

Following yellow arrows on the trees, you come, in 290 metres, to the start of open fields visible off to your right-hand side (you remain in the wood).

At the end of these fields on your right-hand side, cross a minor path to follow yellow arrows straight on, deeper into the wood, your direction 55 degrees. In 320 metres you come *to a crossing* **[8]** *marked in yellow arrows on trees. Here*, 10 metres beyond the first marked tree, *turn right*, your direction 125 degrees.

In 140 metres ignore a fork marked to the left.

In a further 30 metres, you come *to a T-junction, at which you turn left*, again with an edge of forest on your right-hand side, your direction now 135 degrees.

In a further 55 metres, ignore a fork right over a stile and bear slightly left with the main path to a yellow arrow on a tree 30 metres away, with a small crater to its right. In 40 metres ignore the left path to keep onward, now uphill.

In 525 metres, as you are passing a huge industrial corrugated shed off to your right-hand side, *stay on the pathway, not forking off right*. In 80 metres *exit the wood* **[9]** *on to the golfcourse*, coming out between the greens for hole 13 to your left and 12 to your right, to go straight on, your direction 145 degrees.

By green 12, you come to a line of trees, which you thereafter keep on your right-hand side. In 500 metres you come *to a stile (a white metal fieldgate to its right) and cross it, to go straight on, along a tarmac lane with road humps* made of brick and lined with lampposts, your direction 105 degrees.

In 60 metres go over a stile (a wooden fieldgate to its left) to go straight on; then, in 45 metres, past a stile and footpath sign, straight on. In a further 40 metres, you pass the entrance to Lambridge House on the left-hand side.

In a further 40 metres, you pass a folly, screened by fences on your right-hand side. In a further 150 metres, you come to Croft Cottage on your left-hand side **[10]**, where you leave the road, as it veers right, to continue straight on through a dilapidated metal fieldgate, on a signposted footpath, your direction 80 degrees (the late George Harrison's **Friar Park** to the other side of the fence to your right).

In 200 metres you come *to a housing estate road (Crisp Road), where you go right*, your direction 120 degrees.

In 165 metres *turn right uphill into Hop Gardens*, your direction 170 degrees.

In 400 metres you come almost to the main road T-junction – just to your right here is the Victorian Gothic splendour of **Friar Park's lodge house**. You, however, *go left on a minor road, 5 metres before the main road (West Street), which has a one-way sign*, your direction due east.

In 120 metres you pass Row Barge pub on your right-hand side, and keep on, *heading for the church*. Just beyond the church and by the bridge, on the corner of the street, on the right-hand side, is **Crispins**, the suggested tea place. The Red Lion Hotel is opposite.

After tea, *turn right out of Crispins and immediately right again, along the riverfront*, in 50 metres passing **Henley Tearooms** on your right-hand side.

Continue to the Boats for Hire place, where you bend right with the road, *taking the second left* by the Imperial Hotel which brings you to **Henley Station**.

Walk 10

Beaconsfield (round walk)

Milton's cottage & a Quaker hamlet

Length 19.5km (12.2 miles) 6 hours. For the whole outing, including trains, sights and meals, allow at least 9 hours.

OS Landranger Map No.175. Beaconsfield, map reference SU 940 912, is in **Buckinghamshire**, 7km east of High Wycombe.

Toughness 4 out of 10.

Features This walk passes the cottage of the poet John Milton in Chalfont St Giles and comes to Jordans, a hamlet with Quaker links. In between, there is typical Buckinghamshire countryside to enjoy – gently rolling wooded hills – enough to provide interest without being too tiring!

Shortening the walk Instead of completing the loop back to Beaconsfield, you could stop for tea at the Old Jordans Quaker Guest House, and then make the short detour to Seer Green & Jordans Station (see the asterisk **[*]** below), and catch the return train from there. You could also ask at the pub (or phone for information on 0345 382 000) about buses to the stations at Beaconsfield or (going in the opposite direction) Gerrards Cross.

History Bekonscot Model Village (tel 01494 672 919) in Beacons-field is a 1.5-acre miniature 1930s village, mainly for children (admission for adults £3.75; children £12.50). It is open mid-February to October 30th, 10am-5pm daily (including bank holidays).

The village of **Chalfont St Giles** is largely unspoilt, with many listed buildings and lying mostly within a Conservation Area. (It was used as Warmington-on-Sea in the film of *Dad's Army*).

It was a Quaker, Thomas Ellwood, who acquired a cottage in Chalfont St Giles as a refuge for **John Milton**. In London, the plague was a serious threat and, as a high-profile supporter of the republican cause, Milton's liberty was also at risk following the Restoration. It was during the short time that he lived here that he completed his epic poem *Paradise Lost* and was inspired (by a question from Ellwood) to begin *Paradise Regained*. The cottage was probably built in the late sixteenth century, and has an interesting history – it is now a museum, containing the first edition of *Paradise Lost*. Incidentally, Milton was himself a keen walker. **Milton's Cottage** (tel 01494 872 313) is open from March 1st to October 31st, Tuesday to Sunday (plus bank holiday Mon-days), 10am-1pm and 2pm-6pm; admission £2.50.

Old Jordans Farm, now run as a guesthouse, dates back to the Middle Ages, and had close associations with the early Quakers of the seventeenth century; George Fox was one of the many visitors. Meetings here were raided – it was an offence for Quakers to gather in groups of five or more for worship, and informers could earn £50. The

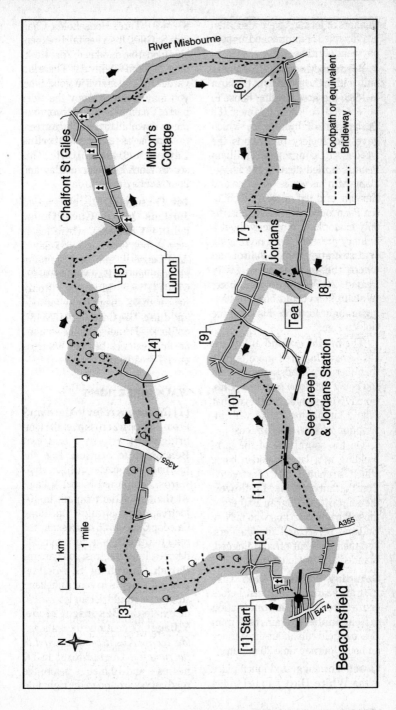

River Misbourne

[6]

Footpath or equivalent

Bridleway

Chalfont St Giles

Milton's
Cottage

Lunch

Jordans

[7]

[5]

[8]

Tea

[9]

[4]

Seer Green
& Jordans Station

[10]

A355

[11]

1 km

1 mile

A355

[2]

[3]

[1] Start

Beaconsfield

B474

N

Quakers at Jordans were also often heavily fined or imprisoned for non-payment of tithes.

Jordans Meeting House was built within the grounds of the farm in 1688, the first meeting house to be erected following James II's Declaration of Indulgence which gave the Society of Friends the freedom to congregate. William Penn is buried next to the house, along with his wives Gulielma and Hannah, and ten of their 16 children. Penn founded Pennsylvania, the only example of a state without a military presence, with no religion or aristocratic group in control, and where the Indians were fairly treated. As Voltaire commented: 'William Penn could boast of having brought forth on this earth the Golden Age.'

The **burial ground** at Jordans has several hundred more burials than there are headstones, the reason being that for a hundred years, from 1766, the Quakers believed that even a simple headstone with inscription was too ostentatious.

On the south side of the farm building is a large wooden barn, which is reputed to be constructed from the timbers of the **Mayflower**, the ship of the Pilgrim Fathers – those Puritan pilgrims who in New England persecuted the Quakers, had their ears cut off and flogged, branded and executed them.

Saturday Walkers' Club Take the train nearest to **9.30am** (before or after) from **Marylebone** Station to **Beaconsfield**. Trains back from Beaconsfield run about three times an hour. Journey time 39 minutes.

Lunch The suggested lunch place is the **White Hart** pub (tel 01494 872 441), Three Households, Chalfont St Giles. It serves fairly expensive food from midday to 2pm weekdays (2.30pm weekends). There is a garden. (If you arrive in good time, you may prefer to enjoy the older part of Chalfont St Giles by continuing on downhill to the village green, to eat at the less expensive **Merlins Cave** pub (01494 875 101). This serves lunch between midday and 2pm Monday to Saturday.

Tea The suggested tea place is **Old Jordans Quaker Guest House** (tel 01494 874 586), where tea is served (but very rarely on Saturday) between 3pm and 5pm. An alternative is the **Bar Med** (tel 01494 672014) in Maxwell Road, Beaconsfield, open all day for food and drink, **The Café** (01494 681137) on Burkes Parade near the station., or other eateries beyond Waitrose on the Broadway.

WALK DIRECTIONS

[1] [Numbers refer to the map.] From platform 2 cross over the footbridge to platform 1 and exit **Beaconsfield Station**. Take the footpath opposite uphill, eastwards, signposted Model Village. At the top of the footpath in 100 metres, carry straight on along Caledon Close. In 35 metres take the road to the left, your direction 345 degrees. In 100 metres, you pass the **Parish Church of St Michael and All Angels** to your right hand side (or you could detour left for 120 metres to the **Bekonscot Model Village**). To continue the walk, *follow the road as it bends around to the right* into Grenfell Road. In 300 metres – and 10 metres before the road curves around to the right into

Wilton Road – *turn left into a road which has no street sign* (Wilton Road), your direction 350 degrees.

[2] In 120 metres you come to the end of what you can now see is Wilton Road, and to a traffic island planted with trees and bushes. Go round the left of this island, straight over the main road (slightly to the right) and down the public footpath dead ahead, your direction 20 degrees initially.

Ignore ways off and keep straight on for 750 metres. 10 metres after the end of the green chainlink fence on your left-hand side, follow the main fork right, into the wood, your direction 350 degrees. Keep to this path and, in 260 metres, by a post with a yellow arrow, ignore the paths you cross to continue straight on, along the same path (due north).

320 metres further on, you come to a point where another path crosses the path you are on. At this juncture, there is a single white arrow on a tree pointing straight ahead. Continue straight on, for another 20 metres, until you come to another tree with white arrow pointing left and right, and here *turn right off the path*, your direction 70 degrees initially. **[3]**

At another (unsigned) path junction in 25 metres, bear right on the main path and keep to it, ignoring ways off, for the next 500 metres, at which point a wide track comes in from the left.

You are now following the edge of the field on your right-hand side, your direction 115 degrees initially. In 250 metres the path takes you over two stile barriers and, in 15 metres, through a metal kissing gate next to a four-armed footpath sign,

with Wood Cottage on your right-hand side.

Turn left into the road and follow it as it immediately curves right and down the hill. Walk down the road for 750 metres until it brings you out on to a road (the A355) with fast-moving traffic.

Once over the road, walk straight ahead along the car-wide track ahead of you, your direction 125 degrees initially. In 125 metres ignore the fork left to a metal fieldgate. 300 metres further on, ignore a stile on your left at a crossroads, and stay on the same track, going straight ahead up the hill. 200 metres brings you out to the top of the hill, with views through gates to left and right. Just follow the path between the hedgerows and underneath overhead cables.

In 200 metres the path brings you down *on to a road* **[4]**, *where you turn left*, your direction 40 degrees, and walk along the road. In 250 metres the road curves sharply around to the right and you *turn left off the road, to go straight ahead*.

In 20 metres you pass a wooden barrier with a Forestry Commission sign next to it. Walk straight ahead into **Hodgemoor Woods**, along the path through the trees, which has a sign in front of it ('Horseriding by permit only'), your direction 20 degrees initially.

Keep to this path, ignoring all ways off and crossings of paths – for instance, at the first junction, in 140 metres, *take the left fork*, more or less straight on – until, in a further 400 metres, you come to a T-junction with a corrugated-iron barn dead ahead. *Here you turn right*. In 30 metres, walk past the entrance to the charcoal burner's yard on your left. 25 metres beyond that, there are two paths going off to the right.

[!] *It is easy to get lost during the next 500 metres or so (this and the next two paragraphs), so follow the notes carefully. Take the first path sharply to the right, signed with a white-topped post showing a 'no horses' symbol* (a red line through a black horseshoe) a car-wide path into the trees, your direction 140 degrees initially.

Carry straight on. In 70 metres, keep ahead at a crossing track. In 15 metres, you pass another 'no horses' post. In 65 metres, bear right, keeping to the car-wide way, due south through a potentially muddy stretch rich with sedges and then, in 45 metres, bear left on this same wide way through a grassier area, your direction now 110 degrees. In 70 metres, *keep ahead (slightly to your left) at the small crossing track*, your direction now 80 degrees. In 25 metres, you pass a post with a yellow band on your left hand side; and in 120 metres, one on your right hand side. In 8 metres, ignore a path to the right (direction 150 degrees) marked with a post with a yellow band and keep on, your direction 50 degrees.

In 100 metres, *at a minor path crossing, by a post to your left hand side with a 'no horses' symbol, go right*, your direction 105 degrees. In 35 metres, *at a T-junction, go left*, your direction 10 degrees, and immediately in 5 metres, *go right, on a narrow path*, your direction 120 degrees, in 5 metres passing on your left hand side a 'no riding' post.

Keep to this main path, ignoring all ways off. In 200 metres, you then join a path that has come in from your right, your direction now 110 degrees. Ignore ways off. In a further 115 metres, leave the wide track as it curves sharply around to the left, going uphill, to *follow the narrower path curving off to your right-hand side*, your direction 140 degrees initially.

Ignore ways off and, in 130 metres, you come *to a T-junction* near to the edge of the wood, and you *turn left* along the path as it follows the tree line, your direction 50 degrees initially.

[5] In 20 metres ignore a fork right. In a further 25 metres, *turn right through the trees*, with the open field visible ahead, following the faint white arrow painted on a tree. This takes you out into the field, round a wooden barrier, where you turn left with the edge of the field on your left-hand side, your direction 20 degrees.

200 metres takes you through a gap in the hedge into the next field.

You are now going to *walk most of the way around three sides of this large field*. In more detail: Follow the footpath as it heads left around the edge of the field. When you get to the corner of the field in 20 metres, turn right along the next field edge. Follow the edge of the field all the way around, 300 metres to the far corner of the field. Ignore a stile in the corner with a footpath going off to the left. Instead, go right, your direction 190 degrees, continuing along the edge of the field for another 40 metres, until you go through a gap in the hedge into the next field.

Continue along the left-hand edge of this field, your direction 175 degrees. In 150 metres go over or past the stile and continue along the track, following the left-hand edge of this field. 350 metres brings you to the far left-hand corner of this field, where you *go left and follow the fenced path*.

In 150 metres you come out beside a metal fieldgate on to the corner of a residential street. *Turn right down this street*, Back Lane, in 50 metres coming up to a T-junction on the main road at **Three Households**, with the entrance to the **White Hart**, the suggested lunch stop, immediately to your right.

Coming out of the pub after lunch, *follow the main road down the hill into the village*. 350 metres further on, you pass on the left the **Milton's Head** pub. 50 metres further on, on your right-hand side, is **Milton's Cottage**. Time permitting, this is worth a visit (for those eating at **Merlins Cave** pub, continue on for 330 metres to the pub on your right-hand side).

The main suggested route is to carry on downhill from Milton's Cottage to the **Feathers pub** on your left-hand side. Opposite it, and 5 metres beyond it, turn right through the beamed archway, leading to the (sometimes locked) **Parish Church of Chalfont St Giles**. Follow the footpath which goes along the right-hand side of the lychgate, along metal railings bordering the churchyard.

130 metres brings you down to the dried-out riverbed, where there is a bridge with metal railings going over the riverbed. 5 metres before this bridge, go over the stile on your right-hand side and head half right across grass (with a terrace of houses on your right-hand side) to go over

the next stile, 50 metres away, your direction 225 degrees. Fork left, once over the stile, and in 10 metres cross another stile. Ignore yet another stile almost immediately left, to continue straight on, your direction 150 degrees, along the footpath between the lines of trees. 125 metres brings you over another stile, and you continue in the same direction as before. In 250 metres go over another stile, and continue straight on.

The path leads out into an open field. You are now going to *walk south for the next 1.5km, through a series of five fields, keeping to the left-hand edge of each field in turn*. This path generally follows the route taken by the **River Misbourne** before it dried up completely due to over-extraction of water from the valley.

In more detail: Follow the path along the field's left-hand edge. In 370 metres, do not follow the tractor tracks as they head off left into the next field through the trees, but continue straight on along the left-hand edge of the field.

Another 100 metres brings you up to and over a stile in the far left-hand corner of the field. Continue straight on along the left-hand edge of the next field.

300 metres takes you past a row of trees going uphill to your right, and into the next field, continuing on in the same direction along the left-hand edge of this field.

350 metres brings you to the far left-hand corner of this field, over another stile into another field, and along a path that follows the left-hand edge of the next field.

Another 350 metres brings you over a stile into another field, and you continue along the left-hand edge of this field in the same direction as before.

70 metres brings you up to a wooden barrier, with the South Bucks Way signposted ahead and left, and a white-painted footpath arrow pointing ahead and slightly to the right. Take the leftmost footpath, continuing along the left-hand edge of the next field. 140 metres brings you to the far left-hand corner of the field, and through a metal kissing gate. Continue on in the same direction, along the path making its way between the trees, your direction 190 degrees initially.

In 200 metres, the trees on the right peter out and the path is bordered by a wooden fence on your right-hand side. In another 130 metres go through a wooden kissing gate and, 10 metres further on, the path splits three ways. There is a tennis club ahead and to the left. *Take the rightmost option, going, in due course, to the right of the tennis courts*, your direction 200 degrees initially. 140 metres takes you beyond the tennis courts, out into an area of playing fields. Continue following the path as it makes its way along the right-hand edge of the playing fields.

[6] In 60 metres *turn right, going up a footpath between houses*, your direction 250 degrees. 70 metres brings you up on to the roadway. Go straight ahead up Boundary Road. In 200 metres, where the road becomes Lovel End, continue straight on up the hill.

In 250 metres, having passed Chalfont St Peter First School on your right, Lovel End curves off to the left. Just before the cul-de-sac

dead ahead, you *turn right down a footpath*, which goes between the school and the houses. This is signed as a public footpath and there is a 'No cycling' sign; your direction is 345 degrees.

Another 320 metres brings you out on to the main road. Go straight across the road and over the stile on the far side, and walk dead ahead through the trees into the grounds of Chalfont Grove. In 30 metres the path forks and you *take the right-hand fork* along the path which follows the line of a chainlink fence, your direction 275 degrees.

In 400 metres you come to a silver-painted metal fieldgate. Instead of going through the gate, *go along the narrow path to the left of the gate*, following the line of the fence on your right-hand side for 25 metres, until you come to a large stile. Cross over this, and *turn right into the field*.

Follow the path which goes off half left, with the 10 foot stump of a tree on your left hand side, your direction 300 degrees. In 80 metres you pass between two large lime trees whose lower branches look as though they've been filled up with twigs for some enormous bird's nest. In another 130 metres, the left-hand fork of the path leads you into the trees, your direction 305 degrees. 45 metres further on, cross over a stile and continue straight on. In another 75 metres, cross over another stile and *follow the white pointer on to the footpath heading to your left*, your direction 265 degrees.

In 140 metres you come to a stile in the left-hand corner of the field **[7]**. Go over this on to a surfaced track. *Turn left, due south, down* *this car-wide track,* following the direction of overhead cables on your right-hand side. 450 metres down this track brings you out on to the roadway, at the entrance to Grove Farm. *Turn right along the road,* your direction 285 degrees.

In 500 metres you pass Welders House and Gate House on your left-hand side. 400 metres beyond that you come down almost to the end of the road, where on your right is the **Friends Meeting House**.

[8] *Enter the grounds of the Meeting House* and, if you have time, ring the bell of the main house and ask for permission to see inside. Continue the walk by *going left up the path around the front of the Meeting House* (not a public footpath, but one that the Quakers allow people to use) then through the **Quaker burial ground**, your direction 10 degrees.

115 metres brings you to the top of the burial ground and through a wooden kissing gate. Continue along the clear path going up the hill ahead.

Another 100 metres brings you out through a wooden gate, alongside a wooden barn. This is the **Mayflower Barn**. *Turn left* here and walk 40 metres up to the road, where you *turn right.*

50 metres up the road is the **Old Jordans Quaker Guest House**, the suggested tea place. Past the guesthouse, in 100 metres, *turn left down the road signed for Jordans Village* ('No Through Road'). 30 metres down this road you pass a house called One Ash on your left side. Ignore ways off and, in 170 metres, at the end of the village green, where the road curves around to the right, continue straight on

down the road dead ahead, your direction, initially, 300 degrees.

170 metres down this road you come to a junction **[9]**. (**[*]** If you want to catch the train back from Seer Green & Jordans Station, turn left down the hill and follow the road for 650 metres for the station.)

To continue the loop back to Beaconsfield, cross straight over on to a car-wide track going steeply downhill, dead ahead. 115 metres brings you to the bottom of the hill, where another path crosses your path. Continue straight on, following the public footpath sign, through the metal railings and along the side of the hedge on your right-hand side. Follow the path up the hill and through a second set of metal railings, and straight on along the path as it leads you through some trees.

In 400 metres the path brings you out on to a car-wide track (going through some wooden gates into a courtyard to the right). *Turn left along this track,* your direction 265 degrees initially. In 50 metres you pass the entrance to Hall Place on your left-hand side. 30 metres further on, you come out to the roadside in the village of **Seer Green**, opposite the parish hall. *Turn left into School Lane,* your direction 210 degrees. 150 metres down the road, you pass Stable Lane on the right. In 130 metres, you walk past the entrance to Seer Green C of E Combined School, which is on your right-hand side.

20 metres further on **[10]** *turn right off the road,* your direction 215 degrees, down the footpath going to the left of Vicarage Close. In 180 metres, cross straight over a residential street, continuing on the

footpath on the other side. 30 metres down the tarmac path going straight down the hill, *take the path going off to the right*, your direction 245 degrees initially. 185 metres brings you down on to the main road, alongside Weathering House on your right-hand side.

Cross the busy road to *go straight on, between fence posts* (the stile is missing) into the trees, your direction 245 degrees.

In 40 metres this brings you out on to a golfcourse, where you follow the direction of the public footpath sign. (Note the warning about 'flying golf balls' – keep watching the direction of play). Head out half right across the fairway, towards the green-and-white striped pole which marks the continuation of the footpath, your direction 225 degrees. When you reach this pole, go straight on towards the footpath sign dead ahead. In 70 metres follow the direction of this sign and *turn right along the side of a fence* which borders the railway on your left, your direction 310 degrees.

[11] In 500 metres you come to another public footpath sign, this time pointing left, and you *follow the path left, over the bridge* across the railway track. Over the bridge, there are three paths and you *take the rightmost path*, which is signposted public footpath, your direction 250 degrees. *Walk straight across the golfcourse for the next 500 metres,* following the directions and the green-and-white striped poles, and also going through trees.

At the edge of the golfcourse, go past a kissing gate into the field beyond. Go straight ahead across the field towards the far side, your direction 245 degrees. 400 metres brings you to the far side of the field and out on to the A355. At the island cross this busy road and go down Ronald Road, straight ahead. This leads into Fernhurst Close.

In 240 metres there is a parking area in the semicircle of houses on the right, and you continue straight on down the road. 90 metres brings you down to the bottom of Candlemas Mead, and you continue slightly left, your direction 280 degrees.

150 metres along here, the road curves sharply around to the left. (If you are interested in visiting the old town of Beaconsfield, follow the road round to the left, turn right at the first T-junction and left at the second one, which takes you on to the road linking the old and new towns.)

To go directly to the station, *turn right here, down the footpath which takes you between the houses*, your direction 10 degrees.

In 80 metres you come out on to a road, which you cross over to walk straight ahead along the left-hand side of the green. 170 metres brings you to the bottom of Ches-terton Green, where you *turn left* into Maxwell Road, your direction 280 degrees.

200 metres takes you past Sainsbury's on the left and the new **Bar Med** (the alternative place for tea) just beyond that on the right, and another 200 metres brings you out on to a junction opposite the Coffee House.

Turn right, then continue straight on over the railway track and *turn right on the far side of the bridge*, going down the road to platform 1, the London platform, at **Beaconsfield Station**.

Walk 11

Tring to Wendover

Reservoir nature reserves & Wendover Woods

Length 21.5km (13.5 miles), 6 hours 30 minutes. For the whole outing, including trains and meals, allow 9 hours 15 minutes.

OS Landranger Map No.165. Tring, map reference SP 952 122, is in **Hertfordshire**, 13km east of Aylesbury. Wendover is in **Buckinghamshire**.

Toughness 6 out of 10.

Features This walk has plenty of variety – completely flat the first half of the day, starting along the quiet tree-lined banks of the Grand Union Canal, then past 'twitchers with bins' (aka birdwatchers with binoculars) beside nature reserves-cum-reservoirs. In the afternoon, the public footpath passes alongside RAF gliders being whipped into the air by a whirling wheel on a stationary lorry. For the last 3km the land changes completely, as you make your way up into a popular part of Wendover Woods (complete with exercise bars and gargantuan signposts), nearly to the highest point in the Chilterns, and then descend steeply into Wendover.

Shortening the walk You could get a bus along the A41 from Aylesbury to Tring (ask at the pub), catching the bus on the main road in Aston Clinton after lunch and then taking the train from Tring (which means you can use a return ticket). Or, before lunch, at point **[5]** on the map, you could turn left along the B489 – this brings you, in 600 metres, to the A41 and the Rising Sun pub for lunch (and the bus to Tring). Or, later in the day, to avoid hills and woods, turn right on to the Wendover Arm Canal after lunch (see the asterisk **[*]** below) and follow it all the way back into Wendover.

History The water from the **Tring Reservoirs** (opened between 1793 and 1805) keeps the Grand Union Canal navigable. The first UK nesting of black-necked grebes was noted here in 1918.

The Church of All Saints, Buckland, was built in 1273. At the time, the Lord of the Manor was Hugh le Despenser who, with his son, was executed by his erstwhile friend, Edward II, in 1326. A later Lord of the Manor, the Earl of Warwick ('Warwick the Kingmaker'), was killed by his one-time friend, Edward IV, at the Battle of Barnet in 1471.

After lunch the route goes through the grounds of the **Halton House estate**, once owned by the Rothschild family – teams of zebras used to take them to their favourite picnic spot – and now given over extensively to the RAF.

Construction of the **Wendover Arm Canal** started in 1793 to supply water to feed the Grand Union Canal at Tring. It became known as the leaky canal – despite partial relinings in 1803 and 1856, it had to be closed in 1904.

Boddington Bank is an Iron Age hill fort overlooking your final destination of Wendover.

Saturday Walkers' Club Take the train nearest to **9am** (before or after) from **Euston** Station to **Tring**. Trains back from Wendover run about twice an hour, and return to Marylebone. Journey time 40 minutes on the way out, 45 minutes for the return journey.

Lunch The **Oak** pub (tel 01296 630 466) in Aston Clinton is 12km from the start, so allow enough time. Excellent and reasonably priced home-cooked food – with some dishes taking 45 minutes to prepare – is served from midday to 2pm Monday to Friday; midday to 3pm winter weekends; midday to 9pm or 10pm summer weekends. Groups of more than ten are asked to book in advance.

Tea The suggested tea place is the **Le Petit Café** (tel 01296 624 601) five minutes from Wendover Station, which is open until 4.30pm weekdays, and until 5.30pm on weekends and bank holidays. Alternatively, the smokier bar of the **Red Lion Hotel** (tel 01296 622 266) in Wendover serves tea all day. There is also the **Gaea tea rooms** (tel 01296 696789) in the Antiques Centre courtyard opposite the war memorial, which is open until 5.30pm, seven days a week.

WALK DIRECTIONS

[1] [Numbers refer to the map.] *Coming out of* **Tring Station** *forecourt, turn left on to the main road, going past the Royal Hotel Posting House. In 300 metres there is a bridge where the road crosses the* **Grand Union Canal**. *Do not cross the bridge. Instead turn right off the road at the start of the bridge, and take the steps going down on to the towpath. You will walk along the towpath for the next 4km, your direction 290 degrees initially.*

In more detail: In 1.2km you come to a stone bridge across the canal. Follow the path up on to the bridge, across to the other side, and down on to the left-hand side of the canal. 900 metres further on, there is a second stone bridge carrying a road over the canal, with the Grand Junction Arms public house next to the bridge. Continue along the path under the bridge, with the British Waterways workshops on your right-hand side.

500 metres further on, a footbridge crosses the junction with the Wendover Arm, going off to the left. *Go over the footbridge* and continue straight along the main canal, signposted 'Braunston 55 miles'. You are now at Lock 45, the top of the Marsworth flight. Counting this as the first set, continue *to the sixth set (Lock 40)*.

[2] Here *leave the towpath and go up on to a higher parallel path on Marsworth Reservoir bank*. In 100 metres, *by a Tring Reservoirs information board, fork slightly right along the right-hand side of the second (Startops End) reservoir,* still parallel with the canal.

Ignore a downwards right fork in 30 metres and continue to the reservoir corner. Facing the **Anglers Retreat** pub ahead (across a road), *turn left to follow the reservoir bank*, parallel with the road. At the next reservoir corner turn left along its third side for 300 metres, then going over a wooden bridge.

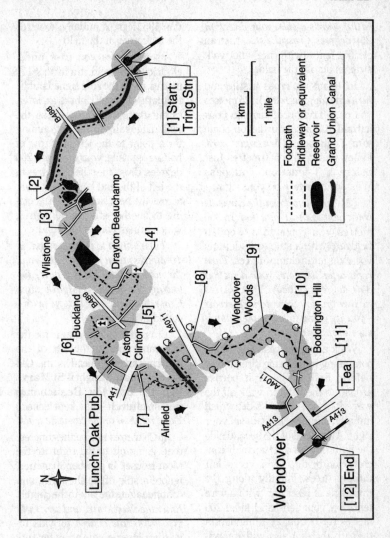

[1] Start: Tring Stn

[2]

[3]

Wilstone

Drayton Beauchamp

[4]

Buckland

[5]

[6]

Aston Clinton

[7]

Airfield

Lunch: Oak Pub

A41

A4011

[8]

Wendover Woods

[9]

[10]

Boddington Hill

[11]

Tea

A4011

Wendover

A413

A413

[12] End

B488

B489

N

1 km
1 mile

Footpath
Bridleway or equivalent
Reservoir
Grand Union Canal

[!] *In 5 metres, ignore some wooden steps on the other side going towards a road.*

Instead turn left with the path, past a 'Tring Reservoirs Walks' guidepost, and, in 15 metres, go up some wooden steps on to the road. With great care, *cross to the other side, where a new path takes you right along another reservoir* (Tringford), your direction 260 degrees initially.

In 50 metres you come to a sign giving information about the area. In another 150 metres, the path reaches the end of the reservoir and continues on in the same direction through some trees, down some steps and curves around to the left. 10 metres further on, *turn right up a path towards a stile, your direction 250 degrees. Cross the stile,* then an electric fence (with care) and walk straight across the field.

In 40 metres cross a stile and *turn left along the road.* In 25 metres you pass Tringford Farm on your left and, 100 metres further on, come to a T-junction. *Turn right here.* Follow this road for 500 metres. Just before a T-junction, you pass Wilstone cemetery on your right.

[3] *Turn left down the car-wide track next to the T-junction.* In 300 metres you come to a wooden fieldgate with a stile to its left, as you come into a clump of trees. *Turn right after the gate, your direction 340 degrees initially. 100 metres further on, you come to a reservoir – you are going to follow the water's edge around two sides.*

Walk along the reservoir bank, continuing in the same direction as before. Follow the first corner around to the left and walk all the way along the second side, which initially parallels a road on your right. At the end of the second side the path crosses over a small concrete footbridge then veers left through trees, initially along the third side of reservoir, with a wire fence on your left-hand side. 200 metres further on, at a junction in the path, there is a sign with information about **Wilstone Reservoir**.

*At this junction take the path to the right, your direction 145 degrees. In 8 metres ignore a stile going off to the right and, 10 metres further on, cross over the stile ahead of you. Immediately over the stile, take the fork going to the right of the tree dead ahead. In 15 metres, branch off right across the field, your direc-*tion 195 degrees initially, towards the far corner of the field.

In 30 metres you pass under electricity lines and, in a further 170 metres, cross the stile signed public footpath. On your right is an interesting thatched house. Cross the field diagonally to the left, aiming for a point to the left of a row of houses opposite, your direction 200 degrees. Cross the stile 60 metres to the left of the end house, and walk across the next field half left, coming to another stile, in 60 metres, which brings you on to a road.

Turn left on to the road and, in 40 metres, turn right off the road through a metal kissing gate, following the public footpath sign. Cross the field half left, your direction 170 degrees.

Cross the stile and aim for the telegraph pole to the left of the church. Directly ahead is the Old Rectory, and to its right is **St Marys [4]**, the **Drayton Beauchamp parish church** – alas, kept locked.) *Turn right on to the car-wide track.*

In 25 metres ignore the concrete road going off to the right (to the Moat House). In another 30 metres, ignore a stile off to the right, and continue along the lane to the church. *Enter the churchyard, and turn right just before the church* to walk towards a kissing gate at its far end. Pass through this, and *cross the field to another kissing gate in its far left-hand corner.*

Beyond the gate, turn left onto a fenced path, which in 20 metres descends steps to a small river. *Turn right on the river,* passing under a bridge and the A41. *On the far side of the bridge, turn right up steps up the river bank.* At the top of the steps, go straight on, ignoring a path to the left, with a wooden fence and the road to your right.

In 100 metres, bear left away from the fence towards a telegraph pole. *You now walk for nearly 1km directly across the fields.* In more detail: cross through a broken hedge into the next field on a car-wide section over a ditch. Cross the next field heading for a 20 metre gap between a telegraph pole and a hedge. Then keep straight on across another very large field, heading for several buildings which are by the corner of a field leading to a road.

Turn right along the road and, in 25 metres, you come to a cross-roads **[5]**, with an old pub sign in the garden to your right-hand side. *You go straight across* the B489 to follow the sign that says 'Buckland village only'.

In 125 metres you pass Neilds farm on your left and, in another 50 metres, you pass Manor Farm on your right. In 200 metres *turn right into Peggs Lane* and, in 10 metres, *go left through the lychgate* of **All Saints Church**, **Buckland**.

After visiting the church, as you come out, turn left and left again, along the side of the church, your direction 330 degrees, to *exit the churchyard into the field beyond*, to go straight on, your direction now 345 degrees.

In 25 metres you pass a timber-framed house, 40 metres away on your left-hand side. In a further 35 metres go over a stile to continue with a field fence on your left-hand side, your direction 315 degrees.

In 12 metres ignore a stile on your left-hand side. In a further 105 metres, go over a stile *on to a tarmac*

road and turn right, your direction 350 degrees, and, *in 60 metres, go left on a signposted public footpath*, hidden by the hedge as you approach it, which goes along the side of Juniper Cottage (to the right of the tall hedge which separates it from Moat Farm), your direction 300 degrees.

In 30 metres, go over a stile, then *half left*, your direction 270 degrees, keeping on *towards the left-hand corner of the field*. At this corner, where this field goes sharp left, *carry straight on*, coming to the hedge ahead. Here you bear left, *with the hedge now on your right-hand side*, your direction 240 degrees.

Ignore on your right-hand side the pair of disused stiles and the gap into a field. 50 metres past these stiles, you go *over a stile and under mini-pylons*. The field hedge is now to your left-hand side, your direction is 235 degreees. In 130 metres, ignore a one plank footbridge with a metal railing, and *turn sharp right*, your direction 335 degrees, walking along the second side of the field.

In 200 metres you cross over the footbridge and stile directly in front of you, into a large open meadow, with the village of **Aston Clinton** on the far side.

Go forward and slightly left to another stile in the hedge ahead. Here cross and go diagonally towards the far left-hand corner of the field to reach a wooden signpost pointing in many directions. **[6]** *Take the path going left*, your direction 255 degrees, signed to Green End Street and the Oak Inn. Go over a wooden footbridge and climb over a small wooden barrier across the path. Walk down this path with a hedge on the right and a wooden slatted fence on the left. 100 metres down the path, you come out next to **Sunny Brook Close**, where you *turn left for 15 metres to reach the road. Across on the other side is the* **Oak** *pub, which is the suggested lunchtime stop.*

After lunch walk through the pub carpark to the road and turn left. Follow this road for 500 metres – ignore College Road off to the right. When you get to the T-junction on to the A41 you will see the village post office straight ahead of you on the other side of the road. There is a pedestrian crossing 20 metres to your left, which you should use to cross the road. Head back to the post office and *walk down the footpath going down the left-hand side of the bungalow which contains the post office.*

In 80 metres the path curves around to the left, your direction 170 degrees initially, and, 70 metres further on, you come out into the yard of a dairy, which you walk straight through, continuing in the same direction as before, with single-storey offices on your left-hand side and some kind of processing plant on your right.

At the end of these buildings you continue on for another 80 metres to a house with a wooden fieldgate (a sign on the gate says 'Beware dogs roaming').

[7] *Turn right at the gate, following the sign for the public footpath,* your direction 250 degrees initially. In 40 metres you come to a wooden barrier which you walk around and into a field. Walk diagonally across this field to its opposite left-hand corner. 50 metres brings you to this corner, where you find another wooden barrier with signs showing the direction of the public footpath. *Walk out into the open. You will see a sign saying 'Caution. Ministry of Defence airfield'. Turn left to follow the public footpath which goes along the edge of the airfield for 750 metres,* your direction 170 degrees initially. A small brook follows the left-hand side of the path. Ignore a first small bridge with a footpath sign to your left, and, at the far edge of the airfield, ignore a small bridge (made of wood and metal) crossing the brook to the left. You follow the path that continues along the right-hand side of the brook, with trees to the right of the path which have been pollarded (possibly to clear a flight path).

In 500 metres you come to the end of an obstacle course on your right, and cross a car-wide track to go straight on (slightly to the left) into the trees, your direction due south. (This path may be diverted around the wood to avoid 'war games' carried out by RAF Halton trainees, but the minor diversion will lead you easily to Harelane Bridge.) In 75 metres go over a stile and turn left on a car-wide track. In 35 metres turn right over a brick bridge (Harelane Bridge), crossing over the **Wendover Arm Canal**.

On the far side of Harelane Bridge, *descend to the left down steps to the towpath.* (**[*]** *At the bottom of these steps, turn left at this point if you want to take a short cut along the canal into Wendover.*) *The main suggested route is to turn right on to the towpath and walk along with the waterway on your left-hand side.*

In 750 metres the waterway narrows markedly and, 100 metres further on, you come to a wooden post with 'Green Park' written on it and a sign entitled 'The Wendover Arm' giving information about Cobblers Pits and the woodland which you are about to enter.

Turn right off the towpath, through a galvanised-iron kissing gate leading you into the wood (due south initially).

Keep straight on, ignoring ways off. In 50 metres you are walking between banks on both sides, then up through a new plantation. Some 200 metres from the canal, your path merges with another path coming in from your right and continues on up the hill. In another 250 metres you come to a stile at the top of the path, and you cross this, coming out on to the A4011.

[8] Directly opposite, a road leads straight ahead up a hill, with a green Forestry Commission sign next to it saying 'Chiltern Forest **Wendover Woods**'. Cross the A4011 and walk straight up the road ahead. In 25 metres turn right off the road on to a path leading into the forest (due south initially).

In 150 metres, *fork left uphill*, following a horseshoe on a post. in 200 metres, *cross a gravel track*, and keep on, again following a horseshoe on a post, your direction 200 degrees initially. In 100 metres a faint footpath crosses your path, going straight up and down the hill. Ignore this and continue straight on. 40 metres further on, you pass on your right a children's pond dipping area bordered by a wooden fence.

Continue and, 300 metres further on, you come to a crossroads with a wider path, which you cross straight over, continuing down for a further 40 metres until you come to a car-wide track.

Turn left on to the car-wide track, your direction 120 degrees initially. In 200 metres the path bends round to the right and starts to go uphill. You are now ascending the eastern flank of **Aston Hill**. After 400 metres of walking uphill, you come to a wooden post indicating footpaths going off to the left, right and straight ahead. Ignore this post and continue walking straight on up the hill.

100 metres further on, you come to a fork with a wooden post indicating a footpath to the left. Take the left-hand fork. 300 metres further on, the path curves round to the left at the top of the climb, and, 60 metres further on, you come to a wooden swing barrier leading out on to a tarmac track.

[9] A wooden post indicates footpaths going to the left and right – *turn right and walk along the tarmac track*. In 60 metres you come to a large two-armed wooden sign pointing left to the Chiltern Hills' highest point, and straight ahead for information and parking. A wooden toilet block is on the left-hand side. Carry straight on along the tarmac track.

In 120 metres you come to a sign saying 'Welcome to Wendover woodland park' and giving information about the park. Above this is another large wooden footpath sign – *follow the direction of the* **Firecrest trail**, down a small footpath at an angle to the main track, your direction 225 degrees initially. In 50 metres you come to a car-wide track and, instead of following the path ahead as it plunges downhill, *turn right on to the car-wide track*, your direction 240 degrees initially. In 20 metres you come to a sign on the left which gives details about the Firecrest trail.

100 metres further on, the track veers sharply around to the right, but two footpaths 10 metres apart continue ahead in the same direction. *Take the footpath on the right*, your direction 220 degrees initially.

In 200 metres you cross another car-wide path and continue on. In 40 metres there is a fork and you take the left-hand path (the right fork goes to a road in 20 metres). In 150 metres you come to an open green space. Here you *turn right and walk 10 metres to join up with the car-wide earth road which runs parallel to the footpath that you have been walking along. Turn left on to this track*, your direction 240 degrees initially, and, in 200 metres, you come to a small grass roundabout and a wooden barrier, dead ahead **[10]**.

Go straight on past this barrier. On your left there is a sign giving information about **Boddington Bank hill fort**. 10 metres beyond it, ignore a fork to the left. In 70 metres there is a path going off to the right diagonally down the hill. To your right, at the top of this path, you will see sit-up exercise benches. *Turn right down this path,* your direction 280 degrees initially. (If time permits, you can continue along the main track to explore the remains of the fort, and in 150 metres enjoy the views from the hilltop over the Vale of Aylesbury, but you then need to retrace your steps to this point.).

After a steep descent of about 300 metres, on a potentially very slippery path, you come to a crossroads with a bridleway, and you continue straight across down the hill, your direction 305 degrees initially. In 30 metres you will see a pair of wooden fieldgates on your right at the entrance to a house.

Turn left on to the car-wide track, your direction 270 degrees initially, with a fine view of Coombe Hill and its monument ahead, to your left. In 300 metres the track comes out into a residential estate **[11]**, and you continue straight on in the same direction along Barlow Road. In 40 metres you cross over Woolerton Crescent to your left and continue straight on. In 100 metres you come to a crossroads, again with Woolerton Crescent to your left (and with Hampden Road going straight on), and you *turn right, by the letterbox in the wall, down an unmarked road* (which is, in fact, Colet Road). In 100 metres this takes you down to a service road running parallel to the A4011.

Cross the service road and *cross the main road (the A4011)*.

Turn left on the A4011, your direction 225 degrees, and, in 15 metres, *turn right on Manor Road*, your direction 310 degrees. Follow this road, ignoring all ways off. In 250 metres cross the bridge over the southern end of the Wendover Arm Canal. In a further 160 metres, at the A413 T-junction, turn left, your direction 150 degrees.

In 200 metres you pass The George Inn on your left-hand side (which serves tea) and, in a further 10 metres, by the clock tower, follow the A413 right, your direction 230 degrees. This is Wendover High Street. In 70 metres you pass the **Red Lion Hotel** on your left-hand side (which serves tea).

Continue up the hill, ignoring a road to the left in 50 metres (signposted 'library'). 70 metres beyond this, the **Gaea Tea Rooms** are on the left. 50 metres on, you reach a road to the left signposted 'A413, London and Amersham'. On the corner is Wendover Book Shop, and just down this turning, on the other side, is the **Le Petit Café**, which is the main suggested tea place. To get to the station, continue on up the High Street and, in 70 metres, you pass the Shoulder of Mutton pub on your right. Immediately after that, Station Approach leads down to **[12] Wendover Station**.

Walk 12

Farnham to Godalming

River Wey, Waverley Abbey & Peper Harrow park

Length 19.9km (12.3 miles), 6 hours. For the whole outing, including trains, sights and meals, allow at least 9 hours.

OS Landranger Map No.186. Farnham, map reference SU 846 465, is in **Surrey**, 15km west of Guildford.

Toughness 6 out of 10.

Features This walk starts and ends along the River Wey. In between, it passes close to the ruins of Waverley Abbey and goes through woods to the suggested lunchtime pub in Charleshill. After lunch, there are further sandy bridleways through woods, before entering the parklands of the Peper Harrow estate, which has its own church and cricket pitch. The tea place is in Godalming's ancient centre.

Shortening the walk Buses run once an hour or so (Monday to Saturday only) from Tilford to destinations such as Farnham, Godalming and Haslemere.

History The town of **Farnham** (the name derives from the Saxon for 'ferny water meadows') prospered through trade in corn, wheat and hops. Its Norman castle was built by Henri de Blois, a grandson of William the Conqueror.

The twelfth-century **Waverley Abbey** – now in ruins – was the first Cistercian monastery to be built in England.

Peper Harrow estate was the home of the Earls of Midleton until the line died out. It became a home for disturbed adolescents, but is presently being converted into flats. Its **Church of St Nicholas** is a Norman church restored by Pugin, the Victorian architect. It contains a memorial to Vice Admiral Thomas Brodrick – he helped court-martial Admiral Byng, who, in 1757, was shot on the quarterdeck of his own ship as a scapegoat for the navy's failure to save a besieged garrison on Minorca or, as Voltaire put it, *'pour encourager les autres'*. The church can only be visited by arrangement a week in advance (phone the rector on 01483 810 328, or the warden on 01483 415 702.)

Godalming is thought to mean 'field (-ing) of Godhelm' (the putative first Saxon to claim the land). It was a coaching town between London and Portsmouth, and a centre of trade in wool, stone-quarrying, timber, leather, paper, corn and brewing. The High Street has many half-timbered buildings.

Saturday Walkers' Club Take the train nearest to **9.30am** (before or after) from **Waterloo** Station to **Farnham** (perhaps changing at Woking). Trains back from Godalming run two or three times an hour. Journey time about one hour.

Lunch The suggested lunch place is **The Donkey** pub (tel 01252 702 124) in Charleshill. It serves simple home-made food at reasonable prices, midday to 2.30pm daily;

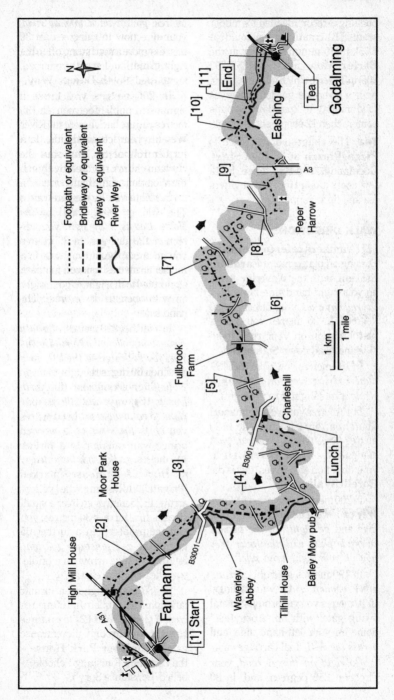

Footpath or equivalent
Bridleway or equivalent
Byway or equivalent
River Wey

N

[2]

[3]

[5]

[6]

[7]

[8]

[9]

[10]

[11]

End

Tea

Godalming

Eashing

A3

Peper Harrow

Fullbrook Farm

Charleshill

Lunch

[4]

B3001

Moor Park House

High Mill House

A31

Farnham

[1] Start

Waverley Abbey

B3001

Tilhill House

Barley Mow pub

1 km

1 mile

booking is recommended for indoor seating. Alternatively, you could eat 2.75km (50 minutes) earlier at the **Barley Mow** pub (tel 01252 792 205) in Tilford, which is by the green, with a riverside garden. It serves food midday to 2pm daily; groups of more than 12 people should book.

Tea The suggested tea place is **Pizza Piazza** at 78 High Street, Godalming. Also **Bay Tree**, just a few doors along High Street, offers tea and light supper items.

WALK DIRECTIONS

[1] [Numbers refer to the map.] Coming off platform 2 at **Farnham Station**, with the Waverley Arms on your right-hand side, *cross over the railway lines*, your direction 330 degrees. In 20 metres you pass a petrol station on your right-hand side and head down Station Hill.

In 100 metres you *cross the A31 dual carriageway and continue straight on* (slightly to the right).

In 40 metres you pass Emmanuel Church on your left-hand side. In 20 metres *turn right on a tarmac path alongside the* **River Wey** *to its left*, your direction 45 degrees (this is the **Borelli Walk**).

In 200 metres *cross over the River Wey* on a wooden bridge with railings and *go right, on the tarmac riverside path, with the River Wey now on your right-hand side*.

In 190 metres go right *over another wooden bridge* with railings. In 10 metres you go through a metal swing gate, with an 'Abbeyfield' home on your left-hand side, and *across the A31* dual carriageway.

Go right on this A road, your direction 250 degrees, and, in 80 metres, *go left on a tarmac road*, your direction 150 degrees. In 30 metres ignore a road going off to the right, to continue left with your road, signposted **North Downs Way**.

In 200 metres you cross a signposted public footpath. In 135 metres you are back beside the River Wey (on your left-hand side). In a further 160 metres, you pass the entrance drive to Snayleslynch Farm on your right-hand side.

In 100 metres, by the gateway to The Kiln, *go right, following the North Downs Way sign*, your direction 120 degrees. In 35 metres you go under the railway line. In a further 85 metres, ignore a footpath signposted to the right, to go straight on with open fields on your left-hand side.

In a further 220 metres, *at a path T-junction, follow the North Downs Way footpath sign to the left*, your direction 60 degrees.

In 65 metres ignore the North Downs Way sign and stile to your right, to go straight on. In 60 metres you *cross the river* on a wooden bridge with railings. In a further 140 metres, go *through the gateway of High Mills House* (marked 'Private'), following the yellow arrow. In 25 metres go over a small stream. In a further 30 metres, you exit the property. In a further 65 metres, *at a T-junction, go right*, following a blue arrow on a bridleway, heading due east.

In 480 metres ignore a tarmac lane uphill to your left. In 160 metres *cross a tarmac road* **[2]** *to continue straight on*, through the entrance gateway to **Moor Park House** – the Campana Finishing School (labelled 'Constance Spry').

In 50 metres – where to fork right would go through the gatehouse – keep straight on, signposted 'School Entrance'. In 80 metres go over a stile. In 610 metres you pass a machine-gun nest on your right-hand side. In 400 metres you pass a cave on your left-hand side. In 85 metres go through a wooden kissing gate. In 40 metres you pass Stella Lodge on your left-hand side to come out on to Camp Hill road **[3]**.

Go right on this road downhill for 20 metres, then left on the road signposted to Godalming, your direction 145 degrees. In 65 metres ignore a way down to the right. In a further 120 metres, by a public footpath sign, *follow the red arrow right, on an earth road*, your direction 185 degrees.

In 200 metres you can see **Waverley Abbey House** away on your right-hand side, and the ruins of **Waverley Abbey**, due west (300 metres to the left of the house).

(If you would like to detour for a closer view of the abbey, in 110 metres take a path down to your right between yew trees; in 45 metres, you are beside the River Wey, with the abbey ruins opposite – at 280 degrees from you.)

Continue on the main path. **[!]** *In 115 metres, where the public footpath is signposted straight on, and there is a metal gate across the path to the left, follow the red arrow sharp right up the hill, your direction 230 degrees.*

In 370 metres you *cross a tarmac road* (with an antique postbox opposite) to continue on a gravel road signposted with a red arrow, your direction 230 degrees.

In 40 metres fork left, your direction 190 degrees. In 10 metres you pass **Sheephatch Farm** (marked on the OS map) on your left-hand side. Keep to this path, ignoring ways off. In 450 metres you pass the entrance drive to Tilhill House on your left-hand side, to continue straight on, now on a tarmac lane.

In 130 metres, by the entrance to Wey Cottage, *fork right off this lane on a signposted public bridleway,* your direction 170 degrees. In 15 metres ignore a stile on your left-hand side. You are back near the River Wey on your right-hand side. In a further 185 metres, ignore a fork going up to the left.

In 285 metres you come *to the main road,* with Tilford Post Office on your left-hand side. (If you want to eat now, turn right, over the bridge, to the **Barley Mow** pub in Tilford, on your right-hand side.)

The suggested route is to *go left,* your direction 45 degrees. In 15 metres you pass the post office, still on your left-hand side. In a further 210 metres, you ignore Whitmead Lane to the right. In 75 metres, *by Caesar's Corner House on your left-hand side, cross over to take the tarmac lane to your right,* your direction 125 degrees, with Marley Cottage now on your left-hand side.

In 75 metres **[4]** *take the public footpath signposted left* (a tarmac road), your direction 60 degrees.

In 150 metres, at the end of this driveway, by the entrance to Archers Hill, *fork right on a public footpath,* following a yellow arrow.

In 400 metres, go through a metal gate in a tall metal fence. Immediately turn left, following the 'Permissive footpath' yellow arrow, and walk through bushes along the edge of the garden of Pooh Corner House to a tarmac road. *Go right on the road*, your direction 190 degrees, downhill, with Highmead House on your left-hand side.

In 240 metres, *by the entrance drive to Whitmead House, fork left* on a vehicle-wide earth road, signposted with a red arrow, your direction 95 degrees, with a timber-framed lodge house on your right-hand side.

In 950 metres you pass the entrance to West Wey House on your right-hand side. In 80 metres, *at a crossing of lanes, fork right*, downhill, your direction 95 degrees. In 30 metres you pass the entrance to Riversleigh Farm on your right. In a further 55 metres, you come to the suggested lunchtime stop, **The Donkey** pub in **Charleshill**, on your right-hand side.

Coming out of the pub after lunch, turn right. In 55 metres you come *to the main road.* Cross this and take the public signposted *tarmac lane straight on* (the entrance to Foxhill on your right-hand side), your direction being 345 degrees.

In 35 metres *turn right, following the bridleway sign*, to go uphill, your direction 65 degrees. In a further 215 metres, your way becomes a tarmac drive. In 210 metres you pass black iron gates on your right-hand side, to *fork left*, your direction 60 degrees, on a tarmac way. There is a column with a 'Three Barrows Place' bell on your left-hand side.

In 80 metres you exit through the Three Barrows Place gateway to *cross the tarmac road* **[5]** *and go straight on*, your direction 70 degrees, along a signposted public bridleway, ignoring fieldgates off to the left and right-hand sides.

In 365 metres, by the entrance drive to Fullbrook Farm, you come out *on to a tarmac road and cross it to continue straight on*, your direction due east.

In 170 metres, by a turning circle or parking area on your right-hand side **[6]**, *go through a swing gate on your left-hand side, following a public bridleway wooden sign, and then go half right*, diagonally across the field. In 25 metres you pass the first oak tree, on your left-hand side, your direction 60 degrees, and keep going in this direction, ignoring all ways off. *Aim for 30 metres to the left of the right-hand corner of the wood, some 400 metres ahead of you.*

Enter the wood by a wooden swing gate, and continue on, your direction 65 degrees, along a potentially muddy way. In 60 metres cross a stream on a bridge with wooden railings. In a further 170 metres, you come *to a tarmac road by a bridleway sign, and you turn right*, your direction 110 degrees.

In 60 metres go over a stream. In 30 metres, opposite Brookside House, *go left on a signposted public bridleway*, your direction now 20 degrees.

In 190 metres you come *to an earth car road T-junction where you go left*, with Kingshott Cottage on your left-hand side, your direction 55 degrees. In 45 metres follow the blue arrow on, ignoring a fork left to Broad Firs. In a further 220 metres, ignore a way off to the right (with a fieldgate also on your right-hand side). In 200 metres ignore ways off to the right and left. In 150 metres ignore a post with a blue arrow to the left (indicating a bridleway) to follow the blue arrow straight on. In 30 metres ignore a way to the right (barred with a wooden barrier).

In 275 metres *(5 metres before a post with red arrows to the left and straight on)*, **[7]** *go right on an unmarked car-wide way*, your direction 190 degrees.

In 60 metres *fork left* (there is a wooden barrier on the right fork).

In 260 metres you come out *on to a tarmac road where you go right*, your direction 215 degrees. In 40 metres you pass the entrance to Prospect House.

In a further 55 metres, *go left on a sandy road, signposted Warren Lodge* and public bridleway, your direction due south.

In a further 240 metres, ignore a more minor fork to the left. In 65 metres cross a stream.

In a further 70 metres, *at a T-junction,* with a cottage on your right-hand side and a wooden fieldgate ahead, *go left*, your direction 80 degrees.

In 240 metres cross a wide way. In 85 metres, *within 20 metres of the end of the wood, at a junction, go right*, your direction 125 degrees – just within the edge of the wood on your left-hand side.

Keep to this main path, ignoring all ways off. In 360 metres you come *to a tarmac road where you turn right*, your direction 195 degrees.

In 45 metres you pass Headlands House on your right-hand side. In a further 240 metres, you come *to the main tarmac road.*

Turn right and, in 40 metres **[8]**, *turn left* off the road, following the public footpath sign down the tarmac road into the **Peper Harrow** estate (which is marked on the OS map).

In 180 metres you pass through a wooden fieldgate. In a further 10 metres, ignore a fork to the right by a postbox. After walking a further 200 metres, you come to the (locked) **Church of St Nicholas**, Peper Harrow.

In 30 metres *take the stile* (with a metal fieldgate to its left) signposted public footpath, *going to your left*, heading due east. In 30 metres you pass close to a wooden farmshed on your left-hand side and *head to the left of the green pavilion* ahead, with no clear path.

In 135 metres you pass the pavilion on your right-hand side and keep parallel to the telegraph poles, some 30 metres to the left of them. *Enter the wood, some 30 metres to the left of its right-hand edge*, going over a stile.

At the other end of the wood, *at a T-junction* **[9]**, ignore a footpath straight on and *go right*, coming in 8 metres *to a small metal swing gate and bridleway sign where you go left*, with the field fence on your left-hand side and your direction 70 degrees.

In 150 metres veer right with the bridleway, a field fence still to your left-hand side.

In 235 metres go through a metal fieldgate to *cross the A3 on a bridge*. On the other side, go right downhill towards a petrol station. In 80 metres *turn left on Lower Eashing Road* (with the petrol station opposite), your direction 120 degrees.

In 45 metres *turn left between Greenways and Lower Eashing Farm Cottage, on a tarmac road,* which is a signposted public bridle-way, your direction 40 degrees.

In 40 metres this tarmac road becomes a concrete road, passing Greenways Farm and Stable on your right-hand side. In 120 metres, by a pillbox on your right-hand side, ignore a path off uphill to your left. In a further 75 metres, you pass under pylons.

In a further 110 metres, you *leave the concrete road to go straight on through a wooden fieldgate, on a car-wide earth bridleway*, your direction 55 degrees – in 10 metres passing a pillbox on your left.

In 230 metres go under pylons (a potentially muddy area). In 110 metres you pass under two lots of pylon cables.

In 145 metres ignore a path to the left, marked by a post. In 30 metres, *by a garden wall and by a post with multiple arrows* [10], *go right*, following a public footpath yellow arrow, your direction 145 degrees.

In 80 metres go through a wooden swing gate (a wooden fieldgate and the entrance to Milton Wood on its right-hand side). In 150 metres go through a metal barrier, now back alongside the **River Wey**.

In 500 metres go through another metal barrier. In 40 metres, *1 metre before the start of a tarmac road* [11], *follow the signpost right*, marked 'Public footpath to Godalming', your direction due south.

In 75 metres go over a concrete bridge, straight on. In 15 metres you *turn left under the pylons*, your direction 140 degrees, with the River Wey on your right-hand side.

In 30 metres you *pass under more pylons and fork left*, your direction 170 degrees.

In 40 metres continue to the left, your direction 100 degrees, *alongside the River Wey on the right.* In 120 metres you again go under pylons; and again in 55 metres.

In 120 metres, by a bench, yours becomes a tarmac path. In 55 metres cross the stream on a bridge. In a further 280 metres, cross a bridge with scaffolding pole railings. In 5 metres go through a metal barrier, *across an entrance drive to offices on your right-hand side, and straight on*, with the stream still on your left-hand side. In 65 metres, *at a tarmac road, go right*, your direction 170 degrees.

In 20 metres *go under the railway line. 10 metres after the bridge, fork right on a signposted public footpath.* In 110 metres, having kept parallel to the road, cross the river on a wooden bridge with wooden railings.

In 35 metres you are *back on the main Borough Road, straight on.* In 65 metres, by the entrance to the Church of St Peter and St Paul, *go left up Church Street*, which is a car road made of bricks and signposted 'To the High Street', your direction 125 degrees. Going uphill, in 130 metres you *turn left into the High Street*, **Godalming**. 140 metres on, you come to the suggested place to have tea, **Pizza Piazza** at no.78.

Coming out of Pizza Piazza after tea, *retrace your steps to the church* – in other words, turn right into the High Street. In 140 metres, by the Old Town Hall, turn right down Deanery Place to go back down to the church – *but then straight on to pick up a passageway leading to the station*, again straight on.

At **Godalming Station**, go under the subway for London trains.

Walk 13

Oxford
(round walk)

Port Meadow, the river,
canal & colleges

Length 15.2km (9.4 miles), 4 hours
40 minutes. For the whole outing,
including trains, sights and meals,
allow as much of the day and
evening as possible – a minimum of
8 hours.

OS Landranger Map No.164.
Oxford is 90km (56 miles) west of
London.

Toughness 1 out 10.

Features The route is easy and entirely level, but can be muddy along
the River Cherwell. It starts as a
walk along the River Isis to Binsey,
a favourite walk for the poet Gerard
Manley Hopkins (the 'wind-wander-
ing, weed-winding bank'), who lam-
ented the felling of aspens along the
towpath here in his 1879 poem
Binsey Poplars ('the sweet especial
rural scene'). You can take a dip
here if you want. Passing the ruins
of Godstow Nunnery, you come to
the Trout Inn at Wolvercote and
take in a bit of Port Meadow before
coming to the suggested lunchtime
pub, the Plough Inn.

After lunch the walk heads south
along the Oxford Canal, past a
community of New Age houseboats,
and across town and via a footbridge by Wolfson College to go
along the River Cherwell through
its Nature Reserve, where butter-

cups are abundant in May. Going
through the University Parks, you
come to the Pitt-Rivers Museum.
From there it is a circuitous route of
small streets and alleyways, past
most of the historic colleges, and
going through Merton Field and
Christ Church Meadow, to tea just
off the Cornmarket.

Shortening the walk There are
buses about every 20 minutes from
near the lunchtime pub back into
Oxford. Or, at point **[4]** below, by
turning right towards the city centre, you could avoid the walk along
the River Cherwell. At any point in
the circuit through the Oxford Colleges, you could give up and make
for the tearoom.

History The Saxons fording the
Thames with their oxen gave this
place the name 'Oxen-ford'. Robert
d'Oilly took over Oxford in 1066,
creating a Norman stronghold.
Possibly the first college to be
founded was **Merton**, in 1264,
although there had been a university for at least a century before
this. A tavern argument between
townspeople and scholars resulted
in a 1354 massacre, in which 14 inns
or halls were ransacked and a
number of chaplains scalped.
Christ Church College in Oxford
was Charles I's headquarters during the Civil War, with **New
College** cloisters used as a gun-
powder store. In the sixteenth century, Cranmer, Ridley and Latimer
were burnt at the stake in **Broad
Street**. Gates at **Balliol College**
still show scorch marks from the
flames, and there is a **memorial** to
these Protestant martyrs in St Giles.
The men's colleges started admit-
ting women in 1974.

There are too many places to visit in one day, but you might like to stop in at the **Pitt Rivers Museum** (tel 01865 270 927) which offers free entrance to 4.30pm and contains shrunken heads and artefacts from around the world. Also free is entrance to **St Johns College** (tel 01865 277 300) and its fine garden (open to 5pm daily, to dusk in winter). Admission to **Christ Church College** (tel 01865 276 151) costs £3 (open to about 5pm daily), but you can get in free any day of the week by attending evensong at 6pm.

Saturday Walkers' Club Take the train nearest to **9.45am** (before or after) from **Paddington** Station to **Oxford**. Journey time 55 minutes. With a Network Card cheap day return, you are not supposed to use the (rare) Intercity trains. There are other trains back two or three times an hour. The last train can be as early as 10.30pm, with a part-bus service later.

Lunch The suggested lunchtime stop is the **Plough Inn** (tel 01865 556 969), Wolvercote Green. This has bar food, a restaurant (which used to be a morgue), a library room, comfortable sofas and armchairs. It serves food from midday to 2pm daily, and in large portions. It is less touristy than the almost equally attractive alternative, 15 minutes earlier in the walk, the **Trout Inn** (tel 01865 302 071) in Wolvercote, which has rushing waters, a dilapidated wooden bridge and some peacocks – including a white one; it serves food all day every day.

Tea The suggested tea place is the **Nosebag**, 6-8 St Michael's Street, Oxford, which serves tea and other drinks, cakes and good food until 5.30pm on Monday; till 10pm on Tuesday, Wednesday and Thursday; 10.30pm on Friday and Saturday; 9pm on Sunday.

WALK DIRECTIONS

[1] [Numbers refer to the map.] Coming off the London train at **Oxford Station**, on platform 2, *exit the station and go out towards Westgate Hotel and Botley Road*.

At the main road (Botley Road), by Mick's Café, *turn right*, your direction 260 degrees, towards the bridge.

In 30 metres, pass the Old Gate House pub on your right-hand side. 40 metres past the pub, *just before the bridge, turn right on the sign-posted riverside footpath ('To Godstow')*, your direction 310 degrees.

The **River Isis** is on your left-hand side, with allotments on the other side of the river.

In 330 metres go over a footbridge with metal railings and straight on, continuing with the river on your left-hand side (ignore the Oxford Canal going off to the right). In 850 metres go straight on over a concrete footbridge with wooden railings, with **Port Mea-dow** now to your right.

In 120 metres turn left to *go on a mini-Brunel-style bridge over the river. Turn right the other side*, following the Thames Path sign to continue, now with the river on your right-hand side, your direction 345 degrees. In 20 metres you pass Bossom's Boatyard on your left-hand side and, in 180 metres, you ignore a fork left towards Binsey. However, in a further 280 metres, if you would like to make a brief de-

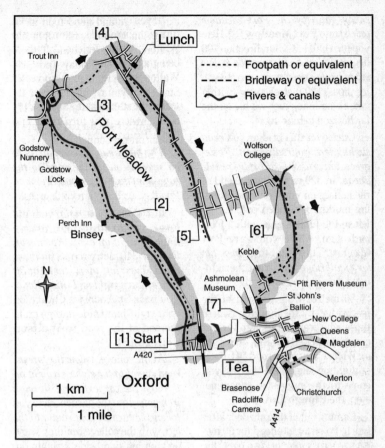

Footpath or equivalent
Bridleway or equivalent
Rivers & canals

Trout Inn

[4]

Lunch

[3]

Port Meadow

Godstow Nunnery

Godstow Lock

Wolfson College

[2]

Perch Inn

Binsey

[5]

[6]

Keble

Ashmolean Museum

Pitt Rivers Museum

St John's

Balliol

[7]

New College

Queens

Magdalen

[1] Start

A420

Tea

Merton

Oxford

Brasenose

Radcliffe Camera

Christchurch

A414

N

1 km

1 mile

tour to **Binsey** and its pub, there is *a path on the left* **[2]** *signposted the* **Perch Inn**, which leads in 50 metres to a gate into its garden that will only be open during the pub's opening hours.

The Old School House in Binsey has a number of doll's houses in its windows, including one with a thatched roof. (If you continue on the tarmac road beyond the Old School House, you come in 750 metres to Binsey Church and St Margaret's Well in the churchyard.)

Return from Binsey to the riverside to continue the walk, in 1.7km

reaching **Godstow Lock**. 100 metres beyond Godstow Lock, you come to the remains of **Godstow Nunnery** (the entrance is round the far side); and, 100 metres beyond the Nunnery, you come *to a tarmac road where you turn right over two bridges* to pass the **Trout Inn**, **Wolvercote**, on your right-hand side.

Cross a bridge 200 metres beyond the Trout Inn and, 50 metres past the bridge, with a carpark on your right-hand side (just where the road bends left by a thatched cottage) *go right through a wooden* swing gate (by the Port Meadow toilets) into **Port Meadow [3]**. Here you turn half left, your direction 105 degrees. You head *towards a low stone bridge* over two concrete water pipes, 120 metres away (with a factory chimney just visible on the far horizon behind it).

Once over this bridge, you *head slightly left, your direction 30 degrees, towards the car bridge visible ahead*. In 320 metres, at the end of the houses on your left, and avoiding muddy or flooded patches, go left to the Jubilee gate with a footpath sign, where you leave Port Meadow. Turn right to *go over the long footbridge* which runs the right-hand side of the road bridge.

80 metres from the end of the footbridge, by the bus stop (where those who want a bus into Oxford can drop out of the walk), *turn right on Wolvercote Green* road **[4]**. Keep straight on and, in 230 metres, you come to the suggested lunchtime stop, the **Plough Inn**.

Coming out of the pub door after lunch, go straight ahead for 50 metres to *cross the bridge* over the Oxford Canal and go down on to the towpath to go back under this bridge (no.236), to *follow the towpath, with the canal on your left-hand side* and the railway line on your right (the railway crossing shown here on old OS maps is now closed.)

In a further 500 metres you go under a railway bridge and come to a whole community of houseboats. In due course, you pass three raisable bridges.

300 metres beyond the last of these, you come to two brick bridges (no.240). *Cross an old brick bridge to get to Anchor Pub* **[5]**.

[If you want to shorten the walk, turn right here and keep on going to Walton Street – Jericho Café there being a possible place to have tea; Walton Street leads into Worcester Street and you rejoin the route towards the station at the asterisk **[*]** below, where you turn right into Hythe Bridge Street.]

The main suggested route is to go straight on up the road to the right-hand side of the pub (Polstead Road), your direction 75 degrees.

In 200 metres *cross Woodstock Road, slightly to the left, to continue straight on along Rawlinson Road*. In 240 metres *cross Banbury Road. Turn left up it, then, in 30 metres, turn right on Linton Road*. You pass St Andrews Church on your right-hand side and go on to the end of the road to **Wolfson College [6]**.

At the college, *follow the tarmac road round to the right, straight on through the carpark, and through iron gates* into the garden. Here you *follow the tarmac lane round to the left*, with the college buildings now on your left-hand side, straight on, to the end of the buildings. The lane bends left to go on an arched metal *footbridge* with metal railings over the **River Cherwell**.

On the other side of the footbridge *turn right*, your direction 195 degrees, on the riverside walk through the **Wolfson College Nature Reserve**, the river on your right-hand side.

In 120 metres you pass the War Memorial Cross on the opposite bank, your way potentially muddy, and go over a stile. In a further 90 metres, go over a stream on a small wooden bridge. Then, in 50 metres, go over a stile and two planks with a wooden railing over a ditch and turn left following the footpath arrow, away from the river, your direction 60 degrees.

In 45 metres go through what can be a very wet and muddy area, on planks and straight on, on a clear path, your direction 145 degrees, thus rejoining the river on your right-hand side.

In 90 metres you come to a sometimes muddy area where the river can flood, with Dragon School on the opposite side of the river. In a further 120 metres, you pass tennis courts on the opposite banks, with Lady Margaret Hall beyond them.

You go over a concrete bridge with metal railings and, in 240 metres, you cross another such bridge and come immediately to a more substantial concrete bridge with metal railings, on your right, over which you *cross the river* to enter the **University Parks**.

The other side of the bridge, go *straight on*, your direction 240 degrees, on an earth path. In 160 metres you cross a path and go straight on. In 100 metres, at another path crossing, continue on with the earth path. In a further 300 metres, you leave the University Parks to *turn left, on Parks Road*, your direction 145 degrees.

You pass **Keble College** on your right-hand side, with its lively yellow-patterned brickwork. Just before the end of Keble College, you pass **Pitt Rivers Museum** on your left-hand side (its entrance is through the University Museum).

At the far end of Keble College, turn right on Museum Road. In 75 metres, *where Blackhall Road goes off to the right, keep straight on* through a wooden barrier, between houses, along a passageway that winds to the right to become the Lamb and Flag Passage, out into the main road of St Giles.

Here you *turn left*, with **St Johns College** on your left-hand side and the **Ashmolean Museum** on the other side of the road.

50 metres past the front entrance of St Johns, you pass the **Martyrs' Memorial** on your right-hand side and, 100 metres beyond this **[7]**, *turn left into Broad Street* [unless you wish to go directly to the tea place, in which case go straight on along the main Cornmarket Street and take the first right into St Michael's Street].

The main suggested route along Broad Street passes **Balliol College** on your left-hand side, the Oxford Story exhibition on your right, and later Blackwells Bookshop on your left-hand side.

85 metres past Blackwells Bookshop, *go right on Catte Street*. Then in 30 metres *turn left on New College Lane*, under its **Bridge of Sighs**, to zigzag round with the lane, and with **New College** on your left-hand side.

This lane becomes Queens Lane, with **Queens College** on your right-hand side, and comes out eventually on to the High Street. Here you cross over the road and *turn left* along it.

You pass Merton Street going to the right. In a further 85 metres, with **Magdalen College** on your left-hand side, *go right on Rose Lane* (that is, after the pink house; the gate is in the wall on your left).

In 120 metres go through gates, with Meadow Cottages on your right-hand side.

20 metres beyond the gates, go right, on Dead Man's Walk (along the side wall of Meadow Cottages), your direction 305 degrees – with walls on your right-hand side and playing fields on your left.

In 20 metres you pass **a notice honouring James Sadler**'s balloon ascent in 1784.

In a further 120 metres, you come to **Merton College** on your right-hand side. *At the far end of Merton College, do not exit by the gates but turn left*, with a wall and **Christ Church College** on your right-hand side, and playing fields still on your left-hand side, your direction due south.

In 60 metres you come *to a broad sandy avenue and turn right*, your direction 265 degrees. In 90 metres you pass a side entrance to Christ Church College, and keep straight on (not the right fork) to go through the **War Memorial Garden**, coming out on the main road, called St Aldates.

Here you *turn right*, your direction due north. In 110 metres you pass the main entrance to Christ Church College. In a further 100 metres, you *turn right*, by the **Museum of Oxford**, *into Blue Boar Street*.

In 90 metres you pass the Bear pub on your left-hand side to continue straight on. *At the next road, King Edward Street, go straight across the bend (Oriel Square) for 30 metres to pick up the passageway (Oriel Street) going to the left*, your direction 5 degrees –

and with **Oriel College** on your right-hand side. In 80 metres you *cross over the High Street to continue on, along a passageway* into Radcliffe Square – passing **Radcliffe Camera** on your right-hand side and the entrance to **Brasenose College** on your left-hand side. 25 metres beyond this entrance, you *turn left, the way signposted to the Covered Market*, your direction 255 degrees, on Brasenose Lane.

In 120 metres *turn right* (on Turl Street). In 20 metres you pass the entrance to **Exeter College** and, in a further 30 metres, *turn left into Ship Street*, at the end of which you pass the **City Church of St Michael** on your right-hand side.

Cross over the Cornmarket and go straight on, along St Michael's Street. 20 metres along this street on your right-hand side, is the suggested tea place, the **Nosebag**, on the first floor at nos.6 to 8.

The station is about ten minutes away. *Coming out of the Nosebag, turn right* along St Michael's Street. In 120 metres *turn right into New Inn Hall Street*, and in 50 metres *turn left into George Street*.

In 160 metres, at the crossroads **[*]**, *go straight across into Hythe Bridge Street*. In 80 metres go over a bridge, past Antiquity Hall pub on your left-hand side.

In 130 metres, *go straight on, slightly to the left* (with the Budget Car & Van Rental depot on your right-hand side), *along Park End Street*, with **Oxford Station** off a turn-off to your right in 70 metres. The London platform (no.1) is on this side of the station.

Walk 14

Gomshall to Guildford

Medieval Shere,
Blackheath & River Wey

Length 14.8km (9.2 miles), 3 hours 50 minutes. For the whole outing, including trains, sights and meals, allow 7 hours 30 minutes.

OS Landranger Map Nos.187 and 186. Gomshall, map reference TQ 089 477, is in **Surrey**, 10km east of Guildford.

Toughness 3 out of 10.

Features There is much that is ancient, beautiful and surprising to be enjoyed on this walk. It starts in Gomshall, passing some of the pleasant buildings on its outskirts, before crossing fields to the interesting church and village of Shere – on the Tilling Bourne stream – a place packed full of fifteenth and sixteenth-century timber-framed buildings. Then the walk continues through the massive gnarled trees of Albury Park and the pine woods of Blackheath Common, and so to lunch in the middle of the forest at the gourmet Villagers pub. From there, the route offers a glimpse of Great Yangley Manor House, and follows the Downs Link path and the River Wey into Guildford, for tea at the Yvonne Arnaud Theatre. Short stretches of the Downs Link can be muddy.

Shortening the walk You could call a taxi from the lunchtime pub. Or you could turn right at the double asterisk **[**]** below, along the A248, to catch a train back to London from Shalford.

History Gomshall Station is where it is because, in the 1840s, the site for a railway station was decided on a given day by whichever shortlisted spot had the greatest number of people waiting. The publican at the Black Horse, Gomshall, provided free beer for those willing to wait at his site, as he wanted the station to be at Gomshall.

Gomshall is detailed in the *Domesday Book* (1086) as having 'land for 20 ploughs, 30 villagers, 8 smallholders with 18 ploughs, 6 slaves'. Of **Shere**, it reports: 'Queen Edith held it… Now it does not pay tax – 19 villagers and 6 smallholders with 12 ploughs. A church. 6 slaves.' By the sixteenth and seventeenth centuries it had grown into a small township of perhaps 40 houses (most of which remain today), housing blacksmiths, wheelwrights, weavers and tailors.

The Church of St James, Shere, was built in 1190 (its lychgate was designed by the architect Edwin Lutyens). It is a rare example of a church in the Early English Transitional Style (with the round Norman arches giving way to pointed ones). The nave pews have numbers – at one time people paid rent to the church for them.

In 1329, anchoress **Christine Carpenter** was enclosed in a cell on the north wall of the church (receiving food through a grating on the outside wall) for three years. She then returned to the world before petitioning to be re-enclosed. The bishop consented: 'The said Christine shall be thrust back into the said enclosure... that she may learn... how nefarious was her committed sin.'

The **Alms Chest** in the church dates from about 1200 and was used to collect money for the crusades fought in the Holy Land.

Guildford Castle, with its impregnable Norman keep, was granted by James I to the Mayor of Guildford for £5 3s 10d.

Saturday Walkers' Club Take the train nearest to **10am** (before or after) from **Victoria** Station – changing at Redhill – that will reach **Gomshall** not later than 11.30am. Journey time 56 minutes. Trains back from Guildford to London run about four times an hour. Journey time 34 minutes.

Lunch The suggested pub is the **Villagers** (tel 01483 893 152), Blackheath Lane, which serves food from midday to 2.30pm daily and under its new management may provide food all day in summer (groups of more than 15 should book). An earlier lunch is possible in a pub or tea shop in **Shere**; or at the **William IV** pub (tel 01483 202 685) in Albury Common, which serves food (good pudding but limiting to vegetarians) from midday to 2pm daily.

Tea The suggested Guildford tea place is the **Yvonne Arnaud Theatre** (tel 01483 569 334), open from 10am to 8pm Monday to Saturday. For Sundays, the suggested place is the **White House** pub (open daily throughout the day, tel 01483 302 006), which is by the river and the Church of St Nicholas.

WALK DIRECTIONS

[1] **[Numbers refer to the map.]** Leave **Gomshall Station** from platform 1 (on the side with the caravans on display) and turn left downhill, on the station approach road, your direction 240 degrees.

In 110 metres, *at the T-junction with the A25*, cross over and turn left under the railway bridge, your direction 155 degrees.

10 metres past the bridge, go right on the signposted public footpath, a lane called Wonham Way, your direction 225 degrees.

In 80 metres go on a bridge over the **Tilling Bourne** stream.

In a further 80 metres, you pass Southbrook Farm Cottage on your left-hand side. In a further 50 metres **[2]**, *turn right on an unmarked bridleway* (just before the gateway of Twiga Lodge, and with the bridleway parallel to an earth farm road on its left-hand side), your direction 265 degrees.

In 200 metres you pass a manor house on your right-hand side and a farm on your left-hand side.

In 40 metres, *at a road T-junction, turn right* and, in 20 metres, go back under the railway line.

In 10 metres, *at a car road T-junction by house no.4, turn left*, your direction 290 degrees.

Ignore ways off and, in a further 190 metres, *at the T-junction, go to the right of the triangle of grass, downhill, cross over the road and leave it, to continue more or less straight on along Gravelpits Lane*, your direction 295 degrees, on a signposted public bridleway (to the right-hand side of the driveway to Monks House).

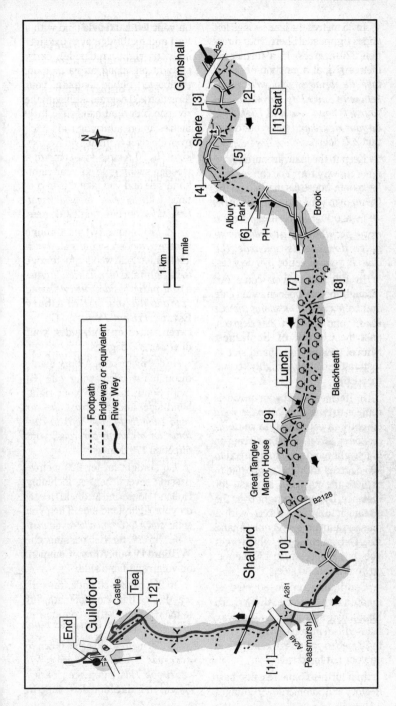

In 35 metres the lane swings left and is signposted Shere, your direction 220 degrees. In a further 65 metres **[3]**, at a junction of paths, *take the bridleway to your right, between Gravel Pits Farmhouse on your left-hand side and Highlands on your right-hand side*, your direction 290 degrees.

Keep to the main arboured way, ignoring ways off. You can see Netley manor house (as marked on the OS map) to your right, northwards.

In 400 metres *turn right on a minor path (through a wooden swing gate) downwards towards the church*, your direction 310 degrees.

In 120 metres you come out through another wooden swing gate and *keep straight on along the car road*, your direction 290 degrees, past the **Church of St James**, **Shere**, on your right-hand side (a visit to the church is highly recommended).

In 100 metres **[4]** your onwards route is to *cross over the main road* (slightly to your right) to *continue on Lower Street*, with the stream on your right-hand side, your direction 305 degrees. (But you might like to explore the village a bit first, for instance, by turning right over the stream into Middle Street, with a tea shop and forge on your left-hand side. Or by turning left, which takes you to the museum, in 130 metres, on your left-hand side.)

Continuing on, in 80 metres, ignore a turn-off to the left (Orchard Road). Go straight on (the way marked 'No entry except for access'). In 20 metres you pass the old prison on your left-hand side.

In a further 65 metres, just past Rectory and Summerdown Cottages on your left-hand side (and with a ford and footbridge over the river on your right-hand side), carry straight on, along an earth road, signposted public footpath, your direction 250 degrees (still with the river on your right-hand side). In 90 metres ignore a turning right back over the river (with an Old Rectory sign). In 20 metres you come to a wooden swing gate on your right-hand side and you take this to continue with *the river on your right-hand side*, your direction 250 degrees.

In 110 metres **[5]** go through another wooden swing gate (with another ford and wooden footbridge to its right) and *turn half left to cross a trail and go beside a disused swing gate ahead of you, marked* **Albury Estate** *Private Property*. Go between fences on both sides, your direction 205 degrees.

In 600 metres exit Albury Estate through a wooden swing gate **[6]** (with South Lodge on your right-hand side) and *go across the car road (slightly to your left) to continue on an earth car road*, your direction 170 degrees.

Go straight on for 220 metres, passing several houses, including Holland House and Midfield House, on your right-hand side. Then you come *down to a road where you turn right*, in 20 metres passing the **William IV** pub, Albury Common, on your right-hand side.

In 225 metres go under the railway bridge (ignoring footpaths off to the right and left) to continue on your car road.

In 320 metres you come down *to a car road T-junction and you go left on Brook Hill*, signposted Farley Green, your direction due south. In

45 metres *turn right on to a broad track* signposted public footpath and also 'Surrey Hacking Centre', your direction 215 degrees.

In 40 metres you pass the horse-riding centre on your right-hand side (bearing uphill and slightly right). In a further 50 metres, keep straight on across a broad track, following the public footpath sign.

In a further 70 metres **[7]**, leave your earth car road to *go right on a footpath*, (there is a public footpath sign here pointing the way you are going), keeping the edge of the field on your right-hand side, your direction 265 degrees.

In 340 metres go over a stile towards pine woods and, in 60 metres **[8]**, you cross over another stile to enter these woods (marked **Blackheath** on the OS map).

Keep straight on this path, ignoring ways off. *In 210 metres go over a stile. In 25 metres, at a junction of paths, keep straight on* (the public footpath post is marked '235'), your direction 285 degrees.

[!] *In a further 160 metres, you come to another multiple junction of paths in a large open area. Imagine this open area as a road junction roundabout and take the second left* (this second left is a quite narrow and inconspicuous way; the third left is within a metre of it and is broader), your direction 245 degrees.

In 40 metres your way merges with one from the other side of the triangle of trees on your right-hand side. You continue on, your direction now 205 degrees. In 40 metres you come *to a T-junction with an earth vehicle-wide bridleway (with a blue arrow on a white background, pointing to the right, on a post).*

Here you turn right, your direction 280 degrees, *your way going straight, off into the distance – as straight as a Roman road.*

Ignore all ways off through **Blackheath Common**. In just under 1km, you *keep straight on through a carpark.* The other side of the carpark, by a group of houses on your left-hand side, *keep straight on again, on a tarmac road (Blackheath Lane),* your direction 255 degrees. In 145 metres you come to the **Villagers** pub on your right-hand side. This is the suggested lunchtime stop.

After lunch, turn right out of the pub into its carpark, and off on a bridleway path (taking the leftmost of three possibilities), previously marked in blue with on a post, your direction 305 degrees.

In 50 metres, again by a post, take the left fork, your direction 295 degrees. In a further 80 metres, you pass a house and its side garden on your left-hand side.

In 55 metres **[9]** *cross over a car road to continue straight on,* your direction still 295 degrees. In 70 metres cross over a path marked 'P5' to continue on. In 25 metres your way merges with an unasphalted car lane marked **Downs Link** to continue on, your direction 280 degrees.

In a further 80 metres you come to Tangley Way – wooden buildings around a courtyard – which you pass on your left-hand side.

In 120 metres *keep straight on at a junction (the left fork; a decorative iron gate on your right-hand side),* your direction 295 degrees.

In a further 360 metres or so, the village of Chilworth is visible away to your right. In a further 280 metres, you pass two giant industrial hay barns on your right-hand side. In 45 metres you come *to a T-junction where you continue to the left (virtually straight on)*, your direction 280 degrees, with **Great Tangley Manor House** visible on your right-hand side. In 80 metres you pass this house's entrance drive (I couldn't resist going down the drive for a closer peek at its approach arcade bridge).

240 metres further along the lane – and shortly before a car road T-junction – *turn right at a two-armed wooden sign saying 'Downs Link'*, your direction 305 degrees. This stretch – churned up by horses – can be muddy.

Until the asterisk [*] below, your route is to follow the Downs Link.

In more detail: Ignoring ways off, in 160 metres, cross over a car road [10] to continue on a bridleway marked 'Downs Link', your direction 245 degrees initially.

In 20 metres you ignore a fork off to the right to continue on past Falcon Cottage on your left-hand side, through another potentially muddy zone. In 275 metres the way straight on heads steeply up to the Tower (as signposted) and to **Chinthurst Hill** (as marked on the OS map), but you fork right on the Downs Link bridleway, your direction 255 degrees.

In 345 metres ignore a stile and footpath off to the right and continue downhill, on a left bend, with your main path, your direction 200 degrees – visible ahead of you are the outskirts of Shalford village.

In 345 metres – amid more potential mud – you pass Southlands

with its horses on your left-hand side, and come down to a car road, which you cross to continue straight on, along a tarmac road (Tannery Lane) signposted Downs Link, your direction 225 degrees.

In 20 metres, *by a Downs Link post, go up left on a tarmac path to the house (no.1A) to continue parallel to the road below you on your right-hand side*. In 40 metres cross Drodges Close to *continue on the tarmac path, and Downs Link, to the left of the phonebox.*

In 80 metres [!] *you go down to the left of the bridge, and in 20 metres fork right to go over a mini-bridge, below and to the left of the main bridge.*

[*] You come to a path T-junction. *Go right, under the bridge*, on a clear path, your direction 330 degrees, with the Tannery industrial building on your right-hand side and the **River Wey** on your left.

It can be more pleasant at this point to *go down to the river and pick up the more meandering riverside path* that runs parallel to your previous path (now on your right-hand side), although this has become populated by tall nettles in recent years.

In 265 metres cross a side stream on some concrete bars. In a further 345 metres, cross a bridge over the river and keep straight on towards the A281, reaching it in 65 metres.

Turn right on this A road and, in 35 metres, *cross the bridge over the river. 80 metres further on (10 metres beyond a brick wall on your left-hand side), take a little unmarked path down off to the left* (opposite Somersway Private Cul-de-Sac) that runs beside the river and moored riverboats (on your left-hand side), your direction 310 degrees.

In 180 metres you come to a stile – by Wharf Cottages which are on your left-hand side – and carry straight on, along a tarmac path (public footpath no.267), your direction 300 degrees.

In 80 metres you continue on a gravel path with moderately ugly modern industrial and office buildings on your right-hand side. In a further 145 metres, you come to the A248 **[11]** and a bridge. (**[**]** If you want to abandon the walk at this point, go right on the A248 to the station at **Shalford**.)

The main suggested route is to *go left over this bridge, and immediately right, to pick up the riverbank path* on the other side by the National Trust sign, the River Wey now to your right, your direction 335 degrees.

Keep straight on along the riverbank, ignoring all ways off, in due course going under a footbridge and, later, seeing the ruins of **Guildford Castle** ahead (to your right, at 15 degrees on the compass). After 2.5km of this riverbank walk, you *cross a mini-weir by a bridge marked 'Danger'.*

Immediately, you turn left **[12]**, with this branch of the river now on your left-hand side, your direction 350 degrees. In 150 metres *go over a bridge with metal railings and an-* *other mini-weir, the canal on your right-hand side* and the river on your left-hand side.

In 80 metres, *just by Millmead Lock, go right over a bridge*. In 70 metres you come out to the entrance of the **Yvonne Arnaud Theatre**, **Guildford**, the suggested tea place for the walk.

After tea, turn right out of the theatre back to **Millmead Lock**. *From the lock, go straight on*. In 25 metres *cross another bridge and turn right*, with the river now on your right-hand side, your direction 335 degrees.

In 130 metres, just past the Riverside restaurant (on the other side of the river), *fork right off the car road to follow the riverside terrace path*. In 75 metres, by the bridge, bear left with the path up beside the **White House** pub on your left-hand side.

Turn right by the Parish Church of St Nicholas and follow the pedestrian sign to the station. **[!]** Keep to the riverbank until you come *opposite the imposing 1913 Electricity Works, then turn left into the crescent of modern office buildings. Take the right fork up steps*, signposted pedestrians to the station, your direction 280 degrees.

In 50 metres you come to an underpass which takes you to **Guildford Station** on the other side of the road, to get the train to London.

Walk 15

Leigh to Tunbridge Wells

Penshurst Place &
Medway Valley

Length 17.5km (10.8 miles) 5 hours 20 minutes. For the whole outing, including trains, sights and meals, allow 10 hours 30 minutes.

OS Landranger Map No.188. Leigh, map reference TQ 546 462, is in **Kent**, 1km east of Tonbridge.

Toughness 5 out of 10.

Features The route of this walk is through a landscape of great beauty, confirming the description of Kent as the Garden of England. It proceeds through the grounds of Penshurst Place, with fine views of the house, taking in a truly pastoral landscape of rivers, lakes, woods and rolling hills; and passes through the lovely village of Penshurst. The walk then makes its way along the River Medway and into historic Royal Tunbridge Wells, through woods and parks which extend right into the heart of the town. The suggested tea place is in the colonnaded Pantiles.

Shortening the walk You can reduce the length of the walk by over 4km, by more or less following the River Medway from point **[5]** to point **[8]** on the map – see the OS map for details – missing out the steepest hill, but also the recommended lunchtime stop and the best

view. This would be a good option if you set out late, and stop for lunch in Penshurst (see the asterisk **[*]** below). Except on Sundays, you can also get a 231 bus about once an hour going to Tunbridge Wells or Edenbridge, from either the bottom of Smart's Hill (a ten-minute walk from the lunchtime pub) or from Penshurst. For bus information phone Traveline on 0870 608 2608.

History The stately home of **Penshurst Place** (tel 01892 870 307) is a perfectly preserved, fortified manor house, which has been the home of the Sidney family since 1552, when Edward VI gave it to his old tutor, Sir William Sidney. The poet Sir Philip Sidney was born here in 1554. The oldest part of the building dates from the fourteenth century, but the present house represents a curious blend of five centuries of architectural styles. The house is open daily from March 31st to October 31st. The gardens are open from 10.30am to 6pm, the house from midday to 5pm (last entry). Admission is £6.

On the south side of **St John the Baptist Church**, Penshurst, are timber-framed cottages, which form part of Leicester Square (named after a favourite of Elizabeth I) and include a post office house from 1850. The church contains the effigy of the top half of Stephen de Penshurst, Warden of the Cinque Ports and Constable of Dover Castle, who died in 1299.

David Salomons' House (tel 01892 515 152) is the former home of civil rights campaigner Sir David Salomons and his nephew (also named David Salomons), the outstanding Victorian scientist and innovator – he developed the first electrically propelled tricycle in 1874 and the house was the first in England to use electricity for cooking. It is open all year round on Monday, Wednesday and Friday (excluding bank holidays) 2pm to 5pm. Admission is free.

The spa town of **Royal Tunbridge Wells** had its beginning in 1606, when a courtier, Dudley, Lord North, discovered an iron-bearing spring which made good the damage to his health from dissolute living. At the town's zenith, William Pitt, Dr Johnson, David Garrick and Sir Joshua Reynolds were regular visitors. Queen Victoria frequented Tunbridge Wells as a child, but the 'Royal' prefix was added in 1909 by Edward VII. The colonnaded **Pantiles** are named from the small clay tiles that Princess Anne paid for in 1698, after her son fell on the slippery ground.

Saturday Walkers' Club Take the train nearest to **10am** (before or after) from **Charing Cross** Station to **Leigh**, changing at Ton-bridge on to the Redhill line – Leigh is the first stop, just 3 minutes down the line. The return train from Tunbridge Wells may be direct back to Charing Cross, but sometimes you have to change at Tonbridge, sometimes at London Bridge. Trains run about twice an hour. You can get a return to Tunbridge Wells and pay the extra from Tonbridge to Leigh for the outward journey. Journey time 1 hour going out, and 1 hour on the return, depending on the connection.

Lunch The suggested lunchtime stop is the **Spotted Dog** (tel 01892 870 253) at Smart's Hill, a large pub with good food, log fires and a superb view across the Medway Valley to Swaylands and Penshurst. Despite being out of the way, this is a very popular and well-known pub, so in season, particularly on sunny days, arrive early to avoid long waits for lunch. Food is served midday to 2pm (sometimes later) daily (on Sunday until 9pm). Alternatively, for late starters, the **Leicester Arms** (tel 01892 870 551) in Penshurst serves lunch from midday to 2pm Monday to Thursday, to 2.30pm Friday and to 3pm weekends; groups of more than 12 people should phone to book.

Tea The suggested tea place is the **Swan Hotel** (tel 01892 541 450) in the Pantiles, which serves tea and coffee, scones, cakes, biscuits and sandwiches at any time. **Café Royal**, opposite the main entrance to the station, is open Monday to Saturday 9am to 5pm, offering home-made cakes, cream teas and other food.

WALK DIRECTIONS

[1] [Numbers refer to the map.] From platform 1 at **Leigh Station**, *take the path down to the road*, your direction 270 degrees. *Turn left and walk up the road*, your direction 200 degrees. In 100 metres, you pass an oasthouse conversion called Paul's Farm Oast. 130 metres further on, to the right of Paul's Hill House, you will see a signpost indicating the start of the Eden Valley Walk and the Link Path, with a concrete public footpath sign at ground level.

[2] *Turn right up this car-wide track, up the hill*, your direction 240 degrees initially. In 120 metres you

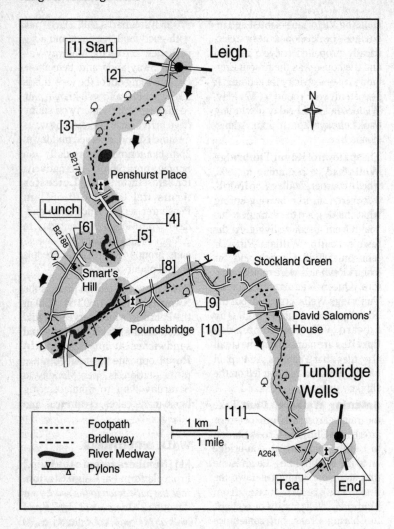

come to a metal fieldgate with a black sign saying 'Penshurst Place Estate Public Footpath'. Cross over the stile to the left of the gate and continue along the track in the same direction as before. In 70 metres you come to a wooden post on the right of the path. Go slightly left here, your direction 240 degrees, to the far left corner of the field, 250 metres

ahead of you. At this point you go down an avenue of plane trees.

In a further 300 metres you come to a metal fieldgate and go through the adjacent stile, which indicates the continuation of the Eden Valley Walk and the Link Path. Continue in the same direction as before. Now, on your left-hand side, you get a fine view of Penshurst Place, Penshurst village church, and the sylvan dales of **Penshurst Park**.

In a further 700 metres, you come to a large post which marks the start of a fence on your right-hand side. Just beyond the post, there is a stile with a path going off to the right. Ignore this path and continue on in the same direction as before.

[3] 30 metres further on, *turn left down the hill, between the trees*, on a broad, grassy path, aiming towards Penshurst Place, your direction 195 degrees. 350 metres down the hill, cross through the stile and continue on in the same direction as before. Walk down through the line of oak trees towards the lake.

In 250 metres, before you get to the wooden palisade fence and gate at the bottom of the hill, look to your right and you will see a very old hollow oak tree with a Y-shaped stile 20 metres to its left.

Go through this stile and follow the lake and fence on your left-hand side until, in 150 metres, the fence veers left, at which point you continue straight on towards the stile in the barbed wire fence 180 metres ahead. Go through the stile (with a black sign for 'Penhurst Estate Public Path' on your right-hand side) and walk straight *towards the right-hand side of Penshurst Place*, your direction due south.

In 400 metres go through stiles across a tarmac road.

Go to the right-hand corner of Penshurst Place's hedge-topped stone wall, 100 metres ahead. *Bear left at the corner* and walk with the wall on your left-hand side. In 200 metres cross the stile leading into the churchyard of **St John the Baptist Church, Penshurst**.

Walk through the churchyard – the church is worth visiting (the second door on your left). Continue out of the churchyard, underneath a cottage which stands on stilts (in a line of remarkable ancient cottages), into **Leicester Square** and down past the 1850 **post office**. Some stone steps take you down to the road.

(For those wanting an early lunch, such as those planning to take the short cut later on, turn right here for the **Leicester Arms**.)

To continue on the main walk, *turn left and follow the road as it curves around to the right*. The entrance to **Penshurst Place** is on your left, on the corner. In a further 25 metres, you cross an offshoot of the Medway on a small stone bridge. 140 metres beyond the first bridge, you cross the **River Medway** itself on a second stone bridge.

[4] 150 metres further on, going slightly uphill, you come to a sign pointing left to the 'Enterprise Centre'. *Turn right off the road*, along a grassy car-wide track, following a metal sign saying 'Public footpath to Poundsbridge', your direction 220 degrees initially.

In 400 metres ignore a metal shack, path and hop poles to your right. In a further 250 metres go to the right on a clear footpath (marked with a yellow arrow SR 454) down alongside a hedge and an old iron shack and a line of hop poles, all on your right-hand side, your direction due west.

In 90 metres, the path curves around to the left, following the line of the trees. 30 metres further on, the path heads quarter right across the field, towards a metal bridge on the far side, your direction 210 degrees. In 140 metres you cross a wood-and-metal bridge over the **River Medway [5]**.

([*] Once over the bridge, you have the option of turning left for a short cut, keeping the river within range on your left-hand side. You rejoin the main walk at **[8]** on the map. In more detail for this short cut: Once over the bridge, take the path over open ground, half left. There is a pillbox under a tree on the left-hand side. You come to a corner of another pillbox and a rough-and-ready footpath sign painted on wood. Go over light humps and a plank through a gap in the hedge into the next field. Bear left, your direction 120 degrees, towards a gap in the trees. Go through this gap and keep the trees on your right-hand side. At the T-junction of paths, turn left along a wire fence to a bridge with high metal railings. Over the bridge, you rejoin the main walk at **[8]** and take the path straight ahead across the field, your direction 120 degrees.)

[5] To continue the main walk: *On the other side of the bridge, turn right along the path*, your direction 300 degrees initially. In 50 metres you come to a large oak tree and pillbox on the right-hand side of the path, where the river curves off to your right. Continue straight on across the field, towards a red-brick building in the distance, your direction 290 degrees.

In 220 metres you come to the far side of the field and see a 'Penshurst Estate public footpath' sign. Cross over the ditch and head up the grassy car-wide track.

In 200 metres you come up *to a T-junction*, an untarmacked car-wide track, with **Ford House** (marked on the OS map) on your right-hand side. *Turn left and walk along this track*, your direction 220 degrees initially.

[6] In 300 metres you come *to a T-junction with the B2188*. Directly opposite you can see the old wooden buildings of South Park Farm, with the house of South Park in the background. *Cross the road and continue up the road on the far side*, signposted 'Smart's Hill, half mile'. In 80 metres you pass the entrance to Gray Leas on your right-hand side.

650 metres further on, having ignored a bridleway to the left, you come *to a T-junction*. *Turn left*, following the sign for Fordcombe and Tunbridge Wells. In 150 metres you come to the **Spotted Dog** on your left-hand side, which is the suggested lunchtime stop.

After lunch, *turn right out of the pub*, retracing your steps back up the road. After 150 metres go straight on past the road going downhill, which you ascended before lunch. 30 metres further on, *turn left* towards Walters Green and Blackham, your direction 225 degrees.

Follow this road steeply downhill, ignoring ways off, for the next 750 metres.

At the bottom of the hill go straight past the turning to the left, signposted Fordcombe and Tunbridge Wells, following the sign for Walters Green and Blackham. In 50 metres *turn left off the road*, where public footpath signs point to both left and right. Cross over the stile and follow the line of the oak trees, your direction 140 degrees.

100 metres further on, you come to the last oak in the row and con-

tinue straight on down the hill, for 120 metres, to a wooden bridge with a scaffolding pole railing, crossing a stream through the hedgerow.

On the other side, head across the field towards the right of the electricity pylon, your direction due south. In 150 metres you come to the banks of the River Medway. *Turn right*, with the river on your left-hand side, until you come, in 200 metres, *to the bridge*. Cross over this wooden bridge with scaffolding pole railings. *Go left along the path*, coming in 150 metres to a metal fieldgate, your direction 45 degrees.

[7] Cross the stile to its right, which brings you out on to the road. *Turn left and, in 20 metres, cross the road and turn right off it, over a stile* (marked with a yellow arrow 471). Head across the field, your direction 70 degrees. In 60 metres cross over a double stile and continue along the side of the next field, in the same direction as before, with oasthouses on your right-hand side.

In 180 metres ignore a wooden plank crossing the ditch going along the right-hand side of the path, with a yellow footpath sign nailed to a tree. Continue straight on in the same direction as before.

200 metres further on, you come to the corner of the field. Follow the path as it bears around to the left. 20 metres further on, *turn right across the wooden bridge with a scaffolding pole railing*, which takes you into the next field.

Follow the path, more or less along the riverbank on your left-hand side, for the next 1.25km, detouring as necessary.

[8] You then come to a bridge with high metal railings, going over the River Medway. Do not cross the bridge. Instead *take a right-hand turn and follow the footpath across the field* towards a row of trees and an electricity pylon in the distance, your direction 120 degrees. In 100 metres you come to the corner of a barbed wire fence, away on your left-hand side. Follow the fence along the side of the field in the same direction as before. As you walk along this path you can see a hop field away on your left-hand side. 170 metres further on, you come to a metal fieldgate. Go through the wooden gate to its right, into the next field, and *turn half right up the hill*, following yellow arrow SR 458, your direction 170 degrees initially.

Ahead of you is a tiny (locked) **chapel** and graveyard (used because Penshurst churchyard is full), and the path goes up the side of a row of oak trees towards the left-hand edge of the graveyard. You come to a metal fieldgate and go through the wooden gate on its left. 40 metres further on, you pass the wooden gate leading into the churchyard and come out on to the road.

Turn left into the road (Coopers Lane) and, in 120 metres, you come *to a T-junction*, with Poundsbridge House opposite. *Turn left, down the hill*. In 150 metres, at the bottom of the hill, ignore a footpath sign pointing off to the left, and go over the bridge crossing a small brook. 50 metres beyond the bridge, you come *to another T-junction*, signposted Penshurst and Leigh to the left. On the corner, on your right-hand side, there is a 1593 house with a walled garden. *Turn right and, in 20 metres, turn left off the road*, over the stile which is marked by concrete and wooden footpath signs. Head straight up the hill, with the edge of the field on your right-hand side, your direction at this point 65 degrees.

For the next 1km you will be walking more or less parallel to the pylons away on your left-hand side.

In more detail: In 320 metres the path goes underneath two parallel sets of overhead cables. Walk along the edge of the pond on your right-hand side, in the same direction as before. 80 metres further on, at the far end of the pond, cross over a stile into the next field. Continue with the field edge on your right-hand side, in the same direction as before. In 75 metres the overhead cables take a sharp right-hand turn, but you continue straight on, to cross a stile which you can see directly 40 metres ahead of you, your direction 95 degrees.

Then follow the path, with another pond on your right-hand side, in the same direction as before. In 30 metres *go over a stile on your left-hand side into the next field and turn sharp right*, heading in the same direction as before, with trees and the edge of the field on your right-hand side.

In 150 metres cross the stile (marked with yellow arrow WT 410) and then cross the small wooden bridge over a ditch into the next field. Go straight ahead across this field in the same direction as before. In 200 metres, over the brow of the hill, you again have the field edge on your right-hand side. Another 120 metres further on, cross over the stile in the corner of the field (with a metal gate on its left-hand side). Follow the footpath which takes you between a fence on your left-hand side and a copse on your right-hand side, in the same direction as before.

[9] 120 metres further on, you come out on to a road. *Turn left down the road. In 35 metres, turn right down a car-wide track*, marked by a concrete public footpath sign and a wooden sign for Squirrelsmead, Barden Mill Cottage and Charlton Cottages. In 180 metres the track veers sharply around to the right. 150 metres further on, go through a gateway with a metal fieldgate. Ignore the turning off to the left and continue straight ahead along the same track. 180 metres further on, the track then curves around to the left, across a running brook.

450 metres further on, you come to the top of the hill, with a barn on your left-hand side and a building with an oast chimney on your right. At the end of the track, just beyond the barn, there is a metal fieldgate. Cross over the stile made of steps next to it and go half right across a concrete yard for 10 metres. On your left-hand side is a horse chestnut tree which has a public footpath sign attached to it, high up and possibly obscured by leaves. Go to the left of the tree and cross over the stile to the right of the wooden fieldgate, and walk straight ahead, with the edge of the field on your right-hand side, your direction due east. In 120 metres cross over the stile into the next field. Follow the path straight across the field in the same direction as before.

In 150 metres you come to the far side of the field, where there is a tree with a white arrow painted on its trunk pointing ahead. There is a wooden fieldgate on its left-hand side and a stile to its right. Go over the stile, which brings you out on to a tarmac lane. *Turn right up the hill.* In 90 metres there is a house on your right-hand side called Hollanbys. Ignoring any ways off, in a further 180 metres you come *to a T-junction.*

Turn left on to the road through the village of **Stockland Green**. In 120 metres you pass Birchetts Lodge on your left-hand side, and a white sign pointing to various other Birchetts. Immediately opposite the drive going off to the left here, there is a concrete public footpath sign on the right-hand side of the road. *Turn right through the metal kissing gate*, down the path leading between the houses. (If you see Birchetts Cottage on your right-hand side, you have missed this path and gone too far down the road.) In 20 metres cross over the stile and walk along the left-hand side of the field, heading in the same direction as before.

In 70 metres you come to the corner of the field and *go over the stile on your right-hand side*, which is marked by a WW (Weald Way) footpath sign, into the next field. Once over the stile, *turn sharp left* for 5 metres (not going into the next field) then follow your previous direction along the edge of the field. In 100 metres go through the kissing gate frame (on the left-hand side of a wooden barrier) in the left-hand corner of the field.

Go straight down the path, between the hedgerows, your direction 80 degrees. In 25 metres there is a wooden post on your left, pointing straight ahead for the High Weald

Walk. *Turn sharp right here* and follow the path (FP72) that heads due south.

[10] In a further 200 metres you come down through another kissing gate on to a road. (At this point, taking a small detour left along the road would bring you to **David Salomons' House**.)

To continue the walk, go straight over the road and, in 10 metres, go through a broken kissing gate, and along the footpath. This is a narrow, potentially muddy little path which makes its way between hedgerows, steeply downhill. In 500 metres you come out on to a road, where you *turn right.*

In 20 metres the road crosses over a small brook, past the Redsheen Kennels at Mill Farm. 200 metres further on, the road curves around to the right, and there is a public footpath sign off to the left.

Turn left off the road, your direction 135 degrees, down the hill, along the car-wide track. In 100 metres cross over a fast-flowing stream and follow the path as it starts to make its way back uphill. 50 metres up the hill, the path forks. *Take the right-hand fork*, your direction 185 degrees initially. In 70 metres you come to wooden fieldgates with signs saying 'Keep Out'. Continue straight on along the track, towards the woods.

80 metres further on, you come to a metal fieldgate and cross through the stile on its left-hand side, into the wood. Follow the woodland path in the same direction as before.

In 200 metres you come to a Forestry Commission sign saying 'No admittance to vehicles'. Ignore the paths to left and right. Go straight on, ignoring all ways off.

In 500 metres you come down to a wooden fieldgate. Go through the kissing gate on its left.

200 metres further on, you come to the end of the public footpath, where there is a brick building dead ahead, with a large metal gate. *Turn left on to the track, which takes you past this gate.* There is a sign on the door to the building, saying 'Southern Water Services Ltd'.

40 metres further on, you come out on to a residential street, on the outskirts of **Tunbridge Wells**. You are on a corner with Coniston Avenue to your left, a footpath straight ahead and Bishops Down Park Road to your right and ahead. *Turn right up Bishops Down Park Road*, your direction 145 degrees. In 150 metres follow Bishops Down Park Road as it goes off to the right, past a house called Charlcombe on your left-hand side. There is a golfcourse on your right as you go.

300 metres further on, *fork right on a path clearly named Manor Park*, your direction 185 degrees.

In 420 metres, with Grange Cote on your right-hand side, you come *to a road T-junction. Turn right*, your direction 240 degrees.

[11] In 90 metres you come to the A484, with the Rookery Arms opposite. *Cross over the road and continue on Major Yorks Road*, but for 5 metres only, *forking left off this road on to a path*, your direction 100 degrees.

In 150 metres cross over a path to go straight on.

In 160 metres go past a scaffolding pole barrier and *over a tarmac road (Fir Tree Lane), to continue on a path straight on*, with a cricket pitch on your left-hand side. Ignoring ways off, in 150 metres you come *to a tarmac path, where you turn right downhill*, your direction 155 degrees. Continue to ignore ways off.

In 350 metres you come *to the A26. Cross this to go down steps to the left of the* **Swan Hotel**. After tea in the hotel, go along Swan Passage *into the* **Pantiles**, *where you turn left*, your direction 35 degrees.

After tea, carry on along the Pantiles, in 65 metres reaching *Neville Street*, with **King Charles the Martyr Church** opposite. Cross Neville Street, by the pedestrian lights on your right-hand side. On the other side of the street, *turn left, then immediately right, down Cumberland Walk. Then turn left, past Gracelands Palace Chinese restaurant* on your right. Go up some steps and a brick alleyway, until you get to the start of the High Street. The White Bear pub is on your left-hand side. Walk straight up to *the top of the High Street*, about 300 metres, to the intersection with Vale Road. On the other side of Vale Road, you can then see signs for **Tunbridge Wells Station**.

You can enter the station from either side, but trains to London depart from platform 1 on the left. **Café Royal**, a suggested tea stop, is opposite the main entrance to the station (on the same side as platform 2).

Walk 16

Balcombe (round walk)

The gardens of Nymans & the ruins of Slaugham

Length 17.5km (10.8 miles), 5 hours 30 minutes. For the whole outing, including trains, sights and meals, allow 9 hours 20 minutes.

OS Landranger Map No.187. Balcombe, map reference TQ 306 302, is in **West Sussex**, 7km south-east of Crawley.

Toughness 5 out of 10.

Features This is a walk full of small delights: a nature reserve and lake with Japanese pagoda down by the stream below the gardens and park of Nymans with its part-ruined manor house; a relatively gourmet inn for lunch in Slaugham (pronounced 'Slaffam'); a churchyard in Slaugham with an 800-year-old yew tree some 10 metres in circumference; the ruins of Slaugham Manor; then a walk down to the River Ouse – suddenly three Roman columns and an arch in a field in the middle of nowhere – and later up through fields and woods to the fine old village of Balcombe. Note though that you need to be nimble to cross the A23 (after Slaugham), it is almost as busy as a motorway.

Shortening the walk The bulk of the walk is after lunch, and the last part is the least interesting in some ways, so you could go as far as the Victory Inn in Staplefield and catch a bus to Haywards Heath or Crawley. Alternatively, you could call a taxi earlier in the day from the lunch stop in Slaugham, or, after visiting Nymans, from the Red Lion pub in Handcross. There are buses from Handcross to Crawley or Gatwick every couple of hours.

History The Japanese pagoda-style aviary in the **nature reserve** was designed by Lord Snowdon, part of whose country estate this is.

Nymans (tel 01444 400 321, or the regional office on 01372 453 401) is a National Trust garden – Ludwig Messel, who bought Nymans in 1890, sought to show that a more exotic range of plants could survive outdoors in Sussex than previously thought. Its manor house was part-gutted by fire in 1947, when the Horsham stone roof, huge slabs of it, fell through three storeys, and the firemen were hampered by bitterly cold weather – ladder extensions and standpipes froze. Nymans garden is open daily from March 1st to the end of October (the café and shop are also open December 1st to the 24th, but the café is closed Mondays). Normally (but not on bank holidays) Nymans garden is closed on Monday and Tuesday. From November to March, Nymans garden is open at weekends. Admission is £6, families £15, groups of 15 and over £5 per person.

St Mary's Parish Church, Slaugham, has a Norman font made of Sussex marble with a fish symbol on it. There is a brass in the church to John Covert, who in his will left 200 marks to his daughters, even if they married without consent to men without land – but only if the men 'have virtue and cunning which seemeth as good as 100 marks' worth of land'.

Slaugham Place, now in ruins, was the residence of the Covert family, who in the sixteenth and seventeenth centuries held land extending from the English Channel to the banks of the Thames.

Saturday Walkers' Club Take the train nearest to **9.50am** (before or after) from **King's Cross Thameslink** station (*not* the main railway station; Thameslink has its own exit from King's Cross tube station, and is on the corner of Pentonville and Caledonian Roads – coming out of the main station you turn left to get to it) to **Balcombe**. Journey time approximately 66 minutes. Trains back from Balcombe run about once an hour.

Lunch The suggested lunch stop, if it is open and you can afford the admissions price to Nymans, is the **Nymans café**, which is open more or less the same dates as Nymans garden (see above) and serves good enough food from 11am to 4pm. An alternative is the **Red Lion** (tel 01444 400 292) in Handcross, which serves food from midday to 2.30pm daily. For the upmarket walker, the **Chequers Inn** (tel 01444 400 239) at Slaugham serves food from midday to about 2pm daily, with the lunch menu priced at £21 for three courses and coffee. The inn does not serve drinks without food.

Tea The suggested tea place is the **Balcombe Tearooms** (tel 01444 811 777), open till 5pm (last orders 4.45pm) Tuesday to Sunday only. They have kindly offered to stay open later if phoned in advance by a group of walkers. When they are closed, walkers could have tea, drinks and cake at the **Half Moon** pub (tel 01444 811 582) in Balcombe, open all day every day – the only food when I was there was chocolate bars and pickled eggs (meals from 6.30pm).

WALK DIRECTIONS

[1] [Numbers refer to the map.] From the London train arriving at **Balcombe Station** on platform 2, *go over the railway line* on the concrete footbridge. Then go 35 metres along the platform the other side, and just before the tunnel, go out through a gap in the fence and *turn left on the station approach road*, your direction due south.

In 130 metres, by a public footpath sign, *take the footpath to the right*, downhill to a stile in 20 metres, your direction 225 degrees. In 25 metres go over another stile and down steps to a road.

Carry straight on towards the cottage for 25 metres (over a stream) and **[2]** *take a signposted footpath to the right* over a stile, your direction 310 degrees.

Go uphill near the field edge on your right-hand side. In 230 metres go over a stile at the top of the field and turn left, your direction 295 degrees, now with the field hedge on your left-hand side.

In 125 metres there is another stile, and you go straight on towards the building just visible ahead. This brings you in 210 metres to a stile (with a wooden fieldgate to its right). Follow the footpath signpost uphill on a car-wide unasphalted road, your direction still 310 degrees.

In 65 metres you pass a wooden shed (which could be seen from a distance earlier). 5 metres beyond

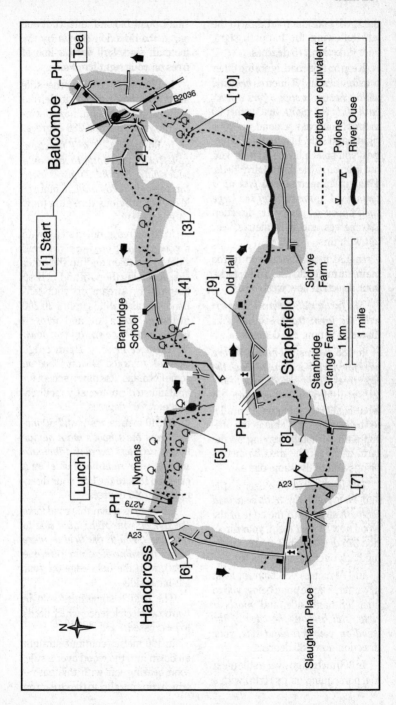

Balcombe

Tea

PH

[1] Start

[2]

[3]

B2036

[10]

Brantridge School

[4]

[9]

Old Hall

Sidnye Farm

River Ouse

1 mile

1 km

Footpath or equivalent

Pylons

Stapleﬁeld

[5]

Stanbridge Grange Farm

[8]

Nymans

Lunch

PH

A279

A23

PH

[7]

A23

Handcross

[6]

Slaugham Place

N

the shed, take the road fork to the left (following the footpath sign), your direction 275 degrees.

Keep on this road, ignoring other possibilities. In 170 metres *bend left with it (where a sign offers a foot-path off to the right)*. In a further 20 metres, you pass a pond on your right-hand side. In a further 70 metres, you pass a house on your left, but keep on towards the barn sheds. Then, in 45 metres, you *pick up a farm road to the right of the large shed ahead of you*, your direction 290 degrees, and, in 20 metres, veer left with this.

In 130 metres you keep to the main farm track (the right fork), your direction now westwards.

In a further 250 metres, veer left with the farm track, so that your direction is now 205 degrees.

In 185 metres, *10 metres before your farm track is about to reach the first trees of the wood, fork to the left*, your direction due south, on what is shortly a footpath parallel to the farm track. (This is the offi-cial path, although staying on the farm track for the next 85 metres brings you to the same place.)

[3] In 85 metres go over a stile and *turn right (by a three-armed footpath sign)* with the edge of the wood now to your right, your direc-tion 275 degrees, in 3 metres cross-ing back over the farm track.

In 170 metres you have, at least in winter, a large pond below you to your left-hand side, and you *bear right, still keeping the edge of the wood on your left-hand side*, your direction now 285 degrees.

In 300 metres go over a stile (next to a horse jump on its right) with a small pond beyond, and continue on, in the direction shown by the footpath sign, still with a line of trees on your right-hand side.

In 175 metres cross another stile (next to a horse jump on its left) to continue along a path, now down-wards, your direction 280 degrees.

In 50 metres, *at a T-junction, go left with the footpath sign on a wider path, but in 25 metres leave this to go right downhill*, in more or less your previous direction (now 240 degrees).

In 20 metres go down steps (with a wooden railing on your right-hand side) to a stream and up the other side, following the path and, at first, keeping the stream on your left-hand side as it winds uphill. In 200 metres go over a stile and *across a tarmac road to go straight on down the entrance drive of* **Brantridge School** (marked Ditton Place on some OS maps, it is now a school for 'maladjusted' pre-teens), your direc-tion now 260 degrees.

In 340 metres, *when still 60 me-tres from the school's main manor house, turn left (there is a footpath sign on your right-hand side)* on a car road fork to the left, your direc-tion now 240 degrees.

125 metres down this road, *take the stile on your right-hand side to continue through the field in more or less the same direction* (now due west), with the field edge on your left-hand side.

The field is sometimes split in two by an electric fence, which needs to be crossed.

In 190 metres continue straight on down into the wood over a stile, soon bearing left with this path – which runs parallel to the stream on your right, and parallel to the pylons beyond the stream.

In 200 metres cross this stream on a wooden bridge to continue in the same direction (170 degrees at present), now on the opposite bank.

[4] In 35 metres *take the right-hand fork uphill (by a public footpath sign)*, your direction 210 degrees.

In 65 metres, at the next footpath sign, continue on (to the left) in your direction, now 170 degrees. In a further 150 metres, *exit the wood by a stile (to the right of a wooden fieldgate) and turn right*, your direction 265 degrees, keeping the field edge on your right-hand side.

In 90 metres, at the end of the field, turn left to follow the field edge on your right-hand side, going parallel to the pylons.

In 90 metres exit the field by a metal gate and turn right, your direction 285 degrees, with the field edge on your right-hand side, to go under the pylons.

In 70 metres, continue to go straight on through another metal fieldgate.

In 50 metres go through a wooden swing gate and *turn left on a concrete farm lane*, as shown by a footpath sign, your direction 235 degrees. (A modernised timber-framed house is on your right-hand side.)

In 90 metres you come *to a junction in the farm track – go across this, slightly uphill and to the right, and go left on the footpath by the three-armed footpath sign*. Go through the metal gate to continue on, your direction 240 degrees.

In 100 metres go over a stream on two planks, then over two stiles, to continue on, your direction now 295 degrees, and with the field hedge on your right-hand side.

In 90 metres, keeping the hedge on your right-hand side, you may have to follow the path dictated by the line of an occasional electric fence.

Head towards the left-hand side of the house ahead of you (the one with a pale green gas storage tank).

In 100 metres follow this house's garden fence (on your right-hand side) and, in 60 metres (with a half-hidden statue of the Virgin Mary on your right-hand side), go over a stile and down steps into the wood, passing **Lord Snowdon's lake with Japanese pavilion** on your right-hand side, to go over a bridge with his 'Private wildlife sanctuary' sign; and so onwards up the other side.

At a T-junction you continue your path (somewhat to the right), your direction initially 315 degrees, *following the footpath sign*.

Keep in this direction at the next junction in 40 metres (with the lakes on your right-hand side), now on a car-wide earth track.

[5] In 300 metres you come to a two-armed footpath sign on your right, and (with the Woodland Walks straight on) you take the footpath fork uphill to the left, your direction 320 degrees – soon with the stream and ponds below you to the right.

Ignore a path off to the left in 400 metres. In a further 240 metres, ignore a fork going uphill to the left. 260 metres further on, *follow the Short Walk sign to the right to cross the streambed, but in 12 metres fork left, uphill*, your direction 310 degrees (there is at this point a small 'High Weald Circular Walk' red arrow on a two-foot-high log on your left-hand side).

In 300 metres you come up to a farm track by a two-armed footpath sign. Cross the farm track (going left here, through a gate 60 metres away, takes you into Nymans Gardens – you could, I suppose, then pay on the way out! But it is neither the main nor the correct entrance) and continue straight on up, your direction 280 degrees.

In 200 metres *you come to Nymans carpark*, with Nymans itself away to your left. In a further 35 metres, go through the wooden fieldgate on your left-hand side into the carpark and to the entrance to **Nymans** (with its café as the suggested lunchtime stop).

Coming out of Nymans, turn right on the main road, the B2114, staying on this road up to the **Red Lion** pub. Here *turn left on a road signposted Cowfold and Horsham* (B2110), your direction 230 degrees.

In 90 metres go over a bridge to cross the A23. All Saints Church is on your left-hand side. In 85 metres keep straight on at the junction (stay on the B2110 towards Lower Beeding and Leonardslee Gardens).

[6] In 125 metres, 5 metres after the **Royal Oak** pub on your right-hand side, *turn left* up a signposted car-wide road, your direction 165 degrees.

45 metres up this lane, *turn left by a two-armed footpath sign*, with fences to your left-hand side and allotments to your right-hand side. In 50 metres, bend right with the path. In 30 metres, go through a wooden swing gate and continue straight on between hedges in your previous direction, now 140 degrees.

In 75 metres you *come out on a car lane and turn right*, your direction 220 degrees.

Ignore a left fork in 90 metres.

In a further 450 metres, you pass what looks like a strange horse/car wash on your left-hand side, but which is in fact a couple of practice starting gates for horseraces.

Keep on this road, ignoring ways off. In a further 800 metres, continue on down through the village of **Slaugham**, coming to the **Chequers Inn** on your right-hand side.

Coming out of the Chequers Inn *after lunch, turn right* towards **St Mary's Parish Church** and go through its lychgate. The onward route is *straight on past the front door of the church, in 12 metres ignoring a fork to the right* (signposted public footpath). Keep to the right-hand side of the church, and *4 metres beyond the side door, fork right* on a path, your direction 120 degrees, through the churchyard. In 15 metres you pass the 800-year-old yew tree on your right-hand side. In 80 metres go through a wooden kissing gate and follow the footpath sign across a field, down to the right of the ruins of **Slaugham Place**, your direction 145 degrees.

In 180 metres this leads you to a two-armed footpath sign, and into a path between fences, your direction now 160 degrees, with the ruins on your left-hand side.

In 90 metres veer right with the path to circumvent the garden of the cottage ahead of you.

In 185 metres cross a wooden bridge over a stream and, in a further 60 metres, continue on Moat

House's driveway, your direction now 70 degrees, with the stream and the ruins to your left.

[7] In 100 metres *cross a car lane with a 'Bridge ahead' sign to go straight on over a footpath-sign-posted stile*, your direction now 100 degrees, keeping the edge of the wood on your right-hand side for 100 metres or so, until you can clearly see the stile half left on the other side of the field – make for this, your direction now 115 degrees.

In 120 metres go over this stile and carry straight on, following the footpath sign.

In 180 metres go over another stile (underneath pylons) and down steps to cross with care the very busy A23 (to avoid the A23, turn left up the car lane and follow it to the T-junction with the main road. Turn right there and follow the road underneath the A23 at the junction. Continue on this road under pylons, past Home Farm, and rejoin the route at the Victory Inn highlighted below).

Turn right on the A23, your direction due south, along the side of the road. In 260 metres, *by a public footpath sign, turn left*, in 15 metres going over a stile, your direction 75 degrees, and with the hedge to your left.

Ignore a stile to your left in 70 metres. In a further 80 metres, by a two-armed footpath sign, veer half right, your direction now 130 degrees (heading well to the left of the building visible ahead).

Exit by the far corner of the field, over a stile set into a metal fieldgate, to go straight on, your direction 125 degrees, with the field fence on your left-hand side.

In 100 metres go over a stile, to continue on a car-wide grassy path between fences.

In 100 metres, you pass a corrugated barn on your right-hand side. In a further 30 metres, go through a white metal gate and straight on, passing a timber-framed house with twin front doors (Stanbridge Grange Farm) on your left-hand side.

In 60 metres you *come out on to a tarmac road where you turn left*, your direction 25 degrees.

In 80 metres ignore a stile on the left-hand side. In a further 140 metres, you pass the gates to Stanbridge House on your left-hand side.

In a further 150 metres, go over a stream. [8] In 30 metres *take a footpath signposted to the right*, going through a metal fieldgate, your direction 100 degrees, with a stagnant stream to your left. In 150 metres go over two little wooden bridges and *follow the footpath arrow* left (a hedge on your left-hand side), your direction 50 degrees. In 180 metres go over a stile to your left in the hedge, and in 10 metres, at a three-armed footpath sign, go straight on, over another stile, your direction initially 335 degrees and with the field hedge on your right-hand side.

In 525 metres exit the field by a stile and continue straight on down a farm track, coming in 65 metres *to a tarmac road (with open common beyond it) where you turn right*, your direction 80 degrees.

In 100 metres you pass **Staplefield**'s **Victory Inn** (tel 01444 400 463) on your right-hand side. In a further 65 metres, you *cross the B2114 to continue straight on up-*

hill. In a further 200 metres, you pass a (locked) church on your left-hand side.

350 metres beyond the church, you pass Jasmine and Heron Cottages on your right-hand side, to keep on your main road. In a further 190 metres, again keep on your road, signposted Balcombe, ignoring Rose Cottage Lane to your right.

[9] In a further 300 metres – and 5 metres past the entrance drive to **Tyes Place** (marked on the OS map) – by a footpath sign on your right, *turn right into the driveway of North and South Meadow Cottages*, your direction 135 degrees.

In 100 metres stay on the drive, passing the cottages on your right-hand side. In a further 30 metres, you go through a wooden fieldgate marked Old Hall Farm Cottage, keeping to the right to pick up a path out of the cottages' property, and go over a stile to *turn left with the footpath sign* (with the field hedge on your left-hand side and your direction 85 degrees).

The intriguing castle-like **Old Hall** is visible to your left with its own mini-crystal palace beyond it.

In 300 metres note the **arch with Roman pillars** in a field to your left.

In a further 40 metres, the path leads you through the hedge, at the bottom left-hand corner of the field, to continue straight on – a clear path with many blackberry bushes.

In 200 metres your path is following the **River Ouse** (on your right).

In a further 350 metres, cross the river by a wooden bridge, following the footpath sign.

There is a clear path on the other side, your direction 155 degrees,

uphill towards buildings. In 230 metres follow the footpath sign to go through Sidnye Farm (as marked on the OS map) to the left, your direction 120 degrees.

In 30 metres, *at the three-armed footpath sign, turn left* (due east), passing the large corrugated shed for straw on your right-hand side.

Keep left to go straight on past Farm Cottages nos.73 and 72 on your left-hand side.

Keep on the farm's driveway and, in just over 1km, *you come to a T-junction by the entrance to Sidnye Farm, and you turn left downhill*, your direction 350 degrees.

In 100 metres you pass the entrance to Hillside on your left-hand side, and, in a further 140 metres, you cross the River Ouse.

In 8 metres, *by a public footpath sign, take a stile to your left* in order to continue straight on, in your previous direction (now due north, towards a red-brick house visible on the horizon) with the field edge on your left-hand side. In 325 metres *you come up to a tarmac lane, where you turn left*. In 20 metres go up and *over a stile to continue in your previous direction*, between a vast network of fields.

Keep to the left of the tall oak trees. In 280 metres go over a stile and half left, your direction 10 degrees. In 90 metres go over a stile and upwards to the left, following the direction of the footpath sign, your direction due north and the field hedge and red-brick house on your left-hand side. Keep to this path, ignoring ways off.

In 270 metres cross farm tracks to keep straight on (now with Balcombe visible ahead to your north). You are now on a car-wide track going downwards. 50 metres after beginning your descent, *by a rock face split by tree roots on your left-hand side, keep on this right fork downhill,* your direction 345 degrees.

In 60 metres you come to an earth car road T-junction, but you go straight across, following the footpath sign, to go downhill on a path through the wood, your direction initially due north – in 40 metres, bearing slightly right with the path and ignoring ways off (your direction now 45 degrees and a new plantation on your right-hand side).

In 220 metres exit the wood by a bridge over the stream (with wooden V-shaped railings) and by a stile. Here you turn half left uphill, following the direction of the footpath sign (due north).

In 225 metres (ignoring the stile with a crater on its left-hand side), go over a stile with the wooded dell on your right-hand side and, to your left, a metal fieldgate and then a field fence. In 65 metres go over a stile and *turn left on a tarmac road,* the B2036, your direction due north.

In 90 metres, just past a house on the other side of the road, cross the road and *go uphill on a tarmac lane with a footpath sign,* your direction initially 140 degrees.

In 115 metres you enter the drive of **Kemps House** (marked on the OS map), with the house on your left-hand side. In 40 metres, *when the drive bears left, you go right* to continue in your previous direction (now due east).

In 35 metres go over a stile and *over the railway line* to continue on

up the other side. In 135 metres go over a stile and straight on. In 20 metres *take the right fork* to continue on, with the field edge on your right-hand side, your direction initially 35 degrees. Continue on to the houses ahead (due north), ignoring ways off.

Once by the houses, follow the footpath sign long the right-hand edge of the three-house terrace. Go over a stile (beside house no.28 on your left-hand side) and across a tarmac road, straight on, up Jobes Cul-de-Sac, your direction 25 degrees. You find the continuation of your path *where the road bears left,* and you *go straight on,* slightly to the right, to go between hedges to the right of a house, your direction due north, on a tarmac path, with gardens on your left-hand side.

In 100 metres continue on, with playing fields on your left-hand side and the field hedge on your right-hand side. At the far end of the playing fields, continue on a tarmac lane past the pavilion on your left-hand side. In 75 metres you pass Balcombe Parish Church Room on your left-hand side. *On reaching the road, turn left.*

In 75 metres, by a newsagent on the right-hand side, either turn right for the **Half Moon** pub and the church, or *go left for 5 metres and over the road to the main suggested tea place,* **Balcombe Tearooms**.

To get to the station, *continue down past the tearooms.* 180 metres past the tearooms, you come to London Road.

If in a hurry or tired, turn left to the station on this main road, but the most pleasant and more circuitous way is to *cross straight over*

London Road to continue down Rocks Lane (the lane marked '6'6" except for access'), your direction 210 degrees. Keep on this road and go under the railway bridge.

330 metres beyond the railway bridge, you come to the morning's T-junction by the stream, where you *turn left, following the footpath sign,* to go up the steps which you came down in the morning. Go over a stile and, in 25 metres, over another stile, then *turn left on the lane* to reach **Balcombe Station**.

Walk 17

Bow Brickhill to Woburn Sands

Woburn, its park & abbey

Length 17.5km (10.8 miles), 5 hours 30 minutes. For the whole walk, including trains, sights and meals, allow at least 10 hours 30 minutes.

OS Landranger Map Nos.165, 153 and (for the last kilometre) 152. Bow Brickhill, map reference SP 896 348, is in **Buckinghamshire**, 2km east of Bletchley. Woburn is in **Bedfordshire**.

Toughness 6 out of 10.

Features Woburn is the main delight of this walk – the ancient town itself, the deer park, Woburn Abbey (for those wishing to make the detour – a compass can be useful at this stage) and the safari park (from the public footpath, without paying admission, you may be able to see lions, tigers, zebras, elephants, giraffes and hippos). The route reaches Woburn mainly through woods, with impressive redwood trees along the way. The route back is through the pleasant village of Aspley Guise. Note that the train service does not run on Sundays – you could instead catch a cab or bus from Bletchley to the start of the walk, or a bus to Woburn and just do the second half of the walk from there (for bus information phone 0870 608 2608). Beware also that short bits of the route can be very muddy in wet weather, and that there are (relatively easy) uphills

and downhills all day. Be careful not to allow dogs to disturb deer in the park, particularly when they are rutting or giving birth – the deer may leave their newborn calves or give birth prematurely.

Shortening the walk Note that there are still 10km (6.2 miles) remaining to be walked after lunch in Woburn. Buses from Woburn go to Leighton Buzzard and Bletchley. Aspley Guise is a nearer station for the return journey than Woburn Sands, but has no tea place.

History Woburn Abbey (tel 01525 290 666), set in a vast park, about 16km in circumference, is the seat of the Dukes of Bedford, though it was founded for Cistercian monks in 1145 by Hugh de Bolsbec, a Norman whose father came over with William the Conqueror. Both Elizabeth I and Charles I were entertained here. The abbey was rebuilt about 1744 in Totternhoe stone. It is open daily until 4pm (Sunday 5pm; closed mid-winter; and weekends only in October and from January to about March 26th).

Woburn, the town, was almost completely gutted by fire in 1729. **St Mary Old Church**, Woburn, whose tower dates from the twelfth century, is now a 'Heritage Centre' (tel 01525 290 631) covering local history. From Easter to September the centre is open Monday to Friday 2pm-4.30pm, Saturday, Sunday and bank holidays 10am-5pm (plus weekends only in October).

St Mary, the parish church of Woburn, graced with devilish gargoyles, was built by the eighth Duke of Bedford in 1868, and has a memorial window to Mary, Duchess of Bedford.

The village of **Aspley Guise** was originally called Aepslea, meaning a clearing in the aspen, with large herds of swine kept in the surrounding woods. The **Pa-rish Church of St Botolph**, Aspley Guise, has Norman and medieval traces, and a brass from about 1410 of a kneeling priest.

Saturday Walkers' Club Take the train nearest to **9.50am** (before or after) from **Euston** Station to **Bow Brickhill**, changing at Bletchley. Journey time 1 hour. Return from Woburn Sands, again changing at Bletchley. Journey time 1 hour 15 minutes. Buy a cheap day return to Woburn Sands. For the return journey, you could, if you prefer, take the train in the other direction from Woburn Sands, to Bedford, and a Thameslink train from there back to King's Cross.

Lunch There are many places to eat in Woburn, but the suggested lunchtime stop is the **Black Horse** pub (tel 01525 290 210) at 1 Bedford Street, which serves good food at medium to high prices, from mid-day to 2.30pm Monday to Friday, all day Saturday and Sunday. It also has a garden.

Tea The suggested tea place is the **Station Hotel** (tel 01908 582 495) in Woburn Sands, which serves drinks, tea and coffee all day, and food from 6pm (no evening food on Saturday). The alternative at earlier times (Monday to Thursday) is the **Henry Higgins** fish and chip shop in the High Street, which is open from 4.30pm or 5pm Monday to Saturday. Or, going the other way, past the station, in 500 metres you come to **Frosts** (tel 01908 583 511), a garden centre restaurant on your left-hand side. This is open till 4pm in winter, and till 5pm from April to July.

WALK DIRECTIONS

[1] [Numbers refer to the map.] Coming off the platform at **Bow Brickhill Station**, from the Bletchley train, go through a wooden swing gate and turn left, southwards, *back over the railway lines*, on 'V10' Brickhill Street.

In 75 metres ignore a left turn towards Bow Brickhill.

In 80 metres *take the signposted footpath to the left*, due east, with the field edge more or less on your right side and a barbed wire fence to your left-hand side. In 345 metres cross a potentially muddy tractor track to continue straight on, through a wooden kissing gate, on a path between fences and houses.

In 40 metres this path comes out *on to an estate road, and you keep straight on* up this road, ignoring a turn-off to the left.

In 170 metres you come *to a T-junction where you go right*, your direction 150 degrees. In 45 metres **[2]** pick up a signposted path to continue in your previous direction (105 degrees).

In 25 metres go through a wooden kissing gate and straight on, across a field of mounds (a remnant of the old ridge-and-furrow field system). In 55 metres keep to the field edge on your left-hand side, your direction 120 degrees.

In 80 metres go over a stile and straight on between fences.

In 260 metres, *by a three-armed footpath sign, follow a bridleway sign to the right, upwards, on an*

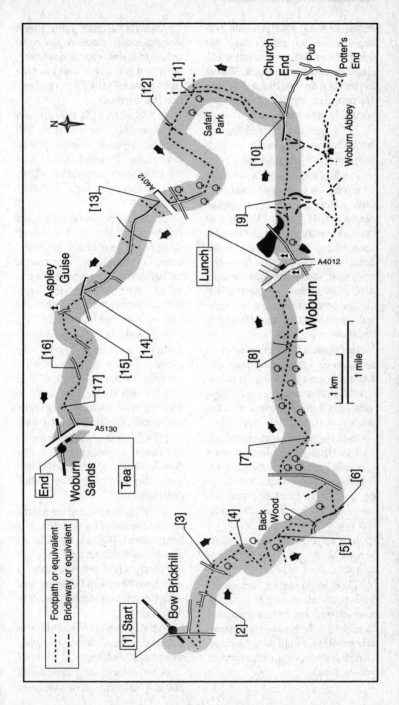

earth car road, your direction 160 degrees. In 30 metres take the leftmost fork [3], your direction 145 degrees, uphill into **Back Wood** (as marked on the OS map). Ignore the first signpost which points implausibly up a steep bank.

In 140 metres you start to have a barbed wire fence with wooden posts on your left-hand side.

In a further 230 metres, *you come to a fence on your right-hand side, with yellow arrows on a corner fencepost* [4]. *Follow the arrow to the right,* your direction 240 degrees, soon with a glade on your right-hand side. 175 metres from the fencepost, ignore a fork to the right and, in 60 metres, ignore another. At this point, you have a fine view out over the valley and Bletchley, unhindered by trees.

In a further 10 metres, you come *to a corner fencepost on your left-hand side, and you follow its arrow left* to continue on through pine trees, your direction 110 degrees, with the fence now on your left-hand side.

In 45 metres ignore the first track to the right and follow arrows onwards (collapsed fencing to your left) and steeply downhill, with gorse on your right-hand side and the tower of the church in Little Brickhill visible away to your south.

In a further 110 metres, follow arrows as the path veers right, now due south.

Then in 80 metres, ignore the path to the right and, in 5 metres, veer left with the path (as indicated faintly by four arrows on a corner fencepost) to go uphill, your direction 70 degrees, with a fence on your left-hand side.

After 220 metres going uphill along a sandy channel, *you come out on to a sandy earth road heading into a golfcourse, and you turn right downhill* on this, your direction 200 degrees.

In 150 metres [5] *take the fork left downhill,* your direction 140 degrees, towards wooden planks soon visible 70 metres ahead. Cross this series of seven sets of two planks over a swampy area, to carry straight on.

200 metres beyond them, cross a yellow arrow path and still keep straight on, your direction 145 degrees. Go straight on, downwards, for 100 metres to a fence, where you follow the arrow right, your direction 250 degrees, with newly planted trees on your right-hand side.

In 215 metres, you come *down to a stream on your left-hand side, which you cross by going left on a car-wide bridleway* (marked with blue arrows) uphill, your direction 135 degrees, towards the **Sierra redwood (Wellingtonia) trees**.

[*] – [This is where those on the less muddy alternative route for the Bow Brickhill to Leighton Buzzard walk should rejoin that walk's descriptions.]

After 350 metres, and ten metres beyond the end of the forest on your left-hand side [6], *take the stairs on your left with railings uphill* (marked to their right by a yellow arrow on a post), your direction 60 degrees, now with the forest again on your left-hand side.

In 380 metres go over a stile *on to a tarmac road. Go left on this,* your direction 20 degrees.

In 340 metres you ignore a possible way into the woods on your right-hand side, but in a further 160 metres – 5 metres beyond the entrance driveway to the golf clubhouse on your left-hand side – go through a kissing gate onto *a signposted gravelled footpath to your right*, your direction at this point 105 degrees.

In 175 metres ignore the arrow on the post to your left to carry straight on, ignoring ways off, with large open fields on your left-hand side and **Little Brickhill Copse** (as marked on the OS map) on your right-hand side.

In a further 420 metres, follow the arrow on a post, straight on, ignoring a path off to the right; and soon with a golf course to your right-hand side.

In 100 metres, *just as the open field to the left is coming to an end* **[7]**, *follow the Woburn Walk (WW) arrow to the left*, on a grassy car-wide way, with the edge of **Charle Wood** (as marked on the OS map) on your right-hand side, your direction 30 degrees.

In 265 metres fork right, *following the WW arrow,* towards a house, your direction 80 degrees.

In 50 metres ignore a car-wide fork to the left and, in 35 metres, a private road right into the forest. In another 35 metres you pass a stile, with the house off to the left.

In a further 95 metres, go through an open gateway and continue with the field to your left and the wood to your right.

In a further 130 metres, by a three-armed footpath sign, carry straight on, along a concrete car-wide way (marked WW). The route is straight on, ignoring all ways off.

In 240 metres you exit the wood and follow the WW sign straight across open fields, along the line of the telegraph poles, with Woburn already visible ahead in the distance, due east.

In 175 metres, at the end of the field, you need to continue on, down, between woods.

In 220 metres you come to a stream T-junction **[8]**, where you follow the WW arrow left, your direction 20 degrees. In 50 metres turn right over the stream, following the WW arrow (your direction 105 degrees) across a field.

In 240 metres follow the WW arrow on through the next field.

In 120 metres go on two planks over a ditch and turn left, following the WW arrow, your direction 5 degrees, now with the ditch on your left-hand side.

In 35 metres follow the WW arrow right to go diagonally across the field, your direction 75 degrees. (There may be future diversions here. If so, follow any WW arrows or get this book's update sheets/ look at the website)

In 400 metres go on a three-plank bridge over a stream and a stile to continue on, following the WW arrow, your direction 100 degrees.

In 80 metres go over a two-plank bridge and stile and go half left, your direction due east.

In 45 metres go over a three-plank bridge and up beside the fence of a house on your right-hand side, coming to the road in 50 metres.

Turn right on this main road, and the **Black Horse** pub, the suggested lunchtime stop, is 260 metres up on your left-hand side.

Coming out of the pub *after lunch, turn left*, due south. In 35 metres *turn left on Park Street*, your direction 70 degrees.

In 100 metres you come to **St Mary**, the church with the dreadful gargoyles.

Coming out of the church, go left to rejoin your road, along which you turn left to continue in your previous direction.

In 65 metres you *enter* **Woburn Park** *by the cattle grid and lodge, and go half right on a signposted footpath*, your direction 115 degrees, with a lake on your left-hand side.

In 450 metres *take the tarmac path to the left of cottages* nos.2 & 3 (the ones with mock-Elizabethan chimneys), to go straight on, your direction 105 degrees.

Go through a swing gate and straight on, with the estate's Bedford office to your right, on a wide tarmac road. On your left-hand side is a timber-framed pavilion protected by its ha ha **[9]**.

[If you have not paid to be in the park, you would officially need to return to this spot afterwards to continue on the main suggested route – those who have paid could try the route described in the paragraph by the two asterisks below. For those who have not paid, this is a point at which an optional detour begins: if you want to take a detour to see the outside of some of the Woburn Abbey buildings and more of the park, or if you want to pay to visit the abbey, veer right with the road, a lake on your left-hand side and stables on your right-hand side, your direction 195 degrees.

You come to the ticket office. You may, if you wish, continue walk-ing – without charge – on a public right of way, heading for a public footpath that is the Greensand Ridge Walk. You may wish to pay the very small fee for the right to walk in the park (see the two asterisks below).

In 90 metres, 5 metres beyond the end of the lake, leave the road to go straight on, following the gravelled farm road marked 'No entry', your direction 210 degrees.

Woburn Abbey is on your left-hand side. Follow the fence on your right-hand side for 600 metres. When you come to the four-armed footpath sign by a metal swing gate, take the path signposted Greensand Ridge Walk, left, your direction 75 degrees, heading well to the left of the abbey, picking up occasional waymark posts on the way.

Head onwards between lakes and across the estate drive, your direction 80 degrees, joining a gravelled road to go straight on, your direction 100 degrees (with the Abbey garden railings on your right-hand side), to the pedestrian entrance to tearooms on your right-hand side.

(**[**]** If you have paid to be in the park and if you have a compass or a good sense of direction, you could go past the tearooms for 300 metres, and there by a No Entry sign, go left, your direction 20 degrees, and you come eventually to the Safari Park fence, to then turn right along it, with the fence to your left-hand side – rejoining the walk directions close to the three asterisks below.)

Otherwise from the tearooms, you can *either* detour for an extra 3.7km by going straight on to join the Greensand Ridge Path – at the end of the fenced garden and 5 metres beyond the ha ha wall, by the 'No entry' signs, forking left with the Greensand Ridge Path – and then find your way, using a map, via Potter's End and Church End, to rejoin the suggested route at point **[10]** below, *or* you can make your way back to point **[9]**.]

The main suggested route from point **[9]** (without any of the above detours) is to *go half left*, your direction 45 degrees, *with no clear path, to the left-hand edge of the lake, and then onwards, parallel to the road that is 100 metres on your left-hand side*. In 1km your footpath joins this road and you continue on it. In 250 metres *you come to a cattle grid* **[10]**, *where you turn left off the road, following the footpath sign*, your direction 10 degrees, and your way marked by regular posts.

In 600 metres your path is parallel to the tarmac road on your left, with lions behind the high fences. **[***]** Nearing the top of the hill, you now pass the tiger section of the **Safari Park** behind the fences.

Go over a stile by a cattle grid, with Trusslers Hill Lodge on your right-hand side. *In 35 metres* **[11]** *fork left*, following the line of the mini-pylons, your direction 310 degrees, downwards into **Hay Wood** (as marked on the OS map), on a grassy car-wide track.

You often pass the zebras on your left-hand side, and *cross over the safari park's entrance drive* **[12]**, *to go straight on*, your direction 310 degrees, on a tarmac road.

In 175 metres, 20 metres past the end of the quarantine area on your right-hand side, *take the signposted public footpath to your left* through a wooden kissing gate, your direc-

tion 210 degrees, going along the edge of the safari park, with (in summer) zebra and water buffalo on your left-hand side and, later, elephants and giraffes.

At the end of the fence *go over a stile ladder and straight on (not the more obvious way to the right)*, your direction 220 degrees, and a fence 5 metres away on your left-hand side.

In 40 metres, by an arrow on a post, follow the footpath to the right, with the streambed on your left-hand side, your direction 285 degrees.

In 450 metres you come *to a tarmac road, where you go right*, your direction 345 degrees.

350 metres down this road (where *the simplest route is to go straight on, which leads directly to the Crawley Lodge exit*, but you are officially meant to detour on a rough and slightly obstructed public footpath, marked with yellow bands), according to the official route, you fork right, your direction 5 degrees, for 220 metres, to a tarmac road.

You cross the road to head straight on, with a not very clear path, through the wood, towards a stile, your direction 315 degrees. In 40 metres you cross a stile and go left, your direction 275 degrees. There is a fence to your left-hand side and right-hand side.

In 125 metres go out over a stile, with a cattle grid and Crawley Lodge on your left-hand side, to exit Woburn Park.

At the main A4012, turn right, your direction 20 degrees. In 40 metres **[13]** *turn left on Horsepool Lane*, your direction 310 degrees, uphill for over 1km towards **Aspley Guise** village, and ignoring ways off.

Over the top of the hill, you pass the Wheatsheaf pub on your right-hand side and, 200 metres further on, you come to a car road T-junction [14] *where you go left* and continue due west.

In 50 metres you pass the thatched Valentine Cottage on your left-hand side, and in a further 60 metres you *go off right, through a metal kissing gate, on a signposted public footpath,* with a garden fence on your left-hand side, your direction 310 degrees.

In 250 metres go through a metal kissing gate out *on to a road T-junction where you go right,* your direction 340 degrees.

In 70 metres, after visiting the **Parish Church of St Botolph**, Aspley Guise, *take the signposted footpath* [15] *opposite the church,* uphill (not into the churchyard), your direction 240 degrees, *with the hedge and the churchyard on your right.*

In 140 metres, you veer right with the path. In 35 metres go through a wooden swing gate and onwards, on a clear path, your direction 235 degrees.

In 180 metres go through a wooden swing gate and straight on, along a car-wide road.

In 140 metres you *go right, through a swing gate marked with a yellow arrow* (a wooden barrier on its left-hand side), your direction 285 degrees, across a playing field, towards Milton Keynes.

In 135 metres go through a wooden swing gate and *follow the yellow arrow through the golfcourse,* your direction 330 degrees.

In 185 metres you come *to an earth car road* [16] *where you go left,* your direction 290 degrees. In 200 metres you pass Golf Course Cottage. Then, in 120 metres, ignore the road (and footpath) going off to the right [17].

In a further 260 metres, you exit the golfcourse and carry straight on, your direction 235 degrees, on Mill Lane. In 80 metres this lane becomes a road between houses on both sides (Burrows Close).

In a further 120 metres, you cross Weathercock Close to continue straight on, along a tarmac path, your direction 230 degrees.

In 50 metres you come to the A5130 and the Weathercock pub on your right-hand side.

(If you turn left at this point, you come in 40 metres to the **Henry Higgins** fish and chip shop on your left-hand side.)

The main suggested route, however, is to *go right on the A5130,* your direction 330 degrees, signposted Wavendon, coming in 250 metres to the suggested tea place, the **Station Hotel**.

30 metres beyond the Station Hotel, you come to **Woburn Sands Station**, with the Bletchley platform 1 on the near side. (To reach **Frosts** garden centre and restaurant, continue on the road over the railway crossing for 400 metres, and it is then apparent on your left-hand side.)

Walk 18

Sunningdale to Windsor

Windsor Great Park

Length 14km (8.7 miles), 4 hours 15 minutes. For the whole outing, including trains, sights and meals, allow 8 hours – or 9 hours if visiting Savill Gardens.

OS Landranger Map No.175 (west London map No.176 covers the walk too, except for a couple of hundred metres near the start of the route). Sunningdale, map reference SU 953 667, is in **Surrey**, 15km south-west of Heathrow Airport. Windsor is in **Berkshire**.

Toughness 2 out of 10

Features Near the start of this walk, you go through Coworth Park, with its polo-playing fields (belonging to a Canadian millionaire), to enter the 4,800 acres of Windsor Great Park (no entrance charge), near the Virginia Water lakes and Valley Gardens. These gardens have a vast collection of rhododendrons and azaleas (best visited in May or June). Lunch is in a restaurant overlooking Savill Gardens (although you have to pay to explore these further). After lunch, the route is up Rhododendron Ride to Cow Pond, which is covered in an array of water-lilies. From there, it is through woods, avoiding as much as possible of the Long Walk: the wearying 4km straight path from the Copper Horse statue to Windsor Castle. Keep clear of the stags in the rutting season (September/October). The suggested tea place is Nell Gwynn's Parlour in Windsor. Then the route is through some of the oldest streets in Windsor to the Thames (with Eton College the other side of the river).

Shortening the walk You could phone for a taxi at lunchtime from the Savill Gardens Restaurant; or walk 2km from there to Englefield Green to catch a bus to Staines or Windsor. A bus can also be caught from the outskirts of Windsor, whilst on the Long Walk (see walk directions below).

History Sunningdale Parish Church was built in 1840 at a cost of a mere £1,600.

The 100-foot-high **Totem Pole** in Windsor Great Park was a gift to the queen in 1958 from British Columbia, and is made from a 600-year-old western red cedar. The giant **Obelisk** in the park was put up by George II to commemorate 'the success in arms of his son, William'.

Savill Gardens (tel 01753 860 222) are named in honour of Eric Savill who, with encouragement from George V, created them on this inauspicious, fast-draining, sandy soil. Later, in 1947, Savill began work on **Valley Gardens**, created on the site of an old gravel pit. Admission costs £5; senior citizens £4.50; children £2 – under 5's free (with slightly lower prices outside April and May).

The **Copper Horse** in the park is a huge equestrian statue to George III, which was commissioned by his son, George IV.

A **castle** was first built at Windsor by William the Conqueror in 1070. Windsor Castle fell to a siege by John, King Richard I's brother, in 1193; and was captured, without a defence being mounted, by the parliamentarians in 1642, the first year of the Civil War. It suffered badly in the fire of 1992, Elizabeth II's *'annus horribilis'*. Windsor Castle (tel 01753 831 118) is open daily and admission is £9.50 (£7.50 on Sundays); last entry is 4pm in summer (March to October) and 3pm in winter.

Saturday Walkers' Club Take the train nearest to **9.50am** (before or after) from **Waterloo** Station to **Sunningdale**. Journey time 45 minutes. Trains back from Windsor & Eton Riverside Station run about twice an hour to Waterloo. Journey time 57 minutes. Or from Windsor Central Station two or three times an hour to Slough, changing there for Paddington. Journey time 31 minutes.

Lunch The suggested lunchtime stop is the **Savill Gardens Restaurant** (tel 01784 432 326) inside Windsor Great Park, serving good and reasonably priced meals. It is open 10am to 4pm daily in winter, and 10am to 6pm in summer (lunch served till 2pm).

Tea The suggested tea place is the **Old Kings Castle** (tel 01753 851708) in Thames Street, down past Windsor Central Station (see directions below), and is one of many possible alternatives for food and drink, as it is open until at least 10.30pm daily. Or there is **The Old Ticket Hall Restaurant** (tel 01753 854 554) which is situated in the old ticket hall at Windsor & Eton Riverside Station, open until late every day (except closed on Sunday and closed daily from 3pm to 5pm outside the tourist season).

WALK DIRECTIONS

[1] [Numbers refer to the map.] Coming out of **Sunningdale Station** (past the ticket office), turn left, your direction 155 degrees. In 25 metres *turn left again to go over the railway crossing*, your direction 80 degrees. *At the other side of the crossing, turn left*, your direction 300 degrees, on a path parallel to the railway lines, (there is a building site to the right of the footpath) back past the station building on your left-hand side.

Ignore all ways off. In 350 metres you cross on a bridge over a stream and *turn right alongside the stream*, which is now on your right-hand side, with a playground and tennis court coming up shortly on your left-hand side.

In 180 metres you come out through a metal barrier *to the B383, where you turn left*, your direction 345 degrees. In 100 metres *turn right on to Station Road*, your direction 10 degrees.

In 200 metres *turn right on Church Road*, your direction 75 degrees.

In 250 metres you come to the entrance of **Holy Trinity Sunningdale Church**, and, *100 metres beyond the church, you go half left* (not the sharp left fork) *up Whitmore Lane*, your direction 355 degrees.

In 320 metres ignore a byway sign to the left, at the bowling club. In a further 200 metres, you pass the entrance to Callaly House on your left-hand side, and then have Tittenhurst Park behind the wall on your left (the park is not yet visible).

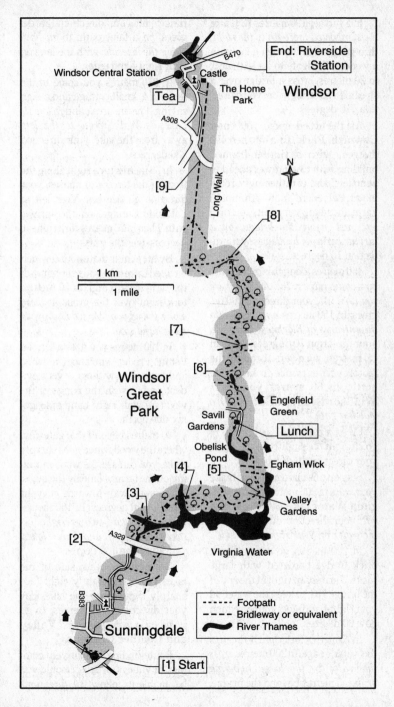

Windsor Central Station

Castle

Tea

The Home
Park

Windsor

End: Riverside
Station

B470

A308

[9]

Long Walk

N

[8]

1 km

1 mile

[7]

Windsor
Great
Park

[6]

Englefield
Green

Savill
Gardens

Lunch

Obelisk
Pond

Egham Wick

[4]

[5]

[3]

Valley
Gardens

[2]

A329

Virginia Water

B383

Sunningdale

Footpath
Bridleway or equivalent
River Thames

[1] Start

In a further 190 metres **[2]**, *take the signposted footpath to the right*, through a small wooden gate (with a wooden fieldgate to its left), and, in 20 metres, cross a bridge over a stream to go straight on, your direction 110 degrees.

As the wood ends, you enter **Coworth Park**. In a further 450 metres, with a timber-framed building with clock tower ahead to your left, and a rather ugly renovated Belvedere (now Ahmibah) Farm ahead to your right, you *turn left, just before the bridge, on a tarmac car-wide bridleway*, your direction 10 degrees.

450 metres along this bridleway, you come out on *the A239 where you turn left*, your direction 290 degrees. In 150 metres *turn right into the entrance of Blacknest Carpark*, your direction 70 degrees. And, in 15 metres, turn left through the motorcycle entrance to head due north. In 60 metres you *enter* **Windsor Great Park** *through a wooden gate*.

Cross a car-wide earth track to go straight on, slightly to the right, your direction 40 degrees.

Stay on this main path and make your way, in 200 metres, *to the* **Virginia Water lake***, where you turn left*, your direction due west, *with the water on your right-hand side*.

In 220 metres go over a small brick bridge bordered with large rocks. Turn sharp right at the end of the bridge **[3]**, to keep the water on your right-hand side, your direction now 20 degrees.

In 75 metres fork right, to keep to the water's edge. In 200 metres *cross the water by the large five-arch bridge*. 5 metres beyond the bridge,

turn right, your direction 125 degrees, on a faint path, to *go back along the lakeside*, with the lake on your right-hand side.

In 270 metres you come to the fence of a small cottage and a sign saying 'Private area', and *follow its Lakeside Walk arrow to the left*, away from the lake, your direction 330 degrees.

In 35 metres turn right along the front of the terrace of houses, your direction 45 degrees. Veer left at Lakeside Cottage, on the tarmac path. Then in 20 metres fork right 40 degrees over the grass.

By the penultimate house, which is called Lakeside, you veer left with the tarmac path and, in 20 metres, fork right over the grass, to *keep along the edge of the wood on your right-hand side*.

In 100 metres you pass a 'Crown Estate. Private' entrance gateway, and keep on – without a very evident path – with the fringe of the wood on your right-hand side, going due north.

80 metres beyond this gateway, where the wood fringe goes sharply right, you can see the wooden railing on the tarmac lane by the lakes. Make your way towards it, your direction 40 degrees. In 160 metres *the tarmac lane swings right, between the upper and lower lakes*, your direction 100 degrees.

Once on the other side of the lakes **[4]**, fork slightly right (not sharply right along the lakeside), your direction 115 degrees, to *go uphill on a way signposted* **Valley and Heather Gardens**.

Route-finding is relatively complex in Valley Gardens. Should you be unable to follow the directions suggested below, simply wander round the gardens to your heart's content, then go down to the lake and turn left, which will lead you in due course to the Totem Pole – or ask for directions to this landmark.

In 70 metres take a left fork, your direction 100 degrees.

In 20 metres ignore the sharp turn downhill to your right, and continue uphill. But in 90 metres, *near the top, with wooden sheds just visible 40 metres ahead of you, turn right downhill on a grassy car-wide track,* your direction 175 degrees (ignore the turn at 120 degrees).

In 6 metres you pass a wooden bench that is 4 metres off to your left. In a further 10 metres, *fork left with your car-wide grass track, uphill,* your direction 155 degrees.

In 40 metres bear right, merging with another car-wide grassy track to go downhill, due south.

In 45 metres, and *30 metres before a sandy lane T-junction below, turn left on a grassy car-wide track,* your direction 85 degrees.

In 15 metres you pass a sign saying 'subsection fulgensia' on your left-hand side.

Carry straight on, ignoring other ways off. In 110 metres ignore a grassy car-wide fork going left (its direction 10 degrees) to keep on down, your direction 80 degrees.

In 15 metres, as you come out into the open, bear half right from the oak tree, your direction 140 degrees, to go downhill, in 80 metres *crossing a wooden bridge with wooden railings.*

At the other side of the stream, carry straight on, your direction 110 degrees.

In 10 metres cross a path and go upwards, straight on, with no clear path, through the open green grass of **Azalea Valley**, between a near bench to your right-hand side and a far bench to your left.

[!] *Once the left-hand bench is facing you, 30 metres to your left-hand side, go half right on a car-wide grassy road, your direction 145 degrees.*

At a crossing of the ways, 60 metres along this road, continue straight ahead. Again, in 30 metres, at another crossing, you join a path coming in from your left to keep straight on. The lake is now visible through the trees on your right-hand side, and your path will be roughly parallel to its edge.)

In a further 100 metres, you come down into a green valley, **Valley Garden**, with the **Plunkett Memorial** – a little pavilion with four columns at the top of the valley – 250 metres to your left-hand side.

Cross the valley to *go up the wide grass and log steps* the other side, your direction due east.

At the twelfth step, ignore the paths you cross to keep on up the main steps. At the top of the steps, keep straight on. Then in 20 metres, *at a T-junction, go left,* your direction 350 degrees.

In 12 metres ignore a faint fork downhill to the right, and in a further 60 metres, ignore another fork downhill to the right. Your path is now a gravelled car-wide track.

In a further 90 metres, *you come to a three-way junction,* all car-wide tracks with tyre marks. *Go sharp right,* on the rightmost one, your direction 130 degrees.

In 35 metres you pass a bench on the left-hand side of the path, and in a further 30 metres, another bench, with the lovely grassy valley of the **Punch Bowl** falling away to your right-hand side.

55 metres past this last bench, ignore a mini-fork off to the right, to keep with the car-wide earth track. In a further 40 metres, cross a car-wide earth road, by a giant wellingtonia tree, to keep straight on.

15 metres beyond this tree, you come to a car-wide earth road, which you take to the right, your direction 95 degrees.

In a further 25 metres, ignore a fork to the left. In a further 400 metres, you come right up to the **Totem Pole [5]**. *10 metres beyond the Totem Pole, go left, with the lake then on your right-hand side*, your direction due north (with no path as such).

In 50 metres cross a stream on four planks, with the lake on your right-hand side. In 110 metres *do not go over the bridge with white railings, but go straight on*, your direction 10 degrees. In 115 metres you come *to a tarmac road* (where to the right is signposted 'Valley Garden exit') and you *go left*, your direction 285 degrees.

In 188 metres, with car wide paths to both left and right and with fingerpost signs in the distance ahead, turn right. In a further 30 metres, *near the brow of the hill, you turn right on an earth car-wide path*, your direction due north.

In 240 metres ignore a small path off to the left. In a further 85 metres, your path crosses a stream (there are wooden railings).

In a further 120 metres, near the top, *go left, your direction 225 degrees, coming to* **Obelisk Pond** in 35 metres. Here you turn right, on a tarmac car-wide path.

In 200 metres fork left, coming in 40 metres to the **Obelisk**.

To continue on, *stand with your back to the side of the obelisk* that says 'This obelisk raised by command of King George the Third', *and go quarter left, your direction 15 degrees, to pick up your previous tarmac path* in 50 metres, by a sign saying 'To Savill Garden and Shop'.

In 200 metres you come to the shop – where you can pay for entrance to **Savill Gardens**, if you wish, or go in without charge to **Savill Gardens Restaurant**, the suggested lunchtime stop, from whose balcony you have a view out over Savill Gardens.

Turn left when you leave the restaurant, to continue in the same direction as previously, 15 degrees. In 70 metres ignore a turn to the right.

In a further 85 metres, *by a distant double-storey greenhouse on your left-hand side, take the right fork*, **Rhododendron Ride**, more or less straight on, your direction 340 degrees, past a sign saying 'No Cycling'.

In 400 metres **[6]**, *at a crossing of paths, go left*, due west, to **Cow Pond** with its water-lilies. *Carry on round the pond*, still keeping it on your right-hand side. **[!]** *At the far end of the pond, where the wide green path comes to an end, you need to turn left, crossing on a tree trunk over the stream* (ignore the first two tree trunks, which have water-channels through them, and take the third with steps) to make your way in the direction of your jump, due west. Keep right on following a path of sorts through the trees, heading in the direction of the car road soon visible ahead, and keeping the bogs and marshes over on your right-hand side.

In 120 metres you *exit the wood and turn right immediately*, to keep the fringe of the wood to your right, your direction due north.

In 100 metres you *turn right on to a car-wide horse ride covered with sand,* your direction 50 degrees.

In 290 metres go left on a faint path, your direction 350 degrees, *heading towards the pink gatehouses of the* **Royal Lodge**.

In 10 metres you cross a ditch, then other paths; in a further 80 metres coming *to a tarmac road where you go right*, your direction 20 degrees.

In 160 metres you *cross the entrance road to the Royal Lodge* **[7]** *and go straight on*, your direction 335 degrees – the road is clearly marked 'Deer park. No commercial vehicles'.

In 75 metres you go through the deer park gates. In 55 metres *fork slightly right, your direction 320 degrees, on a narrow but fairly well-used footpath.*

Keep straight on along this, but, *in 160 metres, go right on a wide sand-and-earth path down into the pine trees*, your direction 40 degrees.

200 metres after entering the wood, *you come to a very wide, sandy avenue for horses. Turn right* on this, your direction 85 degrees.

In 320 metres you ignore a major car-wide fork to the right, in order to keep straight on, your direction now 25 degrees.

[!] *Look out carefully for this next direction: in a further 450 metres, you go left, in 10 metres going between two large oak trees marked 880 and 881, and then you fork half right, your direction 265 degrees, on a narrow bridleway through the forest.*

In 100 metres, with a big tree stump blocking your way, and 40 metres before the wood's valley and stream below, veer right with your path, your direction now 310 degrees.

In 140 metres cross the ditch where it goes through a concrete pipe under your path, and continue on a clear path, now 260 degrees.

In 130 metres *exit the wood and turn right on a car-wide path*, your direction 15 degrees.

In 260 metres you pass the entrance driveway to Scout huts on your left-hand side.

In 40 metres you cross a stream and, *1 metre beyond the stream* **[8]**, *fork left*, your direction 300 degrees; in 75 metres, coming to a notice about fishing/dogs. Now you have a lake on your left-hand side.

Go through some more deer gates and carry on, your direction 255 degrees, along the hedge then fence to your right, but keeping parallel and as far away from the track as necessary to avoid horse-churned muddy zones.

In 300 metres you have a fine view of the **Copper Horse** on the hillock away to the left, and you *follow the bend of the fence to the right*, your direction 310 degrees.

In a further 100 metres or so, *you can see Windsor Castle ahead of you. Head towards it, joining if you wish the* **Long Walk** (a tarmac lane which links the Copper Horse and the castle).

In 1km you exit the park through a metal swing gate to the left of white double gates. In a further 750 metres, you cross the main road, the A308 **[9]**. If you are exhausted at this point, there is a bus shelter ahead to your left, 40 metres after the start of Kings Road; and the Windsor Castle pub, 40 metres beyond the bus stop.

The main route is to go on for another 1.3km up to the castle gates.

Here you turn left to *exit Windsor Great Park on to Park Street,* passing the Two Brewers pub on your right-hand side. In 75 metres *fork right uphill on St Albans Street,* keeping the castle walls on your right-hand side.

In 80 metres you pass the Parish Church of St John the Baptist on your left-hand side.

In a further 25 metres, you pass Church Lane to your left; and then in 50 metres, turn left and walk 10 metres to be by the Henry VII gatehouse entrance to **Windsor Castle**.

Turn left, exactly opposite the gatehouse, to go down Church Street, coming in a few metres to the **Kings Head**, a possible tea place if wished.

Coming out of the tea place, turn left to come to the Highlands (previously the Court Jester pub), where you turn right on Church Lane. Then turn right, by the Three Tuns pub, down the passageway beside Market Street, passing the **Guild-**

hall *on your left-hand side. In 25 metres, by the old leaning Market House, turn left on Queen Charlotte Street,* supposedly the shortest street in Britain.

Turn right in the High Street, (signposted to Central Station and Riverside Station). In 25 metres you pass Queen Victoria's statue to keep straight on. In a further 60 metres, you come to the approach road on your left-hand side to **Windsor Central Station** (for trains to Paddington, changing at Slough).

For Riverside Station, keep straight on, in 75 metres passing the **Old Kings Castle** restaurant on your left-hand side. This is the suggested tea place for the walk.

In 75 metres, ignore River Street to the left, to keep on with the castle walls on your right-hand side. 30 metres on, you pass the Theatre Royal Windsor on your left-hand side. 40 metres on, you pass the statue to Christian Victor, Queen Victoria's grandson.

In a further 40 metres, *cross straight over the main road on to Thames Street, with the William IV pub on your right-hand side,* and in 40 metres you pass Sir Christopher Wren's House on your left-hand side.

In a further 30 metes, *just before the bridge, go down steps on the right-hand side to follow the river-side walk,* along the Thames on your left-hand side.

In 40 metres turn right, by a modern building marked 'Thames-side', up Farm Yard which leads in 80 metres to the entrance, on your left-hand side, to **The Old Ticket Hall Restaurant**, and then to **Windsor & Eton Riverside Station** (for trains to Waterloo).

Walk 19

Hever to Leigh

A Kent castles walk

Length 14.5km (9 miles), 4 hours 20 minutes. For the whole outing, including trains, sights and meals, allow at least 10 hours.

OS Landranger Map No.188. Hever, map reference TQ 465 445, is in **Kent**, 5km east of Tonbridge.

Toughness 3 out of 10.

Features This is a fascinating and very beautiful walk through the 'Garden of England', and includes two castles, a stately home, rivers, ponds, woods, undulating hills and three lovely villages: the National Trust village of Chiddingstone; Penshurst, with its old Tudor half-timbered houses; and Leigh (pronounced 'Lie'), with its large cricket green, dominated by the Church of St Mary. The Medway Valley is prone to flooding, and it is possible that parts of this walk may not be passable in extreme conditions. Note that on Sundays there may be only one train that stops at Hever.

Shortening the walk Penshurst Station is an alternative station to return from – it's about 3km north of Penshurst, one stop to the west of Leigh Station. You could get to Penshurst Station across country after a lunch in Chiddingstone (with good directions locally or OS map).

History Hever Castle (tel 01732 865 224) was erected in 1453 by Sir Geoffrey Boleyn, Lord Mayor of London, and was the childhood home of Anne Boleyn (mother of Elizabeth I). She was courted here by Henry VIII. William Waldorf Astor acquired the estate in 1903, and set about restoring the castle. He employed 1,500 men for five years to divert the course of the River Eden and form a large new lake of 35 acres. He also built a new but surprisingly convincing Tudor-style village on the north side of the castle to accommodate guests and staff. The compact grounds include a maze, topiary and gardens draped on ruins imported from Italy. The gardens are open daily from the beginning of March until the end of November. There are two cafeterias – one by the entrance, one by the lake. Gates open at 11am, the castle is open from midday. Admission is £8; or £6.20 for the gardens only.

St Peter's Church in Hever is a part-Norman church with a fourteenth-century tower topped with a shingle spire. Within the Bullen Chapel is the brass over the tomb of Sir Thomas Bullen, Ann Boleyn's father, showing Sir Thomas in his garter robes.

Chiddingstone Castle (tel 01892 870 347) is not much of a castle compared with Hever – it is more of a country squire's house, masquerading as a fantasy castle. The present castellated structure dates from the seventeenth century. Once the ancestral home of the Streatfield family, it now contains a collection of art and curiosities left behind by its recent owner, Denys Eyre Bower. The castle is open at Easter and from May to September (unless closed for a function). It is always closed on Monday, Tuesday and Saturday. It is open from 2pm to 5.30pm weekdays, and from 11am to 5.30pm Sundays. Admission is £4.

The village of **Chiddingstone** became wealthy as a centre of the iron industry in the sixteenth and seventeenth centuries. The Streatfield family sold the village to the National Trust in 1939, as a consequence of which it remains largely unspoilt. The building that is now a village shop (and tearooms in buildings at the back) was bought, in 1517, by Ann Boleyn's father as the manor house of Chiddingstone.

In 1624, **St Mary's Church** in Chiddingstone, was struck by lightning and extensively damaged by fire. The gazebo in the churchyard covers the vault of the Streatfield family.

The stately home of **Penshurst Place** (tel 01892 870 307) is a perfectly preserved, fortified manor house, which has been the home of the Sidney family since 1552, when Edward VI gave it to his old tutor, Sir William Sidney. The poet Sir Philip Sidney was born here in 1554. The oldest part of the building dates from the fourteenth century, but the present house represents a curious blend of five centuries of architectural styles. The house is open daily from March 31st to October 31st. The gardens are open from 10.30am to 6pm, the house from midday to 5pm (last entry). Admission is £6.

On the south side of **St John the Baptist Church**, Penshurst, are timber-framed cottages which form part of Leicester Square (named after a favourite of Elizabeth I) and include a post office house from 1850. The church contains the effigy of the top half of Stephen de Penshurst, Warden of the Cinque Ports and Constable of Dover Castle, who died in 1299.

Saturday Walkers' Club Take the train nearest to **10.20am** (before or after) from **Victoria** Station to **Hever**, changing at Oxted. Journey time about 51 minutes. Trains back from Leigh run about twice an hour, to Charing Cross (changing at Tonbridge) or to Victoria (changing at Redhill). Journey time up to 1 hour 20 minutes, depending on the connection.

Lunch The main suggested lunchtime stop – assuming you visit at least one of the two castles – is in Chiddingstone at the **Castle Inn** (01892 870 247). Slightly pricey bar food is available all day every day, in attractive and historic surroundings; groups of more than 20 people should phone to book. The **village shop tearooms** in Chiddingstone serve cheaper meals at lunchtime through to late afternoon. Alternatively, you could have lunch later, in Penshurst, at the **Leicester Arms** (tel 01892 870 551), which serves lunch from midday to 2pm Monday to Friday, midday to 3pm at weekends.

Tea The suggested tea place is **Quaintways** (tel 01892 870 272), the sixteenth-century tearooms in Penshurst, serving Kentish cream teas. It is open 10am to 5pm daily in winter (closed on winter Mondays), 10am to 5.30pm daily in summer. Alternatively, the **Leicester Arms** in Penshurst is open for tea and coffee all day and will serve

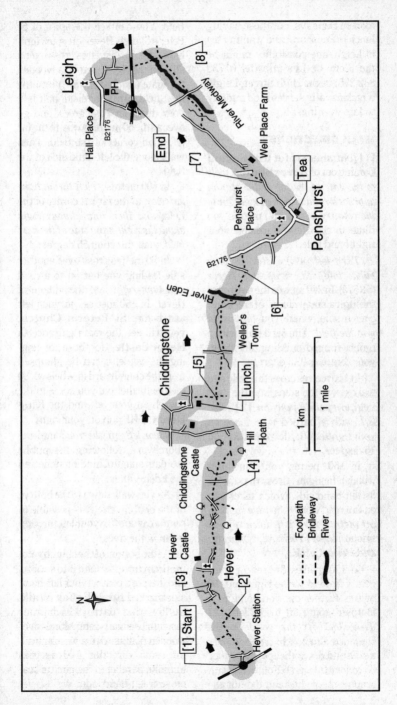

food on Sundays. For those having lunch in Penshurst and wanting tea in Leigh, one possibility might be the Fleur de Lys pub (tel 01732 832 235) in the High Street, Leigh, which usually serves food midday to late evening.

WALK DIRECTIONS

[1] [Numbers refer to the map.] Coming out of **Hever Station**, *walk to the gate at the top of the station approach road and turn right on to the country lane*. In 50 metres you come to Sandfield Farm on your right-hand side.

Turn left over a stile on to a public footpath, signposted Hever (SR575). In 270 metres the path goes through a small clump of trees and over a stile, where you *turn right into the field*. Aim for a stile with a timber-framed building beyond it, your direction 115 degrees.

In 110 metres cross this stile and walk down the steps into the next field, *to a path T-junction*. **[2]** *Turn left*, with a barbed wire fence on your right-hand side, your direction 15 degrees.

In 150 metres you come to a wooden fieldgate. Cross the stile on its left-hand side, which takes you on to a road where you *turn right. In 50 metres, turn left down a road signposted for Penshurst, Tonbridge and Hever Castle*.

In 150 metres the road curves gently around to the right and, 50 metres further on, you come to a footpath going off to the left. **[3]** *Turn left off the road* on the signposted footpath, crossing over a stile and down the footpath, your direction 10 degrees. Follow the path around the right-hand side of the

field. You can see the spire of St Peter's Church, Hever, on your right-hand side. In 75 metres cross over a stile on the right, next to a wooden fieldgate (marked SR 573) into the next field. Cross the field, half left, your direction 70 degrees, and go over a stile 50 metres away in the far left-hand corner of the field. Then walk along the left-hand side of the field.

In 100 metres *go left through the gateway,* at the far left corner of the field, *and then immediately right along the right-hand side of the next field*, your direction 65 degrees.

In 50 metres cross over another stile leading you out on to a road and *turn right* into the village of Hever. In 150 metres, on your left just before **St Peter's Church**, you will see the main entrance to **Hever Castle** – for those not visiting the castle, it can be glimpsed from the churchyard (see below). 30 metres further on, you come to the church on your left and the **King Henry VIII** pub on your right.

Turn left off the road into the churchyard, following the public footpath sign to Chiddingstone and the Eden Valley.

As you walk down to the bottom of the churchyard, it is possible to see the castle off to your left through a gap in the trees.

At the bottom of the churchyard, the path curves around into a copse, and there is a post on your left-hand side marked **Eden Valley Walk**. Follow this path, which goes through a small depression, over wooden planks with a wooden railing, your direction 100 degrees initially, parallel to the tarmac lane on your left-hand side.

In 400 metres you can see the lake belonging to Hever Castle, and the path veers sharply around to the right, your direction 160 degrees. In 300 metres you come to a wooden bridge crossing over a lane. Go over this, continuing in the same direction as before.

150 metres beyond the bridge, you come to another wooden post signed Eden Valley Walk (SR527), alongside the tarmac lane which has now merged in from the right-hand side, straight on.

In 350 metres the tarmac road on your right-hand side comes to a metal fieldgate **[4]**. Pass through a gate in the fence to the left of this, with a pointer for the Eden Valley Walk. Follow the direction of the arrow, *going half right across the tarmac lane,* and continue along the footpath on the other side, your direction 115 degrees initially. There is a cottage on the right-hand side of the path.

In 250 metres you come to a crossing of tracks, where a car-wide track goes left past some houses. Go straight ahead.

In 40 metres you come out on to a road. Cross the road and go over the stile on the far side (marked Eden Valley Walk SR 527). Go straight ahead, between fences, with an open field on your left-hand side and woodland on your right.

In 250 metres cross over a stile (with a metal fieldgate on its right-hand side). Continue along the same path and across a small brook.

[If the directions ahead here have changed, make your way north-east to the road that leads to Chiddingstone from the west, rejoining directions as appropriate]

150 metres further on, go round a sharp left-hand bend (do *not* continue another 10 metres to where the Eden Valley Walk goes left) cross over the stile, and then across a small wooden bridge, which takes you back over the brook. The path then winds its way up the hill through the bluebells in the clearing.

Follow the path through the cleared trees for 170 metres, until you come to a wooden stile next to a high metal-mesh gate on both sides. Go through and in 20 metres you come *to a T-junction* with a track going alongside a tall wire fence bordering a field.

Turn left on to this track, your direction 80 degrees initially. In 130 metres ignore the path that merges in from the left. The path starts to wend gently downhill through trees. The path is cut through sheer rock and the roots of the beech trees overhanging the path make an interesting sight as they find their way through the rock.

In 150 metres the path is bordered by wire-mesh fencing on both sides. 50 metres further on, you come to a metal fieldgate topped with barbed wire, and a choice of stile to right or gate to left. Go straight down the car-wide track ahead, which takes you up to the road, passing an old wood-beamed cottage – part of the hamlet of **Hill Hoath** – on your left-hand side.

In 70 metres you come to a T-junction with the road. Off to the right it says 'Private. No turning'. Opposite, at the junction, a wooden post with an Eden Valley Walk sign points right. Ignore this and *turn left, following the tarmac road towards Chiddingstone.* As you walk along this track you will start to see glimpses of the castle on your right-hand side. In 50 metres pass Keepers Cottage on your left. To your right you can see the tower of St Mary's Church, Chiddingstone, to the right of the castle.

300 metres further on, you come to Garden Cottage on your right-hand side, directly adjacent to the castle walls. 200 metres beyond that, you reach the entrance to **Chiddingstone Castle** on your right-hand side.

From the castle entrance, continue up the road. In 100 metres you come to a crossroads. *Turn right*, following the signpost to Chiddingstone (and the High Weald Country Tour).

In 100 metres follow the road as it curves around to the right. 60 metres further on, ignore the public footpath going off to the left, and go over the stone bridge. From the bridge there is a very fine view across the lake to the castle.

100 metres further on, you pass the tower of St Mary's Church on your left. Ahead of you is the ancient **Castle Inn**, which is the suggested stopping place for lunch (alternative lunch stops are in Penshurst).

From the Castle Inn, walk up the village street. In 40 metres you come to the entrance to **St Mary's Church** on your left, and on your right the village stores and post office. 50 metres further on, you pass the primary school. (20 metres further on, you have the option of taking a diversion to see the Chiding Stone, an outcrop of local sandstone.) 40 metres beyond the Chiding Stone turn-off, just past a tarmac

drive leading to a modern house on your right-hand side, *turn right off the road*, through a kissing gate, down a public footpath indicated by a concrete sign at ground level, your direction 220 degrees.

In 100 metres you come to a stile to the right of a kissing gate. Cross over the stile and walk down the footpath ahead. On your left-hand side there is a playing field and the tops of some oasthouses, and on your right-hand side you get another view across the fields to Chiddingstone Castle.

100 metres further on, cross another stile which brings you out on to a field. Follow the footpath straight ahead across the field, your direction 200 degrees. The path is level at first and then dips sharply down into a valley.

In 150 metres the path curves around to the left, skirting a wooded depression on the right. 30 metres further on, you come down to another stile on the corner of a barbed wire fence. **[5]** *Do not cross this stile. Instead turn left and walk straight across the field towards an oak tree standing alone on the other side of the field*, your direction 80 degrees. In 150 metres you come to the opposite side of the field, past the oak tree and over a stile into the next field.

Cross the field, slightly to the right and downhill, underneath overhead cables, your direction 105 degrees initially. This may be muddy. The oasthouses visible earlier are now away to your left.

Keep straight on, ignoring a fork to the right in 250 metres, going underneath another set of cables, your direction 100 degrees.

70 metres further on, you come down to a metal fieldgate in the bottom right-hand corner of the field, which leads on to a road opposite a sign saying **Weller's Town**.

Turn right along the road. In 25 metres the road crosses over a brook. On the left, on the far side, there is a metal fieldgate. *Turn left off the road* and go over the stile (on the right-hand side of the gate). There is a sign on the stile for Sevenoaks District Council's circular walk. Walk straight ahead along the left-hand edge of the field, your direction 85 degrees initially.

In 250 metres go through a gateway next to a large oak tree. There is a stile to the left-hand side of the gateway, and you ignore a sign pointing out a footpath off to the left. Carry straight along the left-hand side of this next field.

500 metres further on, following the brook along the left-hand side of the path, you come to a stile (with a rusty metal fieldgate on its right-hand side). Cross the stile and continue on along the left-hand side of the next field. 30 metres further on, *turn left over the stile* with a metal fieldgate on its right-hand side. Cross the short concrete bridge going over the brook, and follow the path as it diverges from the brook, your direction 115 degrees, half right, towards the bridge to your right, your direction 155 degrees.

In 100 metres cross this concrete bridge over the **River Eden** (a tributary of the River Medway). Once over the bridge, *turn right along the riverbank. In 50 metres turn sharp left up the hill*, ignoring the path continuing along the riverbank, your direction 120 degrees. Going up the hill, there is a thickly wooded copse with bluebells on your left-hand side and some newly planted trees on your right.

In 100 metres continue straight along the left-hand side of an almost fenceless, large cultivated field. Away on your right-hand side, you can just see the top of an oasthouse peeping above the rounded side of the hill.

In 300 metres you come to two barns at the top of the hill. **[6]** Follow the path straight ahead, your direction due east initially.

300 metres further on, the path comes to the corner of the field and dips down for 20 metres, through some trees. Cross over the stile then go down some steps. You come out on to a road.

Turn right along the road. You immediately pass the entrance to Culver House on your right.

In 300 metres you pass Doubleton Lane off to your right, and 25 metres further on, on the left, a private entrance to Penshurst Place. 60 metres beyond this entrance, *turn left off the road*, over the stile which is signed for the Eden Valley Walk. Follow the direction for the footpath, which heads off half right across the field towards the church, your direction 140 degrees.

There is a fine perspective of **Penshurst Place** as you cross this field. The walk takes you directly alongside the stone wall and manicured hedge surrounding the south side of the house.

In 200 metres cross the stile leading into the churchyard of **St John the Baptist Church**. Walk through the churchyard – the church is worth visiting (the entrance is through the second door on your left). Continue out of the church-yard – underneath a cottage which stands on stilts, in a line of ancient cottages – and down past a very old post office letterbox (not in use). Some stone steps take you down to the road. On your left you can see the stone-arched entrance way to Penshurst Place.

Turn right down the road for refreshments. In 50 metres, where the road curves around to the right, is the **Leicester Arms**. This is the alternative lunch or tea stop. 40 metres further, on the left-hand side, is **Quaintways** tearooms, the suggested tea stop.

Return along the road. 20 metres beyond the entrance to the church-yard, the road bends sharply around to the right. *Go straight ahead through the brick-and-stone arch-way to Penshurst Place*, following the sign which says 'Public footpath to Killick's Bank and Ensfield', as well as 'Eden Valley Walk'.

In 350 metres a fork to the left would take you to the Penshurst Place admissions lodge. The onward route, however, is to keep straight on, ignoring ways off.

In 250 metres you come to a pond on your left-hand side. 250 metres from the end of this first pond, you come to the end of a second, larger one. 50 metres further on, **[7]** *turn left off the track* and cross over the Y-shaped stile (a metal fieldgate on its left-hand side), signposted Eden Valley Walk.

Once over the stile, *turn sharp right* and walk with the edge of the field on your right-hand side, your direction 80 degrees. In 75 metres, up at the top of the field, cross over another Y-shaped stile. Going up-hill, half left, your direction 40 degrees, you come in 150 metres to a post with a yellow footpath mark on it. Looking back, there is a magnificent view of Penshurst Place, the lakes and the River Medway down in the valley, with its backdrop of trees and hills.

In 130 metres, at the top of the field, go through a Y-shaped stile (to the right-hand side of a metal fieldgate). Continue straight ahead. In 50 metres you come to another metal fieldgate. Go over the stile on its right, which brings you out on to a concrete lane. To the right is signed 'Private road to Well Place only'. Carry straight on.

You now have the River Medway flowing through the valley down the hill on your right-hand side, and fields on your left-hand side leading up to some woods.

In 650 metres you come to some red-tiled cottages on your right-hand side, immediately beyond which there is a metal fieldgate with a stile on its right-hand side. *Turn right here, down the concrete track, and in 15 metres cross over the stile on your left*, which is marked Eden Valley Walk SR 427. Set off half right across the field, your direction 90 degrees. Follow the marker posts beneath overhead cables as they lead you down the hill to the river.

In 160 metres cross a wooden bridge with metal pipe stiles, over an offshoot of the Medway. Over the bridge, head very slightly left across the field towards a wooden post with a footpath sign, your direction 95 degrees. In 60 metres you come to the **River Medway**. *Turn left and walk along the* *riverbank*, with the river on your right-hand side. In 450 metres you come to a stone-and-concrete bridge over the river.

Cross a Y-shaped stile on to the road and *turn right across a bridge. 35 metres beyond the parapet of the bridge, take the footpath (SR 429) going off the road to the left.* Cross over a stile and walk along the left-hand edge of the field, your direction 55 degrees.

In 650 metres, walking along the side of the field with the river occasionally visible through the trees on your left-hand side, you cross over a stile. A wooden plank takes you across a ditch. Head slightly left across the corner of the field towards another stile on your left-hand side. In 25 metres *go through this Y-shaped stile* and go straight ahead down the wide track through the trees.

[8] In 30 metres, just before a brick-and-concrete bridge, ignore a wooden signpost indicating the Eden Valley Walk going off sharp right. Go straight ahead across a bridge, which takes you over a tributary of the Medway. Once over the bridge, follow the path round to the left. In 50 metres cross a green concrete-and-metal bridge *over the Medway*. On the other side, follow the path straight ahead across the field, your direction 345 degrees.

You can see a car-wide track going up the hill ahead of you. Walk along the left-hand side of the field, to go through a wooden kissing gate, 5 metres beyond a metal fieldgate, and up the hill on the car-wide track.

In 100 metres go *through a tunnel under the railway,* past a sign which says: 'Warning, by virtue of the flood barrier, this footpath is liable to flooding beyond this point.'

On the far side of the tunnel, the track continues in the same direction. In 100 metres go through a wooden kissing gate leading out into a residential street. The first bungalow on your right is called Hill Crest. In 100 metres you pass Lealands Avenue on your right.

100 metres further on, you come *to a T-junction* leading out on to the village green of **Leigh**. Directly across the green on a small knoll behind and above some picturesque cottages, the **Church of St Mary** (locked) dominates the village. *Turn left and walk around two sides of the village green,* past the village school on your left-hand side, and up to the main road. Across and to the right is the village store. *Turn left along the road* and in 150 metres you come to the **Bat & Ball** pub.

In another 120 metres, you come to the **Fleur-de-Lis** pub on a corner. *Turn left down the road towards the station.*

In 250 metres you come to a brick tunnel under the railway. For trains to London via Tonbridge, take the path going left before the tunnel. For trains to London via Redhill, go through the tunnel and take the path to the left on the far side. Train timetables are at the bottom of each path next to the road – consult these to find out which is the next train, before deciding which platform to head for.

Walk 20

Milford to Godalming

The Greensand Way
& Winkworth Arboretum

Length 16.5km (10.3 miles), 5 hours. For the whole outing, including trains, meals and a church visit, allow 8 hours.

OS Landranger Map No.186. Milford, map reference SU 955 414, is in **Surrey**, 9km south of Guildford.

Toughness 6 out 10.

Features This is a relatively strenuous walk, and bits of it can be muddy in wet weather, but it is rewarding and full of interest. From Milford Station, you come to the lakes and the magnificent timber-framed Enton Mill – one of the many houses on this walk that have seventeenth or eighteenth-century galleting – black pebbles lining the mortar of the walls, a method much used in those days in Kent and the south. Near a pub and church in Hambledon, you join the Greensand Way, a sandy bridleway that runs through The Hurtwood, offering hazelnuts and blackberries in season. Lunch is at the gourmet White Horse pub in Hascombe, a village with a remarkable church covered in wall decoration, so that it looks almost Moorish.

In the afternoon, the walk goes on legitimate rights of way that give free access to the National Trust's Winkworth Arboretum and its lakes – the azaleas and bluebells make this a fine place to visit in springtime – and then along the fringes of its woods to a horse training course and the rich outskirts of Godalming, with its many imposing buildings. The final approach to the town is along the National Trust's River Wey and Godalming Navigations path along the canal, to the Church of St Peter and St Paul and the ancient High Street.

Shortening the walk You could call for a taxi from the Merry Harriers pub in Hambledon. There is a bus at about 3pm from the White Horse in Hascombe to Godalming; or you can get a bus every 20 minutes from the outskirts (near where the Ram Cider House used to be – see below) into the centre of Godalming.

History Timber-framed **Enton Mill** was built in 1757.

St Peter's Church, Hascombe, was rebuilt in 1863, following the old Saxon design, but slightly larger and incorporating older features such as the seventeenth-century font. At the same time, Canon Musgrave had almost every inch of wall space decorated 'to make us aware of God's glory shining through the physical world'. Above the altar is an ornate dome, formed from the decorated undersides of the roof's supporting timbers, and allowing a view through to the hallelujahs painted on the roof. John Betjeman called it 'a Tractarian work of art'. (The white button for the lights is just through the curtains, up on the left.)

Godalming is thought to mean 'field (-ing) of Godhelm' (the putative first Saxon to claim the land). It was a coaching town between London and Portsmouth, and a centre of trade in wool, stone-quarrying, timber, leather, paper, corn and brewing. The High Street has many half-timbered and projecting buildings.

Saturday Walkers' Club Take the *fast* train nearest to **9.40am** (before or after) from **Waterloo** Station to **Milford** (you may need to change at Guildford). Buy a cheap day return ticket to Milford. Journey time 49 minutes. Trains back from Godalming run about twice an hour. Journey time 45 minutes.

Lunch The suggested lunchtime stop is the **White Horse** pub (tel 01483 208 258) in Hascombe, which serves good food from midday to 2.20pm daily (till 2.30pm at weekends). Groups of more than 15 people should phone to book. A lunch earlier on in the walk is possible at the less gourmet but cheaper **Merry Harriers** pub (tel 01428 682 883) in Hambledon, which serves lunch midday to 2pm daily. Groups of more than 15 should book.

Tea The suggested tea place is the **Pizza Piazza** at 78 High Street, Godalming. Also on High Street only a few doors along is **Bay Tree**, for tea and light supper items. A pleasant alternative is to have tea beside the Wey Canal at the **Farncombe Boat House** café (tel 01483 418 769), Catteshall Lock, Godalming. Groups of more than 20 should book. This is open until 5pm or 6pm Wednesday to Sunday during the summer and at weekends in the winter.

WALK DIRECTIONS

[1] [Numbers refer to the map.] Coming out of **Milford Station**, cross the railway footbridge and *exit platform 1 on the station building side by a white gate.*

Cross over the main road to take the signposted footpath opposite between fences, the path that runs parallel to the railway lines on its left-hand side, your direction 200 degrees.

In 425 metres the path bends right away from the railway lines and, in a further 200 metres, you begin to see lakes to the left-hand side. Then in 100 metres your path becomes a farm track to continue straight on.

In 300 metres cross a road (where left is to The Quest and Mill Lane Cottage). Continue on a footpath, your direction 210 degrees.

In 140 metres you come out on a road T-junction, *with Witley Mens Club on your left-hand side,* and you *turn left*, your direction 110 degrees.

In 210 metres bear right with the road, a stream (visible in winter) now on your left-hand side.

In 150 metres you pass the very lovely **Enton Mill** on your left-hand side, to go under a railway bridge and continue on the road.

300 metres beyond the bridge, you come *to a T-junction,* by a barn supported on wooden pillars on your right-hand side **[2]**. *Turn right*, your direction 170 degrees. In 140 metres, *at a T-junction, cross it to go straight on,* your direction 120 degrees, on a signposted footpath.

In 130 metres go over a stile and straight on, slightly to the right, your direction 130 degrees.

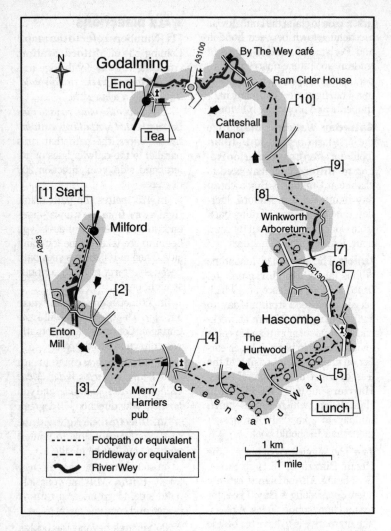

Godalming

End

Tea

A3100

By The Wey café

Ram Cider House

[10]

Catteshall Manor

[9]

[8]

Winkworth Arboretum

[7]

[6]

B2130

[1] Start

Milford

A283

[2]

Enton Mill

[3]

Merry Harriers pub

[4]

The Hurtwood

Hascombe

[5]

Lunch

G r e e n s a n d   W a y

----- Footpath or equivalent
- - - Bridleway or equivalent
〜〜〜 River Wey

1 km
1 mile

In 100 metres you pass a metal barrier (a kissing gate minus tongue) to continue straight on; and straight on again, in 200 metres, when you cross a car lane. At this point you join a car-wide track towards a lake (in winter, this is visible in the distance).

In 150 metres go under mini-pylons. In a further 15 metres, *by the lake, ignore a fieldgate to the left to continue straight on*, with the lake on your left-hand side and your direction due south.

In 160 metres you enter the fringes of the wood through a metal swing gate (which has a wooden fieldgate on its left-hand side).

In 40 metres, *by a mini-pylon, fork left, following a yellow foot-*

path arrow on a post, your direction 160 degrees.

In 75 metres you cross an unmarked path. In a further 20 metres, you come to a post with arrows and go left **[3]**, your direction 100 degrees, initially following overhead mini-pylons.

In 65 metres, at a crossing of paths, keep straight on, your direction 110 degrees. In a further 40 metres, ignore a path from the right.

Then in 50 metres, you come to a potentially muddy zone *by a post with multiple arrows, at the edge of the wood. You go left*, your direction 70 degrees.

In 65 metres you veer right with this wide bridleway, out of the wood, your direction now due east, following mini-pylons.

In 600 metres you come out to a car road T-junction with the **Merry Harriers** pub to your right, offering 'warm beer, lousy food'.

Turn right on the road, your direction 165 degrees. And in 25 metres take the path *opposite the pub,* a signposted public footpath, through a metal kissing gate, your direction 75 degrees.

In 145 metres bend right with this path, and in a further 80 metres, your path becomes a driveway for houses. In 65 metres *you come out on a tarmac road and turn left on this road*, uphill, your direction 110 degrees. In 50 metres you come to **St Peter's Church, Hambledon**, which, alas, is kept locked.

Just past the church, but still alongside its churchyard wall **[4]**, *fork right on a signposted public bridleway* (an earth car road), your direction 125 degrees – and a small parking area on your left-hand side. You are now on the **Greensand Way** (so marked on the OS map).

Keep on this road and, in 450 metres, it becomes a narrower path. In a further 370 metres, you come to a T-junction where you *go to the right,* on a sandy road, your direction 170 degrees.

[!] *In 20 metres turn left up an easy-to-miss public bridleway, your direction 150 degrees (10 metres before a 'steep hill' sign)*, to go along the north fringe of the wood. In 170 metres bend right with the road, down into the wood, your direction 140 degrees, and ignoring ways off.

In 125 metres keep on, following a GW and bridleway sign (with a car road parallel to you on your right). In a further 75 metres, ignore a lesser car-wide way straight on, to fork left with your way, uphill, your direction 100 degrees.

Then in 130 metres, ignore a faint fork off down to the right and towards a house. Keep on the main path, now along the south edge of the wood.

In 85 metres you pass under a mini-pylon. In 650 metres, having enjoyed fine views off to the right, ignore a signposted footpath off to the right.

In 160 metres, at a tarmac road, go left, uphill, your direction 295 degrees. In 85 metres turn right on a bridleway, following the GW blue arrow, your direction 45 degrees, into **The Hurtwood** (as marked on the OS map).

In 80 metres you pass a metal fieldgate to continue onwards.

In 200 metres keep straight on along the main track. In a further

400 metres, cross a car-wide earth road [5] to keep straight on. In 220 metres ignore a fork to the right.

In 150 metres, by a post, turn right, your direction 150 degrees, following a GW blue arrow.

In 25 metres, at a post, follow the GW blue arrow (on a black background) left, your direction 15 degrees. *5 metres later, take the left-hand fork, steeply downwards*, your direction 25 degrees.

[!] *In 160 metres (with – in winter only – a large house and tennis court visible ahead), and by a post with a yellow footpath GW arrow (on a black background), follow the arrow left downhill, leaving the bridleway*, your direction 60 degrees.

In 40 metres you exit the wood by a stile to continue on with the field edge on your right-hand side.

In 130 metres go over two stiles, *straight on towards the* **White Horse** *pub*, **Hascombe**, the suggested lunchtime stop, through a potentially extremely muddy area.

Coming out of the pub after lunch, fork sharp right into Church Road, your direction 25 degrees, in 75 metres coming to the entrance to the delightful **St Peter's Church**, **Hascombe** (it is open to visitors).

Continue on the road past a pond on your right-hand side, and bear left with the road as it passes the School House on your right-hand side. Then in a further 200 metres, *by a cottage* [6], *where one bridleway is straight on, you go left*, on another bridleway, your direction 290 degrees, with the course of a stream still down below you on your left-hand side.

In 75 metres you *fork right to go over a stile* (with a metal fieldgate on its right-hand side), your direction now 305 degrees. Two more stiles, and 130 metres, take you into trees where you *join a footpath and turn right* along it, your direction 345 degrees.

In 80 metres your path merges with an earth road and you carry straight on through a metal fieldgate marked 'The Stables'. There may be a fine garden on your right-hand side of giant wild thistles, lilies and lavatera and in 45 metres you pass a house on your left-hand side. In a further 175 metres, *fork left on a path down between fences*, following a blue public bridleway arrow, your direction 285 degrees. In 120 metres, having negotiated this potentially muddy path, go though a metal fieldgate to *cross the B2130 to continue straight on* up a public bridleway (a gravel driveway signed to Leybourne Cottage), your direction 255 degrees.

In 55 metres you pass Elm Cottage on your left and, in a further 50 metres, Leybourne Cottage, to continue steeply up the bridleway.

In 160 metres ignore an opening and way off to the left. In 145 metres, at the brow of the hill, you pass High Winkworth House on the left-hand side. By a sign for the entrance to High Hascombe House, *turn left on the tarmac lane*, your direction 260 degrees.

In 210 metres, *at a tarmac lane T-junction, go right*, your direction due north.

In 400 metres you come *down to the B2130 where you turn right*, your direction due east.

[!] In 140 metres **[7]** *take a not-very-evident signposted public footpath, sharply to the left (just 1 metre inside Eden House's drive-way, forking left off it)*, your direction 345 degrees.

In 45 metres you pass a part-timber-framed house on your left-hand side, with **Winkworth Arboretum** soon visible beyond the fencing on your right-hand side.

In 500 metres or so, you come to an earth road, with a car park on your left-hand side, and you *follow a public footpath sign to the right*, through a metal fieldgate, your direction 55 degrees, along a car-wide earth road. In 10 metres you pass a cottage on your right-hand side. And, in 60 metres, you pass a wooden ticket kiosk (entrance for those leaving the public footpath costs £2.50).

In 150 metres, at a crossroads, you *follow the yellow arrows* going straight on down towards the Azalea Steps and lakes.

In 75 metres turn left with the yellow arrow, by a wooden sign saying **Fiona Adam Steps**. At the bottom of these steps, turn right, again following the yellow arrow, your direction 110 degrees.

In 130 metres, at a T-junction, follow the yellow arrow to the right, your direction 200 degrees.

In 35 metres, where the steps go up to the right, go left, with a log cabin then on your right-hand side, your direction due east. You pass a lake on your right-hand side.

You come just out of the wood to a T-junction by a National Trust donation pyramid on your right, and you go left with the yellow arrow, your direction 100 degrees, passing a National Trust sign saying 'Hope you enjoyed your visit'.

In 100 metres you *go through the carpark on to a tarmac road where you go left*, your direction 345 degrees.

In 340 metres, *by a public footpath sign and a sign for Phillimore Cottage,* **[8]** *turn left* uphill on a tarmac lane, your direction 340 degrees.

In 100 metres *take a stile off to the right*, marked with an arrow, and once over it, turn left, your direction 300 degrees, with the field edge on your left-hand side. In 200 metres go over a stile, then in 10 metres you pass a sign saying 'Agricultural and sporting pursuits in progress' to go straight on – in 5 metres crossing a path – your direction 310 degrees. In 160 metres you pass a bench on your left-hand side to keep straight on (slightly to the right). Then in 45 metres you cross a path, and in a further 350 metres, having ignored all ways off, you come out through a metal kissing gate *on to a tarmac road where you turn left*, your direction due west.

In 100 metres **[9]**, *by a public bridleway sign, fork right*, your direction 330 degrees. In 25 metres ignore a fork to the right.

In 250 metres, just past a large mansion and garden complex on your left-hand side, cross a bridleway to continue straight on past a metal barrier, between fences.

In 265 metres *cross a tarmac road* **[10]** *to continue straight on*, along a signposted bridleway.

In 1km you pass the swanky gates to Catteshall Farmhouse on your left-hand side. In a further 250 metres, you pass the entrance to Catteshall Manor (with a sign for The Book People) on your left-hand side, and bend right with the road. Then in 80 metres you come to a T-junction, with the ex-pub, the timber-framed Ram Cider House, on your right-hand side, *at a car road junction, where you go left*, your direction 245 degrees.

In 65 metres you turn right by Lawnwood Cottage no.4, your direction 335 degrees. Then in 80 metres you *cross Warramill Road to continue on Catteshall Road*.

In 50 metres, by Brocks Close, you fork left on to the main road to *cross the bridge*, your direction 300 degrees. Stay on the road and, 175 metres beyond the bridge, you *cross another one* by **Farncombe Boat House** café, the attractive alternative place to have tea, on the right-hand side. On the other side of the bridge, turn left, going through a small metal swing gate in 5 metres, to pass Catteshall Lock on your left-hand side, continuing on the National Trust's **River Wey & Godalming Navigations** path, your direction 260 degrees.

In 900 metres you pass the partially converted Godalming United Church to *come out on the A3100 where you turn left*, your direction

210 degrees, to cross the Town Bridge over the River Wey.

At the other side of the bridge, turn sharp right down some steps to get on to the riverside path, meandering with the river on your right-hand side (and Godalming library away to your left).

In 450 metres, beyond the bowling green and before the church, *fork away from the river path towards the back entrance of the churchyard* of Godalming's **Church of St Peter and St Paul** (which is kept locked).

Go through the churchyard and exit it, in 80 metres, *into Deanery Place*, a car road made up of bricks, your direction 160 degrees. Going uphill, in 130 metres, you *turn left into the High Street*, and In a further 140 metres, you come to **Pizza Piazza** at no.78, the suggested tea stop.

Coming out of Pizza Piazza after tea, *retrace your steps to the church* – in other words, turn right into the High Street and in 140 metres, by the Old Town Hall, turn right down Deanery Place to go back down to the church – *but then straight on, to pick up a passageway leading to the station*, still straight on.

At **Godalming Station**, go under the subway for London trains..

Walk 21

Leigh
to Sevenoaks

Knole Park & Kent's
'rolling, tidal landscape'

Length 14.5km (9 miles), 4 hours 20 minutes. For the whole outing, including trains, Knole House and meals, allow 9 hours.

OS Landranger Map No.188. Leigh, map reference TQ 546 462, is in **Kent**, 9km south of Sevenoaks.

Toughness 6 out of 10.

Features You need to start this lovely walk early if you want to be in time for lunch at the pub, as the bulk of this walk is before lunch. The route is through what Laurie Lee described as the 'rolling, tidal landscape' of Kent. The walk starts in the village of Leigh (pronounced 'Lie' from the Anglo-Saxon for 'forest clearing') with its many fine old buildings, goes through the church-yard and parkland of Hall Place, and carries on through a few too many potentially muddy fields, and past many an oasthouse (the coni-cally roofed buildings used for dry-ing hops) to the church and pub in Underriver, the suggested lunchtime stop. After lunch, it is sharply up-hill (and again it can be very muddy – why can't horseriders stick to the middle of bridleways?) to follow the Greensand Way into magnificent Knole Park, passing the front en-trance of Knole and going on a foot-path out of the park into Sevenoaks.

Note that you can also get to Leigh from Victoria via Redhill, in which case you arrive on the opposite plat-form to the one assumed in the walk directions and do not go under the railway bridge.

Shortening the walk There are rare buses (eg 1.30pm Saturdays) from the lunchtime pub in Underriver to Tonbridge station (or vice versa – given that the second part of the walk is the more interest-ing) or there is a 308 bus from Knole House to Sevenoaks station.

History Knole House, built in the fifteenth century (and so huge that it has a room for every day of the year), was visited by Elizabeth I in 1573, who granted it to Thomas Sackville. It remained in the Sack-ville family and was the childhood home of Vita Sackville-West, feat-uring in Virginia Woolf's *Orlando*. The house is open to visitors from April 1st to the end of October, Tues-day to Sunday plus bank holiday Mondays (last entry 3.30pm). Ad-mission is £5; children £2.50. Knole House stands in a park of 1,000 acres. There is no charge for walk-ing in the park, and in any case the route described below follows pub-lic rights of way.

Saturday Walkers' Club Take the train nearest to **9am** (before or after) from **Charing Cross** Station to **Leigh**. Journey time 57 minutes (change at Tonbridge). There are many trains back from Sevenoaks. Journey time 33 minutes.

Lunch The **White Rock** pub (tel 01732 833 112), Underriver, serves food midday to 2pm daily. They prefer to be phoned beforehand if a large group is coming to eat.

Tea The **Brewhouse Tearoom** (tel 01732 450 608) has an entrance in the north wall of Knole House, without the need to pay an entrance fee. It has the same summer-only opening times as Knole House (see above) and serves cream teas. But this walk's suggested year-round tea place is just off the High Street in Sevenoaks: **Coffee Call** (tel 01732 453 580) at 8 Dorset Street serves tea, coffee, sandwiches and cakes, but is rather small; it is open till 5pm Monday to Friday, till 4.45pm Saturday. **Pizza Piazza** (tel 01732 454 664) at 3 Dorset Street, is open daily throughout the day and will serve just tea or coffee as long as the place is not too full. The **Dorset Arms** pub (tel 01732 464 948) nearby at 22 London Road, is also open daily throughout the day for tea, coffee and hot chocolate.

WALK DIRECTIONS

[1] [Numbers refer to the map.] *Exit* **Leigh Station** *down the tarmac path*, your direction 285 degrees, with oasthouses visible to your left.

At the car road turn right under the railway bridge and head towards Proteus garage visible on the right-hand side, 150 metres ahead. Pass the garage and Fleur-de-Lis pub, and *turn right on the main B2027.*

300 metres along this high street (just by a school on your right-hand side and just before a bus shelter on your left), *turn left, northwards, up a tarmac lane to the church.*

Go through the gate into the churchyard. Follow the *path that is to the right-hand side of the church* and out through the lychgate; in 10 metres turn left, *taking the footpath*

indicated with a yellow arrow (SR 414), the direction 345 degrees (past the impressive gatehouse leading to Hall Place to your left) and through a wooden fieldgate (marked Porcupine House).

In 80 metres go through a metal kissing gate and straight on, with the field fence and the ancient trees and parkland of **Hall Place** on your left-hand side. In 300 metres go through another metal kissing gate and straight on, through a potentially muddy area.

In 170 metres ignore the next metal kissing gate at the end of the field and *fork half right over a concrete bridge and stream*, your direction 25 degrees, and continue on. After 100 metres, you continue on the clear onward path across open fields, your direction 15 degrees.

In 260 metres go over a wooden stile to pass through a copse and, in 50 metres, over another stile to follow its yellow arrow (marked FP 414) left down an earth lane, your direction 305 degrees. 20 metres before the end of this lane **[2]** (just before a charming cottage on your left-hand side), follow the footpath sign half right, northwards, with a field fence on your right-hand side.

In 40 metres this path enters the wood on a car-wide earth track. *10 metres into the wood, you turn half right, following a footpath sign, up a wide grassy path, your direction 345 degrees, ignoring a fork right in 15 metres. In 120 metres, at a T-junction of paths, go right*, your direction initially 35 degrees, along a bridleway track.

In 200 metres you exit the wood over a stile and wobbly fence (another potentially muddy area) fol-

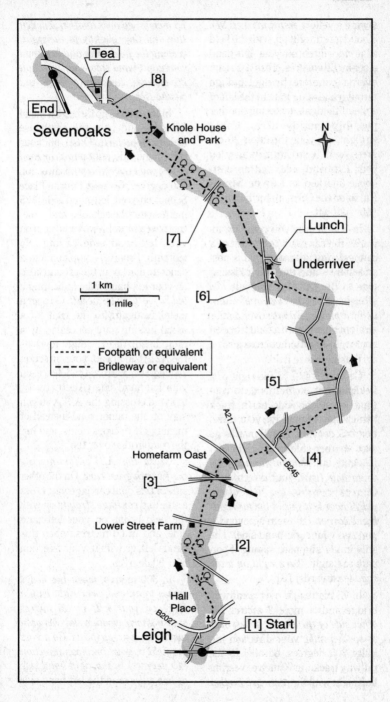

Tea

End

[8]

Sevenoaks

Knole House
and Park

N

Lunch

Underriver

1 km

1 mile

[7]

[6]

----- Footpath or equivalent

--- Bridleway or equivalent

[5]

A21

Homefarm Oast

[4]

B245

[3]

Lower Street Farm

[2]

Hall
Place

B2027

[1] Start

Leigh

lowing a yellow arrow marked MT 30, and go straight on, with the field edge and ditch on your left-hand side. In 120 metres cross a stream over a concrete bridge and go through a kissing gate to the left of a metal fieldgate (entering another possibly muddy area). Carry straight on, your direction 20 degrees, with a stream tributary on your left-hand side, and an oasthouse (marked as **Lower Street Farm** on the OS map) further off to your half left.

In 200 metres you come up towards the car road (to the left of a cottage) – again, more mud is possible here – and through a kissing gate to the left of a fieldgate. *Go straight across the road and continue by a public footpath* over a stile, straight ahead, with a field fence on your right-hand side, across a large agribusiness-size field.

Go over a stile to the right of a fieldgate out of this field, to continue on a car-wide earth track (which may be muddy), your direction 345 degrees. In 120 metres go over another stile to the right of a fieldgate, and *abandon the field edge to go half right*, your direction 35 degrees, *crossing the field diagonally towards a stile in the far right-hand corner* (10 metres beyond a pond on your right-hand side). The stile has a signpost saying 'Footpath to Leigh'. *Turn right on a car road* (eastwards) **[3]**.

In 75 metres go over a railway bridge and, a mere *2 metres the other side of the bridge, go left over a wooden stile*, your direction initially 305 degrees, parallel to the railway tracks, in 90 metres veering half right with the path. *In a further*

75 metres, go over another wooden stile and then slightly to the right, keeping the field fence and hedge on your right-hand side, your direction 25 degrees, towards a farm and oasthouses.

In 150 metres go through a metal fieldgate and past the oasthouse (called Homefarm Oast) on your right-hand side, out *on to a car road where you turn right*, your direction 130 degrees. Go past Bourne Place School on your left-hand side. 125 metres past the school – and 5 metres past a bramble-covered sign on your left-hand side saying 'No footpath. Private' – you come to a concrete marker in the ground (also on your left-hand side) indicating *a public footpath to the left*. Go over a metal fieldgate (to the right of a metal kissing gate concealed by a thorn bush). Head straight towards the A21 road ahead, your direction 70 degrees, with a field fence on your left-hand side. (Alternatively, to avoid crossing the A21, you can stay on the minor road instead of turning off to cross fields, and use the road bridge over the A21).

Cross the A21's fast-flowing traffic with great care. On the other side of this dual carriageway, cross a stile and *continue straight on* with the field hedge on your left-hand side; and in 60 metres, when this bends left, go with it, your direction now 80 degrees.

In 300 metres, *when the hedge comes to an end, veer right with a fence on your left, in 35 metres crossing over wooden slats between two white concrete posts. Go across the field in your previous direction (40 degrees) to the right-hand side of two stiles* (and the left-hand side of wooden sheds) and straight on out to the road in 30 metres, going past Oak Tree Cottage on your left. *Turn left on the B245 and cross the road to turn right in 40 metres, down Mill Lane*, your direction 55 degrees.

In 180 metres, when the road bends slightly to the left, and opposite Meadow House **[4]**, *take the footpath to your right* over a stile, your direction half left (65 degrees), towards a wooden fieldgate visible in the distance.

In 250 metres go over a wooden footbridge and stream, and straight on, your direction 70 degrees, ignoring a footpath marked off to the right. In 130 metres go over a decrepit stile (or through the gate), again ignoring footpath markers off to the right, to go straight on for 120 metres across a field to the stile visible to the right of a fieldgate. Once over the stile, turn half left, your direction then 30 degrees.

In 250 metres you exit this field by its far left corner (near the left-hand edge of the copse) over a stile hidden behind trees, and go slightly left for 20 metres, to leave the copse by a bramble-covered stile or through any less uncomfortable gap. Continue on, your direction 70 degrees, heading well to the left of houses visible ahead (again, across a potentially muddy field).

Exit the field by a stile and in 10 metres go over a wooden bridge and revert to your direction before the stile (70 degrees), following the right-hand edge of the second field.

In 100 metres go over another wooden bridge and stile in the far right corner of the field, then across an earth farm lane, to continue straight on, your direction 70 degrees, past a sand-floored horse training ground on your left-hand side. At the end of this training ground, go over a stile and through a wooden gate, keeping the breeze-block wall on your left-hand side, your direction 55 degrees. In 20 metres go through a gap to the left of a wooden fieldgate, and straight on along the driveway of Brambles House, coming in 60 metres to a car road.

Turn left on this car road, northwards, past a farm shop on your right-hand side.

In a further 120 metres, ignore Vines Lane to your left to keep straight on; but, *150 metres past Vines Lane* **[5]**, *turn left* up a car-wide earth track, with a sign on it saying Woodside and by a public footpath signpost, your direction 325 degrees.

At the end of the track, go between fences and over a stile and through a gap. Follow the fence to your left-hand side, your direction 350 degrees.

At the end of this field to your left-hand side, go over a stile, ignore a way off to the left and continue straight on.

In 150 metres go through a metal fieldgate and straight on across a farm track, heading to the right of a solitary oak tree, to continue straight on, along a farm track, due north.

In 200 metres you leave the farm track as it turns right in order to carry straight on, along a footpath. In 25 metres you go over a stile and half left, your direction 270 degrees, following the direction of the mini-pylons westwards, to the edge of the back garden of a house, where you turn right, your direction 320 degrees, keeping the edge of the gardens to your left-hand side. In 150 metres, exit the field leftwards by a stile and public footpath sign on to a car road.

Turn right on the car road and, in 15 metres, take the car road to the right which is signposted Shipbourne, gently uphill. *In 600 metres or so*, well over the brow of the hill, where a road goes off to the right (again signposted Shipbourne), *you go left (due west) over a stile* signposted public footpath, with a field fence and tennis court on your right-hand side.

Go straight on and in 350 metres go over a stile with a metal fieldgate to its left, and straight on up an avenue of trees, your direction 305 degrees. In 200 metres go over a stile and straight on. After a further 250 metres, across a potentially muddy field, go over a stile and cross a stream to carry straight on, slightly uphill, your direction 315 degrees, with a stream on your right-hand side. Exit the field in 50 metres, *out on to an earth car lane with Green Lane Cottage on your right-hand side.*

[6] *At a T-junction with the tarmac car road ahead, turn right* (due north), in 65 metres passing St Margarets Underriver Church. In a further 75 metres, you come to the **White Rock** pub, **Underriver**, the suggested lunchtime stop.

Coming out of the pub after lunch, turn right on the road and, in 130 metres, ignore the footpath off to the right, to continue gently uphill. In a further 100 metres, opposite a road off to the right signposted

Shipbourne, *take the car-wide lane signposted public bridleway to your left*, your direction 305 degrees.

In 100 metres you pass Black Charles House on your right-hand side to continue up a slightly narrower path. In 315 metres, *with an oasthouse barn just visible ahead and to the right, you turn right up a bridleway*, your direction 345 degrees, to pass to the right of the oasthouse on a path steeply uphill and potentially very muddy and horse-churned in a few places towards the top.

In 400 metres, near the top of this steep alley overarched with trees, you pass a stile marked Greensand Way on your right-hand side, and in 20 metres you fork upwards to the left, in 10 metres going over a stile marked Greensand Way.

In essence you now just *follow the* **Greensand Way** *until you come to a car road*, but here are more details, as the way is not very clearly marked:

Continue on, initially due west, with the field edge on your left-hand side. In 130 metres you bear right with the end of the field, your direction 340 degrees. 100 metres on from this bend, follow the path into the wood on your left-hand side. In 30 metres go over a stile to continue on the Greensand Way, your direction 290 degrees, into the wood. In 200 metres you exit the wood and *go straight across a car road* [7] *to enter* **Knole Park** by a fenced kissing gate (ignore the fenced kissing gate to your right-hand side just inside the park).

Continue straight on, in your previous direction, with the fence on your right-hand side. In 100

metres you come to a junction of tarmac roads, and you take the one straight on, your direction 325 degrees. In 750 metres or so, you come to the third triangle of grass, at the top of a rise, where the track on either side leads in 20 metres to a tarmac path T-junction, but you carry straight on over this, your direction 315 degrees. In 20 metres you are beside fences on your left-hand side and your path becomes a clearly visible car-wide earth path which you can follow towards the walled garden of Knole House, soon visible ahead.

About 100 metres from the walls, *fork left on to a wide grassy path that runs parallel to the walls*, your direction 305 degrees. (You can get a good view of the side of Knole House through the second gap of metal railings along these walls.) At the end of the wall *turn right along the front wall of Knole House* to reach the main entrance tower.

To continue on after going inside Knole House (if you want tea now, go right and right again, to the **Brewhouse Tearoom**'s entrance, otherwise continue as follows): *Coming out of the house's main entrance, turn right on the curved driveway*, due north, and *85 metres from the entrance, you cross another road, and in 1 metre you turn half left to go on the grass with no clear path uphill, heading for the largest oak tree at the top of the hill, your direction 315 degrees* (on a line that is a continuation of the line of the side wall of Knole House behind you).

Once at this oak tree (which you now see is actually two trees), carry on in the same direction (still with no

clear path) downwards, your direction 310 degrees, and in 150 metres keep a crater depression on your right-hand side.

You will now be on a clear path that leads down to the tarmac drive, which you cross to carry straight on, following a very clear path downhill, your direction 300 degrees. In 200 metres you *leave Knole Park by a fenced kissing gate to go steeply uphill* (metal handrail on your right-hand side), your direction 265 degrees. In 5 metres you pass the entrance to **Sevenoaks Environmental Park** on your right-hand side. (If the park is open, a pleasant alternative route is to wend your way up through the park, always choosing the left hand forks, and out to the carpark.)

Following the normal path up, in a further 200 metres, you keep to the tarmac path as you pass the carpark (and Waitrose supermarket) on your right-hand side. Continue on with a wall and houses on your right-hand side and railings on your left, coming out at the carpark entrance **[8]**. *You cross over the carpark road and take the way into town to the right-hand side of the toilets* (Akehurst Lane), your direction 255 degrees. This leads out to **Sevenoaks High Street**.

Turn right in the High Street and, in 60 metres, first left into Dorset Street for **Coffee Call** at no.8, the suggested tea place. Or go to **Pizza Piazza** opposite at no.3, or *continue down the passageway that is Dorset Street* and in 40 metres you have the **Dorset Arms** on your left-hand side, also serving tea. *Turn right downhill for the station* (turning left takes you in 50 metres to the

Curtain Scene Tearooms, which has plenty of seats but not much style).

    Sevenoaks Station *is about 1km away down London Road* at the bottom of the hill, just past the Railway & Bicycle pub on your left-hand side. The station has its own snack bars, and up to eight trains an hour to London.

Walk 22

Haslemere (round walk)

Marley Common & Black Down

Length 14km (8.7 miles), 4 hours 15 minutes. For the whole outing, including trains and meals, allow 8 hours 30 minutes.

OS Landranger Map No.186. Haslemere, map reference SU 897 329, is in **Surrey**, 13km south of Godalming.

Toughness 4 out of 10.

Features The route is through very beautiful countryside. It is mainly National Trust land – mixed woods with blackberries and bluebells and heathlands of bracken, gorse, heather and bilberry, with fine views from Black Down, the highest point in Sussex. It is particularly lovely when the rhododendrons are in flower in late spring, although the heathland is at its most colourful in late summer. The afternoon's bridleways can be very muddy in wet weather.

Shortening the walk There is an hourly bus service from Fern-hurst (the halfway-mark lunchtime village) back to Haslemere (the bus goes from the top of Hogs Hill Road in Fernhurst, along the A286).

History In Tudor and Stuart times **Haslemere** was a centre for the iron industry. With the coming of the railway in the mid-nineteenth century it became a popular spot for literary people. The poet Tennyson's house, Aldworth, is on the slopes of Black Down where he loved to walk; and George Eliot wrote *Middlemarch* in Shottermill.

The town has an interesting **museum** up the High Street, just north of Darnleys tearoom. The museum is open 10am to 5pm Tuesday to Saturday, and has a fine explanatory display of local wild flowers in the foyer.

Saturday Walkers' Club Take the train nearest to **9.20am** (before or after) from **Waterloo** Station to **Haslemere**. Journey time 52 minutes. Get a day return ticket to Haslemere. Trains back run about twice an hour.

Lunch The suggested lunchtime stop is the **Red Lion** pub (tel 01428 643 112), by the village green at Fernhurst, offering quality home cooking. It serves food until 2.30pm daily. Groups of more than 20 people should phone to book.

Tea The suggested tea place is **Darnleys** tearoom (tel 01428 643 048) on Haslemere High Street, which closes at 5pm. The easiest alternative is the **Pizza Express** (tel 01428 642 245) next door, open till at least 10pm daily. The **White Horse Hotel**, also in the High Street, offers reasonably priced food and tea (its serving times are: midday-3pm and 6pm-9.30pm Monday to Friday; midday-9.30pm Saturday; midday-9pm Sunday). There is a bar at the **Haslemere Hotel** opposite the station and **Metro Café** (tel 01428 651 535) is just before the station. This café is open till 6pm weekdays (5pm Saturdays;

closed Sundays). The station is a ten-minute walk from the town centre.

WALK DIRECTIONS

[1] **[Numbers refer to the map.]** *Coming out of* **Haslemere Station***, turn right, cross the main road, and take Longdene Road* (the lane going uphill, to the right of the pub opposite). Your non-tarmac footpath turns off to the right, some 400 metres up this road. Where the road goes sharply left as Courts Hill Road, you continue straight on with Longdene Road, signposted as a dead end.

[2] *Then, in 30 metres, opposite Ridgeways House, take the earth path to the right*, your direction 260 degrees, with an iron gate and kissing gate visible ahead. Once through the kissing gate, keep straight on along the field path and, in 300 metres, again keep straight on, ignoring a fork to the left and keeping the hedge on your left-hand side. Ignoring any further forks off, you come down between farm buildings along a farm track to the main road, the A287.

[3] *Go across the A287 (very slightly to your right), and carry straight on*, through iron railings (by the Sturt Avenue street sign) down a path that becomes a quiet road (heading 260 degrees) between houses. In 150 metres (having ignored a left turn into Orchard Close) take the left fork of this road, your direction 210 degrees, leading on to another main road, the B2131.

Turn right on the B2131 and, in 30 metres, there is a sign on the other side of the road saying Marley Combe Road, with a **Marley Combe** National Trust sign to the

left of it. **[4]** *Go between these two signs and steeply up the steps then a footpath*, your direction 250 degrees, into the woods.

In 50 metres, follow this path round to the left as it becomes a broader track, now 215 degrees. Continue on this main path uphill through the woods, with houses just visible to your right, and the path going gently leftwards, with the direction 140 degrees.

[5] **[!]** Please pay careful attention as the fork in the next paragraph may prove hard to find (if you cannot find it, just keep heading vaguely south, as all such paths take you towards Fernhurst). In 500 metres, at the top of the uphill section, keep going straight – your direction is 165 degrees.

After a level stretch of about 250 metres, the path begins to go downhill, makes a 90-degree bend to the left and starts descending more steeply (its direction 50 degrees). *15 metres down this steep hill from the bend, leave the main path to take a little path that continues in your previous direction (slightly to the right). The path is to the left of a prominent beech tree and has an earthbank on its right-hand side, your direction 140 degrees.* 10 metres down this little path, zigzag with it for 5 metres till it goes in more or less your previous direction (150 degrees), going gently, then more steeply, uphill.

Ignore ways off. In 250 metres, you cross a path signposted Sussex Border Path, but you carry straight on (your path marked with a white footstep on a yellow background on a National Trust wooden post), your direction 160 degrees. Soon you have a small ditch and an earthbank on your left-hand side. *200 metres from the Sussex Border Path sign, the path veers more to the right and then, in 80 metres, crosses another broader path, which you need to take to the left*, your direction 140 degrees. You can further identify this crossing by the houses just visible 100 metres away to your left, at 120 degrees – houses

which become very visible 20 metres further on.

[6] In 100 metres from this crossing, you come to a tarmac road that leads to a small housing estate (you can see the 10mph speed limit signs on the estate's entrance gateposts, 20 metres up the road to your left).

But you *cross straight over this tarmac road and carry on* – there is

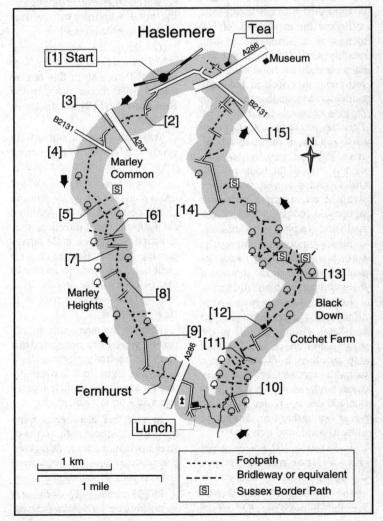

a row of one-foot-high anti-car wooden stumps near the path. Your direction is due south.

In 70 metres, turn right with the waymarked National Trust path, and, in another 80 metres, you turn left on a public road near a National Trust sign for **Marley Common**.

Go along this road for 200 metres, then **[7]** *fork right (initially due south) on to an earth road* that is signposted with a footpath sign.

Follow the earth road for 500 metres as it bends in and out, roughly parallel to the minor power lines on your left-hand side, until you come to a fork in the road, marked by a footpath sign and with za gate on your right-hand side. *Take the fork to the left, still on an earth road,* your direction 170 degrees. **[8]** You come to houses on the left – one of the houses is The Old Orchard – and you carry straight on, along a narrower signposted footpath, initially due south and steeply downwards.

Stick to this footpath as it zigzags *down to a tarmac road. Cross this and carry on down the signposted footpath,* your direction 170 degrees.

In 180 metres, you ignore a turn-off footpath signposted to your left and keep walking parallel to the minor power line on your left-hand side and then, in 80 metres, at a footpath sign, *keep left and downwards on the main fork,* your direction 150 degrees *(going under the power line)* rather than straight on towards a stile and iron gate.

In 50 metres **[9]**, you come out on to a tarmac road by Updown Cottage. *Go to the right down this road,* your direction due south, and, in 350 metres, you come *to an old house and garden called Thrae* (on your left-hand side).

100 metres beyond Thrae's entrance, take the footpath that is signed to the left through a green open space with oak trees, your direction 150 degrees.

In 50 metres, another footpath sign leads you into the woods proper and down shuttered steps across a stream and up the other side (ignoring turn-offs, and now with gardens on your right-hand side).

Go across the main road, the A286, straight over and down Hogs Hill Road, keeping to this tarmac road for 400 metres down to the **Red Lion** pub **[10]**, the suggested lunchtime stop.

After lunch the route is relatively gently uphill for the first 2.5km, on bridleways that can be very muddy.

Turn left out of the pub and left again down the side of the pub and alongside its back garden, *following the footpath sign's direction,* your direction 85 degrees, in 20 metres passing Manesty Cottage on your right-hand side, and in a further 40 metres entering the woods, by a stile next to a wooden barrier on its right-hand side.

Keep to the main path. In 115 metres, you cross a stream and in a further 30 metres you ignore a fork off to the right. In a further 105 metres, ignore two metal fieldgates and a stile off to your left.

In a further 225 metres, bend right with the main path to cross a stream where the water falls down from a storm pipe, with the stream soon on your left-hand side.

In 165 metres **[11]**, *at the next T-junction, with a wooden barn op-*

posite, turn left, following the footpath sign, on a car-wide earth track, your direction 30 degrees.

In 80 metres, at a crossing of paths, by the three-armed footpath sign, take the path, your direction 75 degrees, that is indicated by the footpath sign as straight on upwards (not the fork to the left). *You will be following the overhead telephone cable for some way.*

Soon, ignore a fork to the left.

At the next crossing, again follow the footpath sign straight on, initially 40 degrees.

If it is very muddy at this point, you can normally scramble along the top of the banks to the left or right of the path.

At the next crossroads, follow the footpath sign straight on and up, again the only signed footpath on offer, your direction 75 degrees. Soon you are sharing the path up with a tiny stream coming down it.

You come up to a tarmac lane with a farmhouse on your right-hand side. Leave the overhead telephone cable to take a sharp left, following the signed bridleway to your left, your direction 335 degrees.

200 metres from the farmhouse, at a fork in the bridleways, take the right-hand fork, straight up, due north and, in 30 metres, with a barbed wire fence and a large open field to your left.

Go straight through a fieldgate (it has a bridleway sign on the right-hand gatepost) and down to another fieldgate and a tarmac road.

Turn left on the tarmac road, with the Royal Stables, an Arab stud farm, immediately on your right-hand side (there is a sign in Arabic at the entrance). *Just past the farm, turn to the right on a tarmac road,* signposted bridleway, your direction 20 degrees.

Go on up to **Cotchet Farm**. Here there is a National Trust sign to Black Down on your right-hand side. Go straight on, keeping the farm buildings on your left-hand side, then bending left, and, *at the three-armed signpost, turn right, to follow the bridleway sharply uphill,* your direction 20 degrees.

Follow this bridleway, which is somewhat winding. Continue in a generally north-easterly direction for 800 metres (in due course passing a glorious view out to your left-hand side) until you reach a five-ways path junction. **[13]** Here you *turn sharp left on to the signposted Sussex Border Path,* a car-wide track, your direction 270 degrees, now mainly through the pine forest and the rhododendrons.

From here on, follow the **Sussex Border Path** *signs for 2km almost all the way to Valewood House* down in the valley. But in more detail: at the first fork go left, ignoring the yellow National Trust footpath off to the right.

At the next crossing, a bridleway, carry straight on, your direction 310 degrees. At the next junction, take the Sussex Border Path to the left, ignoring the main yellow National Trust path straight on. Go downhill, and near the bottom of the hill, at the T-junction, the bridleway goes left (downhill) but you take the Sussex Border Path right, initially 10 degrees.

In 250 metres or so, the path veers left. Ignoring a turn-off to the right, and walking through what becomes almost a tunnel of overarching rhododendrons, you soon enter **Valewood Park**, as announced on a National Trust sign. 20 metres past this Valewood Park sign, take the signposted Sussex Border Path to the right across a large open field (initially 300 degrees, in the direction of a large mansion house on the opposite hill).

Go through a very wide gate – a fieldgate on the right-hand side attached to a side pedestrian gate – and you can see down to Valewood Farmhouse below.

The Sussex Border Path continues straight on round the far edge of the field and down, but the suggested route (a short cut) is to take the bridleway car-wide track off to the left, steeply downhill, its direction 285 degrees.

At the T-junction at the bottom of the field, go left, again signposted Sussex Border Path, through another wide farmgate with side gate attached, and down 75 metres, keeping right, to a well-worn earth car track **[14]**. Turn right on this track (heading due north) *to carry on past Valewood Farmhouse* on your right-hand side in 100 metres. *Just past Valewood Farmhouse's white entrance gate and beyond the stream, turn right towards a sign saying 'Stedlands Farm'.*

Then go past the entrance drive on your right that leads to a large new brick house with diamond-paned windows. *At a fork in the track marked with a footpath sign, take the bridleway uphill to the left*, your direction 20 degrees. Then go fairly steeply uphill, ignoring turn-offs. In 500 metres, *you come to a tarmac road at the top* with a house called Littlecote on your left-hand side. *Turn left and, in 20 metres,*

turn right again up a tarmac path marked 'Neighbourhood Watch Area', with an anti-motorbike barrier at its start, the direction 20 degrees, and soon with playing fields on your left-hand side.

In 300 metres, *cross another tarmac road but keep straight on*, down a path with steps between high hedges, *to the main road, the B2131* **[15]**. *Turn left and head straight on to* **Haslemere** *Town Hall in 200 metres, and then turn right into the High Street*. In 40 metres, you pass the **White Horse Hotel** on your right-hand side. And, 100 metres beyond this, you come on your left-hand side to the suggested tea place, **Darnleys** tearoom.

Coming out of the tearoom, turn right and in 25 metres, turn right again *down West Street, signposted to the police station*. In 120 metres, where the main street curves to the right past the police station (which is on your right-hand side), *take the street straight on to the fire station*, but then *not* the tempting path straight on, but rather *turn left in front of the fire station* and take the footpath that goes *down the left-hand side of the fire station* signposted 'to the station', your direction 315 degrees. Follow this path, with a stream to your right and later a playground to your left, till you come *out on to a tarmac road* with Redwood Manor opposite. *Turn left on this road and, in 40 metres, turn right on to the B2131, leading in 260 metres to* **Haslemere Station** on your right-hand side. **Metro Café** is on your right-hand side just before the station.

The London platforms (2 and 3) are over the footbridge.

Walk 23

Otford to Eynsford

River Darent, two castles & a Roman villa

Length 13km (8.1 miles), 4 hours. For the whole outing, including trains, sights and meals, allow 8 hours 45 minutes.

OS Landranger Map Nos.188 and 177. Otford, map reference TQ 532 593, is in **Kent**, 4km north of Sevenoaks.

Toughness 6 out of 10.

Features The walk has three relatively short steep uphill sections. The first half of the walk can be very muddy. The suggested route takes in three villages steeped in history, one palace, two castles and a Roman villa. At times the route runs along the River Darent, at other times through fields and woods. It also comes to Lullingstone Park Visitor Centre (which offers exhibitions and information about the park, serves tea and is open till 5pm in summer; till 4pm October to February) and Lullingstone Park with its (early summer) orchids. There are trains to Otford from both Victoria and Blackfriars.

Shortening the walk To avoid the mud on wet days you could start the walk from the suggested lunch-time stop by travelling directly to Shoreham Station (or you could end the walk in Shoreham). If exhausted by the time you reach Lullingstone

Visitor Centre, you may be able to catch a bus into Eynsford (normally at five minutes past the hour). See also **[*]** below.

History Otford goes back to the sixth century when the Anglo-Saxons called their settlement Ottanford ('Otta's ford'). The Archbishop's Palace in Otford, the remaining fragments of which are on open view, once rivalled Hampton Court for splendour, until Henry VIII forced Archbishop Cranmer to surrender it in 1537.

St Bartholomew's Church, Otford, was founded about 1100 and contains memorials to Cromwell's great-grandsons.

The **Water House** in Shoreham is where the artist Samuel Palmer lived and worked from 1827 to 1834. The poet William Blake visited him there in 1825.

Lullingstone Park was a deer park from the Middle Ages until World War II, when the park was used as a decoy airfield – the heavy bombing so terrified the deer that they escaped. Species of tree that deer would not eat have been planted through the centuries, thus ancient hornbeam pollards remain.

Lullingstone Castle (tel 01322 862 114) is the residence of the Hart Dyke family, having remained in the Dyke family for centuries, with the original house built during the reign of Henry VII. It is open to visitors on Saturdays, Sundays and bank holidays from May to the end of August and on Easter Sunday and Monday. 25 or more people can visit at other times by prior arrangement.

Lullingstone Roman Villa (tel 01322 863 467) was first occupied in

80AD by a rich Roman who practised pagan worship of the local water sprite in a room here, which later became a Christian temple. The ruins include two mosaic floors. It is open daily (not Christmas Eve, Christmas Day, Boxing Day, New Year's Day) from 10am to 6pm in summer; from 10am to 4pm in winter (November to the end of March). Admission is £2.50; concessions £1.90.

The **Church of St Martin of Tours** in Eynsford is unusual in having retained the Norman ground plan with apsidal chancel. In about 1163, Thomas à Becket excommunicated Sir William de Eynsford III, the Lord of the Manor who controlled the patronage for this church. The excommunication was cancelled by Henry II and the issue became part of the quarrel that led to Becket's murder.

Eynsford Castle was built in the eleventh century and vandalised in 1312. John de Eynsford, who lived there, is said to have assisted in Becket's murder.

Saturday Walkers' Club Take the train nearest to **9.40am** (before or after) from **Blackfriars** Station to **Otford**. Journey time 53 minutes. Trains back from Eynsford also go to Blackfriars, about once an hour. Journey time 46 minutes. Note that no cafés are open near Blackfriars station on a Saturday.

Lunch The suggested lunchtime stop is the **Kings Arms** pub (tel 01959 523 100) in Shoreham, which has in its front wall the country's last remaining ostler box (like an enclosed little sentry box, where the ostler used to wait to attend to customers' horses). The pub serves food till 2pm Monday to Saturday, and till 4pm Sunday. Alternatives include the **George Inn** (tel 01959 522017) in Church Street, which serves food midday to 3pm (Sunday to 4pm); and the **Crown** pub (tel 01959 522 903) at 84 High Street, which serves food midday to 2pm (Sunday to 3pm).

Tea The suggested tea place is the **Old Ford Tearoom** (tel 01322 861 733) in Eynsford by the bridge and ford. It is open till 5pm daily October to March, and till 6pm April to September. An alternative is the café at the **Lullingstone Park Visitors' Centre** (tel 01322 865 995) which is open daily to 4pm..

WALK DIRECTIONS

[1] [Numbers refer to the map.] Coming off the London train, go over the railway line and exit the **Otford Station** building. *Turn left into the carpark and, 40 metres inside the carpark, on the right-hand side,* go through the gap in the railings and *take the tarmac path* heading away from the station, your direction 245 degrees, soon with an open field on your left-hand side. Keep to this path through a bend to the right. A wooden kissing gate takes you through to the churchyard and to **St Bartholomew's Church**, which is worth a look inside.

Leaving the church, a detour to the left takes you to the remains of **Otford Palace**.

The walk continues (to the north-west of the church) from the far side of the village pond (the pond is itself a 'listed building' and is home to ducks that occasionally disrupt the traffic). *Take the road left (westwards) by the Crown Inn,* soon passing the Ellenor tea shop on the left and the seventeenth-century Forge House (now a restaurant) on the right.

Keep on this road for 400 metres (passing the Bull pub on the left, part of which dates back to 1500; also on the left, Pickmoss, a medieval open-hall house; on your right the Darent Valley Path; and going over the River Darent). 200 metres or so past the imposing gates of eighteenth-century Broughton Manor to your left, and *10 metres beyond a wooden bus shelter* **[2]**, *turn right over a stile* on to a signposted and well-used public footpath, your direction 330 degrees. In 230 metres, having kept to this main path, go over a stile – a potentially very muddy area – to carry straight on with a hedge on your right-hand side.

In 150 metres go over a stile and continue straight on. In a further 250 metres go over another stile and now continue on with a fence on your left-hand side.

In 130 metres fork left to cross a stream and follow the onward twists in the path, which can be muddy.

In a further 160 metres, ignore a fork down left that goes back over a stream (to a car-wide track beyond) and keep straight on, your direction 315 degrees; ignoring a faint fork off left in a further 40 metres.

Your trail merges with a car-wide farm track by a stream with an arrow on the post marked SR 43. Keep on this farm track.

In 250 metres **[3]** you come to an orchard with, behind it, **Sepham Farm** (so marked on the OS map) and its oasthouses. Here, *by a post on your right with yellow arrows on it, you turn right*, your direction 40

degrees, to go under mini-pylons, along the edge of the orchard.

In less than 100 metres, ignore a left turn through the orchard towards the farm, to continue straight on, along a footpath marked SR10, across a network of open fields (with a stile about halfway) towards **Filston Farm** (so marked on the OS map) visible in the distance.

On nearing the farm, and *by an industrial shed turn left* (a marked footpath) on to a car-wide track and follow this leftwards up to the car road **[4]**.

Turn right on this tarmac road. In 250 metres, turn left up a trackway between hedges, opposite a road going off to the right. Continue over a stile up the public footpath which follows the wood on your right-hand side, up a grassy field. Just before a convenient seat, take the stile on the right. Go straight on, along a wide path, into the wood that is now signposted **Meenfield Wood**.

In less than 700 metres, you come to a crossing, with steps up and down, and you *take the steps down towards Shoreham*, your direction 120 degrees.

In 60 metres go over a stile and continue downwards. In a further 100 metres, go over another stile and down through hedges. In a further 120 metres, go through a metal kissing gate and keep on the main path down past playing fields on your left-hand side.

You come down to the car road. *Turn right and, past the Royal Oak pub on the left-hand side, turn left down Church Street*. In 180 metres you come to the **Kings Arms** pub on the right, which is the suggested

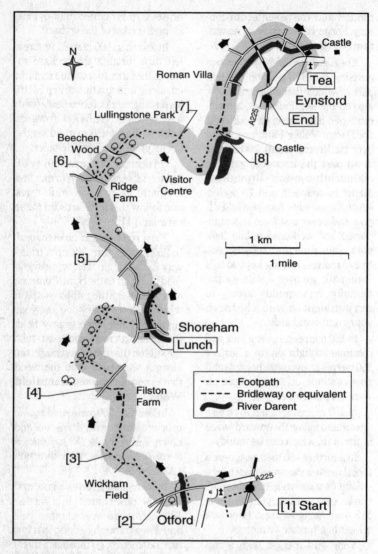

Castle

Roman Villa

Tea

Eynsford

Lullingstone Park [7]

End

A225

Beechen
Wood

[6]

Castle

Ridge
Farm

[8]

Visitor
Centre

[5]

1 km

1 mile

Shoreham

Lunch

[4]

Filston
Farm

Footpath
Bridleway or equivalent
River Darent

[3]

Wickham
Field

A225

[2]   Otford

[1] Start

lunchtime stop in **Shoreham** for the walk.

On coming out of the pub, turn right and cross the river (you can follow the road to the right if you wish to visit the twelfth-century church).

To continue the walk, *once across the river, turn left along Darent*

Way to pass **Water House** on your right-hand side.

Follow the River Darent (on your left-hand side), keeping to the riverside path. In 500 metres you *cross the river by a footbridge* with metal railings.

In 50 metres you leave the Darent Valley Path to *turn left uphill on a* car lane, westwards. At the top of Mill Lane you come to a T-junction with the main road, and you *turn right uphill*, your direction 315 degrees. Ignore a signposted footpath off to the left in a couple of hundred metres and, at the next T-junction, *take the road downhill signposted Well Hill and Eynsford.*

100 metres later, *take the left turn*, Cockerhurst Road, signposted Well Hill and Chelsfield.

After 400 metres of walking uphill between tall beech trees, and opposite a new large bungalow (Combe Vale) **[5]**, *take the footpath signposted to the right*, your direction 15 degrees, to follow an initially fairly clear path steeply uphill, keeping the hawthorn trees and blackberries on your right-hand side, and the open common on your left-hand side.

350 metres from the road, cross a stile made of metal scaffold poles and follow the left-hand field edge northwards, towards **Ridge Farm** (or so it is named on the OS map). Keep on this path, with trees and then hedges on your left-hand side.

In 450 metres the path then bends left beside a small house on the right-hand side. In a further 100 metres, you come on to a concrete car road and continue on, your direction 350 degrees.

200 metres later, *at the T-junction with a car road, turn right down the road*. In 100 metres ignore the car-wide road (with fieldgate) to your left; but then in 8 metres *go left* **[6]** *into* **Beechen Wood** (so marked on the OS map), passing a demolished stile, and *in 5 metres turn right*, your direction 100 degrees. In 40 metres bear left with

this wide path, your direction now 40 degrees. In a further 180 metres, cross a path to carry on (a wooden post, No. 8, has a green arrow saying 'Lullingstone Park').

In 130 metres, by post 13, bear right into a very wide grassy descent, and keep straight on again downhill by post 15 (following its arrow, if it is not buried in nettles), your direction 50 degrees, following down the left-hand side of this avenue.

In 400 metres you cross a bridleway and in 5 metres **[7]** – just before a sign on the right-hand side saying 'Caution. Golfcourse ahead' – *turn left uphill by post 16*, your direction 315 degrees.

In 130 metres, by post 17, follow the path that goes left downhill into the golfcourse.

You then follow these numbered posts and the arrows on them all the way to post 35, which leads you down to the Visitor Centre. Thus you go right at post 18; you leave the wide path to go uphill (due east) on the grass at post 19; at post 23 you ignore the alternative arrow to the right to keep straight on (still due east); and by post 26, where your path crosses the golfers' main track, you go uphill, following the arrow; the path bears right to post 27; go straight on to 28; and turn right to 29 and 30; from post 31, a bearing of 215 degrees leads past the remaining posts to post 35.

From post 35 you go downhill, your direction 115 degrees, in 200 metres reaching **Lullingstone Park Visitor Centre** (which also has a café).

Coming out of the Visitor Centre by the same way you came in, turn right along its northern boundary, to go through a wooden kissing gate and then turn left by the bridge, and continue with the water on your right-hand side. In 600 metres go through a wooden barrier [8] and continue straight on to **Lullingstone Castle**.

Beyond the castle, continue straight on, northwards, on a tarmac lane. In 600 metres or so, you come to a truly hideous green corrugated shed on your left-hand side, courtesy of English Heritage, inside of which is the **Lullingstone Roman Villa**. If you cannot afford the admission fee, you could try peeking in for free through any open windows round the back.

([*] You can shorten the walk by 2km at this point by not going left to the villa but right, over the river, on a track road marked 'Private' – this is in fact a public footpath. Then at the A225 T-junction, go left, coming to Station Road on your right-hand side just beyond the railway bridge.)

Coming out of the villa, go through the metal barrier and turn left on to the car road, to continue on, your direction 10 degrees.

In 600 metres go under the high railway viaduct (built in the nineteenth century with bricks made in Brick Field, just above the east bank of the river) and go straight on, with the river still on your right-hand side.

In 400 metres you keep straight on (signposted Eynsford) at the junction, to go down past the Plough Inn & Restaurant on the left-hand side (which serves food from 5pm Monday to Friday; all day Saturday and Sunday).

80 metres past the Plough Inn, go over the bridge by the ford to the **Old Ford Tearoom**, which is the suggested tea place.

To get to **Eynsford Station** you turn right on to the main road, with the **Church of St Martin of Tours** opposite, and go uphill for 800 metres, to just over the brow of the hill. Trains back to London are on the far platform, over the footbridge. (To visit **Eynsford Castle**, however, turn left on the main road and carry on through the village, and just past the garage, opposite the Castle pub, turn left on a tarmac lane signposted Village Hall.)

Walk 24

Cookham (round walk)

Stanley Spencer, Bisham
& *The Wind in the Willows*

Length 15.8km (9.8 miles), 4 hours 50 minutes. For the whole outing, including trains, sights and meals, allow at least 6 hours 30 minutes.

OS Landranger Map No.175. Cookham, map reference SU 886 850, is in **Berkshire**, 2.5km north of Maidenhead.

Toughness 3 out of 10.

Features The road from Cookham Station passes the very ordinary house where the artist Stanley Spencer lived and worked for some 15 years, until his death in 1959. Later, the route enters Quarry Wood, consisting mainly of beech trees on a thin layer of chalky soil, down to the fourteenth-century Bull Inn in Bisham, a hamlet with its own abbey and church. The Knights Templars, Henry VIII and Elizabeth I all stayed in Bisham – the abbey is now a sports centre. The Bisham lunch pub is 3.8km (2.3 miles), 1 hour 10 minutes, from the start of the walk. After lunch and a peek at the abbey, and a visit to the interesting memorials in Bisham Church, beside the Thames, the walk continues up through woods to Winter Hill, with its views out over the Thames and Marlow's reservoirs. Mole, Ratty and co – of *The Wind in the Willows* fame – inhabited the riverbank and wild woods here; at least, according to their author, Kenneth Grahame, who lived nearby. The last stretch of the walk is alongside the Thames, through the National Trust's marshland at Cock Marsh – an area created by the silting up of the river over the centuries. It contains five ancient burial mounds and provides a home for water voles, redshanks and mallards. The walk returns to Cookham via the churchyard of Holy Trinity Church (where there is a memorial stone to Stanley Spencer) and continues to Stanley Spencer Gallery in the High Street, and to the Kings Arms pub for tea.

Shortening the walk After lunch, you could walk 1km from Bisham to cross the river to the station in Marlow. Or you could miss out the pub at Bisham and stay on the east side of the A404 (see the asterisk [*] below), and perhaps eat a picnic on Winter Hill. Or, 3km before Cookham Station, you could cross the Thames by the railway bridge to catch a train from Bourne End.

History Bisham Abbey was a Tudor residence, granted to Anne of Cleves by Henry VIII. The Hoby family exchanged the title for their house in Kent, and resided at Bisham until 1768.

All Saints Parish Church, Bisham, was founded in the twelfth century. The western tower is built of clunch (chalk). The church is chiefly remarkable for the monuments erected by Lady Hoby for her husband Sir Thomas, Elizabeth I's guardian and ambassador to the Court of France, who died in Paris at the age of 36, 'leaving with child behind his woful wief… The corps with honour brought she to this place.' She commissioned her own tomb, on which she is depicted with all her children, and also a monument to 'two knights' (her husband and brother), lying side by side in their armour.

The Dial Close home of **Kenneth Grahame**, author of the children's classic *The Wind in the Willows*, is now a preparatory school.

Cookham was inhabited by ancient Britons, Romans and Saxons, and in the *Domesday Book* is listed as containing '32 villagers, 21 cottagers, 4 slaves, 2 mills, 2 fisheries and woodland at 100 pigs'. In 1140, a Norman church was built on the site of **Holy Trinity Church**, Cookham. The north wall of the church is built of clunch, probably quarried at Cookham. The artist Sir Stanley Spencer died in 1959, and there is a memorial stone to him in the graveyard of the church.

Spencer was born in 1891, in a Victorian semi-detached house called Fernley, in Cookham High Street. He lived and worked from 1944 to 1959 in a house called Cliveden View (passed on this walk) and attended services at the Wesleyan Chapel in the High Street, which is now **Stanley Spencer Gallery** (tel 01628 471 885). From Easter to October the gallery is open daily 10.30am to 5.30pm; in winter, Saturday, Sunday and bank holidays only, from 11am to 5pm. There is a very small admission fee.

Saturday Walkers' Club Take the train nearest to **11am** (before or after) from **Paddington** Station to **Cookham**. Journey time about 34 minutes, allowing for a change at Maidenhead. Trains back run about once an hour.

Lunch The suggested lunchtime stop is the **Two Brewers** (tel 01628 484140), St Peter Street, Marlow, which is reached through the churchyard of All Saints Church and down an alleyway. To reach the church in Marlow, follow the main road after coming out of the All Saints Parish Church in Bisham. There are other pub options available in Marlow itself.

Tea The reliable place for tea is the seventeenth-century hostelry, the **Kings Arms** (tel 01628 530 667) in the High Street. It is open daily till at least 9pm (with food from 5.30pm, Sunday all day) and has a garden. A pleasanter alternative, just for drinks or a pot of tea, is the **Bel and Dragon** pub (tel 01628 521 263) also in the High Street.

WALK DIRECTIONS

[1] **[Numbers refer to the map.]** Coming out of **Cookham Station**, *turn left*, your direction 15 degrees. In 15 metres *turn left again*, your direction 280 degrees, over the railway crossing. In a further 25 metres, *turn left on High Road*, your direction 185 degrees. In 60 metres bear right with this road.

Ignore ways off. In 350 metres ignore Worster Road to the left – **Cliveden View**, the house on the corner, is where Sir Stanley Spencer lived and worked.

Continue on the High Road, ignoring turn-offs. In 360 metres you come *to a T-junction*. Ignore the footpath sign opposite and *turn right* on this road, due north.

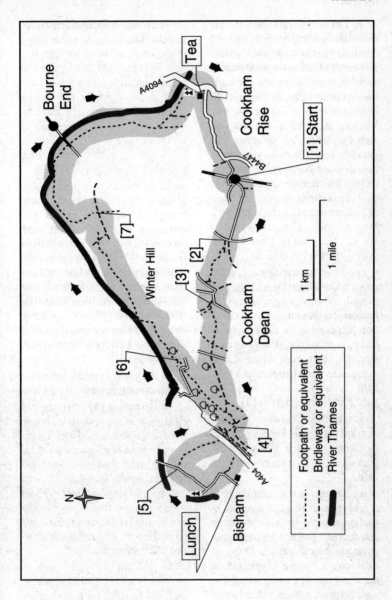

In 80 metres, opposite Whyte Cottage **[2]**, *turn left on a signposted public footpath*, your direction 290 degrees, between fences, with a playing field on your left-hand side.

In 185 metres follow the path around to the left and in 30 metres bear right through the wooden kissing gate, then cross the field, your direction 310 degrees.

In 180 metres you reach the far side of the field and continue straight on along the car-wide track ahead. 100 metres further on, go around a metal barrier – there is a fine view back over the valley at this point. In 75 metres, by Grey Cottage on your left-hand side, follow the footpath sign onwards, your direction 260 degrees. In 110 metres you *join a tarmac road going uphill*, your direction 235 degrees. In 35 metres, by Tuffets House on your left-hand side, bear round to the right with the road and in 35 metres *go left at the Cookham Dean Church sign*, your direction 255 degrees.

In 25 metres *turn right across the green* at **Cookham Dean**, following the public footpath sign *towards the* **Inn on the Green** *sign*, your direction 290 degrees. In 120 metres, *at this sign, follow the left of two public footpath signs*, your direction 250 degrees. In 75 metres *pick up a footpath to the right-hand side of the pub*, going through trees **[3]**.

In a further 100 metres, ignore a sign left to the Jolly Farmer pub and *go right, through a V-shaped stile*, your direction 275 degrees, across a field.

In 300 metres you come down *to a four-armed footpath sign where you go straight on*, your direction 290 degrees. In 6 metres you pass a concrete block with a Duke of Edinburgh Nature Conservation marker, your way being parallel to a gravel road, with an orchard away to your right.

In 135 metres you come *to a tarmac road where you go left*, your direction 205 degrees. In 40 metres *go right, on a signposted public bridleway*, into **Bisham Wood**.

You pass a Woodland Trust field-gate, walking along the inside fringe of the wood. In 160 metres ignore a path off to the right. In a further 210 metres, ignore a yellow arrow footpath to the right. In 130 metres ignore paths to the right and left, but in a further 10 metres *take a fork to the right, more or less straight on*, following a blue arrow, your direction 260 degrees, downhill.

In 55 metres you pass a blue bridleway arrow on a post, to continue on down. In a further 110 metres, you are joined on your downward way by a footpath from the right. **[[*]** If you want to take the short cut avoiding Bisham, turn sharp right on this footpath and follow the instructions from the double asterisk **[**]** below, as after lunch the main suggested route is to come back up the hill to this point and turn left.]

In 105 metres you are joined by a path coming down from your left.

In 140 metres **[4]** you come to a clearing with six options to choose from and a four-armed metal signpost. It is the bridleway offered by the signpost that you want *Go straight across and take the exit opposite (forking half right)* with an overgrown and thus often invisible tree stump on the corner. *5 metres down this track, fork right*, your direction 330 degrees, downhill.

In 100 metres your path is *crossed by a substantial bridleway, and you turn left on this*, your direction 230 degrees, parallel to the noise of the A404 below on your right-hand side.

In 175 metres *turn right on a footpath*, your direction 295 degrees. In 45 metres go over a wooden footbridge with wooden railings, to *cross the A404* (a rambler was killed by traffic here) and go through a lay-by with a tea van (weekdays only) on the other side. Follow the footpath sign and continue straight on over a stile, your direction 300 degrees, and across the field.

In 175 metres go over another stile. In 45 metres you come *to a tarmac road where you continue straight on*. In 65 metres you come *to a T-junction where you turn left*, your direction 200 degrees. In 50 metres this brings you to the suggested lunch place, the **Bull Inn**, **Bisham**.

If you would like a short detour to glimpse Bisham Abbey, either before or after lunch, continue on for 150 metres and turn right into the grounds of **Bisham Abbey**, headquarters of the National Sports Centre – if you go a few metres down their entrance drive, you can see the abbey. This is not a public footpath, but a pressing need to enquire, for instance, about Sports Centre membership, would take you right to it!

Coming out of the pub *after lunch, turn right* and in 50 metres ignore Vansittart Road on your right-hand side. In a further 55 metres, follow the road round to the left. In 40 metres ignore a lane to the right. In a further 145 metres, fork left, more or less straight on, to *enter the churchyard* of **All Saints Parish Church**, Bisham, through its lychgate.

Coming out of the church, turn right out of the lychgate and return *to the main road where you turn left*, your direction 30 degrees.

In 380 metres **[5]**, opposite South Riding House, *take the signposted footpath on the right (by the 'flood warning' notice)*, through a metal kissing gate, your direction 130 degrees, on a possibly unclear path.

In 200 metres go over a stile (if re-erected; otherwise step over barbed wire or take slight detour to where wire has collapsed) following the direction of the arrow, half right, your direction 160 degrees, heading, as you will see later, for halfway between two mini-pylons straddling the A road ahead.

In 250 metres go over a stile into the next field and follow the path straight on across the field. In 200 metres go over a stile and *over the A404, to pick up a footpath on the other side*. Go down steps with a wooden railing and cross a stream on a narrow concrete bridge with a metal railing.

In 85 metres *cross over a bridleway to continue uphill*, your direction 125 degrees – on the morning's path. In a further 140 metres, still retracing your steps, you *take the mid-left (not the leftmost) fork. Yours is a bridleway*, and your direction is 115 degrees. In 20 metres *go straight on, taking the left-hand of the two (blue-marked) paths facing you*, your direction 85 degrees initially. In 35 metres ignore a fork up to the right. In a further 120 metres, *take the footpath to the left* (marked by a yellow arrow on a post), your direction 20 degrees.

[**] In 25 metres ignore a fork down to the left. In a further 110 metres, ignore a fork right, your direction 50 degrees.

In 30 metres you are joined by a track from the right, now a car-wide and potentially muddy path, your direction 40 degrees, with a view out over the Thames, below to your left.

Keep straight on this path, ignoring ways off, for 500 metres, until you come to a clearing. From here you can see Marlow Church behind you to your left (at 310 degrees). You continue straight on, your direction 100 degrees, towards the other side of the clearing. Here *your path is crossed by another, and you go slightly left with this path*, your direction 45 degrees.

In 80 metres you cross a path. In 90 metres, having kept straight on, you come *to a tarmac road which you cross to pick up the signposted footpath on the other side* – with a house called Dormers on its right-hand side – your direction 80 degrees.

In 60 metres you *take the public footpath signposted to the left*, your direction 20 degrees. In 15 metres you pass a 'Private. Keep to path' sign. In a further 110 metres, with a view out to Marlow in the valley below, *at a path T-junction, you turn right*, your direction 40 degrees initially.

In 80 metres **[6]** you are joined by a footpath from behind to the left, and you have a partial view out over the reservoirs below.

In 275 metres you come *into the driveway of Rivendell house*. In 20 metres *follow the yellow arrow on a post left*, on a tarmac road, your direction 80 degrees.

In 30 metres you come to a parking area offering outstanding views, the National Trust's **Winter Hill**.

(To detour to **Kenneth Grah-ame's house**, go sharp right and in 40 metres take the second fork left, by the entrance to Dial Place and Mole End, and then in 120 metres turn left, your direction 170 degrees, on Job's Lane. In 215 metres you come to a road where you turn right, your direction 275 degrees. Up on your right-hand side, in 50 metres, is Kenneth Grahame's old house, now a prep school.)

On Winter Hill, continue straight on. In 250 metres, at the end of the parking space, follow the path off to the left of the road, into the trees, your direction 45 degrees. In 90 metres ignore a faint path to your left. In 5 metres rejoin the tarmac road. In 80 metres *you pass Chiltern Court on your right-hand side. In 6 metres fork left on a path*, your direction 35 degrees.

In 50 metres you cross a tarmac lane and, in 2 metres, another, in order to continue straight on (a private farm road is parallel to your path, on your left-hand side), your direction 55 degrees.

In a further 145 metres, you come *up on to a gravel road T-junction where you go left*, your direction 25 degrees initially. In 145 metres go through a wooden gate (with a metal fieldgate to its right, and a National Trust sign saying 'Dogs must be kept under control').

In 35 metres you ignore a yellow arrow offering a fork to the left, to keep on, your direction 45 degrees.

In 585 metres **[7]** you are back down to the level of the valley, *by a four-armed footpath sign*, where you *go left*, your direction 5 degrees. In 65 metres go over a stile (with a metal fieldgate to its left) to follow a yellow arrow straight on.

In a further 160 metres, *at a two-armed footpath sign, fork right*, your direction 40 degrees, following the sign. In 240 metres you are back beside the River Thames, on your left-hand side.

Your route back into Cookham more or less follows the Thames. But in more detail: In 315 metres go through a wooden gate. In 145 metres fork left to keep by the riverside. In 40 metres go through a wooden kissing gate to pass riverbank houses on your right-hand side. In a further 120 metres, you pass the Bounty Riverside Inn, Bourne End (which has a sign welcoming walkers to lunch, for those wanting a later lunch).

(Those wanting a short cut could go over the Thames, on the footbridge beside the railway bridge, to catch a train at Bourne End.)

The onward route is through the National Trust's **Cock Marsh**. 30 metres beyond the railway bridge, you go through a wooden kissing gate. In a further 500 metres, go through a wooden kissing gate. In a further 520 metres, by a three-armed footpath sign, ignore the path to the right, to keep on along the riverside towards the bridge.

In 120 metres you go through a white metal swing gate, past a sailing club on your right-hand side. In 30 metres go through another such gate. In 40 metres ignore a tarmac path to the right. In a further 250 metres, *take a tarmac path to your right*, your direction 200 degrees, *towards the church visible to*

your right. In 50 metres you enter the churchyard of **Holy Trinity Church**, Cookham, past a metal kissing gate. The church entrance is around the far side.

Coming out of the church, you take the path from the front door, in 25 metres passing **Spencer's memorial stone** (which is to the right of a bench – his ashes were scattered by his wife's grave in a Cookham cemetery). 10 metres beyond the church gates, bear left with Churchgate House on your left-hand side.

In 20 metres you come *to the main A4094, where you turn right*.

In 60 metres you come to **Stanley Spencer Gallery**.

Coming out of the gallery, turn left on the High Street, your direction 260 degrees. Nearly opposite is the **Bel and Dragon** pub.

70 metres from the galllery, you come to the suggested tea places, the **Kings Arms** pub on your left-hand side and, just beyond it, the less walker-friendly **The Bay Tree** tearoom (with garden).

In 90 metres you come to the War Memorial on your left-hand side, and *carry on across* **Cookham Moor**, *on a tarmac lane to the left-hand side of the main street*, your direction 265 degrees, and in 200 metres go over the bridge.

100 metres *beyond the bridge, rejoin the main road and go straight on*. You pass Spencer's and The Old Swan Uppers on your right-hand side, to reach the station 300 metres further on.

Walk 25

Winchelsea to Hastings

Fairlight Glen
& a dip in the sea

Length 19km (11.7 miles), 5 hours 45 minutes. For the whole outing, including trains, meals, sights and a swim, allow at least 11 hours.

OS Landranger Map Nos.189 and 199. Winchelsea, (map 189) reference TQ 899 184, is in **East Sussex**, 3km south-west of Rye.

Toughness 9 out of 10.

Features This is a delightful walk along the south coast, and is best done in summer if you would like to swim, otherwise in spring when the woodland floor is covered in blue-bells and other wildflowers – and, in early May, the gorse is bright yellow. Starting below Winchelsea (once a seaside port, but storms have since stranded it 2km inland), the walk follows the River Brede and canals to an early lunch at a seven-teenth-century pub near the church in Icklesham. Less than 5km (3 miles) of this walk is before lunch. From there, the route crosses two relatively clear streams, both with ill-fitting names: Pannel Sewer and Marsham Sewer. And so to the coast at Cliff End. A detour off the coastal route through the houses of Fair-light is required, as a result of severe coastal erosion (an average 1.4 me-tres of cliff-face is lost annually in these parts). Thereafter the walk is along the coastline through the Hast-ings Country Park, with steep climbs out of the wooded Warren, Ecclesbourne and Fairlight Glens. The latter has a nudist beach where you can drip-dry in fine weather, if you don't happen to have a towel. At low tide (but follow local advice on this) you can also walk along the beach from Fairlight Glen to Hast-ings. Otherwise there is more steep climbing then a descent down steps into the old town of Hastings, with its Net Shops on the beach (tall, black, wooden sheds that were built for hanging out fishermen's nets) and, inland, its lanes and twittens (narrow alleys) of half-timbered cottages. After tea, it is a 25-minute walk along the seafront beneath the Norman castle and up to the station.

Shortening the walk You could get a bus or taxi from near the pub at Icklesham to Hastings, or a taxi from the pub at Pett, or a taxi from a farm tea barn at Fairlight Place (to get to this, turn right at the point where to turn left would take you down to the nudist beach).

History The part-Norman **All Saints Church** at Icklesham contains a variety of architectural styles, and has a nave and chancel that are not aligned with one an-other. A 1592 legacy notice in the church leaves over £3 a year 'for ever' for highway maintenance.

Ex-Beatle Paul McCartney, who lives a few miles from Winchelsea, funded the renovation of **Hog Mill** windmill (see map) which is visible from the walk route.

Iron Age chieftains had fortres-ses on both the east and west hills of Hastings. When the Romans left, the barbarian **Haestingas** tribe gave its name to the place, having to be subdued by King Offa in 771. William the Conqueror built his first **castle** here above the town. In 1287 large parts of Hastings were washed away in the **Great Storm**, the one that left Winchelsea stranded way inland. In medieval times, Hastings was one of the **Cinque Ports**, supplying 25 ships for 15 days a year for the country's defence purposes, in the days before the Royal Navy existed. (the Cinque ports, pronounced 'sink', were Sandwich, Dover, Hythe, Romney and Hastings, plus Rye and Winchelsea).

Saturday Walkers' Club Take the train nearest to **10.30am** (before or after) from **Charing Cross** Station to **Winchelsea** (you may need to change either at Ashford or at St Leonards Warrior Square). Journey time 1 hour 50 minutes. Trains back from Hastings run hourly. Journey time 1 hour 30 minutes. Get a day return ticket to Winchelsea.

Lunch The recommended lunch place is the **Queens Head** (tel 01424 814 552), Parsonage Lane, Icklesham, which serves good food from midday to 2.45pm daily (all day at weekends), but tends to become rather crowded. There is also the **Royal Oak Inn** in Pett (tel 01424 812515) which serves simple food midday to 2pm daily. Groups of more than six people should phone to book.

Tea Since you may arrive in Hastings quite late, the suggested tea place is one that is open daily beyond the normal tea time: The **Swedish Chef Too Café Restaurant** (tel 01424 713 674), 53 High Street, Hastings. This serves interesting food and drink until late and is open Wednesday to Saturday (Tuesday too in summer). Another possibility is **Gannets Café** in the High Street, which is open throughout the year till 7pm Tuesday to Sunday.

WALK DIRECTIONS

[1] [Numbers refer to the map.] Coming off the only platform at **Winchelsea Station**, *at the tarmac road turn right across the railway line,* your direction 170 degrees. There is a tourist information board on the other side of the line, on your left-hand side. Bear left with this road, a waterway to your right. In 440 metres, as you pass under a mini-pylon, ignore a concrete path off to the right beside the River Brede. In 200 metres ignore a stile to the left and cross the River Brede bridge.

Looking back from this bridge, the town of Rye can be seen on a hilltop and, on its right, Camber Castle, built by Henry VIII in 1540.

In 160 metres, *at the A259, turn right on a concrete car lane that is signposted as a footpath,* your direction 310 degrees.

In 40 metres the concrete comes to an end. In a further 70 metres, go over a stile, and in 25 metres go on a platform of planks over a stream.

Carry on with the stream and trees on your left-hand side, your direction 245 degrees.

But in 100 metres, **[!]** *as the wood to your left begins to bear left, fork right, with no clear path, towards an isolated wooden gate visible ahead, at 255 degrees from you.*

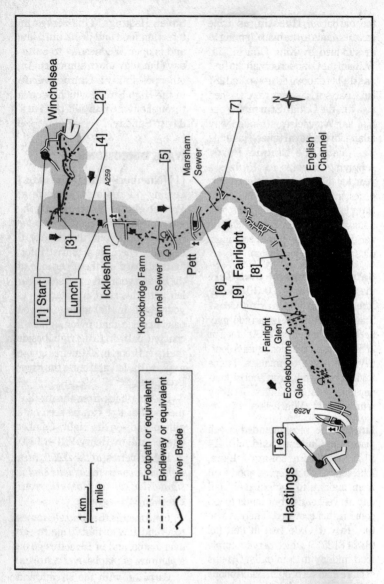

Winchelsea

[1] Start

[2]

[4]

Lunch

[3]

A259

Icklesham

Knockbridge Farm

Pannel Sewer

[5]

Marsham
Sewer

[7]

Pett

[6]

[9]

[8]

Fairlight

Fairlight
Glen

Ecclesbourne
Glen

A259

Tea

Hastings

English
Channel

N

Footpath or equivalent
Bridleway or equivalent
River Brede

1 km
1 mile

In 40 metres you pass a sometimes soggy ditch on your right-
hand side. In a further 50 metres,
climb over the stile to the left-hand
side of the wooden fieldgate you
were aiming for, to cross the stream
and turn left, *following the bank of
the stream on your left-hand side*,
your direction 240 degrees.

In 60 metres, where the main
stream goes left, you *bear right with
the ditch and overgrown hedges on
your left-hand side*, heading 285
degrees. In 180 metres *a stream*

blocks your way. Go right, your direction 20 degrees, for 30 metres, to *cross the stream by a stile* (with a metal fieldgate on its left-hand side).

Although the right of way takes a straight course at 250 degrees for 500 metres, it is easier (and evidently preferred by the land occupier) to *continue with the* **River Brede** *on your right-hand side* [2].

In 600 metres go over a stile and continue on an earth car track.

In 120 metres, by a brick water-pumping hut on your left-hand side, go over a defunct stile (to the right of a metal fieldgate), to carry on with the river on your right-hand side.

In 440 metres go over a stile (a metal fieldgate on its left-hand side). In 210 metres ignore a concrete bridge to the left.

In 140 metres go over a stile; in a further 35 metres, cross on a wooden platform *over the railway line.*

The other side, bear left on a track alongside the river for 25 metres, then go over a stile and turn left along the fence, due west.

In 55 metres [3] *cross a grassy bridge and go through a gateway on your left-hand side and over a stile and again over the railway line.* In 8 metres go over a stile and straight on, with a waterway on your right-hand side and *heading directly for the Icklesham church* already visible in the distance.

Keep on through stiles and fences, and, four fields and 800 metres later [4], you [!] *go over a stile (with a metal fieldgate and a cattle grid on its right-hand side) and ignore the main left fork (a vehicle-wide grassy road) to take a fork bearing right, following no clear path and heading just to the right of the*

leftmost telegraph pole visible on top of the hill ahead, your direction 205 degrees.

In 340 metres, on the brow of the hill, go through a fieldgate with wooden gateposts. You can now see ahead of you the suggested lunch pub, the **Queens Head**, **Icklesham** (its name is painted on the roof tiles). Head for the caravan to its right-hand side in the carpark, your direction 220 degrees. In 85 metres enter the carpark and go to the left-hand side of the pub and to its garden to reach the back entrance.

After lunch, you *go out from the pub on to the passing lane, and turn left* on this lane, coming to the A259 crossroads in 130 metres. The **Oast House Inn** is to your right-hand side. Cross over the A259 into Workhouse Lane, and after 30 metres you turn left on to the driveway of Chantry House (marked footpath) which leads in 130 metres to **All Saints Church, Icklesham**. *Coming out of the church door, turn 90 degrees left to go through the churchyard,* your direction 175 degrees. In 20 metres *ignore a stile 10 metres ahead and fork right through a gap* in the blackberry bushes into an orchard.

Ignoring another stile 8 metres to the left, you fork right to go alongside the orchard fence, with it on your left-hand side, your direction 260 degrees. In 110 metres you come *to a tarmac road where you go left,* heading due south.

(Footpath signs for the following 11 paragraphs of text seem to be missing for now.) In 190 metres, *by a tarmac road right (Laurel Lane), go over a stile* (with a metal fieldgate to its right) on a footpath. *Go 220 degrees* (the old sign, currently missing, pointed the wrong way) *to the bottom right-hand corner of the field*, where the hedge and the wooden fence meet, 130 metres away. Here you go over a stile, continuing with the field hedge on your left-hand side, your direction 280 degrees.

In 40 metres cross a dilapidated stile (with a wooden gate to its left) and carry on, half right, diagonally across the field, your direction 220 degrees, *towards a metal fieldgate visible ahead*, some 100 metres to the right of large farmsheds.

In 200 metres go through this fieldgate and *turn left on the farm's earth drive*. You may now be able to see the sea away to your left-hand side. In 100 metres ignore a fork right to the farmhouse.

Go straight on through the farmyard (one of the readers of this book was bitten by the farmer's dog here). In 80 metres *go through a metal fieldgate and follow the farm track right*, your direction 265 degrees. In 40 metres, *by the farmhouse's back entrance gateway with bobbles, go left*, due south, with the field fence on your left-hand side.

In 80 metres you pass a large crater on your right-hand side. In 55 metres ignore fieldgates to your left and right to continue straight on down the farm track, between hedges. Pett church is visible on the far horizon.

In 110 metres go through a fieldgate and quarter right, *making for a bridge*, your direction 210 degrees.

In 130 metres you go over the **Pannel Sewer** on this bridge and carry straight on, still due south, towards a fieldgate.

In 130 metres *go through this fieldgate* (there is another one 5 metres to its left). *Go right*, your direction 260 degrees, with the field fence on your right-hand side.

In 85 metres, cross a ditch (by an isolated metal fieldgate). *Go left with the ditch on your left-hand side*, your direction 195 degrees.

In 100 metres you come to a fenced wood, where you *go rightwards along the fence*, until, in about 45 metres, you go *left though a metal swing gate* set in the fence and so into the wood, on a track, your direction 225 degrees.

In 200 metres exit the wood by a stile. Go to the left of the tree which faces you in the field and follow the edge of the field, your direction 95 degrees – the wood you have just left is to your left-hand side.

In 70 metres, cross a stile and aim ahead to the far top left corner of the field, your directon 140 degrees. There, in 170 metres, beside a mini-pylon, you go through the blackberries and bracken to come out over a stile on to a tarmac lane.

Cross the lane slightly to the left and **[5]** *take a signposted footpath* (the signpost may be obscured in summer) *over a stile. The paths here may be badly maintained by the farmer*.

Go left for 10 metres, then right, following the hedge on your left-hand side, your overall direction 165 degrees.

In 200 metres, at the bottom of the field, go right, your direction 260 degrees, with the field hedge on your left-hand side.

In 65 metres *go over a stile on your left, and onwards, uphill, your* direction 165 degrees, across the field. Go *straight on towards and past a telegraph pole* (the pole is about 5 metres to the right of the path, although there may be no path maintained in winter).

170 metres past the pole, you come out over a stile and straight on, slightly to the left, your direction 150 degrees, across a field.

In 160 metres you go over a stile and *across a tarmac road to the* **Royal Oak Inn**, **Pett**.

Go around the right-hand side of this pub to carry on, along a tarmac road, your direction 150 degrees. In 40 metres ignore a stile to the right.

In 160 metres you *pass an entrance to Gatehurst Farm* to your right.

In a further 100 metres **[6]**, *go over a stile to the right, which has a post marked to Cliff End.*

Go diagonally across the field, your direction 130 degrees, aiming 40 metres to the left of the brick structure (which was the base of a radar transmitting tower in World War II, used to guide British planes back home).

In 150 metres, with a fine panoramic view to admire, go over a stile signposted to Pett Level, and continue on in the same direction.

In 175 metres you go over a stile and continue in a similar direction, 150 degrees.

In 170 metres go over a wooden bridge (kindly erected by Hastings Rambling Club in 1988) and cross the **Marsham Sewer** to go straight on. In 60 metres cross a stream on another wooden bridge and go straight on, keeping to the left.

In 45 metres you go through a wooden fieldgate (the post marked

with a yellow arrow), *cross a farm track* that leads up to a house and go through a fieldgate on the other side of the track. Then *go diagonally across the field* for 200 metres, your direction 90 degrees, and go over a stile in the opposite corner of the field.

Bear left on the tarmac road for 40 metres. Turn up a driveway to the right for 8 metres, and bear right up four steps on to a path marked 'Cliff Footpath' with the Saxon Shore Way emblem on its post **[7]**. Follow this path for 500 metres, crossing over two driveways (after which you can hear and see the sea below on your left-hand side), and enter the National Trust's land at **Fairlight**.

Ignore a stile to the right – *keep on the coastal path.*

In 220 metres ignore a stile on your right-hand side.

In 180 metres ignore a stile on your right-hand side to go down steps with wooden railings, and then straight on.

In 110 metres go through a wooden barrier to go right with the path, the field fence on your right-hand side. In 80 metres go through a narrow gap between wooden posts and turn right with the path. In 10 metres fork left with it. In 12 metres carry on, your direction 215 degrees, along a gravelled road (with the entrance to Merrie Land on your left-hand side).

In 200 metres (having passed a barrier), *at the first wooden swing gate in a wicket fence across the road (the onward path would lead to Cliff Edge House) you are obliged by cliff erosion to go right, your direc-*

tion 340 degrees. In 45 metres, by Iona House, go left on a gravelled road, your direction 240 degrees.

In 185 metres *take the first turning left (Cliff Way)*, by the 'Sea Road Closed' sign, your direction 160 degrees.

In 100 metres *take the footpath right*, 5 metres before the entrance to Fairhaven on your right-hand side, your direction 250 degrees.

In 150 metres you come *out on to a tarmac road (Rockmead Road) and turn left*, your direction 150 degrees. In 60 metres, by a house called Camellia, you bear right with the road.

At the end of Rockmead Road, in 260 metres, *by the 30mph speed limit sign, you keep straight on, going along Bramble Way*, ignoring all possible ways off. In 170 metres, *at the T-junction, by Tamarisk Cottage opposite, go left*, your direction 170 degrees.

In 100 metres, at a T-junction, *turn right on Channel Way*, your direction 250 degrees.

Ignoring all ways off, you enter a narrower path **[8]**, in 400 metres, by a two-armed footpath sign.

In 70 metres go through a wooden kissing gate, at last leaving the outskirts of Fairlight Cove village behind you, to enter the **Firehills** of **Hastings Country Park**, and fork left, your direction 235 degrees.

Keep on this main path. In 350 metres, *20 metres before a bench ahead of you, fork right uphill with the broad grassy way*, your direction 300 degrees.

Keep along the coastal way as much as possible. In 320 metres you have to head uphill towards the

radar station. Then in 120 metres, by a bench below this station, go left to keep on the coastal way, your direction 245 degrees.

In 30 metres you pass a post saying 'Hastings 3 miles' to carry on downhill.

In 275 metres, by a bench and a multi-path junction, go left down steps. In 150 metres you cross a stream at the bottom of **Warren Glen** to go up the other side on a wide grassy way. Ignore ways off. In 250 metres, by post 13, go uphill up steps.

60 metres from the top of these steps, you pass post 12 (at the top of the steps is a stone slab known as 'Lovers' Seat' – the slab has been dragged back inland from the cliffs where two lovers met in secret in the 1780s; the cliffs have now been eroded and have fallen into the sea).

In 85 metres go down steps. At the bottom of these, follow the post's sign left to Fairlight Glen.

In 340 metres, *by a stream* **[9]**, *the fork left leads to* **Fairlight Glen nudist beach**. (At low tide, we have walked along the beach from Fairlight to Hastings, but it might be as well to take local advice before doing this, access to the beach was recently affected by storms and it may be inaccessible.)

Your eventual onward route is straight on. In 50 metres you pass post 10 to take the leftmost fork (but not the next fork left in a further 10 metres), continuing on a wide grassy way uphill, your direction 225 degrees.

In 240 metres it is steeply up steps again. In 30 metres you pass post 8. 90 metres from the top of the steps, you come to post 7, where you keep left.

In 460 metres ignore a fork to the right (which has a wooden fence on its right-hand side) to keep on along a line of concrete fenceposts, your direction 250 degrees.

In 600 metres *you come to a bench with a view out over the beach ahead, and you go sharp right*, your direction 35 degrees. *In 30 metres, by a post, go left*, your direction 340 degrees, soon down steps.

At the bottom of this (**Ecclesbourne Glen**) you cross a stream, by post 3, and keep straight on upwards, on the main steps, ignoring ways off to the right and left.

At the top of the steps, by post 2, go left, your direction 210 degrees, with a wooden field fence on your left-hand side.

In 320 metres, **Hastings** can be seen at last. In a further 420 metres, you come *to a replica of the old warning beacons* that spread news of the rapidly approaching Spanish Armada in 1588.

15 metres beyond the beacon, you pick up a tarmac path and a paved stepway going downwards, your direction 245 degrees, soon seeing the black wooden **Net Shops** on the beach to your left.

At the bottom, *cross the tarmac Tackleway* and continue on down Crown Lane to the next crossing, All Saints Street, where the *Crown Inn* is on your right-hand side and Willow Room tea shop is opposite you. *Turn right* on All Saints Street.

In 85 metres you pass the Cinque Port Arms pub. 15 metres beyond it, *go left down Bourne Passage*. In 40 metres *cross the A259 to continue on Roebuck Street*.

In 60 metres, by the Duke of Wellington pub on your left-hand side, *turn left into the High Street*, your direction 210 degrees.

In 80 metres you come to the **Rosie Lea** teashop on your left-hand side (which is recommended, if it is open). In a further 20 metres, you come to **Gannets Café** (which is also good). And in a further 40 metres, to the **Swedish Chef Too Café Restaurant** at no.53, the main suggested tea place.

Coming out of this café *after tea, go straight across the High Street and uphill on Swan Terrace*, your direction 305 degrees, passing the Church of St Clements on your right-hand side.

Then *turn left on Hill Street*.

In 80 metres, *at the end of Hill Street, go down steps,* bearing right, past Ye Olde Pump House pub *into George Street, where you go right*, your direction 235 degrees.

In 80 metres you pass, at No. 28, the Hot Potato café (tel 01424 461 941; open until 8pm Monday to Thursday; till midnight Friday and Saturday). In 90 metres continue straight on along Sturdee Place and Pelham Place. In a further 230 metres, you *fork right (by Iceland on your right-hand side) along a pedestrianised street (Castle Street)*. In 35 metres *go down through a tunnel*.

From the other side of the tunnel, you continue on (Wellington Place) and in 140 metres *take the right fork slightly uphill (Havelock Road)* – with the NatWest Bank on your right-hand side – your direction 300 degrees. In 200 metres, *at the top of the road, you take the second fork left*, coming to **Hastings Station** in 110 metres.

Walk 26

Shelford to Cambridge

Grantchester – the Rupert Brooke walk

Length 21.1km (13.2 miles), 6 hours 30 minutes. For the whole outing, including trains, sights and meals, allow at least 12 hours, especially if you want to visit one or two of the Cambridge colleges.

OS Landranger Map No.154. Shelford, map reference TL 465 523, is in **Cambridgeshire**, 6km south of Cambridge.

Toughness 5 out of 10.

Features (Note: There are now trains to Shelford on Sundays.) This walk is long and flat but full of interest, and it's a lovely way into Cambridge. Near the start, you may be able to walk along the River Cam from Shelford and its church, but you need to *write two weeks in advance* to ask the farm for permission (see walk directions below); otherwise there is a 2.5km stretch of road. On leaving the farm, the route passes the old mill at Hauxton, to the pub and church in Haslingfield; and from there you go up near the travelling telescope (on rails) to Grantchester and The Orchard tearooms; then along the meadows and the Backs, to meander down the narrowest Cambridge lanes, past many of the colleges (or you could hire a punt).

Shortening the walk There is

146 bus from Haslingfield to Cambridge (for instance, at the time of writing, leaving Haslingfield at 1.55pm or 3.48pm on Saturdays). Or you could do a shorter version of this walk by taking the 146 or X46 bus from Cambridge – from near the railway station, in Lensfield Road, by the Catholic Church on Hills Road, an hourly service (not on Sundays) – to Hauxton Gap, the lay-by mentioned in the walk directions below, 335 metres beyond the Church of St Edmunds, Hauxton. Or get a bus or taxi to the station as soon as you reach Cambridge – or as soon as you reach the front of Kings College. For bus information phone Traveline on 0870 608 2608.

History Perhaps Friends of the Earth should employ poets. Writing a famous poem must be as effective a way as any of ensuring that a place is preserved forever. Rupert Brooke's poem *The Old Vicarage* – he had rooms as a student at the Orchard, and later, at the Old Vicarage, Grantchester – was written in a mood of nostalgia in a Berlin café, in May 1912. The poem celebrates not only **Grantchester** and the river ('Laughs the immortal river still/ Under the mill, under the mill?'), but the surrounding countryside ('And sunset still a golden sea/From Haslingfield to Madingley'). Augustus John camped in Grantchester meadows with, as Keynes put it, his 'two wives and ten naked children'; Brooke and Virginia Woolf (who dubbed his friends the 'Neo-Pagans') swam naked by moonlight; EM Forster visited to stay with Brooke at the Orchard; Wittgenstein would come there by canoe; AN Whitehead and Bertrand

Russell worked on their *Principia Mathematica* at the Mill House, next to the Old Vicarage. As for the church clock ('Oh! yet/Stands the Church clock at ten to three?/And is there honey still for tea?'), in Brooke's first draft it stood at half past three (the actual time it was stuck at for most of 1911).

The **Church of St Mary the Virgin**, Great Shelford, was rebuilt at the expense of its rector, Thomas Patesley, in the early fifteenth century. It contains a mural of the last judgement which was painted about then, showing the devils, on the left of Christ, dragging away the damned in a chain.

St Edmunds Church, Hauxton, is renowned as one of the oldest and most interesting small churches in Cambridgeshire, with Norman windows, doors and chancel arch; a thirteenth-century font bowl; a fifteenth-century pulpit and nave roof. It also contains a rare thirteenth-century fresco of St Thomas à Becket, which survived Henry VIII's depredations; and, having been previously walled up, this fresco also survived the vandalism of the notorious puritan William Dowsing (who, in 1643, destroyed 'three popish pictures' in this church). St Edmund became King of East Anglia in 856 at the age of 15, and was killed 13 years later by the Danes for refusing to renounce his Christian faith.

The oldest surviving building in Cambridge is **St Bene't's Church**, which has a Saxon tower. **Cambridge University** was founded in the early thirteenth century by students and academics fleeing riots in Oxford, where the townsfolk

felt imposed on by the academics. Within a couple of centuries, the university dominated the Cambridge townsfolk too: in 1440 Henry VI had a large part of medieval Cambridge demolished to make way for **King's College**, intended for students from his new Eton school; in 1496 a twelfth-century nunnery became **Jesus College**; in 1542 a Benedictine hostel was transformed into **Magdalene College**; and in 1596 **Trinity College** was endowed by Henry VIII, with funds from the monasteries he had vandalised. (A few colleges charge for admission, and some charge only from mid-March to September – although often with free admission to evensong. Evensong is the time to visit King's College Chapel, if you get the opportunity. Colleges may well be closed to the public during exams, from late April to mid-June.)

Saturday Walkers' Club Take the train nearest to **9.30am** (before or after) from **Liverpool Street** Station to **Shelford**. Journey time 1 hour 11 minutes. Trains back from Cambridge run about once an hour to Liverpool Street, twice an hour to King's Cross. The last train is about 11pm. Journey time 1 hour 10 minutes. Get a cheap day return ticket to Cambridge.

Lunch The suggested lunchtime pub is the **Little Rose** (tel 01223 870 618), 7 Orchard Road, Haslingfield. The pub serves cheap and simple food from midday to 3pm weekdays, all day weekends; groups of more than 15 people should phone to book.

Tea Whether it is teatime or not, it is worthwhile stopping at **The Orchard** (tel 01223 845 788) in

Grantchester, which first opened as a tearoom in 1897. It is now open daily to about 7pm in the summer, 5pm in the winter. At the end of the day, while waiting for your train at Cambridge Station, there is the quite adequate station restaurant, **Ginghams Coffee Shop**, serving food until at least 9pm daily, with a station kiosk open till 11pm. Some of the many other possible tea places and pubs within Cambridge are marked in bold in the walk directions below.

WALK DIRECTIONS

[1] [Numbers refer to the map.] Coming off platform 2 at **Shelford Station**, *turn right on the main road, Station Road*, your direction 215 degrees. In 40 metres you pass the **Railway Tavern**, which offers morning coffee.

In 115 metres you *cross the A1301, Tunwell's Lane, to continue straight on, on Woollards Lane*, ignoring ways off. In a further 325 metres, you come *to a T-junction* (with house no.90 opposite), where you *go left*, your direction 210 degrees, on Church Street.

In 160 metres you come to the **Church of St Mary the Virgin, Great Shelford**.

In 50 metres you pass Kings Mill Lane on your left-hand side. [2] Now there are two alternatives, but the second requires writing well in advance:

(a) Continue on the main road (Church Street), which becomes Bridge Street for 250 metres. Enter Little Shelford and cross two bridges over the river. Continue for a further 250 metres to a junction. Here go straight ahead, passing to the left-hand side of All Saints Church, Little Shelford. In a further 250 metres, you come to a T-junction by the Sycamore House Restaurant. Here turn right along Hauxton Road. Ignore ways off and in 800 metres you pass over a level crossing and under the M11. In a further 500 metres, you enter the village of Hauxton and pass the bus stop. Continuing along Church Road, ignoring turn-offs, you come in a further 440 metres to the Church of St Edmunds, rejoining the route at the asterisk [*] below.

(b) The alternative: 10 metres beyond Kings Mill Lane, there is *a gravel road to your right, due north, into Rectory Farm*, through double wooden gates, and towards a silo and barns, with an onward route that keeps the River Cam away on your left-hand side. *This is not a public right of way.* [You need to write to the farmer, at least two weeks in advance, saying you would like, if possible, to walk along the river through the farm, stating the date and time you would like to come and how many people there will be, and enclosing a stamped addressed envelope. On many occasions, it may not be possible, due to other activities taking place on the farm, and future building developments may prevent it entirely (see update sheets for this book). Write to: The Farmer, Church Farm, Trumpington, Cambridge CB2 2LG. You must then carry your permission form with you on the day. Please do not abuse the farmer's kindness in making this a possible option. Please stick to the route described below and close all the gates after you.]

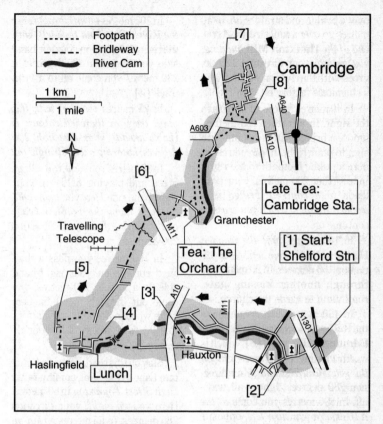

Footpath
Bridleway
River Cam

1 km
1 mile

N

[7]

Cambridge

[8]

A640

A603

A10

[6]

Late Tea:
Cambridge Sta.

M11

Grantchester

Travelling
Telescope

Tea: The
Orchard

[1] Start:
Shelford Stn

[5]

[3]

A10

M11

A130T

[4]

t

Haslingfield

Hauxton

t   t

Lunch

[2]

The route into the farm bears left with the lane as it continues on through the outbuildings.

In 165 metres keep on the concrete road, with wooden fencing on your left-hand side, and ignore a grassy farm track fork left that goes down beside the river. In 45 metres ignore another fork left to continue on, your direction 310 degrees. In a further 180 metres, go through metal fieldgates, *across the railway line*, to continue on.

In a further 750 metres, bend with the road to the left, to continue on, your direction 260 degrees, still with the river on your left-hand side, ignoring a turn-off to the right.

In 305 metres *go under the M11* motorway bridge.

In 730 metres *veer right, with a field hedge on your right-hand side*, your direction 340 degrees, following the main track.

In 290 metres you come *to some farm buildings where you veer left* with the road, your direction 315 degrees, towards the cottage. In 170 metres you pass this building.

In a further 175 metres, you come to *within 25 metres of the A10. But here you turn sharp left on a driveway*, past car-blocking posts, on a signposted public footpath, your direction 175 degrees, towards a timber-framed house. In 65 metres go over a bridge and straight on. In 40 metres go over a mill stream. *At the end of the* **Hauxton Mill** *building, you go left*, your direction 120 degrees, with the river on your left and a chemicals factory on your right.

In 40 metres ignore a footpath to the right. In a further 135 metres, ignore a bridge with a fishing club sign to your right. In 45 metres ignore a public footpath to the right. In a further 200 metres, your path leads *to a concrete bridge with wooden railings, which you cross* to continue on.

In 100 metres *take the wooden kissing gate to your left*, your direction 165 degrees. In 20 metres go through another kissing gate, continuing towards the church.

In 150 metres you come out to the road and to the **Church of St Edmunds, Hauxton [3]**, which is worth visiting **[*]**. *Turn right on this road (Church Road)*, your direction 280 degrees. Ignore all ways off. In 300 metres you come *to the A10 where you turn left*, opposite the bus lay-by (where you can get hourly buses to and from Cambridge), your direction 195 degrees.

In 35 metres *turn right on a public bridleway* signposted to Haslingfield, your direction 285 degrees, on a wide earth road.

In 260 metres ignore a fork to the left towards **Rectory Farm** (marked on the OS map). In 50 metres ignore another fork to the left, to carry straight on, your direction 300 degrees – the church in Haslingfield is already visible ahead to your left.

In 180 metres ignore a turning to the right marked 'Private road'.

In a further 900 metres, *fork right*, your direction 305 degrees.

In 200 metres *go on a bridge over the* **River Cam** *and turn left*, with the river alongside on your left-hand side, your direction 235 degrees. In 230 metres you come on to a farm track **[4]**.

In 25 metres *veer left with this main track (a thatched cottage is visible ahead)*, your direction 200 degrees, ignoring a way straight on.

In 30 metres you come to a village green and playing fields on your right-hand side. Here you *turn right, due west, along the right-hand edge of the playing field*, your direction 290 degrees.

In 100 metres you pass a thatched cottage on your right-hand side. In a further 100 metres, you come out through metal barriers (with wooden posts) *to a road (New Road) where you go left*, your direction 200 degrees.

Stay on this road, ignoring Fountain Lane to the right, coming *to the High Street T-junction* in 80 metres. Here you *go right*, your direction 280 degrees. In 55 metres *go left on Badcock Road* and immediately right, to the modern building that is the **Little Rose** pub, the suggested lunchtime stop.

After lunch *retrace your steps to the High Street and turn left*, your direction 285 degrees. Ignore ways off. In a further 330 metres, *where the High Street veers left, you go straight on, along Church Way*, with a thatched house on your right-hand side. In 80 metres you come to the **Parish Church of All Saints, Haslingfield**.

Coming out of the church door, go straight ahead on a path through the churchyard, your direction 340 degrees. In 110 metres you come *out on to a tarmac road where you continue straight on*. In 25 metres you pass the thatched Oak Cottage on your left-hand side. In a further 35 metres, *fork right on Dodds Mead*. In a further 45 metres, *pick up the tarmac path to the left of a house called Adelaide (no.1)*, straight on, your direction 15 degrees.

In 85 metres you come out *on to a road (New Road)* by house no.118 opposite, where you *turn left*, your direction 320 degrees. In a further 95 metres, you come out *on to Barton Road*, with a thatched house opposite, where you *turn right*, your direction 20 degrees.

In a further 175 metres, opposite house no.31, *take the signposted public footpath to the right* **[5]**, your direction 95 degrees (the pub marked here on old OS maps is closed down).

In 45 metres go on two planks over a stream, through a potentially muddy area. In a further 80 metres, go under mini-pylons. In a further 200 metres, go on a wooden bridge with railings and over a stile, *to the left*, your direction 10 degrees.

In 80 metres veer right with the path, your direction due east.

In a further 240 metres, go on a bridge with railings over a ditch-stream, to go straight on.

In a further 240 metres, you pass a large corrugated shed on your right-hand side (part of Lesania Farm). You come *to a tarmac lane T-junction where you go left*, your direction 25 degrees.

Radio telescopes are visible off to your left-hand side. Ignore all ways off. In 1.75km, by cottage no.6 on your left-hand side, ignore a lane to Catelupe Farm (marked on the

OS map) to your right, to continue straight on, along a concrete lane serving as a bridleway, your direction 20 degrees. In 250 metres you pass the aerials and railway line for the **travelling telescope** on your left-hand side, to continue straight on, on a wide grassy way – with Grantchester Church just visible behind the trees to your right (60 degrees on your compass) and Barton Church away ahead to your left.

In 550 metres go over Bourn Brook, on a concrete bridge with high wooden railings. In 55 metres *fork right*, your direction 65 degrees.

In a further 160 metres, *go over the M11 footbridge* – the top of which offers a panoramic view of the landscape **[6]**. Go straight on with Grantchester Church ahead of you. In 600 metres, *at a footpath sign and crossing of the ways, go straight on, along a path*, your direction 25 degrees. In 60 metres this becomes a tarmac path and you continue on, with buildings on your left-hand side.

In 100 metres you come on to an estate driveway (Burnt Close) and in a further 120 metres, *to the main road where you turn right*, your direction 105 degrees, by the thatched Grant Cottage on your right-hand side.

In 40 metres you pass the **Rupert Brooke** pub opposite. *Turn right on the High Street*, your direction 150 degrees. In 120 metres you pass the thatched **Red Lion** pub on your left-hand side, and also the Green Man pub.

In 100 metres you come to the **Parish Church of St Andrew and St Mary, Grantchester**.

Coming out of the church, go back to the road and turn right, passing the entrance to Manor Farm on your right-hand side, and going in 40 metres through the wooden swing gate into the garden of the suggested early tea place, **The Orchard**.

[One possible detour after tea is to come out of The Orchard front door, going right and out through the carpark, and turning left on the road for 40 metres, to the Old Vicarage, where Rupert Brooke used to lodge, and which is now the home of Jeffrey and Mary Archer. The house abuts the wall, with the huge conservatory where Jeffrey Archer used to write plainly visible from the pathway.]

The main onwards route after tea is to *go straight on (as if coming out of The Orchard front door),* for 40 metres, your direction 100 degrees, *to go over a stile* marked 'To the river', keeping to the right. In a further 100 metres, *detour over another stile on your right-hand side. Follow the path round through the woods* – the **Old Vicarage** can be glimpsed on your right-hand side. Eventually, you come back out over a stile, beside the **River Cam** on your right-hand side, to go straight on. **Trumpington Hall** (marked on the OS map) is visible across on the other side of the river.

Your onward route is more or less to follow the River Cam to the outskirts of Cambridge.

In more detail: In 80 metres go over a stile. In a further 120 metres, go over a stream. In 110 metres go over stile no.19, and onwards, along the bank. In a further 250 metres, go over two stiles. In 80 metres keep left (the way ahead through a fence is by the water's edge but is a blocked and muddy path). In 240 metres go through a potentially muddy patch, and on a single plank over a stream, then through (or over) a difficult barrier.

In 130 metres go through a wooden kissing gate (a cattle grid to its left-hand side) and onwards, going back along the riverside, unless forced by a side stream to rejoin the tarmac path, in 200 metres.

In 400 metres you go through a wooden kissing gate and onwards. In 135 metres you pass Grantchester Meadow on your right-hand side and carry straight on, along a badly made car road, your direction 65 degrees. In 100 metres your way becomes a tarmac road.

In 115 metres, *at a road junction, take the left fork down Eltisley Avenue,* your direction 30 degrees. In 200 metres *turn left* to go northwards *up Grantchester Street.*

In 160 metres, *at the junction with the A603, go straight ahead,* with the A603 on your left-hand side, your direction 40 degrees. Keep to the bike path, parallel and to the right of the pavement and, in 45 metres, by the pedestrian traffic lights, *fork right with the bike path,* your direction 70 degrees, across **Lammas Land** (open grass).

In 240 metres *cross over the main road (Fen Causeway) diagonally to the right, to go across the bridge* and to pick up the path beside the old mill stream on your left-hand side. In 10 metres go through a metal swing gate (with a cattle grid to its right-hand side).

In a further 100 metres, by the Bella Pasta restaurant on your left-hand side, *fork right over a footbridge* with white metal railings, and continue on the tarmac path, your direction 45 degrees – although it can be fun to hire a punt from here up to the Bridge of Sighs and back, a trip that takes leisurely beginners about one and a half hours.

In 70 metres *go over a similar bridge*. In 40 metres you are beside the River Cam on your right-hand side and you continue on, your direction 350 degrees, with the Garden House Hotel on the other side of the river. In 50 metres go over a mini-weir. In 80 metres *cross a bridge to your right*, towards the **Mill** pub. On the other side of the bridge, *turn left, in 15 metres going left down Laundress Lane*, which has bollards at its entrance.

In 50 metres you come *to a T-junction, Silver Street*, with **Queens College** opposite you. *Turn left*, your direction 230 degrees, and in 30 metres *go on a bridge back over the river*.

In 80 metres *fork right following the signpost to 'The Backs'*, your direction 290 degrees.

In 80 metres, by the white pyramid building on your right-hand side, go straight on away from the river, ignoring the fork to the right, your direction now 330 degrees. In a further 180 metres, you come *to the main road, where you turn right*, your direction 345 degrees.

In 25 metres, do not go through the gates on your right-hand side into the grounds of **Kings College**, but keep to the wide path with the river on your right-hand side. In a further 150 metres, you pass the gateway to **Clare College**. In 85 metres **[7]** *turn right on to Garret Hostel Lane*, eastwards, on a long

tarmac lane between railings, with the **Wren Library** away to the left. *Go over the bridge* (with **Clare Bridge** visible to the right).

In 140 metres, *at Trinity Lane T-junction, turn right*, your direction 190 degrees.

In 40 metres, having passed **Trinity Hall** on your right-hand side, *turn left into Senate House Passage*, passing on your left the **Gate of Honour**, topped with sundials (the gateway through which undergraduates pass on their way to receiving their degrees).

At the main street (Trinity Street) turn left, your direction 5 degrees, passing an entrance to **Gonville and Caius College** on your left-hand side and **St Michael's Church** on your right-hand side. In a further 100 metres, you pass the gatehouse to **Trinity College** on your left-hand side.

In 55 metres you come to **St Johns College** on your left-hand side. Here *turn right on All Saints Passage*, your direction 110 degrees. In 30 metres you pass the **Little Tearoom** on your left-hand side.

In 20 metres, *at the T-junction, go left*, your direction 50 degrees. In a further 45 metres, *at the Bridge Street T-junction, go right*, your direction 145 degrees. In 20 metres continue straight on, now on Sidney Street. In 70 metres you pass **Sidney Sussex College** on your left.

In 75 metres you pass Market Passage on your right-hand side. In a further 35 metres, *turn right on Market Street*, your direction 240 degrees. In 35 metres you pass **Holy Trinity Church** on your left-hand side. In 90 metres you come to the back of **Great St Mary's Church**, where you *go left*, your direction 5 degrees, with market stalls on your left-hand side. In 35 metres *go straight on, along Peashill*.

In 25 metres, at the end of the Midland Bank building, *go right*, signposted to 'G David Bookseller', your direction 290 degrees. In 50 metres you pass the front of the **Church of St Edward**, and in 10 metres, *at the T-junction, go right, on St Edwards Passage*.

In 30 metres you come *on to the main Kings Parade, where you go left*, with **Kings College** opposite.

Continuing south on Kings Parade, you pass in 30 metres the **Rainbow Bistro** on your left-hand side. In a further 55 metres, *turn left on Bene't Street*, your direction 85 degrees. In 35 metres you pass the **Eagle** pub on your left-hand side and **Saint Bene't's Church** on your right.

Go right on Free School Lane, your direction 150 degrees. **Corpus Christi College** is on your right-hand side and the **Old Cavendish Lab** is to your left.

In a further 65 metres, you come out *on to the main road, Pembroke Street*, with **Pembroke College** opposite, and you *go right*, your direction 245 degrees.

In 100 metres you come *to Trumpington Street where you go left*, your direction 150 degrees. In 15 metres you pass the entrance of Pembroke College. In 35 metres *go right on Little St Mary's Lane*, your direction 250 degrees, passing **Little St Mary's Church** on your left-hand side.

In 80 metres continue straight on, along a narrow lane. In 50 metres, *at the T-junction (Granta Place)*, by the modern Cambridge University Centre on your right-hand side, *turn left*, your direction 150 degrees.

In 50 metres, with the Moat House Hotel on your right-hand side, *go through the railings and over the cattle grid to fork left*, with the wall of **Peterhouse College** on your left, your direction 130 degrees.

In 120 metres you pass the **Fitzwilliam Museum** (behind the wall on your left-hand side). In 230 metres go through a metal swing gate **[8]** and *across the Fen Causeway (A10) to continue straight on*, through a metal swing gate and across the **Coe Fen**.

In 310 metres, *at a T-junction, go left*, your direction 125 degrees, with a stream on your right. In 190 metres *fork left, due east, with the wall on your left-hand side*.

In 120 metres you come *to the A10 where you go left*, your direction 350 degrees.

In 110 metres *turn right on Bateman Street*, due east. In 70 metres you pass the entrance to the **University Botanic Gardens** on your right-hand side (open daily until 5pm). For the next 450 metres, ignore all ways off.

You come *to the A640 T-junction, where you turn right*, your direction 155 degrees.

In 45 metres you pass the **Oriental Restaurant** and the **Boulevard Pizza Restaurant** on your left-hand side. In a further 15 metres, *fork left on Station Road*, passing the **Bar Moor** on your left-hand side, your direction 105 degrees. In 360 metres you come to **Cambridge Station**, and to the suggested late tea or supper place, **Ginghams Coffee Shop**.

Walk 27

Milford
to Haslemere

Thursley, Hindhead & the
Devil's Punch Bowl

Length 17.1km (10.6 miles), 5 hours
10 minutes. For the whole outing,
including trains, sights and meals,
allow at least 8 hours 15 minutes.

OS Landranger Map No.186.
Milford, map reference TQ 955 414,
is in **Surrey**, 3km south-west of
Godalming.

Toughness 6 out of 10.

Features A long walk along a road
out through Milford is rewarded by
the beauty of the landscape beyond.
Bagmoor Common Nature Reserve's
heathland of purple moss grass and
heather, and woodland of oaks and
Scots pine, leads on to the lakes of
Warren Mere and across to the village of Thursley, which has a fine
old church (the pub has long since
closed). At point [7] below, there is a
300 metre fenced path where the
nettles in summer have made us
grateful for long trousers. Mainly
you are walking through National
Trust land – sandy bridleways
through ancient established woodlands and the heather, gorse and
bilberry of the heathland. After
walking through the Devil's Punch
Bowl, you ascend to the Devil's
Punchbowl Café, the recommended
very late lunch stop, if you have not
picnicked earlier. From there you
follow the Greensand Way with fine

views out towards the South Downs,
with finally a footpath into the High
Street in Haslemere for tea.

Shortening the walk You could
order a taxi from Thursley; or you
could catch a bus from near the café
in Hindhead.

History The **Church of St
Michael and All Angels**, Thursley, has heavy-duty wooden roof
beams, added in Henry VII's time to
support a new tower. Its Saxon
windows up by the altar on the north
wall are the only ones in England
with their original timber frames
(thin horn or oiled linen was used
for window panes).

Legend has it that the **Devil's
Punch Bowl** was formed when the
Devil scooped up earth to hurl at
Thor, the god of thunder, who lived
in **Thor's Lie** (Thursley); the
punch bowl refers to the mist that
seems to flow over the rim of the
bowl.

The **heathlands** here were
among the UK's earliest cultivated
areas – clearings in the forest, that
were abandoned as the nutrients
leached away into the sandy soil.
The spring line between the sandstone top layer and the imperme-
able clay beneath led to erosion of
the sandstone, thus creating the Devil's Punch Bowl.

A sailor in 1786 bought drinks
for three men at the pub in Thursley.
Later, they were seen murdering
him at the Devil's Punch Bowl.
Found guilty, they were hanged in
chains on a hill nearby, now known
as **Gibbet Hill**. The outraged and
doleful headstone erected for the
sailor can be read in the north west
edge of Thursley churchyard.

Only the tower of **St Bartholomew's Church** in Haslemere is ancient, the rest having been boldly demolished by the Victorians. There is a stained-glass window here dedicated to the poet Tennyson.

In Tudor and Stuart times **Haslemere** was a centre for the iron industry. With the coming of the railway in the mid-nineteenth century it became a popular spot for literary people. Tennyson's house, Aldworth, is on the slopes of Black Down where he loved to walk; and the novelist George Eliot wrote *Middlemarch* in Shottermill.

The town has an interesting **museum** up the High Street, 100 metres north of the Georgian Hotel. The museum is open 10am to 5pm Tuesday to Saturday, and has a fine explanatory display of local wild flowers in the foyer. Other highlights include an Egyptian mummy and an observation beehive.

Saturday Walkers' Club Take the train nearest to **8.40am** (before or after) from **Waterloo** Station to **Milford (perhaps changing at Guildford)**. Journey time 49 minutes. Trains back from Haslemere run about three times an hour. Journey time 49 minutes. Buy a day return ticket to Haslemere.

Lunch The **Three Horse Shoes** pub in Thursley has reopened, and may be worth a try. Three quarters of the way through this long walk – at point **[10]** below – you come to the suggested lunch place, the Hillcrest Café, taken back by the National Trust despite much protest from lorry drivers and tarted up under the name **Devil's Punchbowl Café** (tel 01428 608 771). This

is open till 5pm (or till dusk if earlier) and serves hot meals. An alternative is the **Devil's Punchbowl Hotel** (tel 01428 606 565), London Road, Hindhead, which serves food and drinks all day. For those wanting to eat earlier in the day, I suggest buying food at the supermarket in Milford at the start of the walk and eating beside the second lake you come to, a rather lovely spot mentioned in the walk directions below.

Tea The suggested tea place is **Darnleys** tearoom (tel 01428 643 048) on Haslemere High Street, which closes at 5pm. The easiest alternative is the **Pizza Express** (tel 01428 642 245) next door, open till at least 10pm daily. The **White Horse Hotel**, also in the High Street, offers reasonably priced food and tea (its serving times are: midday-3pm and 6pm-9.30pm Monday to Friday; midday-9.30pm Saturday; midday-9pm Sunday). There is a bar at the **Haslemere Hotel** opposite the station and **Metro Café** (tel 01428 651 535) is just before the station. This café is open till 6pm weekdays (5pm Saturdays; closed Sundays). The station is a brisk ten-minute walk from the town centre.

WALK DIRECTIONS

[1] [Numbers refer to the map.] Coming off platform 2 at **Milford Station**, exit by the grey gate and *cross over the railway line to continue on a tarmac road*, your direction 345 degrees, passing the railway station building on your right-hand side. Keep on the road, ignoring all ways off.

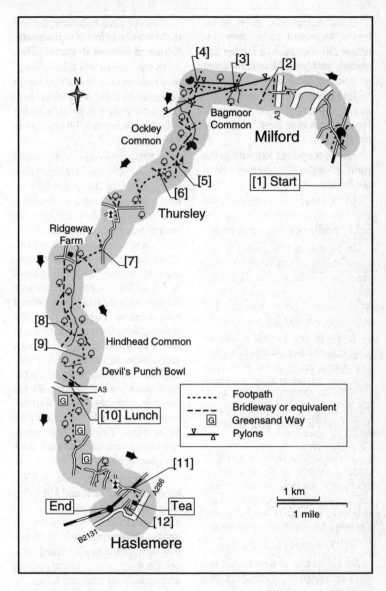

[4]

[3]

[2]

N

Bagmoor
Common

Milford

Ockley
Common

[1] Start

[5]

[6]

Thursley

Ridgeway
Farm

[7]

[8]

[9]

Hindhead Common

Devil's Punch Bowl

A3

G

[10] Lunch

G

G

G

[11]

A286

End

Tea

[12]

B2131

Haslemere

– – – – –	Footpath
– – –	Bridleway or equivalent
G	Greensand Way
▽—▽	Pylons

1 km

1 mile

In just over 1km, *at the T-junction, go right and, in 10 metres go left* on the main road signposted Guildford, your direction 300 degrees, with a grocery store on your left-hand side.

Again, ignore all ways off as you pass through **Milford**, and in 450 metres, at the traffic light T-junction, where right is signposted to Guildford, go left, your direction 230 degrees.

In 50 metres you go right on Lower Mousehill Lane, your direction 280 degrees. In a further 225 metres, you pass Mousehill Court on your left-hand side.

Ignore all ways off and, in 170 metres, you then pass Chimneys House to *continue on a bridge over the A3.*

Ignore the public footpath to the right, immediately the other side of the bridge.

In 100 metres, as the tarmac road becomes an earth road, follow the public bridleway sign straight on.

In 70 metres you pass the entrance to Dairy Farm House on your right-hand side, and in 25 metres you *a fork to the right,* a car-wide track that is a public footpath **[2]** your direction 300 degrees initially.

In 80 metres go over a stile on your right-hand side that has a yellow arrow on it (with a wooden fieldgate to its left) to continue straight on, along a car-wide earth track, along the fence of a house on your left-hand side, your direction 315 degrees.

In 200 metres go over a stile (a metal fieldgate to its left) underneath wooden pole pylons. Follow the line of these pylons straight on, due west, through recently planted Christmas trees (Norway spruce).

In 200 metres go over a stile.

In 150 metres go over a stile and wooden bridge with railings, across a stream.

[!] *Continue straight on across a grassy area with a house away to your right-hand side, and ignoring more obvious ways off to the left,* your direction 285 degrees.

You are soon following the line of the wooden pylons into **Bagmoor Common Nature Reserve [3]**.

In 550 metres you leave the nature reserve over an earthbank, to continue on a not very clear *path that follows the line of the wooden pylons,* avoiding any boggy bits as best you can.

In 175 metres you come to a green sward where the line of pylons bears off to the right. Keep straight on here towards a tarmac road (with a lake beyond). **[!]** *Turn left for a few metres along this tarmac road* **[4]**, *till you are near another minor line of overhead wires, bearing a warning sign (to your right) – you should be beside the concrete slipway into the lake, near the lake's notice board with amusing warnings from the safety officer. Here, on the left-hand side of the tarmac path, is a wooden post. Follow its arrow left, at right angles to the tarmac path, across the open space, your direction 140 degrees. In 30 metres, you will find two waymarks, yellow to the left and blue to the right. Take the blue arrow right-hand fork, a bridleway, your direction 205 degrees.*

In 250 metres go under pylons, keeping to your path and following a blue arrow on a post on your left-hand side. In 12 metres you cross a sandy vehicle-wide track. In 30 metres your bridleway is joined by a vehicle-wide sandy track coming from behind on your right.

In 430 metres go straight on into the **Thursley National Nature Reserve**, ignoring a bridleway to the right. In 170 metres your way is joined by a wide path from behind on your right. In 60 metres *ignore a* *bridleway off to the left* through a metal fieldgate. In 140 metres *fork right, following a blue 'HR' arrow on a post*, your direction 215 degrees, into a pine wood.

In 150 metres, there is a lake 30 metres to your left-hand side. In 70 metres, for a pleasant detour to the lake, fork left, your direction 165 degrees, to *walk beside the lake.*

In 190 metres, at the end of the lake and 25 metres before the end of the wood (with a big polythene greenhouse visible, in winter only, ahead), you bear right with the potentially overgrown path, keeping inside the wood, your direction 235 degrees.

In 80 metres you rejoin the bridleway, still with wooden fencing on your left-hand side. In 75 metres ignore a fork to the right.

In 20 metres you pass under mini-pylons. In 10 metres, *by a post with a blue arrow, fork right*, your direction 215 degrees.

In 50 metres you come to a green noticeboard about Thursley Common (there is a house visible away to your left).

10 metres beyond this noticeboard, turn left on a car-wide earth track **[5]**, your direction 190 degrees.

In 25 metres fork right, your direction 240 degrees.

In 450 metres you come to a bridleway junction with a waymark post ahead. You turn left along a broad sandy track, your direction 155 degrees, to keep on this main way, ignoring a fork left in 5 metres.

In 100 metres **[6]** *turn right* on a way signposted 'No horses. This is not a bridleway', your direction 240

degrees – a sandy way lined with heather on both sides.

In 250 metres ignore a possibly fenced-off path that goes up a hill to your left.

In 350 metres go through wooden fence poles to continue uphill, on a sandy way.

In 110 metres you pass fire paddles on your left-hand side and a fence on your right, to continue on, along a vehicle-wide way.

In 420 metres, by a 'No horses' sign facing away from you on your left-hand side, ignore a blue bridleway arrow to the right. In 6 metres *cross a wide bridleway to go straight on, slightly to the left.* In 15 metres pass to the left-hand side of a wooden fieldgate, to go onwards, your direction 220 degrees.

In 235 metres you come *to a tarmac road T-junction* (with the entrance to Foldsdown Cottage on your left-hand side).

Here you *go right*, passing what used to be Thursley's Three Horse Shoes pub on your left-hand side.

Coming out of the pub *after lunch, turn left.* In 80 metres, by the Old Vicarage, *fork left on The Street.*

In 260 metres *turn right* on a signposted public footpath, leading towards Church Cottages, your direction due west.

In 65 metres *go left into the churchyard* to visit the **Church of St Michael and All Angels**. *Coming out of the church door, go straight on* to exit the churchyard by the wooden swing gates, and *go right uphill on the tarmac road*, your direction 245 degrees.

In 15 metres you pass Hill Farm

House on your right-hand side. Keeping to the left-hand side of the road, your pavement is parallel and above the road. In 100 metres go through a metal barrier, and in a further 100 metres, rejoin the road.

In a further 225 metres, you pass Hill House on the left-hand side.

In 200 metres ignore a public footpath to the right (by a sign for Hedge Farm).

In 35 metres [7] *branch right to take the signposted footpath*, over a stile, your direction 250 degrees, with a field fence on your left-hand side and a hedge on your right.

In 300 metres, having zigzagged with the path (often overgrown with nettles in the summer), go over a stile and continue straight on, now steeply downhill. In 110 metres, having veered left with the path, go over a stile. In 25 metres go on a bridge over a stream to continue on a path uphill, direction 225 degrees.

In 200 metres ignore a fieldgate to the left to go straight on, along an earth farm track.

In 65 metres you pass **Ridgeway Farm** house (marked on the OS map), to continue on its tarmac driveway. In 135 metres, *by the sign for Upper Ridgeway Farm, turn left on a signposted public bridleway*, a sunken path, your direction 175 degrees. In 15 metres ignore an entrance through metal double fieldgates on your right. In 10 metres ignore metal double fieldgates on your left-hand side, to keep straight on uphill.

Ignore ways off and in 440 metres, at a National Trust sign, keep straight on, still uphill. In 200 metres ignore a path to the left. In 125 metres ignore a fork to the left.

In 10 metres, *by a post with four blue arrows on top, turn left*, downhill, your direction 145 degrees, keeping on this main way. In 12 metres ignore two ways off to the left. Your direction is 185 degrees, downhill. In 300 metres you pass a bridle-way down to the left (by a part-timbered cottage).

In 500 metres, *go through a wooden field gate, ignore the second gate, and take a kissing gate beside a third wooden field gate* [8], on a footpath steeply downhill, your direction 105 degrees. In 65 metres go across a stream on a wooden bridge with a railing. In 100 metres, having gone up steps, ignore a defunct fieldgate on your right-hand side and in 12 metres you pass a sign for Hindhead Youth Hostel on your right-hand side. Continue on up with the ditch on your right-hand side.

In 100 metres go through a wooden swing gate and in 12 metres go on to a tarmac lane, where you go straight on, your direction now 100 degrees.

In 100 metres you come to the tarmac entrance driveway to a house on your right-hand side, and carry on uphill, on a tarmac lane, following the red 'HR' arrow on a post.

In 50 metres take *a footpath fork off to the right* by a post with one yellow and two red arrows, and by a yellow grit and salt bin, your direction 185 degrees.

In 40 metres go through a wooden kissing gate. Keep to this main path for 400 metres to go through a kissing gate and on (later keeping straight on at the angled crossing) for 400 metres through the **Devil's Punch Bowl**. You come then to a fork [9] with a small stump on your left-hand side faintly marked '3' and with an arrow pointing back the way you have come. *Branch right here steeply uphill*, your direction 240 degrees.

In 300 metres the path becomes stepped. At the top, with the noisy A3 road only 10 metres to your left-hand side, bear right along a level path, your direction 300 degrees. There are fine views north to the Hog's Back and beyond.

In 200 metres, you go through a kissing gate and, 30 metres further on, fork left, slight uphill, your direction 200 degrees. Follow this path to reach the car park, and then, at the other end of the carpark, the **Devil's Punchbowl Café** in **Hindhead [10]**.

Exiting from the café *to the main road (the A3), cross it and take the footpath, the path nearest to the left-hand side of the Devil's Punch Bowl Hotel*, your direction 160 degrees (direction important here).

In 80 metres, at the end of the fence on your right-hand side, bend left with the main path and stay on it, ignoring all ways off. Continue due south, parallel to the back gardens away to your right-hand side.

In 250 metres you pass the entrance gate to The Shieling on your right-hand side and ignore a path to the left, to go straight on downhill, your direction 130 degrees.

In 180 metres you go through a wooden swing gate and in 25 metres, as you come out to open heathland on your left-hand side, you are joined by a path from behind on your left.

In 200 metres you come to a crosspaths, with a post bearing a number of blue and yellow arrows – and to a wooden swing gate and a fieldgate on your right-hand side. Follow the **Greensand Way** arrow straight on, uphill, on a sandy path, your direction 170 degrees.

In 210 metres you ignore a path crossing (near fire paddles) to keep straight on, going through heather, with a magnificent view out to the south-west.

In 160 metres you cross another path to continue straight on, uphill.

In 110 metres you cross a path to keep straight on, your direction now 170 degrees.

In 145 metres you come out *on to a tarmac road*, with Little Scotstoun House opposite. Here you *go right*, your direction 210 degrees, on this road (Farnham Lane).

In 100 metres ignore a bridleway to the right.

In 255 metres you pass the entrance to Thursley House on your left-hand side, and *turn left on a signposted public byway*, your direction 130 degrees – passing the entrance to Beech House on the right-hand side.

In 85 metres, *at the entrance to Pucksfold House on your right*, keep left downhill along a path in a gully, your direction 120 degrees.

In 150 metres continue straight on, along a tarmac driveway, with Little Stoatley House then on your right.

In 300 metres, having passed a horse farm, you come out *to a tarmac road T-junction*, with Anchor House opposite and a National Trust sign on your left; *go left* on this road, your direction due east. In 40 metres you cross a stream.

In a further 35 metres *you go right on a narrow public footpath,* signposted Greensand Way, your direction 155 degrees.

In 300 metres you cross a stile and a tarmac road to continue on between hedges, the signposted public footpath marked GW.

In 200 metres you come out *on to a tarmac road, with Ventnor House opposite, and turn right downhill,* your direction 140 degrees.

In 180 metres you come to **St Bartholomew's Church, Haslemere,** on your right-hand side. *Keep left with the road* so that the triangular green is on your right-hand side. [For a direct route to the station and the hotel bar opposite the station, you bear right and follow Tanners Lane until you reach the station.]

On the main route, in 80 metres you go over the railway bridge **[11]**. In 15 metres you *follow the public footpath sign right on Pathfields,* your direction 190 degrees.

In 25 metres you pass Haslemere Printed Circuits Ltd on your right-hand side.

In 250 metres *ignore a footpath to the right signposted 'footpath to town'. Keep straight on,* your direction 145 degrees.

In 65 metres *you come out on to the High Street.* Turning left would take you to the **museum,** in 70 metres. *Turning right* takes you, in 80 metres, to the suggested tea place, **Darnleys** tearoom, on the right-hand side (or to other possible tea places in the same street).

Coming out of Darnleys tearoom, turn right and in 25 metres turn right again *down West Street, signposted to the police station.* In 120 metres, where the main street curves to the right past the police station (which is on your right-hand side), *take the street straight on to the fire station,* but then *not* the tempting path straight on, but rather *turn left in front of the fire station* and take the footpath that goes *down the left-hand side of the fire station* signposted 'to the station', your direction 315 degrees. Follow this path, with a stream to your right and later a playground to your left, till you come *out on to a tarmac road* with Redwood Manor opposite. *Turn left on this road and in 40 metres turn right on to the B2131, leading in 260 metres to* **Haslemere Station** on your right-hand side. **Darnleys Café Central** is on your right-hand side just before the station and **Haslemere Hotel,** with its bar, is opposite the station (though it has recently been walker-unfriendly).

The platforms (2 and 3) for London Waterloo are over the footbridge.

Walk 28

Chilham to Canterbury

Canterbury Cathedral & the Great Stour River

Length 17.7km (11 miles), 5 hours 30 minutes. For the whole outing, including trains, sights and meals, allow at least 10 hours 45 minutes.

OS Landranger Map No.179. Chilham, map reference TR 106 553, is in **Kent**, 8km south-west of Canterbury.

Toughness 3 out of 10.

Features (Note: Trains on Sundays go from Charing Cross Station.) This particular pilgrimage to Canterbury starts beside the Great Stour River and its attendant lakes, visits the church and green at Chartham, and passes through hop fields and apple orchards to the suggested lunch pub in Chartham Heath. In the afternoon, the way is through Church Wood and Blean Woods Nature Reserve, to the parklands of the University of Kent, with fine views down over Canterbury Cathedral. The entrance to the city is along the River Stour, through the Norman Westgate and down the medieval high street and alleys, entering the cathedral precincts through its ornate Christ Church Gate.

Shortening the walk There are buses into Canterbury, three times an hour, from near the Plough Inn in Upper Harbledown. There are also buses into the city from near the Hare & Hounds pub on the A290 and from the University of Kent. The route passes near Canterbury West Station on entering the city, for those who wish to go home without visiting the city centre; and there is a suggested short cut in the walk directions (below) once within the city, to Canterbury East Station.

History Attacked by marauding Picts, Scots and Saxons, the Britons could not defend the walled city of **Durovernum Cantiacorum**, once the Romans had abandoned it. When St Augustine and his followers arrived in 397 – at the instigation of King Ethelbert and his French Christian wife, Bertha – the walls were repaired and the overgrown streets cleared. The city was now called Cautwaraburg.

The **cathedral** which St Augustine founded was sacked by the Danes in 1011. It was within the cathedral, on December 2nd 1170, that **Thomas à Becket**, Archbishop of Canterbury, was murdered by four of Henry II's knights. The city became a place of pilgrimage, as celebrated by Chaucer in his *Canterbury Tales*, although these pilgrimages were interrupted in 1538, when Henry VIII had St Thomas declared a traitor and his shrine pillaged and all references to him destroyed.

Entrance to **Canterbury Cathedral** (tel 01227 762 862) is free if attending evensong, which normally takes place at 5.30pm Monday to Friday, 3.15pm Saturday, and 5.15pm Sunday. Otherwise admission is £3. The cathedral is open till 7pm in summer, till 5pm in winter. Entrance to just the surroundings and perimeter of the cathedral is free from 5pm.

Huguenots fleeing France, after the St Bartholomew Massacre of 1572, settled in Canterbury. The **Weavers' House** in the High Street is an example of one their high-gabled houses, with loft doors for lifts.

The **Westgate** is the only surviving gateway into the city, built by Archbishop Sudbury before the Peasants' Revolt of 1381. It was used as a gaol. The **medieval wall** around the city follows the line of the third-century wall in Roman times.

The mainly medieval church of **St Peter's**, in Peter Street, may be of Saxon origin.

Saturday Walkers' Club Take the train nearest to **9.15am** (before or after) from **Victoria** Station to **Chilham**. Journey time 1 hour 46 minutes. Trains back from Canterbury East to London run about twice an hour (you may need to change at Faversham). Journey time between 1 hour and 1 hour 28 minutes.

Lunch The suggested lunchtime pub is the **Chapter Arms** pub (tel 01227 738 340) in Chartham Hatch, which serves food midday to 2pm Monday to Saturday, midday to 2.15pm Sunday; groups of more than eight people should phone to book. Somewhat more interesting than this pub, if you think you could get there in time, is the **Plough Inn** (tel 01227 463 131) in Upper Harbledown, which is 3km (50 minutes) further on in the walk. It serves food midday to 3pm on weekdays and all day on Saturday and Sunday; groups of more than six people should phone to book. Or you could

have lunch nearer the start of the walk at the **Artichoke** pub (tel 01227 738 316) in Chartham, which serves food midday to 2pm Monday to Saturday, midday to 2.30pm Sunday.

Tea There are any number of places to have tea in Canterbury, but if, like me, you like to finish your sightseeing first, the suggested tea place is five minutes from Canterbury East Station: the **White Hart** pub (tel 01227 765 091) in Castle Row. This is open daily till late. The pub will serve sandwiches and ploughmans if requested. There is also a friendly **station snack bar** offering hot chocolate and hot meals, open until 7.30pm daily. Other tea places open late include (in order of nearness to Canterbury East Station): **Il Vaticano** (tel 012227 765 333), mainly a pizza restaurant, at 35 St Margarets, open till 10.30pm daily; and **Café des Amis** (tel 01227 464 390) by the Westgate as you enter the city, open till 10pm daily.

WALK DIRECTIONS

[1] [Numbers refer to the map.] Coming off the platform from London at **Chilham Station**, follow the North Downs Way signpost, your direction 340 degrees, *up the tarmac road away from the station.* In 50 metres you come *to the A28 where you go left*, your direction 240 degrees. (take care on the A28 because there is no pavement to walk on next to the road).

In 80 metres *take the left fork, the A28 signposted to Ashford.*

In 140 metres, just before the Ashford Road service station, *follow the Stour Valley Walk sign left,* your

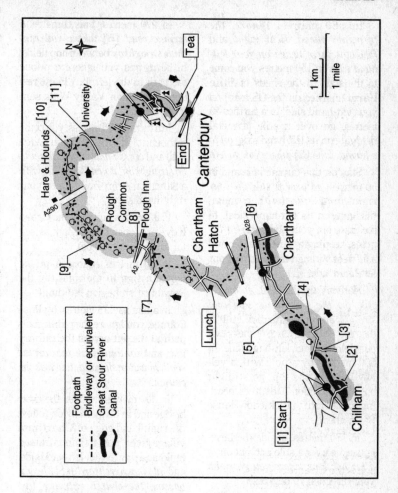

direction 135 degrees, on a tarmac lane to the railway crossing.

In 80 metres *cross the railway lines* and continue on the tarmac lane the other side.

In 80 metres go on a bridge over the clear river and bear right with the lane the other side. In 65 metres you pass **Chilham Mill** on your left-hand side. In 20 metres *go over a second bridge*, with Setford Lake on your right-hand side. The other side of the bridge, *go left*, your direc-

tion 150 degrees, on a gravel car road, then bear left on a path, with the **Great Stour River** on your left-hand side.

In 110 metres, **[2]** at a small wooden barrier marked with a Link arrow pointing straight on, you *turn left*, following a yellow arrow, your direction 30 degrees, with the river below you on your left-hand side. Walk along, following the edge of the trees which are on your left-hand side.

In 560 metres, *ignore the farmgate ahead. Bear right* and *followthe farm hedge on your left-hand side*. In 150 metres you come to the start of the sheds of **Stile Farm** (marked on the OS map) on your left-hand side. In a further 85 metres, go over a stile (a metal fieldgate on its left-hand side) *on to a tarmac lane* [3] *where you go left*.

Stay on this tarmac lane and in 50 metres, *go over a stile on your right-hand side* (with a metal fieldgate on its left-hand side), to continue on, your direction 70 degrees, keeping a band of alder and ash trees 40 metres away to your left-hand side.

Halfway up the field, *go over a stile on the right-hand side and straight on*, your direction still 70 degrees, with the fence of the previous field by your left-hand side. In 500 metres, by a pole with a yellow band at the top, go straight on, your direction 70 degrees, heading to the right of Pickledon House Farm ahead.

In 130 metres, beside the farmhouse, go over a stile and out *on to a tarmac lane where you go right*, your direction 70 degrees.

In 150 metres [4] you *follow the footpath sign, by leaving the tarmac lane to go straight on*, through a wooden fieldgate, with Lake House on your left-hand side, your direction 50 degrees.

Continuing straight on, in 40 metres you start going across a vast open field, with lakes away to your left-hand side. In 280 metres are two t-junctions. Fork left under the pylons, then fork right following yellow footpath arrows.

In 270 metres, you come *to a tarmac road* [5] *where you continue straight on* between hop fields. In 30 metres you ignore a public footpath to the left. In 135 metres, ignore the Stour Valley Walk sign to the left.

In a further 175 metres, you come to the end of this road (Bobbin Lodge Hill) and *cross Shalmsford Street to go straight on, down Bolts Hill*, with a Salvation Army building on your right-hand side.

In 90 metres you pass the **Cross Keys** pub (open 12.30 to 3pm, closed for lunch on Mon/Tue).

In 80 metres ignore a public footpath sign to the right (by the Royal British Legion building).

In a further 115 metres, by Rose Cottage, you ignore the public footpath to the left across the railway line, and *continue with the tarmac road, now Parish Road, towards the church*.

In 300 metres go over the river bridge and in 80 metres you follow the right-hand edge of **Chartham** village green, past a timber-framed building away to your left-hand side, and *into the churchyard of St Mary's, passing the church entrance* (the church is open 3 to 5pm, May to September) *and keeping on, along a tarmac path*. In 40 metres you come *to the road* by a house called Glebe, where you *go right*, your direction 125 degrees.

In 40 metres you *follow the Stour Valley Walk sign to your left*, your direction 65 degrees, the river on your right-hand side. (If you want an early lunch at a pub here, continue over the bridge instead of going left. Pass Chartham Paper Mills on your right-hand side, coming in less than 200 metres to the part-timber-framed **Artichoke** pub.)

In 325 metres go through a wooden swing gate and onwards, with the river still on your right-hand side and a lake on your left.

In 340 metres, *by a derelict bridge on your right-hand side*, and with a wooden kissing gate ahead of you **[6]**, *go left on a grassy car-wide way*, your direction 330 degrees. In 180 metres go through a metal swing gate *across the railway lines.*

In 75 metres you *go across the A28, to go left along it*, your direction 240 degrees.

In 50 metres a discreet concrete *public footpath* marker *on your right-*hand side (to the right of the driveway of Carlton Lodge) and a green footpath sign (potentially overgrown) on a pole indicate your narrow path, marked with a yellow arrow, between hedge and fence, your direction 25 degrees.

In 45 metres go over (the remains of) a stile and on, with an orchard on your left-hand side.

In 40 metres, *at a slight bend left in the path* (when by looking through a terrace of houses, you can see – in winter at least – that you are opposite the lane on which you came out on to the A road), *go left, up between the rows of orchard trees*, your direction 315 degrees. (At the top of the field turn right and almost immediately left into the wood).

In 150 metres you come *to an earth road T-junction, with a wood beyond. Go right*, your direction 45 degrees, for 55 metres, until *you go left by an unstable six-foot iron post on your left-hand side, with a yellow*

arrow, on a clear path into the wood, your direction 305 degrees.

In 80 metres go over a stile and onwards, with the field edge on your right-hand side. In 150 metres go over a stile and up *over the railway lines.* In 20 metres go over a stile on the other side, to continue with the field fence on your right-hand side. In a further 620 metres, go over a stile, with a tall aerial mast on your left-hand side, to carry straight on, your direction 320 degrees.

In 125 metres you come to a stile and *a tarmac road, where you go right*, uphill – this is signposted the North Downs Way, and your direction is 45 degrees.

In 140 metres you come to the **Chapter Arms** in **Chartham Hatch** on your left-hand side, the suggested lunchtime stop.

After lunch, *go straight ahead from the pub door to regain the tarmac road, where you go left*, your direction 25 degrees, on New Town Street.

In 120 metres you come *to a T-junction where you go left on How-field Lane*, your direction 5 degrees.

In 35 metres *take the North Downs Way signposted footpath straight on*, your direction 355 degrees, between fences.

In 100 metres *cross over a tarmac road to follow the North Downs Way sign onwards, up a concrete driveway.* In 15 metres you *fork to the right.* In 8 metres you pass a wooden barrier (a metal gate on its left-hand side) to continue on, following the North Downs Way sign, with a playground on your left-hand side and house fences on your right, your direction 60 degrees initially.

In 145 metres go through a wooden gateway down into **Petty France Wood** (as marked on the OS map), following the North Downs Way arrow and ignoring ways off.

In 310 metres *take the stile on your left-hand side* (at the beginning of a line of poplars, also on your left-hand side), to follow a path quarter right over the top of the hillock ahead. In 125 metres you pass under mini-pylons. In 140 metres go over a stile and on two planks over a stream.

In 5 metres you come *to a track at the edge of the hop field, where you go left*, your onwards direction 310 degrees. In 110 metres you pass under mini-pylons to continue with the field edge on your left-hand side.

In 270 metres you come *to a car-wide earth lane to your right* (there is bridleway off to the left, with a blue bridleway arrow on a well-hidden post). **[7]** Take this bridleway lane to the right, your direction 80 degrees, through the orchard.

In 220 metres, at a crossing of the ways, you pass a primitive water tower on your right, to continue straight on, ignoring ways off.

In 550 metres, *by large sheds on your left-hand side, bear left*, your direction 35 degrees.

In 160 metres you pass the three-storey China Farm Barn on your right-hand side, to bear left with the tarmac road.

In 215 metres you come *to the A2 bridge, which you cross*, ignoring the bridleway sign to the right on the other side.

In 70 metres, *at a T-junction*, **[8]** take the footpath to the right-hand side of St Mary's Hall, **Upper Hambledown**, your direction 320

degrees, into **Church Wood** (marked on the OS map), with a stream on your right-hand side. (But if you want to get to the pub in Upper Hambledown, turn right on this road, and you come in 110 metres to the **Plough Inn**. Just beyond the pub is the bus stop.)

In 185 metres, by a post with a yellow arrow, you *fork right* to keep near the edge of the wood. In 15 metres you cross a ditch on two planks. In 50 metres you pass a ruined stile. In 300 metres the field away to your right ends, and you are walking though a forest with heather beside the path.

In 300 metres go up through a wooden barrier *to an earth road T-junction where you go right*, your direction 75 degrees. In 30 metres ignore the suggestion of a way to your left. In 85 metres, *at a major junction* **[9]**, *turn left*, following a yellow arrow on a post, your direction 30 degrees, with Scots pine trees on your left-hand side, beyond a ditch.

In 85 metres you ignore a path to the right.

In 270 metres you cross a major car-wide footpath to continue on, along a gravel car-wide way into **Blean Woods Nature Reserve**, your direction 45 degrees.

In 150 metres cross a path to continue on your way, signposted short cut. In 385 metres you come to a major junction of paths. You go straight on; in 20 metres you cross over a stile, your direction 70 degrees, following a faint path, your direction 50 degrees.

In 100 metres *go through a gap in the trees, turning right on a path on the other side,* eastwards, with the trees now on your right-hand side. In 110 metres you cross a ditch on a dozen planks and continue on with the edge of the wood on your right-hand side.

For 435 metres follow the hedge straight on, then going past a (decayed) stile and out *to the A290, where you go left*, your direction 325 degrees.

In a further 70 metres (and 50 metres before the **Hare & Hounds** pub), *turn right on a signposted footpath*, down steps, your direction 40 degrees.

Bearing left, in 40 metres you cross a scaffolding pole stile and go through a wooden kissing gate and in 5 metres *fork right*, your direction 130 degrees, away from the stream to your right-hand side.

In 60 metres keep going, now following a fence to your right-hand side, your direction 100 degrees.

In 220 metres, having had a fence to your left-hand side all this way, you go over a wooden bridge with scaffolding pole railings, and 10 metres further on, you follow along the right-hand edge of the field.

In 100 metres you come to a bridge with curvaceous metal railings and an earth road. But you continue straight on, still with a stream on your right-hand side.

In 275 metres go over another wooden bridge, to continue on, your direction 120 degrees, with the stream still on your right-hand side.

In 250 metres you come *to a bridge* on your right-hand side consisting of a dozen planks over the stream **[10]**, *which you cross to go left the other side*, with the stream now on your left-hand side.

In 80 metres fork right under the mini-pylons. In 10 metres *go over a two-plank bridge to fork right, to a sign for the University of Kent* at Canterbury. *Take the main path onwards from this sign, gently upwards along the almost car-wide avenue into the wood, due south.*

Bear left with this path. In 125 metres cross a stream that is piped under the path, your direction now 135 degrees.

In 120 metres you come *to a tarmac road* **[11]**, with the Electronics Department opposite. *Go over this road and carry straight on*, your direction 195 degrees.

In 50 metres you begin to pass the Electronics block (with a large white metal pyramid on its roof) on your right-hand side.

20 metres past the end of the block, fork left to *pass down the left-hand side of the Sports Centre.*

35 metres from the start of the side of the Sports Centre, you come to a little brick, windowless hut on your right-hand side, and *pick up a footpath straight on* (to the hut's left-hand side) into the trees, your direction 145 degrees.

In 90 metres you come *to a tarmac road junction. Go straight across.* In 35 metres you come *to roundabouts at the far side of which, by the Kent Union Venue, you fork right*, towards bus stops (the road is marked 'Caution, Speed Ramps'), your direction 190 degrees.

In 40 metres you pass a bus stop on your left-hand side. In a further 40 metres, you have an unobscured view of Canterbury Cathedral visible below on your left-hand side.

Here you *fork half left off the tarmac road* to follow a clear path across the grass, heading down half-way between the Cathedral and the road you have just left, your direction 170 degrees. In 10 metres you pass a lone oak tree immediately on your right-hand side.

In 400 metres you *cross an earth road to continue straight on*, diagonally across the grass, on a clear path, your direction 155 degrees. In 160 metres you pass through a gap in the hedges. In a further 30 metres you come *on to a tarmac path where you go right*, your direction 225 degrees. In 20 metres, at a path crossing, go left on a path lined with paving stones, your direction 120 degrees. In 150 metres, you continue *straight on, now on Salisbury Road*.

In 250 metres, ignoring all ways off, you come *to a T-junction (Forty Acres Road) and carry straight on*, along a signposted public footpath.

In 110 metres you come to playing fields on your left-hand side, where you keep straight on, with hedges on your left-hand side.

In 85 metres (at the end of the playing fields) go through a metal barrier and *follow the tarmac path to the right*, your direction 175 degrees. In 60 metres *go through a tunnel under the railway*.

Then just before the signal box (which is on the other side of the rails) *turn left* by a house marked '88, 90, 92, 94, 96, 98' on a road with new houses (Station Road West) which goes off at right angles to the rails.

You come out *to the main road (North Lane) which you cross over to continue on a tarmac road*, your direction 165 degrees, past Deans Mill Court on your left-hand side, and *across a mill stream bridge*.

On the other side *turn right, signposted Riverside Walk*, with the water on your right-hand side, your direction 240 degrees.

In 80 metres, with some very fine **tree-trunk sculptures** in the open space on your left-hand side, ignore the lockbridge straight ahead, to *go right on an arched bridge*. Continue on, your direction 165 degrees, now with the water on your left-hand side.

In 80 metres you pass the Watershed Café on your left-hand side, and in 10 metres you pass Guys Bridge. In 80 metres you come to the Westgate, with the Guildhall just beyond and the **Café des Amis du Mexique** opposite.

Go left through the **Westgate** *and straight on*, your direction 130 degrees, on the pedestrianised St Peter's Street.

In 100 metres, you pass St Peter the Apostle Church on your left-hand side. In 75 metres you pass the **Weavers' House** on your left-hand side. [To shorten the walk at this point, continue ahead following signs to Canterbury East Station and the bus station, passing the cathedral entrance to the left-hand side.] In 40 metres the main suggested route is to *turn left on Best Lane*, your direction 60 degrees.

In 80 metres you pass the Thomas Becket pub on your right-hand side. In 15 metres you *cross The Friars to continue on King Street, then take the first tarmac road left* to the old **Blackfriars Gallery**.

At the gallery turn right between terraces of houses, past the second set of concrete bollards. 5 metres beyond these bollards, *take the lane sharp right (Mill Lane)*, your direction 145 degrees.

In 75 metres you come *to a T-junction where you go left* (despite a sign to the right for the cathedral), your direction 35 degrees.

In 40 metres you pass the **Old Synagogue**. In 20 metres ignore Knotts Lane to your left. In 40 metres, with the entrance to **Kings School** ahead, *turn right on Palace Street*, your direction 210 degrees.

In 170 metres, with the Seven Stars pub away to your right-hand side, *turn left on Sun Street*.

In 70 metres you reach the main entrance to **Canterbury Cathedral**.

After *visiting the cathedral* – it is also worth walking round the outside, through the cloisters – *you come out of the same gate to go straight on down narrow Mercery Lane*, your direction 220 degrees.

In 50 metres you *cross the main street (The Parade) to go straight on along St Margaret's Street*.

In 65 metres you pass **Il Vaticano** restaurant on your right-hand side. In 70 metres you pass the Three Tuns pub on your left-hand side and go straight on, walking along Castle Street.

In 140 metres, *by St Marys Street on your left-hand side, you fork left through the bollards to go through the gardens and the old churchyard*, your direction due south. In 60 metres you come to the **White Hart** pub on your left-hand side, the last pub before the station, and the suggested meal stop.

Afterwards, continue on The Crescent, your direction 210 degrees. In 80 metres, with the remains of the Norman Castle to your right, *turn left, opposite Don Jon House*, your direction 120 degrees, with the flint **city wall** on your right-hand side.

In 35 metres, with the **Dane John Mound** ahead of you, go up steps to *cross the bridge*.

Canterbury East Station, with its snack bar, is directly ahead.

For the London trains, go to platform 2 (via platform 1, turning right to go under the tunnel).

Walk 29

Hassocks to Lewes

The South Downs Way via Plumpton

Length 18km (11.2 miles), 5 hours 30 minutes. For the whole outing, including trains, sights and meals, allow at least 9 hours 30 minutes.

OS Landranger Map No. 198. Hassocks, map reference TQ 304 156, is in **West Sussex**, 9km north of Brighton. Lewes is in **East Sussex**.

Toughness 4 out of 10.

Features This is an exhilarating walk along the South Downs Way, a ridge of South Downs chalk grassland with panoramic views inland, and out to the sea by Brighton. This is also an easier walk, with far fewer ups and downs, than Walk 25 from Winchelsea to Hastings. On the way up to the ridge, the route goes through Butcher's Wood and visits a church in Clayton and the still-working Clayton Windmill. The South Downs Way is partly a Sussex Trust Nature Reserve and partly National Trust land, with medieval dew ponds and an Iron Age fort at Ditchling Beacon. After lunch, down below in Plumpton, the final walk into Lewes is along the River Ouse, then up to the Norman castle and through its gateway into the ancient High Street.

Shortening the walk You could abort the walk before lunch by turning left at the asterisk [*] below, which takes you down into Ditchling, where there are pubs and a tea shop (opposite the church). Ditchling is only 2km from Hassocks. From the lunch pub in Plumpton, you could catch a 166 or 124 bus to Lewes, but the buses do not run on Sundays. Or you could catch a bus into Lewes from the tearoom in Offham. Call Traveline on 0870 608 2608 for bus details.

History The Saxon **Church of St John the Baptist** in Clayton has eleventh or twelfth-century wall paintings and an entrance path whose rippled effect comes from stone quarried from the fossilised bed of a sea or a river.

One of the **Clayton Windmills** ('Jill'), a post mill, with its 1852 'Sussex Tailpole' on wheels for changing direction, is normally open to visitors from 2pm to 5pm on Sunday from May to September.

Ditchling Beacon, once an Iron Age fort, with traces of ramparts still visible, was a site for one of the beacons that gave warning of the Spanish Armada.

Lewes Castle (tel 01273 486 290), and the Barbican House Museum nearby, are open to visitors until 5.30pm daily (last entrance 5pm); admission £4. The castle was built by William de Warenne, who fought alongside William the Conqueror at the Battle of Hastings. Its towers were added about the time of the **Battle of Lewes**. In this battle in 1264, the rebel earl, Simon de Montfort, with an army of Londoners and 5,000 barons, defeated Henry III, who had two horses killed under him and was forced to seek refuge in Lewes Priory. The Mise of Lewes was signed next day, and led to England's first parliamentary meeting at Westminster in 1265.

The church at **Lewes Priory** was as large as Westminster Cathedral, but was demolished during Henry VIII's dissolution of the monasteries. Only ruins of the priory remain.

The churchyard of **St John Sub Castro** ('Under the Castle') has an obelisk commissioned by Tsar Alexander II to commemorate the 28 prisoners of war who were captured during the Crimean War and who died in Lewes Gaol in the 1850s.

Tom Paine (1737–1809), author of *The Rights of Man*, lived in Lewes, and his political debating society – the Headstrong Club – often met at the White Hart Hotel. He was forced to leave Lewes for France in 1792 – only to be imprisoned there for opposing the execution of Louis XVII.

Saturday Walkers' Club Take the train nearest to **9.10am** (before or after) from **London Bridge** or **Victoria** to **Hassocks**. You may have to change at East Croydon. Journey time 56 minutes. Trains back from Lewes run once an hour. Journey time 1 hour 7 minutes.

Lunch The suggested lunchtime pub is the **Half Moon** (tel 01273 890 253) in Plumpton, which is friendly and serves simple homemade food from midday to 2pm daily; groups of more than 15 people should phone to book. Those who prefer to take a short cut by keeping straight on along the South Downs Way may be able to buy ice creams from the van which is normally parked at Ditchling Beacon.

Tea There are a number of possible places to have tea in Lewes, so take

your pick. My favourite is the **Garden Room Café** (tel 01273 478 636) at 14 Station Street, near the station, open till 5.30pm Monday to Saturday. Others, in my rough and ready order of preference, include: the **Rainbow** (tel 01273 472 170), 179 High Street, open till at least 10.30pm, with light foods and salads till 7pm; the **Lewes Wine Cellar Café** (tel 01273 471953), 62 High Street, open till 9pm daily (6pm Sunday); the **White Hart Hotel** (tel 01273 476 694), 55 High Street, which has a pleasant lounge and public balcony, and serves reasonably priced tea and food daily till 10pm; and **Ask** restaurant (tel 01273 479 330), 186 High Street, open daily till late.

WALK DIRECTIONS

[1] **[Numbers refer to the map.]** Coming off platform 2 at **Hassocks Station**, go down the station approach road, your direction 105 degrees. In 35 metres you pass The Hassocks pub on your left-hand side, and *take the tarmac path to your right, signposted South Downs*.

In 25 metres you come *to the B2116 and you go right*, due west, back towards the railway bridge. In 40 metres *go left, following the South Downs signpost*, your direction 190 degrees.

Ignore ways off and in 125 metres you cross a tarmac road to go on, slightly to the right, your direction 210 degrees, following a footpath sign.

In 90 metres you come *to a T-junction, where you go left*, your direction 205 degrees, with the railway embankment wall on your right-hand side.

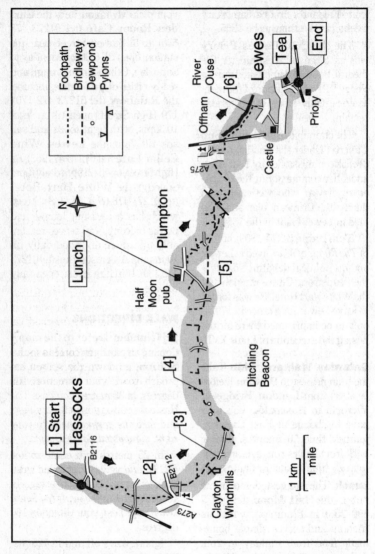

In 150 metres a pleasant detour (unless muddy underfoot) is to go through the unusual metal barrier to your left into the Woodland Trust's **Butcher's Wood** (marked on the OS map) and then to keep on, parallel to your previous route; in 250 metres, crossing over a stile to rejoin this route.

25 metres after rejoining the route, ignore a footpath to the left.

In a further 140 metres, go straight over a path crossroads (where to the right goes over the railway line).

[2] In a further 600 metres, you come *to the A273 where you go left,* your direction 185 degrees. In 25 metres cross over the B2112, and over the stile opposite, heading due south *to the* **Church of St John the Baptist, Clayton**, crossing over to it through a gap in the hedge on the far side of the clubhouse opposite the church.

After visiting the church, you *come out of its lychgate and turn right* on the tarmac road.

In 120 metres *turn right on a signposted public bridleway* through a gap (a wooden fieldgate to its right), your direction 185 degrees, on a car-wide way, uphill towards the windmills.

In 100 metres go though a wooden swing gate and *follow the bridleway sign* straight ahead on the uphill path.

You come to the first **Clayton Windmill** (its entrance is over to the right) and continue on up a bridleway path along the left-hand side of the windmill gardens, your direction 130 degrees.

Veer right with the path beyond the top windmill and cross over a farm track *to an earth road T-junction with a three-armed bridleway sign, where you go left*, your direction 115 degrees.

[3] *In 120 metres take the left fork*, your direction 115 degrees. In 15 metres go through a metal fieldgate. In 750 metres ignore a bridleway to the right and go straight on through a wooden swing gate. In a further 500 metres, at Keymer Post, go straight on, signposted Ditchling Beacon.

In 100 metres, just past a four-armed sign on the left pointing onwards to Eastbourne, go through a

wooden swing gate and continue straight on.

In a further 200 metres, go through another wooden swing gate, and past a **dew pond** on your left, then in 250 metres, another on your right.

[4] [*] 250 metres past this second dew pond, you see a stile 30 metres away to your left, which takes you down to Ditchling, should you wish to bail out of the walk.

The main suggested route, however, is straight on. In 65 metres you enter the **Sussex Trust Nature Reserve**. In 300 metres you come to a footpath post marked 'This is Ditchling Beacon'. Ignore the path going right and continue straight on. In a further 200 metres, you pass a triangulation point on your right-hand side (marked on the OS map).

In 150 metres you come to a stile leading down to a road, carpark, ice cream van and a notice about **Ditchling Beacon**.

Cross the road and go through the gate on the far side, following the sign for the South Downs Way, your direction 115 degrees, with a dew pond on your right-hand side.

In 400 metres ignore a bridleway down to the left, and, 50 metres beyond this, another bridleway to the left.

In 160 metres you may be able to see Brighton and the sea beyond it to your right.

In a further kilometre, ignore way to the left. In a further 250 metres, *cross a tarmac lane to go straight on.*

[5] *In a further 330 metres, fork left* (unless preferring to do without lunch, in which case carry straight on, rejoining the suggested walk at the double asterisk [**] below) on an unasphalted road heading downhill, your direction 75 degrees.

In 440 metres ignore a bridleway to the left and ignore all ways off.

In a further 370 metres, you come to the B2116 where you turn left for the suggested lunch stop, 40 metres away, the **Half Moon** pub in **Plumpton**.

Coming out of the pub after lunch, go left on the B2116. In 40 metres ignore the bridleway you came down on before lunch. In a further 50 metres, pick up the path parallel to the B2116, to its right.

In 70 metres you go over a stile and half right, on a clear path, your direction 140 degrees, heading towards the Downs.

In a further 220 metres, go over a stile. In 80 metres go over another, and into a wood.

In 20 metres you come to a larger path T-junction where you follow the path arrow right uphill, your direction 140 degrees.

In 65 metres fork left, away from the chalk cliff face.

In 150 metres, as you go up the edge of the wood on your right-hand side, do not take the opening with view to your left, but carry on up. In 150 metres ignore the footpath marked with a yellow arrow to your left.

In a further 170 metres, go through a metal fieldgate and on upwards. In 135 metres you cross a vehicle-wide chalk road to go on up, your direction 140 degrees, and continue on, even though the path may not be clear.

80 metres from the road, you come to a bridleway, [**] the South Downs Way again, where you go left, your direction 100 degrees.

In 130 metres you pass a triangulation point (marked on the OS map) on your left-hand side. In a further 60 metres, you take the left-hand fork, your direction 115 degrees (by the post with two blue arrows, and where the right-hand fork would take you towards a cluster of houses).

In 240 metres ignore a fork down to the left.

In 360 metres ignore a way to the left, and continue on, with a field fence nearby on your right-hand side.

In 240 metres follow a blue arrow straight on, slightly to the right. You can now see ahead of you the outskirts of Lewes.

Carry on downwards, your direction 130 degrees.

In 230 metres leave the National Trust land through a wooden swing gate and go straight on, your direction 120 degrees, towards the next post visible, 120 metres away. Once there, follow its blue arrow.

In 110 metres you come through the trees to the next post with a blue arrow and so continue on, in 30 metres passing under pylons.

In 20 metres follow the blue arrow on, your direction 155 degrees (in the direction of the cluster of buildings seen earlier).

In 95 metres ignore a path to the left (with a field fence to its left-hand side) and continue on, with a field fence nearby on your right-hand side.

Keep the edge of the wood on your left-hand side and ignore all ways off. In 220 metres go through a wooden swing gate **[!]** and follow the blue arrow left, still keeping the wood close on your left-hand side, your direction 120 degrees.

200 metres beyond the gate, ignore a blue arrow on a post pointing into the wood. Continue for a further 200 metres, keeping to the edge of the wood close on your left-hand side and then follow the blue arrow on the post down to your left, your direction 30 degrees, into the wood. Shortly you take the way that goes straight on beside the wood, your direction 80 degrees.

In 150 metres go through a wooden swing gate and onwards. In 50 metres ignore a footpath leading to a stile on your right-hand side, and, 60 metres further on, go through a wooden swing gate on your right-hand side to continue on a chalky car-wide road, your direction 35 degrees, with another such road running parallel to its right.

In a further 450 metres, you come *to the A275 where you go left*.

In 35 metres you pass what used to be the Old Post House Tearoom, **Offam**, on your right-hand side.

In 15 metres, by the request bus stop, *go right on The Drove road*. In a further 15 metres, you pass on your left-hand side the entrance to **St Peter's Church, Hamsey** (the church is kept locked). In a further 35 metres, *go to the right of the Old Post House carpark to pick up a path* going due south.

In 30 metres go under pylons. In 25 metres ignore a path to the left. In a further 320 metres, *go left over a*

stile (a wooden fieldgate to its left) and across a waterway, your direction 95 degrees, with a waterway on your right-hand side.

In 280 metres go over a stile (with a metal fieldgate to its left). In 20 metres go under a railway line.

In 15 metres go over a stile and in 15 metres over another stile, then *through two V-shaped stiles, to continue on, along the bank of the* **River Ouse** (the river on your left-hand side).

You can now see Lewes Castle ahead of you.

In 150 metres go through another V-shaped stile to continue on, along the riverside raised path. In a further 200 metres, you pass **Old Malling Farm** (marked on the OS map) on the other bank.

In a further 470 metres, you pass the seventeenth-century **St Michael's Church** (marked on the OS map) on the other bank.

In 120 metres go through a V-shaped stile.

In a further 230 metres, you do not take the footbridge to your left over the river (which would lead to Tesco's), but *go right with a wall on your left-hand side*, your direction due south.

In 80 metres you begin to pass a body of water on your right-hand side. And in a further 80 metres, you pass the entrance to Pells Open Air Pool and a children's park on your left-hand side. At the end of the park, *cross the tarmac road (Pelham Terrace) to continue on up*, your direction 195 degrees.

In 80 metres, keeping to the left, you pass the entrance to **St John Sub Castro Church**. *Go right on*

Abinger Place, towards the Elephant & Castle pub visible ahead.

In 100 metres, by this pub on your right-hand side, cross over the main road and *continue straight on up, along a tarmac lane* (Castle Banks), your direction 220 degrees, with scaffolding pole railings on your left-hand side.

In 80 metres you come to the top of this lane and, *at the T-junction, with the Maltings opposite, you turn right*, your direction 255 degrees. In 15 metres you pass a notice on your right-hand side about the Battle of Lewes. *Follow the tarmac lane going around to the left towards the castle*, your direction 195 degrees.

In 80 metres you pass the entrance to the former Castle Tilting Ground on your left-hand side. In 25 metres you pass through the **Barbican Gate** and then go past the entrance to **Lewes Castle** on your right-hand side and **Barbican House Museum** on your left.

10 metres beyond these, you come *to the High Street*. (Turning right here leads, in 110 metres, to Tom Paine's house and **Crackers** tearoom beyond it on the right-hand side.) The suggested route, however, is to *turn left*.

In 130 metres you come to the **Lewes Wine Cellar Café** and the **White Hart Hotel** on your right-hand side (with the **Rainbow** on the other side of the road, with

Ask restaurant just beyond it). *At the traffic lights, turn right* on Station Street. In 110 metres you come to the **Garden Room Café**, the suggested tea place, on the left-hand side. From there, straight on leads to **Lewes Station**, visible ahead (platform 2 for trains to London).

But if you have half an hour to spend before the train goes, you might care to visit **Lewes Priory**. Coming out of the tearoom, instead of going straight ahead to the station, turn right on Southover Road. Pass Garden Street going off to the left, and immediately go left into Grange Gardens and wander through these (parallel to Southover Road) to emerge again on to Southover Road at the far end.

Then turn left into Keere Street, passing The Grange on your left-hand side. Ignore Eastport Lane to your left, and at the T-junction, turn right, signposted Lewes Priory, soon passing St John's Church on your left-hand side.

Then turn left on Cockshut Road, go under the railway line, and turn left towards the priory ruins. Pass to their right-hand side and go through a gap in the wall on the right, to follow a wall on your left-hand side, passing a mound to your left. Then go left over the railway line and right to the station for trains to return to London.

Walk 30

Wivenhoe (round walk)

To Rowhedge by ferry across the River Colne

Length 14km (8.7 miles), 4 hours 15 minutes. For the whole outing, including trains, sights, meals and ferries, allow at least 9 hours 25 minutes.

OS Landranger Map No.168. Wivenhoe, map reference TM 036 217, is in **Essex**, 5km south-west of Colchester.

Toughness 1 out 10.

Features The full walk is only possible at weekends and on bank holiday Mondays between Easter and the end of October, when the ferry at Wivenhoe is working (although you might be lucky enough to thumb a lift across from a boat at other times). You also need to get there at a time to suit the tides (see Saturday Walkers' Club details below). But it is well worth making the extra effort to fit in this unusual walk. The first half of the walk is 7km, so allow over 2 hours for this.

Wivenhoe, perhaps because of its proximity to the University of Essex, is a remarkable village bursting with community spirit, with volunteers out there constantly, manning the ferry (although its long-term future is under threat), re-roofing the boat house or washing down the slipways. There are al-

ways half a dozen dinghies being made by amateurs in the riverside's Nottage Institute. From the church and town, the morning's walk is along the mudflats of the River Colne past zones of eerie dereliction where new housing is planned, past a £14.5 million flood surge barrier, and past sand-extracting works and lakes created in old extraction craters. Returning to Wivenhoe, catch the ferry over to the village of Row-hedge (the fare is about 50p per passenger – this is less than its upkeep cost, and the ferry relies on donations to keep going). Rowhedge must be the only village in the UK where swans frequently block the main high street. But having circumvented this fearsome obstacle, you go via the church into a wood controlled by the Ministry of Defence and used on occasion as a firing range. The last part of the return journey is, for me, the highlight of the day: passing the lovely Norman Church of St Ouen or St Andrew in Fingringhoe, with its chequerboard design of banded flint, to the disused Fingringhoe Mill and on along the John Brunning Walk – mudflats and saltmarshes beside Roman River, and a haven for heron, redshank, lapwing, sheldruck, kestrels and barn owls.

Shortening the walk Both in the morning and the afternoon, shorten the walk or retrace your steps as necessary to ensure that you do not miss the ferry. A short cut for the morning walk is given in the walk directions (see the asterisk **[*]** below). It is also possible to do just the first or just the second half of the walk. The printed ferry timetable (see below) also contains several suggested shorter walks. Buses from Head Street in Rowhedge leave for Colchester every 15 minutes or so.

History In the fifteenth century, the twelfth Earl of Oxford was **Lord of the Manor** at **Wivenhoe**. He and his comrade-in-arms Viscount Beaumont held out in the last castle to surrender to the Lancastrians. They were imprisoned for over a decade. Beaumont later went insane, was looked after by Oxford, and died. Oxford then married Beaumont's young wife Elizabeth. The fine brasses to Elizabeth and Beaumont lie in the chancel of the parish church.

In the 1750s, there was a **health spa** at Wivenhoe, with fashionable folk taking seawater baths at a fee of one guinea for the season.

An **earthquake** on April 22nd 1884 damaged over 200 buildings, with nearly two tons of brickwork crashing through the roof of Wivenhoe Hall.

In 1916 the army erected a **bridge** over the river, which King George V came to inspect, but it was demolished after the war.

The **Nottage Institute** (tel 01206 823 029) in Wivenhoe was founded in 1896 by Captain Charles Nottage to 'improve navigation skills'. It has information on the area's maritime heritage, and welcomes visitors from 11am to 4.30pm daily from late April until mid-September (or by arrangement at other times).

The **flood surge barrier** was completed in 1993, and is designed to resist the highest tide likely to be seen in a thousand years. Sluices ensure the tidal flow is unchanged except when the barrier is closed.

The north wall of the **Church of St Andrew** at Fingringhoe dates from 1100. The church originally belonged to a French priory in Mersey, and was dedicated to their St Ouen, who was Archbishop of Rouen. St Ouen has since been corrupted to St Andrew. Items hidden within the church at the time of the Reformation have recently been uncovered, including a Trinity crucifix.

Fingringhoe Mill closed in the early 1990s. It was a tidal mill in the sixteenth century, with a wheel underneath, but was converted to steam in the 1800s.

Saturday Walkers' Club The timing for this walk has to be rather complicated because of the need to fit in with the varying tides on the River Colne. To work out the right train to catch, phone the volunteers who run the **Wivenhoe Ferry Trust** (contact Doug Meyers on 01206 824836; Richard Allerton on 01206 824118) to find out the printed timetable times within which the tide allows the ferry to operate for the day you wish to go (for example, between 2.15pm and 6.15pm). Then catch the latest train from **Liverpool Street** Station to **Wivenhoe** that will **arrive at least *two hours* before the official printed timetable start of the ferry operating period** (in this example, by 12.15pm). However, if this would mean catching a train that leaves Liverpool Street before 8am, then catch the latest train that will get there at least *5 minutes* before the official printed timetable start of the ferry operating period (however early this may mean catching a train), and then catch the ferry straightaway on arrival, and do the second half of the walk (on the far side of the river) first, and do the first half later. The timetable is subject to change.

On the trip over, ask the ferry volunteers what times are possible for your return ferry trip from Rowhedge to Wivenhoe. If you miss the ferry back, you could catch a bus or a taxi into Colchester.

If the ferry is not offering a service at all on this particular Saturday, do the substitute Walk 53.

If you plan this walk well in advance, you could obtain a copy of the ferry timetable by sending £1 to: Wivenhoe Ferry Trust (to whom the cheque should be made payable), c/o Doug Meyers, The Nook, Wivenhoe CO7 9NH. The timetable may also be available from the Wivenhoe Bookshop by credit card (tel 01206 824 050).

The train journey takes about 1 hour 9 minutes.

Lunch If the ferry times allow, the suggested lunch place is **Ye Olde Albion** pub (tel 01206 728 972) at Rowhedge Quay, serving food midday to 2pm daily (not Monday and Tuesday in winter). The alternative is the **Anchor** pub (tel 01206 728 382) nearby, with food from midday to 2pm daily. If the tide dictates that you eat on the Wivenhoe side of the river, the suggested place is the **Rose & Crown** pub (tel 01206 826 371) on The Quay, serving food midday to 2pm daily.

Tea The suggested tea place has been the **Café** at 5 High Street, Wivenhoe, but this has new owners

so the position is unclear at present. It used to be open until at least 10.30pm daily (but closed Mondays). Or you can have tea and coffee at the **Station** pub (tel 01206 822 991) – and possibly sandwiches, if you phone to book; or a drink at the **Greyhound** pub (tel 01206 825 573) in the High Street (closed Sunday). In Rowhedge, the **Anchor** pub (tel 01206 728 382) might open at teatime for a group who book in.

WALK DIRECTIONS

[1] [Numbers refer to the map.] Coming off platform 2 at **Wivenhoe Station**, *do not go over the bridge but take the tarmac path* on its left-hand side, your direction 115 degrees. In 30 metres you pass the Station pub on the other side of the railway tracks. 35 metres further on, you go up steps to an earth car road, with King Georges Field opposite. Here you *turn right*, your direction 80 degrees, keeping straight on, ignoring ways off.

In 100 metres, at the High Street T-junction, with the Greyhound pub opposite, you *turn right downhill*. In 85 metres you pass the entrance to **St Mary's Church**. In a further 50 metres, bend right with the main road for 10 metres, to continue on down *to the banks of the* **River Colne**, *where you turn left*.

In 20 metres you pass the **Nottage Institute** on your left-hand side and, in a further 10 metres, the **Rose & Crown** pub.

Continue straight on, along the riverbank, in 50 metres going over a ramp with a crane. In a further 80 sign straight on through a semi-derelict zone (where 300 new houses will in due course be built).

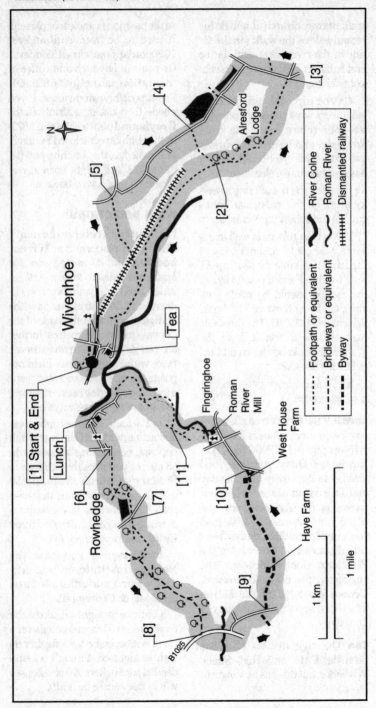

Wivenhoe

Alresford Lodge

[3]

[4]

[5]

[2]

Tea

[1] Start & End

Lunch

Rowhedge

[6]

[7]

[8]

B1025

Fingringhoe

Roman River Mill

West House Farm

[11]

[10]

Haye Farm

[9]

River Colne

Roman River

Dismantled railway

.... Footpath or equivalent

– – – Bridleway or equivalent

▬ ▬ ▬ Byway

1 km

1 mile

In 40 metres you *pass a huge corrugated shed on your right-hand side, coming to a tarmac road T-junction where you go right*, your direction 160 degrees.

In 80 metres you come to a control tower for the flood surge barrier. In 30 metres you are back on the riverbank. In 25 metres you pass the Wivenhoe Sailing Club on your left-hand side. A dismantled railway line runs parallel on your left-hand side. You walk on the newly surfaced sea wall path, in 50 metres going through a wooden swing barrier. In a further 150 metres, you pass the sand extraction workings on the other bank.

280 metres past these workings, you go over a stile and continue on the sea wall path. In 280 metres you pass a bench on your left-hand side. In 270 metres, just as your path is entering the trees, ignore a wooden kissing gate to the left [2]. (If you want a short cut back to town, take this path and in 400 metres you come to a lane T-junction where you go left – see the asterisk [*] below – rejoining the main suggested walk.)

Ignore ways off and in 330 metres you cross a path and continue onwards. In 140 metres, *fork right on a path (between 8"-wide lichen-covered concrete gateposts), your direction 210 degrees, back down close to the riverbank.*

200 metres further on, keep near the riverbank until you rejoin your previous path, between hedges.

In 40 metres you pass a single wide concrete post on your right-hand side. In a further 200 metres, *with the red-brick* **Alresford Lodge** (marked on the OS map) *on your left-hand side, at 50 degrees from*

you, *fork left through concrete posts*, your direction 120 degrees, to continue with a fence and field on your left-hand side. In 125 metres ignore a grassy way to your left. In a further 240 metres, you pass a surreal derelict pier on your right-hand side.

In 100 metres [3] *turn left on an earth car road*, your direction 50 degrees. Go straight on, ignoring ways off. In 170 metres you pass sand extraction works to your left-hand side, and a giant sand extraction crater to your right.

Take the signposted public bridleway left, by a house called Broomlands, your direction 295 degrees. In 80 metres go under a red-and-white archway to continue on a concrete road, with a lake away to your right-hand side. In a further 230 metres, *5 metres before a pedestrians sign, fork left*, avoiding Alresford Lodge Road, to go parallel to the quarry road, going through a metal fieldgate in 25 metres.

In 190 metres, where your road begins to have hedges on both sides, fork left to continue in the same direction, now with the hedges on your right-hand side. In 150 metres [4] *ignore a yellow arrow to the left.* [*] *Rejoin the tarmac lane* and continue on towards town, your direction 335 degrees.

In 400 metres you go through a metal fieldgate. There is a pink house to its left-hand side.

In 200 metres ignore a private road to the left. In a further 270 metres, you *come out on to a main road where you go left*, your direction 305 degrees.

In 110 metres [5], opposite the driveway of a house called The

Chase, *go left on a signposted foot-path* over a stile, your direction 260 degrees. In 280 metres go over another stile and onwards. In 220 metres go over the disused railway line and on towards the riverbank.

In 270 metres you are on the sea wall path and you need to retrace your steps into town, to the Rose & Crown pub. The ferry is 25 metres beyond the pub.

Take the ferry to Rowhedge. Turn left in Rowhedge High Street, to **Ye Olde Albion** pub, which is the suggested lunch place.

After lunch, *turn left out of the pub.* Opposite the **Anchor** pub on your right-hand side, *turn left uphill on Church Street.* In 120 metres you come *into the churchyard* of the **Church of St Lawrence**.

In 45 metres you pass the church on your left-hand side and in 15 metres you *go on out of the church gates on the other side, to continue on, along Church Hill,* your direction 265 degrees. In 50 metres, at a road crossing, *with house no.17 on your left-hand side, go left,* due south.

In 70 metres you come *to a T-junction* [6] *where you go right,* your direction 265 degrees. In 50 metres you go through a metal swing gate on a signposted public footpath, straight on, with a sports field and a line of trees ('each a living memorial to those in the village who died in the war') on your right.

In 200 metres go through a metal barrier into the wood and onwards, ignoring ways off.

In 100 metres, at the start of a wooden fence and houses to your right-hand side, ignore the narrow path down to the left. Then in 50 metres, fork left, 230 degrees.

In 65 metres you come *to a concrete road, with a public footpath signposted right, but you go straight across,* your direction 230 degrees. In 12 metres you pass between two concrete bollards. In a further 65 metres, *fork right (where going left would lead to a burial ground in 35 metres),* your direction 260 degrees. There is a large and rather lovely lake down off to your right-hand side.

In 150 metres *you come to a tarmac road* [7], *which you cross,* into Ministry of Defence land. You nevertheless continue on, following the public footpath sign, your direction 295 degrees.

In 80 metres ignore a fork to the right and keep on the main path, your direction 240 degrees.

In 220 metres *you come to a path crossing where you go straight on, along a more minor path,* marked by a (possibly overgrown) post with yellow paint on top, your direction 260 degrees.

In 60 metres you *ignore the way your path seems to be going right, to carry straight on. Fork right with your main path 35 metres later,* your direction 325 degrees. Keeping straight on, in 50 metres *you come to a car-wide earth road, marked by a yellow post.* Ignore another yellow post 40 metres ahead and *go left* on this road, your direction 265 degrees.

In 30 metres you cross a car-wide road to continue more or less straight on (slightly to your left), your direction 230 degrees and with a fence on your left-hand side.

Ignore all ways off to stay on the main way. In 115 metres ignore a car-wide fork left, to keep straight on. In a further 400 metres, ignore a grassy car-wide fork left to keep on your main road. In 145 metres you cross a path (by a sign warning of the Military Firing Range) to keep on the road. In 200 metres you pass a heavy metal fieldgate, out *on to a lay-by of the B1025* **[8]**, *where you go left*.

In 220 metres cross over **Roman River** to go immediately *left on Haye Lane*, signposted Nature Reserve, your direction 120 degrees.

In 400 metres, towards the top of the hill, **[9]** you need to *go left on a car lane*, to go past the timber-framed Haye Cottage on the right-hand side, sign-posted Byway, your direction 80 degrees.

In 320 metres you pass **Haye Farmhouse** on your left-hand side; and, in 750 metres, **West House Farm** (both marked on the OS map).

In 80 metres *fork left*, your direction 75 degrees, coming *to the main road* **[10]** *in 35 metres, where you go left*, your direction 45 degrees.

In 25 metres you pick up a gravel path parallel to (and to the right of) the road, to continue on.

In 150 metres you rejoin the main road to go onwards. In 120 metres you pass the **Whalebone** pub on your left-hand side, to keep straight on to the **Church of St Andrew/ St Ouen**, Fingringhoe.

In 100 metres *take the public footpath signposted to your left*, your direction 350 degrees, down the private drive to Mill House. In 125 metres you walk down the right-hand side of **Roman River Mill**, on the concrete road. At the end of its garden, on the right-hand side, go over (the remains of) a stile by the power cable warning sign, to go

left downwards on to the **John Brunning Walk**, your direction 10 degrees.

In 60 metres go over a wooden footbridge with two handrails, by Roman River. In a further 110 metres, ignore the stile to the left, to *keep right on the John Brunning Walk, following its arrows and keeping beside the river.*

Ignore ways off. In 300 metres go on four planks over a side stream. In 130 metres ignore a fork to the left. In 70 metres fork right **[11]**, by a plank bridge to the left and (with a sign ahead saying 'Danger. Proceed with caution'). Keep beside the river, your direction 70 degrees, with dock sheds on your left-hand side. You pass a bench and concrete seats.

In 380 metres you are back beside the River Colne, and your right of way is straight along the riverbank, the docks to the left (and the University of Essex high-rise blocks visible on the far horizon to your right). Keep close to the river and, in 160 metres you see a half-hidden *public footpath sign on your right*, behind a raised metal water tank. Go down three steps and continue on, with the river immediately on your right-hand side, your direction 280 degrees.

In 85 metres, by the entrance to Northern Wood Terminals Ltd, go right on their driveway, your direction 335 degrees, and carry on to the ferry in Rowhedge. *Take this ferry back to Wivenhoe.*

At the quay in Wivenhoe, *turn left along the quay and, in 5 metres (by Anchor House) turn right on (unmarked) Anchor Hill*, your direction 30 degrees. In 50 metres you come to **Streets Café** at 5 High Street, the suggested place for tea, on your left-hand side, on the corner with West Street. *Turn* *left on West Street*. In 225 metres you come to **Wivenhoe Station**, with the **Station** pub on your right-hand side.

Walk 31

Glynde to Seaford

Alfriston & the Seven Sisters

Length 23km (14.5 miles), 7 hours. For the whole outing, including trains, sights and meals, allow at least 12 hours.

OS Landranger Map Nos.198 & 199. Glynde, map reference TQ 457 087, is in **East Sussex**, 12km east of Brighton.

Toughness 8 out of 10.

Features Near the start, the route goes through Firle Park and then follows the South Downs Way for much of the day, with not as much climbing as Walk 25's arduous route into Hastings, and with marvellous views across the lush valleys to the north, and down to the sea. There are three lovely villages to enjoy during the course of the day, all with open churches: West Firle; West Dean; and (the suggested lunchstop) the old smuggling village of Alfriston, which likes to call its church a cathedral. There is slightly further to walk after lunch than before lunch. From Alfriston the route follows the riverbank through the Cuckmere Valley and through Friston Forest down to Exceat, an extinct village on the edge of the Seven Sisters Country Park, where there is a relatively interesting small animals exhibition to wander around (fluorescent scor-

pions etc), either before or after tea. The Vanguard Way then leads through the Seaford Head Nature Reserve – hoopoe, bluethroat and wryneck have been seen here – to the beach at Cuckmere Haven. This is a marginally good enough place to take a dip or just to enjoy a front-stalls view of the white cliffs of the Seven Sisters (couldn't they be re-named after seven famous English women?). Finally there is a walk along the coastal path and down into Seaford, a rather grim seaside town whose main pride and joy is its esplanade carparks, but which has been much improved by importing £8 million worth of beach from the Isle of Wight.

Shortening the walk There are occasional buses into Lewes from Alfriston, or you could get a taxi to Lewes Station – there are several firms in Alfriston and the fare is quite cheap. The best bet are the frequent buses from outside the suggested early tea place in Exceat – twice an hour to Eastbourne or twice an hour the other way to Seaford (the frequency is halved on Sundays).

History Firle Place was the seat of Sir John Gage, who helped Henry VIII with the dissolution of the monasteries, despite retaining the old religion himself. The house and its park are still inhabited by his descendants, although from the walk route you can only see Firle Tower, a watchkeeper's residence.

The **Church of St Peter**, Firle, contains an alabaster effigy of Sir John Gage wearing his Order of the Garter and lying beside his wife Philippa. It also has a John Piper stained-glass window in warm colours, depicting Blake's Tree of Life.

Alfriston was once a Saxon settlement. In 1405, Henry IV granted the town the right to a marker, hence the old market square cross (though now without its crosspiece) which was supposed to help ensure honest and fair trading. (There is an interesting free exhibition about the village in the upper storey of Candy Cottage by the market square.) The narrow streets are lined with fourteenth and fifteenth-century houses. In the early 1800s smugglers would run contraband via Alfriston and Cuckmere Haven, with farmers driving their sheep to help cover the smugglers' tracks.

The **Parish Church of St Andrew**, Alfriston – known as the 'Cathedral of the South Downs' – was built about 1360, all at one time and with no later additions. But because there were no local squires and manors, the church is rather bare inside, with few memorials. It has a basin and ewer on the Sepulchre at the north side of the chancel that came from the Holy Land.

The **Alfriston Clergy House** (tel 01323 870 001) was the first building to be acquired by the National Trust, in 1896, for £10 (which makes the £2.60 entrance fee seem rather steep). A Wealden hall house with thatched roof, it contains a medieval hall and has a cottage garden with some rare specimens. It is open from the beginning of April to the end of October until 5pm (closed Tuesday and Friday) and from March 3rd at weekends until 4pm.

West Dean Church has probable Saxon elements, and next door to it is a medieval parsonage with a colourful garden. The parish priest from 1891 was the Revd George Lawrance, who believed in captive audiences – it is said that he used to lock the church door before delivering his sermons.

The chalky cliffs of the **Seven Sisters** developed under the sea, 70 to 100 million years ago – the chalk is mainly made up of microscopic fossils. Later the chalk cliffs dipped beneath the sea again and came up covered in silt and sand, still visible as the top layer. There are also layers of flint – flint being a supercooled liquid leached out of chalk to form globules.

The **Martello Tower**, on the front at Seaford, is the most westerly of a chain of 103 similar fortifications running from Aldeburgh on the east coast. It was built in 1806 against a threatened Napoleonic invasion and now houses the Seaford Museum of Local History.

Saturday Walkers' Club Take the train nearest to **8.45am** (before or after) from **Victoria** Station to **Glynde**. From Monday to Saturday, you will have to change at Lewes, but on Sunday there is a direct service. Journey time 1 hour 17 minutes. Trains back from Seaford run about once an hour, and return to Victoria (changing at Lewes). Journey time 1 hour 29 minutes.

Lunch The suggested lunch place in Alfriston is the **George Inn** (tel 01323 870 319), built about 1397, with a treacherously low-beamed ceiling. It serves lunch midday to 2.30pm daily; groups of ten or more should phone the day before. It has a garden, an amiable host, cheap main dishes and expensive desserts. A viable alternative is the **Wingrove Arms** (tel 01323 870

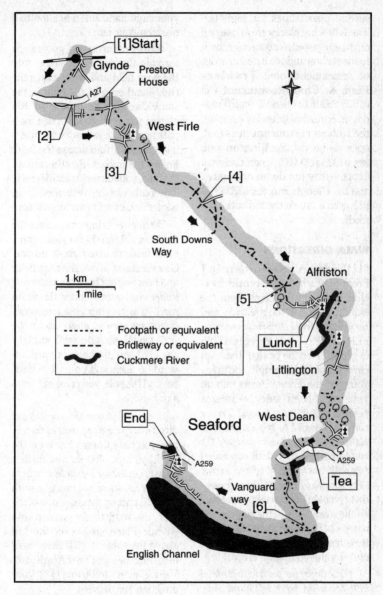

[1] Start

Glynde

Preston House

West Firle

[2]

A27

[3]

[4]

South Downs Way

Alfriston

1 km
1 mile

[5]

Lunch

Litlington

---- Footpath or equivalent
--- Bridleway or equivalent
~~ Cuckmere River

West Dean

Tea

End

Seaford

A259

Vanguard way

A259

[6]

English Channel

N

276), 100 metres down the street towards the sea. It has a garden, and serves food midday to 2pm (Sundays 3pm).

Tea The suggested tea place is the **Exceat Farmhouse** (tel 01323 870 218), set well back from the A259 at Exceat. It offers cream teas and other food and drink until 6pm weekends, 5pm during the week (4pm in winter). It also offers bed and breakfast. Once you reach Seaford, there are several possibilities for high tea. The following places are all passed on the suggested route through town to the station and are listed in order of recommendation: **Trawlers Fish & Chip Restaurant** (tel 01323 892 520) open till 9pm Tuesday to Saturday (Monday 8.45pm); the **Indian restaurant** next to it, open daily; the **Wellington** pub (tel 01323 890 032), open daily till 11pm – they can do tea and coffee; and the **Plough Inn** (tel 01323 872 921) which can do tea and coffee (no food).

WALK DIRECTIONS

[1] [Numbers refer to the map.] From platform 2 of **Glynde Station**, walk up the steps from the station, out on to the roadside, and *turn right across the bridge* over the railway line, your direction 165 degrees. Over the bridge, the road curves around to the right and takes you past the Trevor Arms pub on your right-hand side. 50 metres beyond that, **[!]** *just beyond Trevor Gardens (nos.11 to 16, also on your right-hand side), turn right off the road*, marked by a half-concealed footpath post with a yellow arrow ('Beddingham 1 mile'). [In wet weather, it could be as well to continue on the road to rejoin the route at the asterisk **[*]** below, as the footpaths here tend to be badly maintained and smothered in high crops.]

Walk down the path with a metal link fence on your left-hand side, your direction 260 degrees. In 15 metres you come into a garden where you walk straight ahead along the grass. In another 20 metres you cross a driveway. Over the other side, keep straight on, with a hedge on

your right-hand side and a football pitch on your left.

50 metres further on, go straight through the gap in the hedge into the next field and walk along the right-hand edge of the field in the same direction as before. In 150 metres you come to a wooden footpath post with a yellow arrow pointing straight ahead across the field. Follow the arrow to the other side of the field, your direction 225 degrees. The path can be very muddy in winter and overgrown in summer.

500 metres brings you across the field to a stile on the far side, with a metal fieldgate to its right-hand side. Go over the stile into the next field, and *turn half left towards a concrete underpass*, going under the main road. 70 metres brings you to a concrete passageway going under the A27. On the far side, walk straight ahead through the farmyard towards a telegraph pole. 30 metres beyond the pole, you come out on to a minor road.

Turn left down the road, your direction 75 degrees, and in 60 metres you pass Comps Farm on the left-hand side. 450 metres further on, you come *to a T-junction* (where on your left there is a junction with the A27, and, on the other side of the A27, the road to the station and Glynde Place visible on the hill above the station). **[2]** *Turn right* following the sign ('No through road. Vehicle access to Downs') **[*]**, your direction 195 degrees.

In 300 metres you *turn left down the driveway*, signposted Preston Court, going due east. Keep straight on down the road for 190 metres, then leave the concrete road that bears right, to continue on, slightly to the left, to painted metal field-gates next to each other, and, just to the right of these gates, cross the stile. *Once over the stile, turn three-quarters right into the field*, heading towards a metal fieldgate 200 metres away on the far side, your direction still due east. You go through this gate to walk along the right-hand edge of the field. At the top of the field, go through the small wooden footgate, and straight ahead upwards through the field, your direction 75 degrees initially.

In 150 metres the path, now car-wide, skirts some trees shielding a barn on your left-hand side. Follow the path as it bends around to the left, in 50 metres passing a defunct stile on your right-hand side. 35 metres further on, *turn right on to the concrete car-wide track*.

In 190 metres you pass the entrance to **Preston House** (marked on the OS map) on your left-hand side. Continue along the track for another 100 metres, until you come to the road at a junction, with a road going off to left and right, and two roads ahead (one going half left, the other half right).

Cross the road and take the option going half right, following the footpath yellow arrow. 50 metres takes you through a white wooden gateway into **Firle Park**, with the driveway for **Firle Place** disappearing into the distance ahead of you. Immediately through the gate, *turn right off the road*, following a hedge on your right-hand side, your direction due south. Off to your left, you can see **Firle Tower** on the distant hilltop.

In 100 metres take the stile straight ahead. Once over the stile,

head half left towards the left of the tennis court (and to the left of the church) – in summer you may not be able to see these until you get closer – your direction 145 degrees. 280 metres brings you through a small copse of newly planted trees to a stile, directly to the left of the tennis court.

Once over the stile, go half right to go down a car-wide track between seven-foot-high walls. In 100 metres you come out to the roadside with the **Ram Inn** on your right-hand side. Turn left here along the tarmac road into **West Firle** village, heading due south.

In 110 metres you pass Firle Stores and Post Office on your left-hand side and bear right with the road. 25 metres further on, *turn left off the road up the passageway* leading to the **Church of St Peter, Firle** (the entrance is on the right).

Coming out of the church, go straight ahead to exit the church-yard and *turn right down the car-wide track*, your direction 295 degrees. 65 metres brings you down *to a T-junction*, with the road through the village going off to the right, and a private road going off to the left, with a notice ('Bridleway. No motor vehicles'). *Turn left* into the private road.

In 85 metres you come to the end of the brick farm buildings on your left-hand side. Keep straight on, ignoring ways off until in 150 metres, at a fork in the paths, **[3]** you *fork to the left,* following a red arrow on a wooden post. Follow the track, and in 150 metres you have a stone wall on your left. On your right-hand side you may see hang-gliders floating off from the South Downs.

In 350 metres there is a stone gateway with a wooden gate going off to the left. Ignore the path to the right going off through the trees, and walk the extra 15 metres up to the wooden post on the right-hand side of the track, with a blue arrow pointing to the right. *Go right down this car-wide track*, following the line of the trees on your right-hand side towards the ridge ahead, your direction due south. Firle Tower is now much closer, behind and to your left-hand side.

Ignore ways off and, 550 metres up this track, you go through the wooden gate to the right of a metal fieldgate, and walk straight up the hill ahead of you. 90 metres up the hill, *you follow the slightly wider path as it forks off to the left*, taking a less arduous route up towards the top of the ridge, your direction 170 degrees initially.

Follow the path for 400 metres as it leads you up towards the top of the ridge. Make for the fence that runs along the ridge top. On a clear day, you can see the sea with Newhaven prominent at 220 degrees on the compass, and Seaford just visible at 190 degrees.

Turn left and walk along the ridge top, with the fence on your right-hand side, going east. You will now follow the South Downs Way for the next 5.5km, all the way into Alfriston, where you stop for lunch.

As long as the acorn national trail signs have not been vandalised, you may not need further directions until lunchtime. But here are more details in case you do need them: Go uphill for 400 metres, until you come to a wooden gate which takes you through a barbed-wire fence. On the other side, continue along the path along the ridge top. Another 300 metres brings you to the high point of **Firle Beacon**, where there is an Ordnance Survey triangulation point. This, at 217 metres, is the highest point you reach on the walk.

Continue straight on for 1km and then go through a wooden gate (with a metal fieldgate to its right-hand side). In 50 metres go through another similar gate and straight on, parallel to the tarmac road and carpark on your left-hand side. [4] At the end of the carpark, go through another wooden gate (with a metal fieldgate to its left-hand side) and carry straight on, along a car-wide flinty track.

In 1km ignore a wooden post with a yellow arrow pointing off to the left to Alciston, and all blue arrows, to continue straight ahead over the brow of the hill.

350 metres further on, the path takes you through a wooden kissing gate. Follow the fence on your left, your direction 110 degrees.

In less than 1km the path starts to wend its way downhill – you can see the village of Alfriston nestled in the valley down to your left.

[5] In another 350 metres, you come to a crossroads and follow the direction of the wooden footpath sign marked 'South Downs Way', straight ahead through the bushes. In another 40 metres your way joins a car-wide track and you continue in the same direction as before.

Keep on this road, ignoring ways off, and in less than 1km you come down into a residential street called Kings Ride, and keep straight on down the hill to a crossroads.

Go straight over, with Alfriston Motors on your left-hand side, and walk the 100 metres down to the T-junction. Directly opposite, you will see the **George Inn**, **Alfriston**, which is the main suggested lunchtime stop.

After lunch, *come out of the George Inn and, for a short detour, turn right* down the street to the Market Square and the Candy Cottage exhibition on your right-hand side, above the fudge shop.

Retrace your steps towards the George Inn and continue beyond it.

70 metres beyond the pub, take an alleyway left, with a sign pointing down it to the church ('The Cathedral of the South Downs'). *Turn left down the passageway* and in 35 metres you come out opposite the United Reformed Church Memorial Hall. To the right, across an open space, you can see the **Parish Church of St Andrew**, and beyond that – to the right – the **Alfriston Clergy House**, both of which are worth visiting.

To continue from the gate in front of St Andrew's church, *head half right across the lawn towards the wooden fence on the far side,* where there is a gap in between two small beech trees, your direction 15 degrees. 65 metres takes you through the gap in the fence, next to a sign ('Alfriston Parish Council – Please do not let your dog foul on this green'). 20 metres up the path ahead, *turn right to cross the* **Cuckmere River**. On the far side of the bridge, turn right through the kissing gate by the wooden footpath sign, marked 'South Downs Way'. There is a sign on the gate ('Private land. Access along riverbank only').

You are now going to *follow the South Downs Way for a further 5km, until the suggested tea place.* But in more detail: In 230 metres go through another kissing gate and continue along the raised path with the river on your right-hand side.

In about 1km go through a pair of kissing gates and continue along the riverbank.

450 metres further on, the path follows the river around a sharp left-hand bend, towards the village of Litlington. In 160 metres the path leads through another kissing gate and, on the far side, you continue straight on along the riverbank.

140 metres further on, you come out to a T-junction. **[!]** Ignore the path that heads off right over a bridge across the river. Instead, you turn left, following the South Downs Way sign, which leads through a line of trees into the village of **Litlington**, your direction 120 degrees.

In 130 metres the path leads you out through an alleyway on to the roadside, opposite Holly Tree House. Turn right, in 20 metres passing the **Plough & Harrow** pub on your right-hand side. 80 metres further on, turn left on a road, going up the hill by the side of a house named Thatch Cottage. In 25 metres turn right off the road and head for West Dean, following the South Downs Way sign. 5 metres up the path, go through a kissing gate and straight up the path ahead, in 50 metres coming out into an open field. Go up the hill towards the top left-hand corner of the field, your direction 170 degrees, and go through a wooden kissing gate.

Go straight on, following the line of the telegraph poles, and continue to follow them after crossing the next two stiles, in 260 metres. The hedge is on your right-hand side.

Ignoring ways off, in 650 metres you come to the bottom of the hill and a T-junction. Turn left on to this path, your direction 145 degrees. Ignoring ways off, in 110 metres you come to a wooden footpath post. Ignore a blue arrow pointing along the continuation of the path off to the left. Instead, follow the yellow arrows pointing to the right up some steps going up the hill. At the top of the steps you come to a crossing of the ways and you follow the yellow footpath arrow pointing straight ahead to West Dean.

Ignoring ways off (car-wide paths right and left), in 400 metres the path forks, you take the left-hand fork, which is signposted to West Dean, which goes quickly into trees.

Ignore ways off. In 450 metres you come to a T-junction where you turn right down the hill, your direction 230 degrees, following the footpath post opposite, marked 'South Downs Way'. 65 metres down the hill, continue straight on towards a wooden fieldgate. 45 metres brings you down past the wooden fieldgate and you carry straight on down the hill. 15 metres further on you come out on to the concrete driveway leading into The Glebe on your right. Turn left down the drive, and another 45 metres brings you to a tarmac country lane. Turn left for a 100-metre detour to the fine **West Dean Church and Parsonage**.

Coming out of the churchyard, turn right to go back along the road and continue down the hill. Another 80 metres brings you down to a junction by the side of Forge Cottage on your right-hand side.

Go straight over the road, past the green Forestry Commission sign welcoming you to **Friston Forest**, and past the green phonebox on your left-hand side. Go straight ahead up the steps of the hill in front of you. At the top of the steps, proceed straight on along the path for another 70 metres, up to a stone wall, where you have a marvellous view down over the estuary of the Cuckmere as it meanders its final way down to the sea.

Go over the wall just to the right, by a noticeboard about the **Cuckmere River Meander**, and over the wooden gate leading out into the field. Go straight down the hill towards the river, your direction 245 degrees. 150 metres brings you down to the wooden fieldgate at the bottom, through the kissing gate, and down on to the A259.

On your right-hand side, set back, you come to the suggested tea place, the **Exceat Farmhouse**.

Coming out after tea on to the A259, cross over the road to the bus stop (where buses to Seaford stop) and turn right along the A259, keeping to this main road.

In 500 metres the road comes to Exceat Bridge crossing the Cuckmere River (with a sign 20 metres before it warning you to watch out for badgers!). Walk across the bridge, with the **Golden Galleon** pub directly ahead of you on the far side. *Immediately over the bridge, turn left through the pub carpark.* Walk the 90 metres across the carpark parallel to the river. On the far side there is a stile next to a metal fieldgate ('Footpath leading to Seaford 3 miles'). Go over the stile and along the path between the hedges.

In 270 metres you come to a crossing of paths where there is a signpost announcing the **Seaford Head Nature Reserve**. Continue straight ahead, past the defunct stile on your left, your direction 195 degrees initially.

Ignoring ways off, follow the path for 750 metres to cross over the stile (with a wooden fieldgate on its left-hand side), and continue along the path on the other side in the same direction as before.

After 800 metres, the path appears to fork, where you can see some cottages on the hillside ahead. Continue to follow the left-hand fork along the edge of the fence to your left.

Ignoring ways off, another 200 metres brings you down on to **Cuckmere Haven beach**, where you can have a dip if you are in the mood. There is also a good view to your left of the shoreline of the white cliffs of the **Seven Sisters**, with – at their far end – the lighthouse on the top of Belle Tout.

At this point **[6]** turn right, going uphill behind the cottages which line the seashore, your direction 260 degrees initially. In 150 metres the car-wide track takes you over a cattle grid.

Turn left towards a wooden bench you can just see ahead, and you are now on the edge of the coastal cliff, and you follow the edge of the coastline all the way to Seaford, taking the main path nearest to the cliffs whenever alternatives offer themselves. After 2km following the coast, the path takes

you along the edge of a golfcourse, and soon starts to make its way down the hill towards the town of Seaford. When you get to the brow of the hill looking down into Seaford, again follow the leftmost paths all the way down to the beach.

When you get to the bottom of the hill, walk along the promenade beside the beach with **Seaford** town on your right-hand side. 400 metres along the seafront, you come to the **Martello Tower**, which is the Seaford Museum of Local History. Carry on past the Martello Tower along the esplanade.

In 350 metres, by the new shelter pavilion on the esplanade, *turn right down The Causeway*, heading away from the seafront, your direction 30 degrees. As you walk down this road, you can see the tower of the parish church ahead.

At the bottom of the road is a mini-roundabout, with the **Wellington** pub ahead and, to the left of the pub, a building with white pillars all along its front supporting a wooden balcony. Cross over the road and *go left along the front of this building, and then right into Church Street*.

50 metres up this street, you come *to a T-junction* where you *turn left, going up the hill*, passing the church. Along Church Street you also pass the **Old Plough** pub, **La Mer** restaurant, the **Indian restaurant** and **Trawlers Fish & Chip Restaurant**.

You come to a junction with the A259, a mini-roundabout, with Sutton Park Road to the right and Station Approach Road to the left. *Turn left* for **Seaford Station**, immediately on your left-hand side.

Walk 32

Arundel to Amberley

Arundel Park, River Arun & Burpham

Length 18.8km (11.7 miles), 5 hours 40 minutes. For the whole outing, including trains, sights and meals, allow at least 10 hours 30 minutes.

OS Landranger Map No.197. Arundel, map reference TQ 024 063, is in **West Sussex**, 4km north of Littlehampton.

Toughness 7 out 10.

Features This South Downs walk requires a relatively early start from London if you want to be in time for food at the lunchtime pub – unless you are a fast walker who tends not to dilly-dally visiting churches and other sites en route. Beware that the distance to the suggested lunch stop in Burpham is 9.7km (6 miles), 3 hours. There are several stretches that are steep (with excellent views in compensation); a half-kilometre of the route above Amberley can be very muddy, when churned up by cows; and the marshy Wild Brook meadows beyond Amberley are subject to flooding. The walk starts and ends along the River Arun. It goes up Arundel's old High Street, lined with ancient buildings, to the Duke of Norfolk's castle. The Norfolk family have been Catholic for centuries, hence you pass the only church in the UK that is part-Catholic and part-Protestant (the Catholic part is

their chapel, separated off by an iron grille) and you pass the Catholic cathedral. Entering their 1,240-acre Arundel Park (the park is closed on March 24th each year, but the public footpaths should remain open on that day), you come to the Hiorne Tower, and from there descend steeply to Swanbourne Lake, skirting the edges of the woodlands, and exiting the park through a gap in the wall, to walk along the River Arun again. This leads to the isolated hamlet of South Stoke, with its unusual church, and from there to the church and inn at Burpham. The afternoon's walk, over the chalk downs into Amberley, is short in comparison. Amberley is a lovely, delightful village with many thatched houses, a pub, a village store (closed Wednesday, Saturday and Sunday afternoon), a pottery, a church and a castle. Next to the station is the Chalk Pit Industrial Museum.

Shortening the walk On exiting Arundel Park, you could turn left instead of right along the river (see the asterisk [*] below) to reach Amberley Station in 2km, or to have lunch at the pub in Houghton if desired, and then tea in Amberley. Or you could cross the bridge at South Stoke and take the footpath left instead of right (see the double asterisk [**] below; this is a more complicated short cut and an OS map would be helpful), reaching Amberley Station via North Stoke. Or, on the descent into Amberley, you could stay on the South Downs Way to the station (see the triple asterisk [***] below) without visiting the town. Or you could order a taxi from the lunchtime pub in

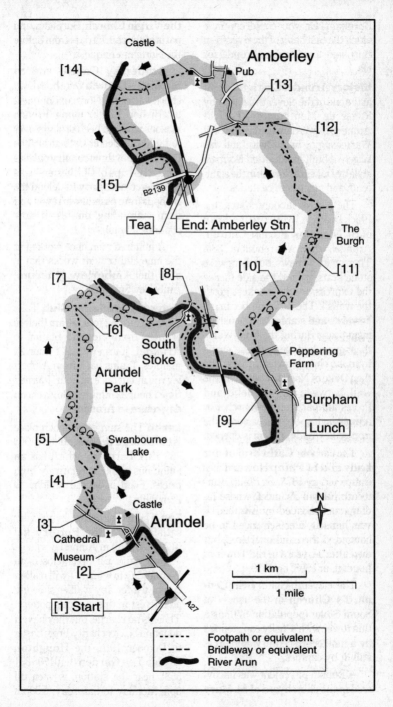

Castle

Amberley

[14]

Pub

[13]

[12]

[15]

B2139

Tea

End: Amberley Stn

The Burgh

[7]

[8]

[10]

[11]

[6]

South
Stoke

Peppering
Farm

Arundel
Park

[9]

Burpham

Lunch

[5]

Swanbourne
Lake

[4]

[3]

Castle

Arundel

Cathedral

Museum

[2]

1 km

[1] Start

A27

1 mile

N

----- Footpath or equivalent
- - - Bridleway or equivalent
━━━ River Arun

Burpham. Or you could continue along the east bank of the river from Burpham, to go back to Arundel for tea.

History Arundel Castle was built at the end of the eleventh century by Roger de Montgomery, Earl of Arundel. It was damaged in the Civil War (changing hands twice) and was largely rebuilt in 'idealised Norman' style by Dukes of Norfolk in the eighteenth and nineteenth centuries.

The lack of labourers after the Black Death in 1349 led to the decay of **St Nicholas Parish Church**, Arundel, which was rebuilt in 1380. There were no pews, but there were stone seats around the side (hence the expression 'the weakest go to the walls'). The building became a barracks and stables for the parliamentarians during the Civil War – their guns laid siege to the castle from the church tower. In 1969, the then Duke of Norfolk opened up the wall between the Catholic and Protestant parts of the church. For ecumenical special occasions, the iron grille dividing them is opened.

The Catholic **Cathedral of our Lady and St Philip Howard** was completed in 1873. St Philip, thirteenth Earl of Arundel, whose father was beheaded by Elizabeth I, was himself later sentenced to be hanged, drawn and quartered, but died after 11 years in the Tower of London, in 1595, aged 39.

The eleventh-century **St Leonard's Church** in the hamlet of South Stoke (population 57) has a thin tower with a 'frilly cap', topped by a nineteenth-century spire. It is still lit by candles.

A Roman pavement was uncovered in the churchyard of **St Mary the Virgin Church**, Burpham, and parts of the church date from before the Norman Conquest.

Amberley Castle and **St Michael's Church** were both built shortly after the Norman Conquest by Bishop Luffa, using French masons who had been brought over to build Chichester Cathedral. The castle – one of three country palaces for the Bishops of Chichester – was considered necessary to defend the Bishops from peasants in revolt and from marauding pirates (it now contains a hotel).

A hundred men once worked at the lime and cement works that is now the **Amberley Museum**, Amberley Station.

Saturday Walkers' Club Take the train nearest to **9.00am** (before or after) from **Victoria** Station to **Arundel**. Journey time 1 hour 24 minutes. Trains back from Amberley run about once an hour. Journey time 1 hour 22 minutes. Buy a cheap day return to Arundel.

Lunch The suggested lunch place is the **George & Dragon** (tel 01903 883 131), Burpham, which has an ambitious menu at relatively high prices. Food is served midday to 2pm daily.

Tea The tea situation is not very satisfactory. **The Pottery** (tel 01798 831 876) in Amberley village – open daily till 5pm (closed on Wednesday in winter) – will make a cup of tea for any walker showing an interest in this working pottery. There is no charge, but they have a donation box for charity. From Easter to October 19th, the **Houghton Bridge Tea Garden** (tel 01798 831 558), near the station, is open till 5pm Monday to Saturday, 5.30pm

Sunday. Another possible tea place is the **Amberley Museum** (tel 01798 831 370), opposite the station, which has a café (open until 5pm Wednesday to Sunday, from about Mar 14th to November 4th; daily in summer holidays). You are, however, likely to be charged £6.50 for entry to the museum (less towards closing time) even if you just wish to visit the café. But assuming your arrival at Amberley Station is on the late side, the main suggested tea place is the **Bridge Inn** (tel 01798 831 619), just by the bridge. This is open for drinks, tea and coffee till at least 10.30pm (food from 7pm except Sunday). The **Black Horse** pub (tel 01798 831 700) in Amberley village is open daily from 6pm in summer, and from 6.30pm to 7pm in winter. For those who want to splash out, the **Country House Hotel** (tel 01798 831 992) within Amberley Castle offers cream teas at the high price of £10.50, from 3.30pm to 5.30pm daily (except weekends). They prefer that people book.

WALK DIRECTIONS

[1] **[Numbers refer to the map.]** From platform 2 at **Arundel Station**, go up the steps to the exit on to the main road. *Go left on this main road*, your direction 40 degrees. In 120 metres you pass Arundel Park Inn on your left. Cross the busy A-road at the pedestrian traffic lights.

In 100 metres *fork right on The Causeway*, signposted Arundel Castle, your direction 315 degrees.

In 160 metres **[2]** *take the public footpath signposted to the right*, your direction 65 degrees. In 60 metres *you come to the* **River Arun** *where*

you turn left, your direction 325 degrees.

In 300 metres the path leaves the riverside. In 10 metres *you follow a two-armed footpath sign between two concrete posts, through a concreted backyard, your direction now 250 degrees*. In 35 metres you come *to the main road where you turn right*, your direction 340 degrees.

Go over the river bridge and *straight on along the High Street (the 'no entry' road)*, your direction 325 degrees.

In 80 metres you pass Tarrant Street on the left-hand side. In 40 metres you pass Arundel Museum and Heritage Centre. Continue up the hill to the castle gatehouse, veering left with the road, and in 20 metres *fork right, keeping the castle walls on your right-hand side*, going due west.

In 90 metres, you pass **St Nicholas Parish Church** on your right-hand side. In a further 100 metres, you pass the entrance to the **Cathedral of Our Lady Philip Howard** on your left-hand side. In 20 metres you pass the St Mary's Gate Inn on your left-hand side.

In 125 metres you pass St Philip's Catholic School on your left-hand side, and here **[3]** you *fork right*, following the wall on your right-hand side, your direction 340 degrees.

In 70 metres you come to a noticeboard about Arundel Park on your left-hand side. Ignore the fork on your right to Arundel Estate Offices. Carry on up the tarmac road, your direction 20 degrees, with the wall on your right-hand side.

Keep straight on, ignoring ways off. In 150 metres go through a gateway (a wooden kissing gate to its left and a turreted lodgehouse to its right-hand side) and carry on along a tarmac road (or along its top right-hand side, for a pleasanter walk) into **Arundel Park**, your direction 10 degrees. In 170 metres you ignore a fork left and continue on the tarmac road. In about 30 metres, you can see the **Hiorne Tower [4]** ahead (so marked on the OS map), and *you make for this tower by forking right off your road*.

Your next 2km will be roughly northwards from the tower, across the valley on your right-hand side.

On reaching the tower, turn 90 degrees right for 30 metres, your direction 30 degrees, to cross a horseride with a surface of wood chips, and so to a fence, from which you can see **Swanbourne Lake** (sometimes waterless) below.

Turn right, your direction 120 degrees, along the fence. In a few metres, *at the end of the fence, go left downhill*, the fence on your left-hand side, your direction 45 degrees.

In 20 metres you come *to an earth car road where you go left* over a stile (with a fieldgate to its left-hand side), your direction 315 degrees. *Once over the stile, leave the road to go right, very steeply downhill, the fence on your right-hand side*, your direction 40 degrees.

In 45 metres you come *to a path, where you go left*, your direction 325 degrees, with a lake below you on your right-hand side.

(Both the next signs may be missing for now.) In 180 metres you come *to a two-armed footpath sign, which leads you away from the lake*, your direction 310 degrees, *towards a three-armed footpath sign*, following the bottom of the valley.

Once at this sign **[5]**, in 160 metres you carry on along the earth car road, bending right with the sign and the valley, your direction now 350 degrees. In about 50 metres it is worth *noticing the sign after the next, on top of the hill*, quarter right ahead of you.

At the next sign, in 230 metres, go right, your direction 25 degrees, steeply uphill on a faint path (*not along an earth car road in the direction shown by the sign, but slightly to left of this road*).

In 160 metres you come to a stile and a two-armed footpath sign. *Go over the stile and straight on, slightly to the left, your direction 5 degrees, uphill, heading for the (not yet visible) left-hand edge of the huge wood* on the far horizon.

In 400 metres, still heading up towards the summit of the hill, you come to two trees and a two-armed footpath sign (attached to an oak tree), and you carry on, still towards the left-hand edge of the wood ahead, your direction due north (and Whiteways Lodge visible at 310 degrees from you).

In 280 metres cross over a stile among oak trees (35 metres to the left of a cluster of half a dozen trees).

Keep on for the left-hand edge of the wood, your direction 5 degrees.

In 270 metres, by a two-armed sign at the wood's edge, continue in the direction of the sign, 355 degrees – chalk cliffs visible far ahead.

At the next footpath sign, in 160 metres, the church of South Stoke on the river is visible to your right-hand side (at 85 degrees from you), and three villages lie below you: North Stoke, the closest, on the right; Houghton to its left; and between and behind these, Amberley, under a cliff, and 40 degrees from you.

Go over a stile (a wooden fieldgate on its right-hand side) *and follow the sign downhill on a potentially slippery chalk road.*

In 225 metres, *at a T-junction* **[6]**, *follow the footpath sign right*, your direction 110 degrees.

In 120 metres, by an old fieldgate and a two-armed footpath sign, *follow the sign left*, with a field fence on your right-hand side, your direction 55 degrees, towards Houghton.

In 225 metres continue down with the park wall on your right-hand side. 60 metres along this wall, *exit Arundel Park through a tall metal swing gate on a brick wall on your right*, with the **River Arun** 30 metres below you. You are at a bridleway junction **[7]** and you *go right*, your direction 190 degrees **[[*]** Going left is an easy short cut – simply follow as close to the river as possible all the way to Amberley]

Continue with the river on your left-hand side and the wall on your right. In 600 metres you come to a fieldgate and stile, and a two-armed footpath sign. Continue on.

In 250 metres go through the wooden fieldgate (to the right of a hidden stile) and follow a footpath signpost left, along a farm track, your direction 120 degrees.

In 340 metres keep with the farm track, rather than forking left on a cement road through a shed.

In 100 metres you come *to an earth road, where you go right*, your direction 145 degrees. In 55 metres you leave **South Stoke Farm** (marked on the OS map) and *turn left on a tarmac lane*, your direction 55 degrees.

In 25 metres you fork left on the road, your direction due north. In 50 metres you pass house no.38 (which used to be an inn) and *come on your right-hand side to the entrance of* **St Leonard's Parish Church**, **South Stoke**. After visiting the church, retrace your steps to the road and continue onwards.

In 150 metres you *cross on a bridge* over the River Arun.

In 5 metres from the other side of the bridge [**[**]** where going left on the footpath would be a short cut, leading you via the hamlet of North Stoke to Amberley Station], the main suggested route **[8]** is to *go over a stile on your right*, to follow the River Arun, with the river on your right-hand side, your direction 115 degrees, the railway line on your left-hand side.

Ignoring all ways off and having gone over two stiles, in 1.3km you *cross railway lines* and go over a stile the other side to continue alongside the river. In 270 metres go over a stile and *keep to the right of a ruin*, your direction 170 degrees. In 15 metres go over a stile and continue beside the river. In a further 300 metres, *fork left* **[9]** *(below the church) on a path that heads steeply uphill*, your direction 130 degrees.

In 70 metres go over a stile and in 10 metres, *at a two-armed footpath sign, you fork left (not right as shown on the sign)*, your direction 55 degrees. In 150 metres you come to the **George & Dragon**, **Burpham**, the suggested lunchtime stop.

Coming out of the pub door, turn right, due north, going to the left of Burpham House and *through the gateway of* **St Mary the Virgin Church**, which is worth a visit.

Coming out of the church, go sharp right through the churchyard, your direction 345 degrees, to exit it through a metal swing gate, out *on to a tarmac road where you go right*, your direction 330 degrees. There may be bison in the field on your left-hand side.

In 400 metres you come to **Peppering Farm** (so marked on the OS map) and *a tarmac road T-junction. Follow the public bridleway sign straight on*, your direction 350 degrees, passing barns and sheds on your left-hand side. Ignore ways off.

In 400 metres go over a stile with a metal fieldgate on its right-hand side. In 70 metres ignore a stile to the left, to stay on your earth road.

In 50 metres, with a chalk cliff on your right-hand side, ignore another stile to the left.

In a further 120 metres, you pass under mini-pylons. In 350 metres you go through a metal fieldgate.

In 5 metres **[10]** *go over a stile on your right-hand side to go very steeply uphill* by a path and steps (this can be tricky when muddy), your direction 100 degrees, up more steps and over a stile. In 6 metres go over another stile. In 80 metres go over a stile (you should see a post with blue and yellow arrows) and out *on to a bridleway (a flint-and-chalk road) where you go left*, your direction 20 degrees.

In 1km **[11]** *fork right* by a three-armed footpath sign, your direction 30 degrees, still on a car-wide way.

In 150 metres, by a three-armed footpath sign, *leave this bridleway to go left*, on a possibly overgrown footpath, due north, into trees.

In 60 metres, by a four-armed footpath sign, *cross the bridleway to continue straight on*, soon with a hedge of blackberries on your right-hand side.

In 330 metres you come to a four-armed footpath sign: cross an earth road to continue straight on, slightly to your left, also on an earth road, your direction 350 degrees.

In 75 metres go through a metal fieldgate and head downwards.

In 300 metres, at the bottom of the combe, *fork right to go due north, through a wooden fieldgate (a metal fieldgate tp its right) and a two-armed bridleway sign, 65 metres away*.

Once over the stile, you go left, your direction 290 degrees, a potentially very muddy patch, on an earth car road uphill.

In 365 metres go through a wooden gate with a metal fieldgate to its right-hand side, and onwards, with a fence on your left-hand side. In 10 metres ignore an earth road fork to the left.

In a further 285 metres, leave your main earth road which forks right and take the left fork, still with the fence on your left.

In 180 metres your way merges with a farm track from behind on your right-hand side; and in 40 metres it is joined from one behind on your left-hand side; there is a pond below you, also to your left, and **Downs Farm** (marked on the OS map) off on the other side of the valley. In 80 metres you come to a three-armed footpath sign **[12]**. *Go left on the* **South Downs Way**, due west.

15 metres from the footpath sign, go through a metal fieldgate (with a stile to its right-hand side).

In 45 metres *fork right* (where left leads to the farm), your direction 280 degrees, with Amberley visible below on your right-hand side, with its church and castle.

Go downhill for 240 metres then through a wooden swing gate. In 50 metres you come *to a tarmac lane where you go right*, your direction 320 degrees.

In 100 metres ignore the South Downs Way forking left on a tarmac road[[***] You can take this way if you want a short cut to Amberley Station – go down the road for 750 metres, turn left on the B2139, coming to the station in 400 metres.] The main suggested route is to *fork right, signposted Village Shop*, downhill on the tarmac road.

In 500 metres you cross the B2139 to go straight on. In 190 metres ignore a road to the left. In 40 metres you pass the **village shop**, **Amberley**, set back from the road.

In 35 metres you pass the **Black Horse** pub. *Turn left at the pub*, your direction due west, walking past thatched cottages on both sides.

35 metres beyond these, ignore a footpath down to the right.

In a further 80 metres, passing the side of the thatched Old Place House on your right-hand side, and you *go right here at the T-junction*, your direction 300 degrees, passing the front of Old Place.

In 60 metres you pass **The Pottery**, a possible place for a cup of tea, on your left-hand side.

In a further 100 metres, you may wish to enter **St Michael's** churchyard. Exit the churchyard by the same entrance you came in, and continue on the tarmac road, in your previous direction.

In 80 metres you are below the start of **Amberley Castle** walls.

In a further 100 metres, continue straight on (at the end of the castle walls) along a footpath, your direction 260 degrees. In a further 160 metres, go over stiles across railway lines and onwards, with Bury Church visible ahead. (You need to aim about 100 metres to the left of the church.)

In a further 210 metres, go over a stile and quarter left (ignoring the leftmost fork), to the next footpath sign, 120 metres away.

In a further 130 metres, go over a stile and across a stream.

In 100 metres you come up on to a raised path (having gone over a ditch), alongside the River Arun, by a three-armed footpath sign **[14]**, with Bury Church just the other side of the river.

Go left on this raised path, your direction 220 degrees.

In 1km, *cross the substantial South Downs Way footbridge* **[15]** *and turn left along the riverside* towards houses visible ahead.

In 600 metres you come to the B2139 and *go left over the bridge*, your direction 75 degrees. On the other side of the bridge, by the old turnpike hut, is a lane on your left leading to the summer **Houghton Bridge Tea Garden** in the caravan carpark. On your right-hand side is the Boathouse restaurant, with, beyond it, the **Bridge Inn**, the main suggested tea place.

Continue along the main road under the railway bridge and in 40 metres turn right uphill to the **Amberley Museum**, with **Amberley Station** opposite.

Walk 33

Mortimer to Aldermaston

The Roman town of Calleva

Length 13.1km (8.2 miles), 4 hours. For the whole outing, including trains, sights and meals, allow at least 7 hours.

OS Landranger Map No.175. Mortimer, map reference SU 673 641, is in **Berkshire**, 10km south-west of Reading. Aldermaston is also in Berkshire. Silchester and the Roman town of Calleva are in **Hampshire**.

Toughness 3 out of 10.

Features Gumboots might be a good idea for this walk, which can be very waterlogged on Papworth Common (even in relatively dry weather) and muddy by Papworth. From St Mary's Church in Stratfield Mortimer, the route follows a clear stream – Foundry Brook – eventually to the amphitheatre and to the 2.5km of Roman walls surrounding the 107-acre site of the Roman town of Calleva; and to the whitewashed twelfth-century church at its entrance. Lunch is at a pub on Silchester Common, and the afternoon is mainly through woods of Scots pine, and commons of gorse and birch trees. Aldermaston, the teatime destination, is reached over the weirs of the River Kennet. Trains back can be rare. If your group faces a long wait in winter, when the tea place is

closed, you can call for a minibus-size taxi on 01635 862 002.

Shortening the walk There are buses about every half-hour from near the lunchtime pub, going to either Reading, Mortimer or Basing-stoke.

History The layout of the **Roman town of Calleva** has survived intact, having been completely abandoned when the Romans withdrew from Britain (the Saxons hated walled towns). However, all the buildings, carefully excavated, have now been reburied to protect them from vandals and the elements. Only the town walls and the amphitheatre are visible. The **amphitheatre** was built in about 50AD, with space for up to perhaps 9,000 spectators. It would have been used for public executions and shows with wild animals, but only sparingly for gladiatorial contests, since gladiators, dead or alive, were expensive. The town walls required some 160,000 wagon-loads of flint and bonding stones, and were built about 260AD as part of a general move to protect the Roman Empire from mounting unrest.

The tiny **Calleva Museum**, half a kilometre beyond the site, is open every day during daylight hours, without charge – but many of the exhibits from Calleva are on display in Reading Museum.

The earliest part of **St Mary the Virgin Church**, **Silchester**, dates from about 1125, with the walls reusing old Roman bricks – there are two Roman temples underneath the church and graveyard. It has been suggested that John Bluett may have contributed to the building of the church, as the price of

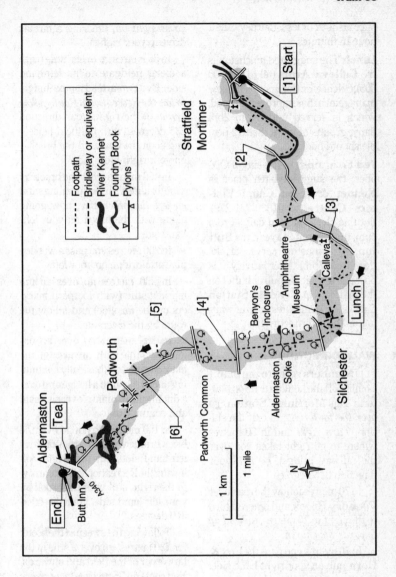

escaping a vow to join the crusades. Records reveal that the church had half a dozen rectors in 1349 – with most of these probably killed by the plague, although one was removed for 'trespass of vert' (the taking of timber from Pamber Forest).

Saturday Walkers' Club Take the train nearest to **9.30am** (before or after) from **Paddington** Station to **Mortimer** (changing at Reading). Journey time 1 hour. Trains back from Aldermaston to Paddington (changing at Reading) run about once an hour or less. Journey time 1 hour 15 minutes.

Lunch The suggested lunchstop is the **Calleva Arms** (tel 0118 9700 305), Silchester Common. The new management has improved the food, which is served midday to 2pm daily; groups of more than 12 people should book.

Tea From April to the end of October, the suggested tea place is **Kennet & Avon Canal Visitors' Centre** (tel 01380 721 279), but this closes at 5pm daily. From 6pm, throughout the year, the **Butt Inn**, Aldermaston, serves drinks (food from 7pm). Alternatively, it is possible to visit the pub or buffet on the platform at **Reading Station** during the 15 minutes or so of waiting on the return journey.

WALK DIRECTIONS

[1] [Numbers refer to the map.] Coming off the London train on platform 1 at **Mortimer Station**, *go over the footbridge* to exit the station. *Turn right* and in 50 metres (where to go right takes you over the railway bridge), *go left*, your direction 315 degrees.

In 70 metres follow the road over **Foundry Brook** and ignore a turn to the right in 20 metres, to *head up towards the church*.

In 70 metres you pass the **Fox & Horn** pub on your right-hand side. In 165 metres, by a red two-armed byway sign, turn left, your direction 210 degrees.

In 75 metres you pass the lychgate entrance to (locked) **St Mary's Church**, **Stratfield Mortimer**, on your right-hand side. In 25 metres you *cross Foundry Brook again and*

go straight on, ignoring a tarmac drive to your right.

In 35 metres go over a stile (with a metal fieldgate to its left-hand side). By a two-armed footpath sign, *follow the Recreational Route yellow arrow* to the right, your direction 235 degrees, with the field fence – and soon the banks of the brook – on your right-hand side.

In 400 metres cross the brook by a footbridge with metal railings and *go left the other side*, now going along with the brook on your left-hand side.

In 200 metres you pass a wooden platform bridge on your left.

In 230 metres go over an unmarked stile (with footpath markers on the far side) and follow the route by the riverside.

In 365 metres go over an unmarked stile with arrows on the back on your left (basically continuing ahead through a hedge and over a ditch) and on planks over a stream and continue on.

In 100 metres do not go over the brick bridge with two stiles on your left-hand side, but turn right, following the Recreational Route arrow to the right, still with the brook on your left-hand side, your direction 310 degrees.

Following the sweep of the brook for 320 metres, go over a stile in the far corner of the field and onwards. You come, in 35 metres, *to a tarmac road* **[2]** *where you go left, over a bridge and onwards*, your direction 230 degrees.

In 400 metres ignore a road to the right to keep straight on, past **Brocas Lands Farm** (as marked on the OS map).

In 100 metres *leave your tarmac road (which veers left) to go straight on, along an earth road*, your direction 240 degrees.

In 200 metres, where this earth road bears left (and 30 metres before a concrete pillbox), *follow the footpath sign straight across the fields towards pylons*, your direction 275 degrees.

400 metres along this path, and *85 metres before going under the pylon cables, turn left*, directly opposite a stile in the hedge, 55 metres away, on a path that goes due south. *Go over the stile, slightly to the right*, your direction 215 degrees (towards a timber-framed house on the hillside; the stile may be obscured by maize crop).

In 45 metres you pass under pylons. In 80 metres you go on one plank over a stream and over a stile the other side.

Once over the stile, *you go straight across the field, aiming about 100 metres to the left of the timber-framed house*, your direction 190 degrees.

In 175 metres go through the V-shaped wooden exit from the field, by the number 26 on a post and a public footpath sign, *on to the earth car road where you turn right uphill*, your direction 205 degrees.

In 85 metres you pass the entrance driveway to The Mount thatched cottage.

In 90 metres, although your onward route is straight on, *detour right on Wall Lane*, your direction 340 degrees, and *immediately go through the wooden kissing gate on your right-hand side*, to visit the **Calleva amphitheatre** (next to The Mount Cottage).

Retrace your steps and *continue on your previous road, southwards*, on the tarmac road. In 100 metres ignore a road to the left and carry straight on, your direction 215 degrees, on Church Lane.

In 80 metres you come to the **Roman walls of Calleva** and a pond on your right-hand side, and beyond it is the **St Mary the Virgin Church** in **Silchester [3]**.

Before visiting the church, you might like to *go along the Roman walls for 30 metres or so to the notice* about the history of the site.

After visiting the church, return to the church's wooden swing gate and, just before it, you turn right along the top of the walls, your direction 205 degrees, through the churchyard.

In 40 metres turn right for 20 metres, to exit the churchyard between two wooden sheds, and to go through a wooden swing gate, to continue on, following the path along the top of the Roman walls.

In 85 metres *go down steps and continue on, below the wall*.

At the next gap in the wall, go back again on top of the walls to continue on. In 265 metres you have another opportunity to *come down off the walls*, to continue on below them. In 300 metres the contours of the old **Iron Age ramparts** are visible on your left-hand side.

In 350 metres go through a wooden swing gate (with a notice about the site implanted in the trunk of an old tree ahead on your right). *Go left here, through a wooden swing gate with a pink arrow on the far side*, direction 285 degrees, and with a fence on your right-hand side.

In 135 metres ignore a stile on your right-hand side.

In a further 200 metres, go over a stile (a wooden fieldgate on its left-hand side) and onwards.

In a further 350 metres, you come to a little green wooden hut which is the **Calleva Museum**.

Coming out of the museum, turn right, your direction 255 degrees, and in 5 metres *cross the tarmac lane to continue on a gravel road*.

In 60 metres you come *to a tarmac road and cross over it to continue on a path*. In a further 120 metres, you come *to a gravel path,* with Silchester Primary School on your right-hand side, *where you turn left and in 5 metres keep left*, your direction 190 degrees, *across the common*.

In 250 metres you reach the **Calleva Arms**, the suggested lunch-time stop.

After lunch, retrace your steps across the common, your direction due north from the pub, passing the pavilion on your left-hand side.

30 metres from the end of the open common, having ignored a first fork left, *fork left, your direction 345 degrees, on a gravel lane*. In 30 metres, *turn left, with a school fence on your right-hand side*, your direction due west.

In 30 metres, at the end of the school fence, do not take the forest track to the right of the fence, but *fork left on a more substantial bridle-way*, your direction 265 degrees.

In 135 metres *follow the main fork to the right*, your direction 300 degrees. In 15 metres you pass a fire paddles' stand on your right-hand side, amid a landscape of gorse and silver birch.

In 80 metres your way is joined by another path from behind, on your left-hand side, and you continue on, your direction 10 degrees.

In 100 metres, you come *to a tarmac road. This you cross to go on an earth car-wide road*, guarded by a wooden field-gate, into **Aldermaston Soke woods** (as marked on the OS map), your direction 5 degrees, and Heather Brae House on your right-hand side.

Go straight on through these woods of Scots pine, ignoring all ways off. *In 1.6km* **[4]** *you come out on to a tarmac road. Turn left* on this, your direction 265 degrees. In 40 metres you pass an electricity substation. In a further 35 metres, you pass under mini-pylons, and, 5 metres beyond these, *take the foot-path over the stile to your right*, your direction 5 degrees, with the edge of the field on your right-hand side, and following the line of the mini-pylons.

Immediately turn left and cross a second stile following a yellow arrow. Walk along a path parallel to the road with a wire fence and embankment to its right and newly planted trees to its left. At the far end of the field, with a road gate to the left, cross a stile and turn right to follow a car-wide path and on before returning to the line of pylons. (Directions for this perimeter diversion due to quarrying are approximately left for 400 metres, your direction 225 degrees, then north for 300 metres, then right for 430 metres, your direction 315 degrees, before returning to the pylons and the route below at the asterisk **[*]**.)

In 500 metres, *when you can go no further because you meet a line of gorse,* **[*]** *go right over a stile, along the edge of this gorse* on your left-hand side, your direction 70 degrees, and with pine trees on your right-hand side.

In 160 metres, with gorse directly ahead, you cross a stile and fence on your left-hand side, and in 2 metres you go on three planks over a ditch. **[!]** Direction is marked by a yellow arrow over the ditch. *2 metres beyond the ditch, bear right* (but not the faint path sharp right that follows the ditch), *your direction 20 degrees, and follow a winding path for 200 metres, ignoring ways off until you reach a T-junction where you turn right,* your direction 55 degrees. (If you get lost, head for the traffic noise; you can go straight over the junction above and cross planks over a ditch to get to the road.)

In 65 metres you come *to Birch Cottage, where you go out on to the main road. Here you turn left,* your direction 260 degrees.

In 65 metres **[5]** *take a signposted bridleway to the right,* marked 'The Croft', your direction 350 degrees, along a rough road.

In 50 metres you ignore a turn to the left (to The Croft, House & Stables). In a further 80 metres, you pass the thatched Yew Tree Cottage. In 300 metres, with a pond on your left-hand side, ignore a fork to the right to *follow to the left.*

In 35 metres you pass The Croft Cottage on your left-hand side and continue straight on. In 45 metres *fork right with the main path,* your direction 345 degrees.

In 270 metres your way is joined by a path from the right, and you keep straight on, slightly to your left. In 30 metres there is the start of a high fence of barbed wire on your right-hand side, guarding a buried BP petrol depot.

In 340 metres you come *to a tarmac road where you turn left,* your direction 235 degrees, uphill. (If the way is not too overgrown, you may prefer to walk by the fence that runs parallel and to the right of the road.)

In 65 metres you pass the entrance drive to the Jubilee Day Nursery on your left-hand side.

In 240 metres, by Upper Lodge Farm **[6]**, *turn right on an earth road,* your direction 345 degrees.

In 20 metres you pass a public footpath sign on your right-hand side, to keep straight on.

In 35 metres you pass a white metal fieldgate, to continue on.

In 300 metres you pass a wooden fieldgate to come out *on to a tarmac road, opposite Padworth College. Turn left on this road,* your direction 225 degrees.

In 80 metres *take the earth road, which is a signposted footpath,* to **Padworth Church**, your direction 315 degrees.

Enter the church grounds through the lychgate and at the entrance to the (locked) church, you *fork left,* your direction 280 degrees, *to go through the churchyard,* in 30 metres exiting by the metal kissing gate.

In 40 metres go through a potentially muddy patch, go through a swing gate and across a tarmac road, out on to an earth road, where you continue straight on, your direction 250 degrees, towards five concrete mushrooms. *By these mushrooms, you turn right, on a signposted footpath*, your direction 335 degrees.

In 65 metres go over a stile (a wooden fieldgate on its right-hand side) and through a potentially very muddy, horse-churned field, with the fence on your right-hand side.

In 190 metres go over a stile (with a wooden fieldgate on its right-hand side) to continue on, your direction 290 degrees, on the path which is the left fork.

In 210 metres go over a bridge with metal railings and onwards, your direction 295 degrees. In 160 metres, by a four-armed footpath sign, go on two planks over a stream and straight on.

In 100 metres go over a stile made of corrugated pipes and on a bridge over **River Kennet Weir**.

You then cross several other bridges in quick succession and continue on a path between fencing. You come out *on to an earth car road*, by a three-armed footpath sign

where you *go left*, your direction 310 degrees. In 400 metres you pass the Rudolf Steiner **Alder Bridge** centre. In 130 metres you come *to a lock and the main road*. Here, if going to the Butt Inn for tea (open from 5.30pm), you go left, your direction 210 degrees. In 120 metres you come to the **Butt Inn**.

Or, if going to Aldermaston Wharf Visitors' Centre for tea (open in summer till 5pm daily), go with the road over the bridge, your direction 355 degrees, and turn right, signposted Padworth Bridge. The canal is then on your right-hand side, and you come in 80 metres to **Kennet & Avon Canal Visitors' Centre**.

Otherwise, if you're going directly to the station, go with the road over the bridge and turn left, your direction 320 degrees. In 60 metres fork right, signposted **Aldermaston Station**. In 120 metres you need to cross over the footbridge to platform 1 for trains to Reading (where you can get a cup of tea while changing trains) and onwards back to London.

Walk 34

Balcombe to East Grinstead

Wakehurst Place, Priest House & Weir Wood

Length 16.5km (10.3 miles), 5 hours. For the whole outing, including trains, sights and meals, allow at least 9 hours.

OS Landranger Map No.187. Balcombe, map reference TQ 306 302, is in **West Sussex**, 7km south-east of Crawley.

Toughness 7 out of 10.

Features This walk has a fair number of relatively gentle uphills and downhills, but is well worth it. It starts in the old village of Balcombe, passes Balcombe House, and then goes through the woods and by the lake of Balcombe Estate, up to a farm that can be extremely muddy in wet weather, to reach the National Trust gardens and Tudor mansion at Wakehurst Place around mid-morning. From there the route passes through further woods to the Priest House Museum, Norman church and the lunchtime pub in West Hoathly (which is less than halfway and is the second highest point in Sussex).

After lunch, the route is through Giffards Wood then past the Stone Arm climbing rocks (sandstone rocks formed from the bodies of plants and invertebrates, and used as shelters in mesolithic and neolithic times), leading to the shoreline of the Weir Wood Reservoir and nature reserve (home to the great crested grebe, heron, osprey etc) – the very energetic could at this point detour to the National Trust estate at Standen – finally reaching the station via a walk along a stream and through potentially very muddy fields that mark the outer edges of East Grinstead.

Shortening the walk There is a bus about once an hour from West Hoathly (the suggested lunchtime stop) to either East Grinstead or (the next hour) to Crawley (the bus goes from the shelter just on the right as you come out of the Cat Inn, the lunch pub).

It might also be possible to get a taxi three miles to Horsted Keynes Station to catch a Bluebell Line steam locomotive towards East Grinstead (the fare is £4.20; phone for details on 01825 723 777).

History The poet **Shelley** lived for a time in Balcombe's Highley Manor. The present queen was a brides-maid at a wedding in Balcombe Church before the war. **Balcombe House**, privately owned, was part-gutted by fire in 1995.

Wakehurst Place (tel 01444 89 4066) dates from Norman times, but the Tudor manor house with its sandstone walls was built in 1590 by Sir Edward Culpeper, a distant relative of Nicholas Culpeper who published the famous herbal compendium in 1651. The gardens are divided into geographical themes, such as Himalayan, Chinese and North American; and are linked to Kew – plants and trees suited to high altitude and extra rainfall can be grown at Wakehurst Place (which won a £10 million lottery award for its seed bank plans). Admission is £5; £3.50 concessions. Opening hours are 10am to 5pm daily in February; 10am to 6pm daily in March and October; 10am to 7pm daily April to September; and 10am to 4pm daily in November, December and January.

The timber-framed **Priest House Museum** (tel 01342 810 479) in West Hoathly is managed by the Sussex Archaeological Trust, and the house and garden are open from March 1st to October 31st 11am to 5.30pm Monday to Saturday, 2pm to 5.30pm Sunday. Admission is £2.50.

St Margaret's Church in West Hoathly has a magnificent coffin-shaped chest, probably thirteenth-century, which was used to collect money for the crusades; it also has a brass memorial to Ann Tree, the last woman to be burned at the stake in England.

The **Cat Inn** once had a tunnel under it, which a past murderer is said to have used to reach the pub for refuge.

Saturday Walkers' Club Take the train nearest to **9.50am** (before or after) from **King's Cross Thameslink** station (*not* the main railway station; Thameslink has its own exit from King's Cross tube station, and is on the corner of Pentonville and Caledonian Roads – coming out of the main station, you turn left to get to it) to **Balcombe**. Trains back from East Grinstead run about twice an hour. Journey time approximately 57 minutes.

Lunch The suggested lunchtime stop is the **Cat Inn** (tel 01342 810 369) West Hoathly, about 8km (5 miles) from the start of the walk,

which serves pricey pub food from midday to 2.30pm daily. Or you could opt for an earlier lunch at **Wake-hurst Place**, about 5km (3 miles) from the start, although entrance to Wakehurst Place costs £5. Alternatively, have a late breakfast at the **Balcombe Tearooms** (tel 01444 811 777), open 10.30am to 5pm Tues – Sun.

Tea The only place near to the station is the quite adequate café at East Grinstead **Sainsbury's** (tel 01342 303 167). The café is open until 7pm daily (Friday 7.30pm, Sunday 3pm). Orders for hot food must be made at least half an hour before these times.

WALK DIRECTIONS

[1] [Numbers refer to the map.] This route has a slight detour at the outset, to avoid the main road: Coming off the London train at **Balcombe Station**, *go over the footbridge and down the platform the other side, exiting to the right just before the tunnel, then down the station entrance road, due south. Take the signed footpath to the right,* in 100 metres, your direction 250 degrees; over a stile in 15 metres, and 20 metres later, another stile. Then go down steps *to a junction of small roads where you turn right* up the road, due north initially, with the first house on your left called Parkers. Go up on this lane, back past the station on your right-hand side and under the railway line, steeply up, *in 250 metres crossing diagonally over the main road* (the B2036). Continue straight on up Bramble Hill, signposted with an arrow to the Tearooms, your direction 40 degrees.

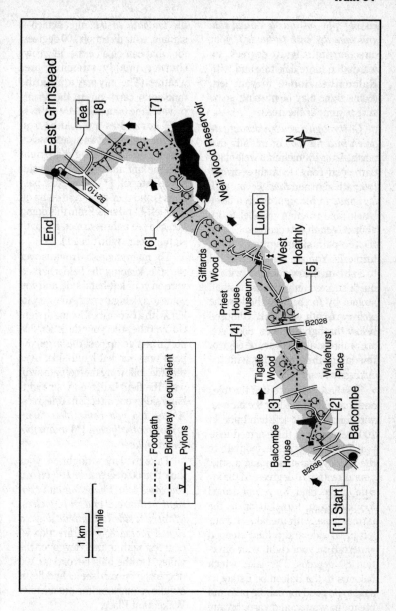

East Grinstead

[Tea]
[8]
[7]

[End]

B2110

Weir Wood Reservoir

N

[6]

Giffards Wood

[Lunch]

West Hoathly

Priest House Museum

[5]

[4]

B2028

Tilgate Wood

Wakehurst Place

[3]

[2]

Balcombe

Balcombe House

B2036

[1] Start

Footpath ·········
Bridleway or equivalent – – –
Pylons △ ▽

1 km
1 mile

Go up into the village, past the
Balcombe Tearooms on your left,
to the crossroads, *second left, with
the Half Moon Inn then on your left-
hand side*. At the end of this road is

a gate marked 'Balcombe House.
Private' **[2]**. *Turn right down a
signed footpath*, your direction 60
degrees. In 100 metres, *by a two-
armed footpath sign, go through the*

kissing gate on your left-hand side and take the path to the left, your direction initially 10 degrees, towards the large oak tree and with **Balcombe House** to your left. (Some signs may be missing, so be sure to aim for the tree.)

Go through a wooden kissing gate down into the woods, initially due north. After 100 metres of well-made path, you come to a three-armed footpath sign and *take the footpath it signals to the right* (with a large black pipe running parallel to it), your direction 120 degrees. Follow the footpath signs, ignoring other turn-offs. You are walking parallel to a stream below you and twice in quick succession you cross a small stream by footbridges. Follow the well-worn path, with a lake glimpsed below through the trees. Soon you are walking along near the edge of this lake (which connects with the Ardingly Reservoir).

A stile takes you out of the trees and into a field. Follow the barbed-wire fence on your left-hand side. In 100 metres, by a three-armed footpath sign, you take the footpath to the left, over a stream and a stile, your direction 70 degrees. At the far side of the field, by a four-armed footpath sign, turn left on to the tarmac lane, with the lake on your left-hand side and a loud stepped waterfall on your right, your direction 80 degrees. The lake, which belongs to the Balcombe Estate, is said to be good for fishing pike and bream in winter, and carp, bream, tench and roach in summer.

Carry on up this lane and *about 450 metres beyond the lake, you come to a two-armed footpath sign on your left-hand side and you take*

the footpath to the right which it signals, your direction 100 degrees, for what can be an extremely cow-churned muddy stretch in wet weather. (The only way to avoid the mud is to carry on up the farm's private lane for a kilometre – this is NOT advised as it would be trespassing, unless advance permission were secured – bending sharp right with the lane and rejoining the walk at the asterisk **[*]** below, just past houses and then a car-tyre dump on your left-hand side. From this dump you can see a three-armed footpath sign to your right, ahead.)

The main suggested route is over the stile, keeping the field's barbed wire on your left-hand side, and you come to a fieldgate and stile on your left, with a two-armed footpath sign. Go over the stile, your direction due north, and go up past the large cow barn on your left-hand side, over the stile, following the footpath sign, with the field hedge on your right-hand side, your direction 50 degrees. *At the top you come to a three-armed footpath sign* **[*]** *and rejoin the farm lane*.

Take the lane straight on, your direction 60 degrees. *In 100 metres you come to a T-junction and turn right on this road and, in 10 metres, left over a stile to continue down a signed footpath*, your direction 70 degrees, with a fine view over the valley. On the hills beyond (at 100 degrees) you can see a huddle of buildings marking the outskirts of Wakehurst Place.

Keep the fence and a large house on your right-hand side. In 400 metres, at the very bottom of the field, are the woods. **[3]** *Follow the footpath sign* to your left, with the edge of the woods now on your right-hand side and your direction 25 degrees.

In 150 metres the footpath sign directs you to the right, through a kissing gate and down a gully and small stream into **Tilgate Wood**, through a large wooden gate (your direction from this gate 120 degrees) and down a path that is bare rock at the outset. Soon it is steeply downhill with a stream visible below you.

Cross two wooden bridges (the second over a main stream) and go up the other side, following the footpath and sign as the path veers to the right in 50 metres. In a further 50 metres, there is another wooden platform over a stream and the route is upwards, in 50 metres going over a series of wooden planks with railings, and then through a wire-mesh kissing gate into **Wakehurst Place** gardens (with only a notice to discourage walkers from gaining free access to these National Trust gardens and the mansion house to the right). The permitted footpath route is clearly signed, your direction 140 degrees, coming in 200 metres to a stile and another wire-mesh kissing gate, now with a path between high electrified fences on both sides (to keep the deer in) – the path soon becomes a wide avenue.

You come out on to a car lane with cottages on the left behind you, and carry straight on, with garden walls on your right-hand side. In 200 metres **[4]**, when this access road bends sharply left, follow the footpath sign. For those not visiting the garden and mansions, this walk's route is straight up the road for 200 metres, through a wooden gate to the right of a cattle grid and,

after a further 200 metres, *exiting by 1 Yew Tree Cottage on your left-hand side, bringing you to the main road (the B2028), where you turn left* – and skip to the asterisk **[**]** below.

Many walkers with time to spare, however, will be tempted to look in at **Wakehurst Place**, in which case continue on the path that goes up from the pedestrian crossing and is signposted 'carpark and exit', to the National Trust information hut at the top (right at this T-junction leads to the house and restaurant, but first go left to the ticket office).

Those visiting the house can rejoin the main walk by going eastwards down the lane from Wakehurst Place's exit to the B2028 T-junction, turning left on to this main road and then in 300 metres coming to the main walk's exit on to the B2028, by 1 Yew Tree Cottage (mentioned above). Ignore a footpath marked back and to the left.

[**] Carry on along the busy B2028 for 200 metres (the left-hand side of the road seems safer). You pass Stonehurst Nurseries (famous for its camellias in early spring) on your right-hand side, *turning right down a signposted bridleway through a wooden gate set between cottages*, your direction 135 degrees, and so into the woods.

In 150 metres turn left on to a car-wide mud track following a bridleway sign, and in 80 metres follow the bridleway sign again, this time to the right, your direction 125 degrees.

In 100 metres *you come to a three-armed sign and take the left bridleway between ponds*, your direction 70 degrees. In 100 metres you have thin bamboo growing on the right-hand side of the path. In a further 100 metres, a stream tumbles noisily under the path, then it can be treacherously muddy uphill.

In 500 metres or so **[5]**, *you come to outhouses and a house, with your path running in front of the house (ignoring a turn-off to the left below the outhouses), then between houses and out left on to a car-wide lane signposted public bridleway*, your direction 105 degrees.

In 40 metres you fork left (following another bridleway sign), your direction now 65 degrees. *Following this lane in roughly the same direction will lead you in just over 1km to West Hoathly*, with the village's church spire soon visible on the horizon. You pass Philpots Quarry on your left-hand side and at the road junction, by Barn Cottage, you ignore the road to the right and keep straight on, your direction 105 degrees. You pass **Priest House Museum** on your left, and the **Cat Inn** pub, the suggested lunch stop, is ahead of you, opposite **St Margaret's Church**.

After lunch, *turn right out of the door of the pub and right again by the bus shelter on the left-hand side, and carry on up this tarmac road for 400 metres*, your direction 20 degrees, past the village school on your right-hand side and ignoring a public footpath off to the left.

When you come to the main road, cross straight over into the entrance to West Hoathly Garage (with its collection of vintage cars). *Go immediately left, following a public footpath sign down a narrow lane*, with the garage on your right-hand side, your direction 355 degrees.

In 200 metres, the lane becomes unasphalted and at the fork in this lane, you continue *straight on* into the wood through a kissing gate 15 metres ahead, ignoring other possibilities. Your path is now 15 degrees. In 70 metres you come to a three-armed footpath sign and you take the fork straight on and down (not the one up to the left), ignoring a further left fork soon after, your direction 40 degrees.

You need to *keep on this main path through Giffards Woods for over 1km*. In more detail: In 110 metres from the fork, you have a pond on your left-hand side. 50 metres after the pond, you come to a broad avenue to the right, but you keep straight on, following the footpath sign, still 40 degrees. It is a dead straight path and can be very muddy.

At the end of this straight section, two more footpath signs lead on to an earth car track. Turn left on this, your direction 30 degrees.

[!] In a 100 metres *take the footpath half right* (it may not be marked), your direction 45 degrees (not the unsigned car-wide track further to the right at 120 degrees).

In 150 metres this path exits the forest and a further 100 metres down, you cross a car-wide grass track and continue straight on, following the footpath sign, your direction still 45 degrees, now with young pines to the left and right.

Carry on down and in 200 metres you go over a stile and across an open field, keeping more or less in the same direction – now 30 degrees, with a line of trees and a stream on your left-hand side, and a couple of houses off to the right.

Over the stile you are on a car lane and you follow the sign to the left, your direction 330 degrees, parallel to the Bluebell railway line embankment, 70 metres to your right. In 40 metres *you come to a three-armed footpath sign set back from the lane on your right-hand side, and you take the footpath to the right*, your direction 40 degrees. Then in 90 metres you go up the embankment and over the railway line, with a (wintertime) view beyond, and down the other side and over a stile into the woods, following the path, your direction 35 degrees, parallel to the stream below you to your right.

In 100 metres follow a footpath sign towards an electricity pylon 150 metres away. Just to the right of this pylon, you *cross a wooden stile and bridge over a stream and take the path half left uphill*, towards the gap in the tree line 40 metres away, your direction 80 degrees (rather than the sharp left path).

From the gap, you bear left, your direction 30 degrees, uphill, along the edge of the wood on your left-hand side ahead, but not following the well-worn path actually into the wood. 150 metres from the gap, where the edge of the woods bends left, *you come to a three-armed footpath sign and take the right fork*, your direction 65 degrees, *towards another three-armed footpath sign visible further uphill* on the edge of the wood, 100 metres away **[6]**.

Once there, *take the bridleway to the right over a stile next to a wooden swing gate*, your direction from the gate 85 degrees. Then keep to this main path, ignoring all possible turn-offs.

About 300 metres from this fieldgate, you come to **Stone Arm Rocks**: these are soft sandstone rocks used for rock-climbing; they are covered with an acne of climbers' bolts and are lined with rope marks; and they provide platforms for fine views of the valley below, soon with the **Weir Wood Reservoir** below to your left.

The path comes to a notice warning climbers not to damage the rocks. 100 metres from this notice, *you come to a car road (with Stonehill House opposite you) and you turn right downhill on this road and, in 50 metres, left on a side road above the reservoir* (your direction 105 degrees) – *you will be more or less following the side of the reservoir for the next 1.5km, until your turn-off to the left)*.

350 metres after leaving the main road, you pass under pylons. In a further 50 metres, follow the footpath sign left (the only open way) and you are now almost at the reservoir shore. Follow the heavy link fence. Ignore turn-offs and in 250 metres, just before going under the pylons again, you come to a Countryside Commission poster describing Standen Rocks and Weir Wood and to a footpath off to the left (which you could take if wanting to visit **Standen House**). The main walk route, though, continues straight on.

In nearly 300 metres, and again almost under the pylons, ignore a footpath sign to the left to stay on the Sussex Border Path.

In 50 metres go over a stile with the Countryside Stewardship badge on it, and continue on, following the reservoir shore.

In 350 metres you again cross a stile with a similar Countryside Commission poster, again nearly under the pylons.

Continue straight on, ignoring in 30 metres a red-and-white marked metal gate offering a way to the left. Head back towards the reservoir, away from the pylons, your direction now 150 degrees, ignoring in 50 metres a second red-and-white marked metal gate to the left.

180 metres from this gate, your path is again by the reservoir shore, running parallel to it. 40 metres after joining the reservoir shoreline, you come to a three-armed footpath sign, offering a footpath 90 degrees to the left, but you carry straight on with the Sussex Border Path.

In 70 metres cross a stile and go into a field with the hedge and reservoir shore on your right-hand side.

The far wall of the reservoir comes into sight in the distance.

In 270 metres **[7]**, *at the end of the field, a three-armed sign offers the Sussex Border Path straight on, or a footpath to the left. Do not go over the stile, but take the footpath to the left instead, your direction 300 degrees and with a barbed-wire field fence on your right-hand side (3km of this path, more or less in the same direction, will lead you to East Grinstead's outskirts).*

You pass just to the left of a pylon ahead of you and through wide metal gates straight on, your direction 355 degrees. In 200 metres go slightly left over a footpath-signed stile, your direction 320 degrees, ignoring the Toll Riders main path straight on, and ignoring in 5 metres a further stile to your left.

Keep the edge of the wood on your left-hand side and in 150 metres there is a pond on your left. 70 metres from this pond, go over a stile into the woods, by a two-armed footpath sign, your direction due north initially.

In a further 50 metres, as you exit this wood, East Grinstead is visible on the far horizon to your north. Go north across the open field to a stile visible 150 metres away that enters the wood again.

Enter the wood by the stile and a three-armed footpath sign, continuing straight on, your direction 340 degrees, and ignoring the footpath to the right.

In 200 metres you come down to a plank over a stream and go up steps the other side. In 35 metres you exit the wood by a stile and follow the footpath sign to the right, your direction 10 degrees, with the field hedge and later a fence on your right-hand side.

In 300 metres you follow a kink at the end of the field to the left, and exit the field to the right by a car-wide track with a footpath sign, your direction 345 degrees.

Then in 40 metres go over a fieldgate and across a field, straight on (25 degrees), your direction just to the right of the church on the hill in the distance. In 150 metres, as you cross the field, you join the edge of the trees surrounding the pond on your right-hand side (the edge marked by a footpath sign). 170 metres from the edge of the trees, go over a stile and a plank over a stream and head straight on, your direction 35 degrees, following a footpath sign.

In a further 150 metres, *go over a stile by a four-armed footpath sign* **[8]**. *Do not go down to the wooden bridge 10 metres to your right. Instead, once over the stile, go immediately sharp left* (a direction not accurately indicated by the sign) and keep the fence of the field you have just exited on your left-hand side. In 30 metres there is a plank over a small stream and then you pass under a mini-pylon.

Follow the field edge to a two-armed footpath sign. Cross the stream. 50 metres further on, you have a wooden fence on your left-hand side and playgrounds, and you are now on a tarmac path. *You come to a road with Dunnings Mill opposite you, and cross over (slightly to the left) to continue on the signed footpath* (next to a sign saying 'Dunnings Mill Snooker Club and Millstream Suite'), your direction initially 275 degrees.

Follow the footpath up to the left of Dunnings Mill Club House and the footpath sign at the end of this building straight on. In 60 metres there is another footpath sign, as you cross the stream, with a new building on your right-hand side. In 100 metres go over a stile, keeping the field edge fence on your right-hand side. In a further 150 metres, go over another stile. And then in 170 metres, go down to and over the stream, then with mini-pylons running along your path. There follow five further stiles within 600 metres, some leading into potentially muddy fields. The last 90 of these 600 metres are enclosed between a low-rail fence and a hedge, which is accessed by an unsigned stile over the low rail-fence.

Finally, you come *out on to the main road (the B2110), where you turn right and in 50 metres left, following the sign saying 'Station'. Keep uphill on this Brooklands Way* (the right fork at the phonebox in 30 metres), and you need to go to the top of this hill, ignoring turn-offs. **Sainsbury's** supermarket, on your left-hand side, is the easiest place to stop for a cup of tea at this point. *Coming out of Sainsbury's, turn right along the edge of the building, then at the car road turn right and* **East Grinstead Station** *is in 70 metres.* (The bus stand is to the right of the station, just beyond the carpark.)

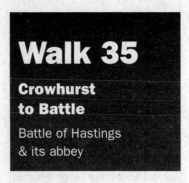

Walk 35

Crowhurst to Battle

Battle of Hastings & its abbey

Length 19km (11.7 miles), 5 hours 45 minutes. For the whole outing, including trains, sights and meals, allow 11 hours.

OS Landranger Map No.199. Crowhurst, map reference TQ 760 128, is in **East Sussex**, 5km north-west of Hastings.

Toughness 4 out of 10.

Features Down the road from the station is the church and ruined manor of Crowhurst, and from farmland nearby – on a clear day – you can see Beachy Head and the sea. The potentially muddy route goes through the woodlands and golfcourse of Beauport Park, to the church and lunchtime pub in the village of Westfield. It is 8.5km (5.3 miles) to this lunch stop.

In the afternoon the route is mainly alongside streams or the River Brede, and passes through the parkland of the Pestalozzi Children's Village. Soon the town, church and abbey of Battle are visible ahead, lining the horizon. You may like to end the day wandering over the site of the Battle of Hastings, by the ruins of the abbey that William the Conqueror built in honour of his victory, and so to the tree marking the spot where King Harold is supposed to have been slain.

Shortening the walk You could get a bus or taxi from near the lunchtime pub in Westfield (turn left out of the pub on Main Road and walk 50 metres), or from near the pub in Sedlescombe (4km further on). For bus information phone 0870 608 2608. A short cut to the station, as you enter Battle, is detailed in the walk directions below.

History The **churchyard in Crowhurst** has a perhaps 2,500-year-old yew tree. Next to the church is a **ruined manor house**, built in the twelfth century by Walter de Scotney, supposedly a gentleman of substance, who made do with this dwelling that was a mere 6 metres by 12 metres.

In 1100, **St John the Baptist Church** in Westfield, along with a pit for the ordeal of trial by water, was given into the care of Battle Abbey. Some of its church bells are thought to have been cast in a pit dug in the churchyard – so as not to have to transport the finished bells. The church lost its stained-glass windows in World War II.

The **Battle of Hastings** was fought on October 14th 1066, starting at 9am, with Harold's forces unmounted on top of Senlac Hill (Battle), under attack from William's mounted knights, protected by infantry and archers. The Normans feigned a retreat to get the English to break ranks, and at dusk King Harold was killed (see www.historylearningsite.co.uk/hastings.htm for more info). The abbey site (tel 01424 773792) is open daily until 6pm in summer (from about April 1st to September 30th), till 4pm in winter. Admission £4.30.

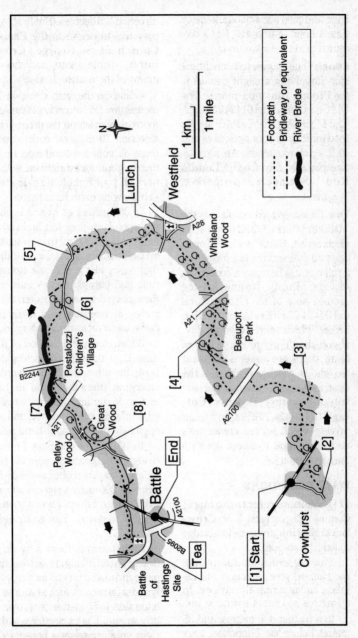

Lunch

Westfield

Whiteland Wood

[5]

[6]

A28

A21

Beauport Park

[3]

Pestalozzi Children's Village

[4]

A2100

B2244

[7]

Great Wood

[8]

Petley Wood

End

Battle

A2100

Tea

B2095

Battle of Hastings Site

[2]

[1] Start

Crowhurst

Saturday Walkers' Club Take the train nearest to **8.40am** (before or after) from **Charing Cross** Sta-

tion to **Crowhurst**. Journey time 1 hour 28 minutes. Trains back from Battle run about twice an hour until

6pm, and then one an hour. Journey time 1 hour 18 minutes. Get a day return ticket to Crowhurst.

Lunch The suggested lunchtime stop (involving a slight detour) is the **Plough Inn** (may now be The Old Courthouse) (tel 01424 751 066), The Moor, Westfield, which serves food midday to 2pm weekdays and to 2.30pm weekends. An alternative place to buy food is **Londis Red Square** supermarket, Westfield.

Tea The suggested tea place is the **1066** (tel 01424 773 224) pub at 12 High Street, Battle, which is open daily all day, serving tea, coffee and a full menu. The many alternatives include **Simply Italian**, on the ground floor of the George Hotel (tel 01424 774466) also in the High Street, which serves food all day. If you should get to Battle before 5pm, there are several pleasant tea shops to choose from – the first, as you enter town, is the seventeenth-century **Bayeux Cottage** (tel 01424 772593) in Mount Street, which serves cream teas and other food to about 5pm (to 3pm in winter).

WALK DIRECTIONS

[1] [Numbers refer to the map.] Coming off platform 2 at **Crowhurst Station**, cross the footbridge to exit the station.

Take the tarmac road away from the station, your direction 145 degrees, and ignoring all ways off. In 80 metres you pass Crowhurst Inn.

In a further 450 metres, and 35 metres before the T-junction, your onward route is **[2]** *left uphill on a concrete farm drive, a footpath* (with collapsing and illegible sign), your direction 125 degrees. (But first, you may like to detour to the **Parish Church of St George, Crowhurst**, visible ahead, and the remains of the **manor house**.)

Going up the farm drive, in 35 metres you follow a privately made footpath sign left off the drive, your direction 70 degrees, with a field fence on your left-hand side. In 45 metres continue straight on, with a barn on your right-hand side, on a vehicle-wide earth farm track.

In 380 metres go over a bridge with ponds to your left and right-hand side. In 200 metres go under an isolated, disused railway bridge that looks like a majestic Roman ruin, and only 80 metres later, go through its degenerate modern alternative: *a corrugated-iron drainpipe tunnel under the working railway lines*.

8 metres beyond the end of the tunnel, go through concrete gateposts the other side and onwards, emerging from the wood in 180 metres, to continue with the wood's edge on your left-hand side, and an open field on your right-hand side.

In 190 metres you pass a metal fieldgate and continue, with the sea far away on your right-hand side. In a further 200 metres, *you come to an earth roads crossing (where you cross a public footpath). You go straight on.*

In 180 metres there may be a flimsy metal fieldgate across the path, and in a further 25 metres, you ignore a farm track fork to your left-hand side. In 55 metres cross over a tiny stream. The track curves to the right uphill towards a house. In a further 80 metres, your way is joined by a farm track from behind on your left.

In 150 metres you pass this house on your left-hand side, and in 15 metres go through a fieldgate and on *through the farmyard of* **Park Farm** (marked on the OS map), with a stable block on your left-hand side, your direction 130 degrees.

In 100 metres you come *to an earth lane T-junction* [3] *where you go left*, your direction 35 degrees, along a lane, ignoring a stile and public footpath ahead. You should pass a labelled entrance to Park Farm on your left, and pass Breadsell Fram on your right. Soon Beachy Head is sometimes visible behind you on your right-hand side. In 1.25km you come out *to the A2100 T-junction, where you cross the road and go left* alongside the walls of **Beauport Park**.

After 450 metres of this unpleasant road, and *30 metres before the water tower on the left-hand side, by a wooden footpath fingerpost on your right-hand side, go right*, your direction 40 degrees, past a metal fieldgate on a wide gravelled track (not the wooden fieldgate and track parallel to yours, to its left).

In 50 metres you pass a corrugated shed on your right-hand side.

35 metres *past the shed, take the left of the two tracks*, with the fencing on your left-hand side.

In a further 75 metres, *fork left by a public footpath sign*, your direction 30 degrees. (Westfield village, the lunchtime destination, may already be visible ahead at 65 degrees, although the walk takes longer than you might imagine to get there.)

The suggested route through the golfcourse is fairly complicated. (The correct right of way is generally in the belts of trees between fairways, and has to some extent now been cleared, but tends still to have very high nettles in some places. In the meantime, the following precise directions work, if you follow them carefully.) In 25 metres *fork right*, your direction 55 degrees (the left fork goes sharply downhill and then off in the opposite direction).

Keep on remaining parallel to the fairway on your right-hand side and ignoring ways off until, in a further 150 metres, [!] *you fork right on a faint path*, marked by a yellow marker on a wooden post, where the main path forks left and sharply downhill (where it continues to go left). Your direction is 80 degrees and *you come out on to the golfcourse fairway, where you bear slightly left, keeping the edge of the wood on your left-hand side*, your direction 55 degrees. In 30 metres you pass under a sizeable oak tree, with a dozen main branches.

In a further 50 metres, you pass a green with a flag on your right-hand side. *Fork right around the back edge of this green*, your direction 115 degrees.

In 40 metres you come to a golfcourse track by the large stump of a beech tree and a bench, where you *go left on the track*, your direction 95 degrees.

In 12 metres you pass a golf tee, to continue down the gravelled track. In a further 40 metres, you pass another tee.

In a further 60 metres, you pass a green on your right-hand side.

The road bends left and in 25 metres, in the middle of a thin line of trees, you go right off your track across two planks and a ditch, down the middle of the line of trees, marked by a post and yellow marker, with the fairways to both sides of you, your direction 75 degrees.

In 80 metres you pass a tee on your right-hand side and in 10 metres you cross a golf track. In a further 20 metres, *you come to a T-junction (a path covered with shells) where you go left*, your direction 10 degrees.

In 15 metres you come *to a fairway, which you cross over* (with a green just on your right-hand side). In 25 metres you come *on to a path where you go right*, your direction 40 degrees.

In 25 metres you pass the same green on your right-hand side.

In 30 metres *you come out to another fairway* (with a seven-foot-high black-and-white pole in the middle of the fairway, 30 metres ahead of you). *You go right, your direction 70 degrees, along the wooded edge of this fairway*.

In 110 metres ignore a fork going off to the right.

In a further 40 metres, you pass a tee and come *to a T-junction, where you go right*, your direction 175 degrees. In 10 metres you pass a public footpath sign (which may still point right into impenetrable blackberry bushes!) and in 5 metres you *go on 10 wooden planks over a stream and immediately left on a path*, due east (the public footpath sign may be hidden in the bushes).

In a further 70 metres, go over a stream which comes out 5 metres underneath you on your left-hand side. Keep on the main path.

In 220 metres you come *to an earth road T-junction* **[4]** by a house with ground-floor lattice window shutters (you are now by the first letter 'o' of Stonehouse on the OS map) you *go left* on this earth road, downhill, your direction 80 degrees.

In 55 metres you ignore a fork to the right (underneath mini-pylons) and the yellow-arrow marked footpath, but in 25 metres *follow the wide path to the right* on a potentially muddy way used by horses, your direction 120 degrees initially. (There may be a footpath sign on the ground.)

In 110 metres, *at the main fork in the ways, go left*, due east, with rhododendrons on both sides.

In 120 metres, at a path junction, you *pass a spreading beech tree on your right-hand side (it has a plastic yellow arrow on its far side) and take a mild right fork*, your direction 75 degrees. In 30 metres *ignore the minor fork left*, your direction now 100 degrees. Head towards the traffic noise.

In a further 160 metres, *at a path T-junction, go right*, your direction 165 degrees. In 45 metres go over a stream on a five-plank bridge.

In 150 metres you come out *on to a mossy open space and, on its left-hand edge, you exit the wood by a wooden swing gate*, next to a public footpath sign, on to the A21.

Cross this A road to continue on Moat Lane, your direction 55 degrees. In 110 metres, just before Cherrycot House on your right-hand side, *you go right into the park* (by a stile and a concrete footpath marker, with a metal fieldgate on your left-hand side), your direction 95 degrees, to follow the left-hand edge of the park.

In 375 metres you enter **Whiteland Wood** (as marked on the OS map) on a bridge with wooden railings over a stream, keeping the fence on your left-hand side. In 200 metres, ignore a way off to the right.

In 145 metres the fencing on your left-hand side comes to an end.

In a further 170 metres, you cross a car-wide way. In 150 metres you cross another way. In 25 metres you ignore a way to the right.

In 30 metres, having crossed a stream, you exit the wood through a wooden fieldgate and carry on, along a farm track, between a hedge on your right-hand side and a fence to your left-hand side, your direction 30 degrees.

In 180 metres you come out *on to a tarmac lane where you go right*, uphill, your direction 140 degrees.

In 100 metres, immediately after a road leading left into a housing estate, you go quarter left up a grass bank *towards a churchyard*, and in 30 metres go through its metal swing gate to **St John the Baptist Church**, **Westfield**.

In 100 metres you come *to the church's entrance on its right-hand side. Continuing onwards brings you out on the A28*, opposite the bus stop, where you *go left*, your direction 15 degrees.

Walk up for for 180 metres before reaching the crossroads with Wheel/Moor Lane. **The Plough Inn**, for lunch, is down Moor Lane (turn right). Retrace your steps after lunch and head down Wheel Lane.

In 450 metres you ignore Vicarage Lane to the left. In 15 metres you pass the thatched Wheel Cottage on your right-hand side. In a further 25 metres, on the other side of the stream, passing between poles to the right of a diagonal metal car gate, *you go right through Wheel Farm business park*, keeping alongside a stream on your right-hand side.

In 240 metres *ignore a wooden bridge with railings on your right-hand side, to go slightly left away from the stream*, your direction 290 degrees. In 45 metres, you pass a pond. In 25 metres, go over a stile with a yellow footpath arrow (and a red "1066 country walk" marker) with a metal fieldgate to your left, to continue straight on, your direction 340 degrees.

In 95 metres you rejoin the side of the stream on your right-hand side, as you pass under mini-pylons.

In 80 metres go over a stile with a 1066 walk marker (a metal fieldgate on its left-hand side).

In 240 metres ignore a grassy vehicle-wide bridge on your right-hand side to go on with a metal fieldgate to its left-hand side. Carry straight on, with a stream on your right-hand side.

In 80 metres, by a mini-waterfall on the right-hand side, you go over a stile (with a metal fieldgate to its left). There is a three-armed footpath post here. Follow this on, ignoring a possible left.

In a further 180 metres, go on a wooden bridge, with wooden railings and a stile at both ends, over a stream. Keep to the right-hand side of the field to reach a footpath T-junction with a 3-arrow footpath fingerpost. Go left here, direction 320 degrees across the field.

In 210 metres you come to a wooden footbridge (with a metal

scaffolding pole railing). Carry straight on from the other side, with the field fence on your right-hand side, towards a line of pylons, your direction 320 degrees.

In 110 metres, you go over a stile. In 45 metres you then pass under mini-pylons. In a further 240 metres, you may have to negotiate an electric fence (its insulated section – a proper stile has been requested) to cross a farm track, slightly left, continuing on over a stile, with a field hedge on your right-hand side.

In 100 metres you pass under pylons. In 45 metres go over a low wooden stile into a wood (with a pond, visible in winter, away on your left-hand side), your direction 350 degrees.

In 45 metres you come *on to a tarmac road* **[5]** *where you go left*, your direction 280 degrees.

In a further 290 metres, you pass an entrance to Westfield Place on your left-hand side.

In 190 metres *ignore a parking area signposted Brassets Wood*, on your right-hand side, with an inviting track leading off it.

In 180 metres you pass another entrance to Westfield Place and a lodgehouse on your left-hand side.

In 25 metres, *as the road bends slightly left, take the path to the right, by a concrete footpath marker* **[6]**, *into a wood* (opposite the entrance to the Lodge Nursery). 4 metres *inside the wood, go left*, your direction 265 degrees.

In 120 metres you veer right with the path. In 10 metres you *cross a path to go through a wooden kissing gate into the parklands of* **Pestalozzi Children's Village**,

your direction now 295 degrees, *aiming towards the left edge of the woodlands below you* (and well to the right of the house visible ahead).

In 215 metres you come to the fence below you, where *you go over a stile in the fence with a public footpath yellow arrow on it* (there is a metal fieldgate in the fence 100 metres away to your left) *and go left into the trees*, your direction 310 degrees. The path may be somewhat overgrown.

In 75 metres go over a stile with a green arrow on and over two planks with a wooden railing to continue in a similar direction (315 degrees). In a further 250 metres, go over a stile and in 15 metres you come out of the trees to carry straight on, direction 300 degrees.

In 55 metres you pass a little hut on your right-hand side. In a further 85 metres, go over a stile in the fence on your right-hand side, under an oak tree, to *cross a stream and go left the other side*, your direction 280 degrees.

In a further 110 metres, go over a stile, with the clean waters of the **River Brede** *down below you on your right-hand side*. Go straight on towards the village of Sedlescombe.

In 110 metres go over a stile to follow the river on your right-hand side. In 280 metres leave **Sedlescombe** sportsfield by a wooden kissing gate and *go right, over a bridge*, your direction 345 degrees. In 70 metres (where straight on takes you to a bus stop and, beyond that, to a pub, should you wish to drop out at this point), you *turn left by a concrete footpath marker* **[7]**, *just before a garage*, on a gravelled road, your direction 250 degrees.

In 70 metres, by the entrance to a private garden, you *fork left*, your direction 220 degrees. In a further 65 metres, go *over a wooden bridge with railings, through a bridleway metal gate and turn right* to continue with the river on your right-hand side, your direction 275 degrees.

In a further 520 metres, *go over the A21* and over a stile (with a metal fieldgate to its left-hand side) *to continue on a path* with a stream on your right-hand side.

In 400 metres you fork left away from the stream (to short-cut a bend in the stream), your direction 240 degrees. In 110 metres go over a stile (the path may be somewhat overgrown with nettles at this point) and in 4 metres go on a plank over a tributary stream, to continue with a stream on your right-hand side.

In 40 metres you come to a fence on your right-hand side – a potentially very muddy area.

In a further 150 metres, you come *to a T-junction where you go left for 5 metres, then go right, between telegraph poles marked 'Danger of death'.* In 6 metres go on two planks with a wooden railing across a stream to continue on, your direction 225 degrees, with a stream on your left-hand side. In 30 metres you pass under mini-pylons.

In 250 metres you come to the first of *seven stiles at the bottom of private gardens, which you cross, keeping the stream on your left-hand side.*

The last of the seven houses is a thatched barn-house away on your right-hand side. The owner has positioned his fence beside the stream, so that immediately after crossing the seventh stile you cross an eighth,

and continue on the line you have been following, with the stream still on your left-hand side, to a stile ahead of you (15 metres from the corner of the field). *Ignore a stile beside a metal fieldgate on your left* (which takes another path across the main stream) and *go across a stile and over the tributary stream* on unsafe wooden planks. *Then go half right*, your direction 250 degrees.

In a further 200 metres, you come *to a tarmac road* **[8]** (with a sign for Great Wood on your left-hand side). There is a concrete public footpath marker pointing back the way you have come. *Turn left* on this main tarmac road, your direction 240 degrees.

In 145 metres *take the farm track fork off right*, your direction 285 degrees. In 15 metres, by a concrete public footpath marker (half-hidden in summer), *go over a stile* to continue on, your direction 250 degrees.

In a further 170 metres (when you reach the end of the field, the path goes too far right, so you may have to go left with the hedge on your right to find the stile), go over or past a stile, and onwards with a fence on your left-hand side and an overgrown hedge on your right-hand side.

At the end of the sewage farm fence on your left-hand side, at the footpath crossroads, you go straight on, slightly to the left.

In 70 metres go through a metal fieldgate and in 30 metres through a tunnel under the railway line.

In a further 25 metres, you go through a metal fieldgate and onwards, your direction 250 degrees, with a stream on your left-hand side and the buildings of Battle visible on the horizon ahead.

In a further 80 metres, go over a stile without steps and on, with a field hedge on your right-hand side. In 200 metres go on a plank over a stile and straight on, ignoring the track up to the house. In 70 metres, continue to go over a stile.

In 40 metres you pass **Little Park Farm** (so marked on the OS map) on your right-hand side and keep straight on.

In 40 metres go over a stile and on a wooden bridge with a railing over a stream. Take care here as the bridge planks are broken.

In a further 70 metres, you come out *on to a farm road. Go left* on the road, your direction 255 degrees. In 20 metres ignore a stile to the left (although the path southwards from this stile would be a short cut to the station, should you need to get there in a hurry: at a fork, after 100 metres, take the left-hand path; follow the lower edge of the hill; then cross on a long line of wooden planks and go uphill, slightly to your right, coming out by the fork right to the station on the A2100 mentioned in the last paragraph).

The main suggested route, though, otherwise continues on the farm road. In 320 metres, as you go uphill, you cross over a footpath by a footpath sign and continue on, with a Battle Town Council garden on your right-hand side.

In 60 metres you come out on to the London road *(Mount Street), where you go left*, your direction 190 degrees.

In 35 metres you pass **Bayeux Cottage**, which serves cream teas. In 35 metres you pass the King's Head. In 30 metres, *at the T-junction, turn left into the High Street*, your direction 150 degrees.

In 25 metres you pass the Bull Inn & Wine Bar on your right-hand side. In a further 25 metres you pass the **George Hotel** on your right-hand side.

In a further 90 metres, you come to the suggested tea place, the **1066** pub (the suggested route is to come back to this after sightseeing, if the castle is about to close for the day).

In 65 metres you come *to the gateway of Battle Abbey School.* Sometimes admission to the **Battle Abbey** grounds and to the **Battle of Hastings site** is through this gateway.

Alternatively, turn right here on a tarmac lane, passing the Pilgrim's Rest pub on your right-hand side, your direction 260 degrees.

In 40 metres you come to a carpark on your left-hand side and another entrance to Battle Abbey. (There is a wooden swing gate into the abbey grounds beyond the entrance tills, which sometimes remains open after official opening hours – one that is possibly intended for use by local people?)

After visiting the abbey and battlefield, *retrace your steps to the 1066 pub*. To get to the station, *coming out of the pub, turn right*, in 150 metres passing the **Parish Church of St Mary the Virgin** on your left-hand side.

In 120 metres *fork right to the station*, on the A2100. In 200 metres, *just before the Senlac Inn (the last place for refreshments), turn left* for **Battle Station**, 200 metres away, your direction 60 degrees, for trains back to London.

Walk 36

Borough Green to Sevenoaks

Plaxtol, Ightham Mote
& Knole House

Length 15.5km (9.5 miles), 4 hours 40 minutes. For the whole outing, including trains, sights and meals, allow at least 8 hours 30 minutes.

Toughness 4 out of 10.

OS Landranger Map No.188. Borough Green, map reference TQ 608 573, is in **Kent**, 9km east of Sevenoaks.

Features Nine of the 15.5km are before lunch: the walk goes south from Borough Green through woods and along streams and past several interesting houses, to the old village of Plaxtol with its Cromwellian church. Then through the park of Fairlawne House and past its Japanese garden to Ightham Mote, a beautiful moated medieval manor. The route onwards is up a potentially muddy bridleway and through orchards to lunch at a gourmet 'bar and brasserie', The Snail at Stone Street. After lunch, the walk is through orchards and woods leading to the 1,000-acre Knole Park and its 365-roomed Knole House, and then up by footpaths off to tea in Sevenoaks, with the station 1km downhill from the centre.

Shortening the walk You could order a taxi from Plaxtol; or from The Snail pub in Stone Street at lunchtime. There are also occasional buses to Sevenoaks.

History The Cromwellian **church at Plaxtol**, built in 1649, and has a fine seventeenth-century hammer-beam roof that was originally painted blue. Thomas Stanley of Hamptons, later beheaded for his part in the execution of Charles I, contributed money for repairing the church. There is a slab in the nave floor recording the death, within one month in 1771, of four young children of the Knowles family.

Knole House (tel 01732 450 608) was a palace of the Archbishops of Canterbury from 1456 until it was seized by Henry VIII in 1532. In 1566, Elizabeth I granted it to the Sackville family. It is described as a calendar house, with 365 rooms, 12 staircases and seven courtyards. The house, with its tapestries, paintings and collection of seventeenth-century furniture, is open to visitors from approximately April 1st to the end of October, Tuesday to Sunday (plus bank holiday Mondays) with last entry at 4pm. Admission is £4.50, children £2.25. The house stands in a park of 1,000 acres. There is no charge for walking in the park, and in any case the route described below follows public rights of way.

Ightham Mote (pronounced 'item') is a lovely Tudor and medieval moated manor house and garden (tel 01732 810 378), and can be seen close to from the public way, without paying to go in. It is, anyway, only open to the public from 11am to 5pm, from April 1st to October 31st (closed Tuesday and Saturday). Tickets cost £5, children £2.50. It also has a tea pavilion for light refreshments.

Saturday Walkers' Club Take the train nearest to **9.45am** (before or after) from **Victoria** Station to **Borough Green**. Journey time 45 minutes. There are many trains back from Sevenoaks to Charing Cross, Waterloo or Blackfriars. Journey time 25 minutes.

Lunch The Snail bar and restaurant (tel 01732 810 233) in Stone Street provides gourmet food at relatively gourmet prices. It serves lunch until 2.30pm daily (not Monday). Or try the **Black Head** or the **Padwell Arms**, at the other end of Stone St.

Tea The **Brewhouse Tearoom** (tel 01732 450 608) has an entrance in the north wall of Knole House, without the need to pay an entrance fee. It has the same summer-only opening times as Knole House (see above) and serves cream teas. But this walk's suggested year-round tea place is just off the High Street in Sevenoaks: **Coffee Call** (tel 01732 453 580) at 8 Dorset Street serves tea, coffee, sandwiches and cakes, but is rather small; it is open till 5pm Monday to Friday, till 4.45pm Saturday. **Pizza Piazza** (tel 01732 454 664) at 3 Dorset Street, is open daily throughout the day and will serve just tea or coffee as long as the place is not too full. The **Dorset Arms** pub (tel 01732 464 948) nearby at 22 London Road, is also open daily throughout the day for tea, coffee and hot chocolate.

WALK DIRECTIONS

[1] [Numbers refer to the map.] *Turn right uphill (eastwards) out of* **Borough Green Station**'s *ticket hall to a T-junction (Wrotham Road) and follow this road to the right,* over the railway bridge (205 degrees initially). In 60 metres you need to cross with care the main Western Road turn-off to the right, to carry straight on. In a further 150 metres, *cross over the A25* (there is a pedestrian crossing nearby) to a fish and chip shop on your right-hand side, to continue straight on, signposted Church & Hall, *now on Quarry Hill Road*, your direction 220 degrees.

In 50 metres, opposite the church on your right-hand side, **[2]** *take Landway, the signposted public footpath on the left-hand side,* a tarmac car lane, downhill, your direction due south. In essence, you *keep heading south on this footpath, or its successors, for the next 3km until you come to a T-junction.* But in more detail: In 175 metres you come down to a car road and you cross over this to continue straight on, along a public footpath, now just a path between fences, soon going gently uphill. In 280 metres you cross a car road to carry straight on between wooden fences. In 275 metres your very straight path bends left, going steeply downhill for 160 metres, to cross a stream by a brick-and-concrete bridge.

80 metres further on **[3]**, you come up on to a car road. Continue on, leftwards (due south initially) with, on your left-hand side, a wide grassy bank, a lake and then a long line of new housing built on an old industrial site.

Beyond all the new houses, you pass Bridge House on your left-hand side, to stay straight on (Basted Lane). In a further 20 metres **[4]**, take the right-hand fork (Mill Lane), your direction 205 degrees, past Orchard Cottage on your right-hand side and with the stream on your

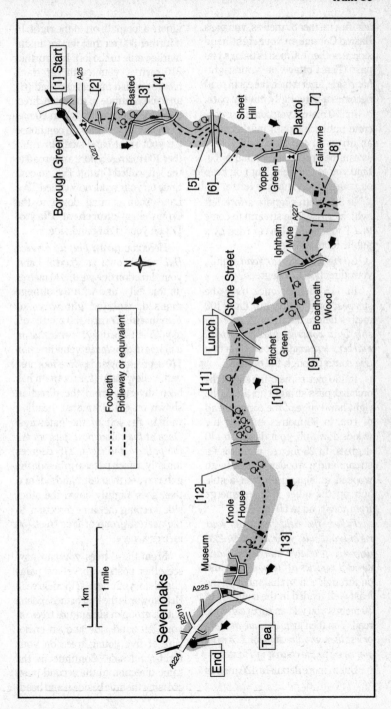

Borough Green

A25

A227

[1] Start

[2]

Basted

[3]

[4]

[5]

[6]

Sheet Hill

Plaxtol

[7]

Yopps Green

Fairlawne

[8]

A227

Ightham Mote

Broadhoath Wood

[9]

Stone Street

Lunch

Bitchet Green

[10]

[11]

Knole House

[12]

Museum

[13]

Sevenoaks

A225

B2019

A224

End

Tea

Footpath

Bridleway or equivalent

N

1 mile

1 km

left. In a further 80 metres, you pass Basted Cottage on your right-hand side. Another 130 metres brings you past Glen Cottage on your right-hand side, after which the earth road becomes a potentially muddy path.

In 350 metres you come to a concrete public footpath marker with an arrow to the right and a tiny stream behind it, and orchards behind you to the right, but you keep on your path as it bends left.

In 325 metres ignore a fork left (which crosses the stream) to come to a T-junction [5], a car road by a public footpath sign.

Go right on this car road, uphill, your direction 275 degrees.

In 115 metres, once over the steepest part of the hill (and 100 metres before the pylons), *take the stile by a concrete public footpath marker, leftwards,* your direction due south through the orchard.

In 150 metres, near the end of the orchard, pass straight on, along the right-hand edge of the copse ahead of you, in 30 metres entering the woods downhill, your direction 140 degrees. In 25 metres you cross a stream and a wooden bridge (with wooden rails), and go over a stile and up the other side to emerge from the wood in 50 metres.

Follow the field fence on your right-hand side, your direction 220 degrees, probably still with many derelict vehicles off to your left, and on through a farm that must be the least well-tended in the country. In 50 metres you join an earth car-wide road. You then just *continue in more or less the same direction for 1.5km till you come to the church in Plaxtol.*

But in more detail: In 420 metres

ignore a footpath off to the right. In a further 300 metres, ignore an unmarked stile to the left. In a further 210 metres, your earth car track merges with a tarmac car road [6] and you continue in the same direction (due south initially). In 80 metres you carry on past an oasthouse (on your right-hand side). In a further 100 metres, ignore a car road to the left, called Grange Hill, to continue on your road, now called Tree Lane, soon coming down to the Cromwellian **church at Plaxtol** [7] on your right-hand side.

Here you *turn right, up Church Hill*, also known as Plaxtol Lane, your direction due west. 300 metres up this hill – and with the strange disused, isolated gateways of **Fairlawne Estate** 150 metres off to your left – *turn left over a stile on a signposted footpath,* your direction 170 degrees, towards a five-foot post with yellow paint (the footpath has been diverted from the direction shown on old OS maps), heading well to the left of the gateways. *Once at the yellow post, pick up the footpath to the right*, 215 degrees initially, which passes up beside the gateways on their left-hand side and then goes slightly down the other side, keeping the same direction, to the nearest group of four trees (50 metres away).

From these trees you can now see other posts with yellow paint ahead to your left (215 degrees). Head towards the first of these posts, with a group of six mature trees on your left-hand side and an enclosure of five young trees on your right-hand side. Continue in the same direction to the second post, crossing the stile beside it and heading towards the third post, some 150 metres away. Impressive **Fairlawne House** is away on your right-hand side, inside its walled garden. (The Queen Mother's horses used to be trained at Fairlawne, which is now Arab-owned.)

About 15 metres before you reach this post **[8]**, *you do not cross the bridleway (that runs parallel with the front of the walled garden) but rather take this bridleway to the right,* westwards, for 200 metres, soon curving right with it, and then going through a wooden swing gate (with a wooden fieldgate to its left). *Go down a tarmac lane towards a pond and buildings, but then in 20 metres you turn left* on a tarmac lane away from the houses, your direction 205 degrees, with a screened **Japanese garden** on your left-hand side.

In 70 metres, *by the wooden bridge on your left, turn right uphill* on a tarmac lane, your direction 290 degrees. In 225 metres you exit by a wooden swing gate (a wooden fieldgate to its left) and *cross the A227 with care to keep straight on*, along the earth road opposite, your direction 290 degrees.

In 150 metres turn right on a car-wide earth road, your direction 15 degrees, in 30 metres going through a wooden swing gate (a wooden fieldgate to its right) to continue straight on. In 150 metres *go left over a stile with stone steps* (next to a wooden fieldgate on its left-hand side) to go on a bridleway, your direction 280 degrees.

In 260 metres you pass a National Trust sign for **Ightham Mote**. In a further 400 metres, you come on to a tarmac road which leads down to this extraordinary manor house (may be covered by plastic sheeting due to renovation).

Going onwards, continue left-wards up the driveway, your direction 170 degrees, away from the house. In 50 metres go *out through the gateway and turn right on the car road,* your direction 300 degrees, passing the renovated cottages and the gardens of Ightham Mote on your right-hand side.

450 metres along this car road, and just before a cottage on your right-hand side, *turn left* on a signposted car-wide public bridleway, your direction 285 degrees. In 600 metres or so **[9]**, at the first cross path, and with your onward path barred *by a wooden barrier, turn right* up a steep and potentially muddy, slippery path, marked 'Permitted Footpath', your direction 330 degrees – a way can be found parallel to the bridleway, a metre or so above it to its right, which can be slightly less muddy.

In some 400 metres, you emerge from the wood and continue straight on, your direction 350 degrees, on a car-wide track, through the orchard and ignoring all ways off. In 750 metres *you come out on a car road and take its right-hand fork* uphill, your direction 70 degrees. *350 metres uphill, you come to* **The Snail** *bar and brasserie restaurant in Stone Street*, your suggested lunchtime stop.

After lunch, retrace your steps for 350 metres, downhill, to where you left the orchard and where a car road fork comes in from your right behind you. *Go over a stile on your right to take the footpath* through the orchards, a path half left, your direction 280 degrees (*not the signposted public bridleway* on the more major earth car-wide fork to the right, 330 degrees; of the three possible forks, yours is the middle one, to the left of a sign saying 'Caution. Sprayed orchards').

Ignore all ways off. In 400 metres you exit the orchard over a stile and *go across a car road* [10] *to continue straight on*, along an earth car road signposted public bridleway, your direction 280 degrees, past Lord Spring Farm Cottage on your right-hand side, and in a further 100 metres, past Lord's Spring Oast also on your right-hand side.

About 1km further on, you come to two small houses on your right and you carry straight on, on these houses' earth driveway. In 90 metres ignore a fork off to the left (which is by a large solitary oak with a yellow footpath arrow on), but in a further 50 metres, *opposite some wooden stables, take the footpath left into the woods* [11] (it too has a concrete public footpath marker), your direction 220 degrees.

Go more or less straight on for the next 500 metres. In more detail: in 160 metres you cross a path, and then another in a further 185 metres; continuing straight on, you have black chainlink fencing on your right-hand side for 180 metres; you then come out on a tarmac driveway and follow this for 50 metres to a car road.

Turn right on this car road, your direction 345 degrees, and *in 100 metres turn left on a signposted public footpath across the playing fields of* **Sevenoaks Preparatory School**, your direction 260 degrees, between two sets of pitches and passing just to the left of an isolated oak tree.

In 275 metres, turn right along the blackberry bushes to the cornere of the playing field and exit between the three posts to the road. *On this gravelled car track* [12] *you turn left*, your direction 210 degrees, gently downhill.

In 200 metres you pass a house called Bowpits on your left-hand side, and, bearing right uphill for a further 100 metres, you enter **Knole Park** through a fenced kissing gate.

Take the wide earth path to the right (along the fence), heading uphill, your direction 265 degrees (not the path to the extreme right, through the metal gate). *In 75 metres leave the fence to fork left on an unclear path just before the third large tree on your left-hand side (they are oak, beech and oak),* your direction 245 degrees – there is immediately a wide swathe of grassland on your left-hand side.

In 85 metres you come to a tiny pond (winter only) and a huge half-dead beech tree on its right. Keep straight on, along the path from the tree, your direction still 245 degrees. You can just see the garden wall of Knole House (at 260 degrees) at the top of the far hill. *Note your onward path to the house that leads steeply downhill from you, then uphill towards the house*.

175 metres down from the tree, cross a wide avenue and continue up the other side, on your car-wide grass route (going due west). 160 metres up from the avenue, take a left fork to continue straight on (due west). In 35 metres you will pass under a cluster of ten small oak trees.

In a further 85 metres, you cross a tarmac path to continue straight on, despite a 'Danger. Golfcourse' sign on your right-hand side. In 90 metres you cross a fairway (beware of golf balls coming from the right), at the other side of which, in 50 metres, you begin to have Knole House's garden walls parallel to you on your left. *Carry on along these walls.* You pass the way in to the **Brewhouse Tearoom**. *At the end of the walls, either turn left for the* **Knole House** *entrance or continue straight ahead on to the grass, heading with no clear path for the largest oak tree at the top of the hill, your direction 315 degrees* (on a line that is a continuation of the line of the side wall of Knole House behind you).

Once at this oak tree (which you now see is actually two trees), carry on in the same direction, still with no clear path, downwards, your direction 310 degrees, *and in 150 metres keep a crater depression on your right-hand side. You are now on a clear path that leads down to the tarmac drive* **[13]**, *which you cross to carry straight on, along a very clear path* downhill, your direction 300 degrees.

In 200 metres you *leave Knole Park by a fenced kissing gate to go steeply uphill* (a metal handrail on your right-hand side), your direc-tion 265 degrees. In 5 metres you pass the entrance to Sevenoaks En-vironmental Park on your right-hand side. In a further 200 metres, you keep to the tarmac path as you pass a carpark (and Waitrose super-market) on your right-hand side. You continue on with a wall and houses on your right-hand side and railings on your left, coming out at a carpark entrance. *Cross over the carpark road and take the way into town to the right-hand side of the toilets* (Akehurst Lane), *your direc-tion 255 degrees. This leads out to* **Sevenoaks High Street**.

Turn right in the High Street and in 60 metres take the first left into Dorset Street, to **Coffee Call** at no.8, the suggested tea place. Or go to **Pizza Piazza** opposite (no.3), or *continue down the passageway that is Dorset Street* and in 40 metres you have the **Dorset Arms**, 22 London Road, on your left-hand side, which also serves tea. *Turn right downhill for the station* (turning left leads in 50 metres to the **Curtain Scene Tearooms**, which has plenty of seats but not a great deal of style).

Sevenoaks Station *is about 1km away down London Road* at the bottom of the hill, just past the Railway & Bicycle pub on your left-hand side. There are about four trains an hour to London.

Walk 37

Southbourne to Chichester

A Chichester Harbour walk

Length 15.5km (9.5 miles), 5 hours 40 minutes. For the whole outing, including trains, sights and meals, allow at least 11 hours.

OS Landranger Map No.197. Southbourne, map reference SU 770 050, is in **West Sussex**, 9km east of Chichester.

Toughness 3 out of 10.

Features There are no hills at all on this walk. On a clear day you can enjoy marvellous views for miles – inland to Chichester Cathedral and south across the harbour. Birdwatchers should bring binoculars. The lunchtime stop is the popular old village of Bosham (pronounced 'Bozzum'), which appears deceptively close quite early on, except that there is a long detour around the water to get to it (we sometimes have a swim before lunch, on the outskirts of Bosham). In the afternoon, you pass a number of elm trees and you may need gumboots, depending on the tide. The walk goes via Fishbourne (there is a Roman palace nearby) and approaches Chichester Cathedral through the lovely Bishop's Palace Gardens.

Shortening the walk A 2km walk north along the road out of Bosham after lunch will take you to Bosham Station, which is on the line back into Chichester, and thence to Lon-don. Or you could end the walk in Fishbourne, visit the Roman Palace there, have a cup of tea and take a bus into Chichester to see the cathedral.

History The **Parish Church of St Mary**, **Chidham**, which dates from the twelfth century, was built on the site of a wooden Saxon church. The Saxon font once had a locked cover (obligatory in the thirteenth century), to prevent witches from stealing the holy water. In 1847, the vicar destroyed a six-teenth-century tomb within the church because no descendant was willing to pay for its repair.

Bosham is traditionally the site of a villa belonging to the Roman Emperor Vespasian, and was an important port in the medieval period. **Holy Trinity Church**, Bosham, is the oldest site of Christianity in Sussex. According to tradition, King Canute's daughter was buried in the church, which also appears in the Bayeux tapestry, where King Harold is shown entering Bosham Church prior to sailing to Normandy in 1064. There are cross marks on the inner porch where crusaders, returning from the holy land, ritualistically blunted their swords.

The **Roman Palace** (Salthill Road, Fishbourne; tel 01243 785 859) is the largest Roman building to have been found in Britain – the remains include mosaic floors and underfloor heating systems. In summer it is open daily till 5pm (August till 6pm); winter weekends to 4pm; and there is a cafeteria (which is not open in December and January). Admission is £4.50. There are three buses per hour from here into Chichester.

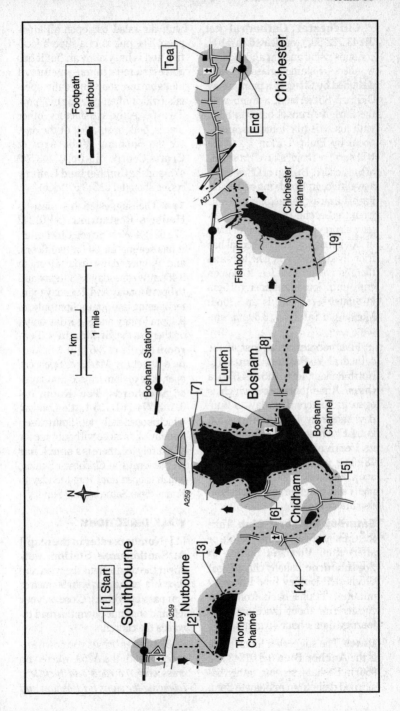

Chichester Cathedral (tel 01243 782 595), dedicated in 1108, contains many ancient and modern wonders: a stained-glass window designed by Chagall; a painting by Graham Sutherland; a tomb with the Earl of Arundel hand in hand with his wife (the tomb inspired a poem by Philip Larkin ' …What will survive them is love'); a shrine of St Richard, Bishop of Chichester; a twelfth-century carving of the raising of Lazarus; and a Roman mosaic from the second century (Chichester was previously the Roman town of Noviomagus). The cathedral has friendly and welcoming helpers and there is no entrance fee. It is open daily until 7pm in summer, till 5pm in winter; evensong is at 5.30pm Monday to Saturday, 3.30pm Sunday.

Five minutes south-east of the cathedral is **Pallant House** (9 North Pallant, tel 01243 774 557), a Queen Anne townhouse which is open to visitors Tuesday to Sunday; last entry 4.45pm. Admission is £4. Chichester is also famous for its **Festival Theatre** (tel 01243 781 312), for those wanting to see a show after the walk; there is normally a late-night train back to London afterwards.

Saturday Walkers' Club Take the train nearest to **9am** (before or after) from **Victoria** Station to **Southbourne**, usually changing at Chichester. Journey time 1 hour 50 minutes. Trains back from Chichester run about twice an hour. Journey time 1 hour 45 minutes.

Lunch The suggested lunch place is the **Anchor Bleu** (tel 01243 573 956) in Bosham, serving rather basic food daily from midday to 2pm, with the salad bar open all afternoon. The pub is in a superb location and is busy all year, but it has a restricted lunch menu of ploughmans, soup and daily specials (which often run out by 2pm). Two perfectly satisfactory other places, both open most of the day, are the **Bosham Walk Arts & Crafts Centre** café (tel 01243 572 475) and the **Cumberland Gallery** coffee shop (tel 01243 572 960).

Tea The suggested tea place is **Hadleys Restaurant** (tel 01243 771 631), 4 West Street, Chichester; it has seating for 50 on two floors, and is open daily from 10am to 9.45pm Wednesday to Sunday and to 6pm Monday and Tuesday (winter opening is to 5pm or 6pm only, to 9.45pm Friday and Saturday only); or there is the **St Martin's Tearoom** (tel 01243 786 715), 3 St Martin's Street (by Marks & Spencer), open 9am to 6pm (closed Sundays); or **Shepherds Tea Room** (tel 01243 774 761), 35 Little London, which is open daily until 5pm (closed Sunday). For those without time for a leisurely tea, there is a **snack bar** on platform 1 at Chichester Station, which is open until 7pm Monday to Friday, 5pm Saturday and Sunday.

WALK DIRECTIONS

[1] [Numbers refer to the map.] At **Southbourne Station**, walk down the platform to the road and *turn left, going south*. In 90 metres you pass Lodgebury Close on your left and continue down the road towards the church.

270 metres brings you down *to a junction* with the A259, where you *cross over the road and turn left, following the signs for Bosham and*

Chichester. On the corner, on your right-hand side, is the **Parish Church of St John the Evangelist**. In 50 metres *turn right off the road*, following the public footpath sign, with the Southbourne Farm Shop and, soon, a tall hedge on your left-hand side, and a ditch on your right-hand side, your direction 205 degrees.

In 200 metres you come to the end of the hedgerows and out into an open field. At the three-armed footpath sign to your right, ignore the way to the left. Carry on straight ahead and in 30 metres follow the footpath as it curves around to the right, with the edge of the field on your right-hand side.

In another 60 metres, there is another three-armed footpath sign on your right-hand side, and a stile facing you.

Turn left, 5 metres before the stile, and continue in a southerly direction. 260 metres brings you to the far right-hand corner of the field and you follow the path as it continues on through some trees between fences, carrying on south.

In another 60 metres, **[2]** you come to another public footpath sign, and out on to the edge of the harbour. *Turn left, take the path on the raised bank and follow the water's edge*, your direction 170 degrees initially.

In 600 metres you come to a wooden barrier with a stile, which you cross over and continue walking along the water's edge, in the same direction.

In 270 metres cross over a stile and continue along the water's edge. In another 300 metres, there is a footpath going off to the left, but you continue straight on along the water's edge.

In another 270 metres, there is a three-armed footpath sign on the left-hand side of the path. Ignore this path and continue straight on along the water's edge, your direction 170 degrees initially.

In 220 metres **[3]** you will find a wooden rail to the left of some steps, going down off the track to the left. *Go down these steps and, at the bottom, follow the path as it parallels your original course*, continuing in a southerly direction along the edge of the field. There is a drainage ditch on your left-hand side.

In 120 metres you come to the corner of the field and *turn left*, following the footpath sign. You walk along the right-hand edge of the field, going inland away from the harbour, your direction 85 degrees initially.

In 300 metres the path takes you over a wooden footbridge, across a drainage ditch, and you continue straight on across the next field, in the same direction as before.

In 170 metres the path comes up to a line of Lombardy poplar trees, and you carry straight on with the trees and a barbed-wire fence on your left-hand side.

In 250 metres the path brings you out on to the road where you *turn right*, your direction 185 degrees. In 35 metres you pass the entrance to Chedeham House on your left-hand side. [!] *Watch out for a path*, 20 metres beyond that, where you *turn left off the road*, just before the drainage ditch. Follow the path along the edge of the field as it parallels the road. In 30 metres there is a short three-armed public footpath sign, pointing to the left and straight ahead. You continue straight ahead, along the right-hand side of the field, your direction 190 degrees initially. You can see the steeple of Bosham Church off to the left across the fields and creek.

After 380 metres of walking around the edge of the field, the path brings you out on to the roadway, and you continue walking straight ahead along the road, past Manor House on your right-hand side. In 90 metres the road curves around to the right, past the Old Rectory dead ahead. 35 metres further on, you then come to the **Parish Church of St Mary, Chidham**.

30 metres past the church, there is a road going off to the left. **[4]** *Turn left off the road just before this turning*, down a grassy path marked by a public footpath sign, your direction 145 degrees initially.

The path takes you around the back of the houses, and in 125 metres it curves around to the right, due south initially.

In 240 metres stay on the same path as it takes you through some trees, and then around to the left, your direction 105 degrees initially. In another 25 metres, you come up on to the edge of a field, and continue along this edge, in the same direction. Follow the direction of the overhead cables on your right-hand side. Through the bushes on your left-hand side, you can catch glimpses of a lake.

In 270 metres the path goes down away from the field, through some trees to the left, and another 40 metres brings you out on to a narrow country lane.

Turn right and walk along the road, with an orchard on your left-hand side. In 90 metres you come to a turning off to the right, signposted to 'Cobnor House and Farm. Private road'. *Turn right on to this tarmac drive*. 60 metres up this drive, *turn left off the drive, and go around to the left and then right*, following the public footpath sign, going along the left-hand side of the hedge, your direction due east (where you turn off the track, you will find an information board describing Chidham and Cobnor).

To your half left across the field, and across the water, you can see Bosham Church – the suggested lunchtime destination.

[5] In 400 metres the path takes you to the water's edge. *Turn left here*, heading for Bosham Church.

In 700 metres follow the path along the edge of a fence – which can be a bit tight if the tide is in. In 50 metres you come to a two-armed public footpath sign where you *turn left* along the side of the garden of the large thatched house to the right of the path, due west.

In 70 metres this brings you out by a grass roundabout, outside the entrance to Grey Thatch. Walk across to the other side of the roundabout, and down the road opposite, in the same direction as before. In 90 metres you pass the thatched Rithe Cottage on your right-hand side.

[6] 300 metres further on, you come out through a wooden gate *at a T-junction* on to a road. *Turn right here*, and in 35 metres you *follow the narrow, unmarked track going up the bank on the right-hand side of the road, up to the water's edge*. Walk along a gravel path with the water on your right-hand side, parallel to the road on your left.

In 140 metres you come down to the corner of a field and *turn right,* following the public footpath sign, continuing along the water's edge, your direction 50 degrees initially. *Follow the water's edge for the next 1.3km* until it brings you out on to the main road, the busy A259.

On the far side of the road, by the property 'Water Edge', *turn right along the pavement and in 30 metres go left up the old road.* Brookside Cottage is on your left-hand side. 200 metres down here, you pass the entrance gate to Neptune House on your left-hand side, and 30 metres further on you go straight over the crossroads into the dead end.

In 150 metres you go past a metal barrier in the road and past Colnor House. [!] *250 metres further on, before the old road comes back up to the main road, there is a small clump of trees on your right-hand side, at the edge of the field. Turn right here, cutting across some land, back to the A259.* 15 metres brings you up to this A road, where you cross straight over.

[7] On the far side of the road, you will see a public footpath sign which you follow, *down some stone steps.* Cross a small wooden bridge out into the field and follow the public footpath sign, taking you straight across the field towards the water on the far side, your direction 190 degrees initially.

150 metres brings you across to the other side of the field and over the stile, up to the edge of the water. *Turn left,* following the path around the water's edge. 150 metres brings you past another stile and you

continue along the path as it heads off right, along the right-hand edge of a field. You are still following the water's edge on your right-hand side, but there is now a hedge between you and the water. 550 metres brings you out to a long plank leading you over a stile by a three-armed footpath sign. *Take the right-hand fork,* continuing along the water's edge.

In 200 metres – some of the route is right along the very edge of the water – you come to a pair of footpath signs and continue straight ahead along the car-wide track which is parallel to your previous waterfront path, slightly on your left-hand side.

In 150 metres you walk through a metal fieldgate which has a number of signs on it (such as 'Please keep your dog on a lead whilst on our premises'). Walk straight past this gate into the boatyard, and straight across to the far side. *Turn left up the car-wide gravel track going into the village.* In 175 metres you come out on to a residential street where you *turn right* down the street, in 40 metres passing the entrance to the **Mill Stream Hotel** on the left. 35 metres further on, you come out on to the main road (Bosham Lane) through **Bosham**.

Turn right, in 25 metres passing the United Reformed Church on your right-hand side. 200 metres brings you down past **Bosham Walk Arts & Crafts Centre**, with its café, on your right-hand side. 90 metres beyond that, *turn right* by **Mariners Coffee Shop** and you pass the **Cumberland Gallery**, with its coffee shop. 70 metres down here, on the left, is the **Anchor Bleu** pub, which is the suggested lunch place. If you continue on up the road, you can visit Bosham's **Holy Trinity Church**.

To continue the walk after lunch, *turn right out of the pub and retrace your steps back to the junction with Bosham Lane. Go straight across the road into the alleyway opposite.* Walk all the way along this footpath. This is raised above the roadway on your right-hand side, along the water's edge (an area that is prone to flooding).

In 550 metres you come to the end of the path, with the long, white 1834 National School building ahead of you, and you turn left into The Drive (underneath the dead end sign, it says 'public footpath'). 35 metres down this cul-de-sac, *turn right off the road*, following the public footpath sign along a path between hedgerows, your direction 110 degrees initially.

In 200 metres the path brings you out through the driveway of a cottage (Byways) and you cross straight over the road on to the footpath on the other side.

[8] *You follow this path going east for the next 1km, until you come to another road.* In more detail: From the road, go straight across the field ahead of you. In about 300 metres, the path bends right and then left over a couple of small footbridges, returning to its original course along a car-wide track, following the two-armed footpath sign. When the track leads up to a house on the left, you follow the footpath which continues straight ahead.

Another 500 metres brings you out on to the road. Just before this, on your left-hand side, there is a metal public footpath sign pointing straight over the road.

Cross the road and carry on along the path on the other side, in the same direction as before (a path not marked on some OS maps).

In 650 metres you come *to a T-junction* with a three-armed public footpath sign. Here you *turn right*, your direction 185 degrees initially.

In 270 metres, you come to a three-armed public footpath sign, and here **[9]** you *turn left*, walking along the next side of the field, with a hedgerow on your right-hand side, your direction 80 degrees initially.

After 400 metres going straight along this path, you come to a two-armed public footpath sign, next to some planks taking you across a small creek, which makes its way out into the channel on your right-hand side. Once over the footbridge, follow the path as it wends through woodland around to the left, following the distant edge of the water.

From here, you can see Chichester Cathedral across the water on your right-hand side.

In 200 metres you climb up a short slope with a step, and then the path proceeds along a ridge which becomes the sea wall ahead. In 60 metres you get to the sea wall and continue on along its top. The sea wall has been rebuilt in places and can be very muddy.

In 700 metres you come to a two-armed public footpath sign and some steps down, immediately after which you cross a small creek on a wooden footbridge with metal railings. (This footbridge and the next one are where you may need your gumboots, depending on the tide.) Continuing along the path for another 40 metres, you then cross a delightfully clear stream on a larger wooden footbridge with metal-and-wood railings, going through reeds. 50 metres further on, go across a plank bridge with a metal railing.

80 metres further on, the path brings you out besides a picturesque duck pond with weeping willows and a thatched cottage on its far side. This is the village of **Fishbourne**. Another 30 metres brings you out by the entrance to The Mill on the right, and a road going off to the left. Go straight across the road and follow the sign for the public footpath ('Fishbourne Church'), through a metal kissing gate. Follow the path along the bank of a stream to your left, and in 80 metres go through a metal gate and continue along the path. 20 metres further on, to your left, there is a sign giving information about Chichester Harbour and Fishbourne Meadows.

Cross over the wooden planks and *follow the path as it heads around to the left*. Do not go towards the new wooden bridge straight ahead, but keep close to the hedgerow on your left-hand side, your direction 110 degrees initially. In 20 metres you go over another new wooden bridge and walk straight ahead, keeping the stream on your left-hand side, going in the same direction as before.

In another 100 metres, cross a concrete bridge with a metal railing, and walk straight ahead for 25 metres, and then turn left through a wooden kissing gate (with a wooden fieldgate on its left-hand side), following the two-armed footpath sign, going initially along the right-hand edge of the field, and then

straight across the field towards the road on the horizon.

In 35 metres the path forks and you *take the left-hand fork* continuing straight ahead towards the far left-hand corner and a four-armed metal footpath sign. Then *take the left-hand path* going through a wooden kissing gate, and into the trees, which form a tunnel, your direction 355 degrees initially. In 75 metres a concrete bridge with metal railings takes you over a small brook. 100 metres further on, you come out through another kissing gate on to a main road. Cross the road carefully. On the far side, *turn right* along the pavement.

(However, if you want to detour to visit the **Roman palace**, go straight ahead, following the public footpath sign, instead of turning right. This soon becomes a tarmac cycle path. In 250 metres, ignore a stile on your right-hand side and follow the path as it bends sharp left. In a further 250 metres, go through a swing gate on your left – with a wooden fieldgate to its left-hand side – and follow the tree line past the café to the museum entrance. Afterwards, retrace your steps to the main road.)

In 100 metres, keep to the pavement. It leads into a footpath to Fishbourne Road East, *through the tunnel under the A27 Chichester bypass*, next to a cycle path. On the other side of the tunnel continue walking straight ahead down Fishbourne Road East.

Follow the roads for the next 1.75km, straight into the heart of Chichester. In more detail: 500 metres after the tunnel, the road curves around to the right and you stay on the left-hand pavement going straight ahead. Cross the railway line ahead.

On the other side of the tracks, walk straight down the road ahead. In 40 metres you see a sign on your right-hand side (to the city centre and station). 200 metres further on, you come to a crossroads with a mini-roundabout at the end of Sherborne Road, and you go straight over into Westgate, in the same direction as before.

Keep straight on down this road until you come to Westgate roundabout. *Turn right here into Avenue de Chartres, cross straight over the road and go right, past the Old Cottage Indian Restaurant* on your left-hand side. 40 metres down the road, there is a tall brick-and-flint wall with a small black plaque pointing off to the left (to Bishop's Palace Gardens). *Turn left down the footpath by the side of the wall and then right through the gate into the gardens.* If the gardens have closed for the day, retrace your steps to the roundabout and turn right to get to the cathedral along the roadside.

Once through the gate into the garden, walk straight ahead, your direction 150 degrees, along the path taking you through the gardens, with the cathedral away on your left-hand side. Keep to the path ahead for 150 metres, as it curves around to the left, between low hedges, and go through the doorway in the stone wall ahead. *Follow the path around to the left, and then in 10 metres follow it around to the right.* In another 20 metres, there is a view of the **Bishop's Palace** through the wrought-iron gate on your left, and 20 metres further on

you *go left through the wooden gate* into the grounds of the palace. *Go immediately right through a stone archway*, and walk straight down the street, your direction 105 degrees, with the cathedral on your left-hand side. 40 metres down here, you will see the Deanery on your right-hand side. *Turn left down St Richard's Walk*, which leads you into the cathedral cloisters. *Here you turn immediately left and walk outside to go around to the West Door*, where you can enter **Chichester Cathedral** itself.

Out of the West Door, continue on up to the road, past the Bell Tower on your right. *Turn right into West Street* and walk along the north face of the cathedral.

The **Dolphin & Anchor Hotel** is on the other side of the street, just before the Market Cross at the main crossroads. Just beyond it is the **Roussillon Coffee House** and the suggested tea place, **Hadleys Restaurant**, at 4 West Street.

The station is eight minutes away. Coming out of the tea place, cross over the road and go down the left-hand side of the cathedral to the first exit on the left (The Close), which brings you into South Street, where you turn right. (The next left, West Pallant, would take you to **Pallant House**, should you want a slight detour.)

Continuing on the main suggested route down South Street, in 200 metres you cross over a busy road, using a pedestrian crossing. Continuing in the same direction, in 100 metres you come to the station approach road on your right-hand side, and so to **Chichester Station**.

Walk 38

Hanborough to Charlbury

Blenheim Palace & Cornbury Park

Length 21km (13 miles), 6 hours 30 minutes. For the whole outing, including trains, sights and meals, allow at least 12 hours.

OS Landranger Map No.164. Hanborough, map reference SP 433 142, is in **Oxfordshire**, 7km north-west of Oxford.

Toughness 6 out of 10.

Features The River Evenlode and its soft, easy hills and fertile countryside inspired Tolkien's Hobbit Shire. At lunchtime you could take a dip in the river and picnic in the meadow by the Stonesfield Ford and the old slate quarries. Before lunch, there are the 2,000 acres of the Great Park leading to Blenheim Palace and its lake, and the Column of Victory that the first Duke of Marlborough had placed on the horizon so that he could see it from his bedroom. Once over the wall out of the park, the route is along Akeman Street, the old Roman road from Alchester to Cirencester, with big stone slabs from the old road still visible in places. Stonesfield, Finstock and Charlbury are the delightful stone villages on this walk, with every front garden seemingly competing for some award. The walk enters Charlbury along a footpath beside Lord Rotherwick's deer park, Cornbury Park. This is a newish footpath for which Lord Rotherwick lost his claim to over £1m in compensation from the Oxfordshire County Council – the claim included loss of shooting rights calculated at £10 per duck.

Shortening the walk At point **[7]** below, you can, if you are tired, turn right to go directly into Stonesfield for lunch, without going down to the riverbank. After lunch, you can walk straight along the Oxfordshire Way into Charlbury (see the double asterisk **[**]** below). Or follow the walk directions below to Finstock station, if you would like to drop out of the walk there. Alternatively, you could take a bus into Charlbury (or Banbury) from outside the lunch pub. Buses are infrequent, so make sure to check the times before you have lunch.

History The royal estate of **Woodstock** was granted to the first Duke of Marlborough in 1704. The old medieval palace had been the birthplace of the Black Prince in 1330, and Elizabeth I was imprisoned there during Queen Mary's reign. It was extensively damaged by the Parliamentary army in the Civil War. **Blenheim Palace** was built for the first Duke in recognition of his victory over the French at the battle of Blenheim in 1704 – the **Column of Victory** has some 6,000 words engraved on it in honour of the Duke. Designed by Vanbrugh, the palace is a fine example of English Baroque, set in parkland, landscaped by Capability Brown. The palace was the birthplace of **Sir Winston Churchill** in 1874, and there is a permanent exhibition of Churchilliana. It is open mid-March to October 31st, and visitors are admitted between 10.30am and 4.45pm daily. Admission £9.50 (tel 01993 811 091/recorded information 01993 811 325).

The village of **Stonesfield** is the home of Stonesfield slates: the stone roof tiles which are characteristic of villages and towns in Oxfordshire and of many of the Oxford colleges. The tiles are no longer mined, so only second-hand tiles can be obtained at great expense.

Cornbury Park is a private estate, whose deer park was carved out of the Wychwood Forest (as was Blenheim). **Wychwood Forest** was once a vast royal hunting ground that extended over much of western Oxfordshire; in pre-Norman times, it extended all the way to London. Now, the sole surviving remnant of the forest lies within the Cornbury Park estate. The imposing seventeenth-century mansion was built for Edward Hyde, who was Viscount Cornbury and the first Earl of Clarendon. As one of Charles II's chief advisors, and Lord Chancellor, he became the virtual head of the government in 1660.

Saturday Walkers' Club Take the train nearest to **8.45am** (before or after) from **Paddington** Station to **Hanborough**. Journey time 1 hour 20 minutes. Trains back from Charlbury to Paddington can be as much as two hours apart. Journey time 1 hour 25 minutes. Buy a cheap day return to Charlbury.

Lunch The suggested lunch stop is the **Black Head Inn** in Stonesfield (01993 891616), opposite the church, which has welcomed walkers in the past (management has changed). They did serve lunch from 12.30pm till 2.30pm, though this may have changed: ringing ahead recommended. Picnicking by the river may be the best option if the weather is suitable.

Tea The suggested tea place is the **Bell Hotel** (tel 01608 810278) in Church Street, Charlbury, which has comfy sofas and serves tea and biscuits at any time throughout the day. Or there are shops in Sheep Street. There is also a pub on the corner, just beyond the hotel and almost opposite it, which serves tea.

WALK DIRECTIONS

[1] [Numbers refer to the map.] Coming out of **Hanborough Station**, walk the 100 metres up the access road to the A4095), dead ahead. *Cross over the road and turn left* along the pavement. You will see a house called Windrush on your left-hand side. Down in the valley on your right-hand side, you can just make out the River Glyme. In 100 metres you come to a bridge over the railway line.

300 metres further on, you pass a large stone house called Hillside Cottage (no.153) on your right-hand side. 100 metres beyond that, you come to a turning on your right-hand side (Park Lane), which is a dead end **[2]**.

Turn right into Park Lane, your direction 345 degrees.

In 220 metres you come to the end of the houses, where a blue-and-white sign ('Highways Act 1980') gives notice that the path on the right has not been dedicated as a footpath. Continue straight on along the path ahead, indicated by the bridleway sign, your direction 325 degrees initially.

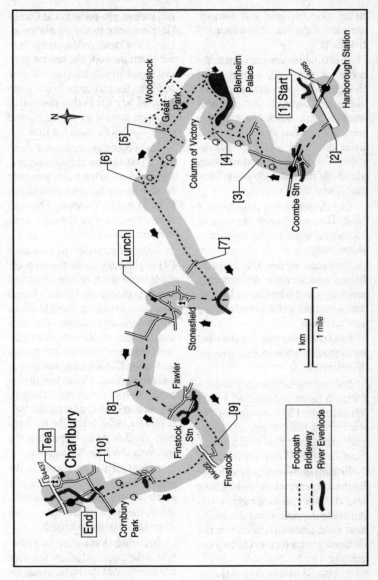

In 15 metres you pass on your left the entrance to High Thatch. Over the wall, ahead on your right-hand side, you can see the tower of Combe Church.

In 100 metres the path brings you out into a field and you follow

the path along the right-hand edge of the field, going downhill in the same direction as you were just previously.

In 150 metres, on approaching a wide gap in the hedge ahead, turn right through a narrow gap in the hedge to your right and immediately left along the left hand edge of that field.

In 300 metres you come to the far corner of this field, with a metal fieldgate on your left-hand side. *Turn left through the adjacent wooden gate*, down the car-wide track with a stone wall on your left-hand side, your direction 250 degrees. The **River Evenlode** runs alongside the track, down on your right-hand side.

In 115 metres you come up to a road. *Turn right along the road*, in 15 metres crossing the river on a stone bridge.

Continue under the railway bridge and straight on, ignoring ways off – and with Combe Church visible on the horizon ahead on your left-hand side.

In 600 metres you come to the top of the hill, where there is a house on your right.

250 metres further on, there are footpath signs pointing off to the left and right. **[3]** *Turn right off the road*, over a stile, following the footpath sign ('East End half a mile'), your direction 85 degrees initially.

In 200 metres you come to the far left-hand corner of the field. Cross over the stile and turn right, walking along the right-hand side of the next field towards a house in the distance, your direction 110 degrees initially.

In 320 metres you come to the far side of the field. Cross a stile and continue straight across the next field, to cross a stile 50 metres away, next to a stone building. *Turn left up the drive to the road.*

Turn left along the road, your direction 340 degrees initially. In 225 metres you come to the Combe Gate entrance to the Blenheim estate. *Turn right, following the footpath sign through the kissing gate*, and go straight ahead down the road. In 50 metres you come *to a T-junction* and *turn left*. Follow the road as it bends around to the right, and down the hill through the trees.

In 350 metres you come to a clearing; if you stop just before the treeline and look to the right, you may be able to see the top of Blenheim Palace through the trees. The road now runs downhill through some conifers.

300 metres further on, you come **[4]** to the edge of the trees on the right-hand side, where the road ahead goes around to the left and down to a cattle grid. Straight ahead on the hillside opposite are half a dozen copper beeches. On your right-hand side here, there is a green-and-white sign ('Visitors are welcome to walk in the park. Please keep to the public footpath and road'). *Turn off the road* and walk around the treeline to the right, following the path as it parallels the metal fence on the left, your direction 55 degrees.

In 200 metres you come to the edge of the lake. *Go left over the stile* and follow the path beyond the stile, along the edge of the lake, your direction 70 degrees initially.

In 70 metres you come to a junction in the track and follow the wide track around to the right, along the side of the lake.

In 600 metres the path curves sharply to the left and up a rise. From this point, you have a fine view across the lake to the Great Bridge and your first real view of Blenheim Palace – a view which will slowly unfold as you continue along this path, around the lake towards the bridge.

Keep to this path for the next 600 metres until it brings you up *to a T-junction* with a tarmac drive.

(If you want to visit **Blenheim Palace**, which is highly reommended, go right here, over the bridge.) The suggested continuation of the walk is to *cross over the drive and to go half left uphill to the just-visible* **Column of Victory**, your direction 335 degrees.

At the column turn right and walk across the field on an unmarked path. Where the field begins to descend, follow it down to the private car road in the valley below. Turn left along this road. Follow the road as it rises to the left, then turns right. The column is behind you, and you are between two avenues of young trees with a fence away to the left. Continue until the end of the fence which has a stile with a footpath marked with a yellow arrow. **[5]** *Go left to this stile and cross it.*

Continue with a wooden fence on your left-hand side, your direction 210 degrees.

In 250 metres you come to a copse of trees surrounded by a wooden fence. *Turn right and follow the fence around the trees.*

In a further 75 metres you should be able to see the Park Farm buildings through the copper beech trees straight ahead on the far side of the field. At this point, *head half right across the field.* Aim for the stile in the fence, between you and the right-hand side of this copse of trees (which separate you from the buildings), your direction 235 degrees initially.

In 110 metres cross over the stile and follow the direction indicated by the yellow footpath arrow across the next field. You are aiming for a stile in the wooden fence on the far side, to the right of the clump of trees in the middle of the field, your direction 320 degrees.

In 330 metres you come to the far side of the field. Cross the stile and go straight across the next field, heading in the same direction as before. In 30 metres you cross over another stile on to a car-wide track. *Turn right*, away from the double wooden fieldgate, going through a narrow band of coniferous trees. In 50 metres, on the far side, *turn sharp left,* following the yellow arrow along the car-wide track, your direction 235 degrees.

[!] *In 200 metres look out for the easy-to-miss footpath pole on the right-hand side of the track, and you follow the direction of the yellow footpath arrow across the middle of the fields (unfenced) to your right,* your direction 300 degrees initially.

In 400 metres follow the edge of some woodland on your left-hand side, following a yellow footpath arrow in the trees. In 30 metres you *turn left through the trees* on an unmarked path; in 30 metres follow a yellow footpath post over a wooden bridge with wooden railings. 15 metres further on, you come to a stony car-wide track. *Turn right,* your direction 350 degrees.

In 200 metres you come to another track at a crossroads. *Turn left on to a footpath* and, in 25 metres, up wooden steps over a high stone wall **[6]**, and leave the Great Park down the steps on the far side into the field beyond. Walk straight ahead along the right-hand side of the very ancient hedgerow (at least 500 years old), your direction 260 degrees, along a path that was once the Roman **Akeman Street**.

You are now *on the* **Oxfordshire Way**, *which you will follow straight ahead for the next 2km.* But in more detail: In 500 metres you go straight over a road and continue along the footpath on the opposite side. At this point, you can see the rooftops of the village of Stonesfield, the suggested stopping place for lunch. 1.5km further on, you come to another road **[7]**. (If you are in a hurry to get to the lunch pub, a short cut is to turn right up the road here, to rejoin the main suggested route, by going to the village centre and turning right into Pond Hill, at the asterisk **[*]** below.)

Cross over the road and continue straight on, keeping a hedge and valley on your left, (At the end of the field, pass a stone wall and turn right, then immediately left to continue following the hedge and valley on your left). Still following the Oxfordshire Way, ignoring all ways off, and in 650 metres you go through a metal kissing gate to the **Stonesfield Ford** meadows by old stone quarries, beside the **River Evenlode**. In 100 metres, go through a metal kissing gate and *turn right – where to go left takes you over the Evenlode footbridge* (30 metres further along the river, on this side and right of the footbridge, is a good spot to swim. This whole area is good for a picnic.)

Your onward path into Stonesfield is relatively steeply upwards, away from Stonesfield Ford, your direction 10 degrees. *You come up*

into the outskirts of **Stonesfield**. Where the Oxfordshire Way goes off to the left, you keep straight on, along Church Street.

In 180 metres you pass the **Black Head** pub (the suggested lunch spot) on your right-hand side. In 45 metres you come *to a T-junction where you continue more or less straight on, slightly to the left, along Pond Hill.* **[*]**

After lunch, *turn right out of the pub* toward Pond Hill to the t-junction with the bus stop. Turn left and follow the sign to Fawler and Charlbury. In 160 metres ignore the Boot Street fork to the left, and 125 metres further on down the hill, you pass a 1722 house called Clockcase on your right-hand side. 30 metres further on, *turn right off the road down a car-wide track*, rejoining the Oxfordshire Way, your direction 330 degrees initially. Note the traditional slates on the building on your right-hand side, at the start of the track, and looking back, on other buildings in the village.

In 350 metres you come to the top of the hill next to a barn with a sign on it (Highfield Farm). 100 metres further on, you come to a crossroads where you can look back for a panoramic view of the village of Stonesfield. Take the tarmac lane going straight ahead, with telegraph poles along the left-hand side of the lane, heading in the same direction as before.

In 500 metres you come to a building on the right-hand side, where the lane curves sharply around to the right ahead. *Turn left off the track*. In 15 metres you come to a wooden fieldgate and *turn right through the wooden gate* next to it, which has a blue (faded) Oxford-shire Way arrow on it. Continue straight ahead, along the left-hand edge of the field, following overhead cables, your direction 290 degrees initially.

In 150 metres you come to the far side of field. Go through the wooden gate and *turn right up the car-wide track*, following the sign for the Oxfordshire Way.

In 750 metres you come to a crossroads, **[8]** where the Oxfordshire Way goes straight ahead through some trees (**[**]** To take the short cut, continue straight on at this point, along the Oxfordshire Way, all the way into Charlbury. When the path comes out on to a road, turn left along the road into the village, and follow the instructions below for getting to the station via the churchyard.)

The main suggested route is to *turn left on to the car-wide track going into a field on your left*. Walk along the right-hand edge of the field, initially with a hedgerow and later a stone wall on your right-hand side, your direction 220 degrees. Ahead, on the hillside opposite, you can see the village of Finstock, which is on the route of the walk (and further to the right, on the horizon, the Wychwood Forest).

In 900 metres you come *to a T-junction* with the main road (to drop out of the walk by heading for **Finstock station**, some 500 metres away, turn right, fork left and then turn left over the river). For the main walk, *turn left*, going down the hill into the village. In 70 metres you pass Manor Barn, a recently restored farm building, on your right-hand side.

200 metres further on, you pass a postbox on your right-hand side.

40 metres beyond the postbox, *turn right down the tarmac lane going past Corner Cottage*, your direction 160 degrees. In 125 metres go over a stile by a padlocked wooden fieldgate (marked 'Private. No parking'). Head for the stile between you and the dark red ironstone railway bridge straight ahead. Cross over the stile and walk straight ahead, along the right-hand edge of the field towards the stile on the far side. In 55 metres you go over the stile or through the fieldgate and under the archway *beneath the railway*. 10 metres beyond the archway, cross the bridge over the **River Evenlode** and turn right along the riverbank, your direction 245 degrees.

After 150 metres along the riverbank, cross over a stile. 20 metres further on, *follow the path as it bends sharp left*, away from the river, your direction 240 degrees.

In 250 metres you come up a gentle incline and cross over a stile. 20 metres further on, go through a wooden barrier, up to a meeting of paths. *Turn left for 5 metres and then turn right on to the wide valley track going uphill*, in the same direction you were going in before, your direction 245 degrees, between barbed wire fences.

After 400 metres straight up this track, you pass under mini-pylons, and 30 metres beyond, you come to a wooden fieldgate. **[9]** *Turn right before the fieldgate*, crossing over the stile into the field. Follow the path going up the left-hand edge of the field, your direction 315 degrees, steeply uphill. In 100 metres you follow the path straight ahead between hedgerows. In 40 metres you come up to a white farmgate. Cross over the stile to its left-hand side, and follow the path around to the left as it becomes a car-wide track going into the village of **Finstock**, your direction 255 degrees.

In 50 metres you pass a cottage on your right called Madeleine. 200 metres further on, you come to a T-junction, the main street going through the village. *Turn right into School Road*, your direction 5 degrees, in 20 metres walking past the Village Store and post office on your right-hand side. 150 metres further on, you come to the **Crown** pub on your right-hand side, and 20 metres beyond that, *to a T-Junction* on the B4022. On the opposite side of the road is the Manor House. *Turn right*, following the sign for Charlbury and Chipping Norton, your direction 45 degrees. 50 metres down this busy and sometimes dangerous road, *you go over the unusual stone stile to your left*, marked by a footpath sign which says 'To Charlbury'. Go through the hedge archway beyond, across to the far right-hand corner of the lawn, to the left of two wooden fieldgates.

Go through the leftmost of the two fieldgates. Walk straight down the track ahead, your direction 315 degrees, ignoring all ways off. In 650 metres, following the track as it curves around to the right, you come on to a car-wide track with a stone wall to the right. There are newly planted saplings on either side of the track, your direction 30 degrees initially.

In 90 metres the track curves around to the left. *Turn half left off the track*, not following the track all the way around, and then going straight ahead down the avenue of trees 60 metres ahead of you, down the hill.

In 330 metres you come down and follow the path indicated by a yellow arrow, going dead ahead down the hill. In 180 metres you come down through the trees on to a tarmac road [10]. *Turn left on this road, along the side of the trout lake*, your direction 340 degrees.

In 115 metres you come to a green wooden gate marked 'Cornbury Park. Private'. *Go through the gate on the right*, into the fisheries carpark. Walk along the left-hand edge of the carpark, following the metal railing to the top. In 90 metres you come up to the top of the carpark, go over a stile, and follow the footpath going between a metal railing and trees, continuing along the side of the railing on your left.

In 450 metres you come to a stile at the end of the trees on your right. Cross over the stile and continue straight on, with the metal rail fence on your left-hand side, in the same direction as before. Deer can be seen in the park on your left-hand side. On your right-hand side, as you walk along, you will see the village of Charlbury.

In 350 metres you come to the end of the path, and cross over a stile with a metal fieldgate on its left-hand side. Walk along a flag-stoned path for 25 metres, then through a wooden gate, which brings you out by the main entrance to **Cornbury Park**. To your left you have a view of the house. *Turn right down the drive*, towards the village. In 90 metres you cross over the **River Evenlode**, way below. 150 metres further on, the drive crosses over the railway line. On the left you can see the tower of Charlbury Church. 100 metres further on, you come up on to the road. Cross over the road to the pavement on the far side, and *turn left towards the village*, your direction 330 degrees.

In 600 metres you come up past **St Mary the Virgin Church, Charlbury**, where the road curves sharply round to the right. You can take a short cut through the churchyard down to the station, or *turn right up Church Street* to find tea. In 80 metres you come to the suggested tea place, the **Bell Hotel**,

on your right-hand side. To get to the station, coming out of the Bell Hotel, go left then go into the churchyard, and *follow the tarmac path around the back of the church to the right.* Follow the path straight out the other side of the churchyard, past the Old Rectory on your left-hand side, and down the road ahead. In 150 metres you come down *to a T-junction* with the main road. *Turn left down the hill* towards the station. In 130 metres the road crosses over the river. 85 metres further on, turn left on the station approach road for the train to London. **Charlbury Station** is a listed building, designed by Isambard Kingdom Brunel.

Walk 39

Manningtree (round walk)

River Stour – Constable country

Length 15km (9.3 miles), 5 hours. For the whole outing, including trains, sights and meals, allow at least 9 hours 30 minutes.

OS Landranger Map Nos.168 and 155 (or Explorer Map No.196 covers the whole walk on a larger scale). Manningtree, map reference TL 094 323, is in **Essex**, 10km north-east of Colchester. East Bergholt, in the second half of the walk, is in **Suffolk**, 3km north-west of Manningtree.

Toughness 4 out of 10.

Features This is a walk through the Stour valley that Constable loved, passing by the settings of some of his most famous paintings – a landscape now protected as the 'Dedham Vale Area of Outstanding Natural Beauty'. Lunch is in the Arts & Crafts Centre in the beautiful village of Dedham. Some of the houses here are painted Suffolk pink (traditionally, the paint mix included buttermilk and pig's blood). After lunch, the route goes past Dedham Lock and Mill, and from Essex into Suffolk, along the River Stour to Stratford St Mary and its church; and from there to East Bergholt, Constable's birthplace, which has a church with an unusual bell cage and an old friary that is now an organic farming community. Nearby is Flatford Mill and a museum of objects from Constable's time. (After heavy rain, the river may overflow; you may need to detour to avoid flooded meadows.)

Shortening the walk You could get a bus or a taxi from Dedham; or from Stratford St Mary (which has buses to Colchester or Ipswich about once an hour); or from East Bergholt. You could cut out 5.25km of the walk by not going to Stratford St Mary after lunch – which is anyway perhaps the least interesting part of the day. This short cut involves crossing over the bridge at Dedham, as in the main walk (see the asterisk **[*]** below), but then turning right along the River Stour (instead of left). In 1km you come to a lane T-junction, where you go left to the East Bergholt church in 800 metres, there rejoining the main walk.

History John Constable was born in 1776. At the age of 33, he met Maria Bicknell, granddaughter of the rector of East Bergholt. As a lower-class miller's son, he had to wait for her parents' deaths before he could marry her. Maria died of tuberculosis in 1828, leaving him with seven children. Constable died in 1837, at the age of 61. He never went abroad, concentrating on painting landscapes in Suffolk, Hampstead, Salisbury and Brighton (they moved south for the sake of Maria's health). The walk passes the grammar school houses in Dedham where Constable was a pupil, and the scenes for many of his paintings, including those entitled *The Hay Wain*, *The Cornfield*, *Dedham Vale*, *Dedham Mill*, *Flatford Mill* and *The Valley of the Stour*.

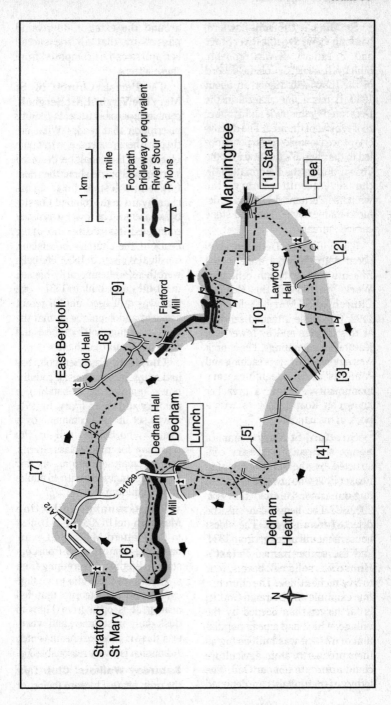

St Mary's Church, Lawford, has long views over the River Stour and its estuary. It was probably built by Sir Benet de Cokefield, Lord of the (Lawford) Manor, in about 1340. It has a fine chancel in the Decorated Gothic style and a timber roof typical of the area. The discovery of treasonable correspondence led to the church's forfeiture by the Crown during the Reformation. In the seventeenth century, the wretched Puritans destroyed or defaced its medieval glass and stone carved statuary.

The village of **Dedham** prospered with the wool trade in the fifteenth and sixteenth centuries. Work started on the **Parish Church of St Mary**, Dedham, in 1492. Constable attended services at this church, and its tower is a feature in his paintings. The church was renowned for its preaching and contains a seventeenth-century monument depicting a preacher known as 'Roaring Rogers' with a book in his hands.

Stratford St Mary contains a **henge**: a circular sanctuary constructed by the sun-worshipping Beaker Folk who invaded Britain in dug-out canoes around the year 2000BC. The henge can only be detected from the air. The oldest house in the village dates from 1334, and the timber-framed **Priest's House** has solid oak beams, four to five inches thick. The church, a fine example of Decorated Gothic, is far larger than needed by the village, which had a peak population of 673 – it was built as big as their prosperity from agriculture could afford, to honour God. The letters of the alphabet are depicted around the exterior, to remind passers-by that all the sacred scriptures can be composed from these letters.

The **Parish Church of St Mary the Virgin, East Bergholt**, contains a possibly fifteenth-century inscription that reads: 'What ere thou art, here reader see, in this pale glass what thou shalt be, despised wormes and putrid slime, then dust forgot and lost in time.' In its churchyard is the tomb of Constable's parents. The tower was never completed, it is said, because of the death of the church's benefactor, Cardinal Wolsey, in 1530. The bells were therefore 'temporarily' housed in a **bell cage**, built in 1531 – one that was still used until a recent accident and is unique, in that the bells are rung, not by wheel and rope, but by force of hand.

Old Hall, East Bergholt, has had many incarnations: a country house (painted by Constable), a nunnery and then a friary. In 1972, it was set up as a commune by a group who advertised in the *Guardian* for middle-class Greens, and has matured into an organic farming community with 40 adults and 20 children.

The **Granary Collection Museum** (tel 01206 298 111), next to the Flatford Mill Field Centre, has a collection of objects from Constable's lifetime – everything from a Vickers machine-gun to vintage cycles and a meteorite that fell nearby. It is open from 11am to dusk daily in summer, and whenever there is good weather in winter. Admission is a very reasonable 30p.

Saturday Walkers' Club Take the train nearest to **9am** (before or after) from **Liverpool Street** Station to **Manningtree**. Journey time 61 minutes. Trains back from Manningtree run about twice an hour.

Lunch There are a number of acceptable lunch places in Dedham, but the recommended one is the **Josephine's Restaurant** in the Arts & Crafts Centre (tel 01206 322 666). The restaurant serves vegetarian food midday to 2pm daily (groups of more than ten should phone to book), although it is closed on Mondays from January to March. At such times, alternatives include the **Sun Inn** (good gourmet food; tel 01206 323351), and the **Millstream Restaurant** (tel 01206 322 066) by Dedham Mill, which is open Wednesday to Sunday midday to 2pm (summer 4pm); it is also open Monday and Tuesday during school holidays.

Tea A reliable tea place is the excellent **Manningtree Buffet**, the station pub-cum-café on the platform at Manningtree (tel 01206 391 114). It is open Monday to Saturday until 11pm (closing at 3pm on Sunday). It serves hot food until 9pm, but cakes, teas, hot chocolate, sandwiches and snacks until 11pm. An alternative is the **Flatford Shop & Tea Garden** (tel 01206 298 260; or regional office 01263 733 471). It is – unreliably – open till 5.30pm daily, from March 1st to October 31st; till 3.30pm the rest of the year (closed Monday and Tuesday in March, April, November and December; closed Christmas and New Year).

WALK DIRECTIONS

[1] [Numbers refer to the map.] Coming off the London train, go under the tunnel to exit **Manning-tree Station** and *turn right, downhill*, towards the carpark, your direction 255 degrees. *At the bottom of the slope, follow the wooden signpost's direction left to Flatford and Dedham, on a path that in 25 metres takes you down to an earth car road lined with black poplars. Turn right*, your direction 275 degrees, signposted Flatford.

In 50 metres, *turn left uphill on a footpath*, signposted Lawford Church, with a field fence on your left-hand side and a ditch on your right, direction 190 degrees.

In 215 metres make a small zigzag with the path to the right. In a further 400 metres, you come to the churchyard. At the start of the churchyard, ignore a stile on your left-hand side. **Lawford Hall** (marked on the OS map) is away on your right-hand side. Your path enters the churchyard.

8 metres inside the churchyard, fork left to *go down the left side of* **Lawford Church**, to its entrance.

Coming out of the church door, turn right, westwards.

In 45 metres you *go out by the wooden swing gate beside Church Clerk's Cottage, to cross the tarmac road. Take the footpath to the right*, signposted the Essex Way, your direction 285 degrees.

In 30 metres you go over a stile, following an Essex Way sign. In 12 metres go over another stile and onwards, half right. In a further 100 metres, you go over a stile (with a metal fieldgate on its left-hand side) to *go left on a tarmac lane*, your direction 255 degrees.

In 240 metres go through a defunct wooden kissing gate (with a wooden fieldgate on its left-hand side) to *go left on a tarmac road* **[2]**, your direction due south.

In 150 metres *take the footpath to the right*, to go slightly to the right across the field, your direction 265 degrees. (This path may be ploughed over, in which case, aim for the point midway between the two nearest pylons.)

In 450 metres you pass under two lines of pylons and over a stile to continue with the field edge and tall trees on your left-hand side, a fence to your right-hand side. In 160 metres go past a wooden pole and *to an earth car road and continue in your previous direction*.

In 40 metres ignore a turn to the left **[3]**. In 25 metres you pass a corrugated hay barn on your right. In a further 60 metres, bear right with the road downhill, continuing and passing a house entrance in 40 metres.

8 metres beyond the clapboard barn, *fork right* on a path marked with a yellow arrow, your direction 315 degrees.

In 20 metres you pass a wooden shed on your left-hand side and keep on down through the wood. Bear right, following on downwards, picking up a potentially muddy path next to a stream on your right-hand side.

At the bottom, go on a wooden bridge covered with chicken wire over the stream and over a stile. In 40 metres go *over the railway lines* and three stiles, and straight on, your direction 310 degrees.

Go up the middle of the field. In 215 metres go over a pair of stiles and onwards between the fences of home paddocks.

In 110 metres go over a stile. In 55 metres you come *to a tarmac road and cross it, slightly to the right*, and go over a stile on a sign-posted footpath, and turn half left, your direction 305 degrees, with a view out to the River Stour valley on your right-hand side.

In 140 metres go over a stile hidden in the far corner of the field, *to a tarmac road where you go right*, your direction 340 degrees.

In 35 metres you pass Frostwood House on your left-hand side.

In 220 metres, *where the road veers right* **[4]**, *carry straight on*, along a signposted footpath, over a stile, uphill, your direction 250 degrees. In 65 metres you go over a stile and straight on with the field edge on your left-hand side.

In 60 metres go over a stile and onwards, with Dedham church now visible ahead, to your right.

In a further 80 metres, go over a stile, and again over a stile in 160 metres, and straight on.

In 230 metres go through a field-gate out on to a driveway, beside a pantiled clapboard shed – with round poles used for its rafters and posts (part of Winterflood House).

Carry straight on for 75 metres, *to a car road T-junction where you go right*, due north, towards the Lombardy poplars.

In 80 metres **[5]** *go left over a stile*, your direction 280 degrees, and go downhill, slightly to the right. In a further 125 metres, go over a stile at the bottom, among the trees, and go along the Essex Way, along a narrow path with a private garden on your left-hand side, and down through the front garden of a house called The Orchard. Then go out on The Orchard's gravelled drive *to a tarmac road where you turn right*, your direction 20 degrees, uphill.

In 200 metres you *take the tarmac lane, signposted public footpath, to your left*, by a cottage called Homestead, your direction 320 degrees.

In 20 metres you pass the renovated, timber-framed Old House. In a further 30 metres *fork right to go through a wooden swing gate* (a metal fieldgate to its right) and across the tarmac front garden of a house. Just in front of a metal fieldgate on the far side, turn right through a metal swing gate, your direction 30 degrees.

In 8 metres go over a stile and keep the farmyard close on your left-hand side.

In 30 metres you pass a notice in memory of two horses, Fred and Shem – 'Now forever in Trapalanda'.

In a further 90 metres, you go over a stile and on a three-plank bridge with a scaffolding pole railing over a stream, to go straight on, your direction 325 degrees (half right is a possible short cut). In 65 metres you come *to a footpath crossing where you go right*, your direction 55 degrees.

In a further 110 metres, go on a two-plank bridge (with a wooden railing) over a stream and onwards, your direction 20 degrees, through **Lower Park** (marked on the OS map) towards an old oak tree.

In 135 metres go through a metal kissing gate and onwards.

In 115 metres go through another metal kissing gate (with a timber-framed pink house away on your right-hand side) and continue with the fence on your right-hand side.

In 110 metres go over a stile and *into a playing field, where you turn left*, your direction 280 degrees.

In 80 metres, past the children's roundabout, *exit the playing field and immediately go right*, with a breeze-block wall on your right-hand side, your direction 350 degrees.

In 60 metres you come out on to a gravel lane and go onwards, in 20 metres passing the Old School House on your right-hand side. In a further 60 metres, you come out on to a tarmac road by the timber-framed Dedham Gourmet, and *turn right on the road*, your direction 55 degrees.

In 80 metres you pass the **Sun Hotel** on your left-hand side. In a further 30 metres, you come to the **Parish Church of St Mary, Dedham**. In a further 35 metres, you pass the **Essex Rose** and the B1029 turning on your left-hand side, and the war memorial on your right-hand side. Continue straight on, and, just beyond the war memorial, are the buildings on your right-hand side that were once the **grammar school** where Constable was a pupil. *120 metres past the war memorial, you come to the Arts & Crafts Centre* and the **Dedham Centre Restaurant**, the suggested lunchtime stop.

Coming out of the centre *after lunch, turn right*, your direction 85 degrees. In 70 metres, where the road veers right, *take the first left fork, a tarmac lane* between fences, your direction 25 degrees, towards a pink house (Dedham Hall on the OS map; it has a high-class restaurant called Fountain House). But, in 65 metres, *go left over a stile*, along a signposted public footpath, your direction 335 degrees, beside a pond on your left-hand side. In 130 metres go over a stile with a stream on your left-hand side.

In 30 metres you pass the **Dedham Vale Family Farm** (with a steep admission fee) to go straight on, alongside the stream. In a further 75 metres, you come to a road which fords the stream. You go left, crossing over the streams on two footbridges, your direction 275 degrees. In 30 metres you come *to the main road (the B1029)*, opposite a converted mill. *Turn right.* In a further 75 metres, just beyond the **Millstream Restaurant** on your right-hand side, *go over a watercourse, and in 2 metres, follow a concrete public footpath sign by going left*, your direction 245 degrees.

In 50 metres, with a converted millhouse on your left-hand side, *go on the bridge over the weir*, and in 20 metres *go over the lockbridge* of **Dedham Lock**. The main suggested route is to go straight *down the steps*, in 17 metres going though a metal kissing gate, to *turn left*, with the field edge nearby on your left-hand side, your direction 245 degrees. (**[*]** Turning right here is the short cut outlined in the introduction: possibly overgrown)

In 90 metres, *at the end of the lock-keeper's garden, turn left*, your direction 225 degrees. In 17 metres you are walking along the banks of the **River Stour**, with the river on your left-hand side.

In 150 metres, as you pass a jokey or pretentious boathouse on the other side of the river, you go through a metal kissing gate, to keep by the riverside, your way marked as the Stour Valley Path. In 40 metres you pass the first of the pollarded Crack Willows.

In a further 185 metres, go through a metal kissing gate and onwards. In a further 420 metres, go over a small bridge and through a metal kissing gate. Keep alongside the river and you come to another metal kissing gate, and, 20 metres beyond it, you go *through a tunnel under the A12* **[6]**. 20 metres further on the other side, go through a metal kissing gate and *on to a tarmac road, where you turn right*, due north, into Suffolk. In 200 metres, you come into **Stratford St Mary**, with a timber-framed house on your left-hand side. In 200 metres you pass a petrol station on your left-hand side and come to the River Stour, also on your left-hand side.

In 25 metres you pass a footpath signposted left (which goes to a lock which Constable painted).

Keeping to the road, in a further 70 metres you pass Valley House, with its glass lookout roof chamber. In a further 80 metres, *turn right immediately beyond the Swan pub to go down an earth road to its left-hand side*, your direction 100 degrees. In 200 metres go *straight through the garden of the house at the end of the road*.

Going through the garden, you come *to a T-junction on its far side, where you turn left*, northwards. In 5 metres ignore a stile on your right-hand side to go straight on through a (defunct) metal kissing gate.

In 115 metres you come *to the main road, where you go right*, your direction 100 degrees. In 125 metres you pass the Tudor timber-framed **Priest's House**.

In a further 80 metres, you pass the Anchor pub on your left-hand side. In 220 metres you ignore a turning left to Higham, to carry straight on, parallel to the A12 which is on your right-hand side, *on the B1029 (signposted Dedham)*. In 200 metres you *go under the A12* and come, in 115 metres, to the **Church of Stratford St Mary**.

In a further 60 metres, *at the T-junction, turn right on the B1029* (signposted Dedham). In a further 230 metres, you pass Haywards Cottage on your left-hand side. In a further 115 metres, *you pass Ravenys on your left-hand side, and immediately go left* **[7]** *on a tarmac lane* (soon a track), your direction 105 degrees.

In 500 metres, by a three-armed footpath sign, *ignore the East Bergholt sign to your left, to continue straight on*, your direction 115 degrees, with a hawthorn hedge on your right-hand side.

You are skirting the water meadows, which stretch away to Dedham in the distance.

In 340 metres you come *to a potentially muddy T-junction where you turn right, following a yellow arrow*, due south. In 40 metres you turn left and go on two planks over a stream. Ignore a stile to the right on the other side, to continue straight on, with the field edge on your right.

In 30 metres go over a stile and onwards. In 100 metres go over a farm track and in 8 metres over a stile, to go onwards, your direction 130 degrees, through a water meadow, with a field fence on your left-hand side. Ackworth Manor House (which Randolph Churchill used to own) is visible ahead to the left.

In 90 metres *ignore a path continuing to the right and go over a stile into the field*. In 215 metres *go over a stile and turn left, uphill* (a river backwater is on your right-hand side), with the field edge on your left-hand side, towards a cottage, your direction 105 degrees.

In 40 metres you come *to an earth road, where you go left*, your direction 50 degrees.

In 110 metres you pass a fork to the left (which would take you into a field – going 10 metres into this field takes you to the spot where Constable painted *The Cornfield*, although the stream is now gone). Carry on up the road, and in 240 metres you come *to a road T-junction* **[8]** *where you go left*, your direction 320 degrees.

In 135 metres you pass a private back entrance to **Old Hall Community** on your right-hand side.

In 110 metres you come to the **Parish Church of St Mary the Virgin, East Bergholt** and to the **bell cage** in the churchyard.

Coming out of the church, retrace your steps southwards (down the lane opposite the church beyond the war memorial) for 250 metres. Ignore the private road on your right-hand side, marked 'Public footpath to Dedham and Stratford'. In a further 15 metres, *take a signposted public footpath left*, your direction 160 degrees, to go alongside the road. In 265 metres you rejoin the road, and in 15 metres start again following a footpath alongside the road.

In a further 65 metres, you cross a footpath.

In a further 155 metres, you cross a driveway to a sewage works and go straight on. In 130 metres you come down to the road and continue on this road, with a stream on your left-hand side.

In 170 metres you come *to a road junction,* with a tourist carpark on your right-hand side. *Go left uphill,* your direction 70 degrees, past the thatched Hay Barn on your right-hand side.

In 100 metres **[9]** *go right on a signposted footpath,* over a stile (with a metal fieldgate on its left-hand side), the path now between fences, again passing the Hay Barn (on your right-hand side). In 80 metres go over a stile to enter the National Trust Flatford estate, to go straight on, with a field fence on your right-hand side. (Manningtree Station is visible half left, away in the distance.)

In 80 metres you zigzag 5 metres to your right to continue on. In 280 metres you come *to a car road T-junction, where you go left,* your direction 135 degrees.

In 35 metres you come to the thatched and black timber-clad **Granary Collection Museum**. In a further 50 metres, you pass the timber-framed Valley Farm. In a further 10 metres, you come to **Flatford Mill**, where Constable painted *The Hay Wain* (now a field centre for nature studies).

Turn back, retracing your steps. Carry on beyond the Granary Collection and you come to the **Flatford Shop & Tea Garden** on your left-hand side, a good place to have tea and should be open. *Turn left beyond this tea place, over the bridge,* your direction 210 degrees. On the other side *turn left* with the River Stour on your left-hand side, your direction 140 degrees.

In 50 metres you come to **Flatford Lock**, the subject of another Constable painting.

In 500 metres you ignore the earth road to your left, to go straight on, your direction 175 degrees, *across the concrete* **flood defence barrier**, in 40 metres crossing over the stream and floodgate. There is a sign for the National Trust's Lower Barn Farm on your right-hand side.

In 80 metres, *at the end of the barrier, turn left*, due east, with a brook on your right-hand side.

In 280 metres, go through a wooden kissing gate. In a further 70 metres, you pass under pylons, and along the estuary defence dyke, with the River Stour on your left-hand side.

In a further 300 metres, go through a wooden kissing gate, *with the upright timbers of a ruined bridge in the river on your left-hand side. Turn right, away from the river* **[10]**, following the signposting to the station, your direction 150 degrees.

In 30 metres go through a wooden kissing gate. In a further 70 metres, veer left with your track, *following a yellow arrow*, your direction 105 degrees.

In 300 metres veer right with this track and follow it under the railway tunnel, 275 metres away. *Through this tunnel and 15 metres beyond it, turn left*, parallel to the railway lines on your left-hand side, due east. In 600 metres you come to **Manningtree Station**, for the last 150 metres retracing the morning's route, and then to the excellent station **buffet** on the platform, the reliable (and therefore recommended) place for tea.

Walk 40

Gerrards Cross to Cookham

Bulstrode Park, Burnham Beeches & Spencer

Length 14.8km (9.2 miles), 4 hours 30 minutes. For the whole outing, including trains, sights and meals, allow 7 hours 30 minutes.

OS Landranger Map Nos.176 and 175. Gerrards Cross, map reference TQ 002 887, is in **Buckinghamshire**, 9km north of Slough and 12km east of Cookham, which is in **Berkshire**.

Toughness 2 out of 10.

Features Near the start, this walk crosses Bulstrode Park to its manor house, now a Christian centre. From there, it goes past woods and lakes to a cratered moonscape where the route crosses the M40. Then it goes through the Hedgerley Green Nature Reserve to the church at Hedgerley, and on through Egypt Wood and Burnham Beeches to a pub in Littleworth Common. 8.3km (5.2 miles) of this 14.8km walk is covered before lunch. After lunch, there are more woods and fringes of woods, with a detour to the hilltop Church of St Nicholas in Hedsor, with a magnificent view out over the Thames Valley and across to a late eighteenth-century folly, a ruined castle. The walk ends alongside the Thames, over Cookham bridge to Cookham Church and Stanley Spencer Gallery, with tea at

a seventeenth-century hostelry, and then across the National Trust's Cookham Moor to Cookham Station.

Shortening the walk Buses run twice an hour from the Yew Tree pub by Egypt Wood to Beaconsfield. From the Jolly Woodman pub (the lunchtime stop), there are buses every 20 minutes or so to High Wycombe, Beaconsfield or Marlow.

History The 400 acres of **Bulstrode Park** were bought by Judge Jeffreys in 1686, who built a house here. It was confiscated when he was sent to the Tower of London. The present manor was completed by the twelfth Duke of Somerset in 1870. Since 1963, it has been the headquarters for 120 missionaries and admin staff of the Worldwide Evangelization Crusade.

Egypt Wood is thought to be so called because it was an oft-used encampment for gypsies prior to 1880 (the name 'gypsy' derives from 'Egyptian', although gypsies probably originate from India). Since 1880, Egypt Wood (which is a part of Burnham Beeches) has been owned and managed by the Corporation of London.

The **Church of St Nicholas** was referred to in land records in 1218 and is unusual in that it is entirely set within the grounds of the landowner, Lady Wantner, with the only right of access being for walkers. Groups of walkers up to 12 in number may be able to arrange viewing of the interior of the church by prior arrangement with Revd John Slater (tel 01628 523 046). The church is often open on Sunday (pm).

Cookham was inhabited by ancient Britons, Romans and Saxons. In the *Domesday Book* it is listed as containing '32 villagers, 21 cottagers, 4 slaves, 2 mills, 2 fisheries and woodland at 100 pigs'. In 1140, a Norman church was built on the site of **Holy Trinity Church**, Cookham. The north wall of the church is built of chalk blocks, probably quarried at Cookham. The artist Sir Stanley Spencer died in 1959, and there is a memorial stone to him in the graveyard.

Spencer was born in 1891 in a Victorian semi-detached house in Cookham High Street, and he attended services at the Wesleyan Chapel in the High Street, which is now **Stanley Spencer Gallery** (tel 01628 471 885). From Easter to October the gallery is open daily 10.30am to 5.30pm; in winter, Saturday, Sunday and bank holidays only, from 11am to 5pm. There is a very small admission fee, or you can get an impression of the place by buying a postcard at the desk.

Saturday Walkers' Club Take the train nearest to **10.45am** (before or after) from **Marylebone** Station to **Gerrards Cross**. Journey time 21 minutes. Trains back from Cookham to Paddington run once an hour, changing at Maidenhead. Journey time 47 minutes.

Lunch The suggested lunchtime stop is the **Jolly Woodman** pub (tel 01753 644 350) in Littleworth Road, Littleworth Common, which has a good menu and quick service, from midday to 7.30pm daily (Sunday to 3pm). Groups of more than seven people should phone to book, as it gets busy. You could get lunch 2.7km earlier in the walk at the **Yew Tree** pub (tel 01753 643 723) by Egypt Wood. It serves good food all day. Those wanting a much ear-

lier lunch stop (or a morning coffee) might like the **White Horse** (tel 01753 643 225) at Hedgerley Village, a family-run freehouse with excellent food.

Tea The reliable place for tea is the seventeenth-century hostelry, the **Kings Arms** (tel 01628 530 667) in the High Street. It is open daily till at least 9pm (with food from 5.30pm, Sunday all day) and has a garden. A pleasanter alternative, just for drinks or a pot of tea, is the **Bel and Dragon** pub (tel 01628 521 263) also in the High Street.

WALK DIRECTIONS

[1] [Numbers refer to the map.] Coming off platform 1 at **Gerrards Cross Station**, go over the footbridge to exit the station building. *Go over the pedestrian crossing* outside the building *and go left uphill on a tarmac path*, your direction 320 degrees.

In 75 metres go straight on, now on a tarmac road, walking parallel to the station carpark down below. In a further 140 metres, where this road veers sharply to the right, and there is a carpark barrier to your left, *carry straight on, along a narrow tarmac footpath*, your direction 305 degrees.

In 210 metres turn left to *go on a footbridge back over the railway lines*. This brings you out onto a road (Layters Way), with Little Orchards house on your left hand side, and you *turn right*, your direction 315 degrees.

In 75 metres bear left with this road, which in a further 140 metres, comes down to a tarmac road.

Cross this road, slightly to the left, to pick up a signposted footpath,

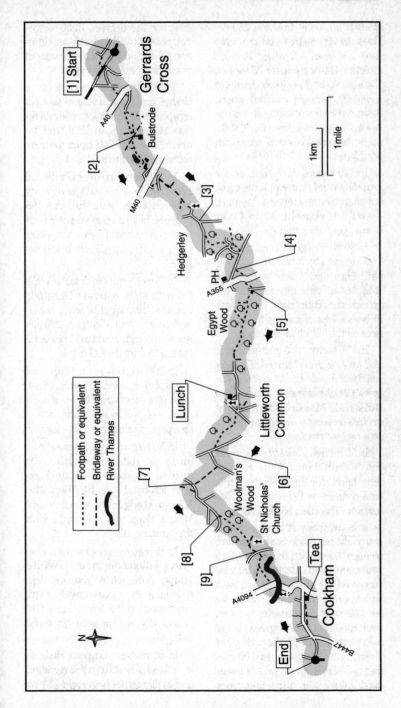

[1] Start

Gerrards Cross

A40

Bulstrode

[2]

M40

[3]

Hedgerley

[4]

PH

A355

Egypt Wood

[5]

Lunch

Littleworth Common

[6]

[7]

Woolman's Wood

St Nicholas' Church

[8]

[9]

Tea

A4094

Cookham

End

B447

1km
1 mile

N

Footpath or equivalent
Bridleway or equivalent
River Thames

straight on, your direction 260 degrees. In 200 metres you *cross the A40 and turn left along it*, your direction 120 degrees, *for 25 metres. Then go right (by a green footpath signpost), between concrete posts, down ten concrete steps, on an unmarked lane*, your direction 220 degrees, between wooden fences on both sides.

In 110 metres, *turn right on the gravelled road* that you have come out on to, heading towards the park – you are opposite Main Court House, your direction 255 degrees.

In 30 metres go through a metal kissing gate by a two-armed footpath sign and *follow a footpath straight on,* your direction 255 degrees, across **Bulstrode Park**, with Bulstrode Manor just visible behind trees on the hillock ahead of you.

In 730 metres you go over a stile and *on to a gravel car road, where you turn right. In 20 metres you cross* [2] *the entrance driveway* to **Bulstrode Manor** and go straight on. In 8 metres go over a cattle grid on a tarmac road.

In 50 metres, *fork left over a stile* onto a path with a fence to your right-hand side. In 225 metres, this path comes to a T-junction. You *go left*, your direction 255 degrees.

In 80 metres you have a lake to your right-hand side. Soon your path reenters trees, with the lake still to your right-hand side. In 340 metres, you come out of the trees to a field with young trees planted. *Go under the pylons at right angles to them*, your direction 245 degrees. In 50 metres, bear left with the path, your direction 225 degrees. In 100 metres, go down steps *to a tarmac road, where you turn right*, your

direction 315 degrees. In 50 metres you pass Moat Farm on your right-hand side, and 120 metres beyond it you *cross the M40 bridge*.

1 metre from the other side of the bridge, cross over a stile to *take the signposted footpath left*, your direction 100 degrees. In 12 metres go over a stile and half right, your direction 145 degrees.

In 45 metres go over a stile and *turn right on a car-wide grassy way* between fences, your direction 195 degrees. In 40 metres you come out *on to a tarmac road T-junction where you go left*, your direction 100 degrees.

In 75 metres, at the Circular Walk footpath sign, opposite Bulstrode Cottages, *turn right on an earth car-wide road*, your direction 220 degrees, through a **nature reserve** (so marked on the OS map).

In 200 metres, *when your road bends left towards Sherley Close, leave it to carry straight on, along a bridleway*, following a blue arrow on a post, your direction 230 degrees.

In 500 metres you ignore a stile off to the right. In a further 200 metres, you come to a church on your left-hand side, **St Mary the Virgin, Hedgerley**, which is kept locked. Here, you veer right with the tarmac path.

In 85 metres you *come out on to a road, Village Lane* (near the **White Horse** pub), *where you turn left*, following the circular walk sign, your direction 195 degrees, past Old School Cottage on your left-hand side.

In 80 metres you pass Hedgerley's 'Bucks' Best Kept Village' sign, and in 60 metres *turn right* [3] by the Brickmould pub, on to Kiln Lane, your direction 265 degrees.

In 200 metres *you turn left through a wooden barrier on to a footpath* signposted Circular Walk, your direction 240 degrees, upwards into a wood and through a temporary coppicing enclosure. Exit the temporary enclosure, bearing leftwards between fences, walking on blocks of wood and paving stones, your direction 190 degrees. Soon you go over a stile and onwards, with a wooden fence to the left-hand side. In 145 metres *turn left on a signposted narrow public footpath* to the right of Old Nursery Court, your direction 155 degrees. Where the footpath begins, there is a yellow water marker in the ground to its left, marked 'H100/8', and a brick wall to its right.

In a further 70 metres, go over a stile. *In 40 metres ignore the Circular Walk arrow on the post and fork right,* your direction 230 degrees.

In 40 metres *choose again the right fork, straight on*; in 40 metres passing through a more open area of the wood, again straight on.

In 25 metres go through a wooden barrier and onwards, in 100 metres coming out on to the road junction, with Andrew Hill Lane on your right-hand side and Christmas Lane straight on, but you *go right, on the main road*.

In 110 metres you pass Top Farm on the right-hand side.

In a further 85 metres, you pass on your right-hand side a metal fieldgate with a 'Pond's Wood, Private' sign. In 130 metres [4] you *go left over a stile, signposted Circular Walk*, into the wood.

(Or, if you would like to detour to an early lunch, carry on up the road to the **Yew Tree** pub, up ahead.)

The main route is straight on beyond the stile, your direction 190 degrees. In 170 metres you *cross the A355, slightly to the right,* to continue on a Circular Walk signposted footpath. In 3 metres you go over a stile, your direction 230 degrees initially, into **Egypt Wood** (so marked on the OS map).

In 250 metres you go over a stile and *across a road* [5], *Egypt Lane (on a Corporation of London signboard), to go straight on, slightly to the right,* signposted Circular Walk, on a concrete lane, your direction 295 degrees.

In 150 metres you pass concrete garages on your left-hand side to keep straight on, along a broad and obvious earth track running roughly east-west for 800 metres through the wood. Ignore all ways off and keep straight ahead – your onward direction is twice confirmed by Circular Walk arrows on posts at junctions – until in 200 metres, after the second of these posts, you *ignore the Circular Walk arrow on a low wooden notice, going to the right, to keep straight on*, slightly left, now with woods on your left-hand side and open fields to your right.

In 140 metres go over a stile (with a wooden fieldgate to its left) to exit the wood, with a field hedge now on your right-hand side.

In 160 metres go over a stile (a wooden fieldgate to its right), to go straight on, along an earth road.

In 100 metres *go straight on, along a tarmac road,* due west.

In 160 metres *keep straight on, at a junction* (your direction signposted Burnham and Taplow), on Boveney Wood Lane.

In 260 metres you pass Boveney Wood Farm on your right-hand side, and ignore a fork left, to go straight on. In 15 metres ignore a bridleway to the right. In a further 80 metres, *you come to a bridleway to the right which, in 50 metres – having passed a large bungalow – brings you to the* **Jolly Woodman** *pub*, the suggested lunchtime stop.

Coming out of the pub door after lunch, go straight on, along a bridleway opposite the front door, your direction 205 degrees.

Having taken the right of two forks, in 45 metres you come *to a tarmac lane and turn right*, your direction 265 degrees.

In 40 metres you come *to the front gate of the (locked)* **Parish Church of St Anne**, **Dropmore**. *Turn left here on to a path into the wood*, between two upright wooden logs, your direction 170 degrees.

Bear right and, *in 40 metres, at a bridleway T-junction, go right*, your direction 295 degrees.

In 55 metres *turn right on Dorney Wood Road*. In 25 metres you come to a car road T-junction, signposted Burnham and Taplow to the left. *Cross this T-junction, slightly to the left, to pick up a* **Beeches Way** *signposted footpath* to the left of Brissels Wood Cottage, through a wooden kissing gate, your direction 295 degrees.

In 460 metres you leave the edge of the wood to your right to go over a stile, on a clear path across open fields, your direction 280 degrees, aiming to the left of the house visible across the field.

In a further 360 metres, go over a stile, coming in 80 metres to a car road **[6]**. *Turn right on this road*, your direction 320 degrees. In 45 metres you pass the entrance to Hales Cottage on your right-hand side. In a further 140 metres, *take the left turn, signposted Taplow*, your direction 245 degrees.

In 310 metres *you take the bridleway signposted Beeches Way going to the right*, on a car-wide road (without tarmac after 25 metres), your direction 290 degrees.

In 150 metres you pass a cottage on your left-hand side and continue on a narrow bridleway. (If muddy, keep close to the fence on your right-hand side, above the path).

In 370 metres you come out *on a tarmac road* **[7]** *where you follow Beeches Way, signposted to the left*, your direction 255 degrees.

In 80 metres ignore a bridleway to the right. In 210 metres you cross Wash Hill Road to your right, and Hedsor Lane to your left, to go straight on.

In 180 metres, where the main road bends right, *you fork left on Branch Lane* **[8]**, which is marked 'Unsuitable for motors', *following the Beeches Way arrow*, your direction 230 degrees.

In 200 metres fork left, signposted Beeches Way, past a metal fieldgate on a car-wide gravelled road, your direction 225 degrees, into **Woolman's Wood**.

In 80 metres fork right, following the Beeches Way arrow on a post and the Church path arrow.

In 620 metres go through a metal kissing gate and straight on, along Beeches Way, with Lord Boston's eighteenth-century mock-castle folly up on the hill to the right.

In 200 metres *it is worth detouring up steps and through a kissing gate on your left-hand side, to take a path across the field steeply uphill,* your direction 125 degrees, heading to the right of the church and through a kissing gate into the churchyard of the **Church of St Nicholas** (locked, alas). From the top, the view over the valley makes the climb worthwhile.

Back on the road below, in 110 metres you *cross the main road* **[9]** past an unusual thatched house with columns on your right-hand side, to *go through green wooden gates,* (pedestrian gate to the side of a vehicle one), direction 235 degrees.

In 60 metres, by the entrance to the manor, take the Beeches Way public footpath signposted to the right, your direction 290 degrees. In 20 metres, at the end of a wall and by the first pine tree, you go over a stile. In 120 metres go over a stream on a large wooden bridge with railings that lean outwards. At the other end of the bridge, fork left, following the Beeches Way arrow, your direction 235 degrees. In 45 metres you go past the stile and onwards, in 35 metres passing an obelisk behind the fence on your left-hand side.

In a further 40 metres your path is beside the **River Thames** on your left-hand side. Then in 130 metres, go over a stile and follow the path slightly to the right, away from the Thames, your direction 235 degrees.

In 300 metres go over a stile, marked by the last of the Beeches Way signposts, and *turn left on the busy A4094, due south, to cross the bridge* into **Cookham**. 20 metres beyond the bridge, ignore steps on the left to the Ferry Inn; instead *go right down steps with wooden railings* (a signposted public footpath) and then straight on, along a gravelled path (looks like dead end) your direction 285 degrees.

In 25 metres you come into the churchyard of **Holy Trinity Church**, Cookham, through a wooden swing gate. The church entrance is around the far side.

Coming out of the church, take the path from the front door, in 25 metres passing **Spencer's memorial stone** (to the right of a bench – his ashes were scattered by his wife's grave in a Cookham cemetery). 10 metres beyond the church gates, bear left, with Churchgate House on your left. In 20 metres you come *to the A4094, where you turn right.*

In 60 metres you come to **Stanley Spencer Gallery**. Coming out of the gallery, turn left on the High Street, your direction 260 degrees. In 70 metres you come to the suggested tea place, the **Kings Arms** pub on your left-hand side and, just beyond it, the less friendly **Two Roses** tearoom.

In 90 metres you come to the War Memorial on your left-hand side, and *you carry on across* **Cookham Moor**, *on a tarmac lane to the left-hand side of the main street,* your direction 265 degrees, and in 200 metres you go over the bridge.

100 metres *beyond the bridge, you rejoin the main road and go straight on.* You pass Spencer's pub and The Old Swan Uppers pub on your right-hand side and so reach **Cookham Station**.

Walk 41

Bow Brickhill to Leighton Buzzard

The Greensand Ridge & River Ouzel

Length 13.8km (8.5 miles), 4 hours 10 minutes. For the whole outing, including trains, sights and meals, allow at least 6 hours.

OS Landranger Map No.165. Bow Brickhill, map reference SP 896 347, is in **Buckinghamshire**, 9km north of Leighton Buzzard, which is in **Bedfordshire**.

Toughness 2 out of 10.

Features This is a short and straightforward walk. It has a potentially muddy bridleway near the start. In wet weather, you may prefer to begin on the more strenuous but less muddy route described in Walk 17 (Bow Brickhill to Woburn Sands), starting at the same station and joining Walk 41 by the sequoia trees in Back Wood (see the asterisk [*] in the walk directions below). After Back Wood and its sequoia trees, this walk goes south through Duncombe Wood to a pub for lunch in Great Brickhill. After lunch, the route joins the Greensand Ridge Walk, with fine views out over the River Ouzel, and so to a pub for tea on the Grand Union Canal. (Note that Bow Brickhill Station may be closed on Sundays – although Leighton Buzzard, the end station, is open. On Sundays, you could join the walk by taking a taxi for the brief ride from Bletchley Station to Bow Brickhill.)

Shortening the walk There are buses about three times a day from the lunchtime pub in Great Brickhill to Leighton Buzzard or Bletchley. Alternatively, you could call a taxi from Great Brickhill or from the teatime pub near Leighton Buzzard.

History **Lower Greensand** is very different from the surrounding claylands, and consists of marine sands with few fossils – a terrain that supports a tree population dominated by pine.

Great Brickhill was a centre of the curious coprolite industry: the mining of fossilised phosphatic nodules used to manufacture super-phosphatic fertiliser.

The **Globe Inn**, the suggested teatime stop, was first licensed in 1830 as a beer shop, to serve passing trade on the Grand Union Canal.

Saturday Walkers' Club Take the train nearest to **9.20am** (before or after) from **Euston** Station to **Bow Brickhill** (changing at Bletchley on to the Marston Vale line, which is an hourly service). Journey time about 1 hour. Trains back from Leighton Buzzard run about four times an hour. Journey time 50 minutes.

Lunch The suggested lunch stop is the **Old Red Lion** pub (tel 01525 261 715) in Great Brickhill, serving food from midday to 2pm daily (closed on Mondays in winter). This is a friendly pub and its garden has a fine view out.

Tea The suggested tea place is the **Globe Inn** (tel 01525 373 338) on the Grand Union Canal, about half

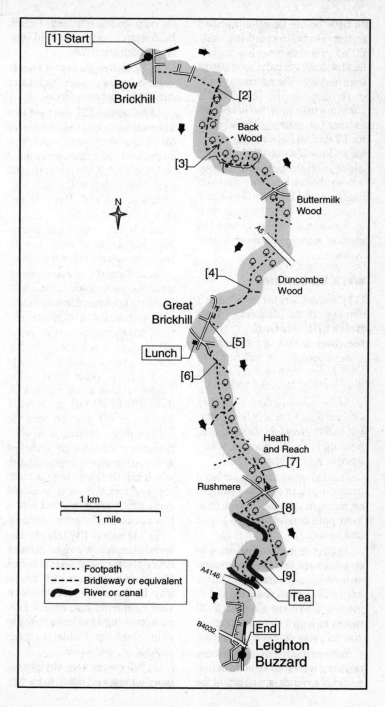

[1] Start

Bow
Brickhill

[2]

Back
Wood

[3]

Buttermilk
Wood

N

A5

[4]

Duncombe
Wood

Great
Brickhill

[5]

Lunch

[6]

Heath
and Reach

[7]

Rushmere

1 km

1 mile

[8]

---- Footpath
-- - Bridleway or equivalent
~~ River or canal

A4146

[9]

Tea

B4032

End

Leighton
Buzzard

an hour before Leighton Buzzard Station. The pub serves drinks daily till late and sometimes has tea, coffee and snacks (Sunday food all day from midday). The alternatives are: carry on along the Grand Union Canal towpath, past the Globe (with the canal on your right-hand side), for 1.75km, to have a cheap cream tea at **Tesco's** (tel 01525 250 400) which is on the canalside on your left, just before you reach the main road bridge at Linslade (Tesco café is open until at least 7pm daily, 4pm on Sunday); or make do with the **station snacks counter** (closed Sunday).

WALK DIRECTIONS

[1] [Numbers refer to the map.] Coming off the platform of **Bow Brickhill Station** (from the Bletchley train), go through a wooden swing gate and turn left, southwards, *back over the railway lines*, on 'V10' Brickhill Street.

In 75 metres ignore a left turn (Station Road) towards Bow Brickhill. In 80 metres *take the signposted footpath to the left*, due east, with a fence to your left-hand side.

In 345 metres cross a surfaced tractor track to continue straight on, through a wooden kissing gate. Your path is now between fences and houses.

In 40 metres you come out *on to an estate road, and you keep straight on* up this, ignoring a turn-off to the left. In 170 metres you come *to a T-junction where you go right.* In 45 metres pick up a signposted path to your left, your direction 105 degrees.

In 25 metres go through a wooden kissing gate and straight on, across a field of mounds (a remnant of the old ridge-and-furrow field system). In 55 metres keep to the field edge on your left-hand side.

In 80 metres go over a stile (a metal fieldgate to your right) and straight on, between fences.

In 260 metres **[2]**, you meet, at a three-armed footpath sign, *an earth car road where you go right on a bridleway.* In 30 metres ignore forks off to the left, to bear right with your road, with a view to the right over Bletchley, and with **Back Wood** on your left-hand side.

In 290 metres ignore an avenue off to left and go straight on, with woods (some cleared) on both sides.

In 270 metres ignore a yellow arrow footpath, uphill to the left. In 50 metres ignore an unmarked earth road turning, going off left uphill.

In 220 metres, as you go downhill through a potentially muddy stretch, ignore a possible way off to the left (by a corner fencepost) to follow the blue arrow straight on downhill. In 80 metres, at what seems like a T-junction near the bottom (and ignoring a wooden fieldgate, stile and footpath, marked with a yellow arrow, 5 metres ahead, which exit the wood to go straight on), *you turn left on a bridleway going gently uphill*, marked with a blue circular walk arrow, due east.

In 200 metres **[3]** *take the blue arrow sharply to the right, through newly planted trees*, your direction 200 degrees, on a car-wide bridleway. In 475 metres, with ponds on your right-hand side, cross a footpath (ignoring a footbridge away to your right-hand side) to keep straight on, eastwards.

In 185 metres keep straight on, ignoring ways off uphill to the left, with sequoia trees now visible ahead on your right-hand side.

[*] In 60 metres ignore a yellow arrow footpath uphill to your left, and go right, continuing on the bridleway, over a stream and up steps (to the left-hand side of the main track).

In 50 metres you can touch the soft and furry sequoia trees on the right-hand side of the path. In a further 80 metres, past the last of these sequoia trees, ignore a grassy avenue up off to the left. In 75 metres ignore a footpath stairway up to the left.

In a further 230 metres, you go through a wooden swing gate (with a metal fieldgate to its left) out *on to a main road, where you turn left*, your direction 125 degrees. Ignore a road to the left which is signposted Woburn Golf.

Continue on the main road and in 40 metres *go right on a signposted footpath*, over a stile, your direction 200 degrees, through a pine wood.

In 210 metres you cross a grassy path to keep straight on. In 130 metres cross a stile (a wooden fieldgate to its left) to leave the wood. Continue straight on along the field edge, in 55 metres passing a pond and a stile to the right-hand side which you ignore.

In a further 250 metres (the field edge having continued parallel to the A5 for some 100 metres) you go through a 12' gap in the hedge, following the hedge on your right-hand side to reach a public footpath sign beside the A5 dual carriageway.

Turn left, alongside the fencing on your right-hand side, your direction 155 degrees. In 175 metres go over a stile to your right, signposted public footpath, *crossing the A5* with extreme care.

On the other side (where there is an interesting milestone) go straight on across a stile to cross a minor road. Go straight on through a gateway, on a signposted footpath, your direction 230 degrees.

Go through a wooden swing gate into **Duncombe Wood** (as marked on the OS map) to go straight on, following a yellow arrow. (The Duncombes used to be the most important family in the area.) In 280 metres go to the right-hand side of a fenced-in pond. Keep straight on, ignoring a fork to the right.

In 165 metres you ignore a fork to the right to bear slightly left with the main path, following a yellow arrow, your direction 195 degrees.

In 175 metres [4] go through a wooden kissing gate *on to an earth car road, where you go straight on*, your direction 205 degrees.

In 400 metres you pass the entrance to a farm on your left-hand side. In 160 metres you enter the outskirts of **Great Brickhill**.

In 30 metres, by a public footpath sign, and *20 metres before the main road T-junction, turn left on an estate road*, your direction 210 degrees.

In 210 metres, at the end of this road, *take the concrete pathway with railings, down to the right. Continue straight on uphill*, on the more main road, your direction 215 degrees.

In 40 metres [5] ignore a footpath to the left and Rotten Row to the right, to go over the brow of the hill and down to the **Old Red Lion** pub, visible 270 metres ahead at the bottom of the hill, on the right-hand side of the road.

Coming out of the pub *after lunch, cross straight over the main road to continue on Heath Road*, signposted to Heath and Reach.

In 55 metres *fork right on Cuff Lane*, your direction 140 degrees.

In 150 metres follow the public footpath sign straight on, your direction 155 degrees.

In 190 metres you pass the entrance to a sewage treatment plant on your left-hand side. In 55 metres go over a stream. In 15 metres **[6]** *go straight on through a wooden swing gate*, your direction 195 degrees, on a way marked 'CW', into woods, ignoring a fork to the left.

In 350 metres ignore a fork to the left to *follow the Millennium Walk arrow* straight on. In 25 metres you cross another path to go straight on. In 130 metres you cross another path to go straight on downhill, following the CW arrow. In 115 metres, at a four-armed footpath sign, *follow the yellow arrow ahead for the Bucks Circular walk* (or the Greensand Ridge Walk (GRW) sign). (The common markings for the Green-sand Ridge Walk are either the letters 'GRW' or the muntjac deer symbol.)

In 160 metres you pass a pond on your left-hand side to go over a stream. Ignore a fork left to go straight on, following a CR arrow. In 15 metres you go over a stile. In a further 170 metres, ignore a fork to the left to follow GRW and CW arrows straight on.

In 160 metres you ignore a way-marked stile to the right, and in a further 150 metres you go over a stile to leave the woods for a time,

with a fine view out over a rural scene on your right-hand side.

[!] In 390 metres **[7]** fork right, following a green deer arrow, your direction 175 degrees (miss this fork and you come to a tarmac lane).

In 220 metres you pass sequoia trees and a lake on your left-hand side. In 90 metres you come out through a kissing gate on to a tarmac road and follow the CW arrows and deer signs left, your direction 135 degrees, walking on Bragenham Lane.

In 25 metres you come *to the main road*, with the gateway to Rushmere Park then on your left-hand side.

At the main road, turn right, then in 15 metres, go left, opposite Rushmere House, *to pick up the Greensand Ridge signpost,* up wooden steps past a barrier, into the beech woods, to follow the path right, your direction 235 degrees, parallel to the road below on your right-hand side.

In 340 metres exit the woods through a wooden swing gate (with wooden posts to its right) to *follow the deer sign left*, uphill, your direction 135 degrees, with the edge of the wood on your left-hand side.

In 135 metres ignore a turning left by a post back into the wood. In 15 metres, at the end of the field, *bend left, with your main path, up into the wood*, your direction 85 degrees. In 20 metres, *by a post on your left-hand side, take the path going downhill towards the river*, your direction 150 degrees.

In 70 metres **[8]** you come down to within 50 metres of the River Ouzel. Then you turn left and go through a wooden kissing gate (next to a wooden barrier on its right), to continue straight on, your direction 120 degrees.

Stay on this path, ignoring all paths off, and in 160 metres go through gateposts (a kissing gate to their left) and straight on.

In 400 metres you come out on to a driveway and go uphill, your direction 160 degrees.

In 150 metres *go right over a cattle grid, the way signposted Greensand Ridge Walk*, and marked Corbetts Hill Farm. In 100 metres *ignore a short cut path straight on, along a line of telegraph poles, to stay on a tarmac lane*, bearing left.

In 85 metres **[9]** *fork off on the path marked GRW to the right*, your direction 310 degrees, with old Linslade Church visible ahead.

In 190 metres you *cross the* **River Ouzel** *on a bridge* – on the other side *turning left along its banks*, your direction 240 degrees.

In 50 metres you cross a streambed on three planks to carry on with the river on your left-hand side.

In 220 metres you come to a sinuous streambed, 15 metres before a derelict bridge to your left. *Turn right along the banks of the stream for 200 metres, to a wooden plank bridge in the field corner. Cross this and follow the path, with a field hedge on your right-hand side, towards the pub*, due east. In 160 metres exit the field by a stile on your right-hand side, *on to a tarmac lane. Turn left*, coming in 80 metres to the suggested tea place, the **Globe Inn**.

After tea, retrace your steps for 80 metres, to *cross the Grand Union Canal* bridge. *Turn right down concrete steps, following the Cross Bucks*

Way sign, your direction 280 degrees, with the canal on your right-hand side.

In 140 metres *(10 metres before the railway embankment) fork left on a tarmac path uphill*, with the railway alongside you on your right-hand side, your direction 150 degrees. In 85 metres go on *up to the A4146 and turn right, over the railway bridge*. On the other side of the bridge, *turn left to go uphill, parallel to the railway lines*. In 5 metres go through a metal kissing gate to head due south.

In 115 metres ignore a turning to the right, keeping left with the path, to turn sharper left past a wooden barrier (the remains of a kissing gate). In 25 metres go through another kissing gate, to go straight on, uphill, due south. Note the railway tunnel ventilation shaft to your left.

In 75 metres, at the top of the hill, there is a panoramic view. In a further 30 metres cross a wide way to go straight on.

In a further 110 metres, you go through a wooden swing gate and *down to a tarmac road. Cross this to go straight on*, marked 'Footpath leading to Knaves Hill'. Keep straight on, ignoring ways off.

In a further 150 metres, you come to a brick wall and follow the path left for 15 metres, then right, in your previous direction. This brings you *out on to St Mary's Way, and you keep straight on.*

In 240 metres ignore ways off, and you come *to the main road, the B4032. Cross over this to continue straight on*, along a one-way street (Leopold Road).

In 110 metres, *when your road goes left, keep straight on, along an alleyway* with Linslade Lower School to its right-hand side.

In 85 metres *go straight on, along Southcourt Road*. In 130 metres *turn left*. In 80 metres you come to **Leighton Buzzard Station**. Go over the left-hand bridge for trains to London (usually platform 4).

Walk 42

Holmwood to Gomshall

Leith Tower, its woodlands & heathlands

Length 15.5km (9.6 miles), 4 hours 40 minutes. For the whole outing, including trains, sights and meals, allow at least 8 hours 30 minutes.

OS Landranger Map No.187. Holmwood, map reference TQ 175 437, is in **Surrey**, 6.5km south of Dorking.

Toughness 6 out of 10.

Features Much of this walk is through National Trust land, the broadleaf woods and heathland of Coldharbour, Leith Hill and Abinger Common. Leith Hill, with its tower, is the highest point in south-east England, with views out across the Weald to the English Channel. The hamlet of Friday Street is the suggested lunch place, and then the walk follows the Tilling Bourne stream to within sight of Wotton House; from there it goes through the National Trust's Deerleap Wood, and so to the picturesque village of Abinger Hammer and for tea to the mill at Gomshall, with its functioning waterwheels oxygenating the water and attracting the trout. Short parts of the walk are very steep, but mostly it is easy going, mainly on sandy ways.

Shortening the walk You could catch a bus from Coldharbour; you could catch a 21 or 22 bus (operated by London & Country) from opposite the lunchtime pub in Friday Street, going to Guildford or Redhill; or you could catch a taxi from the Wotton Hatch pub in Wotton. You could have tea slightly earlier, in Abinger Hammer, as detailed below (then simply turn right, westwards, and stay on the A25 to Gomshall Station).

History Leith Hill, the highest point in south-east England, is based on a 70 million-year-old sandstone bedrock, one formed by a cementing amalgam of sand and the silica from seashells. It was on the summit of Leith Hill, in 851AD, that **Ethelwulf** (father of Alfred the Great) defeated the Danes who were heading for Winchester, having sacked Canterbury and London.

In 1765, **Richard Hull** built Leith Hill Tower with the intention, it is said, of raising the hill above 1,000 feet. He had himself buried under the tower. The Tower is open for people to clamber up it from 11am to 3.30pm on weekends and bank holidays; admission £1. It has drinks for sale, and maps and information about the area.

The **Stephan Langton Inn** in Friday Street takes its name from the Archbishop of Canterbury who was born in 1150 and is said to have spent his childhood in this hamlet. Archbishop Langton was a subscribing witness to the *Magna Carta*, supporting the barons against King John and refusing to publish their excommunication by the pope.

The **Church of St John the Evangelist**, near Wotton (open Sunday only), is of Saxon origin. It contains the tomb of John Evelyn, the essayist (author of, among other works, *Fumifiguim, or the Inconvenience of the Air and Smoke of London Dissipated*) who was born at Wotton House in 1620. His diaries were discovered in an old clothes basket there in 1817.

Abinger Hammer village is named after the Hammer Pond, which enabled the working of the iron industry furnaces here from Tudor times. The commemorative iron master's clock (seen on this walk) has Jack the Smith striking the hours. John Evelyn inveighed against the widespread felling of trees as fuel for iron works. In *Sylvia*, first published in 1664, he suggested exploiting the developing world instead: 'Twere better to purchase all our iron out of America, than thus to exhaust our woods at home.'

Gomshall Mill is mentioned in the *Domesday Book*, but the present mill dates from the seventeenth century. The **Tilling Bourne** stream (which springs out of the north slope of Leigh Hill) passes directly under the mill.

Saturday Walkers' Club Take the train nearest to **9.30am** (before or after) from **Victoria** Station to **Holmwood**. Journey time 55 minutes. Trains back from Gom-shall run about once every two hours, either to Waterloo (change at Guildford) or Victoria (change at Redhill). Journey time approximately 1 hour 5 minutes.

Lunch The suggested lunch place is the **Stephan Langton** pub (tel 01306 730 775) in Friday Street, serving food from midday to 3pm daily. This pub is 8km (5 miles) from the start of the walk. If you do not think that you will get there in time, you could go to the **Plough Inn** (tel 01306 711 793) in Coldharbour, by continuing 750 metres up the road from point **[4]** in the walk directions below. The Plough serves food midday to 2pm (2.30pm at weekends).

Tea The suggested tea place is Blubeckers at **Gomshall Mill** (tel 01483 203 060), which plans to be open all day for food from Easter 2001, serving cream teas, etc. An alternative, next door, is the **Compasses Inn** (tel 01483 202 506), which is friendly and serves food daily till at least 9pm, including tea and hot chocolate. Or slightly earlier in the walk there is the **Clockhouse Tearooms** (tel 01306 730 811) by Abinger Common, although the future of this teashop was unsure at the time of writing.

WALK DIRECTIONS

[1] [Numbers refer to the map.] *Leave* **Holmwood Station**, *platform 2, not by the stairs but by the white swing gate halfway along the platform*. In 5 metres *turn left on a quiet lane*, your direction 65 degrees initially. In 105 metres you come *to the main road, where you turn right*, your direction 125 degrees, with a pond on your right-hand side.

In 75 metres, *at the other end of the pond, turn right* by the phonebox, on Merebank, your direction 220 degrees. In 40 metres ignore the fork right to the village hall. In 35 metres ignore Leith Road to the right, bearing left with the road, your direction 145 degrees. In 40 metres, ignore Leith Grove to the right. Then, in a further 140 metres, *turn right on Woodside Road*, your direction now 240 degrees.

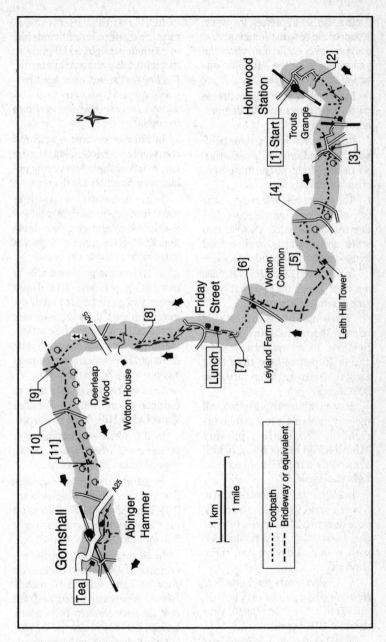

Ignore all ways off. In 160 metres, at the Highland Road T-junction **[2]**, *carry straight on, following a signposted footpath*, your direction 210 degrees. In 50 metres you ignore a path off to the right.

In a further 25 metres, go over a wooden bridge with railings, across a stream, over a stile, and follow the yellow arrow to the left, your direction then 145 degrees.

In 60 metres fork right with the path, your direction 240 degrees, across fields.

In 575 metres, having ignored all ways off and crossed three stiles and a farm drive, you go up steps to *cross the railway line*.

The other side, you cross a stile to continue on, your direction 285 degrees. In 65 metres go over two stiles and upwards, with a field hedge on your left-hand side.

In a further 125 metres, you pass a manor house on your left-hand side (**Trouts Grange**).

In 80 metres go over a stile beyond the tennis court (a metal fieldgate to its right-hand side) and in 15 metres *turn right on a tarmac driveway*, your direction 300 degrees.

Stay on this tarmac driveway all the way, ignoring a footpath to the right in 330 metres, passing **Minnickfold** manor house (which is marked on the OS map) on your right-hand side.

In 240 metres you come out on to a tarmac road [3] which you cross, your direction 240 degrees, to *enter Bearhurst estate*, on a public footpath, with its lodge on your right-hand side.

In 35 metres take the footpath to the right (the signpost may be half-hidden in a hawthorn bush), your direction 310 degrees.

In 100 metres *go over a stile and turn half left*, uphill, a field fence on your left-hand side, your direction due west.

In 240 metres go over a stile (a metal fieldgate on its left-hand side) to continue straight on (slightly to the right), following a yellow arrow, *heading for the top right-hand corner of the field, your direction 300 degrees (not the stile due west into the wood).*

In 170 metres cross a stile and then another (a metal fieldgate to its left) to follow the yellow arrow uphill, your direction 255 degrees.

In 215 metres go over a stile (a metal fieldgate to its right) and follow the yellow arrow on, your direction 305 degrees, aiming 50 metres to the right of the house ahead.

In 250 metres go over a stile (a metal fieldgate to its right) and in 20 metres you go through or around a metal fieldgate to *cross a tarmac road*, slightly to your right, continuing on a public footpath uphill, your direction 265 degrees. (The footpath signpost may be overgrown.)

In 12 metres you cross a path to continue on up into the National Trust **Leith Hill Area** woodland.

In 300 metres you come *to a tarmac road where you go right*, your direction 25 degrees.

In 120 metres a sign indicates that you are entering Coldharbour. [[4] There is a pub 750 metres up the road, should you want an early pub for lunch.]

In 80 metres you pass the entrance to Mosses Wood Cottage on your left-hand side. In 20 metres *take the signposted public footpath (not the path through the wooden barrier, but the less clear path to the left of it), due west and very steeply up* into the National Trust's **Coldharbour Common**. [This is a 1 in 3 path. An alternative is the less steep route up past the wooden barrier. Ignore ways off and in 280 metres you come to a major path crossing and go left, following the Coldharbour Walk arrows. In 260 metres you then rejoin the main suggested route at the asterisk [*] below.]

In 40 metres or so, your path is now a gully, still going very steeply upwards. *At the top of the gully, in 40 metres, you follow a less steep, clear path, straight onwards, keeping due west.* In 40 metres you come *to a path crossroads where you go left*, your direction 190 degrees; there is a yellow arrow on a post here.

In 10 metres [*] you *follow the National Trust Coldharbour Walk arrow to the right*, your direction 250 degrees.

Following the NT arrow, *take a left fork in 20 metres, by post 7*, through chestnut trees.

In 60 metres your path is joined by one from the right. In another 60 metres *follow the arrow by forking right*, your direction 245 degrees.

In 10 metres, *at the T-junction, keep on to the right*, your direction 265 degrees. You are now on a ridge path, with a view out over the Weald and the far line of the South Downs on your left-hand side.

In 50 metres follow the arrow on, your way joined by a wide earth road from your right.

In 270 metres, *by post 8, you go right, and at the next post, 10 metres further on, you follow its arrow towards Leith Tower*, due west, the middle of three paths.

In 150 metres you pass a sign on your right-hand side saying 'Dukes Warren', and you ignore a car-wide

wooden bridleway barrier straight ahead, to go left uphill, your direction 240 degrees; and so to **Leith Hill Tower**.

Just *10 metres beyond the tower, continuing westwards, you fork right on a bridleway*, with a sign on its left-hand side saying 'Mountain bikes, please ride slowly', your direction 320 degrees.

In 8 metres you pass a bench, 10 metres away on your right-hand side. In a further 75 metres, ignore a lesser fork to the left.

In 25 metres you cross a path.

In a further 60 metres [5], *while going downhill, take the left fork, gently uphill*, your direction 310 degrees (the right, equally main way, would have made your direction 5 degrees). 450 metres from this fork, your path having bent left, you come *to a T-junction where you go right*, your direction 5 degrees.

In 100 metres ignore a car-wide earth road to the right.

In 150 metres your way is joined by another earth car-wide way from behind on your right.

In a further 250 metres, *at a three-way fork (where the right fork has a car-wide wooden barrier marked footpath), take the middle fork*, your direction 355 degrees.

[!] In 250 metres *your way crosses a small unmarked footpath, where the path to the right goes off your way 2 metres beyond the path to the left. Take the clear but zigzag path to the left uphill*, your direction 285 degrees.

In 40 metres you come to a tarmac road, with Leylands Farm opposite. *Go right on the road*, your direction 25 degrees.

In 35 metres **[6]** *go left on a signposted public footpath*, your direction 280 degrees.

In 150 metres you come *to wide open fields, where you turn right*, with the field edge on your right-hand side, your direction 5 degrees.

In 65 metres, by the public footpath sign, veer left with the path to keep a field hedge on your right-hand side, your direction 275 degrees.

Keep to this path and in 100 metres you pass a house on your right-hand side. In 35 metres *follow a yellow arrow right, into the wood*, your direction 330 degrees.

In 35 metres (where the fork right heads to a driveway in 10 metres) *fork left*, following the two-armed footpath sign, downhill, your direction 285 degrees. In 100 metres you then pass sheds on your left-hand side.

In 50 metres you continue on a tarmac house driveway, downhill. In 50 metres you come *to a road T-junction – the end of a loop of road – and you go left, downhill*, with Spring Cottage on your left-hand side, your direction 305 degrees.

In 70 metres ignore a bridleway signposted to the left, and a footpath signposted straight on, to carry on with a tarmac road, your direction due north.

In 70 metres, by a car entrance to St John's House on the left-hand side **[7]**, you *fork right on a bridleway marked by a post with dragon and oak leaf symbols*, your direction 15 degrees.

In 35 metres ignore a footbridge to your right. You *keep the stream on your right-hand side, all the way to Friday Street*.

In 400 metres ignore another foot-bridge to your right.

In 140 metres your way becomes a lane between houses, leading in 50 metres to the **Stephan Langton** pub in **Friday Street**, on your right-hand side, the suggested lunchtime stop.

After lunch, *coming out of the pub, turn right to carry on up the lane*, due north. Ignore other ways off. In 110 metres you have a pond on your right-hand side. In 40 metres you *come to a T-junction which you cross over, going slightly to the right to follow a public footpath sign*, on a tarmac driveway downhill, your direction 35 degrees.

In 25 metres you pass Pond Cottage on your right-hand side. In a further 75 metres, you cross a stream by a low footbridge, where cars ford it.

In a further 65 metres, by Yew Tree Cottage on your left-hand side, keep left with your road, joined by a driveway from the right, with the stream on your left-hand side.

In 140 metres cross a path, with a bridge on your left-hand side, to keep on over a stile (with a wooden fieldgate to its left-hand side) into the parkland of Wotton Estate and to a series of ponds created by dams.

In 320 metres you pass wooden fieldgates to your right and left, both marked 'Private'.

In 65 metres **[8]** *take the unmarked footpath fork to the right, steeply up a gully into the woods*, your direction 25 degrees, between fencing.

In 320 metres cross a car-wide way marked 'Private', to carry on downwards, your direction 30 degrees. In 160 metres go over a stile to exit the wood, **Wotton House** visible away on your left-hand side.

In 65 metres go over a stream. In 30 metres go over a stile and up into the wood. In a further 85 metres go over a stile (with a road 5 metres below on your left-hand side) and carry straight on towards the left of the house ahead, your direction 5 degrees.

In 240 metres go over a stile (a metal fieldgate on its right-hand side) and in 12 metres *carry straight on across a carpark towards the A25* – the entrance to the **Wotton Hatch** pub is to the left.

In a further 60 metres, *you cross the A25 and continue on the lane* to the **Church of St John the Evangelist** in **Wotton**.

In 80 metres ignore a stile on your right-hand side. In 200 metres you come to the (locked) front door of the church, and *fork left through the churchyard*, in 25 metres passing the tombstone table supported by griffins. In 15 metres exit the churchyard by a stile on your left-hand side. *Go right on the other side, on a clear path downhill*, your direction 320 degrees.

In 140 metres go over a stile. In 80 metres you enter **Deerleap Wood** (marked on the OS map).

In 200 metres you exit the wood over a stile and continue straight on across a field. In 120 metres go over a stile *on to earth road crossings* **[9]**, *where you fork left (but not sharp left)*, your direction 210 degrees – in 30 metres passing a timber-framed barn (held up by logs) on your right-hand side; and in 20 metres passing the entrance to Park

Farm Cottage, also on your right-hand side.

Keep straight on, following a blue arrow, with the edge of Deerleap Wood on your left-hand side.

In 700 metres veer right with the path. In 65 metres continue in your previous direction (due west).

In 190 metres you come *to a tarmac road* **[10]** *where you go left for 25 metres, your direction 220 degrees, and then take the public bridleway signposted to the right*, past a metal fieldgate, your direction 250 degrees. In 25 metres you pass the National Trust sign for **Abinger The Roughs**. In a further 80 metres, ignore a fork to the left to follow the blue arrow onwards.

In 70 metres you pass a **monument to Samuel Wilberforce**. Keep to the main path. In 360 metres *ignore a sharp turn left and ignore a fork left in a further 18 metres*, to bear right uphill, following the main trail.

Keep on this, ignoring ways off. In 550 metres, at the other end of an open section, with a multiplicity of ways on offer **[11]**, ignore the fork left, with its white arrow, and keep to the way that is to the right of this (the main blue arrow car-wide trail), your direction 260 degrees.

In 10 metres ignore a way to the left, marked with a green arrow.

In 125 metres cross a path to continue on, a field fence now on your right-hand side and a farm visible down on your right-hand side (marked Hackhurst Farm on the OS map).

In 145 metres you cross a road (which leads to the farm) to carry straight on, following the blue NT arrow, through a wooden swing gate (to the right-hand side of a wooden fieldgate), still due west, with a hedge on your left-hand side.

In 160 metres go through a wooden swing gate. In 15 metres you come *to a tarmac lane where you go left, downhill*, your direction then 185 degrees.

In 300 metres you come down *to the A25*, the Abinger Arms pub on your right-hand side.

Turn right, your direction 300 degrees. In 200 metres, just past the red-brick, timber-framed house, *turn left on a signposted public bridleway* (a car-wide earth road), your direction 220 degrees.

In 80 metres you pass The Willows on your right-hand side. In a further 105 metres, you go over the Tilling Bourne stream. In 45 metres *fork left (not sharp left) off the concrete road*, your direction 265 degrees *(following the right of two blue bridleway arrows)*.

In 190 metres you come out on to an earth road driveway. In 30 metres you come *to an earth road T-junction*, where *you go right*, your direction 285 degrees.

In 225 metres you pass the entrance to Twiga Lodge on your left-hand side, and, in 10 metres you *take the second left, a narrow bridleway heading due west*. In 150 metres you pass a farmhouse on your left-hand side. In 60 metres you pass a manor house on your right-hand side. In 60 metres you come *to a car road T-junction where you go right*, your direction 340 degrees, on Tower Hill Road. In 20 metres you *go under a railway bridge, to the T-junction, by timber-framed house no.4, where you go right* (on Goose Green Road), your direction 40 degrees.

In 260 metres you come to **Gomshall Mill** on your right-hand side, the suggested tea place.

After tea, *coming out of the mill, turn right on the A25*, your direction 135 degrees. In 225 metres fork left uphill, your direction 60 degrees. In 160 metres you come to **Gomshall Station**. Cross over the railway to platform 2 for Guildford, or stay on this side for Redhill.

Walk 43

Otford
(round walk)

Romney Street, Shoreham
& the Darent Valley

Length 11.3km (7 miles), 3 hours 30 minutes. For the whole outing, including trains, sights and meals, allow 7 hours 30 minutes.

OS Landranger Map No.188. Otford, map reference TQ 532 593, is in **Kent**, 4km north of Sevenoaks.

Toughness 2 out of 10.

Features This would make a good, brisk, shortish autumn or winter walk, with a late start possible. The route at the outset is steeply uphill, for a time following the North Downs Way, with views back over Otford and the valley, then going through Greenhill Wood, with a glimpse of Hildenborough Hall, before heading north to the pub in Romney Street. On reaching Shoreham there is the Shoreham Countryside Centre to visit, should you want to learn more about the history of the area and about its wildlife (the centre is closed from the end of October to the beginning of April). Shoreham Village itself is worth visiting too, with its five pubs and twelfth-century church. The route onwards is the Darent Valley Path, which leads into Otford. The village of Otford offers a tearoom, a palace (in ruins), a church and many ancient buildings. There are trains to Otford from both Victoria and Blackfriars.

Shortening the walk It is possible to get a train back to London from Shoreham.

History Shoreham is the remote village that the painter Samuel Palmer chose as a refuge from London's pollution. He was visited there in 1826 by William Blake.

Otford goes back to the sixth century, when the Saxons settled the place and called it Ottanford (Otta's Ford). Offa and Canute fought battles here. The village pond, with the duckhouse, is a listed building and was the main source of water for local people until the early twentieth century.

The **Bull** pub in Otford has magnificent fireplaces, brought there from the ruined Otford Palace. Opposite the Bull, is the Arts and Crafts-style **Church Hall**, designed by Edwin Lutyens who waived his fee, as it was commissioned by his brother William who was then vicar of Otford.

The craft shop by the pond in Otford sells a leaflet entitled 'A Look Around Otford' should you have an hour to spend at the end of the walk in which to admire the village's ancient past.

Otford Palace once occupied four acres, but it fell into decay after Archbishop Cranmer was forced to surrender it to Henry VIII in 1537. The **Church of St Bartholomew** in Otford was founded about 1050 and contains murals to the great-grandsons of Oliver Cromwell.

Saturday Walkers' Club Take the train nearest to **10.15am** (before or after) from **Victoria** Station to **Otford**. Journey time approximately 34 minutes.

Lunch The **Fox & Hounds** pub (tel 01959 525 428) in Romney Street, serves simple food from midday to 2.30pm daily (Saturday and Sunday 3pm, closed Monday); groups of more than ten should phone to book.

Tea The suggested tea place is the **Ellenor Tea Shop** (tel 01959 524 322), 11a High Street, Otford. It is open until 4pm Monday to Friday (till 5pm from April to October), and till 5pm Saturday. Profits from the tearoom are used to support the Ellenor Romanian Hospice.

WALK DIRECTIONS

[1] [Numbers refer to the map.] *From the middle of platform 2* at **Otford Station**, *exit up steps* with blue-painted metal handrails, then go on a tarmac lane for 30 metres, at which point you *turn left on an unasphalted public footpath*, a metal fieldgate to its left-hand side, in 30 metres passing a **Chalk Pits** sign on your left-hand side.

Bend left with the path, passing a playing field on your right-hand side and then go up steps to pass through a wooden kissing gate. *Turn right on the main road, for 10 metres, then left on a signposted footpath, the* **North Downs Way**, *uphill, your direction 40 degrees;* and soon steeply uphill, to a bench, with views back down to Otford and its valley.

Carry on up the path and near the top, where it levels out, follow the right-hand edge of the large open common. In 350 metres you pass a chest-high Ordnance Survey Marker 200 metres over on your left-hand side, and in another 100 metres you go over a stile **[2]**. *Leave the North Downs Way to turn right downhill on a tarmac road* signposted Otford and Kemsing.

In 100 metres you *go left over a stile* with a public footpath sign (a metal fieldgate to its left-hand side), your direction 75 degrees, past Rowdow mini-reservoir on your left, and parallel to the vale below. Keep to the main path. In 650 metres go through a wooden barrier and across a path to carry straight on through another wooden barrier, following the yellow arrow, your direction 130 degrees.

In 150 metres, at a T-junction, go left (virtually straight on), your direction eastwards.

110 metres from this junction, you ignore a faint turn-off uphill, to continue straight on over the roots of a 15-foot beech tree stump. Keep on this main path, ignoring a faint fork right, 15 metres from the tree. 150 metres past the tree stump, you come to a path crossing marked North Downs Way, with *earth steps going up to the left. But you go down to the right, in 30 metres coming to a wooden bench* overlooking the vale.

Turn left by the bench along the hillside, your direction 70 degrees, *keeping to the main path (the North Downs Way)*. In 70 metres go over a stile (or through a gap to its right) and straight on. 250 metres past the stile, at a fork, go left following the North Downs Way sign slightly uphill, your direction 115 degrees, in 100 metres re-entering the wood.

In a further 15 metres, *your route crosses a main path with the fainter North Downs Way continuing up the hill*, your direction 140 degrees. *But here you leave the North Downs Way*

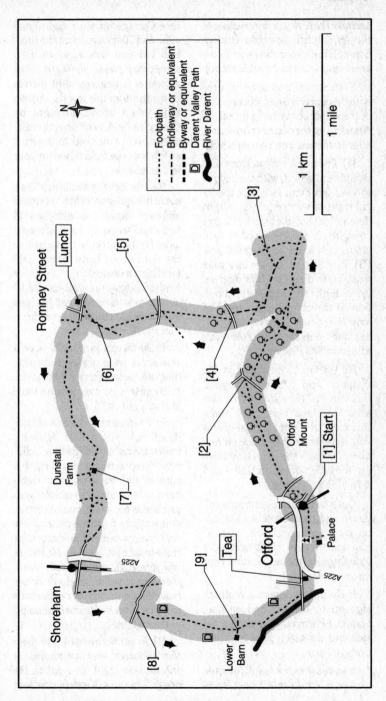

Footpath
Bridleway or equivalent
Byway or equivalent
Ⅾ Darent Valley Path
River Darent

1 km

1 mile

N

Romney Street

Lunch

[5]

[6]

[3]

[4]

[2]

Otford Mount

[1] Start

Dunstall Farm

[7]

Shoreham

A225

[9]

Tea

Otford

A225

Palace

Lower Barn

[8]

and take the path you are crossing to the left, uphill towards Hildenborough Hall, your direction 25 degrees (and a roof just visible ahead).

Keep straight on, over a drive with the courtyard and wooden part of the manor away on your left. In 40 metres go over another drive and, after 50 metres, you go over a stile.

[!] The quick way at this point would be to go left, with the hedges to your left-hand side, but the legal right of way requires a slight detour. Instead of going left, *carry straight on for 200 metres to a yellow arrow on an isolated pole* [3], then *sharp left back into your field*, your direction 265 degrees (in roughly the oppposite direction to the arrow), on a right of way *diagonally across the field*, heading for its far-left corner, your direction 345 degrees.

Go towards a fieldgate in the distance, and 10 metres beyond this you *exit the field on to a car-wide lane*, and bear right along this lane. In 100 metres *go over a stile on your left-hand side on to a tarmac road* – the driveway leading to Hilden-borough Hall – and *turn right*, due west.

Out past the drive's entrance columns, and past Thatched Cottage on your right-hand side, at a T-junction you go right (virtually straight on) up the tarmac road, your direction due north.

In 70 metres ignore a footpath sign off to the left and go past Shorehill Farm on your right-hand side with its black pigs, and past Cottage Farm.

You *come to a road T-junction and turn left downhill*, past Primrose Cottage on your right-hand side, and 70 metres from the junction [4] you *turn right on to a signposted public footpath*, your direction 5 degrees. 400 metres down through the woods, cross a stile to go uphill, straight on through a field, your direction due north. Soon you need to ignore a stile out of the field down on your left-hand side.

Exit the field by a stile (with two metal fieldgates on its left-hand side) and carry straight on, with the field fence and wood on your left-hand side. Then go down across a field to the right of the house ahead, still heading northwards. Exit by a stile (with a fieldgate to its left-hand side) *out on to a tarmac road* [5] *and then turn left downhill*, your direction 305 degrees.

In 20 metres *turn right over a stile uphill on a signposted public footpath*, your direction 10 degrees. In 50 metres go over another stile and straight on.

In 100 metres go over a (dilapidated) stile into a field. Ignore a path to the right towards farm buildings. Keep straight on along the edge of the wood on your right-hand side, or any less muddy way just inside the wood, your direction still roughly northwards. *Exit the field by a stile* (a metal fieldgate to its right-hand side) *and in 10 metres you fork right off the main track, following a yellow footpath arrow* (your direction initially northwards towards a timber-framed building in the distance).

[!] *In 60 metres* [6] *you leave this bridleway over an unobvious stile on your right, at a gap in the hedge. Then go half left over the field towards two white buildings*, on a clear path that is a short cut to the pub, the **Fox & Hounds** in **Romney Street**, the suggested lunchtime stop.

Coming out of the pub, you see a bridleway sign in front off to your right (Romney Street Farm entrance is to its right) and you follow that over a stile, your direction 290 degrees. You pass a large shed on your right-hand side (one that sometimes shelters a small aeroplane) and a grass runway in the distance. 130 metres from the pub, when a turning offers itself to the left, you carry straight on and over a stile signposted 'Public footpath to Shoreham'.

In 50 metres go over a stile, ignoring a yellow arrow to the right, and you are then away from the last building, and carrying straight on downhill, your direction initially 300 degrees, with a **golfcourse** visible in the distance. Keep to the right of a copse (a small island of trees in the field) 120 metres downhill. Exit the network of fields by a stile, cross a car-wide earth track, and continue steeply down towards the golfcourse.

Go over a stile, your direction westwards, and at the bottom of the field you go over two tree-trunk stiles to continue up through the golfcourse between hedges. Exit the golfcourse by a stile and continue uphill to enter the wood, then in 70 metres go over a stile and onwards.

Exit the wood by a stile to carry on, your path being across a field, your direction 245 degrees. In 100 metres you go through a gap in the field to the left of a disused stile, to carry on across a field, your direction now 230 degrees, still on a clear car-wide path.

At the T-junction of farm tracks by a stile with two concrete steps, take the right-hand option to carry virtually straight on, downhill, your direction 255 degrees. Keep on this farm track when it then goes uphill through a farm (Dunstall Farm) **[7]**. Then go more or less straight on, keeping to the right of the corrugated hay barn, and at the end of the far barn, go across a farm track to continue straight on across a field, your direction 260 degrees.

180 metres from the barn, you go down into the wood, crossing a path, in 70 metres to carry on down earth steps. 100 metres from the end of the steps, ignore paths off to continue on the main path. In a further 300 metres, your path merges with a bridleway at a T-junction and you carry on downwards, slightly to the right, your direction 330 degrees.

In 200 metres or so, you come to a road junction where you carry straight on across the A225, on to the road signposted Golfcourse and Shoreham Village.

In 70 metres you come to pedestrian steps up to Shoreham Station. Detour up these (but not in winter – see the introduction above) to visit the **Shoreham Countryside Centre** in the station building.

Carry on by going under the railway bridge. In 130 metres you ignore the main entrance left into the Darent Valley golfcourse. But in a further 80 metres **[8]**, your onward route is to *turn left past a metal barrier on to a footpath signposted Darent Valley Path*, your direction 170 degrees.

I recommend, however, a further detour to visit **Shoreham Village**: staying on the car road brings you, in 200 metres or so, to the Church of St Peter and St Paul and to the George Inn, and beyond that to the Kings Arms and the River Darent. Coming back to the footpath: this leads through the golf-course and, in 550 metres, through a metal kissing gate; and so onwards, now with a playing field and a clubhouse on your right-hand side, to follow a path between fences, your direction 175 degrees.

In 125 metres turn sharply right, *following the signposted Darent Valley Path*, on a tarmac lane, your direction 305 degrees.

In 300 metres, by a crossing of many paths, turn left through wooden barriers, following the Darent Valley Path, signposted 'Footpath to Otford', your direction 200 degrees, and with the golfcourse on your left-hand side.

Carry straight on, following the Darent Valley Path signs. Once you are past the golfcourse, the route is over stiles and over the driveway of **Lower Barn** (so marked on the OS map) **[9]** to carry on towards Otford, now visible in the distance, your direction 150 degrees.

In 230 metres go over a stile to continue on with the River Darent now on your right-hand side, bending left with the river's fork (by a house on the far bank with unusual round brick chimneys). Go through a wooden swing gate to pass between gardens and houses *to the main road and turn left* down the main street of Otford, towards the village green and station.

You pass Pickmoss, a medieval half-timbered yeoman's house, on your right-hand side. Immediately next door is the old Baptist Chapel (at which Samuel Palmer's father was minister); and, a bit further on, the (partly sixteenth-century) **Bull** pub. Beyond this, you come to the **Ellenor Tea Shop**, also on your right, the suggested tea place (opposite Lowries pet food shop). [If you wish, you can take the footpath opposite the Ellenor Tea Shop for 200 metres, cross a stile to your left into a field with sports pitches. There is a scale model of the solar system here in the near corner of the field]

Beyond the tea shop, you come to the village pond and, the other side of that, to the **Church of St Bartholomew**. To the right of the church is **Otford Palace** (ruins).

To get to the station without going on the main road, *take the tarmac path through a kissing gate to the church's front door, and go along the right-hand side of the church*, keeping to the path, soon with a brick wall to your left and the churchyard to your right, and so through a wooden kissing gate. You go eastwards, in about 300 metres reaching the carpark of **Otford Station**. The station's near platform is for London trains.

Walk 44

Witley to Haslemere

Chiddingfold
& the Crown Inn

Length 15.5km (9.6 miles), 4 hours 40 minutes. For the whole outing, including trains and meals, allow 7 hours 40 minutes.

OS Landranger Map No.186. Witley, map reference SU 948 379, is in **Surrey**, 12km south-west of Guildford.

Toughness 2 out of 10.

Features This is an easy but interesting walk from Witley (where walking sticks used to be made – hence the local copses of ash and sweet-chestnut), passing Lockwood Donkey Sanctuary (open 9am to 5.30pm daily, with free admission; it is also a sanctuary for rabbits, pigeons, geese, llamas and deer) and passing Combe Court manor house and its fifteenth-century farmhouse, through the churchyard of St Mary's Church to the medieval village of Chiddingfold, with the Crown Inn as the suggested lunch stop. After lunch the walk is through Frillinghurst Wood and various National Trust estates, coming out into Haslemere High Street near a tearoom.

Shortening the walk Buses run, approximately once an hour, from outside the lunchtime pub in Chiddingfold to Haslemere.

History Chiddingfold's main splendour is the lunchtime pub, the twelfth-century **Crown Inn**. In the late fourteenth century, the publican was convicted of selling ale 'contrary to the assize' (courts tested ale by pouring some on to a wooden bench, then sitting on it – if it had a sticky quality, it was pronounced good). In 1552, Edward VI stayed at this inn, while his 4,000-strong retinue camped on the green.

Chiddingfold was the centre of the stained glass industry between the thirteenth and seventeenth centuries, but the foreigners who ran it were driven out by an edict of Elizabeth I, in response to local petitions. The village was isolated enough to be able to keep working through the plague years, supplying stained glass for St Stephen's Chapel at Westminster in the 1350s.

In the churchyard of thirteenth-century **St Mary's Church** in Chiddingfold, there is a 1776 epitaph to Arthur Stedman, blacksmith: 'My fire is out, my forge decay'd…'

The town of **Haslemere** is lucky to be surrounded by National Trust land in almost every direction – thanks to the campaigns in the early 1900s of Sir Robert Hunter, one of the National Trust's founders, who lived in Haslemere.

In Tudor and Stuart times **Haslemere** was a centre for the iron industry. With the coming of the railway in the mid-nineteenth century it became a popular spot for literary people. The poet Tennyson's house, Aldworth, is on the slopes of Black Down where he loved to walk; and George Eliot wrote *Middlemarch* in Shottermill.

The town has an interesting **museum** some way further up the High Street beyond Darnleys tearoom. The museum is open 10am to 5pm Tuesday to Saturday, and has a fine explanatory display of local wild flowers in the foyer. Other highlights include an Egyptian mummy showing the toes of one foot and an observation beehive.

Saturday Walkers' Club Take the train nearest to **9.40am** (before or after) from **Waterloo** Station to **Witley**. Buy a cheap day return ticket to Haslemere. You may need to change at Guildford. Journey time 53 minutes. Trains back from Haslemere to Waterloo run about twice an hour. Journey time 52 minutes.

Lunch The suggested lunchtime stop is the **Crown Inn** (tel 01428 682 255) in Chiddingfold, which serves lunch midday to 2.30pm daily; groups of more than ten people should phone to book. The **Swan** pub and the **Old Bakery** also both serve food at lunchtime.

Tea The suggested tea place is **Darnleys** tearoom (tel 01428 643 048) on Haslemere High Street, which closes at 5pm. The easiest alternative is the **Pizza Express** (tel 01428 642 245) next door, open till at least 10pm daily. The **White Horse Hotel**, also in the High Street, offers reasonably priced food and tea (its serving times are: midday-3pm and 6pm-9.30pm Monday to Friday; midday-9.30pm Saturday; midday-9pm Sunday). There is a bar at the **Haslemere Hotel** opposite the station (though it can be walker-unfriendly) and **Metro Café** (tel 01428 651 535) is just before the station. This café is open till 6pm weekdays (5pm Saturdays; closed Sundays). The station is a ten-minute walk from the town centre.

WALK DIRECTIONS

[1] [Numbers refer to the map.] On arrival at **Witley Station**, cross the footbridge to platform 1. At the bottom of the steps, keep straight on to the end of the platform, where you join a public footpath, your direction 265 degrees, shortly bending right, your direction 5 degrees.

100 metres from the bend, immediately after passing a house called Inglewood (on your right-hand side), at a crosspaths you turn left, your direction 265 degrees.

Then in 550 metres you come to a road with a National Trust sign for **Sandhills Common** behind you. *Cross the road, slightly to your right*, to a post marked **Greensand Way**, to go up an entrance drive towards a multicoloured pyramid and wall, your direction 300 degrees. *In 15 metres turn right uphill on a path marked GW*, your direction 350 degrees. But, 25 metres up the slope, ignore a GW sign to the right, to go left, your direction 260 degrees.

In 120 metres your path merges with a driveway, and in 30 metres it comes out on to a road, by a red phonebox. *Turn right on this road*, your direction 280 degrees.

In 60 metres *turn left by Doon Cottage*, on Hatch Lane **[2]**, a tarmac lane signposted public bridleway, your direction 190 degrees.

In 150 metres you pass **Lockwood Donkey Sanctuary**, which is worth a look. In a further 150 metres, as you enter the wood, keep straight on, ignoring a possible way to the left.

In 110 metres, by a post offering a public footpath or a public bridleway, follow the public bridleway

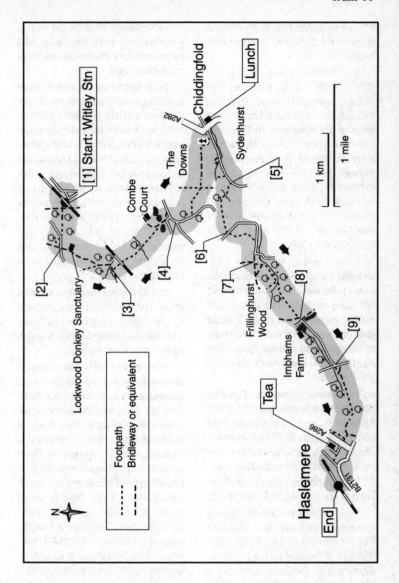

[1] Start: Witley Stn

Combe Court

The Downs

Chiddingfold

Lunch

Sydenhurst

A282

[5]

[6]

[4]

[2]

[3]

Lockwood Donkey Sanctuary

[7]

Frillinghurst Wood

[8]

[9]

Imbhams Farm

Tea

A286

Haslemere

End

B2131

1 mile

1 km

N

Footpath

Bridleway or equivalent

straight on. In 200 metres bear right with your path as it crosses a stream by a wooden footbridge.

100 metres from the bridge, *you come to a fork where you go left uphill* **[3]**, your direction southwards; in 80 metres crossing a ditch

on two concrete sleepers, to go straight on across a field, your direction 140 degrees.

In 160 metres you cross a stile and a plank bridge, then the railway lines, and you go over a stile the other side, then across an earth road and over another stile, to go straight on, with the field fence on your left-hand side.

In 135 metres you go over a stile, still straight on. In a further 230 metres, down in the wood, you cross a stream by a well-made brick bridge to go up the other side. In 35 metres you cross a car-wide earth track to keep straight on, your direction 130 degrees. In 175 metres cross a stile to leave the wood, going straight on across a field, your direction 160 degrees, with **Combe Court** (marked on the OS map) visible ahead to your left.

In 120 metres go over a stile, straight on, your direction 145 degrees, passing Combe Court on your left-hand side, and in a further 200 metres coming to a metal kissing gate in a long metal fence by a cedar of Lebanon and to a car road. *Turn right on this road*, your direction 185 degrees.

In 200 metres your road crosses a bridge over ponds and in a further 150 metres, you leave Combe Park by a metal gate, in 20 metres *reaching the main road, where you turn right*, your direction 250 degrees.

In 235 metres *take the first car road to the left* [4], called Pook Hill.

Follow this road for 300 metres, ignoring ways off, to Langhurst Manor (on your right-hand side). Then in 50 metres turn left, *following a public footpath sign over a stile*, your direction 80 degrees.

In 300 metres cross a stile to go straight across the driveway (a modern cottage on your left-hand side) and *continue straight on across the grass, with a fence to your right-hand side*, your direction 145 degrees, *heading to the right of a*

wooden garage shed. In 30 metres you fork left, with the hedge of a more substantial house on your right-hand side.

In 60 metres go through a metal kissing gate and straight on. 25 metres beyond that, go over a stile and straight on (with the field boundary near to your left). In 300 metres ignore a stile off to the left and cross its footpath. In 130 metres go over a stile and onwards, with fences to both sides. In a further 100 metres, continue on, now on a tarmac road with houses on both sides. In 230 metres, when this comes to an end, continue straight on through a metal kissing gate.

In 130 metres you pass a burial ground on your right-hand side and go through a metal kissing gate, with a metal fieldgate and a wooden swing gate to its right.

Turn right at this point through the wooden swing gate into the burial ground and straight on, your direction 195 degrees, with some of the paving stones underfoot made of old headstones. In 110 metres you turn left, with a wall on your right-hand side, in 80 metres coming to **Chiddingfold**'s **St Mary's Church** (open). *Beyond the church, in 20 metres you go through the lychgate, and opposite is the* **Crown Inn**, the suggested lunch stop. (The **Old Bakery** and the **Swan** pub in Chiddingfold also serve food at lunchtime.)

Coming out of the Crown Inn *after lunch, turn left on the busy A283*, your direction 170 degrees. *In 10 metres, cross the road with care to go up Mill Lane*, your direction 260 degrees.

Continue along this road for 900 metres, to pass the Ukrainian Home,

Sydenhurst, on your left-hand side. In 230 metres, at Upper Sydenhurst (a tile-hung house with a white gate on your left-hand side) and just beyond the end of Orchard Cottage's garden on your right-hand side **[5]**, *go over a stile to your right* (with a metal fieldgate to its right-hand side), your direction 310 degrees, following the right-hand edge of the field.

In 150 metres cross a stile to continue half left, your direction 280 degrees. Keep the fence on your right-hand side. In 85 metres you come to a stile on your right-hand side, which you go over into the wood, a garden fence to your right for 20 metres; then bending sharp left with the path (by the garden door marked 'private'), your direction now 310 degrees.

In 160 metres cross a stile with a yellow arrow, keeping the field fence on your right-hand side, your direction 260 degrees.

In 400 metres you pass a house on your right-hand side and, in a further 50 metres, where the edge of the field goes sharp right (as you pass under mini-pylons) you continue straight on across the field towards another part-timber-framed house visible ahead.

In 120 metres **[6]** *go across a road via stiles to continue half left*, your direction 195 degrees, towards a stile visible in the distance. In 200 metres you go over stiles to continue on (quarter right), your direction now 205 degrees.

In a further 300 metres, you go over a stile (hidden in the right-hand corner) into the wood; in 30 metres, go down *on to a tarmac road where you turn right*, your direction 265 degrees.

In 125 metres ignore a left turn over a bridge, to continue straight on, towards Frillinghurst Mill, Manor and Farm.

In 280 metres, and some 40 metres past a huge corrugated barn on your right-hand side **[7]**, you *go left over a stile*, your direction 200 degrees, *towards a stile visible in a wooden fence* (some 50 metres to the right of where the fence comes out of the wood). Once over it, carry on in the same direction (200 degrees) to the edge of the forest, which you then follow along, with the edge on your left-hand side.

In 80 metres you pass a three-armed footpath sign and a stile to your left; in 20 metres go over a stile into **Frillinghurst Wood** (marked on the OS map), straight on, your direction 250 degrees.

In 35 metres ignore a fork uphill to the right and *keep to the main path*. In a further 100 metres, cross a stream by a wooden bridge. In a further 300 metres, the path continues straight on along the right-hand edge of open land (a ladder to a lookout post in a tree is 40 metres on your left-hand side). In a further 300 metres, you enter a field, with the field hedge on your left-hand side, towards a house visible ahead.

In 260 metres, some 40 metres away from the cottage ahead, you go on to continue on in the same direction as before, but now with the field hedge on your right-hand side, and your footpath now a bridleway. In 100 metres you come down *to a car-road T-junction* **[8]** *where you turn left*, your direction 140 degrees, and *in 20 metres turn right*, your direction 220 degrees, with the lake on your right-hand side.

In 125 metres bear right with the road, the barns of **Imbhams Farm** (marked on the OS map) on your left-hand side.

575 metres beyond these barns, you come out *on to a car road* **[9]** *which you cross, slightly to the left, to continue on a signposted public footpath*, through a wooden kissing gate, with Holdfast Cottage on your right, your direction 235 degrees.

In 220 metres *go over a stile and turn right (not sharp right)* along a track, keeping a house called Silver Trees on your left-hand side.

In 100 metres you enter the National Trust's **Swan Barn Farm** by a wooden kissing gate to the right of a wooden fieldgate, and keep the field edge on your right-hand side. In 110 metres you go through a wooden barrier, over a stream and up through another wooden barrier.

In 100 metres go through a wooden barrier and over another little bridge over the stream, and through another barrier the other side. In 145 metres go through a wooden barrier to enter the National Trust's **Witley Copse** and **Mariners Rewe**.

In 200 metres bear right (with the fence on your right-hand side). In 20 metres cross the stream by a wooden bridge and keep left, your direction due west.

In 350 metres fork left downhill **[!]**, where the main path turns right uphill, for 15 metres to a small wooden bridge, which you cross to enter a field. Cross this field as indicated by the NT waymark, going gently uphill, your direction 260 degrees.

In 100 metres you go through barriers to leave the field, and bear right on to the main track, your direction 290 degrees.

In 80 metres, where the track bends left, you turn right at the National Trust sign and pass through barriers into a field, your direction 280 degrees. In 150 metres you enter the National Trust's **Swan Barn Walk** by its sign and a wooden kissing gate, and turn right along a gravel path, your direction 10 degrees, with fine views across the meadows to wooded slopes. In 80 metres bear left between buildings to reach **Hasle-mere High Street**. *Turn left in the High Street* for 40 metres to **Darnleys**, the main suggested tea place, on the other side of the road. (Or you could go to the **White Horse** further down the High Street on the left-hand side.)

Coming out of Darnleys, turn right and in 25 metres, turn right again *down West Street, signposted to the police station*.

In 120 metres, where the main street curves to the right past the police station (which is on your right-hand side), *take the street straight on to the fire station*, but then *not* the tempting path straight on, but rather *turn left in front of the fire station* and take the footpath that goes *down the left-hand side of the fire station* (signposted 'to the station'), your direction 315 degrees. Follow this path, with a stream to your right and later a playground on your left, till you come *out on to a tarmac road* with Redwood Manor opposite. *Turn left on this road and in 40 metres turn right on to the B2131, leading in 260 metres to*

Haslemere Station on your right-hand side. **Metro Café**, a possible tea place is on your right-hand side just before the station and **Haslemere Hotel**, with its bar, is opposite the station. The London platforms (2 and 3) are over the footbridge.

Walk 45

Princes Risborough to Great Missenden

The Chilterns, a windmill & Bryant's Bottom

Length 14.5km (9 miles), 4 hours 30 minutes. For the whole outing, including trains, sights and meals, allow 7 hours.

OS Landranger Map No.165. Princes Risborough, map reference SP 799 027, is in **Buckinghamshire**, 11km south of Aylesbury.

Toughness 5 out of 10.

Features This walk across the Chilterns – the walker's heaven –is through sloping fields and beech woods and hamlets, past upmarket farms and upgraded cottages. It is easy, but has two short steep hills (with fine views) near the lunch stop (the walk directions offer an alternative route avoiding one of these). Small sections of the route can be muddy in wet weather, particularly before the lunch stop. Stiles and gates are often renewed.

Shortening the walk You could order a taxi from the suggested lunchtime stop, the **Gate Inn** in Bryant's Bottom (after 9.5km of walking) or from the **Polecat Inn** 2.5km further on. Both places also have rare buses pass by (none on Sunday; but on Saturday, for example, there tends to be one at 1.45pm from the Gate pub and one at 4pm passing the Polecat Inn).

For bus information phone Traveline on 0870 608 2608.

History Princes Risborough derives its name from the Black Prince who is said to have been lord of the manor there in 1343.

The **windmill** in **Lacey Green** is the oldest smock mill in the country, built in 1650 and moved to this site in 1821. It was in use until 1918, milling corn, wheat, oats and barley. It is open for internal viewing from 2.30pm to 5.30pm, only on Sundays and bank holiday Mondays from May to September.

Saturday Walkers' Club Take the train nearest to **10.15am** (before or after) from **Marylebone** Station to **Princes Risborough**. Trains back from Great Missenden run about twice an hour. Journey time 45 minutes there and back.

Lunch The suggested lunchtime stop is the **Gate Inn** (tel 01494 488 632) in Bryant's Bottom. Note that the bulk of the walk – 9.5km – is before lunch, so allow time. The pub serves food midday to 2.30pm daily.

Tea The suggested tea place is the **George Inn** (tel 01494 868 455) in Great Missenden, which offers tea and hot chocolate. It is open daily, but on Sundays is often closed between 3pm or 4pm and 7pm. A receommended alternative is **The Cross Keys** (tel 01494 865 373).

WALK DIRECTIONS

[1] [Numbers refer to the map.] *Coming out of* **Princes Risborough Station**, *turn left*. In 65 metres *veer right with this road away from the station*. At the T-junction in 90 metres, *turn right on Summerleys Road*.

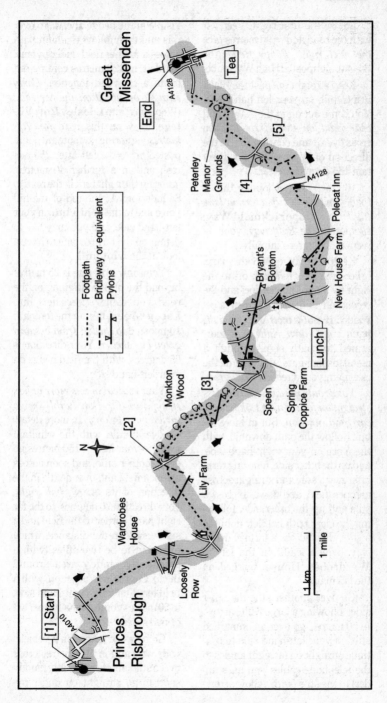

Ignore the first right. Veer left with the road and in 90 metres *take the next right, Poppy Road* (the B4444), signposted High Wycombe.

Keep straight on, past the Black Prince pub on your left-hand side. You come out on to the A4010 and *bear right on this A road*. Then cross over it and continue on, in the direction of Wycombe, your direction 155 degrees.

160 metres after joining this A road, you *turn left up a tarmac lane (the historic* **Upper Icknield Way**) *signposted the Ridgeway*, your direction 60 degrees initially.

Keep straight on up this lane. Ignore the first footpath off to the right by a mini-power line; and the second off to the left, 20 metres beyond it. But *500 metres up from the main road, turn right* at a four-armed footpath sign, through a metal kissing gate, and walk on the clear path, your direction 150 degrees.

Your route remains more or less straight on for the next 1.5km to the car road junction. But in more detail: Follow the path downhill, with the fence on your right-hand side, and up the other side, ignoring turn-offs, over a stile and straight across an open field, and down to cross a stile and up the other side, following the clear path half left uphill to a stile, then across a tarmac driveway (which leads on the left to **Wardrobes House**, marked on the OS map).

Go over another stile the other side, following a large white arrow. In 50 metres, go over an unmarked stile on your left-hand side to continue straight on (at right angles to the telephone cables you pass under) to the stile (with yellow arrow)

visible in the hedge ahead; go over this and then follow the faint path across a further field under pylons, half left, in 120 metres coming out on to a car road junction. *Carry straight on uphill on the car road* (Woodway) into **Loosley Row Village**. Stay on this road *for 750 metres*, ignoring a footpath signposted off to the left after 250 metres; and in a further 40 metres, ignoring the right fork in the road to Saunderton. At the top of the hill you come to the **Whip Inn** on your left-hand side, and you may like to detour on the tarmac lane to have a look at the **windmill**.

Your onward route is 25 metres beyond the pub (continuing on the road you came up earlier) into **Lacey Green**, taking the footpath signposted *to the left from beside a green bus shelter*. Your direction is 65 degrees, with the field hedge on your left-hand side.

Your route remains more or less straight on for 1km (until you go under some pylons). In more detail: Go over a stile, with the windmill away to your left; in 150 metres go over another stile, and soon across an open field and over a stile in the direction of its arrow, *half right*, your direction 70 degrees, to the far right-hand corner of the field and a stile visible in the distance, which turns out to be two stiles (with a potentially muddy area around them). Continue straight on, with a field fence on your right-hand side, in 50 metres going over a further set of two stiles.

Go between fences on a vehicle-wide way and in 100 metres cross over a stile (another possibly muddy spot) to go straight on under pylons, but keeping the field hedge to your left-hand side. In 300 metres you come to the end of this field with a fieldgate on your left-hand side. Ignore this and *turn right along a hedge that marks the far end of the field*, your direction 100 degrees, and, *in 100 metres go over the stile to your left*, half right, following the arrow and clear path, your direction 80 degrees. In 160 metres go *over a stile down into a wooded avenue, a bridleway where you turn left*, your direction 25 degrees. 100 metres down this bridleway (on the line of Grim's Ditch; muddy in wet weather), you pass **Lily Farm** (marked on the OS map) on your right-hand side, to come to a car lane **[2]**.

Turn left and in 15 metres turn right on a car-wide track, signposted public bridleway (in the hedge on your right-hand side), your direction 60 degrees, into **Monkton Wood**. In 50 metres, by the first of two two-armed signs, *take the footpath half right*, your direction 100 degrees, to pass through a wooden barrier in 10 metres.

Your route is more or less straight on along the edge of this mainly beech wood for about 2km. In more detail: After 1km you come to a major crossing of paths, but keep straight on along the edge of the wood. In 500 metres you pass through a wooden swing gate and go straight on past Cedar Cottage on your right-hand side, now on a car-wide track. In 80 metres cross over a car road (the sign at this point says 'Coleheath Bottom') and go straight on, along a car-wide lane signposted as a bridleway, for 500 metres.

Just past Ringwood House on your right-hand side, and *30 metres before a road T-junction*, **[3]** *turn left on a signposted footpath*, in 5 metres passing beside a stile, your direction 50 degrees, uphill into the woods for 350 metres, to come out on to a car road by **Spring Coppice Farm** (marked on the OS map). *Turn left on this road.*

In 150 metres turn right on a signposted footpath over a stile, your direction 85 degrees. In 130 metres go over a stile (between the two copses of trees, but nearer to the left-hand copse of hawthorn trees) to carry straight on, with the fence on your left-hand side. Go downhill under pylons, and 5 metres past the pylons you cross over a stile to go straight on to the right of a house called Balnakeil and through its private garden, to exit by its driveway. In 50 metres *you come down to a car road.*

At this point, if the ground is muddy or you are feeling weary, a short cut is to turn right along the road to the pub 1km further on.

The suggested route, however, is to go straight *across the road and over a stile into the wood*, to go up a very steep and potentially very muddy hill, your direction 65 degrees. In 100 metres, ignoring forks off, keep on uphill over a stile (faint yellow arrow). In 150 metres go over another stile and *turn right on a car-wide earth track*, your direction 160 degrees.

In 100 metres you pass **Denner Farm** on your left-hand side to go over a stile, and continue straight on, following a line of poles and (carefully) crossing an electric fence. In 200 metres you go through a metal gate to the right of a metal fieldgate and go straight on, with a hedge of blackberries on your left-hand side. In 150 metres exit the field by a metal gate in the hedge on your left-hand side to carry on half right, your direction 105 degrees.

In 80 metres *you pass through a metal kissing gate on to car lanes and turn right and take the right fork*, which is a car-wide lane signposted bridleway, its direction 170 degrees, to go past a shed to your left-hand side. In 300 metres you come *to a renovated flintstone cottage on your right-hand side, and turn right along its far wall* to go steeply downhill, your direction 250 degrees.

This clear path comes down to the car road again, with the **Gate Inn** in **Bryant's Bottom**, the suggested lunchtime stop, on your left-hand side.

Coming out of the pub after lunch, turn left on the road for 250 metres to a two-armed sign on your left-hand side. Go over the stile (to the right-hand side of a metal fieldgate) and go uphill for 300 metres, crossing a stile and some fenceposts, your direction 105 degrees; then through a fieldgate or over the stile to its right-hand side, to go straight on, half right across a field, to exit by a stile *on to a car lane. Turn right*, your direction 135 degrees, *in 50 metres going through metal gates marked 'Private – Denner Hill House' and bending left past a substantial house on the right-hand side. 50 metres past its main front gates (marked 'Hughenden Chase'), turn left* following a footpath sign, over a stile, turning immediately right, your direction 80 degrees (ignoring

the direction shown by the sign) to *follow the path downhill parallel to the drive and with the field fence close on your right-hand side*.

In 150 metres go over a stile hidden in the field corner to carry on down. In a further 250 metres, veer left with the hedges to go on down to the hamlet below. Over a stile at the bottom – under pylons – *turn right on the car road* [turning left instead of right here may be worth a detour in summer, to visit the **Prestwood Local Nature Reserve** – the entrance is on the right in 50 metres – a fine piece of chalk downland rich with butterflies]. Having gone right on the car road, *in 20 metres go left on to a car road signed Perks Lane*, your direction 70 degrees.

Go up this straight road for 600 metres, and just past the last house on the right-hand side (White Lodge) where the road veers right, *go over a stile on the left* following the footpath sign, your direction 70 degrees, half right uphill across a field. Go under a mini-pylon and carry on uphill, your direction now 55 degrees, initially parallel to the other set of power cables going your way. With a fine view back over your route, exit at the top left-hand corner of the field by a stile that is 20 metres to the left of a telegraph pole in the hedge.

Carry on with blackberries on your left-hand side. In 100 metres go through a wooden fieldgate and past the **Polecat Inn** on your right-hand side. *Turn right on the A4128 and in 30 metres cross this road to take the footpath signposted over a stile*, your direction 60 degrees. In 90 metres go over a stile to continue on, still walking between fences and a hedge.

In 170 metres go over a stile and slightly leftwards down *into the wood, for 20 metres, then go left on a wide bridleway*, your direction northwards, keeping to the main track. **[!]** *In 70 metres your track merges with a still wider track and in a further 60 metres you come to a deep crater* with exposed beech tree roots on your right-hand side. *Go partway round the right-hand edge of this crater and take the path heading off*, your direction 30 degrees. *40 metres past the crater, at a T-junction, take the path to the left,* virtually straight on (there is then the edge of an open field nearby on your right-hand side, to which your onward path will remain more or less parallel), your direction 25 degrees. In 40 metres ignore other possibilities to keep on in your direction on the main path (there is a white arrow on a tree on your left-hand side). In a further 30 metres cross a path and again keep to your direction, reassured by another white arrow on a tree. In 40 metres ignore a fork off to the left to keep to your path directly towards the houses.

Soon your path is parallel to these houses (70 metres away on your right-hand side) leading you *out of the wood by a three-armed footpath sign, to the left of the end house* (called Woodcot). Continue on the earth driveway parallel to the houses on your right-hand side, your direction now 35 degrees. In 250 metres *you come to a T-junction* **[4]** *where you turn right on to a car road. In 15 metres you go left* on a signposted footpath. In a further 10 metres, you

go over a stile to continue on a clear path, your direction 45 degrees, going across a network of flat open fields.

In 450 metres *you enter a wood, on a path, your direction 100 degrees, keeping the edge of the wood on your right-hand side. In 300 metres go over a stile* **[5]** *and turn left, uphill*, your direction 60 degrees.

In 100 metres ignore a yellow arrow pointing right to continue straight on, past a stile to the left in a further 15 metres, and then along a wooded trail with fields to the left and right. In 250 metres you come out on an earth farm road by a sign saying 'Airton Herd'. Carry straight on, with fine views ahead across the Misbourne Valley, in 40 metres *passing the smart* **Angling Spring Farm** *on your left-hand side. 25 metres past the farm's entrance, fork left off the tarmac driveway on to a gravel path* going along the right-hand side of the farm's property, your direction 320 degrees. *In 35 metres fork right downhill* past a Chiltern District Council woodland management sign and map, your direction 5 degrees.

Keep to the edge of the (part-felled) wood, in 130 metres keeping to the right-hand fork and to the edge of the wood. At the bottom of the hill, *exit the wood over a stile to the right of a wooden fieldgate and take the earth lane towards Great Missenden*, due east.

In 400 metres go over a stile and straight on past a small cemetery on your right-hand side and then *to a T-junction*, and *right on an earth car road*, your direction 65 degrees. *In 30 metres turn left on a narrow tarmac path under a railway arch,* your direction 65 degrees. Carry straight on, along a gravel drive between houses, to a T-junction, with the carpark of the George Inn facing you.

Turn left on a lane. Then in 30 metres turn right on a tarmac path between walls, to arrive by the front door of the **George Inn**, the suggested tea place.

Coming out of the George Inn, turn left into the High Street and, in 350 metres, left on Station Approach (signposted High Wycombe and Prestwood). **Great Missenden Station** is on your left, in 80 metres.

Walk 46

Wakes Colne to Bures

The Colne valley

Length 18km (11.2 miles), 5 hours 30 minutes. For the whole outing, including trains, sights and meals, allow at least 9 hours 30 minutes.

OS Landranger Map No.168. Chappel & Wakes Colne Station, map reference TL 897 288, is in **Essex**, 11km north-west of Colchester and 5km south of Bures.

Toughness 5 out of 10.

Features Many walkers associate Essex with flat landscape, surly pubs and badly maintained footpaths. This walk suffers only from this last failing – in summer, one 400-metre stretch near the end (just past point **[8]**) can be invaded by almost head-high nettles or vegetation, so wear long trousers and take a stick and a compass if possible. For the rest, the walk is delightful. Chappel & Wakes Colne, the station where the walk starts, is a railway museum on every side, with old carriages on display. The village and church at Chappel are a foretaste of the lovely architecture to come, along the Colne valley, such as fine thatched barns and cottages and the neo-Tudor mansion of Colne Priory. The lunch pub at Colne Engaine is just past the church, and then the route follows the side of a huge fishing lake (not marked on old OS maps, as it was only created

in 1995). Brooks, farms, woods and undulating hills lead into tea at the pub in Bures. Note that the train to Chappel & Wakes Colne and from Bures does not run on Sundays in winter (September 29th to June 1st) and is irregular on Sundays in summer (there are trains to Marks Tey, a 7km taxi ride away).

Shortening the walk It is a short walk after lunch down to the main road (the A604), where there are hourly buses going via Wakes Colne viaduct, which is just down the road from the station at which you began the walk.

History 'Colne' is an old English word meaning 'roaring river', and thus there are Colne (or Calne) rivers in various parts of the country.

The station at Chappel & Wakes Colne forms the **East Anglian Railway Museum** (tel 01206 242 524). It is open Monday to Friday 10am to 4.30pm, Saturday, Sunday and bank holidays 10am to 5pm (closed Christmas Day). You get to see a lot of it just coming off the train, otherwise entry costs £3. There is also a bookshop selling everything for railway enthusiasts.

The impressive **Chappel Viaduct**, adjacent to the station, is the longest in East Anglia, with 7 million bricks and 75 feet high. It opened in 1846.

The small church in **Chappel** dates from 1352, although it may incorporate earlier Norman work. In the fourteenth century, the local bishop granted indulgences – remissions of punishment for sins – to all who contributed to the church's repair. It has a tiny wooden steeple and is constructed of stone in the Early English style, with walls of flint rubble and dressings of cement and local materials.

Margery Allingham, the crime novelist, lived in the Chappel area.

Colne Priory in Earls Colne was rebuilt with its high neo-Tudor chimneys by the enterprising local vicar in the 1940s.

The sarsen stones in the tower of **St Andrew's Church** in Colne Engaine are sandstone boulders brought down by ice in the glacial period, and were probably previously used as ritual marker stones in a Stone Age temple on the site. Some of the other building material came from a Roman villa nearby. The church dates back to the early twelfth century and the reign of Henry I.

Saturday Walkers' Club Take the train nearest to **9.15am** (before or after) from **Liverpool Street** Station to **Chappel & Wakes Colne**, changing at Marks Tey. Trains back from Bures run about once an hour, again changing at Marks Tey. Journey time 1 hour 7 minutes going out, and a few minutes longer on the return.

Lunch The suggested lunchtime stop is the **Five Bells** pub (tel 01787 224 166) in Colne Engaine. Lunch is served from midday to 2.30pm daily. There is a wide selection of homemade food. Slow walkers should aim to leave the pub by 2pm in Winter to avoid walking in the dark. Lunch is possible 3km earlier at the **Carved Angel** pub (tel 01787 222 330) in Upper Holt Street, Earls Colne, which serves food from midday to 2pm daily.

Tea The suggested tea place is the **Swan Inn** (tel 01787 228 121) in Bures, which on Friday and at weekends is open all day, serving food from 7pm. On other days the pub closes at 3pm. Phone in advance if your group has special requests for sandwiches, scotch eggs, etc, in case they can provide these.

WALK DIRECTIONS

[1] [Numbers refer to the map.] After looking round the museum, exit **Chappel & Wakes Colne Station** via the booking hall (with adjacent bookshop; if the booking hall is closed, follow the 'Way Out' sign at the far end of the platform). Walk down the approach road. In 120 metres you come *down to the road T-junction where you turn left, going downhill into the village*, your direction 205 degrees.

In 300 metres you come to a crossroads with the A604, with the railway viaduct on your left-hand side and the general store opposite. Cross straight over the main road into the village of Wakes Colne, on a road called The Street. In 30 metres cross the bridge over the **River Colne** and immediately beyond the bridge you pass the **Swan Inn** on the left-hand side.

130 metres further on, at the end of the houses on the right-hand side, ignore a concrete public footpath sign pointing off to the left towards the viaduct. Opposite the sign, *turn right off the road*, down the surfaced car-wide track alongside Raynham House.

In 40 metres you pass the entrance to **St Barnabas Chapel** on the right-hand side. 100 metres further on, ignore a wooded garden and concrete footbridge on your right-hand side, going over the river. Continue straight on, following the arrow marked 'River Colne Coun-

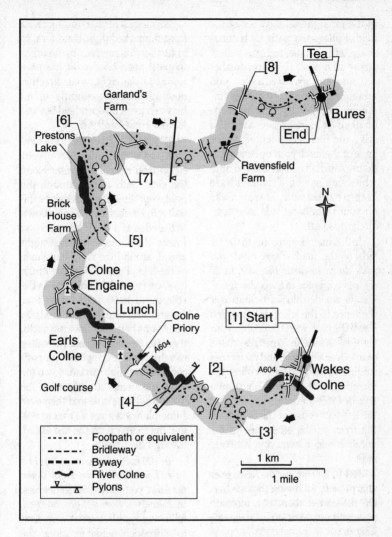

Tea

[8]

Garland's
Farm

[6]

Prestons
Lake

[7]

Bures

End

Ravensfield
Farm

Brick
House
Farm

[5]

N

Colne
Engaine

Lunch

Colne
Priory

[1] Start

Earls
Colne

A604

[2]

A604

Wakes
Colne

Golf course

[4]

[3]

--- - - - Footpath or equivalent
– – – – Bridleway
▄▄ ▄▄ ▄▄ Byway
〜〜 River Colne
▽ Pylons
△

1 km

1 mile

tryside Project' public footpath. 50
metres further on, you come to a
metal fieldgate, and cross the stile
to its left-hand side, into a field.
Continue straight on, along the left-
hand edge of the field, your direction 250 degrees.

In 170 metres cross the stile at
the far side of the field, which takes
you left into the next field. Follow

the path towards the far side of the
field, in the same direction as before. In 75 metres you come to a
footpath post, indicating the continuation of the path straight ahead,
with the hedge on your right-hand
side. 60 metres further on, cross the
stile at the far side of the field and
go straight on in the next field.

In 200 metres cross over the stile

in the far right-hand corner of the field. Follow the path as it turns sharp left, as indicated by a yellow arrow on a post. 15 metres further on, another arrow directs you around to the right. 10 metres further on, go right again across some planks over a stream, over a wooden stile, and then sharp left along the edge of the field, your direction 270 degrees initially. Note the red-and-white sign saying 'Private. Please keep to the footpath'. There is a lake on your right-hand side as you go along this path.

In 200 metres you come to the far side of the field. *Turn right and walk down towards the lake*. In 25 metres you come to a wooden fence. Use the wooden blocks to climb over the fence to the lakeside. *Turn left* down the path with the lake on your right-hand side. In 50 metres cross a plank over a stream, and then cross a stile into the next field. Follow the direction for the 'River Colne Countryside Project' straight ahead along the left-hand edge of the field, with the trees on the other side of the wirelink fence now on your left-hand side.

[2] In 200 metres the fence goes sharply left, following the tree-line. On the corner there is a footpath post, and you *turn left over the stile next to it*.

Walk up the footpath going along the edge of the wood, your direction 220 degrees initially. In 120 metres you come *to a T-junction* with another path. *Turn left on to this path*, following the yellow arrow on the footpath post through the trees, your direction 210 degrees initially. In 100 metres you pass another footpath post.

20 metres further on, ignore a faint unmarked right-hand fork. In a further 25 metres, by another foopath post, *bend with the path round to the right*, your direction now 195 degrees, slightly uphill between trees, an open field beyond to your right-hand side.

[3] In 200 metres, there is a footpath post with many arrows on your right-hand side. *Turn right* along the clear path going through the field, your direction 310 degrees initially. In 100 metres you come down to the edge of a small lake and you follow the footpath sign straight ahead, around the right-hand side of the lake. Past the far side of the lake, carry straight on towards the stile ahead. In 90 metres cross over the stile and into the next field. On your right-hand side, looking north, there is a fine view across the valley to a distant church spire. Your path continues straight ahead, down the field. 100 metres straight down the hill, go over the stile and then over some planks across a stream. Follow the footpath up the hill ahead, through the trees.

In 100 metres you come out *to a lane T-junction. Turn right down the lane*, your direction 30 degrees. In 25 metres *turn left off the road*, following a public footpath sign next to a wooden fieldgate, along the track into the trees, your direction 295 degrees initially. In 70 metres you go through a wooden fieldgate which has a sign on the gatepost welcoming walkers to **Chalkney Wood**. In 70 metres the wide track through the trees forks, and you go straight ahead, ignoring a way to the left, your direction 320 degrees initially.

In 150 metres you pass a sign on the right-hand side of the track, which provides information about the management of the forest. In 80 metres ignore a fork right marked by a post with a red band. 20 metres further on, you come to a crossing of car-wide tracks. *Take the right fork, gently downhill*, your direction 340 degrees initially.

In 250 metres you come down the hill towards a wooden fieldgate into a farmyard, with a white wooden farmhouse directly ahead. *Immediately before this fieldgate, turn left by a red marker post*, to take the track through the woods along the edge of the field. Follow this track for about 150 metres, until you reach the hedge at the far end of the field. *Turn right over a ditch*, via some planks, and use the stile to climb into the next field and carry straight on, your direction 355 degrees, keeping the hedge on your right-hand side.

In 100 metres, on reaching the far corner of the field, ignore the other path coming in from the right. *Turn left here* and continue along the right-hand edge of the field, your direction 250 degrees initially. In 170 metres you walk underneath an electricity pylon. 30 metres beyond the pylon, go through into the next field and continue straight on along its right-hand edge.

In 60 metres you come to the far right-hand corner of this field and *turn right over a wooden plank fence (the remains of a stile, a metal fieldgate to its left-hand side)* into the field on your right. Walk straight ahead, along the left-hand edge of the field, your direction 30 degrees. In 40 metres *turn left using any easy way you can find to cross over a stream* (or further down) **[4]** and then go over a (broken) stile with a metal fieldgate to its left-hand side, into the next field. Walk straight ahead, your direction 315 degrees, in 45 metres picking up a hedge on your left-hand side. In the distance, you can see the tower of the village church of Earls Colne, ahead and to the left of your path.

In 250 metres you come to the furthest left-hand corner of the field, go through a small metal swing gate and continue along the left-hand edge of this next field, in the same direction as before. In 230 metres you come to a metal fieldgate on your left and *turn left over the wooden fence* (stile substitute) to its left-hand side, into the next field. Walk straight ahead across the field towards the row of houses on the far side, your direction 215 degrees.

In 120 metres you come to a stretch of hedge sticking out into the field, where the path forks. *Take the right-hand fork*, following the path as it curves around the edge of the field to your right, and underneath overhead cables. In 40 metres you come to the corner of the field and follow the path around to the right, continuing along the edge of the field. 200 metres further on, you come to the far left-hand corner of the field and *follow the car-wide track as it curves around to the left*. In 80 metres you come out on to a residential street, where you *turn right into the village*.

In 100 metres you come *to a T-junction* with the main road (the A604). The **Carved Angel pub, Earls Colne**, is on the corner on your left, and **Colne Priory** is dead ahead. *Cross with care straight over* *this busy road, and follow the public footpath sign* along the side of Colne Priory. Walk along the footpath with a metal railing fence on your right-hand side and a hedge on your left. Soon you can see the church of Earls Colne on your left-hand side. In 130 metres you ignore a path going off up the hill to your left. Continue straight on through the kissing gate ahead, with a stile to its right-hand side (and a view back to Colne Priory).

In 120 metres you come out on to a **golfcourse**. The next section of the route takes you *across this golfcourse* (beware of flying golf balls). Walk straight ahead across the course towards the right of a large oak tree dead ahead, your direction 315 degrees.

In 120 metres you pass the oak and continue straight on towards the line of white marker posts indicating the route ahead. 60 metres further on, you pass under overhead cables and up the slight rise ahead.

250 metres further on, you ignore a concrete lane going off to the left, towards the road. You go under some more overhead cables and continue straight on up the track along the left-hand edge of the golfcourse, following the line of the cables overhead.

In 200 metres you bear right, with the edge of the golfcourse, not following the fork left with the edge of the houses.

100 metres further on, you come to a finger of hedgerow sticking out into the golfcourse, and take a path that has come down from the road on the left, to *go straight down the hill towards and over the footbridge* 200 metres away at the bottom. Once

over this metal bridge and across the river, ignore the path which you can see going off through the trees when you look half left. *Turn sharp left along the riverbank* towards the stile which you can see ahead, your direction 315 degrees initially.

In 110 metres you cross the stile. Going straight ahead under the metal barriers would be the simplest short cut (under the old dismantled railway bridge), but the official way is to go slightly right and up *over the dismantled railway line*. Then go down again and over the next stile back to the riverbank on your left-hand side. The old railway line is now managed as a nature reserve.

In 100 metres you pass a mini-weir, and 120 metres beyond that you ignore a left-hand fork going towards a metal fieldgate, to go straight on, heading to the right of an oak tree. In 30 metres you go across a plank through the hedgerow into the next field. Continue straight on along the left-hand edge of this field, your direction 310 degrees. In a further 140 metres, the path crosses over into the next field and you follow the left-hand edge of this field, heading in the same direction as before.

On your right-hand side, up the hill, you can now see the tower of St Andrew's Church in Colne Engaine. In 100 metres ignore a stile on your left-hand side, where the fence turns sharp left, to follow the clear path straight across the field, towards the right of a copse of trees dead ahead, aiming for the red house on the far side of the field. 150 metres further on, you come to the corner of the copse, and follow the path as it bears round to the left, along the edge of the wood.

In 300 metres you come out on to a road at a T-junction. The road opposite is signposted to Buntings Green. *Turn right up the road.* (This is the official way, although there is a pleasanter, well-used local footpath that runs parallel to the road – to its right-hand side – and brings you to the church via a climb up a bank and through a football pitch.) But following the road uphill, ignoring ways off, you come into Church Street, following the sign for Pebmarsh and Bures. 10 metres further on, you *turn right off the road*, through the entrance to **St Andrew's Church, Colne Engaine**.

Walk straight through the churchyard, past the church entrance, and straight down the path on the far side, down on to the road. To your right and across the road is the **Five Bells** pub, the suggested lunchtime stop.

After lunch, come out of the pub and *turn right*. This is Mill Lane. In 80 metres you pass a turning on the left for Halstead and Earls Colne. Go straight on and in 60 metres you pass the village store and post office on your left-hand side. 20 metres beyond that, you come to the village green. *Walk across the middle of the green and cross the road on the far side. Walk straight down the path ahead*, to the right of a horse chestnut tree and between houses, your direction 15 degrees initially. The path is indicated by a concrete public footpath sign, which may be obscured by a bush.

In 150 metres you come out into the corner of a large, flat field, and follow the clear path straight ahead

along its right-hand edge. 300 metres further on, the path curves to your right, down on to a road. *Turn left along the road*, in the same direction as before.

In 270 metres there is a footpath post, 30 metres before the lime green brick farmhouse. *Turn right off the road*, cross over the stile and go straight across the field towards the stile on the far side, your direction 100 degrees. In 60 metres go through a wooden fence into the next field, and follow the wooden fence and horse training ground on your left-hand side. 65 metres further on, *turn left over a stile in the corner of the field*. Follow the path along the line of overhead cables, around the back of the farm buildings.

In 40 metres *turn right past the stile* into the next field. Follow the path ahead along the right-hand side of the field, gently downwards, your direction 85 degrees.

400 metres downhill, you come to the bottom of the field and go over a concrete footbridge with metal railings across a stream. Go straight on through the trees, and 15 metres further on, you come out into a field next to a footpath post pointing to the left and right.

[5] *Turn left*, following a path along the left-hand side of the field, as it goes up the hill beside trees. In 25 metres, around the edge of the field, there is another footpath post. *Turn left into the trees*, your direction 340 degrees initially. In 340 metres, along a clear path through the trees, occasionally clambering over fallen tree trunks, you come out into a large field. There is a wooden footpath post on your right-hand side. Ignore the path to the

right and follow the path ahead, along the left-hand side of the field, your direction 340 degrees initially.

In 140 metres, ignore a footpath post to the left. In a further 20 metres, *go left by another footpath post over a plank across a stream* into the next field. Walk along the left-hand edge of this field. In 120 metres you come to the end of the trees on your left-hand side. *Turn right up the hill,* as per the footpath post on your left-hand side. Aim for the footpath post halfway up the hill, your direction 60 degrees.

50 metres up the hill, *turn left,* following the yellow arrow, your direction 340 degrees initially. Your path parallels the edge of the large new fishing lake, called **Prestons Lake**, down on your left-hand side, and follows the line of the upper row of newly planted trees, *above and parallel to a car-wide track.* In 230 metres cross the car-wide track which goes uphill, to continue straight on along the original course. 400 metres further on, you come to the far edge of the field. *Turn right*, following the direction of the yellow pointer along the hedgerow. In 40 metres *turn left through the trees,* your direction being 10 degrees initially.

For the next 600 metres, follow this newly diverted footpath (No. 19) which is intermittently fenced on both sides, until you nearly reach a post with many yellow arrows on it. (The far side of the post has arrows numbered 14 pointing to both left and right.) 5 *metres before this post, go right through a metal fieldgate* (its left-hand side hinged on another metal fieldgate) out of the wood to follow a footpath with a hedge on

your left-hand side, your direction 90 degrees.

200 metres further on you come to a yellow arrow pointing you to the right of the hedge.

150 metres beyond this **[6]**, you come to another footpath post and *turn right*, following the direction of the arrow numbered 28. Walk with the edge of the field and trees on your left-hand side, your direction 140 degrees.

In 160 metres you come to the far edge of the field. Cross over the stile (with a metal fieldgate to its right-hand side), into the next field, and ignore the track straight ahead to follow the yellow arrow slightly to the right across the field towards another footpath post 60 metres away on the far side, your direction 140 degrees. Continue following the direction of the arrow numbered 28, along the left-hand side of this field, your direction 130 degrees initially. In 200 metres the path curves around to the left and takes you out *to a road T-junction.* **[7]** *Turn left along the road*, your direction 350 degrees.

In 300 metres, where the road curves around to the left towards a pretty thatched cottage, *turn right along the road signposted Valiants and Garlands Farms only.*

In 170 metres you pass the entrance to Valiants Farm on your right-hand side. Follow the road as it continues around to the left. 350 metres further on, ignore a public footpath sign pointing off to the left. 180 metres further on, you pass Garlands Cottage on your right-hand side.

Keep on this track, following it round to the right, with ponds on your left-hand side, a drive lined with lime trees, until within 80 metres of the very substantial **Garlands Farmhouse**, at which point you *turn left away from the track*, opposite the first farm building, *along the right-hand side of the farmhouse front garden*, your direction 75 degrees. In 25 metres *bear right on a car-wide grassy path*, your direction 145 degrees, with a row of trees separating the path from the farmhouse on your right-hand side. 60 metres further on, you come out into open fields and follow the grassy track as it continues along the left-hand edge of the field, your direction 105 degrees initially.

Ignore ways off and 340 metres further on, you come underneath overhead cables to the left-hand corner of the field. Go straight ahead for 10 metres through the trees into the next field and walk straight ahead along the right-hand edge of the field, your direction due east initially. Do not go down the track to the right into the trees.

In 280 metres you come *to the far right-hand corner of the field and cross over the ditch, via a grassy bank, into the trees*. Following a yellow arrow on a post, *go left through the trees* and in 15 metres go on two planks across another ditch. *Turn left*, following the direction of the footpath post with hedges to your left-hand side, your direction 55 degrees.

In 25 metres you come out into an open field, and you walk straight ahead along the left-hand edge of the field.

200 metres further on, with a pretty thatched barn ahead of you on your right-hand side, you come

to the left-hand corner of the field, down a couple of steps, across some planks and out on to a narrow country lane *T-junction. Turn right along the road*, your direction 195 degrees. In 40 metres you pass the thatched barn and the entrance to a pink farmhouse on your left-hand side.

50 metres further on, *turn left following the footpath sign*, your direction 75 degrees, between new trees, on an alleyway between two fields. In 200 metres you bear left, your direction 90 degrees, a brick hut is to your left-hand side. You make for the footbridge that is 70 metres ahead of you. *Cross this wooden footbridge* (the metal railing is on its left-hand side).

Go over the stile on the far side into a field. *Go half left*, your direction 60 degrees, across the field and over a horse jump gap in the wooden fence into the next field. In 10 metres, go over another horse jump gap on your right-hand side, and continue up the hill, the hedges to your left-hand side, towards a large farmhouse at the top of the hill, your direction 55 degrees initially. 150 metres up and over the brow of the hill, you can now see a metal fieldgate on your right-hand side. *Turn right across the field*, towards the gate, your direction 120 degrees. In 60 metres cross the stile which is to the right of the gate, and walk through the gap in the wooden fence ahead.

Go straight ahead through the farm buildings of **Ravensfield Farm** (marked on the OS map) towards double metal gates on the far side. When you get to the gate, turn right along the drive down *to the road T-junction*. There may be peacocks in the garden on your right.

Turn left into the road and in 10 metres turn left again, with a sign saying 'Public byway', a car-wide path, your direction 300 degrees.

In 200 metres you come out into a field and continue along the track on the right-hand side of the field, in the same direction.

650 metres further on, you come out *to a road T-junction* where you *turn left,* past the gateway into Horne's Green Cottage, a very pretty 1821 thatched cottage on your left-hand side. In 5 metres *turn right* down the road signposted to Lamarsh, your direction 20 degrees.

In 300 metres **[8]** *turn right off the road,* following the direction of the concrete public footpath sign, down a grassy car-wide track between two hedgerows, your direction 120 degrees.

In 370 metres you come to a wooden footpath post pointing you straight ahead into the trees. Follow the narrow, potentially very boggy and overgrown footpath through the trees in the same general direction as before (140 degrees).

400 metres further on, however lost you may have felt wading through a sea of vegetation, you come out on to the edge of a field and follow the direction of the tree-line on your right-hand side towards a farmhouse.

25 metres further on, you come out through a gap in the fence on to the corner of the field, and you carry on along the right-hand edge of the field, in the same direction as before, but now with the fence on your right-hand side.

350 metres further on, you come out on to a road at a *T-junction.* There is a grassy triangle at the junction and you *follow the right-hand edge of the triangle* to pick up the blue bridleway arrow pointing down the road dead ahead, your direction 75 degrees.

125 metres further on, you come *to another T-junction,* with a horse chestnut tree in the middle of the junction. *Go right on a track down-hill,* signposted Ferriers Barn, your direction 140 degrees. In 50 metres you pass Ferriers Barn on your right-hand side and carry straight on down the road.

100 metres further on, you ignore the footpath going over a bridge to your right.

450 metres further on, you come down to the bottom of the track and out to a residential street T-junction. The sign on your left says 'Lamarsh Hill'. *Turn right,* going into the hamlet of **Bures**. In 50 metres you pass a turning on the right signposted White Colne, and go straight ahead under the railway bridge. After the bridge you pass Water Lane on your left. 25 metres beyond that is the turning on the right which takes you up to the station.

Continue straight on down the road. 100 metres further on, you pass the other end of Water Lane on your left. After another 40 metres further on, the **Swan Inn**, the suggested tea place, is on your right-hand side. Coming out of the Swan Inn, *turn right, back down the road,* retracing your steps to return to **Bures Station**.

Walk 47

Ockley to Warnham

Woods & rural delights

Length 17km (10.6 miles), 5 hours 10 minutes. For the whole outing, including trains and meals, allow at least 8 hours 40 minutes.

OS Landranger Map No.187. Ockley, map reference TQ 165 404, is in **Surrey**, 9km north of Horsham and 6.5km north of Warnham, which is in **West Sussex**.

Toughness 3 out of 10.

Features This is a beautiful walk through an unspoilt countryside of fields, woods and gentle hills. In this sleepy corner on the Surrey-Sussex border, it seems as if nothing exceptional has happened through the ages. You go through no bustling towns, pass no grand country houses, and there are no particularly interesting historical events to relate. Just mile after mile of oak woods and rural delights. Note that it is over 1km to the station from the village of Warnham, if you are trying to catch a train after tea. Also note the last train back is often between 6.30pm and 7.15pm; and there are no trains to Ockley on Sunday.

Shortening the walk You could call a taxi from the lunch pub to Warnham Station.

History The **Parish Church of St John the Baptist** in Okewood has thirteenth century wall paintings and an unusual arrangement of roof beams.

Warnham's best known son is the poet **Percy Bysshe Shelley**, who was born at Field Place, just south of the village, in 1792. Expelled from Oxford for his pamphlet *The Necessity of Atheism* and eloping with 16-year-old Harriet Westbrook, he was forbidden by his father Sir Timothy Shelley even to visit the family seat, in case he might corrupt his sisters.

Saturday Walkers' Club Take the train nearest to **9.30am** (before or after) from **Victoria** Station to **Ockley**. Journey time about 58 minutes. Trains back from Warn-ham run about twice an hour (some go direct, but some require a change at Horsham or Three Bridges). Journey time 1 hour 10 minutes. Get a cheap day return ticket to Warnham.

Lunch The suggested lunch place is the **Scarlett Arms** pub (tel 01306 627 243) in Walliswood. This is a small, friendly and unmodernised pub, with an inglenook fireplace for cold winter days, and a garden for sitting outside in the summer. It has a fairly standard pub menu with some vegetarian options. Food is served midday to 2pm Monday to Saturday, midday to 2.30pm Sunday. A (larger) alternative is the **Punch Bowl** pub (01306 627 249) via a detour beginning in the woods in Walliswood; the walk can then be rejoined by Rosehill Cottage.

Tea The suggested tea place is the **Sussex Oak** pub (tel 01403 265 028) in Warnham. It serves drinks, tea and coffee. Phone in advance if you are a large group with special requests. The **village store** in Warnham is open until 6pm daily and has two benches for sitting outside.

WALK DIRECTIONS

[1] [Numbers refer to the map.]
Come out of **Ockley Station** and *go through the carpark, and down the tarmac station approach road.* In 100 metres you come down *to the road, where you turn right under the railway arch. 10 metres beyond the railway arch, turn left off the road,* following the public footpath sign, your direction 200 degrees initially. In 150 metres go over the metal bridge across a brook. 250 metres further on, you come out on to a narrow road. *Turn right on to the road.* In 25 metres you come to the entrance to a house called Weavers, on your left-hand side. *Turn left off the road along the path,* following the public footpath sign on the corner of the driveway, your direction 250 degrees initially. In 230 metres the path takes a sharp left turn, going around the back of the garden of the big house on your left. 25 metres further on, it goes right again and continues in the same direction as before.

100 metres further on, you come to the edge of the trees and follow the path alongside a barbed-wire fence, in the same general direction as before. 300 metres further on, on the far side of the field, ignore a track which crosses your path. Continue straight ahead, going slightly downhill, with a recent plantation of trees on your left-hand side. 90 metres down the hill, go over the wooden bridge across the stream. Ignore a fork off uphill to the left in 10 metres, to continue along the footpath as it makes its way through the trees.

Ignore ways off and in 340 metres go through a metal fieldgate into the field beyond. *Walk across the field,* your direction 240 degrees, for 100 metres, to a strange, metal contrivance in the middle of the field *(an old water pump).* Then head to the stile visible in the fence ahead, your direction 300 degrees. Over this stile, in 50 metres, having crossed an underground gas pipeline, you go over another stile and turn left, with the fence to your left-hand side, your direction 190 degrees.

In 100 metres you go over a stile in the corner of the field, into the next field. Walk along the right-hand edge of the field, your direction 195 degrees initially. In 90 metres cross a stile and walk along the edge of the next field, in the same direction as before. Ignore the path going off through the woods to your right. In 25 metres follow the path as it bends sharply around to the right into the trees, your direction 260 degrees initially. **[!]** *In 15 metres take the left-hand fork,* initially 240 degrees, and in 40 metres you come down to a lane, leading up to a wooden fieldgate on your left-hand side, with the gate marked 'Private'. **[2]**

Go straight across the lane, following the public footpath sign on the right-hand gatepost, past the large oak tree, your direction 200 degrees. In 40 metres go through the metal fieldgate and walk ahead along the left-hand edge of the field, following the public footpath sign on the gatepost. On your right-hand side, you can now see the village of **Ockley**. In 120 metres go over a stile, a metal fieldgate to its right-hand side, and walk along the left-hand edge of the next field.

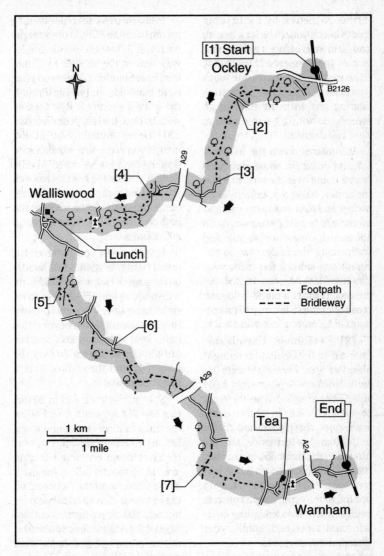

[1] Start
Ockley

B2126

[2]

[3]

N

A29

[4]

Walliswood

Lunch

[5]

[6]

A29

1 km

1 mile

Tea

End

A24

[7]

Warnham

Footpath
Bridleway

In 15 metres, you go over another stile (again with a metal fieldgate to its right-hand side). In 45 metres, you go over a stile (again with its accompanying fieldgate). In 150 metres, you come to a wide-way T-junction.

[!] At this T-junction, with an open area off to its right, and a

beech tree 10 metres to its left (with 'Anthony Annette Adam' carved on it, 6 ft up) *go right*, your direction 255 degrees, entering Birches Wood. Careful inspection of the bushes is needed to find the footpath.

In 45 metres, *keep to the left-hand fork* (a cypress tree marks the start of the right-hand fork). In a further 25 metres, by the first big tree (a beech) since the fork began, and 10 metres before a major junction of paths, *turn left, downhill*, on an easy-to-miss path, due south (towards the sun); in 10 metres bearing left with the path to go steeply downhill, your direction now 150 degrees.

110 metres down the hill, *fork left and cross the wood-and-metal bridge* going over the stream. Over the bridge, *follow the path left for 15 metres and then around to the right up the hill,* heading southwards. In 150 metres cross over the stile and walk along the hedgerow on the right-hand side of the field, your direction 190 degrees. In 200 metres you come to a metal fieldgate; cross over the stile away to its left-hand side, on to a car-wide track.

[3] **Eversheds Farmhouse** (marked on the OS map) is straight ahead of you. *Turn right with the farm buildings to your right hand side.* *Then simply follow the track through its bends:* in 90 metres the track goes sharply around to the left; 140 metres further on, sharply around to the right; 350 metres further on, you come down to the bottom of a slight incline, sharply around to the right, over a concrete bridge (with a wooden railing on its left-hand side) and uphill, your direction 305 degrees.

300 metres further on, you come up on to a concrete road and bear right with it between some farm buildings, with an open barn on your immediate right-hand side, your direction 340 degrees. In 80 metres go through a wide metal fieldgate and straight on along a car-wide track.

In 250 metres you come out on to a main road (the A29). Cross straight over and follow the public bridleway sign on the far side. In 15 metres, East Standon Lodge is on your right-hand side, and you go through the white iron gate. Follow the car-wide track to the left, your direction 230 degrees initially, and in 450 metres you come to a wooden gate (leading to a house called Middle Lodge). *Follow the house's wooden fence round to the left.* In 70 metres, at the end of the fence, keep on the path as it bears left, your direction 200 degrees.

In 100 metres, you go through a metal fieldgate with a tall handle on the edge of Oakwood Mill Farm, with another metal fieldgate on its right-hand side. *Turn right,* down the car-wide track just beyond this gate, your direction 265 degrees initially. In 40 metres go over the river [4] and through or over a metal fieldgate.

Stay on the track and in 20 metres *take the left-hand fork.* Follow the track as it curves around to the left, in the same general direction as the river down your left-hand side. In 70 metres follow the track sharply around to the right and up the hill, your direction 290 degrees initially. 100 metres further on, there is a metal fieldgate directly ahead at the top of the hill. *Follow the track around to the left*, your direction 220 degrees initially. Follow the line of the fence on your right-hand side, with the river down below on your left-hand side.

In 300 metres, the next turning can be easily missed [!]: *Turn sharp right, on to a path going up the hill with a fence to your right-hand side,* your direction 300 degrees initially. In 60 metres you come up into a field. Walk alongside the barbed-wire fence on the right-hand edge of this field, your direction due west initially. In 200 metres cross over the stile into the wood and follow the woodland track, in the same general direction as before. In 50 metres you come to a footpath post and *fork left*, your direction due west. 30 metres further on, there is another footpath post, where you ignore the forks left to continue straight on (bearing right, still due West). In 400 metres the path leads you down through the trees to the **Parish Church of St John the Baptist** in **Okewood**. Go through the wooden gate into the churchyard and walk around to the front entrance of the church, which is worth a visit. *Coming out of the church, go down the path with stepping stones directly opposite the entrance to the church*, your direction 260 degrees. In 25 metres go through the gate in the wooden fence, and follow the yellow footpath arrow into the wood.

Go down some steep steps into the trees, in 100 metres crossing over a wooden bridge across a stream. Once over the bridge, walk straight along the path ahead, your direction 340 degrees initially. 30 metres further on, ignore a path off to the right (going to two bridges) and *turn left along the stream*, your direction 285 degrees. 35 metres further on, *go straight over the wooden bridge with railings dead ahead* (ignoring a similar bridge on your right). On the other side of the bridge, follow the path as it goes slightly to the left and up the hill, your direction 280 degrees.

Ignoring ways off, in 480 metres you come to a footpath post on your left-hand side. Ignore the way ahead into a field, which is anyway fenced and gated. *Turn right here*, following the arrow on the post, your direction 305 degrees initially.

Go straight on for 550 metres, ignoring ways off, to come out through a wooden kissing gate on to a road, where you turn right into the village of **Walliswood**, your direction 15 degrees. In 50 metres, on your right, is the **Scarlett Arms** pub, the suggested lunch stop.

Coming out of the pub after lunch, *turn left, back down the road*. In 60 metres you pass a turning on the right to Ewhurst. 120 metres further on, you pass a dead-end turning on the left called Oakfields. 60 metres beyond that, *turn left*, following signs for Oakwood Hill, Ockley and Dorking. You pass a house on your right-hand side called Charles Copse.

In 400 metres you come to Rosehill Cottage on your right-hand side. Just beyond this, on the left-hand side of the road, there is a public bridleway sign pointing to the right. *Turn right off the road*, along a car-wide gravel track, your direction 200 degrees. In 70 metres go through a wooden fieldgate, following the blue public bridleway arrow straight on. 25 metres further on, go through a metal fieldgate into a field. Follow the blue bridleway arrow along the left-hand edge of the field.

On the far side of the field, you go through a gap in the hedgerow into the next field. Walk straight ahead along the edge of this field, with the wood on your left, direction as before. In 250 metres you come to the corner of the field. Follow the yellow arrows, along the barbed-wire fence on your right-hand side, with the edge of the wood on your left, direction as before. This path may possibly be quite overgrown.

In 150 metres you come out into an open field on the edge of the wood, and here **[5]** you turn sharp left along the edge of the field, your direction 120 degrees initially. In 100 metres you come to the far side of this field. *Turn sharp right.* Many walkers have difficulty finding the next turning **[!]**: *Follow the edge of the field for 40 metres, until you are parallel to the wooden pole sticking up in the fence on your left, which is your handhold for the stile into the next field. Cross over the brook on a small brick bridge, which may be very overgrown* and hidden, and go straight *over the stile into the next field and straight ahead*, your direction 135 degrees.

In 200 metres you come up to the trees, where you will see that there is a barbed-wire fence going all around the copse. You should come up to the right-hand corner of this copse. Walk straight on, with the barbed-wire fence and trees on your left-hand side, in the same direction as before. In 100 metres you come to the far side of the copse, where the fence goes sharply off to the left. Continue straight on, across the field ahead, in the same direction as before. Aim for the gap in the hedgerow – a line of small trees ahead. In 20 metres you walk underneath overhead cables. 80 metres further on, cross over the concrete bridge through the gap in the trees into the next field. *Aim half right towards*

the metal fieldgate on the far side of the field, your direction 210 degrees.

In 130 metres go through the gate and out on to the road. *Turn left along the road*, your direction 80 degrees. In 300 metres you will see a postbox on your left-hand side, and on your right-hand side North Lodge, the gatehouse for Tanglewood. On the left-hand side of the road is a wooden footpath sign pointing out the Sussex Border Path, which goes to Tanglewood. Ignore this and *turn right down the tarmac lane*, signposted Monks Farm and Honeybush Farm, your direction 205 degrees initially.

In 250 metres you come to a four-armed signpost on your right-hand side. Follow the public bridleway straight ahead through a metal fieldgate. In 450 metres you pass between two farmhouses, and up *to a T-junction* **[6]** where there is a three-armed signpost, by a huge oak tree. Ignore the Sussex Border Path 1989 which goes left at this point, along the course of Stane Street (which is an old Roman Road). *Turn right* down the public bridleway.

In 40 metres *follow the track sharply around to the left*, with a wooden fence on your left-hand side. 50 metres further on, there is another three-armed signpost. Follow the public bridleway sign going straight ahead. 30 metres further on, there are two metal fieldgates. Go through the left-hand gate and down the bridleway, your direction 75 degrees initially. In 150 metres follow the bridleway sharply around to the right, your direction 190 degrees initially. 170 metres further on, where there is a metal fieldgate directly ahead, follow the bridleway as it curves around to the left, your direction 155 degrees initially.

60 metres further on, there is a three-armed signpost. Follow the public footpath sign and **[!]** *turn right due south through a wooden gate*, and down the footpath to the left-hand corner of the field, where you can see another footpath sign. In 100 metres you come to the far side of the field and go through the wooden fieldgate on the left. Walk down the path through the trees, which is signposted public footpath, your direction 145 degrees.

In 300 metres, following a clear path through the trees, you come to another two-armed signpost. *Follow the public footpath, going slightly round to the right.* 35 metres further on, look out for the three-armed public footpath signpost on your left-hand side. Go to it and follow its direction due east to go over a stile in 30 metres. Walk straight ahead, your direction due east, with a field fence on your left-hand side.

In 150 metres you come to a two-armed footpath sign on your left-hand side. Follow the direction of the footpath, *going left towards some farm buildings*, your direction 10 degrees. In 40 metres cross a stile in a fence. In 40 metres, having passed the barn on your right-hand side, go over another stile. 20 metres beyond this stile, there is a two-armed footpath sign. *Go right*, following its direction (85 degrees) towards another footpath sign 200 metres away, 100 metres to the right of the red farmhouse.

Once at this three-armed wooden footpath sign, go through a wooden fieldgate. Follow the sign for the public bridleway, going straight ahead, your direction 100 degrees initially. In 150 metres you pass metal fieldgates on both sides of the path and continue straight on down the hill. 125 metres further on, cross over a wooden bridge over North River. On the other side of the bridge, *turn right along the riverbank*, following the direction of the public bridleway sign. In 60 metres cross over a stone bridge with wooden railings going over a stream, and continue straight on up the path on the other side.

In 250 metres you go through the wooden gate on to the main road (the A29). Cross straight over the road and follow the public bridleway sign up the car-wide track on the other side. In 150 metres, where the track goes around to the left through a metal fieldgate, *take the fork to the right*, along the bridleway through the trees, in the same direction as before. In 100 metres you pass Pear Tree Farm on your right-hand side. 250 metres further on, you come out on to a road, alongside a rather sinister old building of mixed styles called Maltmayes, on your left-hand side. *Turn right on to the tree-lined road* and walk up the hill. In 20 metres ignore the public footpath going off the road to the left. 300 metres further on, you pass a driveway on the left-hand side, leading up to a very tall clock tower (an old water tower, built in 1891 for the Warnham Lodge Estate, and redundant since the mid-1930s).

200 metres beyond the tower, the road curves sharply around to the left. Ignore the first way off to the right, but just beyond it you *turn right off the road*, following

the bridleway sign on the corner, going straight ahead, due south. Follow a path to the left of the bridleway, making its way through the trees, beside a railed fence along the left-hand edge of the wood.

After 500 metres along this winding, narrow path – keeping near to the railing on your left-hand side, whenever there is a choice – the path goes steeply downhill. 25 metres from the start of this hill, your way is rejoined by the muddy bridleway coming in from the right. Follow the bridleway straight across the bottom of the depression, and straight up the far side, your direction 235 degrees initially. Ignore a path that forks off to the right.

In 200 metres you come over the hill and down to a four-armed sign. *Turn left off the bridleway* [7] on to a footpath going along oak trees lining the left-hand edge of a field, your direction 125 degrees initially.

In 400 metres you come to the far side of the field, where there is a three-armed public footpath sign, going past a (collapsed) stile, with a metal fieldgate to its right-hand side, to *bear left,* following the path along the left-hand edge of the field, your direction 70 degrees initially. In 80 metres you come to another three-armed public footpath sign and go right, carrying on around the field, your direction 105 degrees initially.

In 80 metres you come to a two-armed public footpath sign. Follow the sign, half right across the field, towards Warnham, your direction 120 degrees. (In the past, we have complained about rape seed up above head level on this path, so that passing along it was like going through a scratchy, wet car wash). In 140 metres go through a gap in the hedge and continue in the same direction. 120 metres further on, you come to the edge of this field, and continue straight on through the gap in the hedge and trees. When you come into the next field, you can see a new development of red-brick houses on your right-hand side. Continue on, with the fence surrounding this development on your right-hand side, down the hill, in the same direction as before. In a further 100 metres, you come to the edge of this field. Follow the path ahead through the trees. The path takes you down through the trees and out on to a road.

Cross straight over the road and walk down Lucas Road opposite. In 150 metres you pass a turning on the right (Hollands Way). 100 metres further on, you come to a dead end, with the Warnham Church of England Primary School at the end. *Go down a footpath to the right of the school.* 150 metres down this footpath, you pass a three-armed footpath sign on the right-hand side, and continue straight on. 100 metres further on, you come out on to the road opposite the church. 50 metres down the road, on your right-hand side, is the village store and post office, which can be relied on for ice cream, cakes and snacks. In the opposite direction, on the left-hand side of the road, is the **Sussex Oak** pub, the suggested tea place.

To get to the station, *walk down Bell Road,* directly opposite the Sussex Oak, signposted 'Horsham 2 miles'. In 500 metres you come *to a T-junction* on to a major road (the A24). Cross straight over the road and *turn left*, in the direction of London and Dorking. In 30 metres turn right, following the sign for **Warnham Station**. As you walk along this road, you can see the brickworks up on the left. Just walk straight up the road until you come to the station. The platform for trains to London is the one on the left before the level crossing.

Walk 48

Whitchurch to Andover

Longparish, thatched cottages & River Test

Length 17km (10.6 miles), 5 hours 10 minutes. For the whole outing, including trains, sights and meals, allow 9 hours 10 minutes.

OS Landranger Map No.185. Whitchurch, map reference SU 464 489, is in **Hampshire**, 16km north of Winchester.

Toughness 3 out of 10.

Features This is a longish walk that is neither steep nor particularly liable to mud. At lunchtime it comes to so many thatched cottages that an alien arriving here might suppose thatch to be a most popular roofing material for twentieth-century earthlings. The route initially follows the line of a dismantled railway and passes the Church of All Hallows in Whitchurch to go along the River Test – 'England's most famous trout stream' – to a pub specialising in fish dishes, in the village of Longparish. The church at Longparish, with punishment stocks beside it, is the first stop after lunch, then the walk goes via a hamlet of more thatched cottages along the River Test and up into Harewood Forest, past a vast piggery and eventually on a straight footpath all the way into Andover itself, with its tearooms, pubs, church and museum.

Just before Longparish is a three-storey brick-built working flourmill (Longparish Upper Mill) on the River Test. If you give the owner a call (and some warning; tel 01264 720 344), they may open it up for a guided tour, which is not normally available to the public. One walker described it as "fascinating and well worth the detour".

Shortening the walk The first part of the walk is perhaps the more interesting, so you could catch one of the hourly buses to Andover, at lunchtime (after 8km of walking) from the Plough Inn at Longparish.

History Whitchurch has a working **silk mill**, still powered by a waterwheel – visiting this involves a 1km detour from the main route. The mill (tel 01256 892 065), at 28 Winchester Street, is open 10.30am to 5pm daily (closed Monday). Admission is £3. **All Hallows Church**, Whitchurch, has Norman arches and pillars with Victorian embellishments, and a gruesome 1602 story picture about those who disobeyed the commandments (for instance, 'one stoned for gathering stocks on the Sabbath Day').

St Mary's Church, Tufton, has a late Saxon chancel arch and an 800-year-old wall painting of St Christopher, depicted unrealistically so as not to infringe the commandment 'Thou shalt not make any graven images'.

Stocks for the punishment of offenders were erected in every village during Edward III's reign. Those in Longparish are among the few still remaining. The **Church of St Nicholas**, Longparish, was perhaps used as a stable by Cromwellian troops. It has a stained-

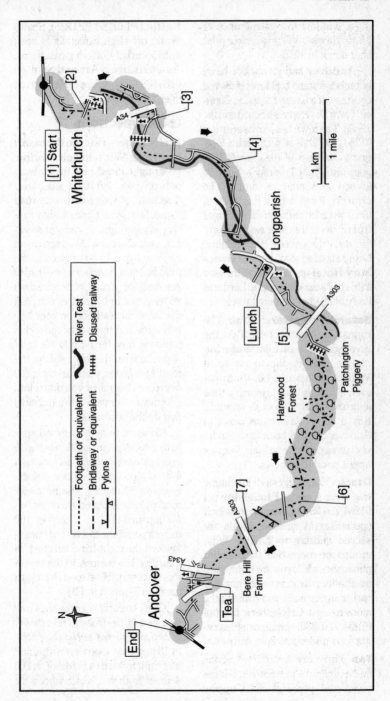

Map legend:

- Footpath or equivalent
- Bridleway or equivalent
- ⋎ Pylons
- River Test
- ┼┼┼┼ Disused railway

1 km
1 mile

[1] Start
Whitchurch
[2]
[3]
A34
[4]
Longparish
Lunch
[5]
A303
Harewood Forest
Patchington Piggery
[6]
[7]
A303
Bere Hill Farm
A343
Andover
Tea
End

N

glass window in remembrance of Major Hawker VC, an air force pilot shot down in 1916.

Andover had its ancient heart of timber-framed buildings removed courtesy of a Greater London Council Town Development Scheme in the 1960s. The town has a **museum** (tel 01264 366 283) at 6 Church Close, just to the east of the church. It is open until 5pm Tuesday to Sunday (closed on Sunday in winter). The **church** closes at 4pm. It is made of Caen stone brought up the old canal from France; the stone was wrongly faced so the church is crumbling. George II used to stay at the **Danebury Hotel** in Andover on the way to his beloved Weymouth. Lord and Lady Nelson also stayed there.

Saturday Walkers' Club The trains may be infrequent. Take the latest possible train from **Waterloo** Station that is due to arrive in **Whitchurch** before **10.40am** (not even a minute later). Journey time approximately 1 hour 3 minutes. Buy a cheap day return ticket to Andover. Trains back from Andover run about once an hour. Journey time 1 hour 10 minutes.

Lunch The suggested lunchtime stop is the gourmet **Plough Inn** (tel 01264 720 358), Longparish, which specialises in seafood. Meals are served midday to 2.30pm daily; groups of more than ten should phone to book. If you are unlikely to reach this pub in time, 20 minutes earlier in the walk you come to the more modest **Cricketers Inn** (tel 01264 720 335), Longparish, serving food midday to 2pm daily.

Tea There are several tea shops and many pubs in Andover, but the suggested place is the **Copper Kettle** (tel 01264 720 335), Shaws Walk, off High Street. It is open until 5pm daily, offering cream teas. An alternative is **Art and Soul** (tel 01264 392 436), 92 Upper High Street, open to 6pm daily.

WALK DIRECTIONS

[1] [Numbers refer to the map.] On exiting **Whitchurch Station**, go straight ahead, past the Railway pub on your left-hand side, your direction 195 degrees, to a car road T-junction by a ten-foot-high railway station sign. *Turn right downhill*, your direction 255 degrees, on Evingar Road. In 200 metres, as the road bends left, *turn right downhill on Ardglen Road*, your direction 260 degrees. In 100 metres you pass the ambulance station on your left-hand side and, just by the end of this building, *take the path to the right* opposite it on the other side of the road, *by a hedge*, your direction 280 degrees. This takes you down into allotments (on your left-hand side) and up the other side.

85 metres from the car road, *your path crosses a car earth track with grass down the middle, and you turn left on this*, your direction 200 degrees, in 80 metres passing under mini-pylons. Keep on this road, ignoring turn-offs. In a further 100 metres you come to a row of bungalows on the right-hand side and, in a further 185 metres, to the end of this driveway (Bloswood Drive) at a car road T-junction **[2]**.

Cross straight over the road and past a metal fieldgate, to take the left of two signposted public footpaths. In 15 metres you go over a stile and half right towards a field exit, at 165 degrees from you, which adjoins the embankment of the disused railway line.

In 200 metres go through a metal kissing gate and onwards, with the embankment on your left-hand side.

In a further 25 metres, ignore a stile to the right and a pedestrian tunnel to the left.

In a further 35 metres, your path goes up on to the embankment and straight on, with the old railway station (now a private house and garden) on your left-hand side.

In 45 metres *turn sharp left, your direction 110 degrees, towards a tarmac lane and buildings.*

In 25 metres you are on this tarmac road and you *turn right* on it (by a house called Mount Flat), your direction 190 degrees.

In 180 metres, at the T-junction, you *enter the wooden gate of* **All Hallows Church**, Whitchurch, to your left. Coming out of the church, you *turn left on the car road* (the B3400), eastwards.

(If at this point you wish to detour to the **silk mill**, continue on this road for 450 metres and then turn right – the fourth turning – at a roundabout on to a road for 150 metres. Coming out of the mill, continue on this road and in 1km rejoin the main route at the asterisk **[*]** below.)

For the main walk route, *20 metres down this B road from the church*, on the corner just past St Cross House on the right-hand side, you *turn right on a signposted footpath*, a car-wide lane, your direction 130 degrees.

In 85 metres veer right with the path, now with the clean **River Test**

(only about 8km from its source in Overton) on your left-hand side.

Keep on this riverside path, ignoring a stile to the right in 150 metres. In a further 250 metres, cross over a concrete bridge with wooden railings. Just beyond the end of the bridge, you pass the entrance to Fulling Mill on your right-hand side and continue straight on, your path parallel and 10 metres to the left of your previous one, your direction 140 degrees. In 15 metres go over a stile and over a stream on two concrete planks, and straight on.

In 70 metres go over a stile and *turn right on a tarmac road*, your direction 210 degrees **[*]**. In 165 metres *turn right on a crescent drive* towards a part-thatched house. In 65 metres you pass this house (Ivy Cottage) on your right-hand side, and in a further 65 metres *go over a signposted stile to your right* (half hidden by cypress trees) to continue on, your direction 200 degrees – *not in the direction shown by the signpost, but diagonally half left, in 240 metres coming to the furthest corner of the field.*

Go over a stile (with a metal fieldgate to its left-hand side) and in 30 metres *turn right on a road to go under a bridge* (and so under the A34), your direction 220 degrees.

20 metres past the bridge, turn right on a signposted footpath, your direction 320 degrees. In 40 metres, by a metal fieldgate to your left-hand side, carry on along a narrow path between fences, your direction 350 degrees. In 110 metres, follow the path to the left, your direction now 255 degrees. In 100 metres, *go over a stile on your right-hand side.*

Go left on a car-wide track, your direction 240 degrees, with a church-yard on your right-hand side and to a phonebox on your left-hand side. [3] Here you *turn right on the road*, your direction 320 degrees, passing **St Mary's Church**, **Tufton**, on your right-hand side (the church is worth a look inside).

There is a way straight on, after bearing left with the road by the River Test, but the owners *do* object to it being used (it is private), so you have to go back past the church, for 150 metres, to the next road crossing and turn right, your direction 240 degrees, and in 650 metres fork right, due west, in a further 350 metres.

You should now be on to a tarmac road, with a sign opposite for Papermill Farm . *Continue straight across* to go along this farm's tarmac road, your direction 165 degrees initially. In 85 metres you pass a large house on your right-hand side, and in a further 100 metres you pass farm buildings on your left-hand side. Veer left with the main lane (following a yellow arrow left on a post) to keep right, passing the farmhouse (on your right-hand side).

In 150 metres fork left, again following a yellow arrow, and away from a wooden bridge over the river, your direction now 165 degrees, past watercress beds below you on your right-hand side.

165 metres from this last fork, *turn right on a tarmac road*, your direction 210 degrees. In 450 metres you pass Garden Cottage. In a further 100 metres you pass the rather beautiful **Britwell Priors** and garden on your left-hand side. In 1927, a colonel and his wife had these timber-framed farm cottages moved here from Oxfordshire, with (in those days) unhealthy water piped in directly from the River Test – at the cottages' previous site the well came up into the dining room.

60 metres past the front gate of Britwell Priors [4], *fork right on a signposted footpath*, your direction 235 degrees, back alongside the river on your right-hand side. In 400 metres you come out on to a tarmac road and follow it alongside the river, your direction 280 degrees.

In 145 metres *fork left with the road, ignoring a path to the right leading to a footbridge*. In 325 metres, by a mini-weir and a farmhouse to the right-hand side, follow your road over a bridge with white railings, and in 45 metres go over a second such bridge, with the farmhouse and old mill closer now on your right-hand side. In 20 metres go over a third (smaller) bridge with white railings.

At the far end of the millhouse, 5 metres beyond it, *go through a gap by a post with a Neighbourhood Watch Area sign*, on a signposted footpath, to the right of a sign saying 'Private road'. *In 30 metres you ignore a car-wide bridge to your right*, to continue on the path, with the river on your right-hand side, your direction 315 degrees.

In 40 metres go over a two-plank bridge with a wooden railing on its right-hand edge, and in 2 metres go over a stile. In a further 55 metres, go over another stile to continue with the field fence on your right-hand side, due west. In 140 metres go over a somewhat ancient three-plank bridge with railing in the middle of a field, past the moderately imposing **Longparish House** (marked on the OS map) away on your right-hand side.

In 100 metres you go over a 40-metre-long wooden bridge between wooden railings (the bridge can be slippery), over the full River Test, and over a stile at the end of the bridge. Then *head for the stile that is the further to the right of two stiles that are less than 100 metres ahead of you*, your direction 260 degrees – in the direction of the thatched buildings beyond. Once over the stile, continue towards the thatched buildings, your direction still 260 degrees.

In 130 metres your path bends right, hugging the field edge on your right-hand side, and in a further 90 metres you exit the field by a stile and footpath sign, in 20 metres coming out on to the B3048, by the thatched Yew Cottage.

Turn left on this B road, your direction 225 degrees, in 40 metres passing the **Cricketers Inn** pub, **Longparish**, on your left-hand side (the alternative early lunch stop if you are going to be too late for the Plough Inn). 130 metres past the pub, and by Little Newton thatched cottage on your left-hand side and Aston thatched cottage on your right, *you turn right up a driveway (that runs to the left of Aston Cottage)*, your direction 315 degrees.

In 40 metres, by a garage shed, *go left on a clear footpath*, your direction 240 degrees, with the field edge now on your left-hand side. In 385 metres ignore a stile on your left-hand side to continue straight on. In a further 155 metres, go over a stile (a wooden kissing gate to its right-hand side) to continue straight on, in 100 metres passing a long

wooden shed on your left-hand side, still straight on. In 50 metres go through a wooden kissing gate *on to a tarmac road, where you turn left*, your direction 130 degrees.

In 10 metres turn right on a signposted footpath (opposite Lower Farm House), passing a terrace of houses on your right-hand side, your direction 205 degrees. *In 110 metres, still 15 metres from the end of the football field, turn sharp left almost back on yourself, by a green arrow on a post*, to find a wooden gate behind the yew trees, your direction now 55 degrees. This is the garden of the **Plough Inn**. Go straight on for 40 metres, with the yew trees on your left-hand side, and then turn right to the carpark and pub – the suggested lunch stop.

Coming out of the pub, turn right on the main road, your direction 210 degrees. In 150 metres *fork left*, your direction 235 degrees, on the driveway leading to the **Church of St Nicholas**, Long-parish; in 65 metres you go through the lychgate into the churchyard – but before going through the gate, note the punishment stocks 3 metres to its right.

Take the left fork through the churchyard. *Leave the churchyard by the other lychgate and pick up the clear footpath* going right (past a thatched barn on your right-hand side), your direction 255 degrees. In 90 metres you go through a wooden kissing gate and continue on.

In 225 metres go through a wooden gate following the Test Way long-distance path (a TW green arrow) to the left, on a tarmac road, your direction 215 degrees. *Your onward route is to follow these Test Way green arrows until the triple asterisk* **[***]** *below.* **[!]** Recently the Test Way has been diverted to cross the A303 on a roadbridge, which is recommended, rejoining at Smallwood Lodge (see below). This is probably permanent, but, if not, follow the directions in brackets below.

(In 30 metres you pass a part-timber-framed building on your right-hand side, and soon a haven of more thatched cottages. 440 metres along this tarmac road, you come to a farm courtyard, with a herring-bone thatched barn and the road veering right. Here you fork left on a car-wide earth road, your direction still 215 degrees.)

(In 75 metres you come to a fork in the road, and on your right-hand side a Test Way two-armed post suggests a turn to the right. Follow this path, your direction 305 degrees, in 130 metres crossing a farm track. In a further 200 metres, go over (or around) a stile and straight on. In 50 metres this leads you down to the busy A303 **[5]**. Cross this dual carriageway with care, slightly to the left, picking up the tarmac lane straight on, your direction 205 degrees and with the river away on your left-hand side.)

(In 430 metres you come to a junction and a house on your right-hand side (with a front porch rather like a church's lychgate), and a fragile wooden bridge visible to your left. Here *turn right on a car-wide road (there is a tennis court on your right-hand side)*, your direction 305 degrees.)

Keep on this road, ignoring any ways off, and in 450 metres you come out on to the B3048, with **Smallwood Lodge** opposite.

Turn left down this B road, your direction 220 degrees. In a 100 metres, by a sign saying Patchington Piggery, you turn right on an earth road, your direction 295 degrees.

In 20 metres you pass through the old railway embankment into **Harewood Forest** (so marked on the OS map) and 20 metres beyond you follow the Patchington Piggery sign and green arrow by forking left on a car-wide road, your direction now 220 degrees.

In 200 metres you come to **Patchington Piggery** on your left-hand side, and soon on your right-hand side. 40 metres beyond six green tanks on your right-hand side, bear left with the concrete road, your direction now 260 degrees.

In 120 metres ignore a turn-off to the right (with a metal fieldgate across it). In a further 270 metres you come to more piggery sheds on your right-hand side, with three Calor Gas propane tanks and two tall Uttley Ingham metal silo-like constructions (after the first shed) also on your right-hand side. After the last of these sheds, you continue straight on.

In 130 metres you come to a junction of paths, just after a metal cable barrier which you need to walk around. Continue straight on, taking the middle path, following a footpath sign, your direction 255 degrees. In 35 metres you pass a wide wooden barrier across your car-wide track. In a further 480 metres, *you come to multiple forks in the road* **[***]**, *but you leave the Test Way at this point and take the rightmost fork*, a car-wide track, your direction due north.

In 150 metres *you come to a fork in the concrete roads and you go left* (there is a five-foot concrete pillar by the right fork), your direction 330 degrees.

In about 800 metres, you come to a junction of paths with a four-armed footpath sign. *Go left on the foot-path signposted concrete road*, your direction 255 degrees. In 185 metres ignore a fork off to the left. In a further 160 metres, you ignore a fork off to the right. Then, in 30 metres, ignore one to the left. In a further 50 metres, you cross a path (with a view out of the woods to your right, to a large red-brick building in the green fields beyond) and continue on, in 20 metres passing two dilapidated sheds made of corrugated arches to your left and right-hand sides.

In 115 metres, with a view of a converted farmhouse away over fields on your right-hand side (marked **Cowden Farmhouse** on the OS map) ignore a fork to the left to keep straight on down your path. In a further 350 metres **[6]**, *veer right up out of a tree-lined avenue and go immediately left* (near a tele-graph pole on your left) keeping the field boundary on your left-hand side, your direction 280 degrees.

In 100 metres veer right with the path and keep on it, with the field edge on your left-hand side. In 145 metres ignore a path to the left and continue on with the field edge to the left, your direction 350 degrees, a roughly similar direction to the line of pylons.

In 135 metres *you cross a tarmac road to continue straight on*, with the field edge on your left-hand side – *it's more or less straight on all the way to Andover now*. At the end of this field in 425 metres, you con-tinue straight on, slightly to the left, between two fences, a copse of low trees on your left-hand side, your direction 330 degrees.

In 190 metres you pass under the pylons. In a further 525 metres, go over a stile to cross the dual car-riageway of the A303 **[7]**, slightly to your left, to pick up your onward path, over a stile, your direction 300 degrees, with the field fence on your right-hand side.

In 160 metres go over a stile to the right of corrugated hay barns to continue straight on (a potentially muddy area), with Andover and its church now visible ahead of you.

In 50 metres you pass **Bere Hill Farm** (marked on the OS map) away on your left-hand side (beware a scarcely visible low electric fence that may be across the path here) and continue on. In 120 metres you cross over an unusual metal pipe stile with metal footplates, and go over a footpath to continue straight on downhill.

Keep straight on all the way to the main road (Eastern Avenue). In more detail: Ignore all ways off and in 125 metres you have allotments on your left-hand side. 60 metres past the end of the allotments, you come to a tarmac estate road and cross this, your onward path now visible for hundreds of metres dead straight ahead, your direction 335 degrees. In 100 metres a sign tells you that this is Dene Path. In a further 280 metres, Dene Path comes to an end, but you continue straight on, along a tarmac road towards the church visible in the distance. In 100 metres your road (Dene Road) comes to an end at a T-junction with Eastern Avenue.

Cross Eastern Avenue by the lights and go down London Street (slightly to the left on the other side of Eastern Avenue) past the Savoy Cinema, Café & Bar on your left-hand side, and in 100 metres passing the Forresters Arms pub on your left-hand side.

In a further 30 metres, *turn right into the High Street*, in 40 metres passing Mount Stevens Bakery & Coffee Shop on your left-hand side, and 10 metres further on, *turning left under the archway of Shaws Walk* to the **Copper Kettle**, which is the suggested tea place.

Coming out of the Copper Kettle, you turn left into the High Street and *carry on upwards towards the church*, taking the slightly right-hand fork in the High Street, coming to a **Norman arch** on your right-hand side, with steps up to the **church**. (If you have time for more sightseeing, turn right at the church to get to Church Close, then left to the **museum** at 6 Church Close.)

To get to the station, however, carry on up the High Street to *turn left into Chantry Street*, just 15 metres before the church. Carry on down this road, but for a quieter and more interesting route, 25 metres past the left turn (West Street) ignore the pedestrian footpath sign to the station, and *go right into Andover Leisure Centre and then, in 50 metres, left* (with Cricklade College and Theatre on your right-hand side). Then go *straight on over the river and under the underpass*. 60 metres beyond it, *at a T-junction with a car road, go right, following the pedestrian sign to the station*, your direction 315 degrees. In 40 metres turn left up Bishopsway. In 400 metres or so, at a T-junction, turn left uphill on Cross Lane, and in 20 metres you fork right for **Andover Station**, now visible ahead. Go under the tunnel for trains to London (platform 1).

Walk 49

Boxhill to Leatherhead

River Mole, Happy Valley & White Hill

Length 11.5km (7.1 miles), 3 hours 30 minutes. For the whole outing, including trains, sights and meals, allow at least 6 hours 30 minutes.

OS Landranger Map No.187. Boxhill & Westhumble Station, map reference TO 167 518, is in **Surrey**, 5km south of Leatherhead.

Toughness 7 out of 10.

Features Boxhill derives its name from the box trees there – yew trees are also found on its chalky slopes, with beech and oak up on top, where the ground is clay and flint. The suggested route involves crossing the River Mole on stepping stones (or detouring if these are under water), before going up on the North Downs Way, with views out over the valley. Then it follows the Happy Valley path northwards, below Lodge Hill and Juniper Top (a valley of moss and lichen-covered trees); then up White Hill to Mickleham Downs, and down to lunch opposite the church in Mickleham. After lunch, the route is along the River Mole valley, through Norbury Park, into the centre of Leatherhead. This route can be slippery at times when wet and has two steep climbs, one up to the top of Boxhill and one, very steep, up White Hill.

Shortening the walk You could call for a taxi from the Boxhill Tavern, the pub at the top of Boxhill. Or you could catch one of the buses that go once every two hours (once an hour on Sundays) from near the pub in Mickleham to Leatherhead. For bus information call Traveline on 0870 608 2608.

History **Boxhill & Westhumble Station** was built in 1867, in polychrome brick with stone dressings, as part of an agreement with the landowner that it should be 'of an ornamental character'.

Boxhill, 172 metres above sea level, contains Bronze Age burial mounds. Daniel Defoe described scenes of drinking, dancing and debauchery on Boxhill; Jane Austen placed the picnic scene in *Emma* here; John Keats climbed Boxhill by moonlight whilst composing *Endymion*; and John Logie Baird conducted his TV experiments from the summit. The area was given to the nation by Leopolds Solomon of Norbury Park, in 1914, and is now in the care of the National Trust. Box trees used to be in demand for making woodcut blocks and mathematical rulers – box wood is heavy and does not float in water.

St Michael's Church, Mickleham, has Saxon and Norman origins and was renovated by the Victorians. Its chancel is noticeably out of alignment with the nave – 'a weeping chancel, to suggest the head of Christ leaning on the cross'.

The poet and novelist **George Meredith** lived at Flint Cottage in Mickleham.

The **River Mole** is thought to have got its name from a tendency to disappear underground in dry weather near Dorking. It rises near Crawley in Sussex, to join the Thames near Hampton Court.

Thorncroft Manor was completed in the 1770s, when Capability Brown worked on the gardens, creating a bridge and island on the river. It was used by Canadian troops during World War II.

Saturday Walkers' Club Take the train nearest to **10.30am** (before or after) from **Victoria** Station to **Boxhill & Westhumble**. Journey time about 45 minutes. Trains back from Leatherhead to Victoria (or Waterloo) run several times an hour. Journey time 47 minutes. Buy a cheap day return ticket to Boxhill.

Lunch The suggested lunchtime stop is the **Running Horses** pub (tel 01372 372 279), Old London Road, Mickleham, which has a log fire in winter. It serves good food from midday to 2.30pm daily. Those wanting lunch earlier in the walk could stop at the less appealing **Smith and Western** bar grill (tel 01737 841 666), an American-style restaurant with steaks, salads, snacks and a children's menu.

Tea The suggested tea place is **Brennans Restaurant** (tel 01372 363 050) in the Swan Shopping Centre, Leatherhead. It is open until 5pm daily, re-opening at 7pm on Friday and Saturday (closed all day Sunday). An alternative is the **Café Roj** (tel 01372 363 237), 7 Bridge Street, Leatherhead, which is open to 6pm, Monday to Saturday, or **Annies Restaurant** (tel 01372 373 399), just beyond the entrance to the shopping centre.

WALK DIRECTIONS

[1] **[Numbers refer to the map.]** Coming out of **Boxhill & Westhumble Station**, *turn left up the concrete steps*, your direction 345 degrees. In 30 metres *turn left over the bridge* to cross the railway line, your direction 295 degrees.

Carry on uphill on this main road (Chapel Lane). In 25 metres you pass a plaque on your right-hand side (dedicated to Fanny Burney, diarist and novelist) and the timber-framed Westhumble Chapel. In a further 30 metres, you *fork left on a tarmac lane by Chaucer Cottage*, which runs parallel to the road to its right-hand side.

In 115 metres you *rejoin the main road*, passing by Pilgrims Way on your left-hand side. **[!]** *In a further 25 metres, take a signposted although somewhat concealed public footpath left*, between fences, your direction 220 degrees.

In 150 metres cross a tarmac lane by a house called Kearsney, to carry straight on.

In 200 metres go through a wooden kissing gate and straight on, across a field. In 50 metres go through another wooden kissing gate. In 15 metres, by a four-armed footpath sign **[2]**, with a large vineyard ahead of you, *turn left on a car-wide way, signposted North Downs Way*.

Ignoring paths off, in 450 metres you go under the railway bridge. In a further 165 metres, you *cross the A24, slightly to the left, to pick up the continuation of the North Downs Way* straight on, down into the carpark area. *At the other end of the carpark, you fork right, marked towards 'Stepping Stones'*, your direc-

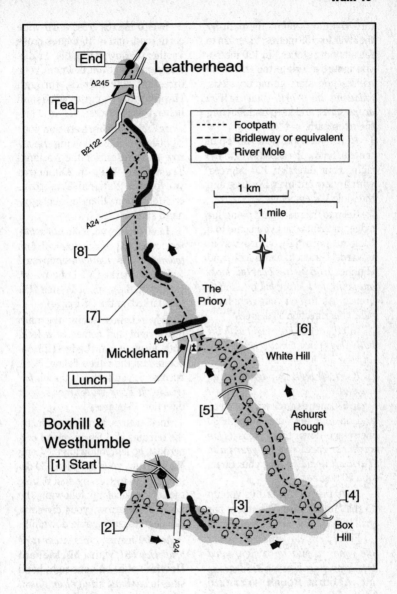

tion 115 degrees. Carry on, straight down. In 100 metres go over the **River Mole** on these **stepping stones**. Carry straight on the other side, on the main path, your direction 120 degrees.

[If the river is running high, and there is a danger of it flooding and covering the stepping stones, retrace your footsteps to the carpark. Take the left-hand fork marked 'footbridge'. Having crossed the bridge, turn right and follow the path by the river for 150 metres, to return to the stepping stones.] In 120 metres you ignore a fork to the left. In 60 metres you start going up steps, *following the North Downs Way acorn signs*, and keep on following the main path.

At a T-junction, near the top of the hill, follow the acorn sign to the right, your direction 120 degrees, with a view out over Dorking and the Mole Valley below.

Keep to the main path along the ridge. In 225 metres you come to a **lookout point [3]**, with views out towards Gatwick, Leith Hill and Hindhead. *65 metres past this lookout point, fork left uphill,* by a multi-branch oak tree on your right-hand side, your direction 35 degrees.

In 110 metres *bear right with the path (there is car parking and a road on your left-hand side).*

Keep straight on, ignoring all ways off.

In 570 metres go down four steps and up four the other side. In 30 metres go down three steps *to an earth car road crossing your path. Turn left uphill on this,* your direction 70 degrees.

In 40 metres this brings you up to the **Smith and Western** bar grill **[4]**, a possible early lunch stop.

From here, *go leftwards across the road, to pick up a signposted bridleway,* your direction 325 degrees, into **Ashurst Rough** (so marked on the OS map).

Ignore all ways off. Thus in 220 metres, keep on the main path, your direction 320 degrees, ignoring a car-wide earth way forking off to the right.

In 210 metres cross a car-wide earth road, and in 15 metres cross another. Follow the public bridleway sign straight on, downhill, your direction 300 degrees, through **Happy Valley** – mossy woods and lichen-covered trees.

In 1.2km, ignore a stile on your right-hand side, following the arrow straight on for the National Trust Long Walk. In 200 metres you pass a National Trust concrete donation pillar on your right-hand side.

In 60 metres you come *to a tarmac road* **[5]** *which you cross to follow the public footpath* signposted walk (also marked NT Long Walk), steeply up the steps of **White Hill** (so marked on the OS map).

Beyond these steps, the path bears right and comes to a fork, with views out to Lodge Hill opposite and the valley below. Here, by post 5, you fork left uphill, *following the Long Walk arrows*, your direction 45 degrees.

In 45 metres, at a T-junction, by the remains of a fence's metal cornerpost, go left, following the Long Walk arrow, your direction 330 degrees. In 40 metres, by post 6, take the left fork, again following the Long Walk arrow, your direction 325 degrees, soon going downhill.

In 200 metres *cross a car-wide bridleway* **[6]**, with a **Mickleham Downs** notice on your right-hand side, to *continue straight on down*, following the Long Walk arrow, due west.

In 310 metres you pass a tennis court on your right-hand side. In 80 metres you come on to a gravel driveway towards the church.

In a further 120 metres, you *enter the churchyard*, and in 40 metres, at the other side of the churchyard, you turn left towards **St Michael's Church**, to its front door (the walk returns this way, should you prefer to visit the church after lunch), and from the church to the **Running Horses** pub, **Mickleham**, which is the suggested lunchtime stop for this walk.

After lunch, *go back into the churchyard and follow its wall on your left-hand side*. In 80 metres *go left, following the NT Long Walk arrow*, your direction 20 degrees. In a further 110 metres, cross a tarmac road to go straight on. In 100 metres, by a green wooden house, *ignore the NT Long Walk arrow to the right, and go straight on*.

In 65 metres you come down to the A24 dual carriageway by St Michael's Restaurant on your right-hand side. Go straight across both carriageways, then slightly left, to *pick up a tarmac lane bridleway* going to the right, opposite Boxhill School. Cross the **River Mole** on a bridge, your direction 345 degrees, into **Norbury Park**.

Ignore all ways off and in 380 metres *you pass Mickleham Priory on your right-hand side. In 100 metres fork left*, your direction 300 degrees, on an earth car road.

In 40 metres go through a wooden fieldgate and straight on. In a further 215 metres, you are back alongside the River Mole on your right-hand side. You more or less follow the river all the way into Leatherhead. In more detail: *When you see a cottage 90 metres ahead of you on your left-hand side, go over the fence on your right-hand side*

[7] *and follow the river* on your right-hand side for 40 metres, until it bends off to the right. You can see, straight ahead of you, a fieldgate on a lane (which you would have come to if you had simply gone to the cottage and turned right, but the above route is the official right of way). *Head towards this fieldgate*, your direction 330 degrees.

In 240 metres you go through a kissing gate to the right-hand side of the wooden fieldgate, to *continue on the lane*.

In 95 metres carry straight on, along a path near the river, your direction 15 degrees. In 400 metres you exit this large field by a kissing gate (with a fieldgate to its left-hand side), and (by a three-armed footpath sign) carry straight on, with the river on your right-hand side.

In 75 metres go over a metal barrier and then onwards *under the concrete bridge carrying the A246* **[8]**.

In 45 metres ignore a fork to the left. In a further 85 metres, go through a kissing gate, with a vineyard then on your left-hand side. In 30 metres you pass a bridge carrying pipes. In a further 320 metres, you go through a metal kissing gate (with a metal barrier to its left-hand side). In 20 metres you come to an earth car road and, by a four-armed footpath sign, you *turn right on the road, signposted Gimcrack Hill*, your direction 65 degrees. In 175 metres you pass the entrance to **Thorncroft Manor** on your left, and you are back alongside the River Mole.

In 100 metres, *5 metres before a bridge, by a three-armed footpath sign, you go left, signposted Town*

Bridge, alongside the River Mole on your right-hand side.

In 500 metres *go right over the town bridge*, your direction 60 degrees. Carry straight on, up Bridge Street, into **Leatherhead**. You pass the **Café Roj**, a possible tea place, on your right-hand side and end up in the High Street. From there, in 45 metres *go into the Swan Shopping Centre on your left*, to come in 80 metres to the suggested tea place, **Brennans Restaurant**, on your right-hand side.

Coming out of Brennans after tea, *exit the shopping centre northwards, through the alleyway, keeping Sainsbury's on your right-hand side*. In 55 metres go up steps on to the main road (the A245).

Cross this A road, slightly to the left, to pick up a tarmac lane (Middle Road) and go straight on between houses, your direction 330 degrees (with house no.4 immediately on your right-hand side).

In 100 metres you come *to a tarmac road T-junction, where you go left*, your direction 230 degrees. In 70 metres, *at the far end of the carpark, turn right*, your direction 345 degrees, with Wesley House, a large building, just ahead of you. In 15 metres *you come to a public garden, where you take the right fork*, a tarmac lane downhill.

In 50 metres take the second fork right, your direction 25 degrees, now parallel to the main road below on your left-hand side, and still within the garden.

In 80 metres you come down *to the main road, which you cross to go straight on*, your direction 290 degrees, on Randalls Road.

In 145 metres, *turn right* to go to **Leatherhead Station**, your direction 15 degrees. After a further 70 metres, go under the railway lines to reach platform 1 for trains to return to London (which go back to Victoria).

Walk 50

Yalding to Borough Green

Mereworth & the Kentish Weald

Length 13km (8.1 miles), 4 hours. For the whole outing, including trains, sights and meals, allow 7 hours 20 minutes.

OS Landranger Map No.188. Yalding, map reference TQ 685 502, is in **Kent**, 10km north-east of Tonbridge.

Toughness 3 out of 10.

Features This is an easy walk through the woods and fields of the Kent countryside, without too much in the way of hills – a good walk for a brisk winter or autumn outing, or for eating blackberries. You will, however, need gumboots in muddy weather, and long trousers/sleeves in summer for the long stinging nettles. The walk starts beside the River Medway, follows the Greensand Way to Roydon Hall (the self-styled Maharishi's 'Capital of the Age of Enlightenment'), and then goes on to the lunch stop in Mereworth, a village dominated by its massive Palladian church, the steeple of which is visible for miles around. After lunch, the walk is principally through the vast Mereworth Woods, on the Wealdway, then up following a stream to the tearoom in Borough Green.

Shortening the walk You can get a bus about once an hour to either Maidstone or Tunbridge Wells from a stop on the way into Mereworth near the church.

History **Roydon Hall** is a Tudor manor house, built in 1535, which has changed ownership only twice: in 1834 from the Roydon/Twysden family to William Cook, a city merchant who accepted it in settlement of debts; and in 1974 from the Cook family to the Maharishi, for his Transcendental Meditation centre. In the nineteenth century, a water diviner told the Cook family to dig into the lawn – where they found a collection of large silver dishes, probably buried in the Civil War.

The **Church of St Lawrence**, Mereworth, has been described as 'one of the most remarkable neoclassical churches in Europe', with a portico supported by six Tuscan columns, and a steeple 'so tall', wrote Horace Walpole, 'that the poor church curtsies under it'. Admiral Charles Lucas, who won the first Victoria Cross in 1854 for throwing overboard a live shell that hit his ship, is buried in the churchyard.

Saturday Walkers' Club Take the train nearest to **10am** (before or after) from **Charing Cross** Station to **Yalding**, changing at Tonbridge or Paddock Wood. Journey time 59 minutes. Trains back from Borough Green to Victoria run twice an hour. Journey time 44 minutes. Buy a cheap day return to Yalding.

Lunch The **Queen's Head** (tel 01622 812534) in Butcher's Lane does unpretentious food at low prices from midday to 3pm daily. Groups of more than 12 people should book in advance. They are under threat of closure. An alternative, requiring a detour, is the **Beech**

Inn, 501 Seven Miles Lane, Mereworth (tel 01622 813038), serving food midday to 2.30pm daily (closed Mondays).

Tea The **Henry Simmonds** pub, Wrotham Road, Borough Greeen, by the station, is open daily till at least 10.30pm, with food till 8pm (not Mondays, and to 6pm Sundays).

WALK DIRECTIONS

[1] [Numbers refer to the map.] Coming off the London train, go over the bridge and exit **Yalding Station** by a gap in the fence. Go out through the station car park to the main road, and *turn left* (where to turn right goes over the railway crossing) your direction 75 degrees, *past Zeneca Agrochemicals*. In 120 metres, just before the bridge over the **River Medway**, *turn left on a signed Medway Valley footpath on the left-hand bank of the river*, your direction 15 degrees. Note: *Your route will follow the Greensand Way and its arrows (as far as the church beyond Roydon Hall)*.

In 110 metres fork left away from the river, following the Greensand Way arrow, your direction 340 degrees, and between concrete fences. In 100 metres cross the railway line and go up the steps the other side, over a stile and then straight on, slightly to the right, your direction 325 degrees, across a large field.

In 380 metres two stiles lead to another field, where you go half left **[2]**, your direction 280 degrees. Follow a barbed-wire fence on your left-hand side, and in 230 metres you exit over a stile and go straight across the B2015, to *continue straight on to the left of no.1 White Cottage*, your direction 290 degrees.

In 55 metres go over a stile and straight on across a field of ponies, donkeys and ducks, exiting the field in 160 metres, by a stile in its top left-hand corner, to continue in your previous direction (280 degrees) towards the woods.

In 160 metres you have an edge of the wood on your right-hand side. In a further 150 metres, you come to a large wood-enclosed field and continue straight across it, your direction 310 degrees. Exit the field in 450 metres, over a stile, straight on into **Moat Wood** (marked on the OS map).

In 275 metres bend sharp left with your main path (following the Greensand Way arrow). In a further 175 metres, the wood becomes a dark pine forest, your direction now due west. In a further 75 metres, you step across a tiny stream; in a further 100 metres, exiting the wood by a stile to go straight on.

In 80 metres you continue straight on along a car-wide grass road, your direction 295 degrees initially, between blackberry bushes.

In a further 150 metres, you get a first sight of **Roydon Hall** ahead to your right, your path following the fence on your right-hand side. At the end of this fence go straight on, ignoring the path off to the right (a detour down this, for 100 metres, would give you a close-up view of Roydon Hall and its garden). In 80 metres you are down on a tarmac road where you turn right, your direction 40 degrees. In 110 metres you pass a side entrance to Roydon Hall and, in a further 120 metres you come to the front entrance and a sign announcing the 'Capital of the Age of Enlightenment'.

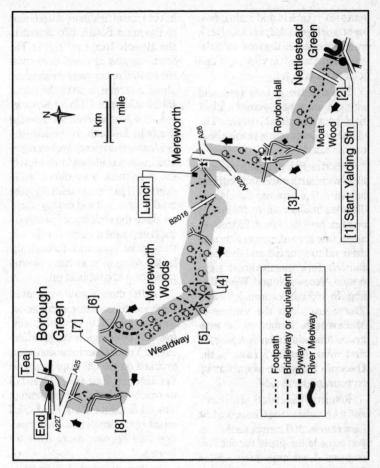

Those with an interest in Transcendental Meditation (or in architecture) can go up the drive, take their shoes off in the front hall, and visit the shop just inside on the right, where almond massage oil, Vedic teas and postcards of flying meditators are for sale.

Your onward path is opposite the front entrance, a Greensand Way footpath going 305 degrees, in 90 metres becoming a path between fences. In a further 120 metres, go over two stiles, with a pond on your right-hand side. You exit the next field by a stile leading to a path that runs outside the churchyard as far as the opening into the churchyard. Go along the left-hand side of the church, past its front door, to *exit the churchyard by a stile* in its far corner, down steps and straight on *downhill on a car road (the one with a dead end sign)*, your direction 320 degrees.

200 metres down the road **[3]**, by the end of the wood (and just before gravelled approaches to field-

gates to your left and right), *turn right on a signposted public footpath*, your direction 25 degrees, with the edge of the wood on your right and a fence on your left.

In 300 metres go over a stile and straight on, a path across a giant field, your direction 25 degrees. The church in Mereworth is visible ahead to your north.

In 500 metres your path becomes a car-wide earth track, and you bend left with this towards the church. This leads *down on to the A228, and you turn right* on it. 200 metres along this A road, ignore a tarmac drive off to your left and then take the left fork (northwards) signposted Mereworth and West Malling. In 165 metres *turn left on to The Street* into the village of **Mereworth**. Detour to the suggested lunchtime stop by *taking the first right, Butcher's Lane*, to the **Queen's Head** pub (some way up on your left-hand side).

Return to Mereworth after lunch and turn right to the **Church of St Lawrence.** 100 metres further on, you come to the site of the old Torrington Arms pub (now called Torrington House). *Turn right on a signposted footpath*, a tarmac lane, your direction 325 degrees. You go into a narrow path between fences by house no.103. In 180 metres you ignore a fork up to the right (going north). *Continue on the main path* (now 265 degrees). In 130 metres go over a stile to continue straight on (275 degrees) on a car-wide earth track through a network of fields.

Take the left fork in 250 metres, by a corrugated water mini-reservoir, your direction now 230 degrees. In a further 100 metres, a stile (to the left of a metal fieldgate) leads out on to the main B2016. (To detour to the **Beech Inn**, turn right.) The main suggested route is to *cross the B2016 to continue straight on*, along a tarmac lane to the left of Libbits Cottage. **[!]** *In 50 metres go left, by a post marked 'FP'*, to take the faint footpath to the left of a fieldgate, with a fence on your right-hand side, parallel and to the left of the main track, your direction 175 degrees. This is a potentially very muddy area – if too muddy, carry on along the wide track (parallel to the path) until it curves to the left, then make your way through the hedge down to it, or carry on and rejoin near the rubbish tip.

In 180 metres go over a metal fieldgate to continue straight on, your direction 210 degrees initially, towards buildings, with the chimneys of **Yotes Court** mansion house (marked on the OS map) visible in the distance. Exit the field in 175 metres, by its far left corner, through a metal fieldgate. *Turn right uphill on an earth farm road, your direction 320 degrees, away from the houses.*

In 30 metres take a footpath to the right of metal fieldgates, your direction 350 degrees. In 20 metres you are between hedges on both sides. In a further 270 metres, your path crosses over a stream, and then the path follows the stream (with the stream to its left). In 160 metres you come to what looks almost like a low wooden horse jump and you go over this, leaving the stream banks, to continue straight on, with a fence on your left-hand side, your direction 285 degrees. In 130 metres there are duck ponds on your left.

Go over a mini-stile, part of another 'horse jump', and in 10 metres you are *on a tarmac road, where you turn left,* your direction 210 degrees. *Opposite Yew Tree Cottage, in a few metres, turn right* on an earth car road (there is a pond on your right-hand side), your direction 295 degrees.

Keep straight on. In 100 metres you pass a cottage on your left-hand side. In a further 100 metres, go out through their metal fieldgate and continue straight on, slightly to the right, your direction 295 degrees, on a wide avenue. In a further 250 metres (guided by 'Keep dogs on leads' signs), go left up through a metal fieldgate on an earth car road, your direction 300 degrees.

In 100 metres this road has an avenue of small redwood trees on both sides of the road. You are now in **Mereworth Woods** (as marked on the OS map). In 650 metres you cross a bridleway and continue straight on (due west). In a further 375 metres, *you come to a T-junction of paths and turn left,* your direction 245 degrees, and in 15 metres you ignore an unofficial bridleway off to the right (310 degrees) to continue straight on.

In a further 150 metres you come to *a post with blue arrows* **[4]**, *and here you turn sharp right,* your direction 330 degrees, on a path marked with a public bridleway concrete marker.

It is normally possible to skirt the muddy areas ahead by little detours into the woods. In a further 200 metres, keep to the main path, your direction 300 degrees, ignoring a fork off to the right. In a further 110 metres, ignore another slight suggestion of a fork off to the right (due east) to keep to the main path, your direction 315 degrees. In 80 metres you come out on an earth road with a wooden post covered with yellow arrows. *Go right on this earth road (MR 315),* your direction 355 degrees.

In 65 metres, at a road junction **[5]**, *take the middle fork with the WW arrow indicating the* **Wealdway** (so marked on the OS map), your direction 330 degrees.

Your route for the next 2km or so is more or less straight on, following the Wealdway, till you come to a tarmac car road. In more detail: In 275 metres you cross paths to continue on, following the WW arrow on a post. In a further 360 metres, you come to a three-way fork and take the leftmost fork (the one that is most straight on for you), your direction 330 degrees.

In a further 200 metres, you ignore a fork off to the right, to continue straight on, your direction 325 degrees. In 300 metres you ignore a footpath going left, marked MR 316 on a post, and keep straight on, your direction 340 degrees, with the field fence (and oasthouse beyond) on your left-hand side and the wood to your right.

In 275 metres, ignore a turn to the right and follow the WW arrow straight on. In a further 140 metres, you cross a path that goes off left into orchards (and right into a field for horses).

In a further 800 metres **[6]**, you come out on to a car road (by a WW arrow on a post) and *turn left on this car road. In 1 metre you go left again on to a public bridleway* (with a concrete marker), your direction 285 degrees.

A green way, soon running parallel to your path in a field to the left, and with regular openings from your path, offers an unofficial refuge from the potentially muddy bridleway. You come out by a wooden fieldgate, in 400 metres, *on to a car road where you turn left uphill*, your direction 230 degrees. *In 200 metres, turn right, downhill, on Crouch Lane* (signposted to Borough Green and Ightham), your direction 325 degrees. (If it is getting dark, you can follow this road all the long way to the A25, then turn left into town.)

In 250 metres you pass Sotts Hole Cottage on your left-hand side. **[7]**. [!] DO NOT GO DOWN THE DRIVE or GARDEN OF SOTTS HOLE COTTAGE [!] *Carry on down the road for 100 metres* **or** *so*, be**fore** joining the clear, narrow bridleway by turning left further up (well beyond the cottage and its environs). Th*en continue parallel to the grass car road on your left-hand side.*

Follow this path for 1km. In more detail: In 70 metres you follow the way through two zigzags to the right. 90 metres beyond these, you pass a wooden fenced gate (marked 'Private') on your right-hand side.

In 110 metres you come out to an open glade, ignoring a minor fork straight on, to fork right on the main bridleway.

In a further 600 metres or so, having passed through a housing estate site, you reach a car road. Turn right here. There is a small waterfall visible on your right hand side.

[8] Continue on, now with a lake on your right-hand side.

[!] In 450 metres, *just beyond the end of the green open space on your right-hand side*, you *fork right on an unmarked path*, your direction 5 degrees.

In 50 metres you pass a small orchard on your left-hand side and immediately go over a stream on a concrete-and-brick bridge (if you forked right off the tarmac road 50 metres too soon, you will have come to the wrong bridge, consisting of three wooden planks).

The route is then steeply up the other side. In 450 metres you cross a car road to continue on your path between fences, your direction 15 degrees.

In 260 metres, having passed a telephone exchange on your left-hand side, you cross a housing estate road to carry straight on, still uphill, your path now tarmac. In a further 185 metres, *you come up to the Church of the Good Shepherd and a car road, where you turn right*, your direction 55 degrees.

In 40 metres you pass a fish and chip shop on your left-hand side and cross the A25 to go straight on, now in **Borough Green** High Street. In 220 metres you come to the railway bridge. 5 metres before the bridge, a tarmac lane to the left leads down between metal railings to platform (no.1) of **Borough Green Station**. But check carefully: some trains to London go from the other platform. On the other side of the bridge is the recommended tea stop, the **Henry Simmonds** pub.

Walk 51

Henley to Pangbourne

River Thames, beech woods & a vineyard

Length 18.5km (11.5 miles), 5 hours 40 minutes. For the whole outing, including trains, sights and meals, allow at least 9 hours 30 minutes.

OS Landranger Map No.175. Henley, map reference SU 764 823, is in **Oxfordshire**, 10km north-east of Reading. Pangbourne, map reference SU 633 766, is in **Berkshire**, 8.5km north-west of Reading.

Toughness 6 out of 10.

Features This walk could almost make an all-day pub crawl, with a dozen pubs en route. The walk starts beside the Thames in Henley, goes down one of Henley's most ancient streets, out into a broad valley, to the church and pub at Rotherfield Greys – probably the best pub of the day, but too early for lunch, for most walkers. Then the walk goes to the church at Rotherfield Peppard, and thereafter it is fields, beech woods, mild hills and small villages. The suggested lunchtime pub in Cane End comes after 11.8km (7.3 miles), 3 hours 30 minutes. The walk also goes down to Bozedown Vineyard (tel 01734 844 031; open till 6pm Saturday, till 5pm Sunday) where award-winning English wines can be tasted. Then to the Whitchurch parish church beside the Thames and to the tollbridge

over the Thames, and so into Pangbourne for tea.

Shortening the walk You could get a bus from near the Red Lion pub in Peppard Common to Reading, or from near the Unicorn pub, 1km further on. They run about once an hour; for bus information phone 0870 608 2608. There is also a bus at rare intervals (for example, at about 2.30pm and 5.30pm) from the King Charles' Head pub in Goring Heath to Goring or Reading. Alternatively, you could order a taxi from any of the other pubs en route.

History Henley, with its 300 listed buildings, is said to be the oldest settlement in Oxfordshire.

St Nicholas' Church in **Rotherfield Greys** seems to be unlocked nowadays. It contains the ornate tomb of Robert Knollys, counsellor to Elizabeth I and friend of Mary Queen of Scots.

The building of **All Saints Church**, **Rotherfield Peppard**, began in the twelfth century. It has early twentieth-century stained-glass windows designed by Meredith Williams, son of a rector of the parish. At the start of the twentieth century, Mirabel Grey, another local artist, made the Last Supper picture behind the altar, and the other panels of inlaid wood.

St Mary's Church, Whitchurch, dates from the twelfth century. St Birynius is said to have landed at the ferry crossing at Whitchurch and, on seeing how fine the place was, decided to build a church.

An act of parliament in 1792 allowed the building of **Whitchurch Toll Bridge**, to replace the ferry. The ten proprietors were given the right to charge tolls – for instance, one halfpenny for every sheep and lamb. The present iron bridge (built in 1902) replaces two previous wooden tollbridges.

The earliest mention of **Pangbourne** is in a Saxon charter of 844 as Paegingaburnam (meaning 'streams of sons of Paega'). In 1919, DH Lawrence stayed in Pangbourne, commenting: 'Pleasant house – Hate Pangbourne – Nothing happens.' Kenneth Grahame, author of *The Wind in the Willows*, lived in Church Cottage, Pang-bourne, just off this walk's route.

Saturday Walkers' Club Take the train nearest to **10.05am** (9.05am during winter) from **Paddington** Station to **Henley**. Change at Twyford. Journey time 54 minutes. Trains back from Pangbourne to Paddington run about twice an hour (some require a change at Reading). Journey time 55 minutes.

Lunch The recommended (very late) lunch stop is the **Fox Inn** (tel 0118 9723 116), Cane End. It is part of the Brewers Fayre chain, so the food is very uninspired, but it serves food all day, the prices are reasonable and it can cope with groups. Groups of more than 25 people should phone to book. A small group might prefer to have lunch earlier. The options include (in the order that you reach them): the gourmet **Maltster's Arms** pub (tel 01491 628 400) in Rotherfield Greys, serving food midday to 2.30pm daily, although the pub can be very full; the **Red Lion** pub (tel 01491 628 329) in Peppard Common, serving food all day every day (except until 5pm only on Mondays); the **Unicorn** pub (tel 01491 628 452) near Peppard Common, although this

may be closed in the future to become private housing; and the **Reformation** pub (tel 0118 9723 126) in Kidmore End, serving home-made food all day.

Tea The suggested tea place is the cheerful **The Ditty** (formerly Ducks Ditty) (tel 0118 984 3050) 11 Reading Road, Pang-bourne, open Monday to Saturday until 5pm, serving teas and hot food. Or there is the **Copper Inn** on the A329 just before the station or the **George Inn** nearby. Both just provide tea, coffee, nuts and crisps, until they start serving dinner at 7pm daily.

WALK DIRECTIONS

[1] [Numbers refer to the map.] Coming out of **Henley Station**, turn right, your direction 305 degrees, and walk 50 metres to the main road. Here, *with the Imperial Hotel opposite you, turn right on the road*, your direction 45 degrees, towards the Boats for Hire place. In a further 120 metres, you are walking alongside the Thames with the water on your right-hand side.

In 120 metres *turn first left, up Friday Street*, due west, with the Anchor Inn on your left-hand side. Go straight on, ignoring turn-offs. In a further 180 metres, you *cross Reading Road to continue on Greys Road*, with the Queens Head on your right-hand side. Go straight on. In 200 metres you pass the Bird In Hand pub on your left-hand side.

In a further 20 metres, you *fork right on to Deanfield Avenue*, your direction 275 degrees. In 15 metres you *fork left on a car lane, signposted as a public footpath*, your direction 230 degrees. Go straight on, ignoring ways off. In 350 metres, you

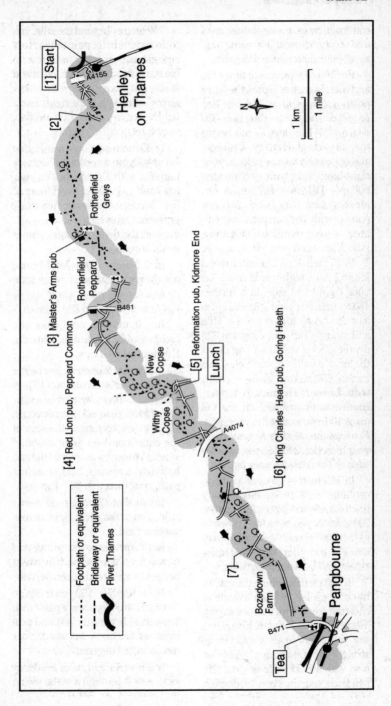

[1] Start

A4155

Henley on Thames

[2]

Rotherfield Greys

[3] Malster's Arms pub

Rotherfield Peppard

B481

[4] Red Lion pub, Peppard Common

New Copse

Withy Copse

[5] Reformation pub, Kidmore End

Lunch

A4074

[6] King Charles' Head pub, Goring Heath

[7]

Bozedown Farm

Pangbourne

B471

Tea

N

1 km
1 mile

········· Footpath or equivalent
– – – – – Bridleway or equivalent
〰〰〰 River Thames

come out *on to a wide tarmac road and carry straight on along this road*, your direction 245 degrees.

For 160 metres, ignore turn-offs, and then 50 metres before the letter postbox, *turn right on Tilebarn Close (a cul-de-sac)*, your direction 330 degrees. **[!]** In 85 metres, just before the carpark of **Henley College**, and opposite a tarmac path on your right-hand side with two wooden bollards **[2]**, *turn left on an unmarked path, due west, between fences*, with the car park immediately on your right-hand side and a hillock ahead on your left-hand side.

In 45 metres go through a metal kissing gate, with tennis courts on your right-hand side. In a further 480 metres, go over a stile and cross a bridleway to go over another stile and straight on, your direction 320 degrees. Soon you are going down the left of a valley of vast fields. In a further 550 metres, go over a stile, with **Lower Hernes**, a timber-framed farm (marked on the OS map), 100 metres ahead to your right. *Continue on, slightly to your right*, your direction 295 degrees, *with the edge of the copse on your left*.

In 125 metres go over a stile to continue on a potentially muddy tractor track, straight on. In a further 200 metres, you come *to a junction of tractor tracks and you carry straight on*, your way now more grassy and between open fields.

In 300 metres, where the tractor track bears left into an avenue of chestnut trees, with a notice saying 'Hernes Estate. Private. Keep Out', *you fork right over a stile* to go straight on, following a yellow arrow, with a field fence on your left-hand side, your direction 280 degrees.

240 metres beyond the stile, you follow a white painted arrow straight on, ignoring an arrow to the right. In 55 metres *go left over a stile in the fence* to follow its yellow arrow's direction to the right, with a field hedge on your right-hand side, your direction 275 degrees.

In 85 metres *go over a stile, and left uphill*, your direction 210 degrees initially, with a field fence on your left-hand side. (Note the difference here between the flower-rich chalk grassland on which you are walking and the disturbed agricultural fields around.)

In 520 metres, bear left to come out through a wooden swing gate *on to a tarmac road, where you go right*, your direction 290 degrees.

In 20 metres you pass the lychgate of **St Nicholas' Church, Rotherfield Greys**.

In a further 25 metres, just before the **Maltster's Arms** pub **[3]**, *by William's Cottage, turn left on a signposted public footpath*, your direction 185 degrees, keeping to the edge of the churchyard on your left-hand side. In 70 metres go over a stile and half right across the field, on a clear path, your direction 220 degrees.

In a further 220 metres, go over a stile, then make a half right, across another field.

In 135 metres *go over a stile and turn left* on a wide path between hedges, your direction 185 degrees.

In a further 150 metres, go through a wooden swing gate (with a metal fieldgate to its left), and *turn right on an earth car road*, your direction 280 degrees.

In 80 metres, *by a public bridleway sign, go left* through a metal swing gate (a metal fieldgate to its right), your direction 160 degrees, on a potentially muddy path on the fringe of the wood.

In a further 225 metres, *take a stile to the right*, to go through new trees due west across vast fields. In a further 540 metres, go over a stile and onwards, between the fences of Rectory Farm.

In 190 metres go over a stile *on to an earth car road, where you go right*, your direction 300 degrees.

In 130 metres you come to a fine little church, **All Saints Church, Rotherfield Peppard**.

Coming out of the church, *carry straight on along the road (Church Road)*, ignoring ways off.

In 270 metres you come to a school on your right-hand side and Slaters Farm on your left-hand side, and you *fork right*, still on a tarmac road, your direction 330 degrees. Head towards the **Red Lion** pub **[4]**, **Peppard Common**, visible 240 metres ahead, and reached after crossing the main road.

At the pub, turn left on the minor tarmac road, your direction 240 degrees. In 270 metres ignore a road coming in from your left. In 155 metres ignore a bridleway off to your right, to stay on your road, soon steeply uphill.

In 300 metres, near the top of the hill, ignore a signposted footpath off to the left. In 200 metres you come to the **Unicorn** pub on your right-hand side.

Your route is straight on at this road crossing. In 35 metres *go over the main road to carry on, along Wyfold Lane*, your direction 240 degrees. In 200 metres you pass a

Woodland Trust sign saying 'Visitors welcome to walk in our woods'. In 50 metres ignore an earth road to the left, by a house called Greenmarch. In 40 metres you *take the signposted footpath over a stile to your left*, to go due south, with a field hedge on your right-hand side. In 180 metres go over a stile with angle-iron edges.

In 140 metres *go over another stile with angle-iron edges. Here you go sharp right*, your direction 310 degrees, with the field hedge on your right-hand side.

In 150 metres you go over a stile to enter a beech wood, **New Copse** (so marked on the OS map). In 10 metres *fork right*, due west. In a further 15 metres, keep straight on, ignoring a white painted arrow to the right.

Keep straight on, ignoring ways off. **[!]** *In 640 metres you come to a multiple junction with four possible ways onwards, and marked as a footpath T-junction on the tree (with a fieldgate and the edge of the forest to your right, 35 metres away). Here go left*, your direction 165 degrees.

In 265 metres, at a crossroads, keep straight on; likewise in 10 metres at the next crossroads. Your way is now car-wide, your direction 170 degrees.

In a further 185 metres, and about 100 metres from the nearest house, ignore a faint path to the left, to bear right with the main path.

In a further 175 metres, having ignored all ways off, you come out through wooden barriers *on to a car lane lined with houses, where you go left*, your direction 110 degrees.

In 120 metres you pass the cog-wheels of an interesting well on your left-hand side, and in 15 metres you come *to the main road, where you go right*, your direction 250 degrees. In 50 metres this brings you to the **Reformation** pub in **Kidmore End [5]**.

In a further 270 metres you pass Wyfold Road to the right, and in 10 metres you pass Wood Lane to the left. In 120 metres you pass sheds and a house on your right-hand side. In 60 metres, at the end of the fence on your right-hand side, *there is a scaffolding pole barrier on your right-hand side, and you go right on a signposted footpath into the wood*. 6 metres into the wood, you follow a faint white arrow marked on a tree, by *forking left*, your direction 270 degrees.

This is **Withy Copse** (marked on the OS map).

In about 500 metres carry straight on along a narrow path when the main walk veers to the left. In 200 metres you are *on a public footpath through a private back garden. Go straight through the garden* to come out, in 45 metres, to the road, with a house called May Lodge on your right-hand side.

Turn left on this tarmac road, your direction 165 degrees. In 140 metres *take the signposted footpath over the stile to your right*, your direction 220 degrees. Keep the field hedge on your left-hand side at this point (a timber-framed thatched cottage is visible ahead of you to your right.)

In 145 metres *take a stile to your left in the fence*, to continue on an entrance driveway. In 35 metres *turn left on the A4074*, by a thatched cottage on your left-hand side, your direction 130 degrees.

In 105 metres you come to the suggested late lunch stop, the **Fox Inn**, **Cane End**, on your left-hand side. *Coming out of the pub, turn left on the A road verge. In 40 metres*, where a lane comes in from the left, *cross carefully to an earth track opposite, leading to a stile* by a green metal fieldgate. Cross the stile and ignore the stile ahead to *follow the blue arrow bridleway half left*, your direction 170 degrees.

In 40 metres go through a metal swing gate and go half right, your direction 205 degrees. In 30 metres, go through another metal swing gate. Keep straight on, a fence on your right-hand side, ignoring stiles off to your right.

In a further 200 metres follow the path to the right. In 20 metres you enter the wood, your direction then 215 degrees.

Keep on the main path. In 150 metres, at a signed path junction, follow an M3 (this stands for Mapledurham Footpath 3) arrow to keep straight on, along a car-wide earth track, along the edge of the wood to your right, your direction 295 degrees.

In 110 metres you cross a farm track to continue on into the wood, following the white arrows on the trees.

In 230 metres, with forks left and right indicated by white paint on a tree, *take the left fork*, your direction 250 degrees.

In 20 metres keep straight on, ignoring a fork to the left.

In 135 metres, at a car road junction, *go straight on, along a tarmac road*, your direction 240 degrees.

In 10 metres you pass Crossways Cottage on your left-hand side. In a further 160 metres, by concrete bollards on your left-hand side, *take the signposted bridleway to your right* into the wood, your direction 280 degrees, on a wide muddy track (part of the Hardwicke Estate). Ignore an equally wide track going off to the right.

In 65 metres ignore a fork to the left, and again in 40 metres. In a further 80 metres, your track crosses another and you take this new track downhill slightly to the left, your direction now 240 degrees, following intermittent white arrows on trees.

Ignore ways off. In 150 metres, you way goes gently uphill. Then in 250 metres, near the top, follow a white arrow on a tree straight on, your own way now slightly narrower.

In a further 460 metres, you come *to a tarmac road where you turn left*, your direction 120 degrees. In 115 metres you come to the **King Charles' Head** pub **[6]** in **Goring Heath**, on your left-hand side.

Opposite the pub, you *go right on a footpath over a stile*, signposted Path Hill, your direction 230 degrees, across a paddock. In 80 metres *go over a stile on your right-hand side to follow the edge of the wood on your left-hand side*, your direction 250 degrees, through a small paradise for rabbits.

In 125 metres go over a stile. In 45 metres you come out on to a driveway, between fences, past a flint cottage on your left-hand side. In a further 145 metres, *cross a tarmac lane to go straight on*, along a very wide earth avenue.

In 130 metres *turn left on a car-wide earth road*, signposted public bridleway to Mapledurham, your direction 190 degrees.

In 40 metres you pass a turn to the right to a house and shed. In a further 10 metres, by a yellow arrow on a cornerpost (on your left-hand side), you *go right, between sheds*, your direction 290 degrees. Then in 20 metres pass to the right of a metal fieldgate and go forward on a narrow enclosed path (with truly free range chickens to your left-hand side) at the end of which you *go over a stile and half left*, downhill, across the field, your direction 250 degrees.

In 80 metres you go over a stile straight on into the wood. In a further 110 metres, you exit the wood over a stile, to continue on downhill across a field, due west.

In 80 metres *go over a stile and left, uphill*, your direction 245 degrees, with the edge of the wood fairly near you, on your left-hand side. In a further 145 metres, go over a stile and straight on, through a potentially muddy field. In 60 metres you come to a tarmac road, with Path Hill Farm and its Farm Shop opposite.

Go over the road and straight on, along a tarmac lane **[7]**, signposted footpath, your direction 220 degrees. In 200 metres you pass the entrance on your left-hand side to a house with turrets and a Lego-brick ground floor. In 35 metres you *take the stile ahead and slightly right (level with the house's garden gate)*, offering a view out over the Thames, to go downhill with the fringes of

Bottom Wood (marked on the OS map) on your left-hand side.

In 265 metres you come *to a tarmac road which you cross* to continue straight on, over a stile (with a metal fieldgate to its right) and so onwards, with a field fence on your left-hand side and a view to the Thames away to the left.

In 160 metres you go through a metal kissing gate. In 25 metres, by a painted arrow on a post, *turn left, downhill,* your direction 165 degrees, with a field hedge on your left-hand side. In 150 metres you go through a metal kissing gate (to the left of a metal fieldgate) *on to a tarmac road, where you go right*. In 410 metres you have the start of vineyards on your right-hand side.

In 100 metres you come to the **Bozedown Vineyard** and wine-tasting shop.

Just past the vineyard, you can get off the road on a path parallel to and above it, to its right.

In 340 metres, the path rejoins the road, and where the tarmac pavement starts, 35 metres past the 35mph sign, you *turn left on a sign-posted footpath* beside a wooden fieldgate, an earth car-wide road, your direction 170 degrees, going past playing fields on your right-hand side.

In 265 metres *turn right on the tarmac driveway* of a primary school, your direction 235 degrees. In 50 metres bear right on a lane (Eastfield Lane) and, in a further 400 metres,

you come *to the main road*, with the **Greyhound** pub, **Whitchurch**, on your right-hand side. *You turn left*, due south.

In 35 metres *take the footpath right to the church*, signed Thames Path, on the tarmac driveway of Walliscote House. In 15 metres you *fork left*, your direction 225 degrees. In 65 metres you *enter the lychgate* of the **Parish Church of Whitchurch-on-Thames**, which is worth visiting. *Turn right out of the church*. In 45 metres go on a lane between brick walls. In 30 metres *turn left on a gravel road by a millhouse*, with the Thames on your right-hand side.

In 65 metres you come back to the main road and turn right to *cross* **Whtichurch Toll bridge** over the Thames. Keep on this main road. In 250 metres you go under the railway bridge. In 45 metres, with the **George Hotel** on your right-hand side, you come *to the main road T-junction* . You *turn left* and in 35 metres you come to **Ducks Ditty** on your left-hand side, the suggested tea place.

Coming out of the tearoom, turn right. In 125 metres you come to the **Copper Inn**, where you *turn right*, your direction 340 degrees, on the A329. In 145 metres, just before the bridge, *turn left up the lane* to **Pangbourne Station**. You need platform 2, on the other side, for trains to return to London (back to Paddington).

Walk 52

Princes Risborough to Wendover

The Ridgeway Path through Chequers

Length 16km (10 miles), 4 hours 50 minutes. For the whole outing, including trains, sights and meals, allow 8 hours.

OS Landranger Map No.165. Princes Risborough, map reference SP 799 027, is in **Buckinghamshire**, 11km south of Aylesbury.

Toughness 6 out of 10.

Features This walk is easy to follow, being mainly along the Ridgeway, and is very much uphill and downhill, but not strenuously so. The way is predominantly through high beech woods and chalk downlands, including the Grangelands Nature Reserve, and has views out from Coombe Hill over the Vale of Aylesbury and surrounding counties. The walk ends by descending into the pleasant old town of Wendover.

Shortening the walk There are buses back to Princes Risborough, several times an hour, from near the lunch pub in Great Kimble. You could also shorten the walk by staying on the Ridgeway and not detouring via Dunsmore.

History The town of **Princes Risborough** derives its name from the Black Prince who, in 1343, was lord of the manor.

This area was first settled by farmers in neolithic times, around 4,000BC, and was defended by a line of hilltop forts linked by the broad **Icknield Way** (which can be traced from Dorset to Norfolk, and on this walk survives as the narrow Ridgeway). Remains of such forts can be found on **Pulpit Hill** and **Coombe Hill**.

Whiteleaf Cross, carved into a hillside, is thought to commemorate a victory over the Danes.

Chequers, the prime minister's country retreat, was given for this purpose to the nation by Lord and Lady Lee of Fareham in 1921. Even the state, with all its power, has not been able to divert the public footpath from this land, where the PM is at the mercy of any sniper.

Lady Mary Grey, sister of Lady Jane Grey, was imprisoned in Chequers in 1566, and the house was later owned by a grandson of Oliver Cromwell.

Wendover's name comes from the Anglo-Saxon 'wand' (winding) 'ofer' (bank). In 1600, the town had one pub for every 50 inhabitants. Wendover became the property of the crown and was given by Henry VIII to his wife Catherine of Aragon. It had John Hampden as its MP during the five parliaments leading up to the Civil War. He was one of the MPs whose attempted seizure by Charles I led to the Civil War.

Saturday Walkers' Club Take the train nearest to **10.15am** (before or after) from **Marylebone** Station to **Princes Risborough**. Journey time 45 minutes. Trains back from Wendover run about twice an hour. Journey time 48 minutes.

Lunch The suggested lunchtime stop is the **Bernard Arms** pub (tel 01844 346 172) in Great Kimble, which serves food until 2.30pm daily; groups of more than ten should phone to book. This is the pub which Yeltsin and other foreign dignitaries tend to visit, when at Chequers. For those starting late or not wishing to detour off the Ridgeway to this pub, an early lunch could be had at the **Plough** (tel 01844 343 302) in Lower Cadsden. It serves food midday to 2pm daily; groups of more than 15 people should book. Both of these pubs are open on Christmas and Boxing Day, although the Plough only serves food on Christmas Day to groups that pre-book.

Tea The suggested tea place is the **Le Petit Café** (tel 01296 624 601) five minutes from Wendover Station, which is open until 4.30pm weekdays, and until 5.30pm on weekends and bank holidays. Alternatively, the smokier bar of the **Red Lion Hotel** (tel 01296 622 266) in Wendover serves tea all day and is open throughout the Christmas period. There is also the **Shoulder of Mutton** pub (tel 01296 623223) next to the station.

WALK DIRECTIONS

[1] [Numbers refer to the map.] *Coming out of* **Princes Risborough Station**, *turn left*. In 65 metres *veer right with this road away from the station*. At the T-junction in 90 metres, *turn right on Summerleys Road*. Ignore the first right, Picts Lane. Veer left with the road and in 90 metres *take the next right, Poppy Road* (the B4444), signposted High Wycombe.

Keep straight on, past the Black Prince pub on your left-hand side. Join the A4010 and *bear right on this A road*. Then cross over it and continue on, in the direction of Wycombe, your direction 155 degrees. **[2]** In 160 metres you *turn left up a tarmac lane (the historic* **Upper Icknield Way**) *signposted the Ridgeway*, your direction 60 degrees initially.

Keep straight on up this lane for 1km, ignoring footpaths off to the right and left.

Just past the playing fields on your right-hand side, *cross over the car road you come to and continue straight on*, along the Ridgeway Path (still called the Upper Icknield Way). Keep on this lane, ignoring a footpath sign off to the left.

[3] In 350 metres, *by the football field on your left-hand side, at a three-armed footpath sign, take the Ridgeway footpath to your right*, your direction 95 degrees, uphill, now with the Whiteleaf Cross visible on the hillside to your left (at 40 degrees on the compass). Keep on this main way all the way up, with a field fence on your right-hand side. Ignore a fork to the left at the top right-hand corner of this first field.

At the top, *follow the acorn sign* (the Ridgeway Path symbol – and the symbol for all National Trails) up steps into the wood. In 15 metres you ignore a footpath sign to the left, to keep on up the steps of the Ridgeway Path.

Near the top of the hill, go through a kissing gate (with a view back over Princes Risborough). In order to stay on the right of way (not the most direct route), follow the

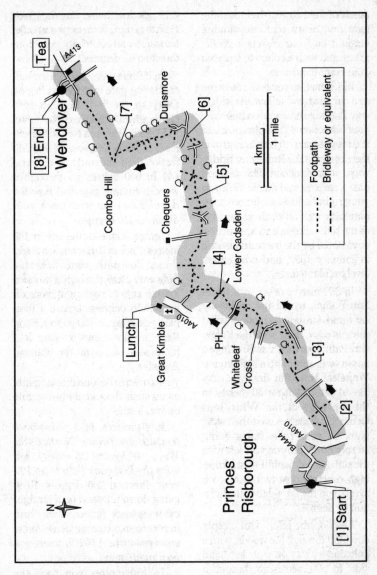

acorn straight on upwards, eastwards (less leftwards than the arrow by the kissing gate might lead
you to believe), *going between
bushes 15 metres up from this gate.*

In 200 metres, at the top right-
hand corner of the field, there is a

car lane on your right. But just before the stile out on to this tarmac
lane, you follow the Ridgeway Path
sign to your left, staying within the
field, close to its right-hand edge,
your direction 15 degrees. Go
through a potentially churned-up

patch of field to exit by a kissing gate and acorn sign, continuing straight on, your direction 25 degrees, and with a concrete fence on your right-hand side.

In 125 metres you come down on to a car road and follow the Ridgeway Path sign upwards on this road, your direction 115 degrees. In 15 metres go sharp left by a four-armed sign, up on to the Ridgeway bridleway, your direction 345 degrees, past a carpark and picnic tables on your right-hand side. Ignore footpath signs off. Follow along the ridge of the hill – through an area nearly devastated by the tremendous gale in January 1990, and now extensively replanted.

In 350 metres or so, at a three-armed sign, where the bridleway continues straight on, your onward route is to go right with the Ridgeway Path, your direction 80 degrees, past a swing gate and a sign saying Whiteleaf Hill. (But first you may like to detour left for 50 metres to the top edge of the **Whiteleaf Cross**.) 100 metres past the swing gate, as your path starts going steeply downhill, you veer left with the main path downhill, past a knee-high concrete post (with an acorn symbol on the far side), your direction 60 degrees.

Keep on the main path steeply downhill through the woods, with a golfcourse away on your left-hand side. In 500 metres go through a metal kissing gate (next to a metal fieldgate to its left).

In 70 metres *turn left on a tarmac road*, passing the **Plough** pub in **Lower Cadsden**. 110 metres beyond the pub, you cross a more substantial road. 10 metres beyond

this junction, *leave the Ridgeway Path to turn right through a wooden barrier*, by an electricity pole, your direction 45 degrees.

In 150 metres go through a wooden kissing gate (not the bridlegate away to the left) and up into **Grangelands Nature Reserve**. In 15 metres ignore a fork to the left. *Keep to the path upwards*, your direction predominantly 35 degrees. **[4]** In 500 metres go through a wooden kissing gate and *turn left downhill on a car-wide track*, your direction 310 degrees.

Ignore a stile to the left in 130 metres. Then in 70 metres, at a three-armed footpath sign, *take the Ridgeway Path* through a wooden kissing gate to your right, your direction 15 degrees. Ignore a footpath you cross in 150 metres. Soon there are fine views on your left-hand side out over the Vale of Aylesbury.

400 metres beyond this footpath, go up steps through a kissing gate or over a stile.

In 40 metres, *by a four-armed footpath sign (saying 'North Bucks Way – Wolverton 35 miles'), you leave the Ridgeway Path to go left*, your direction 260 degrees. Keep going downhill, soon on a straight car-wide track. Ignore all ways off, in 800 metres coming *down to the main road (the A4010), where you turn right*, uphill.

In 150 metres you pass the **Church of St Nicholas** and reach the suggested lunchtime stop, the **Bernard Arms** in **Great Kimble**.

After lunch, *retrace your steps*: Go right out of the pub, 150 metres downhill on the main road, then left up the lane as before, signposted

North Bucks Way and public bridle-way, passing a well with a thatched roof on your right-hand side.

400 metres up this path, take the footpath to the left, by a post with two blue arrows on it, going through a metal kissing gate and taking a right fork to go *half right, uphill,* towards four tree stumps (180 metres away), your direction 110 degrees.

Keep to the main path that goes just to the left of the hilltop ahead. 500 metres from your fork off the lane, *you come to a T-junction, the well-trodden Ridgeway Path, where you turn left,* eastwards. The Ridgeway Path is marked with acorn posts in both directions.

65 metres after crossing a gully, go past a three-armed footpath sign, ignoring a footpath to left, and keeping on the Ridgeway Path, along the top of an old rifle range valley on your left-hand side.

In a further 110 metres, ignore a stile and footpath off to the left, and go on for 75 metres up to a metal kissing gate (next to a metal field-gate and a stile off to the left). Go straight on, along the Ridgeway Path, due east.

In 250 metres, by a three-armed footpath sign, go out through a kissing gate (a wooden fieldgate to its right), and go to your right, following the Ridgeway sign, your direction 140 degrees, with the wood's edge on your right-hand side.

You now have your first glimpse of **Chequers** to your left (at 70 degrees). In 500 metres you turn left by a two-armed footpath sign and a stile, towards the Chequers gate-house, your direction 115 degrees, through kissing gates, over the

Chequers entrance drive and straight on the other side, through another kissing gate.

In 350 metres, leave Chequers through a kissing gate. Carefully cross the car road and continue straight on, following the Ridgeway bridleway sign, your direction 75 degrees.

In 130 metres you pass a barn on your right-hand side.

Go up into a narrow strip of woodland, following the acorn and blue arrow on a post. *In 100 metres fork left* (the right fork merges again with your way in 100 metres).

A further 45 metres beyond where these ways merge, by a four-armed footpath sign, ignore the South Bucks Way to your right and carry straight on up the Ridgeway footpath.

[5] In 250 metres you come to a three-armed footpath sign, more or less at the top of the hill, a poten-tially muddy patch. The suggested route is to *leave the Ridgeway Path here (which goes left) and to carry straight on, following the footpath sign, on a car-wide track,* your direc-tion 65 degrees.

Carry on, soon downwards, through the woods, ignoring ways off. In 450 metres you ignore a foot-path that crosses yours, staying on your car-wide track. In 300 metres ignore a yellow-signed footpath up to your left. Go down past the house and stables on your left-hand side, to *go over the road,* at a four-armed footpath sign.

Carry straight on, along a signposted footpath, uphill, over a stile, your direction 70 degrees, be-tween fences. Then go over a stile into a field, following the path half left to the next stile. Go over this stile towards the upper left-hand corner of the field, which you *exit just to the left of a mini-pylon* **[6]**.

Turn right on a car road. In 80 metres, just past a pond on your right-hand side, *turn left*, signposted 'Dunsmore Village only'.

Ignore a footpath sign off to the right in 60 metres. In a further 60 metres, a bridleway sign points your continuing way, straight on up the tarmac car lane.

In 50 metres continue past Apple Tree Cottage on your right-hand side and the converted (now closed) ex-Fox Inn on your left-hand side (which is marked as a pub on some OS maps).

In a further 90 metres, ignore a stile off to the left.

The path has by now narrowed somewhat, and in 100 metres you *fork left on a wide path, between fences to your left and right, through woods*. Continue on for 50 metres.

In a further 450 metres, cross a bridleway. In a further 70 metres, go over an earth car track (a cattle grid and private property are to your right, a bridleway to your left).

Go straight on, along a public footpath, your direction 320 degrees, *following a fence on your right-hand side*, and parallel to the driveway beyond.

Ignore a footpath off to the left, and (100 metres away, on the other side of the fence to your right) you pass a small house with a conservatory. In a further 250 metres, at the point when the fence ends, you continue straight on between the rusted remains of a fence, your direction 315 degrees.

In 250 metres **[7]** there is a tree on your left-hand side with a railing partly embedded in it. Go straight on through a gap in the bank to cross a wide track and continue ahead (in more or less your previous direction, 320 degrees) on a **[!]** narrow winding path.

In 90 metres, *at a footpath T-junction painted in yellow on trees, go right*, your direction 15 degrees.

In 65 metres *go left*, your direction 295 degrees, following a yellow sign on a tree.

You pass the back of a National Trust sign (saying 'Footpath only' on the other side) and in 40 metres you go through a wooden kissing gate, and *past a National Trust sign saying* **Coombe Hill**. Carry straight on, your direction 285 degrees, with barbed wire on your left-hand side. In 450 metres you come to a **Boer War** monument.

At the monument, there is a concrete pillar indicating directions to distant points. Follow more or less the direction it marks as Ellesborough Church, *to your right, to pick up the Ridgeway Path* (marked with acorn posts) down towards Wendover, your direction 80 degrees. Exit the Coombe Hill grounds by a wooden kissing gate, to go over a bridleway and straight on along the Ridgeway Path, your direction 70 degrees.

In 300 metres, as you enter the woods, by a sign for **Bacombe Hill**, you fork left, following the Ridgeway Path down, in 100 metres passing through a wooden kissing gate, straight on, your direction 70 degrees. There are fine views out on to the Vale of Aylesbury below.

Keep to the main path. Further on, a fine view of Halton House appears ahead on your left-hand side. 680 metres from the wooden kissing gate, ignore a fork to the left and, by a bench, carry straight on, now more steeply down, your direction 60 degrees.

In 190 metres go through a metal kissing gate marked with the acorn, and carry on down.

In 80 metres *turn right on the car road and carry on down under pylons into Wendover,* passing the station off to your left and *coming to South Street on your right,* where you find the suggested tea place, **Le Petit Café**. If this is closed, the **Red Lion Hotel** is further down the road on your right-hand side.

After tea, to get to the station, turn left out of the café, retracing your steps as you go. In 70 metres you pass the Shoulder of Mutton pub on your right, and take the road to the right (Station Approach), which leads down to **[8] Wendover Station**. The platform nearest to you is the one for London.

Walk 53

Wye
(round walk)

Substitute walk on the
Crundale Downs

Length 17.3km (10.7 miles), 5 hours 15 minutes. For the whole outing, including trains, sights and meals, allow at least 9 hours 30 minutes.

OS Landranger Map No.189. Wye, map reference TQ 048 470, is in **Kent**, 6km north-east of Ashford.

Toughness 7 out of 10 (8 out of 10 in muddy weather).

Features Start early from London if you want to get to Sole Street in time for lunch. The walk goes high up on the Crundale Downs ('crun' in Old English meant chalk, and 'dala' meant dell or valley), with breathtaking views. The walk comes to an isolated Norman church at Crundale, and to a fifteenth-century inn for lunch. It then passes Crundale House and the manor of Olantigh, crosses the River Stour and returns to Wye through its churchyard, to the tea shop in Church Street. (Beware that parts of the route can be very muddy in wet weather, so be prepared.)

Shortening the walk You could call a taxi from the lunchtime pub. Or you could save 2km by not having lunch and descending on a byway from the Crundale church, your direction 290 degrees, to rejoin the main suggested route beside Crun-

dale House. On the return journey to Wye, 2.5km before getting there, you could call for a taxi from the phonebox in Bilting. Or you could turn left at the T-junction just after point [9] below and walk in to Wye itself.

History The large Edward VII **Crown Memorial** was cut into the hillside outside Wye in 1902, and is made of flintstones.

The **Church of St Mary** in **Crundale** is thought to be on a Roman site and still retains Norman parts. Inside is a nearly life-sized memorial slab commemorating the Reverend John Sprot, who died in 1466 and is depicted in his full vestments.

The **Church of St Gregory and St Martin** in **Wye** dates from the twelfth or early thirteenth century and was larger than it is now – its tower collapsed in 1686. **Wye College**, next to the church, was founded in 1447 by John Kempe, the Archbishop of York, and is now part of Wye Agricultural College, University of London.

Saturday Walkers' Club Take the train nearest to **9.15am** (before or after) from **Victoria** Station to **Wye**. You may need to change at Ashford. Journey time about 1 hour 39 minutes. Trains back run about once an hour.

Lunch The recommended lunchtime stop is the **Compasses Inn** (tel 01227 700 300), Sole Street. It serves home-cooked hot food from midday to 2.15pm, and cold food till 3pm daily. Groups of more than 15 should book. Walkers are permitted to eat their sandwiches in the garden. (The more accessible pub in

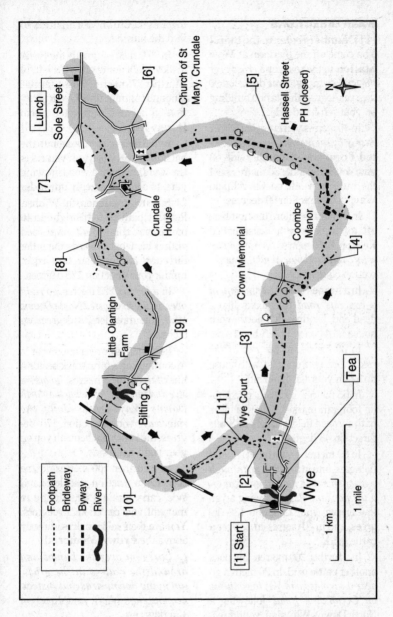

Hassell Street, marked on old OS maps, has closed.)

Tea The recommended tea place is the **Tickled Trout** pub (tel 01233 812 227), next to the station, which serves food all day in the summer, and from 12 to 2.30pm in winter. In winter the pub is closed between 3pm and 6pm.

WALK DIRECTIONS

[1] [Numbers refer to the map.]
You come off the platform at **Wye Station** to the road, and *cross over the level crossing*, your direction 90 degrees, to pass the station building on your left-hand side.

In 40 metres you *cross the* **River Stour** *by bridge*, passing the **Tickled Trout** pub on the other side, on your left-hand side. 30 metres past the pub, turn left on Churchfield Way, your direction 60 degrees.

In 80 metres ignore the first lane off to the left by a house called Kelston. In 55 metres *turn left on an estate road (Abbots Walk)*, your direction 55 degrees.

In a further 115 metres, *go left on a concrete road* that looks like a dead end, heading due north, with house no.44 on your left-hand side.

In 30 metres, *at the end of the road, turn right*, due east, with house no.52 on your left-hand side.

In 55 metres, by a concrete public footpath marker, follow a clear path across a field, straight on, your direction 45 degrees.

In 80 metres go through a metal fieldgate, and in 5 metres go *through a wooden swing gate to go right on a tarmac lane* **[2]**, following a yellow arrow, your direction 130 degrees, and in 40 metres cross over a cattle grid.

In a further 200 metres, you pass another cattle grid. In 20 metres go *over a tarmac road* **[3]** *to continue on Occupation Road*, following a North Downs Way sign, your direction 100 degrees, straight on.

In 320 metres you cross Wibberley Way (a 'permissive path') to continue straight on, steadily upwards, towards the Crown Memorial carved into the hillside.

In 270 metres ignore the Stour Valley Walk going off to the left. In a further 275 metres, cross a tarmac lane and continue uphill, your direction 85 degrees, signposted North Downs Way.

In 250 metres there is a fine view back over the valley, as you enter the wood, through a wooden swing gate, to continue steeply upwards.

In 100 metres ignore the Wibberley Way path off to the right. In 40 metres you come *to a tarmac road* with a view out towards the other direction (north). You *turn right*, uphill, your direction 125 degrees.

In a further 225 metres, *go right over a stile, signposted North Downs Way*, your direction 220 degrees, up steps.

In 30 metres go over another stile to continue on a farm track beside a line of trees. In 60 metres, *go over a stile and turn left, following the North Downs Way arrow along the ridgeway*, your direction 170 degrees, the valley out beneath you on your right-hand side.

In a further 100 metres, at the corner of a fence on your left-hand side, carry straight on, slightly to the right, your direction 215 degrees. You are then, in 35 metres, directly above the **Crown Memorial**.

Carry on over the bumps and around the craters in the grass, not going downwards, but instead bearing slightly left, your direction 125 degrees.

In 165 metres you *go over a stile, following the North Downs Way arrow*, with the fence on your left-hand side, your direction 145 degrees.

In 250 metres **[4]** *leave the North Downs Way to go through a metal kissing gate to your left*, marked with a yellow circular walk arrow, your direction 80 degrees, to cross a field. In 120 metres go down into the wood on a footpath used by horses, your direction 135 degrees.

In 115 metres, *at the other end of the wood, go straight on with the edge of the wood now on your right-hand side*, and **Coombe Manor** ahead on your left-hand side.

In 275 metres you come *to a tarmac lane where you go left*, your direction 25 degrees.

In 145 metres, *turn right uphill* following a footpath sign. In 120 metres, *at the top of the field, turn left*. In 50 metres, ignore a stile ahead of you and *turn right* up the hillside, with the edge of the wood on your left-hand side.

In a further 225 metres (15 metres before a metal fieldgate with a blue bridleway arrow), *go left over a stile into the wood*, your direction 25 degrees. In 35 metres go over a stile to continue on, with the edge of the wood on your left-hand side, your direction 60 degrees.

In a further 140 metres, go over a stile and onwards. In a further 340 metres, go over a stile and then on to an earth lane.

Go left, and then immediately fork right, by a four-armed footpath sign **[5]**, along a byway (a car-wide earth lane), your direction 350 degrees. Stay on this byway, uphill, through the wood of beech and chestnut trees, ignoring other ways off.

In 680 metres, as you go through a potentially muddy patch, you have a view out over the valley to your west. In a further 150 metres, you come to an open field on your right-hand side and continue on.

In 160 metres ignore a stile on your right-hand side.

In 20 metres you go through a metal fieldgate and straight on, your direction 345 degrees, with a field fence on both sides. In 640 metres go through a metal fieldgate. In 45 metres you come to the **Church of St Mary, Crundale**, on your right.

After visiting the church, *leave the churchyard by its main gate, by the war memorial, and turn right on the tarmac lane, downhill*, your direction 105 degrees.

In 500 metres, *at the T-junction* **[6]**, *follow the Compasses Inn sign to the left*.

In 750 metres, having climbed steeply for the last part, you come *to a T-junction where you turn right*, due east. In 275 metres this brings you to the suggested lunch pub, the **Compasses Inn**.

After lunch, turn right out of the pub. In 275 metres ignore the fork to the left that you came up before lunch. In 125 metres ignore the dirt road that forks to the right uphill.

In a further 170 metres, ignore a path to the right marked with a blue arrow. But then in 40 metres **[7]**, *fork left through a tractor-wide gap in the hedge to go downhill on a path, half right across a field*, your direction 235 degrees.

In 150 metres, at the edge of this field, cross an old hedge line and continue straight on, your direction 250 degrees.

Ignore ways off, and in a further 450 metres the path leads you along the left-hand edge of a wood.

In 80 metres, just before the field corner, turn right and cross a stile into the wood. In 10 metres ignore a stile straight ahead into a field and bear left, downwards, through the wood, your direction 290 degrees. In 70 metres you come out *on to a tarmac road where you go right.* In 110 metres *go sharp left on the driveway of Crundale House,* your direction 175 degrees.

In 10 metres *fork left on a footpath* (the way has been overgrown at times in the past) by a public footpath concrete marker, your direction 120 degrees.

In 25 metres go over a stile between two metal fieldgates and follow the path with a field fence on your right-hand side.

In 85 metres ignore a wooden gate on your left-hand side.

In 160 metres, *by a stile on your left-hand side, go right, steeply downhill,* your direction 280 degrees. In 15 metres go over a stile and across a field, your direction 250 degrees.

In 65 metres *go through a metal fieldgate and over a concreted farm road, with a stables on your right-hand side, to continue straight on,* your direction 260 degrees.

In 10 metres you go through a metal fieldgate, with a field hedge on your right-hand side.

In 80 metres you go over a stile (there may be an electric fence here). In 5 metres you come *out on to a road, which you cross to continue straight on, uphill,* on an earth road, your direction 240 degrees initially.

In 35 metres, at the end of the fence on your right-hand side, *follow the yellow arrow to the right,* your direction 320 degrees, *along the line of the telegraph poles,* with the hedge and then the back garden of **Crundale House** on your right.

At the end of the hedge, keep on across the field, still following the poles, your direction 310 degrees.

In 180 metres, when the path reaches the garden ahead of you, veer left with it, your direction 250 degrees, with the garden fence on your right-hand side.

In 80 metres, *8 metres beyond the house, you go right, following the yellow arrow through a wooden fieldgate,* your direction 335 degrees. In 25 metres go straight on, now on the driveway of Farnley Little Barn.

In 40 metres *you come to a tarmac road where you go left uphill,* your direction 255 degrees.

In 120 metres **[8]** *take the signposted footpath left.*

In 15 metres, ignore footpaths off to the left, and continue straight on up the hill, following *the rightmost fork of those on offer, up into the wood,* your direction 260 degrees (not the Stour Valley middle fork).

Crossing over any logs that may block the path, *continue on up to a fence where you make your way to the left for 10 metres or so, to a gap in the fence, to come out on to a bridleway where you go right,* your direction 300 degrees.

In 35 metres you come *to a tarmac road, which you cross to go through a kissing gate and then to go left,* your direction 210 degrees, *with the field fence on your left-hand side.*

In 150 metres you *bear slightly to the right, to make for the far right-hand corner of the field.*

There, you go over a stile and across, slightly to the left, aiming for a footpath post on the far side of the field, your direction 275 degrees.

In 200 metres go into the wood. In 15 metres you come *to a path where you go left*, due south.

In 40 metres you come *to the exit from the wood, where you go half right across fields*, your direction 230 degrees.

In 340 metres, by a footpath sign, you come out *on to a car road where you go right*, your direction 300 degrees.

In 280 metres you pass Olantigh Garden Nurseries on your left-hand side. In 20 metres **[9]** ignore a fork left to Brook and turn right, signposted Wye.

In 300 metres *you come to a T-junction where you go right, signposted Crundale*. (A shortening of the walk is to go left on the lane into Wye.)

In 30 metres *go left through a wooden swing gate, on a signposted footpath*, your direction 320 degrees, making for the footbridge.

The **chapel and manor of Olantigh** (as marked on your OS map) are visible, away on your left-hand side.

In 215 metres you *cross the River Stour by footbridge to go straight on*, your direction 320 degrees.

In 145 metres you go over a stream and continue slightly left, your direction 300 degrees.

In a further 200 metres, you pass Finches House on your left-hand side. In 25 metres you go through a wooden kissing gate to *cross the railway line*.

Continue on through a kissing gate the other side. In 120 metres you come *to a T-junction by Home Farm House, where you go left*, your direction 260 degrees.

In 200 metres (30 metres before a **phonebox** and the A28) **[10]** go left on an earth car road, your direction 200 degrees.

In 40 metres you come to the edge of the field and go straight on across it, your direction 205 degrees.

In 250 metres you come to a field fence the other side, at the left-hand corner of a wood, and you go over a stile to continue in your previous direction (205 degrees), now with a fence and the wood on your right-hand side.

In a further 255 metres, you go over a stile with a three-step ladder the other side, and continue onwards, slightly right, your direction 220 degrees.

In a further 385 metres, *cross a stream on a plank bridge*, 15 metres north-west of a hedge corner, *and then fork left*, due south. In 100 metres go through a gap in the hedge and onwards across another field, your direction 140 degrees.

In 215 metres go down to *cross the river and a tributary on two bridges*. On the other side you *turn right along the riverbank*, your direction 165 degrees.

In 120 metres go over a stile and *across the railway line, and on a concrete bridge over the River Stour. Go half right the other side*, your direction 160 degrees.

In 60 metres go through a wooden fieldgate in the top right-hand corner of the field, and onwards, keeping the field edge and drain on your left-hand side, your direction 145 degrees.

In 300 metres you *cross a drain on a concrete tractor-wide platform, to follow a yellow arrow half right*, your direction 170 degrees, towards a house. In 160 metres [11] *go along the side of this house and then right, with the house on your left-hand side*. In 50 metres *exit the field by its far left corner*, through a wooden swing gate. Go slightly left, along a tarmac lane, your direction 155 degrees. In 35 metres ignore a path off to the right (through a wooden swing gate). In 35 metres go over a cattle grid. In a further 60 metres, *go through the wooden swing gate to your right*, with a hedge on your left-hand side and a fence on your right, your direction 220 degrees.

In 135 metres *you come into the churchyard* of the **Church of St Gregory and St Martin** in **Wye**.

To continue, go straight on to the main road, where your turn right, coming to the **Tickled Trout** pub, the recommended stop for refreshments, on your right-hand side and to **Wye Station** – the platform on your near side is for trains to Ashford and return journeys to London.

Updates, news & credits

The original editor of this book, Nicholas Albery, sadly died in a car accident while returning from a country walk in June 2001; he is greatly missed, but not forgotten, by all those who walked with him, in the country and in life. To learn more, see the information on the web: www.alberyfoundation.org

Updates are added periodically to the Saturday Walkers' Club website at www.walkingclub.org.uk If you have **any** information about blocked paths, errors and changes, please send an e-mail to walks@alberyfoundation.org.

The Nicholas Albery Foundation (tel 020 7359 8391) is the charitable project which benefits from bookshop and credit card sales and any royalties from this book. The Foundation's activities include: the on-line think-tank, Global Ideas Bank (www.globalideasbank.org), the Natural Death Centre (www.naturaldeath.org.uk), the Poetry Challenge (www.poetrychallenge.org), and many innovative publications (including a walking guide to the Canary Island of Gomera: see www.gomera.org.uk).

Walk checkers

Huge thanks to all those who have helped check or update information in this book, including: David Allard, James Anderson, Peter Barbour, Jens Bammel, Julia Bardos, Wendy Baron, Tim Bassett, JM Baugié, William Benn, Fiona Bernard, Peter Boon, Clive Bostle, Tom Brooks, Fabian Bush, Tony Campbell, Margaret Chambers, Jim Cheetham, Sue Clark, Terry Clyne, Miss M Collin, Harry Comber, Peter Cocks, Peter Conway, David Cooke, James Dixon, Andrew Duncan, Richard Evans, Mrs AP Farley, Jane Feinmann, Tim Foster, Father Alan Green, Jason Greeves, Susan Gunning, Martin Haggerty, Sheila Hale, Derek Halls, Geraldine Hay, Mr Henderson, Susan Hoffman, Mrs J Hussey, Nick Imison, David Johnson, Derek Keeble, Orsolya Lelkes, Pat Lonergan, Tony McLaughlin, Edward Masters, Scottish Catriona, Bob Matthews, RA Mercer, Joe Merriman, Michael Monk, Andrew Murphy, Nancy Noël, Anette Nuebel, Mark Parker, Mike Powell, John Pestle, Doug Pugliese, Derek Purcell, Robert Puzey, Marianne Rice, Sue Richards, Frankie Rickford, Melanie Robinson, Peter Savage, John Sephton, Katy Shaw, Steve Small, Mr P Smith, John Squibb, Michael Stokes, Joan Thompson, Roy Treacher, Ross Urquhart, Lynne Wallis, Marian Watkinson, Bill Webster, Peter Whitestone and William Wingate.

The Ramblers

The Ramblers Association (1-5 Wandsworth Road, London SW8 2XX, tel 020 7339 8500; web www.ramblers.org.uk) takes decisive action on blocked paths and helps to keep the path network open. Annual membership costs £20.

Index